Ecumenical Documents IV

BUILDING UNITY

Ecumenical Dialogues with Roman Catholic Participation in the United States

Edited by
Joseph A. Burgess and
Brother Jeffrey Gros, FSC

Preface by
Reverend John F. Hotchkin

PAULIST PRESS
New York/Mahwah, N.J.

The publisher is grateful to the following for permission to include their documents in this publication: the United States Catholic Conference, the Executive Council of the Episcopal Church, the North American Baptist Federation, the Home Mission Board/Southern Baptist Convention, the Council on Christian Unity of the Christian Church (Disciples of Christ), Lutheran World Ministries, the United Methodist Church, the Greek Orthodox Church of North and South America, the Ecumenical Department in the Office of Cardinal O'Connor, the Coptic Orthodox Church in North America, the Office of Ecumenical Coordination/Division of Corporate and Social Mission/Presbyterian Church (U.S.A.), and the National Council of the Churches of Christ in the U.S.A./Commission on Faith and Order.

Library of Congress Cataloging-in-Publication Data

Building unity.

(Ecumenical documents ; 4)
Bibliography: p.
Includes index.
1. Christian union—History—20th century—Sources.
I. Burgess, Joseph A. II. Gros, Jeffrey, 1938–
III. Series.
BX6.5.B85 1988 282 88-28890
ISBN 0-8091-3040-8 (pbk.)

Published by Paulist Press
997 Macarthur Boulevard
Mahwah, New Jersey 07430

Printed and bound in the
United States of America

Contents

Dedicated to
John Sheerin, C.S.P. and John Hotchkin
under whose leadership
this volume emerged

and to the memory of
Arthur Carl Piepkorn
and
W. Jerry Boney
whose spirituality
inspired this generation of
ecumenical scholarship
in the U.S.A.

Preface

The second thousand years of Christianity, the "millennium of divisions," has been dotted by periodic efforts, always courageous, often brilliant, but all in some way ill-fated, to restore unity to the Christian people. Thomas Aquinas died on his way to the Second Council of Lyons (1274), but giants like Albert the Great and Bonaventure did take part in this Council which sought, without success, to unite the Christian East and the Christian West. The Council of Florence (1438-1445) brought together a still larger number of Eastern and Western bishops with the same purpose, and even formally approved three decrees of union. Again, these failed to gain acceptance by the churches at large.

The Regensburg Colloquy (1541) is remembered as what proved to be a last ditch attempt to stave off a definitive split between Rome and the Reformation. It was led by outstanding figures: Philip Melanchthon and the reform-minded Cardinal Gaspar Contarini, with others such as the Emperor Charles V and John Calvin in attendance. After one month it was jubilantly announced that agreement had been reached on the crucial doctrine of justification. However, neither Rome nor Luther proved so sanguine; events overcame the efforts of the collocutors, and abiding division ensued.

More recently, the second quarter of the nineteenth century saw fresh efforts mounted to overcome the division between Anglicanism and Rome. The Oxford Movement, with its orgins in the 1830s, laid the basis on patristic foundations, developing thereon a theology of the unity of Christianity. Still, the way forward was hardly free of setbacks. Within the Church of England Protestant opposition materialized against the "Romanizing" tendencies of the movement. In 1864 Rome forbade Catholics to continue membership in the Association for Promotion of the Unity of Christendom (APUC), a league founded by Anglican and Catholic leaders devoted to prayer for the corporate reunion of the Anglican, Orthodox and Roman Catholic Churches. In 1870 the First Vatican Council pronounced the infallibility of the pope when he defines dogmas of faith. Nonetheless, by 1895 Lord Halifax tematic approach, reflecting the particular theological muscularity of the two traditions which meet here.

The carefully measured, succinct and sober reports of the Orthodox-Catholic Consultation demonstrate how utterly serious any agreement quickly becomes between sister churches. Nearly every word counts and is weighed. In the Anglican-Roman Catholic Consultation one can usually detect the resonance of their worldwide communions humming in the background. It is particularly interesting to compare the Catholics' dialogue with the Disciples of Christ and that with Southern Baptist scholars. In both one catches the note of discovery, almost a sense of surprise, but the discoveries unfold along somewhat different lines. In the dialogue with the United Methodists one observes the careful, uncertain yet persistent Catholic search for the "distinctives" of their partners. To this rich and varied world of U.S. bilaterals, the Faith and Order Commission adds its own far-reaching multilateral endeavors.

Reverend John F. Hotchkin
Executive Director
Committee for Ecumenical and
Interreligious Affairs
National Conference of Catholic Bishops

Feast of Francis of Assisi, 1988

Introduction

Through the formal acts of the Second Vatican Council (1962–65), especially its *Decree on Ecumenism,* the Roman Catholic Church officially became an active participant in the already developed ecumenical movement. Thus began for Catholics the experience of a new tradition of attitudes, theological understandings, activities and structures.[1] That tradition, now but twenty-some years old, remains both blessed and burdened more by discontinuity than continuity with the past. Yet that tradition is already harvesting an abundant early growth to be shared between the Christian Communions.[2]

Catholic Principles of Ecumenism

The *Decree on Ecumenism* had broadly sketched the Catholic ecumenical agenda as an integral part of the post-Vatican II renewal—"an increase of fidelity to the Church's own calling": (1) spiritual ecumenism, the soul of the whole ecumenical movement, a change of heart and holiness of life, along with public and private prayer, also with other Christians, for the unity of Christ's one and only Church; (2) collaboration in mission through common witness in service, social action and evangelization; and (3) dialogue as a means of resolving those theological and ecclesiological issues of faith and order that hinder full communion.

Development of the Dialogues

In addition to these explicitly ecumenical principles, there are two other items of Catholic renewal that shape this "agenda": the understanding of "local or particular" churches emerging from Vatican II, including the collegiality implicit in this self-understanding, and the challenge of "reception" that has emerged as a result of ecumenical progress in theological dialogue.[3]

Structural developments have taken place on the regional and national levels. In 1967 Paul VI approved and ordered the publication of the Secretariat for Promoting Christian Unity's (SPCU) *Directory Concerning Ecumenical Matters: Part One.* This directed that each national episcopal conference set up "a commission of bishops for ecumenical affairs, assisted by experts." One of the commission's functions is "dialogue and consultation with the leaders and ecumenical councils" of other Christian Communions in the nation.[4]

Personal and organizational contacts with other Christian Communions during Vatican II, especially through their delegated observers to the Council, helped to initiate a variegated series of international and national *bilateral* theological dialogues with Orthodox, Anglicans and Protestants, and *multilateral,* conciliar faith and order studies with Catholic participation.

On the international level, the Vatican SPCU established joint dialogue commissions with the Lutheran World Federation (1965), the Anglican Communion (1966), the World Methodist Council (1966), the World Alliance of Reformed Churches (1968), some Pentecostal Churches (1970), and the Disciples of Christ (1977). Upon the joint initiative of Pope Paul VI and Patriarch Dimitrios I, preparatory commissions were established (December 1975). Their work led to a Joint Catholic-Orthodox Commission for Theological Dialogue, which first met in plenary, May 1980.[5]

The first annual meeting of the Joint Working Group between the World Council of Churches and the Roman Catholic Church was held in 1966, and by 1968 twelve Catholic theologians had become full members of the WCC Faith and Order Commission.

In the United States, the Catholic hierarchy had already taken such initiative in 1964, when it established the Bishops' Committee for Ecumenical and Interreligious Affairs (BCEIA). Besides its general functions of fostering relations with other Christian Communions and of advising and assisting dioceses in developing ecumenical policies and programs, the BCEIA has engaged in several bilateral dialogues, most of them ongoing: with Anglicans (1965), American Baptists (1967–72), Southern Baptist (1978), Disciples of Christ (1967–73), Lutherans (1965), Eastern Orthodox (1965), Oriental Orthodox (1978), United Methodist (1966), Presbyterian and Reformed (1965), and the Polish National Catholic Church (1985). Roman Catholic theologians have been full members of the Faith and Order Commission of the National Council of Churches since 1968.[6]

As these U.S. dialogues progress or conclude, joint statements are issued and published, but these are scattered in various brochures and books, or are isolated in journals. This volume in the series *Ecumenical Documents* collects, for the first time, most of these statements, with references to more complete findings elsewhere.

Theological Context

The Catholic development is informed by biblical and historical understandings of the nature of the Church as the people of God, the sacrament of Christ's presence on earth, and the communion of the faithful by the power of the Spirit. The experience of Orthodox, Anglican and Protestant Christians in the World Council of Churches is also an important resource for clarifying these ecclesiological principles of the tradition found in Scripture and Christian history.[7] For the Catholic Church, theology and church union have a unique priority, as they did in the founding of the World Council, without prejudice to spiritual and missional ecumenism. This means that church-to-church ecumenism and bilateral dialogue is as important as conciliar collaboration in multilateral dialogue and mission.

As the documents in this volume show, both of these approaches have been fruitful. They not only support church unity efforts, but they also reconcile differences in the approaches to mission, ethics, and ecumenical priorities.[8] Both conciliar and bilateral dialogue are resources for the Catholic spiritual and educational renewal that will be necessary for full participation in the ecumenical movement.[9]

The question of how the Roman Catholic Church will respond to ecumenical proposals has been an element in its ecclesiological development. Three moments describe a trajectory in the evolution of the Catholic Church's response to its ecumenical responsibilities.

(1) The Roman Catholic Church has come to understand itself as a communion of churches in full communion with each other and in communion with the Bishop of Rome. Although the role of the Bishop of Rome is central in the communion, by the principle of collegiality local churches and their bishops have an integrity within that communion. Bishops' conferences, the Synod of Bishops, and a new code of canon law (1983) attempt to move toward the conciliar theology of communion and collegiality. In the ecumenical sphere, the local bishop and the Bishop of Rome have special, differentiated responsibilities for supporting and promoting the unity of the Church. Over thirty-three national and regional councils of churches include Roman Catholic participants.[10] In the early 1970's a recommendation was

made by representatives of the Vatican and the World Council that bishops' conferences (and WCC member churches) be involved in evaluating proposals for Catholic membership in the World Council. At that time bishops' conferences were not involved, and the decision was deferred.[11]

(2) When the Anglican Roman Catholic *Final Report* was issued in 1981, there was some discussion as to whether the evaluation would be made solely in the Vatican or whether bishops' conferences also would be involved. Bishops' conferences have been asked to respond to this international dialogue, and some, like the U.S. bishops, have asked for a Synod of Bishops on the ecumenical issue. Before the bishops' conferences had the opportunity to formulate their responses, the Congregation of the Doctrine of the Faith provided its initial contribution to the process.

(3) When the World Council of Churches' document *Baptism, Eucharist and Ministry* (1982) was submitted to the Catholic Church for response, it was distributed for response to the bishops' conferences. The formulation of the final, unified Roman Catholic response to the World Council has included all appropriate elements of the Roman Curia.[12] This evolution itself indicates a certain level of reception of both the ecumenical commitment and the role of renewed collegial structure in the Catholic Church.

Ecumenism and the U.S. Church

The documents in this volume indicate another aspect of the experience of collegiality emerging in the theology of the local church. In various contexts around the world the Catholic community experiences different manifestations of the unities and divisions among churches. For this reason, initiatives of individual theologians, of local ecumenical groups, and of bishops' conferences in communion with Rome all provide resources for the worldwide Catholic Church in its quest for visible unity.

The U.S.A. provides the stimulus for certain initiatives, such as common theological labors, the experience of pluralism and liberty, and a polarized ethical context. Europe, the home of the Reformation and Counter-Reformation, where decades of war have forged a common mind, creates a different set of resources and challenges. The third world, with very different experiences in Asia, Africa and Latin America, inheriting mission histories and approaching the present situation with a variety of different problems, tensions and possibilities, shows other areas of reconciliation. The differences in ecumenical style within local and regional churches not only indicate different content but also illuminate the diversity of methodologies which can potentially contribute to church union. Already some of the documents included here have led the way to progress in World Council and international bilateral discussion.

Response and Reception

For the use of this volume, we offer a few reminders:

1. Before Roman Catholics became partners in bilateral interconfessional dialogues, others had already taken place; for example, between Anglicans and Orthodox, Anglicans and Old Catholics, and Old Catholics and Orthodox. But beginning in the 1960's, a sudden increase of such international and national dialogues joined those which had Roman Catholic participation. The same period witnessed an increase also of faith and order discussions, especially in national and regional councils or conferences of churches, e.g., the National Council of Churches in the USA, the East Asian and All Africa conferences of churches. In these conciliar multilateral studies, Roman Catholics are most often present as members or as consultors.[13]

In their lengthy general introduction to *Growth in Agreement* (Ecumenical Documents II), Harding Meyer and Lukas Vischer outline the reasons and motivations for this increased number of dialogues and the resulting complex network, the principal features and aims of bilateral dialogues, and the needed interaction between these and multilateral conciliar dialogues.[14]

2. Although these church-to-church dialogues are authorized by the respective church authorities who appoint official delegates, the results are not official, that is, they have no authority on their own. They must be submitted directly to the church authorities for their response. These authorities, in turn, differ in the self-understanding of their function, whether on the national or the worldwide levels, e.g., between the United Methodists in the USA and the U.S. Conference of Catholic Bishops; between the World Methodist Council and the Holy See in Rome.

3. Because the Roman Catholic Church believes itself to be spiritually and structurally united as a worldwide communion of local churches in full communion with each other and with the Bishop of Rome, there is a unique bonding between the various national dialogues among themselves and with those which the Holy See directly

and officially sponsors. This relationship is called for especially in those issues which touch upon the faith and order of the Church.

For more than two decades, Roman Catholic attention has focused almost exclusively on the contents of the dialogues, insofar as one could have access to them in their entireties or in brief, often poorly nuanced quasi-summaries in the religious or secular press. The flood of results, even of the U.S. BCEIA-sponsored dialogues, with various degrees of consensus, convergences and agreements about disagreements of historically divisive issues, has only been trickling into the constituencies. "Too much has come too soon for too many." Pastoral leaders themselves are afflicted by the "too much." So now there is far more concern about "reception," that is, the process of disciplined digestion and ownership at all levels of the church's life, thought and practice. Reception is thus far more than an initial response or final approval "from above."

Cardinal Johannes Willebrands, president of the Vatican SPCU, has helped to describe a Roman Catholic understanding of the reception process:

> In Catholic understanding reception can be circumscribed as a process by means of which the People of God, in its differentiated structure and under the guidance of the Holy Spirit, recognize and accept new insights, new witnesses of truth and their forms of expression because they are deemed to be in the line of the apostolic tradition and in harmony with the *sensus fidelium*—the sense of faith living in the whole People of God—of the Church as a whole. Because such witness of new insights and experiences are recognized as authentic elements of apostolicity and catholicity, they basically aim at acceptance and inclusion in the living faith of the Church. The Decree on Ecumenism of Vatican II says that divisions among Christians make it more difficult for the Church to express in actual life her full catholicity in all of its aspects. In its full form reception embraces the official doctrine, its proclamation, the liturgy, the spiritual and ethical life of the faithful, as well as theology as systematic reflection about this complex reality.[15]

Fundamental Consensus

In recent years both Catholics and other Christians have been taking up once again the old question of fundamental consensus—fundamental differences. This had been a Protestant way of looking at the ecumenical situation, but now prominent Roman Catholics are addressing the issue. After all these years of discussion, why have we not made more progress in our ecumenical efforts? Some very hopeful things can be said. When everything is considered, it would seem that more unites us than divides. We are Christians. We hold to common creeds and common sacraments. We have a fundamental consensus. At the same time we admit that differences do exist which seem to reach to the very heart of Christian faith. Yet these differences may have other causes. There may be historical reasons or deep misunderstanding at the root of our divisions. By facing these issues directly we may discover the profound unity that unites us all in Christ and in his Church.

Use of the Dialogues

Each dialogue is unique for each develops out of a unique context. For this reason comparisons between dialogues must be tentative and may often be misleading: (1) Only official documents count. Surveys and individual experiences do not determine the faith. (2) Dialogues do not need to repeat what other dialogues have already investigated. A dialogue may work on the basis of what others may already have discovered in another context with another tradition. (3) Certain traditional phrases are not necessary. Modern phrases may say the same as traditional doctrines but in other words. (4) Dialogues do not intend to legislate for the churches. If read that way, they mislead. They speak *to* the churches, not *for* the churches.

By themselves the documents produced by the dialogues can be abstract and remote. Helps, such as study guides with study questions, are essential. It also makes a great difference if the persons from the dialogue can be present to discuss the materials. Most of all, prayer makes a qualitative difference.

Those who use these documents either by themselves or guiding others will want to be aware of three major resources:

(1) Other volumes in this series:
  - (i) Thomas Stransky and John Sheerin, eds., *Doing the Truth in Charity* (Ecumenical Documents I; New York: Paulist Press, 1982)
  - (ii) Harding Meyer and Lukas Vischer, eds., *Growth in Agreement,* Reports and Agreed Statements of Ecumenical Conversations on a World Level (Ecumenical Documents II;

New York/Ramsey, Geneva: Paulist Press/World Council of Churches, 1982)

(iii) E.J. Stormon, S.J., ed., *Towards the Healing of Schism:* The Sees of Rome and Constantinople (Ecumenical Documents III: New York: Paulist Press, 1987)

(2) J.F. Puglisi and S.J. Voicu, eds., *A Bibliography of Interchurch and Interconfessional Theological Dialogues* (Rome: Centro Pro Unione, 1984)

(3) Ruth Rouse and Stephen Charles Neill, eds., *A History of the Ecumenical Movement,* Vol. I, 1517–1948 (Geneva: World Council of Churches, 1987); Harold E. Fey, ed., *A History of the Ecumenical Movement:* The Ecumenical Advance, Vol. II, 1948–1968 (Geneva: World Council of Churches, 1987)

Other dialogues have contributed internationally. They are not included here in order to make available the widest spectrum of dialogues produced in the United States.[16]

A word of appreciation is in order for John Hotchkin and John Sheerin who began this project, and to Robert Huston, Robert Torbet, Robert Welsh, Thomas Stransky, and Richard Harmon who contributed background materials.

Footnotes

1. Thomas Stransky and John Sheerin, eds., *Doing the Truth in Charity* (New York: Paulist Press, 1982); Johannes Willebrands, "Vatican II's Ecclesiology of Communion," *Origins,* 17:2 (May 28, 1987) 27–32.

2. Thomas Stransky, "Surprises and Fears of Ecumenism: Twenty Years After Vatican II," *America,* 154:3 (January 25, 1986), 44–48; Jeffrey Gros, "Ecumenism: Steps Forward, Steps Backward," *The Priest,* 43:3 (March 1987) 11–19.

3. *The Local Church: Proceedings, Catholic Theological Society of America,* Thirty-Sixth Annual Convention, Cincinnati, OH, 1981, Vol. 36, *In Each Place: Toward a Fellowship of Local Churches Truly United* (Geneva: World Council of Churches, 1977); Robert Schreiter, *Constructing Local Theologies* (Maryknoll, NY: Orbis Books, 1984).

4. Thomas Stransky and John Sheerin, *op. cit.,* p. 44.

5. E.J. Stormon, S.J., ed., *Towards the Healing of Schism:* The Sees of Rome and Constantinople (Ecumenical Documents III; New York: Paulist Press, 1987).

6. "Ecumenical Dialogues," *Catholic Almanac* (Huntington, IN: Our Sunday Visitor Press, 1987) pp. 281–290.

7. W.A. Visser't Hooft, *The Genesis and Formation of the World Council of Churches* (Geneva: World Council of Churches, 1982); Hans-Georg Link, ed., *Apostolic Faith Today: A Handbook for Study* (Geneva: World Council of Churches, 1985).

8. "The Quest for Christian Consensus: A Study of Bilateral Theological Dialogue in the Ecumenical Movement," *Journal of Ecumenical Studies* 23:3 (1986); *Midstream,* 25:3 (July 1986).

9. National Association of Diocesan Ecumenical Officers (NADEO), *Baptism, Eucharist and Ministry: Initial Reactions from Roman Catholic Dioceses in the United States* (1986); National Association of Diocesan (RC) Ecumenical Officers, *Educating for Unity:* "A Survey Concerning Diocesan Ecumenical Leadership" (1979); "A Survey of Ecumenical and Interfaith Education in Catholic Seminaries" (1982); "A Survey of Professional Roman Catholic Educators" (1983) (Research and Development Committee: 4807 Staunton Avenue, Charleston, W.VA 25304-1951); Episcopal Diocesean Ecumenical Officers (EDEO)/NADEO Standing Committee, *What in the World?* (1987), *Who in the World?* (1986), *Food for the Journey* (1985), *Progress Report* (1984), *The Five Year Report* (1983), *Pastoral Care for ARC Couples* (1982), *ARC Marriages* (1981), *A Study of ARC Covenants* (1980), *A Survey of ARC Covenants* (1979) (1818 Coal Place SE, Albuquerque, NM 87106).

10. "Synthesis of Responses to A Questionnaire on Ecumenical Formation and Collaboration in the Local Church," *Information Service* (IS), 59 (1985) 53–70. (This regular publication from The Secretariat for Promoting Christian Unity provides consistent documentation of official Roman Catholic ecumenical activity worldwide.)

11. Thomas F. Stransky, C.S.P., "A Basis Beyond the Basis: Roman Catholic/World Council of Churches Collaboration," *The Ecumenical Review,* Vol. 37, #2 (April 1985) pp. 213–222.

12. "Baptism, Eucharist and Ministry: An Appraisal" Vatican Response to WCC Document, *Origins,* Vol. 17: No. 23 (November 19, 1987).

13. Among some of these dialogues are: Church of Scotland and the Roman Catholic Church in Scotland, *Inter-Church Marriage* (1980); Lutheran-Roman Catholic Dialogue in Australia, *Sacrament and Sacrifice* (1985); *Reform und Anerkennung kirchlicher Aemter. Ein Memorandum der Arbeitsbemeinschaft oekumenischer Universitaetsinstitute* (Munich: Kaiser, 1973) 13–25; "Final Report of the Joint Ecumenical Commission to Examine the Condemnations of the Sixteenth Century" (Maria Laach, 1985) to be published by Fortress Press; *Ecumenical Dialogue in Europe: The Ecumenical Conversations at Les Dombes (1937–1955)* Ecumenical Studies in History 6 (London: Lutterworth Press, 1966); Pamela Gaughan, trans., Group of Les Dombes, *Toward a Common Eucharistic Faith* (London: SPCK, 1973); Group Les Dombes, "Towards a Reconciliation of Ministries: Points of Agreement between Roman Catholics and Protestants," *Modern Ecumenical Documents* (London: SPCK, 1975) 94–107; Group of Les Dombes, "The Episcopal Ministry: Reflections and proposals concerning the ministry of vigilance and unity in the particular church," *One in Christ* (1978) 14:3, 167–288; F.P. Coleman, "Forty Years on the Groupe des Dombes," *Faith and Unity* (1977) 21, 34–35, Lukas Vischer, *National Gefuehrte Dialogue von Roemisch-Katholischen und Reformiert-Presbyterianischen Kirchen* to be published by the World Alliance of Reformed Churches.

14. Harding Meyer and Lukas Vischer, eds., *Growth in Agreement,* Reports and Agreed Statements of Ecumenical Conversations on a World Level (Ecumenical Documents II; New York/Ramsey, Geneva: Paulist Press/World Council of Churches, 1982), p. 1.

15. Johannes Willebrands, "Address to the Lutheran Church in America," July 3, 1984 (available from the Evangelical Lutheran Church in America, 8765 West Higgins Road, Chicago, IL 60631); "The Ecumenical Dialogue and Its Reception," *Bulletin Centro Pro Unione* 27 (1985).

16. "Agreement Between the Lutheran Church and the Roman Catholic Church, Philippines," *Lutheran World* 20 (1973), 68–70. Felix Neefjes and Jesus Hortal, "25 Anos De Dialogo Catolico-Luterano No Brasil," *Comunicado Mensal Conferencia Nacional dos Bispos do Brasil* 355 (Abril 1982) 395–401, "Ato De Reconhecimento Oficial E Bilateral Da Administracao do Sacramento do Batismo" (Porto Alegre, 12 de Novembro de 1979). Caribbean Conference of Churches, Ecuadorian Episcopal Conference and Latin American Council of Churches, "Communique to Our Churches from the Consultation on Contemporary Religious Movements and Their Challenge to Our Churches" (Cuenca, Ecuador, November 1986). The proceedings of the Ecumenical

Association of Third World Theologians have all been published by Orbis Press, New York: Kofi Appiah-Kubi and Sergio Torres, eds., *African Theology En Route* (1979); Virginia Fabella, *Asia's Struggle for Full Humanity* (1980); Sergio Torres and John Eagleson, eds., *The Challenge of Basic Christian Communities* (1981); Virginia Fabella and Sergio Torres, eds., *Irruption of the Third World: Challenge to Theology* (1983) and *Doing Theology in a Divided World* (1985); cf. James H. Cone, "Ecumenical Association of Third World Theologians," *Ecumenical Trends* 14:8 (September 1986), 119–122. Cf. also Leonardo Boff, *Ecclesiogenesis* (New York: Orbis, 1986); Consejo Episcopal Latinoamericano, *Otra Iglesia en la Base?* (Bogota: CELAM, 1984).

ANGLICAN–ROMAN CATHOLIC DIALOGUES

Introduction

The Episcopal Church entered the colonies as the Church of England with the earliest English settlers in Jamestown, Virginia, 1607. After the American Revolution it became autonomous as "The Protestant Episcopal Church in the United States of America," and adopted that name at its first General Convention in 1789. "The Episcopal Church" has become the official alternate name.

Samuel Seabury of Connecticut was elected the first bishop and in 1784 was consecrated in Aberdeen by bishops of the Scottish Episcopal Church. The Church suffered severe setbacks in the immediate post-Revolution years because of its former association with the British Crown and its number of clergy and prominent laymen who had been Loyalists. Nevertheless, the Church soon established its own identity and mission. It spread westward from the original colonies into the newly settled territories of the United States. The Episcopal Church also undertook missionary work in Africa, Latin America, and the Far East. Today the overseas dioceses are developing into independent provinces of the Anglican Communion, which is the worldwide fellowship of churches in communion with the See of Canterbury.

The beliefs and practices of the Episcopal Church, like those of other Anglican Churches, are both Catholic and Reformed. Bishops in the apostolic succession and the historic Creeds of Christendom are regarded as central elements of faith and order, along with the primary authority of Holy Scripture and the two chief Sacraments of Baptism and Eucharist.[1]

Anglican-Roman Catholic relations take on a unique character as a result of the historic claims of the Anglican Communion, and the contacts between the two churches that predate the initiatives of the Second Vatican Council. The common declarations between the Popes and the Archbishops of Canterbury and their interchange of letters about even very sensitive issues demonstrates the maturity of this relationship.[2]

Since 1965, the U.S. dialogue has met about every eighteen months with up to ten persons on each team. An extensive selection of documents on Anglican-Roman Catholic relationships, including all of the main reports from ARCUSA, have been published in *Called to Full Unity* (1986).[3] We publish here only the key reports. Numerous studies and study guides are also available.[4] An evaluation of Anglican relations with other communions in the U.S. was published in 1979.[5] In preparation for the 1988 Lambeth Conference, the Anglicans have produced a synthesis of their own ecumenical responses, including that to the international ARCIC *Final Report*.[6] The Diocesan Ecumenical Officers of these two churches in the United States have thoroughly studied ecumenical relationships on the local level.[7]

We publish here the careful analysis of ARC's work and its results (the "Twelve Year Report") and a previous report on methodology.

Notes

1. This and subsequent introductions are condensed and drawn from: Constant Jacquet, ed., *Yearbook of American and Canadian Churches* (Nashville: Abingdon Press, 1988).

2. Thomas Stransky and John Sheerin, eds., *Doing The Truth in Charity* (New York: Paulist Press, 1982), 253–268.

3. Witmer, Joseph W. and J.R. Wright, eds., *Called to Full Unity. Documents on Anglican-Roman Catholic Relations 1966–1983* (Washington, D.C.: United States Catholic Conference, 1986).

4. Mullaly, L. and J. Osgood, eds., *Anglican-Roman Catholic Inter-Parish Dialogue: Participant's Guide for Use in Anglican-Roman Catholic Inter-Parish Dialogue* (Garrison, NY: Graymoor Ecumenical Institute, 1979). Mullaly, L. and J. Osgood, eds., *A Call to Communion: Documents of the International Anglican-Roman Catholic Dialogue, 1966–1977 with Study Guides* (Garrison, NY: Graymoor Ecumenical Institute, 1979). Ryan, H.J., "Ordained Ministry in Anglican-Roman Catholic Dialogue," *Diakonia* 7 (1972) 182–191. Ryan, H.J. "The Roman Catholic Vision of Visible Unity," in *A Communion of Communions: One Eucharistic Fellowship* (J. Robert Wright, ed.: New York: Seabury, 1979) 120–29. Ryan, H.J. and J.R. Wright, eds., *Episcopalians and Roman Catholics: Can They Ever Get Together?* (Denville: Dimension Books, 1972). Vogel, A.A., "Epilogue: In the United States," *Rome and Canterbury through Four Centuries. A study of the relations between the Church of Rome and the Anglican Churches, 1530–1973* (New York: Seabury, 1975) 364–87.

5. Griffiss, James E., chair, with Richard A. Norris, John H. Rodgers, J. Robert Wright, and William A. Norgren, "Where Are We Now? The Major Ecumenical Dialogues of the Episcopal Church. Theological Analysis," in *A Communion of Communions: One Eucharistic Fellowship* (J. Robert Wright, ed.; New York: Seabury, 1979) 67–119 (77–88).

6. Anglican Consultative Council, *The Emmaus Report* (Cincinnati: Forward Movement Press, 1987).

7. Episcopal Diocesan Ecumenical Officers (EDEO)/NADEO Standing Committee, *What in the World?* (1987), *Who in the World?* (1986), *Food For the Journey* (1985), *Progress Report* (1984), *The Five Year Report* (1983), *Pastoral Care for ARC Couples* (1982), *ARC Marriages* (1981), *A Study of ARC Covenants* (1980), *A Survey of ARC Covenants* (1979) (1818 Coal Place SE, Albuquerque, NM 87106).

Doctrinal Agreement and Christian Unity:

Methodological Considerations[1]

"We are all to come to unity in our faith and in our knowledge of the Son of God, until we become the perfect Man, mature with the fullness of Christ himself" (Eph 4:13 BJ).

With its call to unity in truth and to living the truth in love, the Epistle to the Ephesians depicts the Christian life as the growth of a body to maturity or, in another passage, as the erection of a building whose cornerstone is Christ. The goal is a completeness, a perfection, a fullness that lies ahead and toward which each Christian and the Christian fellowship as a whole must grow.

Ecumenical dialogue among separated Christians is a part of this process of growth. Its aim is not to produce a statement of minimum essentials by which one Church can measure the orthodoxy of another, but to deepen, strengthen, and enrich the life of both. As Vatican II declares in the Constitution on Divine Revelation: "There is growth in the understanding of the realities and the words which have been handed down. . . . As the centuries succeed one another, the Church constantly moves toward the fullness of divine truth until the words of God reach their complete fulfillment in her" (*Dei Verbum* 8).

Churches coming out of the isolation imposed by the divisions of the past find that they are able to contribute to each other's growth in the fullness of divine truth. But unless the origins and purposes of theological discourse are rightly understood differences in terminology and in modes of conceptualization, due in part to past isolation, can lead to failure of communication and even impasses in doctrinal discussion. Theological discourse must always be interpreted within the horizon of man's experience of the divine mystery because it grows out of that experience. From this it follows that no formal or conceptual statement can ever be fully adequate to the religious data. Because of man's nature, however, his religious experience must come to expression by every means available to him.

Whenever man speaks about the engulfing mystery of God he speaks from within a particular situation—geographical, temporal, cultural, sociological, psychological, linguistic. . . . Because of the transcendence of God's mystery, one must always speak about him symbolically, but these symbols, taken from man's experience of the world, always have the stamp of human particularity. Even statements made by groups of men in representative councils bear this stamp of particularity. For example, when the early councils apply to God and Christ terms such as substance, person, and nature, they are using the terminology and conceptual tools available in a given culture. When these terms in another time and culture take on different connotations their effectiveness for expressing the truths of faith may be impaired. Human discourse even under the working of grace is perspectival and hence also pluralistic.

To acknowledge the relativity of theological statements is not to fall into relativism but to escape it. Because encounter with God always calls man beyond himself it must be recognized that all religious expression may itself be transcended. The abiding presence of the Holy Spirit moves communities of believers to express their life in Christ in ways that may not be abstractly deducible from their previous statements.

The result of the preceding analysis is to recognize that Christians who are orthodox in their faith may express it in varying formulations, as the Bible and the creeds of the early Church so well exemplify. This does not mean that all formulations are equally appropriate. Some may in fact express, and conduce to, a misapprehension of God and his relationship to man, and thus be impediments to the Christian life.

The participants in this dialogue, fortunately, rejoice in the possession of the same Sacred Scriptures, the same creedal formulations of the ancient Church, and a substantial body of shared intellectual and spiritual tradition. They also acknowledge the need for critical scholarship if the meaning of the ancient texts is to be accessible to modern man. There are, however, some other doctrinal formulations which, in the course of a sadly separated history, have been adopted by one communion or the other and are generally seen as obstacles to full communion between the Anglican and Roman Catholic Churches.

In order to promote the cause of full mutual recognition and full ecclesiastical communion, the participants commend the following operative principles in the assessment of whether such divergent formulations do indeed constitute an essential obstacle to full communion:

1. Paradoxical Tension

As previously pointed out, theological language never adequately corresponds to the reality to which it refers. In revelation itself there is always an inherent tension between God's self-disclosure and man's capacity for understanding: human thought and language can never encompass the divine mystery. For this reason there is a peculiar ambiguity in theological statements. The grammatical opposite of a true statement of faith, therefore, may in some sense be also true. E.g., man is—or is not—saved by faith alone; the Bible is—or is not—the word of God.

2. Contextual Transfer

It should be recognized that past doctrinal utterances were made in definite cultural situations that are not our own, and hence that they reflect the presuppositions, terminology, and concerns of their times. This means that a Christian today, in order to be orthodox and to maintain continuity with the tradition expressed in the language of another day, may need to find new language and even new concepts to express the same truth; e.g., the descent into hell.

3. Relative Emphasis

It should be acknowledged that some statements made in the past as "definitions" and imposed under anathema, are no longer insisted upon because, at least today, they do not seem to be of crucial importance in relationship to salvation. E.g., the teaching of the Council of Vienne on the soul as the substantial form of the human body (*DS* 902).

4. Doctrinal Pluralism

(a) Within a single Church one and the same formula often receives different theological interpretations—e.g., the Banesian and Molinist interpretations of the Tridentine canons on grace; the use of the Thirty-Nine Articles in the Church of England. We see these as instances of the principle of comprehensiveness which, rightly understood, involves living in tension and does not admit of easy compromise or superficial syncretism.

(b) Because the same mystery can sometimes be conveyed more effectively by different formulas in different cultural contexts, one may support a variety of theological expressions among different groups of Christians. In Churches entering into full ecclesiastical communion, different creedal formulas are sometimes mutually acknowledged—e.g., the use or omission of the "Filioque" in the agreement between Churches of the East and West at the time of the Council of Florence.

Both these forms of doctrinal diversity should be taken into consideration in assessing the possibilities of overcoming obstacles to union among separated Churches.

5. Empathetic Evaluation

Any Church, in deciding whether it can enter into communion with another, should seek to appraise the role played by the formulations of the other community in the life of that community. One should not condemn all that one would not personally wish to say.

In this connection one may apply the principle of St. Ignatius Loyola, prefixed to the *Spiritual Exercises:* " . . . It is necessary to suppose that every good Christian is more ready to put a good interpretation on another's statement than to condemn it as false. If an orthodox construction cannot be put on a proposition, the one who made it should be asked how he understands it. . . ."

6. Responsive Listening

Since no Church exists by itself in this world, every Church should listen respectfully to what the others find unacceptable in its own formulations, and consider whether its own official doctrinal commitments can be re-expressed in contemporary statements that remove the occasion for offense. In this way the Churches will be of mutual help to one another in their ongoing expression of the faith.

Mindful of the fact that the revelation once for all given to man is the person of Christ present in the Spirit, Christians are called to be faithful to that presence at all times in their living tradition. The foregoing principles should be applied in conformity to that abiding presence, and thus in a way that leads to an ever richer appropriation of the gospel. "So the body grows until it has built itself up in love" (Eph 4:16 BJ).

Notes

1. As part of the work of its eleventh biannual meeting held in New York City, the Anglican-Roman Catholic Consultation in the United States (ARC) unanimously approved this statement on January 23, 1972. The statement is made public in the hope of advancing one of the aims of the *Report of the Anglican-Roman Catholic Joint Preparatory Commission* written at Malta, January 3, 1968. The pertinent section of the "Malta Report" is 5: "We agree that revealed Truth is given in holy Scripture and formulated in dogmatic definitions through thought-forms and language which are historically conditioned. We are encouraged by the growing agreement of theologians in our two Communions on methods of interpreting this historical transmission of revelation. We should examine further and together both the way in which we assent to and apprehend dogmatic truths and the legitimate means of understanding and interpreting them theologically. Although we agree that doctrinal comprehensiveness must have its limits, we believe that diversity has an intrinsic value when used creatively rather than destructively."

Where We Are: A Challenge for the Future

A Twelve Year Report

PREFACE

Having met nineteen times over a twelve-year period, the national consultation of the Episcopal and Roman Catholic Churches in the U.S.A. now issues a report to its sponsoring communities. The report is both a summary of past work and a challenge for future cooperation. The Consultation believes it has discovered a significant and substantial unity of faith between the two Churches, a unity which demands visible expression and testimony now. At the same time, the Consultation honestly recognizes differences which continue to separate the two Churches. In the following pages we present, at this point in our work, conclusions and suggestions to our sponsoring bodies for evaluation, response, and action. We offer direction to the Churches which commission us, but we also seek direction and a continuing mandate from those Churches for the pursuit of the unity God wills for His Church.

The Most Rev. Raymond W. Lessard, Bishop of Savannah
The Rt. Rev. Arthur A. Vogel, Bishop of West Missouri
Co-Chairmen
December, 1977

INTRODUCTION

Since 1965 the Episcopal Church and the Roman Catholic Church have been in officially sponsored dialogue. At the request of these Churches, these meetings have been conducted in this country by the

Anglican-Roman Catholic Consultation in the USA (ARC), whose members have been jointly appointed by the authorities in both Churches. The purpose of these official consultations has been to aid both Churches in realizing together that unity for which Christ prayed.

After 12 years of study ARC contends that the Episcopal Church and the Roman Catholic Church agree at the level of faith on such topics as the Holy Eucharist, Priesthood and Ordination, and the nature and mission of the Church.[1] There is also a common understanding between us of the theological methodology necessary for ecumenical dialogue. Yet agreement even at the level of faith is not always evident in visible expression. The Episcopal and the Roman Catholic Churches differ in their forms of worship, their traditions of spirituality, their styles of theological reflection and in some of their organizational structures of church life. Despite these historically conditioned differences, however, ARC finds after 19 joint consultations that the Episcopal and Roman Catholic Churches share so profound an agreement on the level of faith that these Churches are in fact "sister Churches" in the one *Communio* which is the Church of Christ.[2]

How may this unity in faith be shown? We propose that such unity be given expression in an immediate responding together in the Spirit through Christ to the Father. In this report we suggest specific joint activities which can be undertaken by our two Churches, and we indicate some areas which we think require further investigation.

A. Responding together in the Spirit through Christ to the Father

1. Worship. The ritual patterns in the liturgies of Baptism and Eucharist in both our Churches show that we both understand the Christian life as a response not only to historical events but also to a transcendent reality. In the historical person of Jesus Christ, crucified and risen, the all-holy God is both revealed and glorified by his people on earth. Initiated in Baptism, constantly renewed by repentance, service, and daily prayer, the Christian life finds its core in the worship of the eucharistic community as the apex and source of the Church's mission. Already in 1967 ARC-USA found our two Churches to be in substantial agreement on the meaning of the Eucharistic sacrifice,[3] and in 1972 ARC was happy to record its own endorsement of the ARCIC (Anglican-Roman Catholic International Commission) Windsor agreed statement on the meaning of the Eucharist as the spiritual but real presence of Christ and His sacrifice for us in the consecrated bread and wine.[4] Although there may be occasional differences in secondary matters of theology and practice, we are convinced that the centrality of the Eucharist in the Church's life and work is a major affirmation made by both Anglicans and Roman Catholics in their common faith. A convergence about ritual and worship, as we indicated in our joint statement on the Church's purpose or mission, is evidence in turn of a deeper convergence in faith and doctrine that can readily be discerned from a comparison of our contemporary liturgical texts.[5] It is in the sacrament of the Eucharist above all, and in the eucharistic way of life which flows from it, that we respond together in the Spirit through Christ to the Father.

2. Scripture. Episcopalians and Roman Catholics believe that in the Bible the inspired word of God is expressed: through the Holy Scriptures the living God speaks to us still today. The Bible records Yahweh's self-disclosure throughout Israel's religious history and his definitive revelation in Christ Jesus, the Word made flesh, attested by the living faith of the early Christian communities. Both the Episcopal and Roman Catholic Churches hold that the collection of New Testament canonical writings, properly understood in their literary forms, is historically trustworthy concerning the life, death, and resurrection of Jesus and is permanently normative[6] for the life and faith of the Christian Church. To help comprehend the meaning of Scripture the Episcopal and Roman Catholic Churches endorse and utilize historical, critical methods of exegesis.[7]

However, it is the conviction of both our Churches that the task of understanding the Bible and the biblical faith does not cease with the establishment of the historical context of a given text, section, or verse of the Bible. Biblical faith is a living response to the living God revealed in the Bible. Thus, appreciating how Scripture has been utilized to articulate the Church's living faith in its worship, preaching, spirituality, and outreach is also part of the task of understanding the biblical message.

3. Articulation of the Faith. Both Anglicans and Roman Catholics, we are convinced, share all the basic doctrines of classical Catholic Christianity and view them as normative for the Church's continuous living tradition. Neither of our Churches conceives of doctrine as developing in isolation from scriptural foundation or from historical and cultural forms of thought and speech. We both believe that one reason why the Church cherishes, studies, and teaches the whole canon of Sacred Scripture is so that articulation of the faith may be formed from it and reformed by it. Yet we also both maintain that doctrines do not remain verbally static—in a vacuum, so to speak—apart from the various thought patterns, historical factors, and modes of interpretation that produced them at a given time and that guide the Church, under the Holy Spirit, along its course.[8] The Church fathers, liturgy and devotion, catholic creeds, ecumenical councils, papal statements, theological reflections, scriptural exegesis, "sense of the faithful," and concrete decisions of the Church in every age, among other factors, all contribute to that dynamic process which in both our Churches is collectively called tradition.

Over these past 12 years the agenda of ARC has tended to concentrate on those points of doctrine that have divided us in the past—the Eucharist, the ordained ministry, and the question of authority. But in the process of investigating our respective beliefs on these points, as well as in preparing our agreed statement on the Church's purpose and mission, we have become increasingly conscious of the very great body of fundamental doctrine that our churches have inherited in common and still share with little or no divergence between us. We both affirm the Trinity of God as Father, Son, and Spirit. We both confess Jesus Christ as true God and true man in accord with the formula of Chalcedonian Christology.[9] Much ecclesiology in both our churches is the same: the Church is the mystical body of Christ, its structure of authority is truly episcopal, and its purpose is proclamation, worship, and service.[10] We both recognize Baptism and the Eucharist as the basic sacraments of Christian life, often called necessary to salvation. In both our traditions confirmation, penance, matrimony, orders, and the unction of the sick are also considered to be authentic sacramental means of grace, appropriate to specific situations in life.[11]

Further, the whole Christian view of the world may properly be called sacramental inasmuch as outward and material appearances conceal and at the same time reveal inward and spiritual realities visible to the eyes of faith. We also hold that faith is inseparable from hope, because for the Christian death itself is in the hands of a loving God and the final destiny by all human kind has already been anticipated in the resurrection of Christ. It is in this perspective that many of the faithful in our two Churches have found inspiration in countless holy men and women, among whom are the Virgin Mary, the apostles and the martyrs, and all the saints already sharing the divine glory in the Risen Christ.

We are painfully aware, of course, that no summary of the doctrine which our Churches hold in common can be thoroughly adequate. The foregoing has been only a brief attempt to survey some of the highlights, and our Consultation stands prepared to investigate any other areas which may be of concern to our respective communities. We do both share the conviction that not all doctrinal truths are of the same order of importance,[12] however, and although neither of us has yet spelled out this order with exact precision it is the firm belief of ARC that the doctrines of Trinity, Christology, sacraments, ecclesiology, and eschatology are of the highest order in the faith of each of our Churches. To be sure, our verbal formulations of these doctrines may have differed from time to time over the centuries, but we in ARC judge that the methodological considerations already set forth in our agreed statement on "Doctrinal Agreement and Christian Unity" show that these differences are less important than what our Churches hold in common.[13] The object of our faith is not the earthen vessels but the treasure which they contain, and we have become convinced from our papers, investigations, and conversations over the past 12 years that substantial agreement does exist between us at the level of faith and doctrine.

4. Relations of Bishops to Worldwide Church. The structure of authority as it is understood in each of our Churches is obviously undergoing considerable scrutiny, analysis, and clarification at present. In view of the diversity of Church structures that were operative within the New Testament churches and in view of an imminent expectation of our Lord's second coming at that time, it seems impossible for scholars in both our Churches to prove on historical grounds alone that Jesus himself intended any one particular structure of authority to be determinative and normative for all earthly time. Yet neither of our Churches has been or is willing to conclude from this observation that questions of authority and structure are unimportant. Even the substantial agreement on the Eucharist in the Windsor statement has ecclesial implications for the problem of authority since the Church is there considered as eucharistic community.[14]

In fact, we both share a common tradition of theological reflection, extending over many centuries and rooted both in Holy Scripture and in the ancient fathers, concerning the basic structures of authority necessary for the Church to pursue its mission. We both agree, moreover, that the structure of authority cannot be static, that its renewal involves and always has involved a forward development and not merely a backward return to some pristine *status quo,* and that in every age the Church must conceive its structure of authority not as a self-giving end but rather as a means of proclaiming the Gospel and serving the Church's mission. This measure of agreement, our Consultation believes, led ARCIC to affirm, in its Canterbury statement on Ministry and Ordination in December of 1973, that an essential element in the earliest ministry of the Church is that of the ancient term *episcopé,* meaning "oversight," which involves "fidelity to the apostolic faith, its embodiment in the life of the Church today, and its transmission to the Church of tomorrow."[15] ARC has previously recorded substantial agreement with the Canterbury statement,[16] and we do not propose to reiterate its contents here.

We do note, however, that beginning with the time of the Reformation in the Sixteenth Century, our two Churches placed differing emphases upon the expression and interpretation of this ministry of *episcopé.* For Roman Catholics, this episcopal ministry was increasingly centered in the Bishop of Rome and its nature has appeared to be too authoritarian in the eyes of many Anglicans. For Anglicans, on the other hand, the ministry of bishops has been less centralized and the nature of their authority has appeared too vague and indefinite in the eyes of many Roman Catholics. At the same time, over the past few centuries each of our Churches has continued to grow and develop in its own separate way without the benefit of close contact or conversation with the other.

Yet in the last decade or so, thanks to a movement of change which we are entirely unable to explain apart from the providence of God, deeper understandings and fresh perspectives about the nature of *episcopé* among both Anglicans and Roman Catholics have led many of us to suspect that perhaps we are not so far apart as we seemed and indeed that perhaps we are in fact growing closer together even on this very basic question. We do both affirm, after all, that the fundamental structure of the Church should be "episcopal." In the past many Roman Catholics have seen an Anglican tendency to impose excessive constitutional limitations on the episcopal office. Many Anglicans in the past have seen a Roman Catholic tendency to impose excessive papal controls on the episcopal office. Yet both structures are in their very nature *vere episcopalis,* that is, "truly episcopal." Some Anglicans now seem increasingly convinced of the need for a greater degree of worldwide organization and focus, not only for the sake of doctrinal and liturgical cohesion but also in order to facilitate the Church's work of evangelization and service. Some Roman Catholics seem increasingly concerned to recognize and indeed protect a greater degree of local self-government, individual expression, and plurality of theological affirmation within their various regions, episcopal conferences, and even dioceses and parishes.

Neither of our Churches is entirely certain how present structures will be affected in the future, but ARC-USA is convinced that an empathetic evaluation of our past histories and present situations, an effort to enter into the experience of the other Church and to understand what lies behind its formulations and customs, will enable us both to work together and learn from each other. Our joint statement on "Doctrinal Agreement and Christian Unity: Methodological Considerations" proposes some principles for such a serious effort towards mutual understanding.[17]

In particular, on the question of the way in which bishops in their individual dioceses serve and relate to the worldwide mission of the universal Church, ARC believes that a certain degree of convergence may be developing between Episcopalians and Roman Catholics about the ministry of the Bishop of Rome. It is a ministry of service to his fellow bishops as well as to other Christian churches.[18] The "Synod of Bishops," for example, is a structure of recent evolution in the Roman Catholic Church that encourages us to look at the papal ministry to and with other bishops in new perspectives as a "truly episcopal" office. Among the proposals for pastoral action concluding this report we suggest a study by ARC and also the naming of a joint task force of bishops to facilitate our greater cooperation and mutual understanding of the question: What are the structures of episcopal ministry that will best enable our bishops to care for all the churches by teaching, leading, and serving the Church and peoples in the Christian life for our day?

The relation of bishops to one another and of the Bishop of Rome to other bishops, we may add, should in no way detract from the ministry bishops also share with priests, deacons, and lay people. The co-responsibility of all the people of God, both in the deliberations and in the decision-making process of the Church, which received renewed emphasis for Roman Catholics in the Second Vatican Council, has long been a concept of vital importance to Anglicans and is now another aspect of convergence that both our Churches share.

While the Roman Communion has given increased importance to national and regional councils of bishops, with other forms of decentralization, history has required Anglicanism to develop means of closer communication and cohesion as a world communion. In this further example of convergence, the two churches have moved toward each other from different starting points.

The Archbishop of Canterbury, during the worldwide expansion of the Anglican Communion in the nineteenth century, instituted, as *primus inter pares,* the custom of inviting his brother bishops to Lambeth Palace every ten years to take counsel together on matters of common concern in faith, morals, and the mission of the Church. The first such conference met in 1867.

Though the Lambeth Conferences do not claim synodical authority, they have had great influence on the life of the Communion. As the Anglican Communion grew and separate national churches were formed, more organized ways of maintaining relationships of mutual support and communication were needed. In 1968, 101 years after the first meeting, the Lambeth Conference created the Anglican Consultative Council (ACC) to meet this need.

The ACC includes bishops from all the Anglican provinces and, recognizing that priests and lay people share the ministry of Christ along with bishops, also includes the representatives of these orders in its membership. Each province or national church is encouraged to identify the current goals of mission among its dioceses and to take counsel with representatives of other Anglican provinces for ways of mutual support, providing money and personnel from the stronger provinces for those that need help. These "Partners in Mission" conferences, as they are called, began in the younger churches and then expanded into similar conferences in the older churches concerning help they needed from the younger ones. Carrying out its assigned task of enabling Anglicans "to fulfill their common inter-Anglican and ecumenical responsibilities in promoting the unity, renewal, and mission of Christ's Church,"[19] the ACC assisted inter-Anglican communication among the churches on the question of ordination of women opened by the 1968 Lambeth Conference.

At its most recent meeting, in 1976, the ACC devoted much of its report to current trends in ecumenism. Such new terms as "visible unity" and "conciliarity" seem to be opening a way to a different idea of Christian unity from the older concept of one monolithic church in each city, province, and nation. This line of thought, the report noted,[20] appeared to show convergence with Roman Catholic thinking on the *communio* model of church-to-church relationships.

5. *Ethics of the Christian Community.* The people of the Old Testament were made a unique community by the covenant God established with them. As that community, they led a visible, corporate life of witness to Yahweh. The New Covenant established in Christ, through his life, death, and resurrection, forms of a new community. By Baptism the believer enters this community of visible, corporate witness to Christ. "But you are a chosen race, a royal priesthood, a

consecrated nation, a people set apart to sing the praises of God who called you out of the darkness into his wonderful light. Once you were not a people at all and now you are the People of God; once you were outside the mercy and now you have been given mercy." (I Peter 2: 9–10)

The Christian witness of worship in the Spirit through Christ to the Father involves the entire Church in a corporate response of love and service both to God and to the whole of humankind. Such response is sometimes simply called the "Christian life-style."

The Christian life-style is based on the belief that the Triune God has redeemed all creation in Christ. Because God has first loved us, as a people as well as individually, so must we as Christians corporately and individually express our love for God and for each human being. Upon the corporate or social character of the Trinity's redemptive action for the whole human family the morality of the Christian community is built. Christian life or the Christian life-style begins as a covenant response of a people witnessing to God's love in Christ. Therefore in Christian ethics there is a primacy given to the social or corporate character of life in Christ.

Episcopalians and Roman Catholics agree on the primacy given to the corporate witness of the Christian life-style. Both agree that the Church as Church has a responsibility of compassionate service to the whole of humankind, to manifest in the Spirit the Father's love shown us in Christ Jesus. How the individual Christian appropriates to himself or herself what the Church proposes as the Christian life-style has been and is a source of apparent discrepancies between the Episcopal and Roman Catholic Churches.

Christians living in the world of today are confronted with a confusing array of philosophies and values. These touch upon what it means to be a human person. Consequently new questions have risen in related areas such as human sexuality, marriage, and the family. In this kind of situation diversity in the manner of forming Christian conscience—a traditional difficulty between Roman Catholics and Episcopalians—is exacerbated as both Churches grapple separately to find what is the proper Christian response to the new questions. Though both Episcopalians and Roman Catholics hold that the ultimate subjective norm of morality is the properly informed individual conscience and therefore share the same solution to many moral problems, there is insufficient agreement as yet between them in facing the new and serious questions now before the Christian community. The initial studies made of these questions by Episcopal and Roman Catholic theologians indicate answers that are not in agreement with one another. In this situation for both our Churches pastoral responsibility is all the more arduous as Christians find it increasingly difficult to reach certitude among the conflicting answers suggested to these troubling questions. Thus dialogue between the Episcopal and Roman Catholic Churches is urgently required in this new area of growing disagreement.

6. Personal Life in Christ. Episcopalians and Roman Catholics believe that the relationship of Jesus with his heavenly Father is both the summit and model of the spiritual life. To be a Christian today is to believe that through the Spirit an individual now can also somehow share Jesus' self-giving love leading through the Cross to the glory of the Resurrection.

Because the human nature of Jesus is uniquely related to the Second Person of the Blessed Trinity, Jesus is both true God and true man, "consubstantial" with the Father and "consubstantial" with us. The hypostatic union of the human nature of Christ and the Word or *Logos* in no way prevents Jesus' experience of God from being truly human. It is Jesus' relationship with God that the Christian religion seeks to convey to all human beings. "He became what we are in order that He might bring us to be even what He is."[22]

Jesus' relation with God the Father is communicated to Christians in many ways. Among these are the reading and study of Scripture, meditation on the mysteries of salvation, and the devotional exercises of the Christian life. The eucharistic liturgy, with its renewed emphasis on the proclamation of the word of God, and its celebration of the presence of Christ, is regarded in both our traditions as "the summit toward which the activity of the Church is directed; at the same time it is the fountain from which all her power flows."[23] It is in liturgical worship, and especially in the eucharistic celebration, that the Christian as a member of the community worshipping the transcendent and indwelling God can realize the deepest implications of what it is to be a person, find the impetus for ethical action in the Christian style, and learn the destiny to which one is called by God in Christ through the Spirit.

Human beings live in a world that is ever changing. Christian doctrine and the visible social structure of the Christian Church are therefore necessary in order for Christians living in a world of change to discern, communicate, adapt, and transmit through different times and cultures their historical identity in Jesus as Lord and Saviour. Christians believe that this process of adaptive continuity springs from the Spirit's abiding in the Church and from the charisms that the Spirit brings.

B. Conclusion: Pastoral Recommendations

Part I. Areas for Further Investigation
ARC's Proposals for Future Agenda

ARC asks of its sponsoring bodies whether it should study the following problem areas:

1. In view of the ARCIC statement, "Authority in the Church" and recent papers prepared for ARC on authority, the episcopacy, and papacy, we now see the possibility, after some further investigation, of drawing up a set of mutual affirmations about the ministry of the Bishop of Rome. There are points on which we believe there may well be substantial agreement between the Episcopal and Roman Catholic Churches and which should therefore be drafted on paper for further consideration by our respective bodies and authorities. Should such a statement on authority, however, be limited to more theoretical questions touching the pope and other bishops, or should it extend to more practical realities—such as the way in which Episcopalians are treating the issue of women's ordination and the way in which the recommendations of the Detroit "Call to Action" conference are being handled by Roman Catholics?

2. In view of the growing claims of Christian women for full participation and partnership with men in the life of the church and the world—a fact of contemporary life—we now recommend a study of the new and perplexing questions which arise for both our Churches. Behind the issues of changing sex roles in family and work and the still deeply divisive questions raised around the ordination of women to the presbyteral and episcopal ministries, lie fundamental theological issues. The imaging language of Fatherhood and Sonship in Christian theology and devotion has shaped our experience of God and ordained ministry as well as our experience of ourselves as women and men in relationship to each other and to God. Other images for the Holy are to be found, such as Bride, Queen, Mother, Nurturer. A careful study of the role of Mary, of other female saints, of sexual imagery for God, the Church and its ministries, and the soul, may provide important theological and spiritual guidance for our Churches today as we wrestle with the common perplexities raised by these issues of human wholeness (holiness), what it means to be a woman and a man, and how men and women image God in their being and their callings in the Church and the world.[24]

3. In view of apparent discrepancies concerning the formation of conscience in the Christian community as well as the resolution of certain moral questions in both our Churches, we recommend an inves-

tigation of the relation between normative tradition and individual conscience in our respective Churches. The relative weight that is given to the tradition of the earliest Christian centuries, as well as that given to the faith of the Church at present, in the way that consciences are formed and educated for life in Christ in each of our Churches, should be compared and then related to such current questions as abortion and the right to life, the pastoral approach to ecumenical marriages, and homosexuality.

4. In view of the particularly close relationship that both our Churches share with each other,[25] we recommend a study of the degree of unity that each of us feels necessary as prerequisite to sacramental sharing, and how each Church intends to relate this convergence between us to the ongoing ecumenical relations each of us has in many other ecumenical dialogues.[26] Must a closer relationship and even sacramental sharing between us be delayed until all Anglicans and all Roman Catholics throughout the world agree on every point that the other thinks is important, or is it possible that our growing together and sacramental sharing may be allowed to develop differently in different places? In view of the present situation, what can be said about Pope Leo XIII's *Apostolicae Curae* (1896) and the validity of Anglican Orders that will satisfy both Anglicans and Roman Catholics?

Part II. Joint Task Forces:
ARC's Proposals for Possible Action

ARC asks its sponsoring bodies whether ARC should now proceed to establish, with their authorization, any of the following:

1. Joint Task Force on World Hunger. This problem received the highest priority rating from Episcopalian diocesan ecumenical officers in their survey of February 1976 and was emphatically underlined by Pope Paul VI in his message to the International Eucharistic Congress at Philadelphia in August of the same year. What can our two Churches do together now to face this problem? There could be a joint task force of experts in social witness to be convened by our respective authorities. Possibilities: Joint letter from our bishops to our peoples, posters, conference of experts, raising of consciousness, meatless days every week, periods of fasting and abstinence, congressional legislation, etc.

2. Joint Task Force on the Apostolate of the Church or Evangelism. This task force would embody a common thrust in mission to which Archbishop Coggan and Pope Paul VI have jointly called us.[27] The task force could: 1) look carefully at the mission of the Christian Church to so present "Jesus Christ, in the power of the Holy Spirit, in such ways that persons may be led to believe in Him as Saviour and follow Him as Lord, within the fellowship of His Church"[28]; 2) compare the ways in which this is understood, implemented, and described in both Churches; and 3) recommend ways in which there could be a greater partnership in this common missionary imperative.

3. Joint Task Force on Prayer and Spirituality. The existing calendars of prayer in our two Churches, now based upon very similar liturgical years, might be enriched through the choice of special days for appropriate intercessions that would draw us more deeply into our common mission. Also, opportunities for a shared ministry of the word, through preaching, might profitably be explored. Persons gifted in spirituality, prayer, and liturgy, and other persons placed in positions of leadership might be convened. Perhaps a booklet might be published jointly for widespread distribution and use.

4. Joint Task Force to Survey ARC Covenants. Many of these already exist, between parishes, dioceses, seminaries, etc.[29] Their positive accomplishments, their shortcomings and misgivings, their goals and needs, should be studied. This task force should include clergy and laity from groups already in covenant relationships.

5. Joint Task Force on the Pastoral Role of Bishops. We propose a study and report on the similarities and differences in episcopal ministry between our two Churches. This task force, consisting of six or eight bishops, would be named by the Presiding Bishop of the Episcopal Church and the President of the National Conference of Catholic Bishops. How do our bishops see their roles in worship, evangelization, proclamation of the gospel, and service to the clergy and laity, as well as their relation and responsibility to the universal Church? This report should be published for the benefit of the general membership of both our Churches.

Notes

1. The major printed source for official documentation of ARC-USA and of the Anglican-Roman Catholic International Commission (ARCIC) is the series of three booklets entitled *Documents on Anglican/Roman Catholic Relations* (ARC/DOC I, II, and III), published in 1972, 1973, and 1976 by the U.S. Catholic Conference, 1312 Massachusetts Avenue, N.W., Washington, D.C. 20005. ARC's "warm approval" of the 1971 ARCIC Windsor statement on the Eucharist is recorded in ARC/DOC II, pp. 54–156, and the statement itself is printed in ARC/DOC I, pp. 47–50. ARC's "substantial agreement" with the 1973 ARCIC Canterbury statement on Ministry and Ordination is recorded in ARC/DOC III, pp. 82–84, and the statement itself is printed on pp. 74–81. ARC's own statement on theological methodology for use in ecumenical discussion (1972) is printed on pp. 49–53 of ARC/DOC II, and its statement on the nature and

mission of the Church (1975) is on pp. 1–11 of ARC/DOC III. Much of this documentation is also published in *Ecumenical Trends* (Graymoor Ecumenical Institute, Garrison, N.Y. 10524) and in the *Ecumenical Bulletin* (Episcopal Church Center, 815 Second Avenue, N.Y.C. 10017).

2. Cf. Pope Paul VI, 25 October 1970: "There will be no seeking to lessen the legitimate prestige and the worthy patrimony of piety and usage proper to the Anglican Church when the Roman Catholic Church—this humble 'Servant of the servants of God'—is able to embrace her ever beloved sister in the one authentic Communion of the family of Christ: a communion of origin and of faith, a communion of priesthood and of rule, a communion of the saints in the freedom of love of the spirit of Jesus." (ARC/DOC I, pp. 42–43).

3. ARC/DOC I, pp. 3–4.

4. ARC/DOC II, pp. 54–56.

5. ARC/DOC III, pp. 1–11.

6. Cf. ARCIC 1976 Venice statement on Authority in the Church, para. 2.

7. Vatican Council II, Dogmatic Constitution on Divine Revelation *(Dei verbum)* 12, ed. Abbott p. 120; Decree on Priestly Formation *(Optatam totius)* 16, ed. Abbott p. 451. Cf. *Proposed Book of Common Prayer* (Episcopal Church), pp. 853, 888 ff., 934 ff.

8. ARCIC Venice statement, para. 15; 1972 ARC statement on Doctrinal Agreement and Christian Unity: Methodological Considerations, esp. paras. 2, 3, and 4 (ARC/DOC II, pp. 51–52).

9. Common Declaration of the Pope and the Archbishop of Canterbury signed in Rome, 29 April 1977, para. 2, published, among other places, in the *Ecumenical Bulletin* no. 24 (July–August 1977), p. 9. For the Chalcedonian text, cf. *Proposed Book of Common Prayer,* p. 864. It is acknowledged that some theologians of both our Churches, as well as others, are calling for restatement, reformulation, reinterpretation, or, in some cases, even rejection of the Chalcedonian terminology. For some Roman Catholic views, see W. Kasper, *Jesus the Christ;* Hans Küng, *On Being a Christian;* Gerald O'Collins, S.J., *What Are They Saying about Jesus;* K. Rahner, various articles on Christology in *Theological Investigations* vols. 1, 3, 4, 5, 7, 8, 9, and 10; P. Schoonenberg, *The Christ;* B. Vawter, *This Man Jesus.* For some Anglican views, see William Temple, *Christus Veritas;* Richard A. Norris, "Towards a Contemporary Interpretation of the Chalcedonian Definition," in *Lux in Lumine: Essays to Honor W. Norman Pittenger;* E.R. Hardy, "Chalcedon in the Anglican Tradition," and David Jenkins, "The Bearing of Chalcedon upon the Modern Discussions about the 'Humanum' and the Secular," both in *The Ecumenical Review* xxii:4 (Oct. 1970); Maurice Wiles, *The Remaking of Christian Doctrine;* J.A.T. Robinson, *The Human Face of God.*

10. ARC 1975 statement on the Purpose of the Church, paras. 10–16 (ARC/DOC III, pp. 4–8).

11. *Proposed Book of Common Prayer,* pp. 860–861; Vatican II, Constitution on the Sacred Liturgy *(Sacrosanctum concilium)* 59–82, ed. Abbott pp. 158–163. See also the study entitled *Subscription and Assent to the Thirty-nine Articles* (London, 1968), prepared for the Tenth Lambeth Conference by the Commission on Doctrine appointed by the Archbishops of Canterbury and York.

12. Cf. Vatican II, Decree on Ecumenism *(Unitatis redintegratio)* 11, ed. Abbott p. 354; "When comparing doctrines, *Catholic theologians engaged in ecumenical dialogue* should remember that in Catholic teaching there exists an order or 'hierarchy' of truths, since they vary in their relationship to the foundation of the Christian faith."

13. ARC/DOC II, pp. 49–53.

14. ARC/DOC I, pp. 47–50.

15. Cf. I Timothy 3:1, ARCIC Canterbury statement, para. 9; Arndt and Gingrich, *Greek-English Lexicon of the New Testament,* p. 229; G.W.H. Lampe, *Patristic Greek Lexicon,* p. 532.

16. ARC/DOC III, pp. 82–84.

17. ARC/DOC II, pp. 49–53.

18. See the ecumenical study *Peter in the New Testament,* ed. Raymond E. Brown, Karl P. Donfried, and John Reumann (1973).

19. Lambeth Conference 1968, *Reports and Resolutions,* p. 145 and cf. pp. 46–49.

20. Anglican Consultative Council, *Report of the Third Meeting: Trinidad 1976,* p. 16.

21. Vatican II, Pastoral Constitution on the Church in the Modern World *(Gaudium et spes)* 47–93, ed. Abbott pp. 249–308, and Dogmatic Constitution on the Church *(Lumen gentium)* 11, ed. Abbott p. 29; cf. Lambeth Conference 1968, *Reports and Resolutions,* pp. 78–81.

22. Irenaeus, *Against Heresies,* book V, preface; cf. Athanasius, *On the Incarnation,* 54.

23. Vatican II, Constitution on the Sacred Liturgy *(Sacrosanctum concilium)* 10, ed. Abbott p. 142.

24. Cf. E. McLaughlin, "Christ My Mother: Feminine Naming and Metaphor in Medieval Spirituality," *Nashotah Review* xv (1975), and F. Jelly, O.P., "Marian Dogmas within Vatican II's Hierarchy of Truths," *Marian Studies* xxvii (1976).

25. Common Declaration of the Pope and the Archbishop of Canterbury signed in Rome, 29 April 1977; Vatican II, Decree on Ecumenism *(Unitatis redintegratio)* 13, ed. Abbott p. 356; Pope Paul VI, statement quoted in note 2 above; *Annual Report,* Episcopal Diocesan Ecumenical Officers, 1976 survey of diocesan ecumenical priorities, showed Anglican/Roman Catholic relations "an overwhelming priority in interest and effectiveness" (p. 1).

26. For a survey of these up through 1974 see N. Ehrenstrom and G. Gassmann, *Confessions in Dialogue,* third ed., Geneva 1975. The survey of "Bilateral Conversations between the Roman Catholic Church in the U.S.A. and other Christian Communities" published in the 1972 *Proceedings of the Catholic Theological Society of America* (vol. 27) is now being updated, and a similar survey is under way for the Episcopal Church under the sponsorship of its Standing Ecumenical Commission.

27. Common Declaration, 29 April 1977, para. 9: "Our divisions hinder this witness, hinder the work of Christ, but they do not close all roads we may travel together. In a spirit of prayer and of submission to God's will we must collaborate more earnestly in a 'greater common witness to Christ before the world in the very work of evangelisation.' It is our desire that the means of this collaboration be sought: the increasing spiritual hunger in all parts of God's world invites us to such a common pilgrimage. This collaboration pursued to the limit allowed by truth and loyalty will create the climate in which dialogue and doctrinal convergence can bear fruit."

28. General Convention of the Episcopal Church 1973, definition of evangelism.

29. For specific examples, see ARC/DOC III, pp. 36–58.

BAPTIST–ROMAN CATHOLIC DIALOGUES

Introduction

The many Baptist bodies in the United States have different stories of participation in the ecumenical movement and differing ecumenical priorities.[1] The Roman Catholic Church in the United States has been in dialogue with two of these Baptist bodies.

Originally known as the Northern Baptist Convention, the American Baptist Churches changed the name to American Baptist Convention in 1950, with a commitment to "hold the name in trust for all Christians of like faith and mind who desire to bear witness to the historical Baptist convictions in a framework of cooperative Protestantism." In 1972 it adopted its present name—American Baptist Churches in the USA.

Baptist work at the local level dates back to the organization by Roger Williams of the First Baptist Church in Providence, Rhode Island in 1638. Although national missionary organizational developments had begun in 1814 with the American Baptist Foreign Mission Society and continued with the American Baptist Publication Society in 1924, the denominational body was not formed until 1907.

From 1967 through 1970 the American Baptist Churches and the BCEIA sponsored an annual dialogue. These papers have been published[2] and summarized along with the discussion.[3] Excerpts of a progress report is published here.[4]

The Southern Baptist Convention was organized on May 10, 1845, in Augusta, Georgia. Its purpose is "to provide a general organization for Baptists in the United States and its territories for the promotion of Christian missions at home and abroad and any other objects such as services which it may deem proper and advisable for the furtherance of the Kingdom of God."

Building on a series of regional conferences between Southern Baptists and Roman Catholics between 1974 and 1977[5] and on some local conversations,[6] the Department of Interfaith Witness of the Home Mission Board of the Southern Baptist Convention and the BCEIA sponsored a series of scholars' conversations from 1978 to 1980 on a wide range of issues: Scripture, salvation, spirituality, ministry, evangelization, social action, and eschatology.[7] The second set of conversations (1982–1984) had grace as the theme. The summary of this discussion is published here.[8] The third set (1985–88) dealt with mission. The Southern Baptist Home Mission Board has also published Baptist-Catholic Marriage guidelines.[9]

Notes

1. Cf. W. Jerry Boney and Glenn Igleheart, eds., *Baptists and Ecumenism* (Valley Forge: Judson Press, 1980).

2. John A. Hardon, "Towards an American Baptist-Roman Catholic Dialogue," 150–158, Robert T. Handy, "Areas of Theological Agreement from a Baptist Point of View," *Foundations* (hereafter Fd) (April–June, 1967) 159–172; George Peck, Robert Trisco, "Christian Freedom and Ecclesiastical Authority," Fd (July–September, 1968) 197–226; Robert G. Torbet, John S. Cummins, "The Nature and Communication of Grace," Fd (July–September, 1969) 213–231; Emmet A. Blaes, Lloyd M. Short, "The Role of the Church: A Lay View," Fd (October–December, 1970) 335–353; Robert T. Handy, "Toward a Theology of the Local Church," Robert Trisco, "The Catholic Theology of the Local Church," Fd (January–March, 1972) 53–71; John S. Cummins, L. Doward McBain, "Clergy-Lay Issues and Relations," Fd (April–June, 1972) 146–162; Lloyd M. Short, "Church-State Relations: Viewed by the Baptist Joint Committee on Public Affairs"; Emmet A. Blaes, "The Relationship of Church and State: A Catholic View," Fd (July–September, 1973) 261–278.

3. Robert G. Torbet, *After 450 Years—A New Thing* (Valley Forge, Pa: Office of Ecumenical Relations, American Baptist Churches in the U.S.A., 1973).

4. *Growth in Understanding: A Progress Report on American Baptist–Roman Catholic Dialogue* (Washington: United States Catholic Conference, 1972).

5. Baptist-Catholic Regional Conference, *The Church Inside and Out* (Washington: United States Catholic Conference, 1974); Baptist-Catholic Western Regional Conference, *Conversion to Christ and Life-Long Growth in the Spirit* (Atlanta: Home Mission Board, Southern Baptist Convention, 1976), Southern Baptist-Roman Catholic Midwestern Regional Conference, *The Theology and Experience of Worship* (Washington: US Catholic Conference, 1978).

6. Claude U. Broach, *Issues in Church and State* (Winston-Salem, NC: The Ecumenical Institute of Wake Forest University and Belmont Abbey College, 1976).

7. E. Glenn Hinson, ed., "Issues in Southern Baptist–Roman Catholic Dialogue," *Review and Expositor,* LXXIX:2 (Spring, 1982).

8. James Leo Garrett, ed., "GRACE: Roman Catholic/Southern Baptist Dialogue," *Southwestern Journal of Theology,* 28:2 (Spring, 1986).

9. C. Brownlow Hastings, *Baptist and Roman Catholics in Interfaith Marriage* (Atlanta: Home Mission Board, 1972). A popular summary of all the dialogues (1978–88) with study guides for congregational use is *To Understand Each Other. Roman Catholics and Southern Baptists,* Co-published by *The Theological Educator* (New Orleans Baptist Theological Seminary) and Paulist Press, 1989.

Growing in Understanding

A Progress Report on American Baptist—Roman Catholic Dialogue

We Christians who participated in the dialogue of our respective traditions wish to share with you the experience we have had together over a period of four years. It was an experience that came from the discovery that the same Christ in whom we believe is the Savior to whom others have also committed themselves; and that in Him we share far more than our deeply felt differences would suggest.

This witness to our discovery through dialogue is co-sponsored by the American Baptist Convention's Commission on Christian Unity and the Catholic Bishops' Committee for Ecumenical and Interreligious Affairs, of which we were the chosen representatives. Our full complement was fourteen members whose names appear at the end of this statement for which we alone assume full responsibility.

In order to do some justice to an immense subject, it seemed wise to cover what we consider the five principal phases of our dialogue: its original purpose and summary history, its emerging areas of common understanding and of need for further study, and its effect on us personally and collectively as Christians who are dedicated Baptists and Roman Catholics.

Original Purpose

At the outset it was agreed that our dialogue should enable us to give a more effective witness to Jesus Christ through the removal of misunderstandings and through increased understanding, mutual enrichment and goodwill. Our intention was to share with one another how we understand the Christian faith, its doctrines and certain specific issues from the point of view of our respective traditions. It has not been to press either for consensus or agreement.

A second purpose, but by no means secondary, was to provide

substantive material for our fellow-Christians, to use in local dialogues throughout the country.

Our goal, therefore, was to engage in spiritual and theological conversation with a view to eliminating misconceptions due to a lack of knowledge. It was also to develop fruitful areas of exploration that in the years to come might lead to fuller mutual appreciation and fellowship in the interests of the People of God.

Summary History

Preliminary plans for the dialogue began in 1966 between Dr. Robert G. Torbet, Executive Director of the Division of Cooperative Christianity in the American Baptist Convention and the Most Rev. Joseph Green, then Auxiliary Bishop of Lansing, Michigan, and now the Bishop of Reno, Nevada.

The first meeting was held on April 3–4, 1967, at the Franciscan Retreat House, DeWitt, Michigan. Central to the meeting were two papers, by a Baptist and a Catholic spokesman respectively, each stressing what the two traditions had in common. From the Catholic viewpoint, it was explained that the name "Baptist" is profoundly theological; it expresses the cardinal principle of the Baptist ethos, which is "spiritual liberty" of the person under the leading of the Spirit. Roman Catholicism respects this position. On the Baptist side, note was taken of the shared concern of Baptist ministers and Catholic priests regarding salvation by grace through faith; a marked interest of the Roman Catholic laity in the Baptist stress on the priesthood of all believers; and a growing agreement on the nature of religious freedom.

At our second meeting on April 29–30, 1968, at the American Baptist Assembly, Green Lake, Wisconsin, three topics were explored: a) the relation between believer's baptism and the sacrament of confirmation, b) the nature of Christian freedom in its bearing on ecclesiastical authority, and c) the role of the congregation in the total life of the Church. In each subject, the focus was on the implied dialectic between two different approaches to Christianity, the Baptist and the Catholic understanding of: the initiatory rites for Church entrance and acceptance of responsibility, the exercise and sacrifice of personal liberty, and the biblically or traditionally revealed Christian community.

In the third meeting, at the Holiday Inn, Schiller Park, Illinois, on April 28–29, 1969, we addressed ourselves mainly to a single subject, "The Nature and Communication of Grace." Two papers, one from each perspective, were read and discussed. The Catholic stress was on grace as an objective principle of new life in the soul, communicated through the Church and the sacraments. In the Baptist presentation, grace was described as the spontaneous manifestation of God's mercy, emphasizing the mediation of grace in the word rather than through the sacraments.

In our fourth meeting, April 17–18, 1970, at St. Benedict's Abbey, Atchison, Kansas, two of the lay members of the dialogue presented their side of the ecumenical story. Their papers made clear how devoted are many lay people to the Church, but how minimally their talents and resources have been utilized. The Baptist statement reflected an inter-faith approach and pointed to the current tension between two competing roles of the Church, as sanctuary for the word of God and as activist collaborator in society. The Catholic speaker told what the faithful are looking for: to have priests and religious leaders who are up to date in the spirit of the Second Vatican Council, yet primarily responsive to the people's spiritual needs; and to give the laity far more opportunity to serve the Church in every possible capacity.

Emerging Areas of Common Understanding

There were far more areas on which we found either substantial agreement or the prospect of a wider harmony than we had ever expected. It seems more accurate to speak of areas than of specific doctrines because in many cases it became apparent that our different backgrounds made it next to impossible to express agreement in the same terms. What we often lacked, therefore, was a common vocabulary, even though we sensed that the inner faith was sometimes closer than the words at our disposal could articulate.

Thus we found the source of authority in the Triune God, the Father, Son, and Holy Spirit, who communicated Himself in a unique way to the Church in the Scriptures of the Old and New Testaments. The Baptists are coming to see that there has been a mutual influence over the centuries between the Scriptures and Christian experience. Both of these elements, in turn, have affected our understanding of God's message to His people; they have also been affected by the continual teaching of the Holy Spirit in the community of faith. Catholics, on their part, are realizing better than they had previously understood how fundamental to Christian revelation is the Bible as the inspired *word* of God, where not only the content but also the expression are believed to have been shaped under the influence of the Holy Spirit.

We also discovered common ground in recognizing that there is no salvation except by grace through faith that comes as a gift from God. From a Baptist viewpoint, those who possess the faith are believers and in that sense they are also sharers in the priesthood of Christ. This universal priesthood of the faithful gives the laity a dignity that is becoming more respected in Catholic circles, without threatening the status of the ordained priests and bishops in the Roman Catholic Church.

Moreover, we came to see that having the faith is one thing, but the desire and will to share it is something else. There was a mutual concern with the concept of the Church as mission, as a community of faithful who respond to Christ's sending them into the world to share His riches with others.

In spite of our vastly different histories, we learned that Catholics as well as Baptists have been extraordinarily convinced of Christ's words that we are to give Caesar only what belongs to Caesar, but to God what belongs to God. Religious freedom, which in practice generally means spiritual liberty from political encroachment, is part of both our ancestries. We have both been deeply concerned over the Gospel teaching that the rights of God take precedence over the dictates of man; that Christians "must obey God rather than man." And in both our traditions have been those who have suffered much because of our convictions.

Although we might define grace differently, yet we agreed on the biblical affirmation that grace is a divine favor, somehow far beyond our human claims and undeserving to us as sinners. On the delicate question of how grace is communicated, we came to admit that—along with grave differences on such issues as sacramental efficacy—God uses the community of faith to channel His favor to mankind. Whether the object of this favor is a baptized infant or a baptized believer, the grace each receives is given to nurture and sustain his relationship with God and foster solidarity through charity with his fellow men.

Both communions appear to be seeking a fuller realization of the meaning of the Church. Many Baptists are endeavoring to develop a more corporate, ecclesiastical emphasis; Catholics are striving to develop a larger measure of parochial and personal liberty within the existing church structure. The latter were pleasantly surprised to hear that "the complete independence of a local congregation was foreign to early Baptists," that "in the associations which they formed, they gave expression to their belief in the reality of the church universal to which all true Christians belong, and they confessed their need of the wider fellowship for purposes of mutual assistance, counsel and fulfillment of the Great Commission." The Baptists, on their part, were surprised at the broad understanding of the word "Christian" voiced by the Second Vatican Council. "All those justified by faith," says the Decree on Ecumenism, "through baptism are incorporated into Christ. They therefore have a right to be honored by the title of Christian and are properly regarded as brothers in the Lord by the sons of the Catholic Church."

Areas That Require Further Study

There is a marked difference between us on the meaning of the sacraments. Roman Catholics profess seven sacraments, all believed to have been instituted by Christ, whereas Baptists accept only two, which they prefer to call ordinances. Also, our very understanding of what the sacraments are, and of their role in the economy of salvation differs greatly. In the Catholic tradition, the sacraments are mysteriously effective of the grace which they ritually signify, and in which the faithful have a personal encounter with Christ who confers on them His saving grace. In the Baptist view, the ordinance of baptism is a dramatic emblem to the one baptized of his fellowship in Christ's death and resurrection, and the Lord's Supper is a holy symbol in which bread and wine are used to commemorate together Christ's dying love for mankind. The ordinances do not, however, actually effect or confer the grace which they symbolize.

We correspondingly differ in our approach to the question of how Christ's authority is made explicit in the community of faith. Roman Catholicism sees Christ during His stay on earth as having founded a Church in which He chose twelve apostles, with Peter at their head, and giving these apostles and their successors under the pope the right to "bind and loose" in His name. Baptists, on the other hand, do not so conceive the Church. They do not hold that God delegated to any person or persons in the Church the right to teach infallibly in His name, nor to bind the human conscience in moral matters. Even when they recognize that, "for the Christian, authority in matters of faith and practice has *de facto* always been located in some form of the Church," they do not identify within the Church any hierarchical order which has the divine right to teach and guide the faithful authoritatively in Christ's name.

We also approach the subject of Church membership and incorporation into its body differently. Catholics view membership more as the result of baptism, which explains their practice of baptizing infants. Baptists regard a person's profession of trustful faith and repentance as fundamental to Church affiliation. In the expression "believers' baptism," their stress is on *believers,* since for them the Church is a gathered community of those who believe in Jesus Christ; it is through confident belief in the Savior that a person enters the Church's fellowship.

A further difference between us concerns the Catholic sacrament of confirmation, absent in the Baptist tradition. Baptists find it difficult to distinguish adequately between where baptism of the infant ends and confirmation begins. They wonder whether it would not be possible to restore the ancient catechumenate and the re-linking of baptism with confirmation.

Characteristic of Baptist theology is the view of many scholars who favor a "declared" or imputed righteousness, which comes to those who are justified while they still remain sinners. It was asked whether this concept should not be set alongside of the incarnational view of the Church which sees Christians, once baptized, as a "pilgrim people" in a process of sanctification. Those who favor this view trace its origins to the *devotio moderna* of pre-reformation times.

Touching on the same issue, but in the practical order, Baptists and Catholics face a common problem regarding baptism and dedication to the Church. For Baptists, the problem is the status of the child before baptism. Is the child in the Church or not and, more crucially, what is the Church's responsibility toward those born into Christian families who are not yet baptized? On the Catholic side, there is a crisis affecting those who had, indeed, been baptized in infancy but never perhaps made a personal decision for Christ and commitment to the Church. Might not the two communions seek together a form of baptism (or a ritual of initiation) which would make more meaningful the rite of Christian incorporation into Christ?

An uncharted field for united action between Catholics and Baptists lies open in areas of social concern. Family instability and racism, alcoholism and drug addiction, an escalating crime rate and pornography, abortion and artificial contraception, pacifism and militarism, affluence and poverty, are typical issues. Such issues have deep theoretical presuppositions. How can ecumenical conversations about the theology of these premises strengthen us to cooperate in responsible action to help solve the problems which beset our country?

Summary Statement of the Second Triennium in the Dialogue Between Southern Baptist and Roman Catholic Scholars (1982–1984)

The general topic for this triennium of meetings was the life of grace within us and it consisted of three general areas: (1) an introduction to the issues; (2) beginning in grace; and (3) growing in grace. Particular topics included: [A] Roman Catholic and Southern Baptist conceptions of the notion of grace itself, [B] the ways in which divine grace is communicated to us, [C] Southern Baptist and Roman Catholic understandings of the relationship between divine grace and human nature, [D] the relationship of baptism and the Lord's Supper to the initiation and renewal of the life of grace, [E] discipleship as the unfolding of the life of grace, and [F] the communion of saints as our belonging to a community of grace.

The purpose of the dialogue has been that we might grow in mutual understanding of the relationships between our two Christian traditions. Both groups have learned that, despite the different vocabularies we use in presenting and explaining our beliefs, we share a basic understanding of what it means to be a follower of Jesus Christ. There are also differences which exist among us. For example, we have different views concerning the mediation of God's grace, different emphases in our preaching, different ways of manifesting faith in our forms of public worship, and different evaluations of the presence of God's saving grace within the other world religions. We have not inherited an identical theological language for speaking about grace. The following points describe some measure of the agreement we have reached on the topic of grace, but we also note those positions on which we disagree.

[A] Both groups agree upon the normative role of scripture in coming to understand the notion of grace. We have also found that it is much easier to describe grace in functional terms than to develop a precise theoretical definition. We seem to agree that grace is experienced both through creation and through redemption, and that the personal God meets us in personal ways. We all believe in the pervasiveness of grace. The graciousness of God toward the world is revealed in the work of creation, in the original blessing pronounced upon creation when "God saw that it was good" (Gen. 1:12, 18, 21, 25, 31). That graciousness continues in salvation history and its ultimate triumph will appear when Christ returns in glory.

Salvation is God's gift, and so too is the very offering of salvation to human beings. In offering us salvation, God thereby calls us to obedience. And so, since the possibility of responding to God is also a result of grace, God empowers us to respond to divine goodness through the obedience of faith. In our daily living, we experience grace in many ways, but central to our experience of grace is the awareness that we are loved sinners: We are conscious of our sinfulness and we are also conscious of God's love.

We are unable to agree on the appropriate conceptual language to use in talking about grace. While we agree that the grace which comes to us is the saving grace of Christ, for God's grace comes to us in and through Jesus, we do not have a common understanding of how grace is mediated. We also disagree about the extent to which a Christian may have the assurance of saving grace. Furthermore, we have not been able to develop a mutually satisfying description of what it means to be human both before and after a saving experience of grace.

[B] Since God relates to creation in personal ways, as scripture abundantly testifies, grace can be described as God's self-giving to human beings. God's predisposition toward creation is thoroughly gracious; this has been revealed to us through God's faithfulness throughout human history. Divine fidelity reached its highest expression in the mystery of the incarnation, that is, through the Word which became flesh in the birth and life, the teaching and healing, the suffering, death, and resurrection of Jesus; in short, through the whole Christ-event.

We agree that grace can be described from various perspectives. This description may legitimately draw upon concepts and expressions which are scriptural, historical (i.e., patristic, medieval, reformationist, etc.), philosophical, existential, or psychological. (We came to realize that any discussion of the mediacy and immediacy of grace requires language which is precise and often technical; it may also run into the realm of epistemology or theories of how knowing occurs. For the basic question is not simply whether grace is experienced mediately or immediately; one has to settle whether and to what degree our knowledge of anything can ever be immediate, that is, directly intuited.)

While Southern Baptists and Roman Catholics have their particular vocabularies for describing and explaining grace, together we hold that the experience underlying those categories is the experience of being loved and accepted by God in Jesus Christ. We hold further that the Church, that is, the body of Christ or people of God, expresses the grace of Christ in an important way. Being received into the believing community and taking responsibility for building and perpetuating the community of Jesus are themselves aspects of grace. In the experience of being church, therefore, God meets us in a personal and communal way.

[C] Both groups prefer to speak about the fullness of Christian life in terms of process, for the life of grace involves our continually growing in faith, hope, and love. Christian life, we believe, begins at a particular point in the history of a human being. While Southern Baptists tend to emphasize the individual aspect of sin and grace and Roman Catholics tend to stress the social dimension, both groups struggle to maintain a balance between the individual and the corporate aspects of sin and grace. Both groups emphasize the importance of personal freedom in the human response to grace and the working out of one's salvation. Although we may disagree about the meaning of the sinfulness of all humanity, we hold in common the view that all people share the human condition of alienation from God and yet that each person bears individual responsibility for his or her own rejection or reception of God's saving grace. Jesus Christ, of course, the one who was like us in all things except sin (cf. Heb. 4:15), did not share this condition of alienation. For Roman Catholics, neither did Mary, the one who was "highly favored" (cf. Luke 1:28). But whereas our understandings of the sin of Adam (which is often referred to as "original sin") are different, we agree that this sin does not entail personal guilt. In other words, God does not hold us individually responsible for the sin of our first parents. Both groups insist upon the essential role which Jesus Christ occupies in the mystery of salvation (cf. Col. 1:15–20), although we differ in our understanding of how individual believers actually experience the saving grace which is Christ.

Both groups agree that the baptism of believing people testifies to a prior experience of grace (whether this consisted of a single experience or several), for it is God's grace which prompts a person to faith and to baptism. "No one can come to me," Jesus said, "unless the Father who sent me draws him" (John 6:44). In addition, Roman Catholics believe that baptism, as a sacrament, is also a means of grace. For them, baptism not only confirms that grace is already present in a person's heart, but baptism can also be a moment when grace is experienced in a new way. A complication arises, however, when we consider the question of God's presence within those people of other world faiths. Roman Catholics and Southern Baptists have different opinions of God's relationship to human beings who have never known Jesus. We assess differently the status of those who have not believed in Christ.

[D] Baptism and the Lord's Supper are events in the life of a believing Christian community, and they are celebrated in obedience to the Lord's example and command. Jesus himself received baptism from John (Mark 1:9), Jesus commissioned his followers to baptize in his name (Matt. 28:19–20), and he charged his disciples at the Last Supper to break bread and share the cup in his memory (1 Cor. 11:23–26). Both groups agree that it is not the individual but the community, in fidelity to scripture, which determines the meanings of baptism and the Lord's Supper. While we recognize that salvation begins with God's saving grace accepted in faith, formal entrance into the church is marked by water baptism in the name of the Father, and of the Son, and of the Holy Spirit. Southern Baptists baptize by immersion. Roman Catholics ordinarily baptize by the pouring of water over the believer's head or by immersion; they also recognize baptism by sprinkling. Both groups acknowledge that the paradigm or theological norm of Christian initiation is the baptism of mature, free, responsible believers. Nevertheless, Roman Catholic practice for pastoral reasons allows for the baptism of infants, while Southern Baptist practice does not. Furthermore, both groups hold that authentic Christian baptism, in principle, can be received only once. Roman Catholics will not rebaptize on the grounds that it is Christ who baptizes through his minister; thus the church guarantees the genuineness of baptism, not the individual. Most Southern Baptists defend the practice of "rebaptism" on the grounds that a previous baptism would not be genuine if a person had not truly professed faith.

We attach different significance to the elements of the Lord's Supper, that is to say, to the bread and wine of communion. Both groups agree that the celebration of the Lord's Supper, or eucharist, includes the memorializing of Jesus' passion and death, the proclamation of his resurrection and ascension, and the anticipation of his return for the gathering of the faithful into glory. But Catholics would add that, through the power of the Spirit, bread and wine actually become the body and blood of Christ, thus enabling a unique mode of Christ's real presence to the community.

[E] Together we believe that Jesus continues today to call men and women to be his disciples, just as he did before his death and resurrection. Scripture, as the Word of God, presents the response to Jesus' call which is normative for our contemporary understanding of discipleship. Roman Catholics and Southern Baptists realize that there are various patterns of discipleship, but for both of us discipleship always includes participation in church life, prayer and worship, a distinctively Christian ethic, service to others, and witness to the Gospel. We both speak of discipleship as the following or imitation of Christ. For Catholics, this has represented a tradition of modeling one's life according to the teaching and example of Jesus. For Baptists, the imitation of Christ is used in a more general sense to refer to living the Christ-like life, as, for instance, the Apostle Paul did (cf. 1 Cor. 11:1 and 1 Thess. 1:6). For both groups, central to the imitation of Christ is following the way of the cross.

The term "community of disciples" has been recently used as an additional designation for the church among Roman Catholics, and the term is not commonly used among Southern Baptists. However, "community of disciples" is an acceptable description of the Church for both groups, and this term could serve as a helpful theological category for furthering mutual understanding and communion. We believe that Jesus calls us, as the community of his disciples, to share with each other our practice of discipleship. By such sharing, differences among Christians might eventually be transcended and divisions, where they exist, might be healed so that all people one day should hear more clearly Jesus' call to follow him.

From our discussion of discipleship, we realize that three areas need further investigation: the relation of the Twelve to the disciples of the New Testament, the relation between discipleship and apostleship, and the continuing significance of these relationships.

[F] The life of grace is personal, though not private; it necessarily assumes a corporate dimension. Human holiness, we agree, is a gracious gift of the Spirit of God; this Spirit transforms men and women into the likeness of Christ. Holiness is God's gift not only to individuals but also to the church. Those in whom and through whom God's gracious love has been manifested throughout the ages serve as models and examples to inspire faith and courage among later generations of believers. Those who are drawn into the community of disciples have an obligation to support and to minister to one another in loving service.

Southern Baptists and Roman Catholics do not agree upon the twofold meaning which historically has been attached to the notion of communion. Southern Baptists and Roman Catholics alike use the term "communion" to refer to the Lord's Supper or eucharist. Baptists, however, more commonly use the word "communion" to describe the real, personal union which exists between Christ and his disciples, and among the disciples in his Spirit. For Catholics, the eucharist as sign and source of union both expresses and helps to create personal communion between believers and the Lord, and among believers in the Spirit.

In addition, we disagree on the practice of invoking Mary and the saints in our prayer to God. Catholics believe that this form of piety, as an implication of its belief in the communion of saints, is both sound and meaningful because the saints bring into the heavenly church their loving concern for the welfare of those in the pilgrim church. In giving his mother to the care of the beloved disciple (cf. John 19:26–27), Jesus, according to Catholic sensibility, was giving his mother to each of us and each of us to her. Baptists reject prayer to Mary and the saints on the grounds that it compromises the sole mediatorship of Christ, since "there is salvation in no one else, for there is no other name under heaven given among men by which we must be saved" (Acts 4:12); the invocation of the saints is unnecessary in a relationship of grace with God.

Nevertheless, we agree that the concept of the communion of saints is biblical, although this term is not explicitly used in scripture. The life of grace draws people into a communion or fellowship which is grounded in the union of the people of God with the risen Christ; this communion is brought to expression through the Spirit. Moreover, this communion brings us into a spiritual bond with men and women of every age who truly profess Jesus as Lord, however imperfectly such communion has been manifested.

On the note of communion, then, this second triennium of the dialogue has come to a close. The conversation between Christians of various churches must continue if Jesus' prayer for his disciples which we find in the seventeenth chapter of John's gospel is to be realized. Such conversation, we believe, is a work of faith. One eventually discovers that ecumenical dialogue, much like Abraham's call from God to go "to the land that I will show you" (Gen. 12:1), often winds along paths which one did not initially envision. Insight into one another's faith, the realization of how important Jesus has been for us personally, the desire to join with one another as Jesus' disciples in prayer, in service to the world, and in mission, are all fruits of the Spirit.

The topic of our third triennium of talks is mission, since this seems to follow naturally and appropriately from our consideration of the life of grace. After all, the empowering source of grace for Christians is the Spirit of Jesus, for it was this Spirit whom the early community of disciples was awaiting, the "promise of the Father" (Luke 24:49), the Holy Spirit who empowered the disciples to witness to Jesus "in Jerusalem and in all Judea and Samaria and to the end of the earth" (Acts 1:8). It is the fervent prayer and hope of those of us who have been involved in the Southern Baptist/Roman Catholic Scholars dialogue that the Spirit who has begun such a good work among us will bring it to completion.

DISCIPLES OF CHRIST–ROMAN CATHOLIC DIALOGUES

Introduction

Born on the American frontier in the early 1800s as a movement to unify Christians, the Christian Church (Disciples of Christ) drew its major inspiration from Thomas and Alexander Campbell in western Pennsylvania and Barton W. Stone in Kentucky. Developing separately for a quarter of a century, the "Disciples," under Alexander Campbell, and the "Christians," led by Stone, united in Lexington, Kentucky, in 1832.

This Church is marked by informality, openness, individualism and diversity. The Disciples claim no official doctrine or dogma. Membership is granted after a simple statement of belief in Jesus Christ and baptism by immersion—although most congregations accept transfers of those baptized by other forms in other denominations. The Lord's Supper—generally called Communion—is open to Christians of all traditions. The practice is weekly Communion, although no church law insists upon it. The local congregation remains autonomous.

The dialogues in this volume began in 1967. The background papers have been published, a summary report of which is here.[1] The U.S. experience became the basis for the Roman Catholic dialogue with the International Convention of Christian Churches (Disciples of Christ) in 1977.[2]

Notes

1. "Bilateral Conversations Between Catholics and Disciples," *Midstream* (Winter, 1967–68) 7:2; "Further Bilateral Conversations Between Catholics and Disciples," *Midstream* (Winter, Spring, Summer, 1973) 12:2,3,4.

2. Roman Catholic/Disciples of Christ Dialogue, *IS,* "Report of Dialogue between the Catholic Church and the Disciples of Christ, 1977–1981," 1982, 49:II,III, 65–73; 1985, 59:III,IV, 42. "Papers and Reports for the Disciples of Christ-Roman Catholic International Commission for Dialogue, 1984–1985," *Midstream,* 25:4 (October, 1986) 339–429.

Summary Memorandum

April 29–May 1, 1968
St. Louis, Missouri

At our third consultation, April 29–May 1, 1968, as representatives of the Committee for Ecumenical and Interreligious Affairs of the National Conference of Catholic Bishops and of the Council on Christian Unity of the Christian Churches (Disciples of Christ), we have been meeting in St. Louis, Missouri, to discuss "A Responsible Theology for Eucharistic Intercommunion in a Divided Church." In listening to two papers, one presented by a member of each church, and in frank and extensive discussion we have come not only to a better understanding of each other, but also of ourselves. We can say the following things together:

1. The act given to the Church by our Lord Jesus Christ and variously known as the Eucharist, Communion, and the Lord's Supper, is the highest expression of unity within the Church. Through it we remember the death and resurrection of Jesus Christ, experience his presence among us as the living and saving Lord of the Church, and have a foretaste of the community which God pledges to mankind.

2. Since we all have been baptized into this community, we have a given unity in the Lord Jesus Christ which our unhappy divisions have not been able to destroy. We eagerly press forward to the fullness of unity that Christ desires and its tangible realization in the world which he came to save.

3. Through the bread which he proclaimed to be his body broken for us and the fruit of the vine which he described as "my blood of the covenant, which is poured out for many," we experience a union with him and with one another. Even when we celebrate the Eucharist separately, we are aware that we are in communion with the same Lord, and, therefore, in union with one another.

4. The Scriptures describe the Eucharist for each of us, and we have discovered that our understandings of the Lord's Supper are more similar than we had expected.

5. Each of our churches gathers at least every Sunday around the Table of our Lord. We mutually recognize that the bond of Christian community and the power of Christian life are centered upon Eucharistic celebration. For both of us the nature of the Church is discernible principally in the fellowship of the Lord's Supper.

6. In our respective beliefs and churchly self-understandings, and even within the officially expressed statements of our churches at present, we have found sufficient theological justification *in principle* for some eucharistic sharing. Furthermore, we detect that urgent theological, ecumenical and especially pastoral reasons exist in our country to make some eucharistic sharing desirable. We urge our communions to explore as rapidly as possible the circumstances and procedures for responsible eucharistic sharing.

An Adventure in Understanding

1967–1973

Introduction

Six years ago we embarked on an adventure of understanding which did not seem to have great promise of discovery or excitement. The Christian Church (Disciples of Christ) and the Roman Catholic Church on the surface do not appear to have much in common, and because of the great difference in size, age, and practice did not seem to be able to contribute much to one another.

But we were wrong. We have had an exciting time together, and we would share this with the members of our two communions particularly, and any others who are interested in the whole Church. We have already reported to our respective sponsoring bodies, the Committee for Ecumenical and Interreligious Affairs of the National Conference of Catholic Bishops and the Council on Christian Unity of the Christian Church. The papers from which we began our discussions have been, or soon will be, published.

One thing we know. Wherever the future may lead us we can never think of one another in the same way we did in the past. We have come to an appreciation and understanding, admittedly incomplete, but substantial enough to survive any strains or difficulties we may encounter. We know we are brothers in Christ.

We hope this brief report of our adventure will enable you to share in our discoveries and our trust.

Methodology

Our method of dialogue has been more productive of new understandings than the outline of topics, the papers and this summary statement may indicate. The papers were often a springboard for exploration and discovery and we would hope that the reader may catch some of our experiences by probing the arguments of the papers as they are read.

As we talked over these papers with one another, one difference between our ways of thinking about the faith emerged. Catholics speak from a long historical systematic development of thought. The Disciples, being a much younger body, have not developed a systematic theology of their own, and tend to express the faith through more experimental accounts. A refreshing experience for the Catholics was the anecdotal method the Disciples frequently used to convey their thought. Disciples were surprised at the rich divergence within the present Catholic Church.

It should be noted regarding the topics considered that the order was not planned more than one session in advance. What may seem haphazard was due to the fact that we were probing various areas of our common experiences.

Because our two churches have not had historic battles to undo we found an openness to exploring wide ranges of our faith and practice in a relaxed and friendly context. At the same time our common experience in the wider ecumenical movement enriched our dialogue and broadened its perspective. In particular, the enriched understanding of sacrament and ministry which the Disciples had found through their participation in the Consultation on Church Union met with enthusiasm from the Catholic participants.

We can only highlight here the understandings we have reached in our eight sessions through the discussions which followed the papers.

Topics

We began by discussing the *nature of the unity we seek.* It came as some surprise that all participants agreed that if we believe in the incarnation and in the sacramental principle, nothing less than organic constitutional union can be accepted as the will of Christ. This implies more than a spiritual or invisible union, more than cooperation in a biblical scholarship, social action and missionary activity, or membership in councils of churches. Moreover, our participants are in agreement that the fuller manifestation of unity is to be realized in the ongoing stream of history and cannot be found by the recovery or restoration of past forms. It is something to be aspired to in hope and, with the assistance of the Holy Spirit, to be achieved in the historical future.

Eucharist

In our next session we talked about the *Eucharist* as a symbol and agent of unity. We summarized our thoughts this way: "The act given to the Church by Our Lord Jesus Christ and variously known as the Eucharist, Communion, or the Lord's Supper, is the highest expression of the unity of the Church."

At this juncture we refrained from any extensive consideration of doctrinal elaborations regarding the eucharist. However, our dialogue revealed that, from a Scriptural standpoint, our understandings of the Lord's Supper were more similar than we had expected.

Our primary focus was on the understanding of the eucharist as symbol and agent of unity within our respective traditions. We have become intensely aware of the centrality of the eucharist in the life of both of our churches, and we believe it is central for progress toward ecumenical reconciliation among Christians. For us the eucharist defines the Church. We understand ourselves as eucharistic fellowships. The unfailing celebration or observance of the Lord's Supper on the Lord's day and on other significant occasions in both of our churches shows this.

Intercommunion

Our reflection on the eucharist as symbol and agent of unity provided the context for us to consider the problem of intercommunion, the fellowship of the table or eucharistic sharing.

Our dialogue had brought us to a common appreciation of two theological principles drawn from the New Testament Pauline understanding of the eucharist. For Paul, the eucharist is a sign of the unity of the body of Christ which is the Church. Secondly, it is also a means of grace, that is, it is capable of deepening our unity in Christ.

We felt that these two principles could help our churches overcome our separation at the Lord's table. In our judgment, this two-fold biblical understanding of the eucharist as sign *and* agent of unity provides sufficient reason for our churches to work out a provisional solution to the problem of eucharistic sharing.

We are convinced that neither the restrictive policy of the Roman Catholic Church nor the "no question asked" practice of the Disciples adequately respond to the contemporary ecumenical relationship of our churches. Moreover, we believe that more responsive policies could be developed to meet the pastoral needs of our people. It is time for the unilateral policies of our churches to cede to some reciprocal, albeit provisional, policy. We, therefore, urge our proper church bodies to explore as rapidly as possible the circumstances and procedures for responsible eucharistic sharing.

Christian Marriage

The unresolved problems related to the issue of intercommunion turned our attention to the problems which surround mixed marriages. Thus, we decided to discuss the topic of Christian marriage as a matter of pastoral concern.

Both churches recognize marriage as a divinely instituted covenant union, modeled after the Covenant between God and His people. Both understand marriage as blessed by Christ with the possibility of being a sign of Christ's love for His Church and a means of grace for the married couple and their family. On this basis Catholics consider the marriage of two baptized Christians as a sacrament. Although Disciples do not call marriage a sacrament, they nevertheless see, on this basis, the possibility of Christian marriage having a certain sacramentality. Our dialogue on this point made us realize the need at some future date to explore our various understandings of sacrament and the sacramental principle.

We also discovered that in both of our traditions the officiant priest/minister acts as the Church's official witness to the marriage covenant effected by the man and woman.

Our two churches have a conscientious pastoral desire to be supportive of every marriage. Because of the frequency of mixed marriages this calls for a greater cooperation between us. Such cooperation is especially important in counseling before and after marriage, in arranging and celebrating the wedding service, and serving as a reconciling agent between the respective families of the couple.

Ministry

The pastoral concerns about mixed marriages led us to consider in our next conversation the pastoral role of the ministry.

We both found the concerns of our ministry to be the same; training our people in the nature and practice of our Christian faith, developing high ethical standards, cultivating a devotional life, an increase of charity, an awareness of the need for a decent and just social order, and establishing and maintaining a personal pastoral relationship with the people entrusted to our care. Another experience which we share is the problem of defining the role of the priest/minister in the wider community concerns for social causes. This is often a source of contention between the priest/minister and members of his parish.

We commonly see the pastoral ministry as of divine calling to an apostolic service of witness, prophecy, sacrifice, guardianship and intercession. While Disciples would consider the calling to the ministry as direct from God, Catholics understand it as mediated through the Church. We both would model our ministry on the ministry of our Lord and Savior Jesus Christ.

Whereas in the Catholic Church the various ministries or offices are structured in a hierarchical order (pope, bishop, priest, deacon) with an authority and leadership role proper to each, among the Disciples the various offices (pastor, area minister, general minister, elders) are considered as equal, and their relationship to one another is advisory and consultative.

Whereas the Catholic priest and deacon promises obedience to his bishop, the Disciple minister makes no vow of obedience to any human authority. Both of our traditions understand our ministers as under the authority of the revealed word of God.

However, our dialogue noted that the relationship of ministries within our churches is becoming increasingly collegial and consultative. We also noted the enlargement of the ecumenical spirit of our ministries.

It is in the celebration of the Eucharist that the variety and functional diversity of the ministries proper to our traditions become apparent. In the Catholic liturgy the bishop or priest presides, leads the prayer, preaches, celebrates and distributes the eucharist, a deacon may read the Gospel and assist in distributing the communion, and lay readers may read the first two scripture lessons. In the Disciple service, the minister preaches the sermon, offers the prayers and may preside at the Table, although this is usually done by lay elders, with the elements distributed by lay deacons or deaconesses.

Regarding the post-college training of candidates for the ministry, we noted that our seminary students receive a theological training that is very similar in academic outline. One of the differences considered was that the Catholic seminary assumes the responsibility of fostering the personal spiritual development of each candidate within the context of the community. Disciples manifested a keen interest in the formative aspect of Catholic seminary training. Both of our training programs are placing an increasing emphasis on field education.

Another obvious difference is the requirement of celibacy for the Catholic priest, and the general expectation of marriage in the Disciple ministry. We had a fruitful discussion on the advantages of both a celibate and married ministry and came to see values in each.

Parish

After discussing the pastoral ministry we then decided to consider in greater depth the parish in which the ministry is for the most part carried out. This decision was re-inforced by the publication of the proposed Plan of Union of COCU with its new concept of parish which the Disciples were called upon to examine. Both Disciples and Catholics were concerned about maintaining certain values in the parish. The immediate Christian community should be able to minister to every individual in it. At the same time, there should be communities large enough to enable adequate resources to be commanded to meet the individual and social needs which the local church faces.

The development of parish councils and other forms of consultation in the Roman Catholic communion suggests that in the future the Catholic and Disciple or protestant laity may have increasingly similar ways in which their congregations reach decisions. The paralleling of these patterns in parish life may open the way to more successful collaboration and interaction between the congregations of the future.

Baptism

In considering baptism Catholics and Disciples found that both have the same intention in baptism although the manner of baptizing and age of the candidate are quite different. Disciples immerse. Catholics effuse. Disciples baptize persons of the age of consent. Infant baptisms are general practice among Roman Catholics.

Disciples could respond positively to the Catholic emphasis on baptism as incorporation, liberation and empowerment. We both agree that baptism incorporates the baptized into the Church, remits sin and confers the earnest of the Spirit. We believe that it would be possible for Catholics and Disciples to elaborate a common understanding with regard to baptism.

Sin

Since baptism is for the remission of sins we next took up the respective understandings of sin and reconciliation.

We recognized that there are pastoral crises in both our churches regarding the understanding of sin and reconciliation with a consequent development and change in attitude and thought. Members of both churches have an increased awareness of corporate and social sin and a lessened conviction of individual sin. In both churches there is less reliance on pastors as instructors in morals and more reliance on pastors as counselors.

Initially in our conversation the impression was that Disciples were much more optimistic about the remedy of sin than the Catholics because of the conviction that baptism wiped away all sin, whereas Catholics felt the need for recourse to frequent use of the sacrament of penance for reconciliation of post-baptismal sins. For Disciples post-baptismal sins are understood as being forgiven to the penitent at the Lord's Supper, and also whenever the sinner is truly penitent. However, further discussions showed that with the Disciple participants there had been great influence from Reinhold Niebuhr, Paul Tillich and Karl Barth, so that there was a deep realism about the cure of man's sinfulness.

Conclusion

We cannot end this report without stating from our own viewpoint what we have discovered in the other church. These experiences may not fit neatly into an agenda, indeed are by-products rather than direct conclusions from our conversations. But these convictions may be as important as any agreement on topics we have achieved, if not more so.

For the Disciples there has been a heart-warming discovery that the Catholic Church presently takes Scripture with utmost seriousness. This is contrary to our notion before we began our discussions, but we have seen that we were wrong. There is not only a resurgence of Biblical scholarship but also a very strong emphasis on the preaching of the Word. Along with this we find that our Catholic brothers still take the Church with utmost seriousness. Because of the ferment within the Church as reported in newspapers and journals it is easy to have the idea that the Catholics are trying to overthrow or destroy both the structures and the substance of their Church. We find such is not the case. Rather, the ferment is a sign of vigor and of life. There would not be such a rigorous examination of their Church's life if there were not this serious concern.

We were also moved by the discovery of the depth of Catholic concern for the human predicament, for the fierce necessities that force modern man into strange and tragic circumstances. This pastoral concern was matched by the seriousness with which true piety is regarded as a means of grace and empowerment in the service of God and man. The pastoral concern over social ills has not sprung from any shallow or fleeting emotion but from the depths of vision of what God wills for His people.

There are serious disagreements between our churches which separate us, differences which are unlikely to be resolved in our lifetime. But these differences can be embraced within the bonds of Christian friendship. For we Disciples would add a word of appreciation for our Catholic partners in this adventure in that we have found them to be Christian men of godly and winsome lives. We treasure the friendships that this dialogue has enabled us to find.

From the very beginning of our meetings the Disciples made a very positive impression on their Catholic partners. Their spirit of fellowship and warmth, coupled with their direct and informal manner, not only served to make our dialogue relaxed and frank, but provided a context wherein friendships were born and have continued to grow.

The utmost seriousness with which the Disciples historically have worked toward the goal of a more corporate expression of the unity of Christ's Church was a revelation to many of us. Our experience of their sense of commitment to the idea of unity in the Church stimulated our own ecumenical awareness and enthusiasm.

The Disciples' conviction about the centrality of the Lord's Table in the life of the church struck a concordant note among us Catholics. The Eucharist, for Catholics, represents the summit of the Church's activity and is the supreme manifestation of its corporate life and structure. The old adage that Protestants represent the Church of the Word and Catholics represent the Church of the Sacraments seemed to dissolve as we gained a mutual appreciation of one another's liturgical traditions.

The fact that Disciples emphasize scriptural authority in the Church was a point which Catholics would qualify but with which we are not completely uncomfortable, since we consider the teaching office of the Church as not above the Word of God but serving it. We know that further joint study of the nature of the authority of the revealed Word of God is warranted. However, as Catholics, we were consoled that our Disciple partners recognized the need for some ongoing interpreting function of the Church regarding the message of the Scriptures. Moreover, each side seemed to be relieved that neither of our traditions exegete and interpret the scriptures in a fundamentalist and uncritical way.

Our feelings of unity were intensified by the discovery that our pastoral concerns were much the same as those of the Disciples. This underlined the urgency of our forging a greater unity of our ministries so that we might more effectively collaborate in the Lord's vineyard.

But what made the deepest impression on us Catholics were the genuine Christian faith and simple evangelical piety manifested by the Disciples. We especially cherish the moments of prayer and worship which we shared together, and through which we experienced firsthand the active presence of the Spirit of Christ in our Disciple friends. For us, this experience of the Spirit was the most dramatic and moving sign of the unity which, in His Grace, was already ours. It provides us with the motive to continue our efforts together toward the goal of a fuller unity which in His way will be accomplished.

The Future

We Catholics and Disciples have completed five years of dialogue through which we have developed a deeper understanding of one another's traditions and of the differences between us, as well as a better awareness of the unity with which God has already embraced us. We are convinced that this is no time to rest. We feel compelled by His Spirit to forge ahead in a joint study of the nature and mission of the Church as witnessed by the New Testament. Our method very simply will be an attempt to reflect together on His Word under the guidance of the Spirit. We hope thereby to move our dialogue beyond the stage of comparative ecclesiology to a level which will lead us to a greater degree of common understanding.

In this joint endeavor we humbly seek God's light and commend ourselves to the prayers and support of our brethren in both our churches.

Apostolicity and Catholicity in the Visible Unity of the Church

June 24, 1982

I. Introduction

1. In September 1977 a five-year international dialogue between the Disciples of Christ and the Roman Catholic Church was launched on the theme: "Apostolicity and Catholicity in the Visible Unity of the Church." The 18-member commission had been appointed jointly by the Secretariat for Promoting Christian Unity in collaboration with the U.S. bishops' Committee for Ecumenical and Interreligious Affairs, and the Disciples Ecumenical Consultative Council and the Council on Christian Unity of the Christian Church (Disciples of Christ) in the U.S. and Canada. It's membership included Roman Catholic theologians and pastors from Canada, France, Ireland, the United States and the Vatican, and Disciples theologians and pastors from Canada, England, Puerto Rico, the United States and Zaire. Dr. Paul A. Crow Jr. and Bishop Stanley J. Ott were named as co-chairmen for the commission.

2. In developing the main theme of its work the commission selected four subthemes to focus discussion at each annual meeting: "The Nature of the Church and Elements of Its Unity" (Indianapolis, 1977): "Baptism: Gift and Call in the Search for Unity" (Rome, 1978); "Faith and Tradition in the Life of the Church" (Annapolis, 1979); "The Dynamics of Unity and of Division" (New Orleans, 1980). At its fifth session (Ardfert, Ireland, 1981), the commission prepared a final report to be submitted to its authorizing bodies.

3. Each annual meeting lasted five days and followed a regular pattern of work, of sharing in worship and prayer, and of worshiping with Disciples and Roman Catholics in local congregations and parishes. Four papers, two from each team, were presented and discussed with the tasks of identifying present agreements, convergences, new insights

and continuing tensions or problems for further consideration. An "agreed account" of each meeting was prepared to serve as a common memory for the commission's work. The papers and agreed accounts were published in *Mid-Stream: An Ecumenical Journal* (Vol. XVIII, No. 4, October 1979; Vol. XX, No. 3, July 1981).

4. This final report does not summarize the papers and the agreed accounts from our previous meetings. Rather, it is a statement of shared insights and findings which the commission identified out of its work, its discussion and debate, and its life together in fellowship and prayer during these five years.

II. Our Life Together

5. These five years of the dialogue between Disciples of Christ and Roman Catholics have been the occasion of joy as we have grown together in theological understanding, in fellowship and in the way we approach the problems of doctrine. We have been led to a better understanding of the nature of the one church of God, the situation of our divided traditions and also of the pressure of our common calling to visible unity in Christ.

6. We are aware that we come from two very different Christian backgrounds. Our histories, our cultural journeys, and our theological traditions and methods have in some often important respects been different. Some of the problems between us spring from these differences. Yet the very diversity of our histories and Christian experiences frees us for a new kind of ecumenical dialogue. The Disciples movement was born out of the churches of the Reformation, but has developed its own unique position among them. In particular, there was no deliberate, formal break in communion between the Disciples of Christ and the Roman Catholic Church, although our histories have included the general bias which in the past reflected uncharitable attitudes between Protestants and Roman Catholics. This fact has allowed us to move beyond any initial apprehensions or presumed distance into cordial relationships and to discover that we have more in common than we expected.

7. A significant amount of what we thought initially to be division cannot be so defined. We have begun to discover that when we go beneath the current theological descriptions of our traditions, a convergence becomes evident. As we understand our traditions and our ecclesiologies more clearly, we discover a common source has fed them. The customary vocabulary of division does not exactly describe

our situation, even though there are still some important things we cannot do together or on which we cannot yet be at one.

8. This dialogue has been liberating because both Disciples and Roman Catholics set the fullness of communion at the heart of their understanding of the church. Barton Warren Stone claimed for Disciples: "Let Christian unity be our polar star." Alexander Campbell proclaimed that "the union of Christians is essential to the conversion of the world." The same vocation, inherent in the Catholic tradition, was also claimed for Roman Catholics by the Second Vatican Council: "The restoration of unity among all Christians is one of the principal concerns of the Second Vatican Council. . . . The concern for restoring unity involves the whole church, faithful and clergy alike" (Decree on Ecumenism, nn. 1, 5).

9. Paradoxically, some of our differences spring from the ways we have understood and pursued Christian unity. For example, the Disciples of Christ, called into being as an instrument of unity among divided Christians, have refused to make creeds the definitive faith in order to promote unity and communion among Christians. The Roman Catholic Church, on the other hand, holds to the creeds and the Petrine ministry for the same purpose. Our dialogue has helped us see this and other contrasts in the context of the fundamental commitment of Disciples and Roman Catholics to serve the visible unity of the whole people of God. In this perspective some issues that seem to divide us can be traced to the same roots and certain of our differences appear complementary.

10. The nature of our ecumenical dialogue requires us to listen to each other's theological words while searching for the language of convergence, always in faithfulness to the truth of the Gospel. Our report gives substantial commentary on the issues which have been at the heart of the first phase of our dialogue and gives our churches hope for the future.

III. Spiritual Ecumenism

11. In Christ God has shown his supreme love for the world (Jn. 3:16), destroying the power of sin, reconciling us to himself (2 Cor. 5:18–19) and breaking down the barriers of division in the human family. The Spirit of God is in the church to bring this reconciling work of Christ to completion and continues to gather into it all who are ready to accept the saving Gospel. As human history unfolds, the Spirit of God prepares the coming of the final kingdom. Already in the

church the future unity of the kingdom is anticipated as the Spirit brings together in faith and love those who acknowledge the lordship of Christ.

12. The Spirit of God draws the church toward full unity. God's Spirit also works in the world for a new humanity through the liberation of human beings from the oppression and alienation that comes from sin. Both realms of the work of the Spirit are integral parts of one plan of salvation.

13. The unity God has given and continues to give the church has its origins in God's own life. The Spirit of God is the author of the church's unity. Through the Spirit all who are one in the church are drawn into the loving communion of the Father and Son and in that communion are united to one another. Thus they are being made one in mind and understanding, since through faith they adhere to the one eternal word in whom the wisdom of God is fully expressed. In this unity the divine plan of salvation accomplished in Christ is expressed in the world and is being ever more fully revealed.

14. This theological awareness permits us to affirm that visible unity will come from the one grace of the Spirit of God dynamically present among Christians even in their divided condition. The Spirit calls all Christians to assume responsibility for giving authentic expression to their unity in life, in worship and in mission. The Spirit enables them to overcome obstacles and empowers them to grow together toward full visible unity.

15. The work of Christian unity, then, is profoundly and radically a spiritual one, i.e., it comes from and is a response to the Holy Spirit. We are encouraged that both our churches share a will for unity but acknowledge that, for this unity to be made fully manifest, our will and our commitments must be sustained by what has been called "spiritual ecumenism" (Decree on Ecumenism, 8).

16. Spiritual ecumenism does not permit us to avoid the pain of our separated existence, being content to remain as we are. Indeed, the Spirit gives us the courage to confront our divided state.

17. Spiritual ecumenism does not allow us to leave aside the need to deal with the visible manifestations of the unity of the church. Indeed, we understand that just as the word of God became flesh in Jesus, so in a similar way the power of the Spirit of God is manifested in the church as a visible communion.

18. Nor does spiritual ecumenism relieve us of the gospel concern for the poor, the alienated and the oppressed. Indeed Christians often become truly aware of the bonds that unite them and hear the call to

conversion of heart as they meet the challenge to promote a society of justice, freedom and charity serving the dignity of every human being.

19. Spiritual ecumenism arises from the realization that the one Spirit of God has already brought us into Christ and continues to move us toward full visible unity. Spiritual ecumenism gives us hope that the Spirit will lead us from the imperfect unity we know painfully in our divided condition to a wholeness we shall experience in joy.

20. Spiritual ecumenism implies a clear consciousness of the sinfulness of division among Christians. Through spiritual ecumenism we are set free as communities and as individuals from seeking to justify our divisions, and we are moved to seek a shared life in a reconciled community. Spiritual ecumenism impels us to a quality of evangelical life marked by the will to be faithful to Christ and open to one another. It also implies repentance and renunciation of egoism, as well as newness of mind, humility and gentleness in the service of others, that is, conversion of heart. This *metanoia* thus provides what might be called an "evangelical space"—an arena for the operation of the Gospel—in which we find God's grace newly available to bind us together in praising, blessing and beseeching the God who makes us one. In this evangelical space we discover new possibilities for genuine exchange and sharing and for seeing in a new light these affirmations that find historical expression in our still separated communities.

21. Thus spiritual ecumenism allows us to be open to the grace of God. The Holy Spirit is freeing us to experience together his unifying power in the many ways open to us in the ongoing life of the church, that is, accepting and proclaiming together the word of God in the scriptures, confessing together the same Lord, praying together, attending one another's celebration of the Lord's Supper and having a common mission as the priestly people of God in the whole human community. Although we do not yet fully share these experiences owing to our desire to be authentic and faithful to the church as we have known it heretofore in our communions, we nevertheless realize that God makes the power of his unifying love felt even now. He speaks to us about the contradictions of our divisions when together we open ourselves to him in prayer and worship, in our joint efforts at articulating a common theological language in ecumenical dialogue and in the common struggle for justice and peace in the world.

22. In this evangelical space we are empowered both to grow together and at the same time to pay the price of suffering caused by our present divisions and by the efforts to overcome them. Here we discern a reflection of the present growth in painful struggle that marks

the whole ecumenical movement. But we take hope, knowing that "the whole creation has been groaning in travail together until now and not only the creation but we ourselves, who have the first fruits of the Spirit, groan inwardly as we await . . . redemption." So "we wait for it with patience," confident that "the Spirit helps us in our weakness" and trusting that "the Spirit intercedes for the saints according to the will of God" (cf. Rom. 8:22–27).

IV. Baptism

23. By its very nature baptism impels Christians toward oneness. In baptism a person is incorporated into Christ Jesus and into his body, the church. The fundamental unity which God has given us is rooted in the sacrament and cannot be destroyed. We are called to the one baptism by the Gospel that is the way of salvation for all humanity. Baptism is therefore the fundamental source of our oneness in Christ's life, death and resurrection.

24. Yet we came to the subject of baptism with an awareness of differences in baptismal practice which could not be treated lightly. At first sight these differences might seem to represent divergent understandings which could threaten our fundamental unity through baptism.

25. In fact we have discovered important areas in which our understanding and practice of baptism encourage us to speak truly of one baptism. These areas were found to have varying degrees of significance.

26. (a) We share a common attribution of the origins of baptismal observance to the example of Jesus, the command of the risen Christ and the practice of the primitive church.

27. (b) For both Disciples of Christ and Roman Catholics baptism is with water and "in the name of the Father, and of the Son, and of the Holy Spirit."

28. (c) In both our traditions baptism is ordinarily administered by a duly authorized minister.

29. (d) In both our traditions it is affirmed that we enter into a new relationship with God as his children and as brothers and sisters, one of another in Christ, for in baptism our sins are forgiven and we become a new creation.

30. (e) Since God never revokes the new relationship brought about in baptism, rebaptism is contrary to the Gospel and should never be practiced. Nevertheless, we are aware of the need for contin-

ued repentance after baptism and we experience forgiveness in the ongoing life of the church.

31. (f) Both our traditions maintain the necessity for the role of faith in baptism. For both Roman Catholics and Disciples incorporation into the body of Christ and forgiveness of sins are primarily acts of God that presuppose faith and call for a continuing active response of faith for their full development and fruitfulness.

32. This fundamental agreement must be kept in mind as we seek to interpret anew certain differences in regard to baptism. These differences fall under two headings:

33. *The Relation of Personal Faith to Baptism.* Since believers' baptism is the form of baptism explicitly attested in the New Testament, the conviction of Disciples is that the rite of baptism should be preceded by a personal confession of faith and repentance.

For historical, theological and pastoral reasons, Roman Catholics baptize infants. They see this as the first sacrament in the process of Christian initiation, followed by Christian nurture and instruction, and culminating in the sacraments of confirmation and eucharist, accompanied by a life of continual repentance and conversion.

However, Catholics see the fundamental belief of their church regarding baptism as expressed with new clarity in the revised rite for adult baptism, which includes personal confession of faith.

At the same time Disciples have an increasing appreciation for the place of infant baptism in the history of the church. In part this involves understanding infant baptism in relation to Christian nurture in both the family and the Christian community. Also Disciples have seen that infant baptism has been a pastoral response in a situation where members are no longer predominantly first-generation Christians.

34. *The Mode of Baptism.* Disciples practice immersion, believing it to be the practice of New Testament times and the clearest symbolic representation of our participation in the death and resurrection of Christ. Roman Catholics, on the basis of early Christian tradition, regard pouring as an acceptable mode while acknowledging the symbolic value of descent into the baptismal waters. They have always recognized and sometimes practice baptism by immersion. Disciples are coming to recognize the other modes, while retaining a preference for immersion.

35. Although God's saving power in the world is unlimited, baptism is fundamental in Christian life. By it we become members of Christ's body and participate in the life he gives. Participation in Christ's life calls us to enter his ministry, suffering, death and resur-

rection, as is prefigured in our baptism, for the salvation of the whole world.

36. Because both baptism and the eucharist involve participation in the body of Christ and since the grace of God received in baptism is nurtured and strengthened by participation in the eucharistic meal, the oneness achieved by grace in baptism should find manifestation and completion in the *anamnesis* (memorial, remembrance) of the sacrifice of Christ for all humanity at the table of the one Lord.

37. Baptism is paradoxically a sign of unity and a reminder of disunity. It is a sign of unity inasmuch as it incorporates all Christians into Christ. It is a reminder of disunity in that, as administered, it also initiates Christians into separated ecclesial communities with their special traditions and doctrines.

38. We have been helped in our further consideration of this paradox by distinguishing two affirmations of faith. The one is the fundamental assent of the person to God's gift of grace in Jesus Christ, a gift that is in itself life transforming and that is signified in baptism. This affirmation brings our lives under the determination of God's grace, thereby turning us outward from ourselves and making us one in Christ. The other is the acceptance of the elaboration of the faith as that has come to expression in our separated ecclesial communities. Baptism is also the induction into a particular ecclesial community with its own explication of the one faith. Making this distinction, therefore, has helped us to understand our fundamental unity and to locate the source of our separation.

39. However, in conclusion, we affirm the mutual recognition of baptism administered by Roman Catholics and Disciples, convinced that the oneness we receive by the grace of God in baptism must find its completion in visible ecclesial unity, so that the world may believe that Jesus is the Christ, the Son of the living God, as we together confess him to be. We are determined, therefore, by the same grace to discover more fully the truth that shall set us all free.

V. Faith and Tradition

40. Our two traditions are called to proclaim to the world the fundamental truth of God's reconciliation in Christ, to which both have given assent. This common assent is sealed through baptism in separated ecclesial bodies; nevertheless, in our baptism we are given radical unity. This realization impels us as the church, the body of Christ, to witness to the apostolic faith in our life, teaching, liturgy and service.

41. The church, under the guidance of the Holy Spirit, has developed the means for proclaiming the apostolic faith from age to age as it has sought to defend the faith and communicate it faithfully in different times and circumstances. Scripture and tradition embody these responses to the faith that God gives.

42. Faith is God's gift both to the individual and to the community. In both cases it is through the power of the Holy Spirit that we believe, grow in faith and live by faith. Our faith is that Christ is the risen Lord who is the reason for the existence of the church. This faith begets a new relationship among all who believe. The faith which commits a person to Christ commits that person to the church, which is his body; because faith is given by the one spirit of Christ, it is the one basic faith that binds Roman Catholics, Disciples and other Christians in one fellowship in that Spirit. However, in spite of this radical unity in the body of Christ, we recognize that we have not yet fully achieved the visible ecclesial unity which he willed. While gratefully recognizing the measure of agreement reached on this topic, we also become acutely aware at this point of some serious unresolved issues that need further discussion in our dialogue; these, we believe, should be a major part of our future agenda.

43. The conversion process by which one commits oneself in faith to Christ and to discipleship is a gradual, continuous and difficult one. Christ promised that his Spirit would be present to the individual in and through the community of believers. The Christian community, therefore, calls forth, nurtures, illumines and sustains the faith of the individual in its liturgy and prayer, and its example of Christlike love and service.

44. Christian life is life in community, a community which recognizes the dignity and freedom of human conscience, while also acknowledging the need for the individual conscience to develop in greater obedience to the Gospel. The church is called to guide and enable this process.

45. Each Christian's faith is inseparable from the faith of the community. Personal faith is an appropriation of the church's faith and depends on it for authenticity as well as for nurture. At the same time, bearing witness to personal faith builds up the life of the church and quickens and strengthens the faith of all.

46. Insofar as the church as a community of faith and love is the sign of Christ in the world, believers are called to offer a common witness of faith so that the world might believe that Jesus is Lord. Thus the life of faith, both of the individual and of the community, is expected to manifest a certain quality by which it becomes a "light of

the world," "salt of the earth." Both the individual believer and the pilgrim church are ever called to a deeper conversion to Christ, a more authentic faith. Scripture, mediating the word of God, has a central, normative and irreplaceable role in this process of personal and ecclesial conversion.

47. Together the Disciples of Christ and the Roman Catholic Church acknowledge the important role of tradition in the life of the church. The relationship between faith and tradition has to do with the question of how Christians from age to age come to the knowledge that Jesus Christ is the Lord of life and the way of salvation for the whole world.

48. The apostles were called by Christ and commissioned to a unique position in the life of the church. They attest the presence of the risen Lord and hold a special place in the communication of faith to subsequent generations. In that communication the Holy Spirit is always present in the life of the church, guaranteeing that the church shall not fail to bring about the fulfillment of the divine plan.

49. Under the inspiration of the Spirit, the New Testament expresses the response in faith of the apostolic church to the risen Lord. This response was itself conditioned by God's revelation and promises to Israel.

50. The New Testament scriptures, resting on the authority of the apostles and interpreted with the aid of the Holy Spirit, constitute the inspired record of the tradition which stems from the apostolic era. This tradition reflects the *sensus fidelium* (the shared awareness of the faithful) of the primitive church as a whole. However, the *sensus fidelium* is not fixed in the past, but is ever dynamic and living through the dialectical interaction of scripture and tradition in the ongoing life of the church from age to age.

51. Each generation must come to faith anew through the power of the Holy Spirit and hand on this faith to succeeding generations. At the same time the church in every age inherits the successes and failures of the past.

52. In the process of making explicit the implications of revelation, various traditions arise. This resultant diversity is to be expected and is frequently itself an expression of the catholicity of the church. Problems arise when the ecclesial context in which a baptismal assent is made exercises an influence of such a kind that the communion in faith is compromised. Roman Catholics and Disciples both recognize that they move beyond the fundamental reality of faith in God revealed in Jesus Christ to understandings that have grown out of a diversity of Christian traditions.

53. Roman Catholics hold that the living transmission of the Gospel in and by the church is necessary for a more complete articulation, manifestation and application of the truths that are in scripture than scripture alone affords. They look to the affirmations of faith and interpretations expressed in the church's official liturgical texts, creedal statements, teachings of the episcopal college, especially in councils, and papal teachings which they believe to be formulated with the guidance of the Spirit. While the scriptures are normative and the soul of all subsequent theological investigation, their adequate understanding is possible only within the life of the believing community.

54. Disciples believe that the New Testament is a sufficient expression of the essential faith, doctrine and practice of the individual Christian and the Christian community. Thus while being conscious of standing in the tradition of the church, they have not given a normative position to later expressions of the faith of the church, and in particular have not used creeds and confessions as tests of eucharistic fellowship. Disciples believe their history shows that a church can develop and sustain its own distinctive character without a formal creed, and that the exercise of freedom and diversity in expressions of belief and worship need not threaten its unity. However, where affirmations of faith, both ancient and modern, have been used as a basis for the expression of the essential unity of the whole church (for example, in united churches), Disciples have gladly accepted them.

55. Both Disciples and Roman Catholics are committed to the appropriation in their own lives of all that is good from the traditions of others, both in the past and today.

VI. Affirmations About the Unity We Seek

56. Through a convergence of doctrinal understanding and in the experience of the reality of our oneness in the fundamental assent to God, we are able to accept as a basic principle of ecumenism that there can be only one church of God *(unica ecclesia)* and that this church already exists. It is the accomplishment of salvation, both individually and corporately, for all humanity. This salvation to which scripture bears witness expresses God's purpose for the entire creation.

57. The new humanity in Jesus Christ which God wills comes to exist in the one church of God. The coming definitive form of the church as God's eschatological people can be fully known only to God. Both Roman Catholics and Disciples believe that the church takes visible shape in history and that one sign of this visibility is the common

profession of the Gospel with reception of baptism. This visible community belongs to the very *esse* of the church.

58. Through their common life and fellowship *(koinonia)* the members of this community which is the church witness to salvation as they pray and worship together, forgive, accept and love one another, and stand together in time of trial. Such communion is made possible by a deeper communion, a communion in the good things that come from God, who makes the people of the church his own as a new creation in Christ.

59. We become this new creation through the means of grace which God has given to his church. Thus the church is the visible form of God's grace. It opens the way to salvation through preaching, sacraments and other institutions derived from apostolic authority. Participation in these means of grace constitutes the deeper communion that unites us together in true fellowship in the Spirit.

60. To this one church belong all those who are baptized in water and the Spirit with the authentic confession of faith in Jesus as the Son of God. These persons become members of the body of Christ and receive the seal of the Holy Spirit, which cannot be removed even by schism. Divisions among Christians cannot destroy the one church of God.

61. As we look at differences between Roman Catholics and Disciples we often discover in them elements of complementarity. We see ourselves as having a communion *in via.* The unique unity of the one church of God is the goal. We are already on the way; we have taken the first step in faith through baptism, which is also the call to that final unity. Now we have the task of giving external expression to the communion *in via.* In the very process of our mutual discovery of certain ecclesial elements in each other, we are called in a renewed fidelity to actions that will make our relationship more intense and more profound.

VII. Looking to the Future

62. Our situation as Disciples of Christ and Roman Catholics, discovering each other in this dialogue, is a reflection of what is happening everywhere among Christians as they yield themselves in obedience to what God is doing through the ecumenical movement. We are not yet at the point where we can ask the churches to which we belong to make a definitive judgment on our work or to commit themselves to some decision which could have structural consequences.

63. Yet our experience tells us and we must declare that the relation between the Roman Catholic Church and the Disciples of Christ is in the process of a growth which is deeply important for both partners. This process calls for loyalty and courage as we pursue it toward maturity and, here and now, it challenges and makes demands on us both in a practical and costly way. The Lord is confronting us with these demands. We believe several of them especially require us to give a faithful response and to draw certain conclusions in practice:

64. (a) Catholics and Disciples along with many other Christians are discovering that, in essence, their commitment to Christ and their fellowship in the Gospel are the same. There is already a unity of grace which in some measure is present, bearing fruit, and which is disposing us for visible unity and urging us to move ahead to it. One of the most striking insights we have received in our dialogue is the awareness that the interior communion between Christians across divisions is an essential element of unity and a necessary part of achieving the goal of full visible unity. This is something we have experienced as we have learned to take each other seriously in our theological awareness and in our commitment to the mission of Jesus Christ. Above all, we have experienced it together in our prayer, our reading of the scriptures and the meditation which has seasoned all our work and given a special flavor and substance to this dialogue. We have come to appreciate more deeply also the importance in our two traditions of the renewal of the liturgy and the centrality of the eucharist. It is our immediate task to reflect seriously on what all of this means for the relationship between Roman Catholics and Disciples of Christ in each parish and congregation.

65. (b) Spiritual ecumenism leads to more than the sum of doctrinal agreements. It requires us to "do the truth" of unity by acting together in the name of the Gospel. Our obedience to Christ, the Lord of history, has to be made incarnate as we carry our own responsibility of enabling the kingdom to penetrate the world, its life and its institutions. In its own way it can be as full an expression of the common faith as doctrinal agreement, for action in harmony with the demands of the Gospel makes known Christian truth and reveals its riches. Communion expressed through practice is an important element of the emerging *koinonia* among churches. Joint action, both of individuals and of separated churches, is a factor in unity which reaches to the roots of the ecumenical task. This too has implications now for Disciples of Christ and Roman Catholics in each place.

66. (c) Preparation for visible unity is taking place already through discussion of important doctrinal issues. This is clear from the work

which has been done in our dialogue commission over the past five years. That is a significant beginning. We have now the framework in which it becomes possible and necessary to do further work on unresolved issues, particularly the nature and mission of the church, the eucharist and the ministry.

67. The dialogue commission gives thanks to God that certain doctrinal convergences on some key issues begin to be discernible in our work already. This encourages us to work for no less than visible unity—not a limping compromise achieved by paring away divergences, but nothing less than common witness to the one apostolic faith.

68. The dialogue between Disciples of Christ and the Roman Catholic Church has begun and already we must live in the logic of what is happening. It demands that we begin now, as far as possible, to proclaim together the same Lord Jesus Christ, giving common witness to "the hope that is in us" (1 Pt. 2:13). It demands, even now, that we enter to the fullest extent possible into that process of mutual recognition which is ultimately a worshipful acknowledgment of the one Lord in whom we are baptized, whose gifts we enjoy, to whose service we are called.

Co-Chairmen's Note

Only by the power of God and the guidance of the Spirit can Christians grow together toward unity. In a spirit of thankfulness the theologians and pastors who have taken part in the Disciples of Christ-Roman Catholic dialogue for five years now bring a report of the fruit of their meetings.

Some bilateral theological dialogues have matured to the point of publishing reports of new convergences and agreements in the understanding of the Christian faith. The publication, dissemination and study of such reports is a necessary element in the process toward union. Thus the participating churches will grasp the significance of what is emerging and, with discernment, reach some decisions.

Along the way toward such maturation, the publication of accounts of significant progress can be enlightening. The present 1982 paper from the Disciples of Christ-Roman Catholic Dialogue is of this kind. It contains not an agreed statement on points of doctrine, but an agreed account, written by those commissioned for the dialogue, to record promising developments. The paper describes some convergence in understanding as well as some of the problems which have yet to be faced.

Thus the paper will inform our churches and evoke from them interest and reactions. We desire that what has begun in good faith may end in a unity of faith given visible expression. May the Lord bring to completion the work of his grace.

Dr. Paul A. Crow Jr, President
Council on Christian Unity
of the Christian Church

Bishop Stanley Ott
Auxiliary of New Orleans

LUTHERAN–ROMAN CATHOLIC DIALOGUES

Introduction

The Catholic Church in the United States is in dialogue with what are now two Lutheran bodies: The Evangelical Lutheran Church in America (ELCA) and the Lutheran Church–Missouri Synod.

The ELCA, organized in 1987, brought together the 2.3 million-member American Lutheran Church, the 2.9 million-member Lutheran Church in America, and the 110,000-member Association of Evangelical Lutheran Churches.

The ELCA is both the youngest and at the same time, through its predecessor church bodies, the oldest of the major U.S. Lutheran churches. Its roots stretch back to the mid-seventeenth century when Dutch Lutherans formed a congregation in New Amsterdam (now New York). The first Lutheran association of congregations, the Pennsylvania Ministerium, was organized in 1748.

In 1962, the Lutheran Church in America merged the United Lutheran Church with the Augustana Lutheran Church, founded in 1860 by Swedish immigrants; the American Evangelical Lutheran Church, founded in 1872 by Danish immigrants; and the Finnish Lutheran Church, founded in 1891 by Finnish immigrants.

In 1960, the American Lutheran Church merged with an earlier American Lutheran Church, which was formed in 1930 by four synods that traced their roots primarily to German immigration; the Evangelical Lutheran Church, which dated from 1917 through a merger of churches chiefly of Norwegian ethnic heritage; and the United Evangelical Lutheran Church in America, which arose from Danish immigration. In 1963, the Lutheran Free Church merged with the ALC.

The Association of Evangelical Lutheran Churches arose in 1976 from a doctrinal split with the Lutheran Church–Missouri Synod.

The Lutheran Church–Missouri Synod began in 1847. It is the second largest Lutheran denomination in North America with 2.7 million members.

In 1961, the USA National Committee of the Lutheran World Federation (after 1976, Lutheran World Ministries) initiated negotiations with the National Conference for Catholic Bishops in Washington, D.C., about establishing a theological dialogue. The first dialogue took place in July, 1965. Because Lutherans and Catholics confess the Nicene Creed in common, they began with that subject.

This dialogue process has been productive for several reasons. It had time to develop the methodology and new insights needed to deal with classical issues.

Both sides decided to distribute common statements and supporting papers widely in their constituencies. The dialogue team pushed forward toward more complex and fundamental issues, even dealing with what has been called the most divisive issue of all—the papacy. The partners soon discovered that the materials on this theme are so extensive that they divided the subject in two parts—primacy and infallibility. They commissioned also a team of New Testament scholars to produce *Peter in the New Testament* in order to make a separate investigation in the dialogue itself unnecessary. For its future study on Mary, the dialogue team commissioned another book by Lutheran and Catholic scholars, *Mary in the New Testament.* And when they turned to justification, they commissioned *Righteousness in the New Testament,* by the New Testament members of the team. In August 1986 the Lutheran Church in America, in convention, reacted to the Common Statement on justification; and the American Lutheran Church, in convention, received the report of the ALC Church Council for study. The Catholic Bishops' Committee on Doctrine has also reviewed the earlier stages of the dialogue.

Recommended Readings

Lutherans and Catholics in Dialogue, 7 volumes.

1. *The Status of the Nicene Creed as Dogma of the Church* (P.C. Empie and W.W. Baum, eds.; 1965).
2. *One Baptism for the Remission of Sins* (P.C. Empie and W.W. Baum, eds.; 1966).
3. *The Eucharist as Sacrifice* (P.C. Empie and T. Austin Murphy, eds.; 1967).
4. *Eucharist and Ministry* (P.C. Empie and T. Austin Murphy, eds.; 1970).
5. *Papal Primacy and the Universal Church* (P.C. Empie and T. Austin Murphy, eds.; Minneapolis: Augsburg, 1974).
6. *Teaching Authority and Infallibility in the Church* (P.C. Empie, T. Austin Murphy, and J.A. Burgess, eds.; Minneapolis: Augsburg, 1980).
7. *Justification by Faith* (H.G. Anderson, T. Austin Murphy, and J.A. Burgess, eds.; Minneapolis: Augsburg, 1985).

Volumes 1–4 were originally published by the Bishops' Committee for Ecumenical and Interreligious Affairs, Washington, D.C., and the U.S.A. National Committee of the Lutheran World Federation, New York, NY. Volumes 1–3 have been reprinted together in one volume by Augsburg Publishing House (n.d.), as has volume 4 (1979).

"Bishops' Committee for Ecumenical and Interreligious Affairs Evaluation of the U.S. Lutheran-Roman Catholic Dialogue", *Lutheran Quarterly,* 1 (1987) 125–69.

Brown, Raymond E., Karl P. Donfried and John Reumann, *Peter in the New Testament* (Minneapolis: Augsburg and New York/Paramus/Toronto: Paulist, 1973).

Brown, Raymond E., Karl P. Donfried, Joseph A. Fitzmyer and John Reumann, *Mary in the New Testament* (Philadelphia: Fortress, and New York/Ramsey/Toronto: Paulist, 1978).

Burgess, Joseph A. and George H. Tavard, *Studies for Lutheran/Catholic Dialogue* (Minneapolis: Augsburg, 1980).

Empie, Paul E., *Lutherans and Catholics in Dialogue: Personal Notes for a Study* (R. Tiemeyer, ed.; Philadelphia: Fortress, 1981).

Reumann, John, with Joseph A. Fitzmyer and Jerome D. Quinn, *"Righteousness" in the New Testament* (Philadelphia: Fortress, and New York/Ramsey: Paulist, 1982).

Stone, Glenn C. and Charles La Fontaine, S.A. (eds.), *Exploring the Faith We Share. A Discussion Guide for Lutherans & Roman Catholics* (New York/Ramsey: Paulist, 1980).

The Status of the Nicene Creed as Dogma of the Church

July 6–7, 1965

Summary Statement

Following is the text of the joint statement issued in Baltimore July 7 at the close of the first official theological discussion in the United States between representatives of the Roman Catholic Church and the major Lutheran churches.

In praise to God, and in gratitude for those gifts of His Spirit whereby He steadily draws His people to unity in Christ, we rejoice in this first official theological conversation in the United States between Roman Catholic and Lutheran believers.

Those regularly appointed to arrange for and summon this meeting selected the topic for discussion: The Status of the Nicene Creed as Dogma of the Church.

The main points of the conversation are summarized in the following paragraphs:

1) We confess in common the Nicene Faith and therefore hold that the Son, Our Lord Jesus Christ, who was made man, suffered, died, and rose again for our salvation, is true God; that He is from God the Father as Son, and therefore other than the Father; that the Godhead is one and undivided; and that the Holy Spirit, together with the Father and the Son, is to be worshipped and glorified.

2) The Nicene Faith gathers up and articulates the biblical testimony concerning the Son and His relationship to the Father.

3) The Nicene Faith, formulated by the Council at Nicaea in 325 and developed in the Nicene-Constantinopolitan Creed, was a response to contemporary errors. The Church was obliged to state her faith in the Son in non-biblical terms to answer the Arian question.

4) The confession that Our Lord Jesus Christ is the Son, God of God, continues to assure us that we are in fact redeemed, for only He who is God can redeem us.

5) The Nicene Faith, grounded in the biblical proclamation about

Christ and the trinitarian baptismal formulas used in the Church, is both doxology to God the Father and dogma about God the Son.

6) As we reflect upon the role of dogma in our separated communities, we are aware of the following:

(a) The Nicene Faith possesses a unique status in the hierarchy of dogmas by reason of its testimony to and celebration of the mystery of the Trinity as revealed in Christ Our Savior, and by reason of its definitive reply to an ever-recurring question. This does not imply that the Nicene Faith exhausted the richness of Scripture regarding the person of Christ. For example, the Council of Chalcedon in 451 confessed that He was "in every respect like us, except without sin."

(b) We are agreed that authoritative teaching in the Church serves the people of God by protecting and nurturing the Faith. Dogma has a positive and a negative function. It authoritatively repudiates erroneous teaching, and asserts the truth as revealed in the saving deeds of God and in His gifts to His Church and to His world.

(c) The way in which doctrine is certified as dogma is not identical in the two communities, for there is a difference in the way in which mutually acknowledged doctrine receives ecclesiastical sanction.

(d) Different understandings of the movement from kerygma to dogma obtain in the two communities. Full inquiry must therefore be made into two topics: first, the nature and structure of the teaching authority of the Church; and, secondly, the role of Scripture in relation to the teaching office of the Church.

7) We together acknowledge that the problem of the development of doctrine is crucial today and is in the forefront of our common concern.

One Baptism for the Remission of Sins

1966

JOINT STATEMENT
by
Bishop T. Austin Murphy and Dr. Paul C. Empie

The series of theological conversations in which we are engaged continue to be exceedingly fruitful. We were reasonably certain that the teachings of our respective traditions regarding baptism are in substantial agreement, and this opinion has been confirmed at this meeting.

At the same time, discussions dealing with several aspects of the subject brought to light the fact that although at times we use the same words with somewhat different meanings, we also upon occasion have quite different ways of saying the same things. It has been especially interesting to discover that we have common problems related to the development of doctrine in this and other theological areas, and a comparison of approaches to the solution of these problems has been mutually useful. Some points of misunderstanding have been clarified in the process.

We will be examining subjects in future meetings which present greater difficulties, but are encouraged to proceed in the knowledge that the conversations held thus far have deepened mutual understanding and respect while strengthening the bonds of brotherly affection.

The Eucharist: A Lutheran-Roman Catholic Statement

As a result of our conversations on the eucharist, we Roman Catholic and Lutheran theologians wish to record, chiefly and first of all, our profound gratitude to God for the growing unity on this subject which we see in our day.

Our responsibility is to try to articulate and explain this increasing agreement to the people and leadership of our churches, so that they may test for themselves what we have discussed and draw whatever conclusions in thought and action they find appropriate.

What we have to report is not so much original with us as simply one manifestation of a growing consensus among many Christian traditions on the Lord's supper.[1]

Ours, however, is a specifically Roman Catholic-Lutheran contribution. It attempts to go beyond the more general ecumenical discussion of the eucharist to an examination of the particular agreements and disagreements of our two traditions. While we have considered the biblical and patristic sources of eucharistic doctrine and practice in our preparatory conversations, this statement deals with problems that have become particularly acute for Lutherans and Roman Catholics as a result of the sixteenth-century controversies. It does not try to treat the sacrament of the altar comprehensively.

Our attention has focused on two issues: the eucharist as sacrifice, and the presence of Christ in the sacrament. These issues have been especially divisive in the past and are involved in most of our historical disagreements on eucharistic doctrine and practice. For this reason it seems to us important to enunciate our growing agreement on these two points, even though there are other aspects of the sacrament of the altar we have not yet discussed.

I
THE EUCHARIST AS SACRIFICE[2]

With reference to the eucharist as sacrifice, two affirmations have not been denied by either confession; four aspects of the problem have been major points of divergence.

1. *a*) Lutherans and Roman Catholics alike acknowledge that in the Lord's supper "Christ is present as the Crucified who died for our sins and who rose again for our justification, as the once-for-all sacrifice for the sins of the world who gives himself to the faithful."[3] On this Lutherans insist as much as Catholics, although, for various reasons, Lutherans have been reticent about speaking of the eucharist as a sacrifice.
   b) The confessional documents of both traditions agree that the celebration of the eucharist is the church's sacrifice of praise and self-offering or oblation. Each tradition can make the following statement its own: "By him, with him and in him who is our great High Priest and Intercessor we offer to the Father, in the power of the Holy Spirit, our praise, thanksgiving and intercession. With contrite hearts we offer ourselves as a living and holy sacrifice, a sacrifice which must be expressed in the whole of our daily lives."[4]
2. Historically, our controversies have revolved around the question whether the worshiping assembly "offers Christ" in the sacrifice of the mass. In general, Lutherans have replied in the negative, because they believed that only thus could they preserve the once-for-all character and the full sufficiency of the sacrifice of the cross and keep the eucharist from becoming a human supplement to God's saving work, a matter of "works-righteousness."
   a) First of all, we must be clear that Catholics as well as Lutherans affirm the unrepeatable character of the sacrifice of the cross. The Council of Trent, to be sure, affirmed this, but Lutheran doubts about the Catholic position were not resolved. Today, however, we find no reason for such doubt, and we recognize our agreement in the assertion that "What God did in the incarnation, life, death, resurrection and ascension of Christ, he does not do again. The events are unique; they cannot be repeated, or extended or continued. Yet in this memorial we do not only recall past events: God

makes them present through the Holy Spirit, thus making us participants in Christ (I Cor. 1:9)."[5]

b) Further, the Catholic affirmation that the church "offers Christ" in the mass has in the course of the last half century been increasingly explained in terms which answer Lutheran fears that this detracts from the full sufficiency of Christ's sacrifice. The members of the body of Christ are united through Christ with God and with one another in such a way that they become participants in his worship, his self-offering, his sacrifice to the Father. Through this union between Christ and Christians, the eucharistic assembly "offers Christ" by consenting in the power of the Holy Spirit to be offered by him to the Father.[6] Apart from Christ we have no gifts, no worship, no sacrifice of our own to offer to God. All we can plead is Christ, the sacrificial lamb and victim whom the Father himself has given us.

c) Another historically important point of controversy has been the Roman Catholic position that the eucharistic sacrifice is "propitiatory." Within the context of the emphases which we have outlined above, Catholics today interpret this position as emphatically affirming that the presence of the unique propitiatory sacrifice of the cross in the eucharistic celebration of the church is efficacious for the forgiveness of sins and the life of the world. Lutherans can join them up to this point.[7] They reject, however, what they have understood Trent to say about the mass as a propitiatory sacrifice "offered for the living and the dead,"[8] even though the Apology of the Augsburg Confession concedes with respect to prayer for the dead that "we do not forbid it."[9] We have not discussed this aspect of the problem; further exploration of it is required.

d) In addition to the growing harmony in ways of thinking about the eucharistic sacrifice, there is a significant convergence in the actual practice of eucharistic worship. Doctrine is inevitably interpreted in the light of practice, as well as vice versa, and consequently oppositions on this level can negate apparent doctrinal agreement. For example, the Reformers and later Lutherans have believed that the multiplication of private masses and the associated systems of mass intentions and mass stipends are evidence that Roman Catholics do not take seriously the all-sufficiency of Christ's sacrifice, and this suspicion has been reinforced by such statements of Catholic theologians as "the sacrificial worth of two Masses is just double the sacrificial worth of one Mass."[10] Now, however, the Second Vatican Council in its Constitution on the Sacred Liturgy has declared that the nature of the mass is such that the communal way of celebrating is to be preferred to individual and quasi-private celebrations.[11] As the liturgical renewal progresses in this and other respects, each group in these discussions finds it increasingly easy to understand and approve what the other says about the eucharist in general and its sacrificial aspects in particular.

The question of eucharistic sacrifice is closely related to other issues. The problem of the "real presence" has been the first to claim our attention. Do we, in the eucharist, genuinely encounter Christ in the full reality of his person and sacrificial action? It is therefore to this subject that we now turn.

II
THE PRESENCE OF CHRIST IN THE LORD'S SUPPER

Here, too, there are areas in which this group believes that Roman Catholics and Lutherans can make the same affirmations, and others in which our agreement is not yet complete.

1. *a*) We confess a manifold presence of Christ, the Word of God and Lord of the world. The crucified and risen Lord is present in his body, the people of God, for he is present where two or three are gathered in his name (Mt. 18:20). He is present in baptism, for it is Christ himself who baptizes.[12] He is present in the reading of the scriptures and the proclamation of the gospel. He is present in the Lord's supper.[13]

   b) We affirm that in the sacrament of the Lord's supper Jesus Christ, true God and true man, is present wholly and entirely, in his body and blood, under the signs of bread and wine.[14]

   c) Through the centuries Christians have attempted various formulations to describe this presence. Our confessional documents have in common affirmed that Jesus Christ is "really," "truly" and "substantially" present in this sacrament.[15] This manner of presence "we can scarcely express in words,"[16] but we affirm his presence because we believe in the power of God and the promise of Jesus Christ, "This is my body. . . . This is my blood. . . ."[17] Our traditions have spoken of this presence as "sacramental,"[18] "supernatural" and "spiritual."[19] These terms have different connotations in the two traditions, but they have in common a rejection of a spatial or natural manner of presence, and a rejection of an understanding of the sacrament as only commemorative or figurative.[20] The term "sign," once suspect, is again recognized as a positive term for speaking of Christ's presence in the sacrament.[21] For, though symbols and symbolic actions are used, the Lord's supper is an effective sign: it communicates what it promises; " . . . the action of the Church becomes the effective means whereby God in Christ acts and Christ is present with his people."[22]

d) Although the sacrament is meant to be celebrated in the midst of the believing congregation, we are agreed that the presence of Christ does not come about through the faith of the believer, or through any human power, but by the power of the Holy Spirit through the word.[23]

e) The true body and blood of Christ are present not only at the moment of reception but throughout the eucharistic action.[24]

2. In the following areas our historical divergences are being overcome, although we are unable at present to speak with one voice at every point.

   a) In reference to eucharistic worship:

   a. We agreed that Christ gave us this sacrament in order that we might receive him and participate in his worship of the Father.[25]

   b. We are also agreed that the Lord Jesus Christ is himself to be worshiped, praised and adored; every knee is to bow before him.[26]

   c. We are further agreed that as long as Christ remains sacramentally present, worship, reverence and adoration are appropriate.[27]

   d. Both Lutherans and Catholics link Christ's eucharistic presence closely to the eucharistic liturgy itself. Lutherans, however, have not stressed the prolongation of this presence beyond the communion service as Catholics have done.

e. To be sure, the opposition on this point is not total. Following a practice attested in the early church, Lutherans may distribute the elements from the congregational communion service to the sick in private communion, in some cases as an extension of this service, in some cases with the words of institution spoken either for their proclamatory value or as consecration.

f. Also in harmony with a eucharistic practice attested in the early church, Roman Catholics have traditionally reserved the consecrated host for communicating the sick, which, according to the Instruction of May 25, 1967, is the "primary and original purpose" of reservation.[28] The adoration of Christ present in the reserved sacrament is of later origin and is a secondary end.[29]

The same Instruction repeats the insistence of the Constitution of the Sacred Liturgy that any adoration of the reserved sacrament be harmonized with and in some way derived from the liturgy, "since the liturgy by its very nature surpasses" any nonliturgical eucharistic devotion.[30]

b) In reference to the presence of Christ under both species, a divergence of practice concerning the cup for the laity has been one of the most obvious signs of disunity between Roman Catholics and other Christians. Catholics of the Eastern rites in union with the Roman See have always retained the practice of communion under both species. The Lutheran confessions emphasize the desirability of communion in both kinds in obedience to "a clear command and order of Christ,"[31] but do not deny the sacramental character of communion administered to a congregation in one kind only. At Vatican II the Roman Catholic Church reintroduced, to a modest but significant extent, communion under both kinds for the Western church.[32] The Council thereby recognized that this practice better expresses the sign of the mystery of eucharistic presence. Recent liturgical directives have explicitly acknowledged this principle and have extended this usage.[33]

c) Lutherans traditionally have understood the Roman Catholic use of the term "transubstantiation" to involve:

a. An emphatic affirmation of the presence of Christ's body and blood in the sacrament. With this they are in agreement.

b. An affirmation that God acts in the eucharist, effecting a change in the elements. This also Lutherans teach, although they use a different terminology.[34]

c. A rationalistic attempt to explain the mystery of Christ's presence in the sacrament. This they have rejected as presumptuous.

d. A definitive commitment to one and only one conceptual framework in which to express the change in the elements. This they have regarded as theologically untenable.

It can thus be seen that there is agreement on the "that," the full reality of Christ's presence. What has been disputed is a particular way of stating the "how," the manner in which he becomes present.

Today, however, when Lutheran theologians read contemporary Catholic expositions,[35] it becomes clear to them that the dogma of transubstantiation intends to affirm the fact of Christ's presence and of the change which takes place, and is not an attempt to explain how Christ becomes present. When the dogma is understood in this way, Lutherans find that they also must acknowledge that it is a legitimate way of attempting to express the mystery, even though they continue to believe that the conceptuality associated with "transubstantiation" is misleading and therefore prefer to avoid the term.

Our conversations have persuaded us of both the legitimacy and the limits of theological efforts to explore the mystery of Christ's presence in the sacrament. We are also persuaded that no single vocabulary or conceptual framework can be adequate, exclusive or final in this theological enterprise. We are convinced that current theological trends in both traditions give great promise for increasing convergence and deepened understanding of the eucharistic mystery.

CONCLUSION

There are still other questions that must be examined before we Catholic and Lutheran participants in these conversations would be prepared to assess our over-all agreements and disagreements on the doctrine of the sacrament of the altar. To mention two important omissions, we have not yet attempted to clarify our respective positions on the roles of the laity and the clergy, the "general" and "special" priesthood, in sacramental celebrations, nor have we discussed the pressing problem of the possibilities of intercommunion apart from full doctrinal and ecclesiastical fellowship.

On the two major issues which we have discussed at length, however, the progress has been immense. Despite all remaining differences in the ways we speak and think of the eucharistic sacrifice and our Lord's presence in his supper, we are no longer able to regard ourselves as divided in the one holy catholic and apostolic faith on these two points. We therefore prayerfully ask our fellow Lutherans and Catholics to examine their consciences and root out many ways of thinking, speaking and acting, both individually and as churches, which have obscured their unity in Christ on these as on many other matters.

Notes

1. Various terms are current in the different Christian traditions for this sacrament: e.g., eucharist, holy communion, sacrament of the altar, mass. We shall use them interchangeably. Further, in order to mark the way our statement shares in the growing ecumenical consensus, we shall, on occasion, use language from the documents of the ecumenical movement to express our own convictions.

2. Scripture and the history of theology contain many ways of describing Christ's sacrifice and therefore also the sacrificial character of the memorial of that sacrifice which is the eucharist. The most general meaning of "sacrifice" is broader than any current in contemporary usage—or in that of the sixteenth century. Thus, according to the Second World Conference on Faith and Order (Edinburgh, 1937), "If sacrifice is understood as it was by our Lord and His followers and in the early Church, it includes, not His death only, but the obedience of His earthly ministry, and His risen and ascended life, in which He still does His Father's will and ever liveth to make intercession for us" (L. Vischer, ed., *A Documentary History of the Faith and Order Movement, 1927–1963* [St. Louis: Bethany Press, 1963] p. 57). In what follows, however, no particular theory of "sacrifice" or of related terms such as "propitiation" is presupposed.

3. *Consultation on Church Union: Principles* (Cincinnati: Foreward Movement Press, 1967) p. 50. See also the Montreal Faith and Order affirmation: the Lord's supper is "a sacrament of the presence of the crucified and glorified Christ until he come, and a means whereby the sacrifice of the cross, which we proclaim, is operative within the church" (P.C. Rodger, ed., *The Fourth World Conference on Faith and Order: Montreal, 1963,* p. 73).

4. Rodger, *op. cit.*, pp. 73–74. See also the *Apology of the Augsburg Confession* XXIV, 30–88, esp. 33, 35, 74–75, 87. References to the Lutheran Confessions are based on *Die Bekenntnisschriften der Evangelisch-Lutherischen Kirche* (5th ed.; Göttingen, 1964.)

5. Rodger, *op. cit.*, p. 73.

6. Luther says: "not that we offer Christ as a sacrifice, but that Christ offers us"; but he also holds that this involves a sense in which "we offer Christ": "Through it (faith), in connection with the sacrament, we offer ourselves, our need, our prayer, praise and thanksgiving in Christ, and thereby we offer Christ. . . . I also offer Christ in that I

desire and believe that he accepts me and my prayer and praise and presents it to God in his own person" (A *Treatise on the New Testament,* in *Luther's Works* 35 [Philadelphia: Fortress Press, 1961] 98–101). This agrees with the testimony of the Second Vatican Council, which, quoting St. Augustine, says that the "aim" of the sacrifice offered in the eucharist is that "the entire commonwealth of the redeemed, that is, the community and the society of the saints, be offered as a universal sacrifice to God through the High Priest who in His Passion offered His very Self for us that we might be the body of so exalted a Head" (*Decree on the Ministry and Life of Priests,* no. 2; tr. W.M. Abbott and J. Gallagher, eds., *The Documents of Vatican II* [New York: Guild Press, 1966] pp. 535–36; quotation from Augustine's *City of God* 10, 6). The continuation of this quotation is paraphrased in the 1947 encyclical *Mediator Dei,* no. 125: "in the sacrament of the altar which she [the church] offers, she herself is also offered." The contemporary Catholic theologian Karl Rahner explains this point by saying that the eucharistic offering of Christ inseparably involves "the believing, inner 'yes' of men to the movement of loving obedience of Christ to the Father." He goes on to speak directly to the fears which Protestants have expressed regarding the notion of the "sacrifice of the mass": "The sacrifice of the mass creates no new gracious and saving will in God vis-a-vis the world which did not already exist through the cross (and only through the cross!)." "We can speak of 'moving' God to forgiveness, reconciliation, mercy and assistance through the sacrifice of the mass only in the sense that the gracious will of God, founded exclusively on the reconciliation of the cross, becomes visible in the sacrifice of the mass, comes to man . . . and takes hold of him"—producing, Rahner goes on to suggest, manifold effects in the worshipers and, through their actions and prayers, in the world ("Die vielen Messen und das eine Opfer," *Zeitschrift für katholische Theologie* 71 [1949] 267 and 288).

7. A question can still be raised whether the word "propitiatory," given its usual connotations, correctly describes the Father's action in Christ on Calvary. Cf. C.F.D. Moule, *The Sacrifice of Christ* (Philadelphia, Fortress Press, 1964), pp. vi–viii, 33 f., and the literature cited on p. 46.

8. Denzinger-Schönmetzer 1753 (950).

9. XXXIV, 94.

10. A. Vonier, *Collected Works* 2 (London, 1952) 343. It should be noted that Vonier does not regard such a statement as irreconcilable with his own insistence on the uniqueness and sufficiency of Christ's sacrifice.

11. Cf. *Constitution on the Sacred Liturgy,* nos. 26 and 27.

12. Cf. *Constitution on the Sacred Liturgy,* no. 7; St. Augustine, *Treatise on the Gospel of John* 6, 1, 7 (PL 35, 1428).

13. Cf. *Constitution on the Sacred Liturgy,* no. 7; *Instruction on Eucharistic Worship* (May 25, 1967) no. 9; FC (= *Formula of Concord*) SD (= *Solid Declaration*) VIII, 76–84.

14. 1 Cor. 11:27. Cf. Denzinger-Schönmetzer (hereafter DS) 1636, 1640 f., 1651, 1653. Writing of the eucharistic presence, E. Schlink states: "The divine nature of Christ is not without the human nature and the human nature is not without the divine nature" (*Theology of the Lutheran Confessions* [Philadelphia, 1961] p. 158.) See also FC SD VII, 60; VIII, 76–84.

15. Cf. DS 1636; Ap (= *Apology of the Augsburg Confession*) X, 1, 4; FC Ep (= Epitome) VII, 6, 34; SD VII, 88, 126.

16. DS 1636. Cf. FC SD VII, 38.

17. Cf. DS 1636; FC Ep VII, 16 f.; SD VII, 97–103, 106.

18. DS 1636. Cf. FC Ep VII, 15; SD VII, 63.

19. FC Ep VII, 14 f. In the context of the *Formula of Concord,* it is clear that "spiritual" here is not opposed to "real." Cf. SD VII, 94–106, 118.

20. Cf AC (= *Augsburg Confession*) X; Ap X, 1 ff.; FC Ep VII, 6 f., 26 ff., 34; SD VII, 2–11, 38, 48 f.; DS 1636, 1651.

21. Cf. DS 1651; FD SD VII, 7, 49, 116; *Constitution on the Sacred Liturgy,* nos. 33, 59; *Instruction on Eucharistic Worship,* no. 6.

22. *Consultation on Church Union: Principles,* p. 49.

23. Cf. LC (= *Large Catechism*) V, 9f., 14; FC Ep VII, 9, 35; SD VII, 73–82, 89, 121; DS 1636 f.;1640. See also DS 1612; FC Ep VII, 8; SD VII, 16, 32, 89; LC IV, 52, and V, 4 ff., 15–18. Catholics see in these affirmations of the Lutheran Confessions the essential content of the Catholic doctrine of the *ex opere operato* working of the sacraments. In some of the pre-Tridentine Confessions, Lutherans rejected a concept of *opus operatum* which Catholics do not recognize as their own. Cf. DS 1606 ff., 1612.

24. Cf. AC X, 1; FC SD VII, 14; Ep VII, 6: "We believe . . . that in the holy supper the body and blood of Christ are truly and essentially present and are truly distributed and received *(wahrhaftig ausgeteilet und empfangen werde)*. . . ." In his *Sermon on the Sacrament of the Body and Blood of Christ* (1526; WA [= Weimar edition] 19, 491, 13), Luther declared: "As soon as Christ says: 'This is my body,' his body is present through the Word and the power of the Holy Spirit" (tr. F. Ahrens, American edition 36, 341). Cf. WA 30/1, 53, 122.—Trent (DS 1654) refers to Christ's presence before reception as "ante (usum)." For Trent *usus* means the actual reception by the communicant: "in usu, dum sumitur" *(ibid.)*. Lutherans speak of the whole liturgical action as *usus:* the consecration, distribution and reception *(sumptio)* of the sacrament (FC SD VII, 85 f.). If, therefore, Lutherans do not speak of Christ being present before or apart from "use," this is not to be understood as contradicting Trent; for the Lutheran Confessions agree that Jesus is present *(adesse)* in the sacrament before he is received *(sumi)*, that is, *ante sumptionem.* It is "the body and blood of Christ" which "are distributed to us to eat and to drink. . . ." (SD VII, 82).

25. DS 1643: "(sacramentum) quod fuerit a Christo Domino, ut sumatur, institutum."

26. Cf. Phil 2:10.

27. Cf. DS 1643, 1656; FC SD VII, 126: one must not "deny that Christ himself, true God and man, who is truly and essentially present in the Supper when it is rightly used, should be adored in spirit and in truth in all places but especially where his community is assembled" (ed. T.G. Tappert). See also Luther, WA 11, 447 (Amer. ed. 36, 294); St. Augustine, *On Psalm 98,* 9 (PL 37, 1264).

28. *Instruction on Eucharistic Worship,* no. 49.

29. Cf. *ibid.* As Dom Lambert Beauduin has expressed it, the eucharist was not reserved in order to be adored; rather, because it was reserved, it was adored (cf. *Mélanges liturgiques . . . de Dom L. Beauduin* [Louvain, 1954] p. 265). It should be noted, however, that adoration of the reserved sacrament has been very much a part of Catholic life and a meaningful form of devotion to Catholics for many centuries.

30. *Instruction on Eucharistic Worship,* no. 58; cf. *Constitution on the Sacred Liturgy,* no. 13.

31. AC XXII, 1.

32. Cf. *Constitution on the Sacred Liturgy,* no. 55. It should be noted that some scholars hold that communion under both kinds has not always been the practice within the church even in ancient times. For example, J. Jeremias (*The Eucharistic Words of Jesus* [New York, 1964] p. 115) suggests that "the breaking of the bread" in the New Testament refers to communion under one species. Other scholars disagree.

33. Cf. *Instruction on Eucharistic Worship,* no. 32.

34. Lutherans traditionally speak of the change that takes place in the elements as involving a sacramental union with the body and blood of Christ analogous to the hypostatic union of the human and divine natures in Christ; cf. FC SD VII, 36 f. Coupled with this affirmation is the statement that the bread and wine are essentially untransformed *(unvorwandelten);* cf. SD VII, 35 ff. In Ep VII, 22 the Roman Catholic affirmation of transubstantiation is understood to involve an annihilation *(zunicht werden)* of the bread and wine. It should be noted, however, that Trent's understanding of transubstan-

tiation has nothing to do with the idea of annihilation of the elements. Catholic theologians emphasize today that the substantial change of bread and wine is a sacramental change which involves no change in "the chemical, physical or botanical reality of bread and wine" (E. Schillebeeckx, "Transubstantiation, Transfinalization, Transignification," *Worship* 40 [1966] 337). Further, on the basis of Ap X, 2, which cites with approval the Greek tradition that the bread is truly changed into the body of Christ ("mutato pane"; "panem . . . vere mutari"), there is a certain sense in which "one can stand on Lutheran ground and talk about a transformation of the elements *(Verwandlung der Elemente).* Cf. Fr. Brunstaed, *Theologie der lutherischen Bekenntnisschriften* (Guetersloh, 1951) p. 156.

35. Cf. K. Rahner, "The Presence of Christ in the Sacrament of the Lord's Supper," in *Theological Investigations* 4 (Baltimore, 1966) 287–311; E. Schillebeeckx, "Christus tegenwoordigheid in de Eucharistie," *Tijdschrift voor Theologie* 5 (1965) 136–72.

Eucharist and Ministry: A Lutheran-Roman Catholic Statement

COMMON OBSERVATIONS ON EUCHARISTIC MINISTRY

Introduction

1. The problem of the Ministry[1] is an inevitable item on any agenda of doctrinal discussion between Roman Catholics and Lutherans. In each of our other discussions, we have found ourselves confronted by it.

2. In our treatment of the Nicene creed and the significance of dogmatic statements we saw the necessary connection between dogma (i.e., authoritative creeds and confessions) and the teaching authority of the church.[2] Our dialogue on baptism made it possible for us to confess together our faith that this sacrament is an act of Christ by which God calls his church into being. At the same time we recognized that differences of interpretation of this sacramental act have frequently been rooted in differing understandings of the Ministry of the church.[3]

3. Sessions devoted to the problems of the eucharist as sacrifice and of the presence of Christ in the sacrament showed again a remarkable agreement in these much controverted topics, but also showed us how many matters could be cleared up only by discussion of the question of the Minister of the eucharist.[4] This became even more clear when we devoted one meeting to the problems of receiving communion in each other's eucharistic celebrations. There we recognized that a solution was not possible until the problems of the Ministry were squarely faced.

4. In our sessions dealing with the Ministry, as in our other discussions, we have attempted to clear away misunderstandings, to clarify to each other the theological concerns of our traditions, and to see what common affirmations we can make about the reality of the Ministry. Neither Catholic nor Lutheran participants came to this dialogue with a complete doctrine of this Ministry and we have not formulated

one in our discussions. We have found certain areas that we judge are central to this reality and critical for the unity of the church. In these areas we make common affirmations. We gratefully acknowledge the contribution of the ongoing discussion of the Ministry in the ecumenical movement, both for its clarification of the theological issues and for its service in prodding us to do our thinking about the Ministry in a responsibly ecumenical context.[5]

5. Again we have noted that in our use of the same terms, we have not always meant the same things, and that differing theological language has sometimes masked theological concerns which are similar if not identical. We are convinced that in spite of differing vocabularies and problematics we are both approaching greater agreement on what God is doing in his church, as is evidenced in the following paragraphs.

I. The Ministry in the Context of God's Act in Christ

6. Both the Catholic and the Lutheran traditions confess that God fulfills his promise to his people and definitively reveals his saving love for the world in the life, death, resurrection, and coming again of Jesus Christ. The God of Israel acts and speaks in the deeds and words of his Son.

7. Scripture attests that it was through the work of the Holy Spirit that Jews and Gentiles alike repented, believed, and were baptized. Thus were men united by Christ into the unique community called the church.

8. The Lord of the church, through the Holy Spirit, continues to act sacramentally and to proclaim his teaching through the men whom he has united with himself. The words and acts of Jesus in which the God of Israel has revealed his love for all mankind are the "good news." Under the guidance of the Spirit the first believers proclaimed by deed and word this gospel of the saving presence, activity, and teaching of the Lord.

9. The church has, then, the task of proclaiming the gospel to all, believers and unbelievers. This task or service of the whole church is spoken of as "ministry" *(diakonia).* In the course of this statement, we employ the term ministry (lower case *m,* with or without the definite article) in this sense. The ministry of the church, thus defined, will be distinguished from the (or a) Ministry, a particular form of service—a specific order, function or gift (charism) within and for the sake of Christ's church in its mission to the world. The term Minister in this document refers to the person to whom this Ministry has been

entrusted. We are convinced that the special Ministry must not be discussed in isolation but in the context of the ministry of the whole people of God.

II. The Ministry in the Context of the Church

A. The Ministry of the People of God

10. The ministry which devolves upon the whole church can rightly be described as a priestly service (*hierateuma,* cf. I Peter 2:5, 9), such as that of ancient Israel, whom Yahweh fashioned into "a kingdom of priests and a holy nation" among all peoples (Exodus 19:5–6). We are agreed that in Jesus Christ God has provided his people with a high priest and sacrifice (cf. Hebrews 4:14ff.). All who are united with Jesus as Christ and Lord by baptism and faith are also united with, and share, his priesthood. We recognize therefore that the whole church has a priesthood in Christ, i.e., a ministry or service from God to men, that "they may see your good deeds and glorify God on the day of visitation" (I Peter 2:12). They are thus privileged and obliged to represent the concerns of God to men and those of men to God.

11. To enable the church to be what God intends it to be in and for the world, God bestows within this priesthood various gifts for ministering. In particular, "God has appointed . . . apostles, prophets, teachers," etc. (I Corinthians 12:28–30; cf. Romans 12:6–8, Ephesians 4:7–12). While no single Ministry mentioned in the New Testament corresponds exactly to the special Ministry of the later church,[6] many of the specialized tasks of which we hear in the New Testament are entrusted to that later Ministry: preaching the gospel, administering what the church came to call sacraments, caring for the faithful. We turn now to what we can say in common of this special Ministry in the church (keeping in mind the particular aspect of our study—valid Ministry in relation to the eucharist).

B. The Special Ministry

12. Just as the church is to be seen in the light of God's love, his act in Christ, and the work of the Spirit, so also the Ministry is to be seen in light of the love of God, his saving act in Jesus Christ, and the ongoing activity of the Holy Spirit. This Ministry has the twofold task of proclaiming the gospel to the world—evangelizing, witnessing, serving—and of building up in Christ those who already believe—teaching, exhorting, reproving, and sanctifying, by word and sacrament. For this twofold work, the spirit endows the Ministry with varieties of gifts,

and thus helps the church to meet new situations in its pilgrimage. Through proclamation of the word and administration of the sacraments, this Ministry serves to unify and order the church in a special way for its ministry.[7]

13. The Ministry stands with the people of God under Christ but also speaks in the name of Christ to his people. On the one hand, the Ministry as part of the church's ministry stands under the Word and the Spirit, under judgment as well as under grace. But it also has a special role within the ministry of the people of God, proclaiming God's Word, administering the sacraments, exhorting and reproving.[8]

14. This Ministry is "apostolic." The term "apostolic" has had a variety of references: it has been applied for instance to doctrine, practices, authority.[9] Indeed, the *variety* of ways in which the gospel is expressed in the early church may be recognized as a feature of apostolicity.[10]

15. Apostolicity has usually implied some sort of succession in what is apostolic. For many Catholics the phrase "apostolic succession" has meant succession in the ministerial office as a sign of unbroken transmission from the apostles. The stress for Lutherans has been on succession in apostolic doctrine. Historical studies have shown that in the New Testament and patristic periods there was stress on doctrinal succession; there also arose an emphasis on succession in apostolic office as a very important way of ensuring doctrinal succession and thus providing a sign of unity and a defense against heresy.[11]

16. Entry into the Ministry has been designated by both Catholics and Lutherans as "ordination." This term too has had a variety of meanings. Catholics have seen in ordination a sacramental act, involving a gift of the Holy Spirit, a charism for the service of the church and the world, the designation to a special service in the church, and the quality of permanence and unrepeatability. Lutherans, using a different (and more restricted) definition of sacrament, have generally been reluctant to use "sacrament" with reference to ordination, although the Apology of the Augsburg Confession is willing to do so (13, 9–13). Because of post-Reformation polemics, Lutherans became even more reluctant to use the term. Their consistent practice, however, shows a conviction concerning the sacramental reality of ordination to the Ministry. Lutherans too invoke the Holy Spirit for the gifts of the Ministry, see ordination as the setting apart for a specific service in the church and for the world, and regard the act as having a once-for-all significance.[12] Thus there is considerable convergence between the Catholic and the Lutheran understandings of ordination.

17. The expressions "character" and "indelible" have been used

by Catholics with reference to ordination to describe the aspects of gift, charism, designation, and the qualities of permanence and unrepeatability.[13] Lutherans have objected to these terms because of the metaphysical implications they understand to be involved in them. However, historical studies and the renewal of liturgical and sacramental theology have brought into our discussions an emphasis upon the functional aspect of character and upon the gift of the Spirit.[14] These factors may help us to overcome traditional disagreements and open the way to a common approach to this complex of problems.

18. Having discussed the terms "apostolic," "ordination," and "character," we now affirm together that entry into this apostolic and God-given Ministry is by ordination. No man ordains himself or can claim this office as his right, but he is called by God and designated in and through the church. In reference to what has been called "character," we are agreed that ordination to the Ministry is for a lifetime of service and is not to be repeated.

C. The Structuring of the Special Ministry

19. Although we agree that Christ has given his church a special order of Ministry, we must also acknowledge the diverse ways in which this Ministry has been structured and implemented in the Catholic and Lutheran traditions.

20. In Catholicism, the Ministry of order has been apportioned among three Ministries or major orders: deacon, priest *(presbyter),* and bishop. All are conferred by a rite of ordination that includes the laying on of hands. The distribution of ministerial functions among these orders varies and has varied. In the present discipline, all three are appointed to baptize and proclaim the gospel; only priests and bishops celebrate the eucharist; only bishops ordain to major orders. Without prejudice to their belief that it is the bishop who possesses the fullness of the Ministry conferred by ordination,[15] Catholics note that it is both historically and theologically significant that priests have ordained others as priests.[16]

21. The Lutheran tradition has one order of ordained Ministers, usually called pastors, which combines features of the episcopate and the presbyterate. This Ministry is also conferred by a rite of ordination that includes the laying on of hands. The pastor who has received this Ministry possesses the fullness of that which ordination confers and in general he corresponds in his functions with the bishop in the Catholic tradition.[17] In the Lutheran churches represented in this dialogue, the ordination of pastors is reserved to the district or synodical president

or a pastor designated by him. The ordination of pastors in these churches goes back historically to priests ordained in the Catholic tradition who, on becoming Lutherans and lacking Catholic bishops who would impose hands on successors, themselves imposed hands for the ordination of co-workers and successors in the Ministry. From the Lutheran standpoint, such an ordination in presbyteral succession designates and qualifies the Lutheran pastor for all the functions that the Catholic priest *(presbyter)* exercises, including that of celebrating a eucharist which would be called (in Catholic terminology) valid. It is to be noted, however, that the Lutheran confessions indicate a preference for retaining the traditional episcopal order and discipline of the church, and express regret that no bishop was willing to ordain priests for evangelical congregations.[18]

22. These ways in which the Ministry has been structured and implemented in our two traditions appear to us to be consonant with apostolic teaching and practice. We are agreed that the basic reality of the apostolic Ministry can be preserved amid variations in structure and implementation, in rites of ordination and in theological explanation. As we learn more of the complex history of the Ministry, we begin to grasp the ways in which this gift of God to his church is able to assimilate valuable elements from different ages and cultures without losing its authentic apostolic character. In this context we find that the present moment speaks persuasively to us, urging both the renewal of what is basic in our apostolic heritage as well as openness to the variants that our Christian witness to the world requires. In presenting these common observations on the eucharistic Ministry we are aware of the difficulties implied therein for both of our traditions,[19] as our respective reflections in the following two chapters indicate. That we have not found these difficulties insuperable is indicated by the recommendations which each group has been able to make. We rejoice together at the future prospect of Christian recognition and reconciliation opened by these recommendations.

REFLECTIONS OF THE LUTHERAN PARTICIPANTS

23. Lutherans approach the questions dealt with in this common statement on the basis of the conviction that their churches belong to the one, holy, catholic, and apostolic church. They regard their ordained clergymen as persons validly set apart for the Ministry of the gospel and of the sacraments in the church of Christ. They hold that

the sacraments that these ordained clergymen administer in their midst are valid sacraments. In their confessional writings, the Lutherans claim to stand in the authentic catholic tradition.[1]

24. On the basis of their confessional writings, Lutherans also affirm the churchly character of the Roman Catholic community and the validity of the Roman Catholic church's Ministry and sacraments. For Lutherans the church exists wherever there is a community of believers among whom the gospel of God's grace in Christ is responsibly proclaimed and applied and the sacraments are administered in accordance with our Lord's intention.[2] The responsible proclaiming and applying of the gospel and the administering of the sacraments require that persons be set aside for this office and function.[3]

25. Some Lutherans have had misgivings in the area of Roman Catholic commitment to the gospel. Nevertheless, Lutherans have always held that as long as the gospel is proclaimed in any Christian community in such a way that it remains the gospel and as long as the sacraments are administered in that community in such a way that they are channels of the Holy Spirit, human beings are through these means reborn to everlasting life and the church continues to subsist in these communities. We believe that the Roman Catholic church meets these criteria.

26. Noteworthy in this connection is the insistence of the Lutheran symbolical books that the church never ceased to exist down to their own time. Concretely they declare that St. Bernard of Clairvaux (1090–1153), the most famous son of the Cistercian Order, St. Dominic Guzman (1170–1221), founder of the Order of Preachers, and St. Francis of Assisi (1181?–1226), founder of the Order of Friars Minor, are "holy fathers" *(sancti patres)*.[4] As evidence of the persistence of the church and of the communication of the Holy Spirit within it through baptism, the Book of Concord cites not only St. Bernard, but also, bracketed with him, two late medieval churchmen of quite diverse theological views, John le Charlier de Gerson (1363–1429) of the University of Paris and John Hus (1369?–1415) of Prague.[5]

27. There is no doubt in Lutheran minds that the Roman Catholic church subscribes to the fundamental Trinitarian and Christological dogmas, "the high articles of the divine majesty" (Smalcald Articles, Part One). Lutherans must take seriously the Roman Catholic church's profession of the catholic creeds—including the "for us men and for our salvation" and the "was crucified also for us" of the creed of Constantinople ("Nicene Creed") and the "suffered for our salvation" of

the Symbol *Quicumque vult* ("Athanasian Creed"). The Roman Catholic church affirms its kinship with "those Christians who openly confess Jesus Christ as God and Lord and as the sole Mediator between God and man to the glory of one God, Father, Son, and Holy Spirit."[6] Lutherans are well aware that Roman Catholics pray the same Sunday collects that Lutherans pray (including those that stress man's helplessness and salvation by grace alone, such as those for Sexagesima Sunday, the Second Sunday in Lent, Laetare Sunday, Easter Day, and the First, Third, Eighth, Twelfth, Fourteenth, Sixteenth, and Eighteenth Sundays after Trinity). They know too that the Roman Catholic church affirms the gospel in unmistakable terms in many other places of its liturgy—for example, the *Exsultet* in the Easter Eve office and the *Veni, Sancte Spiritus,* in Whitsuntide.[7]

28. The episcopal structure and polity of the Roman Catholic church does not in itself constitute a problem for Lutherans. Indeed, the Book of Concord itself affirms the desire of the Lutheran reformers to preserve, if possible, the episcopal polity that they had inherited from the past.[8] As long as the ordained Ministry is retained, any form of polity which serves the proclamation of the gospel is acceptable. Within their own community some Lutherans have episcopacy with a formal "apostolic succession"[9] (e.g., Sweden, Finland, and some Asian and African churches). Other Lutherans have episcopacy without the "apostolic succession" (e.g., Norway, Denmark, Iceland, and Germany). Lutherans also have or have had churches governed by synods, by consistories, and by ministeria.

29. Even with the misgivings that sixteenth-century Lutherans had about the papacy,[10] the Lutheran symbolical books recognize the bishop of Rome as the lawful pastor of the church in that city.[11] In fact, the confessional writings do not exclude the possibility that the papacy might have a symbolic or functional value in a wider area as long as its primacy is seen as being of human right.[12]

30. We have no basis in the Book of Concord for denying that Roman Catholic priests are competent Ministers of the gospel and the sacraments. While some Lutherans in times past have doubted that the Ministry of Roman Catholic clergymen is really a Ministry of the gospel, the fact that Vatican II has called the proclamation of the gospel of God to all a "primary duty" of priests in the Roman Catholic church[13] should remove these uncertainties.

31. Within this context, we see no reason for doubting the validity of the sacrament of the altar within the Roman Catholic church.[14] In conformity with the Lutheran confessional writings, we hold that the

distribution and reception of the sacrament in one kind only, conflicts with the biblical injunction, but we do not hold that this invalidates the sacrament that Roman Catholic communicants receive. We note that Eastern Catholics in union with Rome have always received holy communion under both kinds. We likewise observe with joy the increasing frequency with which members of Roman-rite congregations are communicated under both kinds in the Roman Catholic church since Vatican II.

32. There are Lutherans who do not find it easy to overcome their concerns about the inferences that they have heard drawn from the Roman Catholic teaching of transubstantiation, about some of the language in which the sacrificial aspect of the sacrament of the altar has been popularly described, and about some of the attitudes and practices involving the reserved sacrament. But we observe that, in terms of the Lutheran theology of consecration, these things do not affect the *validity* of the sacrament of the altar as Roman Catholic priests celebrate and dispense it. At the same time, we have taken cognizance elsewhere of the official Roman Catholic instruction on eucharistic worship (1967) which asserts that the "primary and original purpose of the reservation of the sacrament is the communication of the sick" and that "the adoration of Christ present in the reserved sacrament is of later origin and is a secondary end."[15] In the same connection we have gratefully recorded the increasing measure of agreement between Lutherans and Roman Catholics on the sacrificial aspects of the sacrament of the altar. We have likewise stated that today "when Lutheran theologians read contemporary (Roman) Catholic expositions, it becomes clear to them that the dogma of transubstantiation intends to affirm the fact of Christ's presence and of the change which takes place and is not an attempt to explain how Christ becomes present."[16]

33. Although we see our common statement as removing some of the obstacles that separate Roman Catholics and Lutherans, there are still problems to be discussed before we can recommend pulpit and altar fellowship. The common statement that precedes these reflections does not provide an adequate basis for the establishment of such fellowship. Nor does it constitute approval by either community of every practice fostered or tolerated by the other community.

34. We Lutherans are conscious of the real and imagined differences that centuries of mutual separation have built up between us and Roman Catholics. We are sensitive to the canonical, traditional, and psychological barriers to eucharistic sharing that are present in both

communities. We are aware of the many doctrinal discussions with other churches that both the Roman Catholic and the Lutheran churches in the United States are conducting, and recognize the magnitude of the theological work that still needs to be done.[17]

35. **As Lutherans, we joyfully witness that in theological dialogue with our Roman Catholic partners we have again seen clearly a fidelity to the proclamation of the gospel and the administration of the sacraments which confirms our historic conviction that the Roman Catholic church is an authentic church of our Lord Jesus Christ. For this reason we recommend to those who have appointed us that through appropriate channels the participating Lutheran churches be urged to declare formally their judgment that the ordained Ministers of the Roman Catholic church are engaged in a valid Ministry of the gospel, announcing the gospel of Christ and administering the sacraments of faith[18] as their chief responsibilities, and that the body and blood of our Lord Jesus Christ are truly present in their celebrations of the sacrament of the altar.**

REFLECTIONS OF THE ROMAN CATHOLIC PARTICIPANTS

Introduction

36. At first glance the Roman Catholic attitude toward the Lutheran eucharistic Ministry would seem easily determinable. A simplified expression of the traditional Roman Catholic outlook is that those who preside at the eucharist do so in virtue of being ordained by a bishop who stands in succession to the apostles who received from Christ the commission, "Do this in commemoration of me." Without such ordination a man can make no claim to a valid eucharistic Ministry. Now, at the time of the Reformation in Germany the bishops did not ordain Ministers for the congregations that professed to follow Martin Luther; and so it came about that priests who had adopted Lutheran beliefs ordained other men to preside at the eucharist,[1] thus perpetuating a presbyteral rather than an episcopal succession. Among most Lutherans there is no claim to an episcopate in historical succession to the apostles.[2] Thus the Lutheran eucharistic Ministry would seem to be deficient in what Catholics have hitherto regarded as essential elements.

37. Yet, as we Catholics in this dialogue have examined the problem, our traditional objections to the Lutheran eucharistic Ministry

were seen to be of less force today, and reasons emerged for a positive reappraisal. We may group our reflections below under the headings of historical arguments and theological arguments.

I. Historical Arguments

38. It is impossible to prove from the New Testament that the only Ministers of the eucharist were the apostles, their appointed successors, and those ordained by their successors. Modern biblical investigations have shown that there were several different concepts of "apostle" in the New Testament.[3] While Luke-Acts is representative of a strain of New Testament thought that would equate the apostles with the Twelve and hence with those whom Jesus commanded, "Do this in commemoration of me," Paul is representative of a wider (and perhaps earlier) view whereby men, like himself, could be apostles even though they had not been disciples of Jesus during his lifetime. There is no clear biblical evidence that the Twelve were the exclusive Ministers of the eucharist in New Testament times or that they appointed men to preside at the eucharist. (On the other hand, we may add that neither is there evidence that all Christians were eligible Ministers of the eucharist.) While in the local churches, founded by apostles like Paul, there were leaders or persons in authority, we are told very little about how such men were appointed and nothing about their presiding at the eucharist. Even in the Pastoral Epistles (which are of uncertain date), in which there is described a church order featuring bishop-presbyters, we are not told that such figures had a eucharistic Ministry. Of course, this argument drawn from the silence of the New Testament has serious limitations, and the eucharistic practice may have been far more definite than the limited evidence proves. We must insist, however, in face of this silence, how difficult it is to make affirmations about what is necessary in the eucharistic Ministry.

39. At the beginning of the second century (but perhaps even earlier), as attested by Ignatius of Antioch, the bishop had emerged as the highest authority in the local church, and either he or his appointee presided at the eucharist. However, we are not certain how the Ignatian bishop was appointed or that he stood in a chain of historical succession to the apostles by means of ordination or even that the pattern described by Ignatius was universal in the church. Some find in *Didache* 10:7 evidence that wandering charismatic prophets could preside at the eucharist.[4]

40. When the episcopate and the presbyterate had become a gen-

eral pattern in the church, the historical picture still presents uncertainties that affect judgment on the Minister of the eucharist. For instance, is the difference between a bishop and a priest of divine ordination? St. Jerome maintained that it was not;[5] and the Council of Trent, wishing to respect Jerome's opinion, did not undertake to define that the preeminence of the bishop over presbyters was by divine law.[6] If the difference is not of divine ordination, the reservation to the bishop of the power of ordaining Ministers of the eucharist would be a church decision. In fact, in the history of the church there are instances of priests (i.e., presbyters) ordaining other priests, and there is evidence that the church accepted and recognized the Ministry of priests so ordained.[7]

41. By way of summation, we find from the historical evidence that by the sixteenth century there had been a long and almost exclusive practice whereby the only Minister of the eucharist was one ordained by a bishop who had been consecrated as heir to a chain of episcopal predecessors. Yet, in this long history there are lacunae, along with exceptions that offer some precedent for the practice adopted by the Lutherans.

II. Theological Arguments

42. The negative appraisal of the Lutheran eucharistic Ministry that has been traditional among Catholics was not based solely or even chiefly on an analysis of the historical evidence favoring episcopal ordination. Theological factors entered prominently into this appraisal. Here again, however, as we Catholic participants in the dialogue examined the difficulties, we found that they no longer seemed insuperable.

43. A. The question of an authentic eucharistic Ministry in a worshipping community is intimately related to an evaluation of that community as part of the church. The unity that is signified and realized by the reception of the eucharistic body of Christ is related to the unity of the body of Christ which is the church. Formerly the Roman Catholic church did not speak of the Christian denominations that resulted from the Reformation as churches; but in the Second Vatican Council these groups were spoken of as "churches or ecclesial communities,"[8] a change that seems to have theological implications.[9] Not all Catholic theologians would conclude that because a Christian community possesses "ecclesial reality," its table fellowship is necessarily graced by the presence of the body and blood of the Lord. Neverthe-

less, our ability to recognize the Lutheran communities as churches removes a barrier to our favorable understanding of the Lutheran sacred Ministry. We are now obliged to reassess whether the Lutheran communities may not be churches that truly celebrate the holy eucharist.[10]

44. B. It may be objected that while the Lutheran communities do constitute churches, they are defective churches in an essential note that has ramifications for the eucharistic Ministry, namely, apostolicity. This charge is true if apostolicity is defined so as necessarily to include apostolic succession through episcopal consecration.[11] However, it is dubious that apostolicity should be so defined. In the first two centuries of Christianity apostolic succession in doctrine (fidelity to the gospel) was considered more important than simple succession in office or orders.[12] The lists of bishops that appeared late in the second century were intended to demonstrate more a line of legitimatized teachers than a line of sacramental validity.[13] Undoubtedly apostolic succession through episcopal consecration is a valuable sign and aspect of apostolicity, for in church history there is a mutual interplay between doctrinal integrity and the succession of those who are its official teachers. Yet, despite the lack of episcopal succession, the Lutheran church by its devotion to gospel, creed, and sacrament has preserved a form of doctrinal apostolicity.[14]

45. C. In the past, Catholics commonly assumed that Lutherans did not believe in the real presence of Christ's body and blood, sacramentally offered in the eucharistic sacrifice, and consequently were presumably not ordaining a eucharistic Ministry in the sense in which Catholics understood eucharist. This assumption of defective intent now appears to us unfounded; for in our joint statement on the eucharist, we Catholics and Lutherans affirmed our agreement on the real presence and on the sacrificial character of the Lord's supper.[15]

46. D. Still another Catholic difficulty about the Lutheran eucharistic Ministry arose from a fear that the Lutheran understanding of the sacred Ministry was defective. In examining a number of points discussed below, we found that, while there are differences of emphasis and phrasing in the theologies of our respective churches, there is also a gratifying degree of agreement as to the essentials of the sacred Ministry.

47. 1) Do Lutherans recognize that the sacred Ministry is of divine institution? We find the Lutheran affirmation: "God instituted the sacred Ministry of teaching the gospel and administering the sacraments."[16] Also, "The church institutes clergymen by divine com-

mand," so that "ordination performed by a pastor in his own church is valid by divine right."[17]

48. 2) Do Lutherans conceive of the sacred Ministry as simply or primarily a Ministry of the word (preaching) rather than of sacrament? We have found a frequent joining of word and sacrament in the Lutheran writings on the subject. It is true that in the sixteenth century the Lutherans gave emphasis to a Ministry of the word in reaction to what they saw as a danger of a purely ritualistic Ministry. In response, Catholics tended to give emphasis to the dispensation of the sacraments lest the importance of that factor in Ministry be denigrated. In the less apologetic atmosphere currently prevailing, both groups see that the task of the Ministry includes both word and sacrament.

49. 3) Do Lutherans see the sacred Ministry as something beyond or distinct from the general ministry of all believers? It is quite clear that the Lutherans have a concept of a *special* Ministry in the church. "The symbolical books see the sacred ministry both as an office *(ministerium; Amt)* and as an order or estate *(ordo; Stand)* within the church."[18] There have been disagreements among Lutheran theologians about the relation of the special Ministry to the universal priesthood of believers.[19] Catholic theologians too have been unable to state this relationship with complete accord; yet we do find the statement made by the Second Vatican Council that the common priesthood of the faithful and the ministerial priesthood differ from one another in essence and not only in degree.[20] On the Lutheran side there is the affirmation: "We say that no one should be allowed to administer the word and the sacraments in the church unless he is duly called."[21] Theologians of both churches need to clarify further the relation between clergy and laity and to analyze the biblical concept of the royal priesthood of God's people in order to see if that concept really tells us anything about eucharistic Ministry.[22]

50. 4) Do Lutherans recognize the sacramentality of ordination to the sacred Ministry? Actually on one occasion in the Lutheran confessional documents,[23] the term "sacrament" is deemed applicable to ordination, but such language is not common in Lutheran theology. The question is obviously affected by the sixteenth century dispute about the number of Christian sacraments, a dispute which reflected differences in sacramental theology and in the criteria for defining the term, sacrament. Despite the difference of terminology in reference to the sacramentality of ordination, we have heard our Lutheran partners in the dialogue affirming what to us would be the essentials of Catholic teaching on this subject, namely, that ordination to a sacred Ministry

in the church derives from Christ and confers the enduring power to sanctify. We heard the affirmation that "The church has the command to appoint Ministers . . . God approves the Ministry and is present in it."[24] "All three American Lutheran churches understand the Ministry of clergymen to be rooted in *the Gospel.*"[25] "Like the Roman Catholic, the Lutheran too sees ordination as conferring a spiritual authority on the recipient in a once-for-all fashion—namely, the power to sanctify through proclamation . . . of the word of God and the administration of the sacraments."[26]

51. E. Perhaps the most serious obstacle standing in the way of a favorable Catholic evaluation of the Lutheran eucharistic Ministry has been the doctrine of the Council of Trent pertinent to sacred orders. In particular, canon 10 of Session VII (A.D. 1547; DS 1610) denied that all Christians have the power of administering all the sacraments; and canon 7 of Session XXIII (A.D. 1563; DS 1777) said that those who had not been ordained or commissioned by ecclesiastical or canonical power were not legitimate Ministers of the word and the sacraments. It would seem, *prima facie,* that in Trent's judgment Lutheran Ministers, since they have not been ordained by bishops, would not have the power of presiding at the eucharist, and that the Catholic church could not change its stance on this question since the doctrine of Trent is permanently binding.[27] Yet cautions are in order. The Council of Trent was not concerned primarily with passing judgment on the sacred orders of the Reformed communities but with defending the legitimacy of the Catholic priesthood against Protestant attacks.[28] The Tridentine assessment of Protestant ideas about the Ministry is detected chiefly through the implications of its condemnations of anti-Catholic theories. In the anathemas formulated against "Those who say . . ." there is no indication of whether Lutherans are meant in distinction from Calvinists, Zwinglians, Anabaptists, etc. Because of these difficulties, it is not easy to determine Trent's attitude toward the Lutheran eucharistic Ministry and the permanent value of that attitude.

52. One approach to the problem is the contention that the Tridentine attitude was not so absolutely negative as has been thought. Some are not sure that the council meant that a Minister "not ordained by ecclesiastical or canonical power"[29] was really incapable of celebrating the eucharist. They emphasize that all that the council said was that this was not a "lawful" Ministry.[30] They further point out that the term "power" is vague in the Tridentine teaching that all Christians do not have the power to celebrate the eucharist, for that word need mean no more than ecclesial authority or authorization.[31]

53. Another approach to the Tridentine position reckons with the likelihood that the council really did mean implicitly to declare invalid Lutheran orders in the sixteenth century but wonders whether the present situation is not so changed that the Tridentine attitude is now only partially applicable.[32] If Trent rejected the Lutheran Ministry, it did so in the context of what it considered the defective Reformation theology of the church, the sacraments, and the eucharist. (While we may admit that the Tridentine assessment of these Reformation attitudes was not entirely adequate or correct, we should point out that some of the polemic of the Reformers against the legitimacy of Catholic practices likewise had its share of inadequacies and incorrect assessments—there were weaknesses on both sides.) As is evident from the theological arguments already discussed, we have found in the course of our dialogue with the Lutherans that in the twentieth century there is a much broader agreement on theological questions related to the eucharist than there seems to have been in the sixteenth. Thus the whole context of the discussion of Lutheran Ministry has changed. There is indeed something of permanent value for the church in Trent's rejection of abuses; but, without settling the question of the past, one might well conclude that the abuses Trent rejected are not present now.

54. The historical and theological reflections made above move us to doubt whether Roman Catholics should continue to question the eucharistic presence of the Lord in the midst of the Lutherans when they meet to celebrate the Lord's supper. And so we make the following statement:

As Roman Catholic theologians, we acknowledge in the spirit of Vatican II that the Lutheran communities with which we have been in dialogue are truly Christian churches, possessing the elements of holiness and truth that mark them as organs of grace and salvation.[33] Furthermore, in our study we have found serious defects in the arguments customarily used against the validity of the eucharistic Ministry of the Lutheran churches. In fact, we see no persuasive reason to deny the possibility of the Roman Catholic church recognizing the validity of this Ministry. Accordingly we ask the authorities of the Roman Catholic church whether the ecumenical urgency flowing from Christ's will for unity[34] may not dictate that the Roman Catholic church recognize the validity of the Lutheran Ministry and, correspondingly, the presence of the body and blood of Christ in the eucharistic celebrations of the Lutheran churches.

55. Lest we be misunderstood, we wish to add the following clarifications:

a. While this statement has implications for the question of Lutheran orders in the past, we have not made that question the focus of our discussions, and we do not think it necessary to solve that problem in order to make the present statement. Nor do we attempt to decide whether recognition by the Roman Catholic church would be constitutive of validity or merely confirmatory of existing validity.

56. b. By appealing for *church* action we stress our belief that the problem should be resolved by the respective churches and not on the level of private action by Ministers and priests, for such private action may jeopardize a larger solution.

57. c. In speaking of the recognition of a Lutheran Ministry not ordained by bishops, we are not in any way challenging the age-old insistence on ordination by a bishop within our own church or covertly suggesting that it be changed. While we believe that the church of Jesus Christ is free to adapt the structure of the divinely instituted Ministry in the way she sees fit (so long as the essential meaning and function of apostolic Ministry is retained), we affirm explicitly that the apostolic Ministry is retained in a preeminent way in the episcopate, the presbyterate, and the diaconate. We would rejoice if episcopacy in apostolic succession, functioning as the effective sign of church unity, were acceptable to all;[35] but we have envisaged a practical and immediate solution in a *de facto* situation where episcopacy is not yet seen in that light.

58. d. We do not wish our statement (no. 54) concerning the Lutherans to be thought applicable to others without further and careful consideration, i.e., to other churches, communities, or movements that have the practice of ordination by priests, or where the congregation ordains, or where there is a spontaneous charismatic ministry. Our outlook on the possibilities of accepting the Lutheran eucharistic Ministry has been greatly determined by our increasing awareness that so much of Lutheran doctrine, practice, and piety is sound from the Catholic viewpoint, particularly in the areas of church, Ministry, and eucharist. Other churches and communities would have to be studied from a similar perspective before one could make a recommendation concerning their Ministries and eucharistic celebrations.

59. e. We caution that we have not discussed the implications that a recognition of valid Ministry would have for intercommunion or eucharistic sharing. Obviously recognition of valid Ministry and sharing the eucharistic table are intimately related, but we are not in a position to affirm that the one must or should lead to the other. At the same time, we note that the *Ecumenical Directory,* promulgated by the

Vatican Secretariat for Christian Unity, states that Catholics in circumstances involving sufficient reason or urgent cause may receive the sacraments of the holy eucharist, penance, and the anointing of the sick from one who has been "validly ordained."[36]

Notes

Common Observations on Eucharistic Ministry

1. For the distinction between *M*inistry and *m*inistry, see paragraph 9 below.

2. *The Status of the Nicene Creed as Dogma of the Church.* Published Jointly by Representatives of the U.S.A. National Committee of the Lutheran World Federation and the Bishops' Commission for Ecumenical Affairs. 1965.

3. *Lutherans and Catholics in Dialogue II: One Baptism for the Remission of Sins.* Edited by Paul C. Empie and William W. Baum. Published jointly by Representatives of the U.S.A. National Committee of the Lutheran World Federation and the Bishops' Commission for Ecumenical Affairs. 1966.

4. *Lutherans and Catholics in Dialogue III: The Eucharist as Sacrifice.* Published jointly by Representatives of the U.S.A. National Committee of the Lutheran World Federation and the Bishops' Committee for Ecumenical and Interreligious Affairs. 1967.

5. *Faith and Order Findings,* Montreal, 1963 (Minneapolis: Augsburg Publishing House, 1963).

6. Development of the Ministry of the Christian church is difficult to trace and much controverted. Cf. Jerome D. Quinn, "Ministry in the New Testament," pp. 69–100. The passages cited in the text above list the following varieties of ministering:
1 Corinthians 12: apostles, prophets, teachers, miracle-workers, healers, administrators, those who speak in tongues;
Romans 12: prophecy, serving *(diakonia),* teaching, exhorting, liberality in giving, zeal in aid, acts of mercy;
Ephesians 4: apostles, prophets, evangelists, pastors, teachers.
Everyone would agree that some of these categories belong in the special Ministry of the church (e.g., apostles, prophets, teachers), and that others reflect the ministry of the people of God (acts of mercy, aid and helping), and that some are hard to categorize (healing, teaching). Of particular interest, in any sketch of the development, would be the Ministry of "the Twelve," the Ministry of the apostles in a broader sense, the Ministry of the presbyter-bishop, the Ministry of those who baptized, and the Ministry of those who presided at the eucharist. Information, however, is incomplete. Neither the Twelve nor the apostles in the Pauline writings seem to have limited their Ministry to a local church as the later presbyter-bishop normally did, nor do we have much evidence of their administering sacraments. In fact, we are told very little in the New Testament about those who did preside at the eucharist. Thus the Ministry in the later church involving evangelism, preaching, sacraments, pastoral care, and administration in a community, combines functions that were not always united in the early church.

7. Cf. the paper given at the Catholic-Lutheran conversations in Nemi, Italy, May, 1969, by George A. Lindbeck, "The Lutheran Doctrine of the Ministry: Catholic and Reformed," in *Theological Studies* 30 (1969), 588–612; also the Common Statement of the Nemi meeting.

8. Warren A. Quanbeck, "A Contemporary View of Apostolic Succession," pp. 185–187.

9. James F. McCue, "Apostles and Apostolic Succession in the Patristic Era," pp. 138–171; and Walter J. Burghardt, "Apostolic Succession: Notes on the Early Patristic Era," pp. 173–177.

10. The variety of ways in which the term "apostolic" is applied is not startling when we note that the New Testament authors employ the term "apostle" to designate persons with a variety of roles in the earliest Christian generations (cf. R. Schnackenburg, *"L'apostolicité: état de la recherche,"* in *Istina* 14 (1969), 5–32, a paper originally prepared for the Vatican—World Council of Churches discussions on "Apostolicity and Catholicity."

The Second Vatican Council Decree on Ecumenism twice adverts to the fact that variety is itself an element in apostolicity. "While preserving unity in essentials, let all members of the Church, according to the office entrusted to each, preserve a proper freedom in the various forms of spiritual life and discipline, in the variety of liturgical rites, and even in the theological elaboration of revealed truth. In all things let charity be exercised. If the faithful are true to this course of action, they will be giving ever richer expression to the authentic catholicity of the Church, and, at the same time, to her apostolicity" (4). This principle finds its first and obvious application in relation to the churches of the East and the council fathers emphatically reaffirmed it when they said, " . . . this Sacred Synod declares that this entire heritage of (Eastern) spirituality and liturgy, of discipline and theology, in their various traditions, belongs to the full catholic and apostolic character of the Church" (17).

Our Lutheran-Catholic dialogue has been conscious of and attempted to implement this principle as we sorted out our answers to the question, "How is the Ministry apostolic?"

11. Burghardt, *op. cit.*

12. Cf. the Lutheran replies to Catholic questions, Baltimore sessions, given by George A. Lindbeck and Warren A. Quanbeck, pp. 53–60.

13. Denzinger-Schönmetzer, *Enchiridion Symbolorum,* 33rd ed. (Hereafter cited as DS) (Freiburg: Herder, 1965), 1609; cf. 1313.

14. Lindbeck, "The Lutheran Doctrine of the Ministry: Catholic and Reformed," cited above, note 7; article *"Ordo"* by Piet Fransen, in *Lexikon für Theologie und Kirche* (Freiburg: Herder), vol. 7 (1962), columns 1215, 1216; article "Orders and Ordination" by Piet Fransen, in *Sacramentum Mundi* (New York: Herder and Herder), vol. 4 (1969), pp. 305–327.

15. The Dogmatic Constitution on the Church *(Lumen Gentium)* of Vatican II states, "This sacred Synod teaches that by episcopal consecration is conferred the fullness of the sacrament of orders *(plenitudinem conferri sacramenti Ordinis),* that fullness which in the church's liturgical practice and in the language of the holy Fathers of the Church is undoubtedly called the high priesthood, the apex of the sacred ministry" (21). The council fathers were first asked whether they wished to say that episcopal consecration constituted the *summum gradum sacramenti Ordinis.* After agreeing upon this, the precise terminology for expressing it was debated. As the *Relatio* of 1964 puts it, *"Potius autem quam supremus gradus sacramenti Ordinis, Episcopatus dicendus est eius plenitudo seu totalitas, omnes partes includens . . . ; plenitudo sacerdotii cui presbyteri deinde participant . . . ; plenitudo sacramenti Ordinis, vel ipsum sacramentum Ordinis"* (Rather than the highest degree of the sacrament of orders, the episcopate should be called its fullness or totality, embracing all its parts . . . ; the fullness of priesthood in which priests then participate . . . ; the fullness of the sacrament of orders, or the sacrament of orders itself).

16. DS 1145–1146, 1290. Cf. Fransen, "Orders and Ordination," in *Sacramentum Mundi,* vol. 4. esp. p. 316; Kilian McDonnell, "Ways of Validating Ministry," *Journal of Ecumenical Studies* 7 (1970), 209–265; Arthur Carl Piepkorn, "The Sacred Ministry and Holy Ordination in the Symbolical Books of the Lutheran Church," pp. 116–117.

17. In Lutheran churches, for pastoral and administrative reasons, one pastor is designated "pastor of pastors," president of district or synod, or bishop. See Piepkorn, *op. cit.* See also the "Reflections of the Lutheran Participants" below.

18. Apology of the Augsburg Confession, Article 14. The critical edition of the Lutheran confessions is *Die Bekenntnisschriften der evangelisch-lutherischen Kirche* (Göttingen: Vandenhoeck & Ruprecht, 6th ed., 1967). The standard English edition is *The Book of Concord: The Confessions of the Evangelical Lutheran Church,* edited by Theodore G. Tappert (Philadelphia: Fortress Press, 1959). Cf. below the Lutheran answer to the Catholic question at the Baltimore sessions. "How do Lutherans evaluate, theologically and practically, episcopally structured churches?" pp. 53–56. Cf. also no. 28 of the Lutheran "Reflections" below.

19. Other aspects of matters treated need further discussion and many other topics are not touched in these common observations. Among the latter might be mentioned the apostolic Ministry and succession of the bishop of Rome and its relationship to the apostleship of Peter and Paul; infallibility, especially as applied to papal infallibility; the distinction between matters that are of divine law and those which are of human law *(jure divino et humano):* the question of a purely charismatic ministry; questions of eucharistic sharing; the specific relations of a presbyterally ordained Ministry to an episcopally oriented Ministry; and finally, the practical problems of mutual recognition of Ministries, including psychological, canonical, and administrative factors.

Reflections of the Lutheran Participants

1. Augsburg Confession, Epilogue to Article 21, 1–5; Preface to Article 22, 1; Postscript to Article 28. See also Apology of the Augsburg Confession, 2, 32; 10, 2–3.

2. "Sacraments" in this connection include at least baptism, absolution—conceived of either as implied in baptism or as an independent sacrament—and the sacrament of the altar.

3. Augsburg Confession, 5, 1–3; 7, 1–4; 14; 28, 5–9, 21–22; Apology, 28, 13.

4. Apology, 4, 211.

5. Large Catechism, Baptism, 50.

6. Decree on Ecumenism, 20.

7. Augsburg Confession, 20, 40, recalls that "the church sings: *'Sine tuo numine / Nihil est in homine, / Nihil est innoxium'"* (Without [the action of] your godhead, there is nothing in a human being, there is nothing that is not destructive), from the *Veni, Sancte Spiritus.*

8. Apology, 14, 1.5.

9. In the technical sense of an unbroken personal succession of members of the episcopal order theoretically going back to the apostles, with each bishop consecrated to the episcopal order by one or more persons already in the order.

10. The focus of Lutheran concern in the sixteenth century (Smalcald Articles, Part Two, 4, 4, 10–12) was the concluding definition of *Unam Sanctam: "Porro subesse Romano Pontifici omni humanae creaturae declaramus, dicimus, diffinimus omnino esse de necessitate salutis"* (Further, we declare, state [and] define that for every human being it is absolutely necessary for salvation to be under the bishop of Rome) (DS 875). We have not discussed the papacy with our Roman Catholic partners-in-dialogue, but we look forward to an examination of this issue at an early date. In the meantime, however, it may be observed that, however widely the cited thesis of Boniface VIII may have been held during the three centuries following its promulgation in 1302, it runs counter to twentieth century Roman Catholic thought (see, for instance, the letter of the Holy Office to the cardinal archbishop of Boston dated August 8, 1949, of which DS 3866-3873 reproduces the essential portions). Similarly, the recognition sanctioned by Vatican II that the "churches and ecclesial communities" that are not in communion with the Roman see are not without "significance and importance in the mystery of salvation," that the Holy Spirit uses these churches and ecclesial communities "as means of salvation," and that Roman Catholics are to regard "all those justified by faith through baptism [as] incorporated into Christ" and as "brothers in the Lord" may be read as a kind of modern modification of the passage in *Unam Sanctum* that Lutherans have found so disconcerting (Decree on Ecumenism, 3). We also note that in the Dogmatic Constitu-

tion of the Church, 15, "communion with the successor of Peter" is not a necessary prerequisite in the case of baptized persons for being "honored with the name of Christian," for being "united with Christ," and for receiving "other sacraments." Again, the entire section on "The Separated Churches and Ecclesial Communities in the West" in the Decree on Ecumenism (19–23) nowhere mentions the papacy as such. At most it speaks of "the churches and ecclesial communities which were separated from the Apostolic See of Rome" and "the ecclesial communities separated from us." Also relevant to this issue is the fact that the Roman Catholic church recognizes as authentic churches the Eastern Orthodox bodies that have consistently refused to acknowledge a divine-right universal jurisdiction of the pope (Decree on Ecumenism, 14–18).

11. Smalcald Articles, Part Two, 4, 1, *"Dass der Papst nicht sei* jure divino *oder aus Gottes Wort das Häupt der ganzen Christenheit (denn das gehoret einem allein zu, der heisst Jesus Christus), sondern allein Bischof oder Pfarrherr der Kirchen zu Rom . . . ."* (The pope is not the head of all Christendom by divine right or according to God's Word, for this position belongs only to one, namely, to Jesus Christ. The pope is only the bishop and pastor of the churches in Rome. . . .)

12. *Ibid.*, 7–8. We have as yet not had the opportunity to discuss with our Roman Catholic counterparts the full significance of the terms *jure divino* and *jure humano.*

13. For example, in the Decree on the Ministry and Life of Priests, 4.

14. In this dialogue, (but cf. *Lutherans and Catholics in Dialogue III: The Eucharist as Sacrifice,* p. 191), we have not discussed the matter of "private masses," which Lutherans have regarded as an abuse (cf. Smalcald Articles, Part Two, 2, 8). We rejoice that current Roman Catholic theology emphasizes the communal aspects of the eucharist.

15. Instruction on Eucharistic Worship (May 25, 1967), p. 49, cited in *Lutherans and Catholics in Dialogue III: The Eucharist as Sacrifice,* p. 194.

16. *Ibid.*, pp. 188–198 (the quotation is from p. 196). This sentence from the conclusion is particularly apposite (p. 198): "Despite all remaining differences in the ways we speak and think of the eucharistic sacrifice and our Lord's presence in his supper, we are no longer able to regard ourselves as divided in the one holy catholic and apostolic faith on these two points."

17. For example, the examination of what the anathemas of Trent and of Vatican I (DS 3055, 3058, 3064, and 3075) and the exceedingly severe judgments on dissenters from the definitions of 1854 (DS 2804) and 1950 (DS 3904) really imply. These are occasions of concern to Lutherans, since they apparently exclude large numbers of sincere believers from the church. Indeed, they exclude so many believers that they seem to some Lutherans to call into question the churchly character of the community that pronounces them. We anticipate a thorough discussion of this problem with our Roman Catholic colleagues.

18. See the Decree on the Bishops' Pastoral office in the Church, 12, and the Dogmatic Constitution on the Church, 21.

Reflections of the Roman Catholic Participants

1. See the Lutheran answers given to Catholic questions at the Baltimore sessions, pp. 53–61. Cf. no. 21 above.

2. We do not wish to discuss here or elsewhere in this document the preservation of pre-Reformation episcopal structure in the Lutheran church of Sweden, Finland, and some missionary churches. See the Lutheran answer at the Baltimore sessions, question 1, section 3, p. 55. In general, what we say in this document of the Lutherans or the Lutheran communities refers to those Lutheran communities with whose representatives we have been in dialogue. Cf. no. 28 above.

3. Cf. R. Schnackenburg, *"L'apostolicité,"* as cited above, Chapter One, note 10.

4. The *Didache* is a work of uncertain date, perhaps even first century. James F. McCue, "Apostles and Apostolic Succession in the Patristic Era," pp. 163–164, inter-

prets Tertullian, *De exh. cast.* 7 (early third century) to mean that in cases of necessity the eucharist might be celebrated by an unordained layman.

5. Arthur Carl Piepkorn, "A Lutheran View of the Validity of Lutheran Orders," pp. 217–219.

6. Session XXIII, canon 7; DS 1777. See Piepkorn, *op. cit.*, p. 220.

7. Piepkorn, *op. cit.*, pp. 220–226; Corrado Baisi, *Il Ministro Straordinario degli Ordini Sacramentali* (Rome: Anonima Libreria Cattolica Italiana, 1935); Yves Congar, *"Faits, problèmes et réflexions à propos du pouvoir d'ordre et des rapports entre le presbytérat et l'épiscopat,"* in *La Maison-Dieu* 14 (1948), 107–128; Piet Fransen, "Orders and Ordination," *Sacramentum Mundi* (New York: Herder and Herder), vol. 4 (1969), p. 316; the full texts of the bulls may be found in H. Lennerz, *De Sacramento Ordinis, editio secunda* (Rome: Pontificia Universitas Gregoriana, 1953).

8. Constitution on the Church *(Lumen Gentium),* 15; Decree on Ecumenism, 3.

9. Kilian McDonnell, "The Concept of 'Church' in the Documents of Vatican II as Applied to Protestant Denominations," pp. 307–324.

10. Constitution on the Church, 15. Speaking of Christian churches that do not preserve the unity of communion with the successor of Peter. Vatican II states, "Many of them . . . celebrate the Holy Eucharist."

11. Cf. note 2, above.

12. Walter J. Burghardt, "Apostolic Succession: Notes on the Early Patristic Era," pp. 173–177.

13. *Ibid.;* see also McCue, *op. cit.,* pp. 156–157.

14. In the joint Lutheran-Roman Catholic document, *The Status of the Nicene Creed as Dogma of the Church* (1965), p. 32, both sides confess that "the Nicene Faith possesses a unique status in the hierarchy of dogmas," and it is that creed which proclaims the church as one, holy, catholic, and *apostolic.*

15. *Lutherans and Catholics in Dialogue III: The Eucharist as Sacrifice,* pp. 192, 188.

16. Cf. Piepkorn, "The Sacred Ministry and Holy Ordination in the Symbolical Books of the Lutheran Church," p. 102, section 4.

17. Cf. *ibid.,* p. 116, section 25.

18. *Ibid.,* p. 105, section 8; cf. pp. 107–108, section 12.

19. John Reumann, "Ordained Minister and Layman in Lutheranism," sections 16–18, 28–30, 44, pp. 235, 239–240, 247–248.

20. Constitution on the Church, 10: *"Essentia enim et non gradu tantum inter se differunt"* (Though they differ from one another in essence and not only in degree); for discussions of these, see *Commentary on the Documents of Vatican II,* Herbert Vorgrimler, editor (New York: Herder and Herder, 1967), pp. 156–159, and John F. Hotchkin, "The Christian Priesthood: Episcopate, Presbyterate and People in the Light of Vatican II," pp. 202–206.

21. Augsburg Confession, 14: *"De ordine ecclesiastico docent, quod nemo debeat in ecclesia publice docere aut sacramenta administrare nisi rite vocatus"* (Our churches teach that nobody in the church should publicly preach or administer the sacraments unless he is regularly called); Apology, 14, 1: *"Dicimus nemini nisi rite vocato concedendam esse administrationem sacramentorum et verbi in ecclesia"* (We say that no one should be allowed to administer the word and the sacraments in the church unless he is duly called); see Piepkorn, *op. cit.,* pp. 113–116, section 23, for a discussion of *rite vocatus.*

22. The concept of royal priesthood is found in Exodus 19:6; I Peter 2:9; Revelation 5:9–10. A recent Lutheran work, John H. Elliott, *The Elect and the Holy,* Supplements to *Novum Testamentum* 12 (Leiden: Brill, 1966), has examined I Peter 2:9 carefully and finds no evidence that the author of that biblical book related this priesthood to the eucharistic Ministry. The Constitution on the Church, 10, says: "The faithful join in the offering of the Eucharist by virtue of their royal priesthood."

23. Apology, 13, 9–13; see Reumann, *op. cit.,* sections 25–26, p. 238; Piepkorn, *op. cit.,* p. 112, section 21.

24. Cf. Reumann, section 26, p. 238.
25. Cf. *ibid,* section 73, p. 265.
26. Arthur Carl Piepkorn, "A Lutheran View of the Validity of Lutheran Orders," p. 215. It should be noted that one who resigns from the Lutheran Ministry and then seeks readmission to the exercise of the Ministry is not re-ordained. Cf. Piepkorn, "The Sacred Ministry . . ." p. 117, section 26.
27. For a variety of possible Catholic reactions to the Tridentine and Counter-Reformation positions, see George H. Tavard, "Roman Catholic Theology and 'Recognition of Ministry,'" pp. 301–305.
28. It argues on behalf of a visible and sacramental priesthood that has a perpetual character, on behalf of an episcopate and the pope's right to appoint bishops, and on behalf of the validity of ordination by a bishop.
29. DS 1777. Note the wording; it is significant that Trent ignored a proposal which stated that only those ordained *by bishops* are legitimate Ministers of the eucharist.
30. Harry J. McSorley, "Trent and the Question: Can Protestant Ministers Consecrate the Eucharist?" especially pp. 291–293. On p. 293, he contends, "It seems to us that Trent is asserting the canonical or juridical illegitimacy (illiceity) of Lutheran ordinations—nor their invalidity in a widely held modern sense."
31. *Ibid.,* pp. 283–285, 294–295. It should be noted that there was disagreement among the Catholic participants in regard to this position.
32. Particularly involved here is the question of hermeneutics, and the nature of the church's grasp of truth in any era.
33. See the Constitution on the Church, 8 and 15 (with the *relatio specialis* to 15), and the Decree on Ecumenism, 19–23.
34. Our intention here echoes the assurance of Cardinal Willebrands, President of the Vatican Secretariat for Christian Unity, when, in speaking of the divisions which still remain, he declares " . . . our firm resolve to do everything possible to overcome them" (*The Position of the Catholic Church concerning a Common Eucharist between Christians of Different Confessions,* January 7, 1970, see *One in Christ* 6 (1970), p. 201, no. 10).
35. See the Lutheran answer to a Catholic question, given at the Baltimore sessions, pp. 56–60.
36. *Directory for the Application of the Decisions of the Second Ecumenical Council of the Vatican Concerning Eucumenical Matters,* published by the Secretariat for Promoting Christian Unity (Washington, D.C.: United States Catholic Conference, 1967), 55.

Differing Attitudes Toward Papal Primacy

PART I
COMMON STATEMENT

Introduction

In the discussions conducted in the United States between Roman Catholic and Lutheran theologians, we have found broad areas of agreement on the Nicene Creed and the christological center of the faith as well as on baptism, the eucharist, and the Ministry of word and sacrament.[1] In the most recent sessions of our dialogue, we have moved to the problems of how that Ministry might best nurture and express the unity of the universal church for the sake of its mission in the world. It is within this context that we have considered papal primacy.

Visible unity in the church has from the earliest times been served by several forms of the Ministry. Some of these forms, such as that exercised in the ecumenical councils,[2] have not been the subject of major disputes between Catholics and Lutherans. By contrast the role of the papacy has been the subject of intense controversy, which has generated theological disagreements, organizational differences, and psychological antagonisms.

In discussing the papacy as a form of Ministry within the universal church we have limited ourselves to the question of papal primacy. No attempt has been made to enter into the problem of papal infallibility. While this issue must be faced in the discussions between our churches, we believe that this limitation of the scope of our present discussion is justified, since papal primacy was a doctrinal issue long before papal infallibility became a major problem.

In these sessions, we have once again found common ground. There is a growing awareness among Lutherans of the necessity of a specific Ministry to serve the church's unity and universal mission, while Catholics increasingly see the need for a more nuanced understanding of the role of the papacy within the universal church. Lutherans and Catholics can now begin to envision possibilities of concord, and to hope for solutions to problems that have previously seemed insoluble. We believe that God is calling our churches to draw closer together, and it is our prayer that this joint statement on papal primacy may make some contribution to that end.

The Setting of the Problem

(1) The church as reconciled and reconciling community cannot serve God's purpose in the world as it should when its own life is torn by divisions and disagreements. The members of the church, wherever they are found, are part of a single people, the one body of Christ, whose mission is to be an anticipatory and efficacious sign of the final unification of all things when God will be all in all. In order to bear credible witness to this coming kingdom, the various Christian bodies must mutually assist and correct each other and must collaborate in all matters which concern the mission and welfare of the church universal. Even within the same Christian communion, local churches or units must be related to the church universal, so that pluralism and pluriformity do not undermine oneness, and unity and uniformity do not destroy a desirable diversity.

(2) As we Lutheran and Roman Catholic theologians turned in our discussions to the need for visible unity in the church universal, we were assisted by the fundamental accord stated in an earlier report on the doctrine of ministry. We there agreed that, by the will of God 1) the general ministry of proclaiming the gospel devolves upon the whole people of God, and 2) "the Ministry of word and sacrament" serves to unify and order the church for its mission in and to the world.[3]

Our previous discussions had centered on the service rendered to the local communities by the Ministry. Now we focus on the unifying and ordering function of this Ministry in relation to the universal church—on how a particular form of this Ministry, i.e., the papacy, has served the unity of the universal church in the past and how it may serve it in the future.

(3) Catholics and Lutherans have in part recognized and employed similar means for fostering the unity of the universal church. Christians of the various communities have been bound together by one baptism and by their acceptance of the inspired scrip-

tures. Liturgies, creeds, and confessions have also been unifying factors. For both traditions the councils of the church have had a significant unifying role. The Reformers affirmed the value of councils; and this has been implicitly acknowledged in a different form by most contemporary Lutheran churches through their formation of the Lutheran World Federation and, on a wider scale, by participation in the World Council of Churches. On the Catholic side, the importance of the conciliar principle has been reasserted by Vatican II in its exercise of conciliar functions, as well as in its emphasis on the collegial structure of the church.

(4) Precisely because large areas of agreement exist on such means of unifying the church, we have focused our attention in this discussion on another unifying factor on which there has been disagreement, namely, the role of particular persons, offices, or officeholders in exercising responsibility for the unity of the universal church. In describing this specific Ministry and its exercise by a person we were naturally drawn, in the light of centuries of development, to the image of Peter.[4] Among the companions of Jesus, he is given the greatest prominence in the New Testament accounts of the origins of the church. He is spoken of in the Gospels in terms relating him to the founding of the church, to strengthening his brethren, to feeding the sheep of Christ. He is a prominent figure in some of the Pauline letters, in Acts, and for two of the Catholic Epistles—a fact which suggests that he was associated with a wide-ranging ministry. Subsequent church history made him the image of a pastor caring for the universal church. And so, although we are aware of the danger of attributing to the church in New Testament times a modern style or model of universality, we have found it appropriate to speak of a "Petrine function," using this term to describe *a particular form of Ministry exercised by a person, officeholder, or local church with reference to the church as a whole.* This Petrine function of the Ministry serves to promote or preserve the oneness of the church by symbolizing unity, and by facilitating communication, mutual assistance or correction, and collaboration in the church's mission.

(5) Such a Petrine function has been exercised in some degree by various officeholders, for example by bishops, patriarchs, and church presidents. However, the single most notable representative of this Ministry toward the church universal, both in duration and geographical scope, has been the bishop of Rome. The Reformers did not totally reject all aspects of the papal expression of the Petrine function, but only what they regarded as its abuses. They hoped for a reform of the papacy precisely in order to preserve the unity of the church. Melanch-

thon held that "for the sake of peace and general unity among Christians" a superiority over other bishops could be conceded to the pope.[5] For many years Lutherans hoped for an ecumenical council that would reform the papacy. They continued to concede to the pope all the legitimate spiritual powers of a bishop of his diocese, in this case, Rome. They even granted the propriety of his exercising a larger jurisdiction by human right over communities that had by their own will placed themselves under him.[6]

The Issues

(6) Nevertheless, the pope's claims to primacy and his exercise of it have occasioned violent disagreements. Lutherans and others have even gone so far as to call the papacy "antichrist."

The disputes have centered, first, on the question whether the papacy is biblically warranted. Roman Catholics have read the New Testament as indicating that Jesus conferred on Peter a unique role of leadership in the whole church for all times and in this sense provided for successors in the Petrine function, the bishops of Rome. In this view, the papacy has remained substantially the same through succeeding centuries, all changes being accidental.

Lutherans, in contrast, have minimized Peter's role in the early church and denied that this role continued in the church in later periods or that the Roman bishops could be considered his successors in any theologically significant sense.

(7) Closely linked to this historical question regarding the institution of the papacy by Christ is the theological issue whether the papacy is a matter of divine law *(ius divinum)*.[7] Roman Catholics have affirmed that it is and consequently have viewed it as an essential part of the permanent structure of the church. Lutherans have held, in opposition to this, that the papacy was established by human law, the will of men, and that its claims to divine right are nothing short of blasphemous.

(8) A third area of controversy centers on the practical consequences drawn from these prior disagreements. Roman Catholics have tended to think of most major aspects of papal structure and function as divinely authorized. The need or possibility of significant change, renewal, or reform has generally been ignored. Most important, it has been argued that all ministry concerned with fostering unity among the churches is subject—at least in crisis situations—to the supervision of

the bishop of Rome. His jurisdiction over the universal church is in the words of Vatican I, "supreme," "full," "ordinary," and "immediate."[8] This authority is not subject to any higher human jurisdiction, and no pope is absolutely bound by disciplinary decisions of his predecessors.[9] This view of the exercise of papal power has been vehemently repudiated by Lutherans and viewed by them as leading to intolerable ecclesiastical tyranny.

In the course of our discussions, however, we have been able to gain helpful and clarifying insights regarding these points of controversy.

Focus on the New Testament Question

(9) Any biblical and historical scholar today would consider anachronistic the question whether Jesus constituted Peter the first pope, since this question derives from a later model of the papacy which it projects back into the New Testament.[10] Such a reading helps neither papal opponents nor papal supporters. Therefore terms such as "primacy" and "jurisdiction" are best avoided when one describes the role of Peter in the New Testament. Even without these terms, however, a wide variety of images is applied to Peter in the New Testament which signalizes his importance in the early church.[11]

(10) It is well to approach the question of Peter's role in the church by recognizing that the New Testament writings describe various forms of Ministry directed toward the church as a whole. These writings show a primary concern for local communities of believers (the churches). There is also ample evidence of concern for groups of churches, for relationships between churches of different areas or backgrounds, and also for *the* church as the one body of Christ. Paul sometimes holds up one local church as an example to another; he seeks to retain fellowship between the Gentile and the Jewish churches; he collects from the churches he has founded for the support of the church in Jerusalem. Both the letter to the Galatians and the book of Acts describe a meeting in Jerusalem among church leaders to settle a major problem facing various communities, namely, the circumcision of the Gentiles. The First Epistle of Peter, the Pastoral Letters, and the Revelation (the Apocalypse), show concern for groups of churches. Colossians and Ephesians speak of the church as the body of Christ, and Ephesians in particular stresses the unity of the body. In the description of the Pentecost scene in Acts, there is a global vision of the Spirit-

filled community reaching men of every land and tongue. In the Fourth Gospel, Jesus speaks of the day when there will be one flock and one shepherd.

(11) What role does Peter play in this Ministry directed to the church at large? There is no single or uniform New Testament outlook on such a question. The New Testament books, written by men of different generations and varying outlooks, living in widely scattered churches, see Peter in a diversity of ways.[12] There are certain features common to or underlying these different pictures of Peter. He is listed first among the Twelve; he is frequently their spokesman; he is the first apostolic witness of the risen Jesus; he is prominent in the Jerusalem community; he is well known to many churches. Yet it is not always easy to tell to what extent he exercises a function in relation to the church as a whole and to what extent his influence remains regional. For instance, Galatians 2:7 attributes to Peter a special role in relation to the gospel addressed to the Jews, while Paul has a similar role in relation to the gospel addressed to the Gentiles. Moreover, the relative silence of the New Testament about the career of Peter after the Jerusalem meeting (ca. A.D. 49) makes it difficult to find a biblical basis for affirmations about his continuing role in the church in his later years. There is increasing agreement that Peter went to Rome and was martyred there, but we have no trustworthy evidence that Peter ever served as the supervisor or bishop of the local church in Rome. From the New Testament, we know nothing of a succession to Peter in Rome. We cannot exclude the possibility that other figures, such as Paul or James, also had a unifying role in relation to the whole church, although the available documents connect them primarily with individual churches or groups of churches.

(12) Although the New Testament gives us limited information about the historical career of Simon Peter, individual writings associate him with different aspects or images of Ministry which have relevance to the church as a whole. It is Peter among the Twelve who confesses Jesus as the Christ (Mark 8, Matthew 16, Luke 9) and as the Holy One of God (John 6); he is listed as the first apostolic witness to the risen Lord (1 Corinthians 15; Luke 24); he is the rock on which the church is to be founded and he is to be entrusted with the power of the keys (Matthew 16); he is the one who is to strengthen his brethren in faith (Luke 22); he is the one who, after confessing his love, is told to feed Jesus' sheep (John 21); he takes the initiative in filling the vacancy among the Twelve (Acts 1) and receives the first Gentile converts (Acts 10). He is also the one who denies Jesus in an especially dramatic way (all four Gospels); who sinks in the waves because of his lack of faith

(Matthew 14); he is sharply rebuked by Jesus (Mark 8, Matthew 16), and later on by Paul (Galatians 2). The fact that these failures were so vividly remembered is perhaps also evidence of his prominence.

(13) How this view of Peter in the New Testament as developed by modern scholarship relates to the papacy might be summarized thus. Peter was very important as a companion of Jesus during Jesus' public ministry; he was one of the first of the disciples to be called and seems to have been the most prominent among the regular companions. This importance carried over into the early Palestinian church, as indicated in the record of an appearance of the risen Jesus to Peter (probably the first appearance to an apostle). Clearly he was the most prominent of the Twelve and took an active part in the Christian missionary movement. Peter had a key role in decisions that affected the course of the church. Thus one may speak of a prominence that can be traced back to Peter's relationship to Jesus in his public ministry and as the risen Lord.

Of even greater importance, however, is the thrust of the images associated with Peter in the later New Testament books, many of them written after his death. While some of these images recall his failures (e.g., Peter the weak and sinful man), Peter is portrayed as the fisherman (Luke 5, John 21), as the shepherd of the sheep of Christ (John 21), as a presbyter who addresses other presbyters (1 Peter 5:1); as proclaimer of faith in Jesus the Son of God (Matthew 16:16–17); as a receiver of special revelation (Acts 10:9–16); as one who can correct those who misunderstand the thought of a brother apostle, Paul (2 Peter 3:15–16); and as the rock on which the church was to be built (Matthew 16:18). When a "trajectory" of these images is traced, we find indications of a development from earlier to later images. This development of images does not constitute papacy in its later technical sense, but one can see the possibility of an orientation in that direction, when shaped by favoring factors in the subsequent church. The question whether Jesus appointed Peter the first pope has shifted in modern scholarship to the question of the extent to which the subsequent use of the images of Peter in reference to the papacy is consistent with the thrust of the New Testament.

Historical and Theological Questions

(14) Historical studies have opened new perspectives not only on the New Testament writings but also on other problems. It is now clear that the question of papal primacy cannot adequately be treated in

terms of proof passages from scripture or as a matter of church law, but must be seen in the light of many factors—biblical, social, political, theological—which have contributed to the development of the theology, structure, and function of the modern papacy.

(15) In the period following the New Testament era, two parallel lines of development tended to enhance the role of the bishop of Rome among the churches of the time. One was the continuing development of the several images of Peter emerging from the apostolic communities, the other resulted from the importance of Rome as a political, cultural, and religious center.

The trajectory of the biblical images of Peter continued in the life of the early church, enriched by the addition of other images; missionary preacher, great visionary, destroyer of heretics, receiver of the new law, gatekeeper of heaven, helmsman of the ship of the church, co-teacher with Paul, co-martyr with Paul in Rome.[13] These images had a theological significance even before they were associated with the bishop of Rome.

(16) A parallel line of development occurred through the early church's accommodation to the culture of the Graeco-Roman world, when it adopted patterns of organization and administration prevailing in the area of its missionary work. Churches identified themselves according to the localities, dioceses, and provinces of the empire. The prestige and centrality of Rome as the capital city, combined with the wealth and generosity of Roman Christians, quite naturally led to a special prominence of the Roman church. Moreover this church enjoyed the distinction of having been founded, according to tradition, by Peter and Paul, and of being the site where these martyrs were buried.

(17) In the controversy with the gnostics, episcopal sees of apostolic foundation served as a gauge or standard of orthodoxy, and the Roman church, associated with Peter and Paul, was especially emphasized in this respect by Western writers. During the first five centuries, the church of Rome gradually assumed a certain pre-eminence among the churches: it intervened in the life of distant churches, took sides in distant theological controversies, was consulted by other bishops on a wide variety of doctrinal and moral questions, and sent legates to faraway councils. In the course of time Rome came to be regarded in many quarters as the supreme court of appeal and as a focus of unity for the world-wide communion of churches.

(18) With Leo I the correlation between the bishop of the Roman church and the image of Peter, which had already been suggested by some of his predecessors, became fully explicit. According to Leo,

Peter continues his task in the bishop of Rome, and the predominance of Rome over other churches derives from Peter's presence in his successors, the bishops of the Roman see. The Petrine function of the bishop of Rome is nothing less than the care for all the churches. It imposes upon other bishops the duty to obey his authority and apply his decisions. Thus Western theological affirmations of papal primacy found an early expression in the teaching of Leo I.

(19) The later development of these claims can now be seen by both Lutherans and Catholics to have had both positive and negative features. On the one hand, this development was furthered by the historical situation of the Middle Ages, when Rome no longer found itself in competition with the other major metropolitan sees in the long struggle against secular, and especially imperial, power. On the other hand, the theoretical interpretation of primacy in the categories of canon law made rapid progress. Among others, Gregory VII and Innocent III, relying on such documents as the False Decretals, depicted the church as a papal monarchy in accordance with secular models available in their day. Documents such as Boniface VIII's *Unam Sanctam* (1302) embodied the claim that the pope had not only spiritual but also temporal dominion over the whole earth.[14] At the same time, some medieval theologians continued to see Rome as the center of unity in a world-wide communion of churches. Some accented the religious and charismatic, rather than the juridical and administrative, aspects of papal primacy.

In the high Middle Ages the mendicant orders and some of their prominent theologians, such as Bonaventure and Thomas Aquinas, tended to exalt the powers of the Roman see. Moreover, the growth of scholastic theology reinforced a pyramidal view of authority in the church. The powers diffused in the body of the faithful were seen to be concentrated in the order of bishops and still further in the one person of the bishop of Rome. Some theologians, for example the conciliarists, interpreted the powers as ascending from the body into the head, while others, for example the papal canonists, saw them as descending from the head into the body. The latter view reemerged with added emphasis after the Council of Basel (1431–37). The Council of Florence in its Decree of Union for the Greek and Latin churches (1439)[15] set forth the doctrine of papal primacy in terms that approximate those of Vatican I.

Within post-Tridentine Roman Catholicism, the polemics of the sixteenth century and the Counter-Reformation strengthened this trend. Several centuries of struggle against nationalistic movements, an upsurge of ultramontane centralism, and the desire to oppose nineteenth century liberalism created the climate for Vatican I. This council taught that the pope as successor of Peter has a primacy of jurisdiction over all individuals and churches. It declared that this jurisdiction is "full," "supreme," "ordinary" (that is, not derived by delegation from another), and "immediate" (that is, direct), and linked this primacy of jurisdiction with papal infallibility.[16]

(20) The theology of Vatican II developed the teaching of Vatican I, giving a more balanced account of the relations of the pope to the bishops and of the bishops to the people of God. The bishop of Rome is head of the college of bishops, who share his responsibility for the universal church. His authority is pastoral in its purpose even when juridical in form. It should always be understood in its collegial context.[17]

(21) We thus see from the above that the contemporary understanding of the New Testament and our knowledge of the processes at work in the history of the church make possible a fresh approach to the structure and operations of the papacy. There is increasing agreement that the centralization of the Petrine function in a single person or office results from a long process of development. Reflecting the many pressures of the centuries and the complexities of a world-wide church, the papal office can be seen both as a response to the guidance of the Spirit in the Christian community, and also as an institution which in its human dimensions, is tarnished by frailty and even unfaithfulness. The Catholic members of this consultation see the institution of the papacy as developing from New Testament roots under the guidance of the Spirit. Without denying that God could have ordered the church differently, they believe that the papal form of the unifying Ministry is, in fact, God's gracious gift to his people. Lutheran theologians, although in the past chiefly critical of the structure and functioning of the papacy, can now recognize many of its positive contributions to the life of the church. Both groups can acknowledge that as the forms of the papacy have been adapted to changing historical settings in the past, it is possible that they will be modified to meet the needs of the church in the future more effectively.

Toward the Renewal of Papal Structures

(22) In considering how the papacy may better serve the church as a whole, our reflections will bear on basic principles of renewal, and on questions facing Roman Catholics and Lutherans in view of the possibilities of rapprochement.

A. Norms for Renewal

(23) *The Principle of Legitimate Diversity.* The ultimate source of authority is God revealed in Christ. The church is guided by the Spirit and is judged by the word of God. All its members share in this guidance and are subject to this judgment. They should recognize that the Spirit's guidance may give rise to diverse forms in piety, liturgy, theology, custom, or law. Yet a variety of ecclesial types should never foster divisiveness. With humility and in self-criticism, Ministers in the church should therefore "test the spirits", and listen to the judgment which may be implied in "the signs of the times".[18] Even the exercise of the Petrine function should evolve with the changing times, in keeping with a legitimate diversity of ecclesial types within the church.

(24) *The Principle of Collegiality.* Collegial responsibility for the unity of the church, as emphasized by Vatican II, is of utmost importance in protecting those values which excessive centralization of authority would tend to stifle. No one person or administrative staff, however dedicated, learned, and experienced, can grasp all the subtleties and complexities of situations in a world-wide church, whose many communities live and bear witness in the variegated contexts of several continents and many nations. It is only through the contributions of many persons and groups that the problems which need urgent attention can be identified, and the talents necessary to deal with them be mustered. The collegial principle calls all levels of the church to share in the concern and responsibilities of leadership for the total life of the church.

(25) *The Principle of Subsidiarity.* The principle of subsidiarity is no less important. Every section of the church, each mindful of its special heritage, should nurture the gifts it has received from the Spirit by exercising its legitimate freedom. What can properly be decided and done in smaller units of ecclesial life ought not to be referred to church leaders who have wider responsibilities. Decisions should be made and activities carried out with a participation as broad as possible from the people of God. Initiatives should be encouraged in order to promote a wholesome diversity in theology, worship, witness, and service. All should be concerned that, as the community is built up and its unity strengthened, the rights of minorities and minority viewpoints are protected within the unity of faith.

B. Roman Catholic Perspectives

(26) The church's teaching office "is not above God's Word; it rather serves the Word."[19] Indeed this is true of all ecclesiastical

authority. The gospel may require that church offices be exercised in very different ways to meet the needs of various regions and periods. New means of exercising authority may have to be discovered to fit the cultural patterns arising out of the changing forms of education, communications, and social organization. The signs of the times point to the need for greater participation of pastors, scholars, and all believers in the direction of the universal church.[20]

(27) Further, it is an important political principle that authority in any society should use only the amount of power necessary to reach its assigned goal. This applies also to the papal office. A canonical distinction between the highest authority and the limited exercise of the corresponding power cannot be ruled out and needs to be emphasized. Such a limitation need not prejudice the universal jurisdiction attributed to the pope by Roman Catholic doctrine. Thus one may foresee that voluntary limitations by the pope of the exercise of his jurisdiction will accompany the growing vitality of the organs of collegial government, so that checks and balances in the supreme power may be effectively recognized.

C. Lutheran Perspectives

(28) If perspectives such as the foregoing prevail, papal primacy will no longer be open to many traditional Lutheran objections. As we have noted (see 3 above), Lutherans increasingly recognize the need for a Ministry serving the unity of the church universal. They acknowledge that, for the exercise of this Ministry, institutions which are rooted in history should be seriously considered. The church should use the signs of unity it has received, for new ones cannot be invented at will. Thus the Reformers wished to continue the historic structures of the church.[21] Such structures are among the signs of the church's unity in space and time, helping to link the Christian present with its apostolic past. Lutherans can also grant the beneficial role of the papacy at various periods of history. Believing in God's sovereign freedom, they cannot deny that God may show again in the future that the papacy is his gracious gift to his people. Perhaps this might involve a primacy in which the pope's service to unity in relation to the Lutheran churches would be more pastoral than juridical. The one thing necessary, from the Lutheran point of view, is that papal primacy be so structured and interpreted that it clearly serve the gospel and the unity of the church of Christ, and that its exercise of power not subvert Christian freedom.

(29) Our discussions in this dialogue have brought to light a number of agreements, among the most significant of which are:

• Christ wills for his church a unity which is not only spiritual but must be manifest in the world.

• promotion of this unity is incumbent on all believers, especially those who are engaged in the Ministry of word and sacrament;

• the greater the responsibility of a ministerial office, the greater the responsibility to seek the unity of all Christians;

• a special responsibility for this may be entrusted to one individual Minister, under the gospel.

• such a responsibility for the universal church cannot be ruled out on the basis of the biblical evidence;

• the bishop of Rome, whom Roman Catholics regard as entrusted by the will of Christ with this responsibility, and who has exercised his Ministry in forms that have changed significantly over the centuries, can in the future function in ways which are better adapted to meet both the universal and regional needs of the church in the complex environment of modern times.

(30) We do not wish to understate our remaining disagreements. While we have concluded that traditional sharp distinctions between divine and human institution are no longer useful, Catholics continue to emphasize that papal primacy is an institution in accordance with God's will. For Lutherans this is a secondary question. The one thing necessary, they insist, is that papal primacy serve the gospel and that its exercise of power not subvert Christian freedom (see section 28).

There are also differences which we have not yet discussed. We have not adequately explored to what extent the existing forms of the papal office are open to change in the future, nor have we yet touched on the sensitive point of papal infallibility, taught by Vatican Councils I and II.

(31) Even given these disagreements and points yet to be examined, it is now proper to ask, in the light of the agreement we have been able to reach, that our respective churches take specific actions toward reconciliation.

(32) Therefore we ask the Lutheran churches:

• if they are prepared to affirm with us that papal primacy, renewed in the light of the gospel, need not be a barrier to reconciliation;

• if they are able to acknowledge not only the legitimacy of the papal Ministry in the service of the Roman Catholic communion[22] but even the possibility and the desirability of the papal Ministry, renewed under the gospel and committed to Christian freedom, in a larger communion which would include the Lutheran churches;

• if they are willing to open discussion regarding the concrete implications of such a primacy to them.

(33) Likewise, we ask the Roman Catholic Church:

• if in the light of our findings, it should not give high priority in its ecumenical concerns to the problem of reconciliation with the Lutheran churches;

• if it is willing to open discussions on possible structures for reconciliation which would protect the legitimate traditions of the Lutheran communities and respect their spiritual heritage;[23]

• if it is prepared to envisage the possibility of a reconciliation which would recognize the self-government of Lutheran churches within a communion;

• if, in the expectation of a foreseeable reconciliation, it is ready to acknowledge the Lutheran churches represented in our dialogue as sister-churches which are already entitled to some measure of ecclesiastical communion.

(34) We believe that our joint statement reflects a convergence in the theological understanding of the papacy which makes possible a fruitful approach to these questions. Our churches should not miss this occasion to respond to the will of Christ for the unity of his disciples. Neither church should continue to tolerate a situation in which members of one communion look upon the other as alien. Trust in the Lord who makes us one body in Christ will help us to risk ourselves on the yet undisclosed paths toward which his Spirit is guiding his church.

PART II
REFLECTIONS OF THE LUTHERAN PARTICIPANTS

(28) Many Lutherans as well as Roman Catholics will be startled by the convergence on papal primacy recorded in the preceding joint statement. This issue is both more sensitive and more difficult than any of those previously dealt with in our national dialogue.[1] It is doubly necessary, therefore, that the Lutheran participants explain their views to their fellow Lutherans more fully than was appropriate in the common statement (just as the Roman Catholic participants will address their fellow Roman Catholics in the third part of this report). We need to explain (1) why we have dealt with this issue, (2) what seems to us the position of the Lutheran tradition on this matter, and

(3) why we believe the time has now come for our churches to consider seriously the possibility of a role for the papacy such as is sketched in Part I.

(29) It would have been impossible to avoid the question of papal primacy in our discussions even if we had wished to do so. The purpose of the dialogue is:

First, to define as clearly as possible the extent and the limits of the common ground between Roman Catholics and Lutherans at this particular time in our respective histories.

Second, and more important, we are called as Christians to give a credible witness to our unity in Christ for the sake of our mission in the world (John 17:21; Ephesians 4:3–6). This unity is not an exclusively spiritual unity. It is true that we have a unity that our one baptism and our one faith in Christ bring about. At the same time Lutheran theologians have insisted that the church is not a Platonic republic that exists only in an ideal realm (Apology 7:20),[2] but that it is an empirical assembly of Christians among whom the gospel is proclaimed and heard and the sacraments are administered.

Third, we must deal not only with problems on which agreement is already visibly developing (such as the eucharist and eucharistic Ministry),[3] but also with such apparently intractable issues as the papacy.

In our previous discussions on the ministry, we had already encountered the issue of the papacy. In those discussions we repeated the traditional Lutheran affirmation that "as long as the ordained Ministry is retained, any form of polity which serves the proclamation of the gospel is acceptable."[4] We also observed that the Luthern confessional writings "do not exclude the possibility that the papacy might have a symbolical or functional value in a wider area as long as its primacy is seen as being of human right."[5] In addition, we joined with our Roman Catholic colleagues in declaring that "the ordained Ministry, through the proclamation of the word and the administration of the sacraments, serves to unify and order the church in a special way for its ministry."[6] We were thus challenged to develop more fully a Lutheran view of the papacy's possible role as a symbol and center of unity in the exercise of a Ministry on behalf of the church universal.

We have not, as our joint report repeatedly mentions, discussed papal infallibility. Our common statement is therefore by no means a complete treatment of the papacy. It addresses itself particularly to the issues of papal primacy. While this fact may be disappointing to some people, it is our conviction that it is by such a step-by-step procedure that we can most responsibly clarify our agreements and differences.

(30) In considering the historic Lutheran position on the papacy, we have become very much aware that the early Reformers did not reject what we have called the "Petrine function," but rather the concrete historical papacy as it confronted them in their day. In calling the pope the "antichrist," the early Lutherans stood in a tradition that reached back into the eleventh century.[7] Not only dissidents and heretics but even saints had called the bishop of Rome the "antichrist" when they wished to castigate his abuse of power. What Lutherans understood as a papal claim to unlimited authority over everything and everyone reminded them of the apocalyptic imagery of Daniel 11, a passage that even prior to the Reformation had been applied to the pope as the antichrist of the last days. The pope's willingness to derive advantage from doctrines and practices that seemed to them to contradict the gospel compelled them to resist such doctrines and practices as antichristian.[8]

The claim that probably rankled most was Boniface VIII's sweeping assertion in the bull *Unam sanctam* (1302) that it is necessary for all human beings for their salvation to be subject to the bishop of Rome.[9] This declaration would probably not have played the role that it did in the sixteenth century if Leo X had not reaffirmed it at the Fifth Lateran Council (1516).[10] Against this teaching Lutherans consistently denied that the bishop of Rome is the visible head of Christendom by divine right, that is, on the basis of the word of God.[11]

Further, the direct involvement of the late medieval papacy in the politics of Europe, the popes' frequent resort to war and to the sometimes devious devices of medieval statecraft made the bishop of Rome in Lutheran eyes only one more secular prince who was ready to use his spiritual authority to achieve political ends.[12] As such he could be resisted in the name of patriotism in the same way any other foreign potentate might be resisted, a principle which was also admitted by Catholic theologians of the period.

Because of these factors, from the 1520s on, Lutherans regarded themselves as in fact outside the pope's spiritual jurisdiction. They saw themselves as being on a par with those parts of the church, especially in the East, which did not recognize the jurisdictional primacy of the bishop of Rome. The Lutheran refusal to submit to the authority of the bishop of Rome was reinforced in succeeding centuries by some of the political strategies employed by the Counter Reformation, by what seemed the defensiveness of the Roman Catholic reaction to intellectual and political liberalism, and by the increasing trend toward centralization of power in the Roman see and the Roman curia. The setting forth of the teachings of universal papal jurisdiction and of papal infallibility in 1870 seemed in Lutheran eyes to make the gulf between the Roman Catholic Church and the heirs of the Reformation virtually unbridgeable.

During the same period Lutheranism had difficulties of its own. It suffered from subservience to state power. Its own ecclesiastical authorities have not always fostered Christian liberty and faithfulness to the gospel. It too reacted defensively to intellectual and cultural movements. Worst of all, in many places it came close to losing the vision of the unity of God's people. In view of this record, Lutherans have no ground for self-righteousness.

(31) Today, after over four centuries of mutual suspicion and condemnation, it is generally supposed that Lutherans have had no place for papal primacy in their thinking about the church. This is not true. We need to remember that the earliest Lutherans hoped for a reform of the papacy precisely for the sake of seeing the unity of the church preserved. Melanchthon held that "for the sake of peace and general unity among the Christians" a superiority over the other bishops could be conceded to the pope.[13] Many Lutherans kept hoping for an ecumenical council to reform the papacy. Despite their often violent antipapal polemics, Lutherans continued to concede to the pope all the legitimate spiritual powers of a bishop in his diocese, in this case, Rome. They even granted the propriety of his exercising a larger jurisdiction by *human* right over communities that had by their own will placed themselves under him.[14] They were ready to grant that the rock on which Christ promised to build his community was Peter in his capacity as a minister of Christ.[15]

Even theologians of the era of classic Lutheran orthodoxy conceded that in the New Testament Peter possessed a preeminence among the Twelve as a leader *(coryphaeus),* spokesman *(os),* chief *(princeps)* and the one "who proposed what was to be done."[16] In rejecting the monarchical authority of the bishop of Rome in the church, they were careful not to exclude a primacy of Peter among the apostles based on honor, age, calling, zeal, or order, nor did they deny that in a broad sense Peter could be called a "bishop" of Rome, and that the leadership of the Roman see devolved upon episcopal successors as happened in other apostolic sees.[17]

Since they felt bound by the gospel to seek the unity of the church, many of our Lutheran forefathers over a period of nearly two centuries negotiated with representatives of the Roman Catholic Church, in spite of deep reservations.[18] Lutherans sent delegations to the second phase of the Council of Trent,[19] and even after the peace of Augsburg (1555) responsible Lutheran leaders were ready to enter into discussion with their Roman Catholic counterparts.[20] Irenic attempts continued late into the seventeenth century.[21] The vision of "one church of the future" was in the minds of a number of prominent Lutherans throughout the nineteenth century.[22] The willingness of Lutherans to engage in serious dialogue suggests that they believed that ultimately the Holy Spirit might point both sides to a solution even of the knotty problem of the papacy.

(32) Ours is an era of change in social structures, in technology, in science, in human knowledge. In some ways these changes have brought all Christians closer together. Furthermore, the return to the sources, particularly the Bible and the church fathers, has helped prepare the way for a greater common understanding of the heritage shared by all Christians.

From our Roman Catholic partners in dialogue we have received a vivid impression of dramatic changes within their church, changes which are throwing new light on the role of the papacy in Roman Catholic thought and life. For instance, Pope John XXIII, by his gesture of "opening the windows," has become for many Christians a new symbol of what the papacy might be. Our partners are careful to point out that for them the pope is neither a dictator, nor an absolute monarch. He does not replace Christ; he represents Christ. His role is primarily that of one who serves. He cannot act arbitrarily but is limited by the same gospel that provides the norm for the life of the total Christian community. The documents of Vatican II, they emphasize, understand the papacy from the point of view of the church, not the church from the point of view of the papacy. These documents also stress the collegial aspect of church leadership.

To be sure, in the texts from Vatican II, as well as in more recent documents,[23] there are also claims for exclusive papal power. During the council, Pope Paul VI reserved certain questions[24] for himself and he has continued to act independently to a degree that at times seems to compromise the principle of collegiality.

We Lutherans have to ask ourselves if the same factors that have contributed to the new situation in Roman Catholicism are not in fact also changing our own perspective on the papacy. In this day of intensified global communication and international cooperation, the concern for the unity of the entire empirical church is being keenly felt. Lutherans in the past have used documents such as those contained in the *Book of Concord* as a device for achieving a common identity within their confessional family. In recent decades the Lutheran World Federation has been increasingly used for this purpose. Lutheran participation in the World Council of Churches, which includes major churches of the East, is also evidence of the Lutheran concern for unity of faith and action among all Christians. We Lutherans consider the need for symbols and centers of unity to be urgent. We believe that we must try more energetically than we have in the past to give concrete expression to our concern for the unity of the whole empirical church. When we think of the question of the church's unity in relation to its mission we cannot responsibly dismiss the possibility that some form of the papacy, renewed and restructured under the gospel, may be an appropriate visible expression of the Ministry that serves the unity and ordering of the church.

(33) The results of biblical research and historical scholarship have placed in a new perspective many of the once intensely debated issues surrounding the papacy. The National Dialogue group has recognized the importance of these findings for a fresh approach to the question by commissioning two independent studies, one on "Peter in the New Testament"[25] and another on "Roman primacy in the patristic era."[26]

The report of the biblical panel makes it clear that "no matter what one may think about the justification offered by the New Testament for the emergence of the papacy, this papacy in its developed form cannot be read back into the New Testament; and it will help neither papal opponents nor papal supporters to have the model of the later papacy before their eyes when discussing the role of Peter."[27] This report quite properly warns against an anachronistic interpretation of the New Testament. Instead, it points out the diversity of the images of Peter in the various strata of the New Testament materials and directs attention to the "trajectories"[28] of these images of Peter, and to their continuation and use in the early church. The view of Peter as the confessor, missionary, repentant sinner, and martyr is as much a part of this tradition as the view of Peter as the shepherd, pastor, teacher, and spokesman.

On the other hand, Lutherans too will find many of their cherished polemical readings of the texts challenged. Exegetically it is hard to deny that Peter enjoyed a preeminence among the apostles during Jesus' ministry as well as in the post-Easter church. He exercised in his time a function on behalf of the unity of the entire apostolic church. This we have chosen to designate the "Petrine function", even though its exercise was not restricted to Peter alone. This "Petrine function" is significantly connected with the images of Peter not only in the book of Acts and the two Petrine epistles but also, less directly, in the Pauline letters. Paul had his own understanding of his special role in and for the universal church, but at the same time room is left for a Petrine function for the sake of unity.[29]

Again, the report of the patristics panel indicates that there is no conclusive documentary evidence from the first century or the early decades of the second for the exercise of, or even the claim to, a primacy of the Roman bishop or to a connection with Peter, although documents from this period accord the church at Rome some kind of preeminence.[30] Both primatial claims and the Petrine trajectories went through a long history in which—as the Common Statement points out—not only religious-theological but also political, social, and cultural factors played a considerable role before these two trends finally merged in the third century. While we are aware of the variety of factors which contributed to this development, we as Lutherans are impressed by the fact that the bishops of Rome were nevertheless able to exercise a Ministry of unifying and ordering the church in the West. Sometimes, as in the contribution of Leo the Great to the resolution of the christological controversies at Chalcedon in 451, this Ministry was extended to the East as well.

Critical as we Lutherans have been in our evaluation of papal history, we can recognize that the existence of the papacy has in many ways been beneficial. While the civilization of the West was emerging, bishops of Rome did in fact express and nurture the visible unity of the church in a world threatened by non-Christian forces and divisive tendencies. Thus the Petrine function was fulfilled in a specific way. As other concrete examples over the centuries we might cite the leadership of Gregory the Great in the promotion and protection of the Christian mission in northern Europe; the medieval popes who successfully asserted the independence of the Western church against the attempts to subjugate it to the will of emperors, kings, and princes; and the serious humanitarian concern exhibited by modern popes in the face of war and social injustice.

(34) To be sure, there is for Lutherans no single or uniquely legitimate form of the exercise of the Petrine function. At every stage, the Petrine function developed according to the possibilities available at that time. Councils, individual leaders, specific local churches, credal statements[31] and the papacy have all in various ways ministered to the unity of the church. Further, the papal form of the universal Ministry has not always involved the centralized, juridical apparatus which now

exists, nor need we assume that it will always continue to do so. Even if it should be desirable that the Petrine function be exercised by a single individual, the question of his powers would still be open.

(35) This brings us to a thorny problem between Lutherans and Roman Catholics which the group has had to discuss. Whatever primacy the Lutheran reformers accorded to the bishop of Rome was seen as a matter of historical development, and therefore of human right *(de iure humano),* rather than something rooted in the teaching of the scriptures. Over against this position the Roman Catholic view of the papal primacy claimed divine sanction *(de iure divino)* for certain papal prerogatives. Lutherans and Roman Catholics alike have often doubted that a reconciliation of the two standpoints would be possible. We have found in our discussion however, through a series of careful historical investigations, that the traditional distinction between *de iure humano* and *de iure divino* fails to provide usable categories for contemporary discussion of the papacy.[32] On the one hand, Lutherans do not want to treat the exercise of the universal Ministry as though it were merely optional. It is God's will that the church have the institutional means needed for the promotion of unity in the gospel. On the other hand, Roman Catholics, in the wake of Vatican II are aware that there are many ways of exercising papal primacy. Some are willing to consider other models for the exercise of the Petrine function. They recognize the dangers of ecclesiastical centralism, and realize the limitations of a juridical description of the Petrine function.[33]

Rather than using the traditional terminology of divine and human right, therefore, both Lutherans and Roman Catholics have been compelled by their historical studies to raise a different set of questions: In what way or ways has our Lord in fact led his church to use particular forms for the exercise of the Petrine function? What structural elements in the church does the gospel require for the ministry which serves the unity of the empirical church?

(36) Structures invested with powerful symbolic meaning cannot be created at will. Therefore we do not anticipate that a concrete Ministry of unity to serve the church of the future will be something completely new. It will have to emerge from the renewal and the restructuring of those historical forms which best nurture and express this unity. We recognize that among the existing signs or structures for the Ministry of unity in the whole church, the papacy has a long history marked by impressive achievements in spite of all the things we have regarded as faulty in it.

(37) Lutherans are convinced that the church lives by the gospel.

Our Lutheran forefathers rejected the late medieval papacy precisely because in their judgment it was obstructing the gospel. With them we believe that it is the task of the church at all times to proclaim the gospel in its fulness and to affirm the freedom of the children of God for which Christ has set us free. This very freedom, however, means that for the sake of the gospel Lutherans today are free to examine with an open mind the opportunities for the exercise of the Petrine function which a renewed and restructured papal office might provide.

(38) Lutherans can see in the papacy both values and what appear to be defects. On the positive side Lutherans can appreciate the papacy's assertion of the church's right to be independent of state control, the serious social concern exhibited by modern popes,[34] the liberating insight into the way in which the Bible should be studied, as set forth in encyclicals such as *Divino Afflante Spiritu,*[35] and the efforts which modern popes from Benedict XV on have devoted to the cause of peace among the nations. Nevertheless, for Lutherans as well as for many Roman Catholics, the present mode of operation of the papacy and the Roman curia leaves much to be desired. It is evident, moreover, that the close tie at the present time between primacy and infallibility has consequences in Roman Catholicism which will need thorough investigation in our future discussions. Again, any form of papal primacy that does not fully safeguard the freedom of the gospel is unacceptable to Lutherans. Many Roman Catholics manifest similar concerns when they insist, for example, that the primacy of the Roman bishop should not compromise the principle of collegiality.

(39) Everything that we have said underlines the fact that the discussion of papal primacy between our two churches has entered a new phase. It is true that the best model for the exercise of the Petrine function through a papacy is an issue that remains to be determined. At the same time, many of the changes decided upon at Vatican II and since are at least in the process of implementation. As examples we could point to the new rules for the Roman curia, the abolition of the index of prohibited books, the creation of an international synod of bishops meeting at regular intervals, and the appointment of an international commission of theologians.

In spite of the delay in implementing other reforms that have been under discussion among Roman Catholics, we Lutherans must maintain our hope that the papacy will continue to be renewed. We owe it to our Roman Catholic brothers to make this optimism evident. We acknowledge our profound indebtedness to them for the insights into their own church that they have mediated to us. They need to know in turn, about our hopes and prayers for a truly evangelical universal Ministry in the church just as we need to know what they are hoping and praying for us. Only thus will we be able to help and encourage each other in our common search for fuller manifestations of the unity that we have in Christ.

(40) We are not prepared in this report to spell out what the Lutheran willingness to recognize the primacy of a renewed and restructured papacy might mean in practice for Lutheran-Roman Catholic relationships. We are keenly aware that we have been speaking of possibilities whose actualization remains in the future. In the meantime, however, we believe that it is important for Lutherans to work for the renewal of the papacy, not only for the sake of their Roman Catholic brothers, but also for their own.

(41) We ask our churches earnestly to consider if the time has not come to affirm a new attitude toward the papacy "for the sake of peace and concord in the church"[36] and even more for the sake of a united witness to Christ in the world. Our Lutheran teaching about the church and the Ministry constrains us to believe that recognition of papal primacy is possible to the degree that a renewed papacy would in fact foster faithfulness to the gospel and truly exercise a Petrine function within the church. If this is indeed what Lutherans hold, ought they not to be willing to say so clearly and publicly? We urge the church bodies that have appointed us to accord high priority to the discussion of this question.

PART III
REFLECTIONS OF THE ROMAN CATHOLIC PARTICIPANTS

In our view as Roman Catholic members of the consultation, the Common Statement, while falling short of total agreement, represents a major advance in the ecumenical discussion of one of the most sensitive issues that have historically divided the Lutheran and Catholic churches.

The Common Statement has positive significance for us as Roman Catholics. Together with the reflections of the Lutheran Participants it embodies a clear recognition on the part of our Lutheran colleagues that the church needs unifying Ministry concerned with the worldwide apostolate, and that this Ministry may be effectively exercised by a renewed papacy, at least as a humanly constituted organ.

The Common Statement, however, does not fully reflect everything that we believe concerning the papacy. The acceptance of the papal office is for us imperative because we believe that it is willed by God for his church. The mission entrusted to the church by Christ is served by the papacy. In it God has given us a sign of unity and an instrument for Christian life and mission. Therefore we affirm the traditional Roman Catholic position that the papacy is, in a true sense, "divinely instituted."

In the course of our discussion in this consultation, we have been able to refine and nuance our own thinking on many points. One important point has been precisely the meaning of the traditional term "divine right" *(ius divinum)*. In earlier centuries it was rather commonly thought that this term involved, first, institution by a formal act of Jesus himself, and second, a clear attestation of that act by the New Testament or by some tradition believed to go back to apostolic times. Since "divine right" has become burdened with those implications, the term itself does not adequately communicate what we believe concerning the divine institution of the papacy.

In the New Testament we have found many indications positively pointing in the direction of the papacy, especially the Petrine texts and the various images of Peter alluded to in paragraphs 12 and 13 of the Common Statement. We have not, however, found a clear and direct affirmation of the papacy itself. This fact does not surprise or disconcert us. We believe that the New Testament is given to us not as a finished body of doctrine but as an expression of the developing faith and institutionalization of the church in the first century.

In many respects the New Testament and the doctrines it contains are complemented by subsequent developments in the faith and life of the church. For example, the statements of faith in the early creeds, though they are in conformity with scripture, go beyond the words and thought-patterns of scripture. The church itself, moreover, had to take responsibility for the selection of the canonical books, no list of which appears in the scriptures themselves. Similarly, the church had to specify its sacramental life and to structure its ministry to meet the requirements and opportunities of the post-apostolic period.

As Roman Catholics we are convinced that the papal and episcopal form of Ministry, as it concretely evolved, is a divinely-willed sequel to the functions exercised respectively by Peter and the other apostles according to various New Testament traditions. In seeking to carry out its mission throughout the Roman Empire the episcopate frequently appealed to the theological judgment and unifying influence of the chair of Peter *(cathedra Petri)* at Rome, where Peter and Paul were believed to have been martyred. Thus the Petrine function, already attested in New Testament times, was increasingly taken up by the bishop of Rome.

In the section of the Common Statement sketching the subsequent historical developments of the papacy, we have singled out the dogmatic teaching of Vatican Council I as especially important. The teaching of this council should be understood according to the context of the times in which it was formulated and the intention of the council fathers. To this end we may now call attention to some principles recently articulated by the Congregation for the Doctrine of the Faith with regard to the historical conditioning of dogmatic formulations. In a declaration dated June 24, 1973, the following four factors are set forth:

> a) The meaning of the pronouncements of faith depends partly upon the expressive power of the language used at a certain point in time and in particular circumstances.
> b) Sometimes a dogmatic truth is first expressed incompletely, but not falsely, and later more fully and perfectly in a broader context of faith and human knowledge.
> c) When the church makes new pronouncements, it not only confirms what is in some way contained in scripture or previous expressions of tradition; usually it also has the intention of solving specific questions or removing specific errors.
> d) Sometimes the truths the church intends to teach through its dogmatic formulations may be enunciated in terms that bear traces of the changeable conceptions of a given epoch.[1]

In confronting the specific problems and errors of its time, Vatican Council I sensed that a concentration on the papacy was crucially important, in order to safeguard the church's evangelical freedom from political pressures and its universality in an age of divisive national particularism. Yet the council tended to accent the juridical aspects of the papacy more than church needs would require in the broader context of our times. It has become apparent that the papal Ministry, as a spiritual and evangelical task, can and needs to find a "fuller and more perfect expression"[2] than was possible at Vatican Council I. Vatican Council II has already begun this process.

Since we have been cautioned by the holy see to recognize the conditioning imposed on church pronouncements by "the language used at a certain point of time and in particular circumstances," we must carefully interpret adjectives such as "full," "supreme," "ordinary," and "immediate," used by Vatican Council I to describe the pope's power of jurisdiction. Similar care must be exercised in detecting the historical conditioning of the affirmation of Vatican Council I with respect to the conferral of a primacy of "true and proper jurisdiction"[3] upon Peter by Christ. This affirmation must be understood in a way that allows for the complex process of gospel development explained in *Dei Verbum,* 19.

A general directive was given by Christ to his disciples: "Earthly kings lord it over their people . . . yet it cannot be that way with you" (Luke 22:25–26). In keeping with this directive, the doctrine concerning the papacy must be understood in ways that recognize the church's total subordination to Christ and the gospel and its obligation to respect the rights of all individuals, groups, and offices both within the church and beyond its limits. Monarchical absolutism in the church would violate the command of Christ. Generally speaking, Christians today are strongly conscious that the Holy Spirit works through all the ranks of the faithful and that a measure of interdependence exists among all who exercise ministry on different levels in the church. By setting the primacy of the pope within the broader context of a people-of-God ecclesiology, and by promoting a collegial understanding of authority in the church, Vatican Council II has called for modifications in the Roman Catholic understanding of papal leadership.

We share the concern of our Lutheran partners in dialogue that safeguards should be provided against violations of Christian rights and freedoms on the part of all ecclesiastical authority, papal included. Simultaneously, we are conscious of the need to proceed with caution. In particular, the effective exercise of the papal Ministry requires a large measure of power—and power, by its very nature, is capable of being abused. It is not yet clear what restrictions are compatible with the very nature of the Petrine function to be exercised by the pope—that is, his special unifying and ordering Ministry with reference to the church as a whole (see the Common Statement, par. 4). What limitations would leave room for the relative independence that the papacy must have in order to discharge its high mission? To impose juridical limits on papal power would presumably involve a transfer of some of that same power to other organs, which would likewise be capable of arbitrary and un-Christian conduct.

Our Lutheran partners in dialogue acknowledge that their independence from the papacy has not freed them from all abuses of ecclesiastical authority. They acknowledge that officers and assemblies on various levels in any church body are themselves capable of violating the rights and freedoms of the faithful and of resisting God's will for his church.

As Catholics we consider that, notwithstanding some human failings, the papacy has been a signal help in protecting the gospel and the church against particularistic distortions. It has served the faith and life of the church in ways too numerous to mention. While we look forward to changes in the style of papal leadership corresponding to the needs and opportunities of our times, we cannot foresee any set of circumstances that would make it desirable, even if it were possible, to abolish the papal office.

To our Lutheran brothers we wish to express our thanks for the wisdom and concern they have shared with us as we have in dialogue with them tried to formulate responsible views concerning the papacy. We have learned that they, as Lutherans, consider the faithful proclamation of the gospel in the Roman Catholic communion to be their concern as well as ours. We ask them to continue to support us by their understanding, counsel, and prayer.

In exploring the possible future relationships between the Lutheran churches and the papacy, as we have done in this consultation, we have been addressing central ecclesial issues raised by the Reformation. These issues have not been solved by the polemical approaches of the past four centuries, but we are bold enough to hope that the kind of collaboration we have experienced in this dialogue may be a prelude to a new relationship between our traditions. In terms of the Petrine function we believe that both Lutherans and Roman Catholics may no longer avoid the question: Could not the pope in our time become in some real way pastor and teacher of all the faithful, even those who cannot accept all the claims connected with his office? In the light of our experience in this dialogue we believe that the Roman Catholic church should take definite steps to face this question.

In view of their own particular spiritual patrimony and, not least, their own firm convictions concerning the papacy itself, Lutherans will presumably not be in a position to adopt the same relationship to the see of Rome that is currently held by Roman Catholics. But we suggest in our Common Statement (par. 33), that a distinct canonical status may be worked out by which Lutherans could be in official communion with the church of Rome. Such a restoration of communion, we believe, would be of great benefit to Roman Catholics, and to Lutherans, enabling them both to share in a broader Christian heritage. In such a wider communion of churches the papacy would be able to serve as a sign and instrument of unity, not simply for Roman Catholics, but for others who have never ceased to pray and labor for the manifest unity of the whole church of Christ.

PART IV
PROCEDURES OF THE NEW TESTAMENT AND PATRISTICS TASK FORCES

In previous discussions and published volumes of the Lutheran—Roman Catholic Dialogue concerning creed, baptism, eucharist, and ministry, we have paid attention to, and have been strongly influenced by, both the scriptures and church history. But in the discussions on the papacy, the amount of biblical and historical data to be reviewed and analyzed was so enormous that it seemed impossible to have the data examined with scholarly precision by experts in each discipline at the bi-annual meetings of the dialogue or to print full treatment of the data in the current volume. Therefore a decision was taken in the dialogue meetings at Miami (February, 1971) and at Greenwich, Connecticut (September, 1971) to commission smaller task forces to study the background of the papacy during two particularly sensitive periods, namely New Testament and patristic times, and to digest the results of these studies for use in the dialogue.

In each instance two members from the National Dialogue, one Lutheran and one Roman Catholic, were appointed to chair these task forces in order to keep the National Dialogue abreast of the results. The New Testament co-chairmen were Raymond E. Brown and John Reumann; the patristics co-chairmen were James F. McCue and Arthur Carl Piepkorn.

The New Testament task force met some fifteen times between October, 1971 and March, 1973. Since it was felt that a study of Peter's role in the New Testament as background for the papacy might serve many purposes, including the needs of other ecumenical dialogues, the membership of this task force was broadened to include Episcopal and Reformed scholars. The results of their inquiry were published in September, 1973 under the title, *Peter in the New Testament,* by a Lutheran (Augsburg) and a Roman Catholic (Paulist/Newman) publishing house.

The patristics task force originally envisaged a joint document analogous to *Peter in the New Testament.* After canvassing for suggestions it met in December, 1971. Arthur Piepkorn and James McCue then prepared drafts covering the pre- and post-Nicene periods respectively. These were discussed at a two-day meeting in December, 1972. After revision the two reports were presented to the dialogue group at San Antonio in February, 1973. Further revisions were then made. Because of the vastness and complexity of the material, it was out of the question for the entire task force to examine the primary and secondary documentation with the kind of detail possible for the New Testament. It was therefore decided that the papers would appear in this volume under the names of their principal co-authors rather than as joint reports.

Since the studies produced by the two task forces have their own integrity, readers of this volume are urged to examine them firsthand. However, the portions of our Common Statement which deal with the New Testament (par. 9–13) and with the patristic era (par. 15–18) have been written in light of the conclusions of the respective task forces. We present here a brief analysis of the thrust of these two task force studies.

Our discussions on the roles of Peter in the New Testament and on the relation of Peter's roles to the status of the bishops of Rome in the first five centuries must not be considered simply as informative background for this volume. Roman Catholicism has presented its claims for the papacy precisely in terms of a relationship of the bishop of Rome to Peter. It was the view of Vatican Council I that Christ constituted Peter chief of all the apostles and visible head of the whole church on earth, and that by Christ's institution Peter would always have successors in that office who are the bishops of Rome. Such a formulation expressed a point of Roman Catholic faith in historical language, and therefore raises at least two questions for contemporary scholars. First, how is the role of the bishop of Rome historically related to the roles of Peter as described in the New Testament? Second, to what degree are the pictures of Peter in the New Testament genuinely historical? To answer the first question requires information from both the patristic and New Testament fields; to answer the second question is a matter of New Testament research.

Since there is a strong element of history in the Roman Catholic claim, it was important that both task forces employ the methods in common use today for scientific historical study. At the same time it must not be assumed that historical criticism can answer with certainty the two questions asked. But such study sometimes changes the perspective of the discussion. In answering the first question, for instance, the Roman Catholic who is conscious of historical criticism will not expect to find Peter in the first century acting in the same manner as the pope in the fifth century. The Lutheran who is conscious of historical criticism will admit that if Peter did not act in the manner of a later pope, the relationship of the papacy to Peter is not necessarily disproved. Both of them must come to terms with the fact of historical development.

Awareness of this historical development on the part of the New Testament task force is illustrated in *Peter in the New Testament:*

> . . . papacy in its developed form cannot be read back into the New Testament; and it will help neither papal opponents nor papal supporters to have the model of later papacy before their eyes when discussing the role of Peter. For that very reason we have tended to avoid "loaded" terminology in reference to Peter, e.g., primacy, jurisdiction. Too often in the past, arguments about whether or not Peter has a "universal primacy" have blinded scholars to a more practical agreement about such things as the widely accepted importance of Peter in the New Testament and his diversified image (pp. 8–9).

Similarly, the reports on the patristic period note that, as institutions are affected by the challenges and needs of the times, the papacy can be no exception. As a clearly identifiable institution the Roman primacy emerged gradually. Some of the elements that would later be combined to constitute the Roman primacy were already in existence before Nicaea. Yet it was in the post-Nicene period that a claim was clearly made by a number of Roman bishops that they succeeded Peter in his responsibility for all the churches. In neither the East nor the West were the responses to this claim without fluctuation and ambiguity.

These biblical and patristic studies have examined the roles of Peter and of the Roman pontiffs in the context of the first five centuries. As a result, they do not directly answer the later questions which the National Dialogue has faced. For instance, Paragraph 13 of the Common Statement portrays Peter as having various roles in New Testament times; attention is drawn in particular to his roles as the great fisherman (missionary), the shepherd (pastor) of the sheep, the martyr, the receiver of special revelation, the confessor of the true faith, the guardian of faith against false teaching. The line of development of such images is obviously reconcilable with, and indeed favorable to, the claims of the Roman Catholic church for the papacy. The same may be said of some images of Peter which appeared in early patristic times. Yet important questions remain: To what extent is the trajectory of these images, as traced by recent scholars, influenced by the events of later history? How do images not so favorable to papal claims, e.g., that of Peter as a weak and sinful man, affect the general picture? One may also ask the further theological question: How should these developments be interpreted in the light of God's providence?

Thus, the studies of the two task forces clear aside some of the obstacles faced in the past. They do not, however, relieve us of the difficult task of evaluating the historical developments of the Petrine image and of the papacy. But a discernment of the hand of God in history is not a matter of historical criticism; it is rather a question for theological reflection. In its work, therefore, the National Dialogue has had to go beyond the results of historical study as presented by the two task forces.

We are aware of the fact that the biblical and patristic reports do not reflect total agreement among scholars. Even within one church, researchers may disagree over the meaning of a text or document. No attempt has been made to gloss over the instances where no unanimous results could be arrived at. Diversity of scholarly opinion, especially in relation to the New Testament, may be misunderstood by those who believe that the interpretation of the Bible should not be subject to the vagaries of human scholarship and should reach divine certainty. Such a simplistic view has sometimes been fostered among Protestants by the assertion that the Bible, being the sole rule of faith, should be immediately clear to all Christian readers. Among Roman Catholics, this simplistic view has sometimes found support in the contention that since church authority is the infallible interpreter of scripture, its meaning has been decided once for all. However, while the members of this National Dialogue clearly accept their respective traditions on the interpretation of scripture, they recognize that scholarly analysis of the documents often blunts the edge of some affirmations found in these traditions. For instance, such a technical question as the exact historical description of Peter's role during his lifetime cannot be answered simply by citing scriptural texts or authoritative teachings of the magisterium.

The recognition of difficulties and the presentation of a tolerable diversity of opinions about the meaning of the sources studied constitute a challenge to the churches to reexamine some past assumptions. Do the positions that seemed clear in the Reformation and the nineteenth century remain equally clear today? Might not new possibilities of agreement be opened by a reconsideration of the relation of the papacy to Peter in the light of modern historical method? The only alternatives to the type of historical criticism that allow for diversity of interpretation are the opposing theses which either affirm or deny that the papacy is found in the New Testament or the patristic documentation. Such theses entail the corollary that those who do not find the clear doctrine, whatever it might be, must be either uninformed or in bad faith. This inference has, over the last four centuries, produced little progress in bringing Christians together. By contrast, the members of the National Dialogue have judged that historical criticism, though by no means the supreme arbiter, must be used as a gift from God in the contemporary discussions among Christians.

Notes

Part I: Common Statement

1. It should be noted that we shall in this report follow the practice established in Volume IV of employing the term "ministry" to refer to the task or service which devolves on the whole church in distinction from the (or a) Ministry (or Minister) which performs a particular form of service—specific order, function or gift (charism) within and for the sake of Christ's church and its mission in the world. "This Ministry has the two-fold task of proclaiming the Gospel to the world—evangelizing, witnessing, serving—and of building up in Christ those who already believe—teaching, exhorting, reproving, and sanctifying by word and sacrament. For this two-fold work, the Spirit endows the Ministry with varieties of gifts, and thus helped the church to meet new situations in its pilgrimage. Through proclamation of the word and administration of the sacraments, this Ministry serves to unify and order the church in a special way for its ministry," *Lutherans and Catholics in Dialogue IV: Eucharist and Ministry,* p. 11; see also p. 9.

2. Martin Luther, "On Councils and the Church," Luther's Works, vol. 41, pp. 9–178. For a commentary, see Jaroslav Pelikan, "Luther's Attitude Towards Church Councils," *The Papal Council and the Gospel* (ed. K. E. Skydsgaard), Minneapolis: Augsburg, 1961, pp. 37–60, and for a full treatment, Ch. Tecklenburg-Johns, *Luthers Konzilsidee in ihrer historischen Bedingtheit und ihrem reformatorischen Neuansatz.* Berlin: Topelmann, 1966.

3. See above, note 1.

4. Cf. *Peter in the New Testament,* Raymond E. Brown, Karl P. Donfried, John Reumann, eds. Minneapolis and New York, Augsburg Publishing House, and Paulist Press, 1973, pp. 162ff.

5. Thus, Melanchthon noted in signing the Smalcald Articles with their anti-papal polemics that if the Pope "would allow the Gospel, we, too, may concede to him that superiority over the bishops which he possesses by human right, making this concession for the sake of peace and general unity among the Christians who are now under him and may be in the future." T.G. Tappert, ed., *The Book of Concord* (Philadelphia: Fortress Press, 1959) pp. 316–317.

6. *The Book of Concord,* p. 298.

7. Carl Peter, "Dimensions of *Jus Divinum* in Roman Catholic Theology," and George A. Lindbeck, "Papacy and *Ius Divinum,* A Lutheran View," see below.

8. Maurice C. Duchaine, "Vatican I on Primacy and Infallibility."

9. The Theological Commission of Vatican Council II rejected a proposed amendment to the effect that the pope, calling the bishops to collegial action, is "bound to the Lord alone" *(uni Domino devinctus).* In support of this reflection, the Commission wrote that such a formula was "oversimplified: for the Roman Pontiff is also bound to adhere to the revelation itself, to the fundamental structure of the Church, to the sacraments, to the definitions of former Councils, etc." (*Schema Constitutionis De Ecclesia,* MCMLXIV, p. 93).

10. *Peter in the New Testament,* pp. 8f.

11. *Ibid.,* pp. 158–68 with detailed discussion in previous chapters of the book. See also "Procedures of the New Testament and Patristics Task Forces."

12. *Ibid.*, p. 166. Cf. Oscar Cullman, *Peter—Disciple, Apostle, Martyr.* Philadelphia: Westminster Press, 2nd ed., 1962.

13. James F. McCue, "The Roman Primacy in the Patristic Era: I. The Beginnings Through Nicaea," see below.

14. George H. Tavard, "The Papacy in the Middle Ages," see below.

15. Denzinger-Schönmetzer, *Enchiridion Symbolorum.* 33rd ed. (hereafter cited as DS) (Freiburg: Herder, 1965), 1307 and 3059.

16. DS 3059–3065.

17. *Lumen Gentium,* Chapter III.

18. *Gaudium et Spes,* 4.

19. *Dei Verbum,* 10.

20. *Lumen Gentium,* 25.

21. *Book of Concord,* Article 14, pp. 214f.

22. *Lutherans and Catholics in Dialogue IV, Eucharist and Ministry,* pp. 19, 20. See also note 5 above.

23. The expressions, "legitimate traditions" and "spiritual heritage", are meant to include the broad span of all the elements that Lutherans have experienced as being the ways in which they and their ancestors have lived the gospel. These ways pertain to different though related levels that may be called, customs and faith, discipline and doctrine, canon law and teaching, etc. The intention of the text is to suggest that structures of reconciliation should extend further than the central patrimony of faith, in order to include also the *adiaphora* that usage has legitimized.

Part II: Reflections of the Lutheran Participants

1. *Lutherans and Catholics in Dialogue IV: Eucharist and Ministry,* 1970, p. 11.

2. *Apology of the Augsburg Confession* 7:20. Theodore G. Tappert ed. *The Book of Concord,* Philadelphia: Fortress Press, 1959, p. 171.

3. *Lutherans and Catholics in Dialogue III: The Eucharist as Sacrifice,* 1967, *IV: Eucharist and Ministry,* 1970.

4. *Lutherans and Catholics in Dialogue IV: Eucharist and Ministry,* p. 19.

5. *Ibid.,* p. 20.

6. *Ibid.,* p. 11.

7. *Schaff-Herzog. Encyclopedia of Religious Knowledge.* New York and London: Funk and Wagnalls, 1908. Vol. II pp 76, 260–262; Vol. XII p. 2.

8. Tappert, *op. cit.* pp. 298, 299.

9. It was this statement that provoked the assertion of the Smalcald Articles that the pope is the real antichrist: Part II, Article IV, 10, 11. Tappert, *op. cit.,* p. 300.

10. For a modern Roman Catholic interpretation and critique of this document, see G. Tavard, *"The Papacy in the Middle Ages,"* below.

11. Smalcald Articles Part II, Article IV, 1; Treatise on the Power and Primacy of the Pope, 1–4. Tappert, *op. cit.* pp. 298, 320.

12. Tappert, *op. cit.* pp. 325, 326.

13. See his note in signing the Smalcald Articles, Tappert, *op. cit.* pp. 316, 317.

14. Smalcald Articles Part Two, 4, 1. Tappert, *op. cit.* p. 298.

15. Treatise 25, Tappert, *op. cit.* p. 324.

16. So, for example, Balthasar Meisnerus. *Disputatio decima de distinctis gradibus ministrorum et usu templorum,* thesis XIII, in his *Collegium adiaphoristicum,* editio altera (Wittenberg: Haeredes D. Tobiae Mevii et Elerdus Schumacherus Johannes Borckardus, 1653), p. 198.

17. For one of the fullest discussions of the question of papal primacy by a 17th century Lutheran author, see Johannes Gerhardus: *Confessio Catholica,* liber II, articulus III, "De pontifice Romano" (Frankfurt und Leipzig: Christianus Genschius Johannes Andreae, 1679), pp. 523–675, especially chapters 1 through 5, pp. 523–581.

18. Such contacts recurred, e.g., at Augsburg during the diet of 1530, at the Leipzig

Colloquies of 1534 and 1539, at the Colloquy of Hagenau of 1540, at the Colloquy of Worms in 1540–1541, and at the Colloquies of Regensburg of 1541 and 1546.

19. Hans Preuss. *Die Vorstellungen vom Antichrist im späterem Mittelalter, bei Luther und in der konfessionalen Polemik,* Leipzig, 1906. Bishop Arnulf of Orleans protested (ca. 991) against the misuse of the papal office in his time, denouncing the cruelty, concupiscence, and violence of a succession of popes, and asking, "Are any bold enough to maintain that the priests of the Lord all over the world are to take their law from monsters of guilt like these—men branded with ignominy, illiterate men, and ignorant alike of things human and divine? If, holy fathers, we are bound to weigh in the balance the lives, the morals, and the attainments of the humblest candidate for the priestly office, how much more ought we to look to the fitness of him who aspires to be the Lord and Master of all priests! Yet how would it fare with us, if it should happen that the man the most deficient in all these virtues, unworthy of the lowest place in the priesthood, should be chosen to fill the highest place of all? What would you say of such a one, when you see him sitting upon the throne glittering in purple and gold? Must he not be the 'Antichrist, sitting in the temple of God and showing himself as God'?" Philip Schaff, *History of the Christian Church,* New York: Scribner and Sons, 1899. Vol. IV pp. 290–292.

20. We may mention the abortive Colloquy of Regensburg in 1557, the Colloquies of Zabern in Alsace in 1562, of Baden (1589), Emmendingen (1590), Aegensburg (1601), and at Torum in Poland (1645).

21. The course that the discussions took in one series of exchanges is instructive. In 1691 the Lutheran Abbot Gerard I of Loccum (Gerard Walter Molanus) in his *Cogitationes privatae de methodo reunionis ecclesiae protestantium cum ecclesia romano-catholica* stated that the Lutherans are willing to concede that by positive ecclesiastical law the bishop of Rome is the first patriarch, the first bishop of the church, and as such entitled to obedience in spiritual matters. If the bishop of Rome wants recognition of his status as of divine right he must be ready to prove it to a general council from sacred scripture. In a later exposition, Gerard sees the primacy of the pope by divine right as one of the nineteen issues that make up the "irreconcilable" controversies. In his detailed discussion he quotes the Roman Catholic theologians of the Sorbonne against the primacy of the pope by divine right, against infallibility, and against the pope's authority to adjudicate controversies inside or outside of a general council. If these views should find acceptance in the rest of the Roman Catholic Community, Molanus holds that the entire business would be resolved. These views, however, did not find much acceptance; indeed, the documents that Molanus quotes were placed on the index of forbidden books.

22. See the recent book by Manfred P. Fleischer, *Katholische und Lutherische Ireniker unter besonderer Berucksichtigung des 19. Jahrhunderts* (Göttingen: Musterschmidt Verlag, 1968).

23. Cf. *Lumen Gentium* 18, 22, 24, 25; the *Addenda* of November 16, 1964; *Christus Dominus* 2, 4, 8. Declaration in Defense of the Catholic Doctrine of the Church against Certain Errors of the Present Day: 3. (1973).

24. For example, the reservation of the question of birth control during Vatican II, and the encyclical *Humanae Vitae* which ignored the advice of a majority of the special advisory commission.

25. Published in 1973 by Augsburg Publishing House, and Paulist Press, cited above Chapter 1, Note 4.

26. See the studies by McCue and Piepkorn in this volume.

27. *Peter in the New Testament,* p. 8.

28. The terminology here takes up a suggestion made by J.M. Robinson and H. Koester in their book, *Trajectories through Early Christianity* (Philadelphia, Fortress Press), 1971.

29. *Peter in the New Testament,* pp. 23–28, esp. 29f., and passim.

30. See the study by James F. McCue in this volume.

31. See the Common Statement above.

32. See Carl Peter, "Dimensions of *Jus Divinum* in Roman Catholic Theology," in *Theological Studies* XXXIV (1973) pp. 227–250; and A.C. Piepkorn, "Ius Divinum and Adiaphoron in Relation to Structural Problems in the Church: the Position of the Lutheran Symbolical Books," below.

33. Peter, *passim.*

34. e.g. The encyclicals of Pope Leo XII (notably *Rerum Novarum*), as well as those of Pope Pius XI *(Quadragesimo Anno)* and Pope John XXIII *(Mater et Magistra, Pacem in Terris).*

35. The encylical *Divino Afflante Spiritu* of Pope Pius XII, 1943, gave papal sanction to the use of historical-critical methods in the study of scriptures. This approval is made more explicit in the instruction *Holy Mother Church* (prepared by the Pontifical Commission for the Promotion of Bible Studies, 1964) and by the dogmatic constitution of Vatican II *Dei Verbum.*

36. Tappert, *op. cit.* pp. 316–317.

Part III: Reflections of the Roman Catholic Participants

1. *Acta Apostolicae Sedis* 65 (1973), 402–403.
2. *Ibid.,* p. 403.
3. DS 3054–3055.

Teaching Authority and Infallibility in the Church

I
COMMON STATEMENT

INTRODUCTION

1. Lutherans and Roman Catholics in the United States have been engaged since 1965 in a theological dialogue dealing with the main issues which have divided their churches since the 16th century.[1] The measure of consensus they were able to reach on the Eucharist and on Ministry[2] was expressed in two joint statements that are of major importance for continuing theological convergence. In approaching the topic of papal primacy, they were aware of special difficulties, since this topic occasioned the most violent antagonisms of the past, and since these antagonisms have left their mark on the mentalities of contemporary Christians. Yet they were also able to agree on many points in a joint statement in which papal primary is regarded as a Ministry to the universal Church.

Because papal infallibility is conceptually distinct from primacy and has had its own, rather more recent, development, the agreed statement on primacy did not include consideration of the question of infallibility. But, as had been planned, the members of the dialogue began discussing this topic as soon as agreement had been reached on the principle of a Ministry to the Church universal. The present statement thus follows logically the previous discussions and joint statements of *Lutherans and Catholics in Dialogue.*

In order to treat the subject adequately, this dialogue had to set the question of papal infallibility in a broad horizon. Papal infallibility is related to several wider questions: the authority of the gospel, the indefectibility of the Church, the infallibility of its belief and teaching, and the assurance or certainty which Christian believers have always associated with their faith. Furthermore, such a question cannot be examined in our day without referring to the contemporary crisis of authority, and without paying attention to the critical questions raised by linguistic analysis and philosophy regarding the use of language to express religious insights.

2. Discussion of papal infallibility on the Catholic side was given its focus by the First Vatican Council when the doctrine was defined in 1870. The Council taught that the bishop of Rome, as successor of Peter in the primacy, is divinely protected from error when he speaks *ex cathedra,* that is, when, "as pastor and doctor of all Christians" and by virtue of "his supreme apostolic authority," he "defines a doctrine concerning faith or morals" to be held "by the universal Church." In such an extraordinary case, the Council specified, the bishop of Rome proceeds with the infallibility with which "the divine Redeemer wanted his Church to be endowed in defining doctrine concerning faith or morals."[3] It was this infallibility which Pius XII invoked when he defined the doctrine of the Assumption of Mary in 1950.

Despite the careful delimitation of papal infallibility by Vatican I, this dogma was frequently understood more broadly in the period between the two Vatican Councils. Often for the popular mind, and also in theological manuals,[4] it was thought to imply that all papal utterances are somehow enhanced by infallibility. Encyclicals were sometimes interpreted as infallibly conveying the true doctrine even when they did not meet the conditions specified by Vatican I for ex cathedra definitions. Piux XII, indeed, pointed out that encyclical teaching may require the assent of Catholics, especially when it reiterates what is already settled Catholic doctrine or when the pope, even without appealing to his infallible teaching authority, expresses his intention of settling what was previously a controverted question.[5]

Following Vatican II and its treatment of infallibility in the Constitution *Lumen gentium,*[6] the climate of Catholic theology has favored reassessing popular assumptions and theological interpretations. The present common statement of *Lutherans and Catholics in Dialogue* is a contribution to this reassessment.

3. On the Lutheran side, there seems at first glance no room for reassessment. The Reformers' attitude toward papal infallibility was strongly negative.[7] They insisted that in proclaiming the Pauline teaching of justification of the sinner by grace through faith they had a biblical and catholic basis. Consequently they regarded the excommunication of Luther as an arbitrary act, an abuse of papal authority. They viewed the division in the Church as a tragic necessity, as the price they had to pay for fidelity to the Word of God. The promulgation of papal infallibility in 1870 appeared to Lutherans as the deepening of

an already serious disagreement. The separation begun by the condemnation of Luther's teachings in *Exsurge Domine*[8] and later widened by the Council of Trent now seemed beyond hope of reconciliation. For while Lutherans share with Catholics the conviction that the Church of Christ is indefectible,[9] they regard the maintenance of this indefectibility as the sovereign work of God. It appeared to them that the dogma of infallibility was an attempt to usurp the Lordship which God has conferred on Christ alone.

Yet Lutherans need not exclude the possibility that papal primacy and teaching authority might be acceptable developments, at least in certain respects.[10] The Lutheran Reformers accepted the legitimacy of developments in the Church except where these denied or subverted the teaching of Scripture. Thus, they retained the liturgy of the Latin rite, making revisions where they judged its formulations to be contrary to the gospel; and they tried to preserve the episcopal structure of the Church and the traditional ecclesiastical discipline.[11] Theoretically, some aspects of the papacy could have been accepted in the same way. For while Lutherans see papal primacy as emerging over a long period of time, rather than something taught in the Scriptures, this function could, under proper conditions, be acknowledged as a legitimate development, maintaining unity, mediating disputes, and defending the Church's spiritual freedom.

This theoretical possibility of seeing papal teaching authority in a more favorable light is now being actualized. Roman Catholics are rethinking their position, and this suggests that Lutherans may well ask themselves whether the Roman Catholic doctrine of papal infallibility, even if not something which they would be able to affirm for themselves, need continue to be regarded by them as anti-Christian and therefore as a barrier to the unity of the churches. Catholics, on the other hand, must ask themselves whether their view of the papal teaching office and its infallibility can be so understood and presented as to meet the legitimate concerns of those Christians who have traditionally opposed the doctrine.

A FRESH LOOK AT DOCTRINAL AUTHORITY IN RELATION TO THE QUESTION OF INFALLIBILITY

4. Two areas of investigation have been especially helpful to us in examining infallibility afresh. First, the topic has been set in the broader horizon of doctrinal authority in the early Church, especially as examined in light of modern historical studies in Scripture and the

Church Fathers. We set forth below not a complete historical survey but pertinent highlights from our discussions. Second, because of insights which arise when the question is examined in light of linguistic and cultural contexts, we have found ourselves able to think in ways which are different from earlier discussion. These influences have enabled us to view our mutual and individual concerns in new ways.

A) Gospel and Doctrinal Authority in the Early Church: Biblical and Patristic Roots

5. God, known to us above all through what he "has done for the salvation of the world in Jesus Christ,"[12] is the source and ground of authority for the Church of Christ. The gospel, the proclaiming of this saving action of God in the person, life, death, and resurrection of Jesus and made present in the Holy Spirit, is an expression of this authority. This gospel (*a*) was proclaimed by witnesses—apostles and others—in the early Church; (*b*) was recorded in the New Testament Scriptures, which have "a normative role for the entire later tradition of the Church";[13] (*c*) has been made living in the hearts of the believers by the Holy Spirit; (*d*) has been reflected in the "rule of faith" *(regula fidei)* and in the forms and exercise of church leadership; (*e*) has been served by Ministers.

1) Jesus Christ as Authority

6. In Jesus' day there were all sorts of authorities. For example, the political authority was that of the Roman Empire. Israel recognized the authority of the law (Torah), of the traditions (Mark 7:8) amplifying the law set forth by the teachers (Matt. 23:2), and of the temple and its cult administered by priests. In the New Testament authority is ascribed to Jesus Christ (John 17:2; 5:27; Rev. 12:10).

The New Testament pictures of Jesus are all influenced by the theologies of various writers reflecting on his earthly life in the light of the Easter event. Yet it is possible to discern, especially because of multiple attestation in our sources, that Jesus' contemporaries associated various kinds of authority with his words and deeds, even before his resurrection.

He was understood to be a prophet (Mark 6:2–4 and par.; Luke 7:39; 13:33–34), to speak and act as one of the prophets of old (Mark 8:28 and par.; Luke 7:16). Jesus was remembered as a man who taught with authority (Mark 1:22). He not only interpreted the law, as the rabbis did, but he did so with definitive authority (Matt. 7:28–29, with reference to the Sermon on the Mount). In the Gospel of Matthew he is depicted as speaking in his own name, in contrast to "the men of old": "But *I* say to you . . . " (Matt. 5:21–48).

Jesus was understood to have the authority of an exorcist because he cast out demons and worked cures (Mark 1:27; Matt. 12:27–28, par. Luke 11:19–20; cf. Luke 9:1 and 10:17). These wonders aroused hopes that he might be the expected King of Israel (John 6:14).

To him, as Son of man, the Gospels ascribe the authority on earth to forgive sins (Mark 2:5–10 and par.) and to interpret the Sabbath (Mark 2:23–28 and par.). In Jerusalem, in the context of his teaching (Mark 11:17) and the cleansing of the temple (Mark 11:15–17), he was asked specifically, "By what authority are you doing these things, or who gave you this authority?" (Mark 11:28).

Thus the New Testament authors see his authority, in various forms, as a feature of his ministry. Here was "something greater than the temple" (Matt. 12:6), greater than Jonah and Solomon (Matt. 12:41–42), and different from the power of "this world" (John 18:36).

7. After his death and resurrection, the authority in Jesus is seen in an entirely new dimension. He is now declared to be risen and enthroned at the right hand of God. He is acclaimed as the Lord, ruling with authority. He is designated Son of God "in power" . . . (Rom. 1:4). To him "all authority in heaven and on earth" is given (Matt. 28:18). He is exalted at God's right hand (Acts 2:34–36), acclaimed as Lord (*kyrios,* Phil. 2:9–11). Now the Holy Spirit is poured forth as the Spirit of Christ (Acts 2:33; Gal. 4:6).[14]

Faith as trust and obedience is the proper response to the Lord Jesus Christ (Rom. 1:5; 10:8–10; Phil. 2:12; 3:21). No one can confess him to be Lord without the Holy Spirit (1 Cor. 12:3). In the perspective of faith all creation is subject to him (Phil. 2:10): he has a role in creation (1 Cor. 8:6; John 1:3) and in the preservation of the world (Heb. 1:3); he will sit upon God's judgment seat (2 Cor. 5:10; cf. Rom. 14:10) as the one designated by God to judge the living and the dead (Acts 10:42). Past, present, and future are under the authority of Christ, in whom all God's promises are affirmed (2 Cor. 1:20).

2) The Gospel as Authority

8. The risen Lord's authority and power in the Christian community are expressed in the gospel, that message of Christ crucified

and risen which his followers proclaimed (1 Cor. 1:21–23; 2:2; Rom. 1:16, 4:25; Matt. 26–28). It includes what Jesus himself had taught,[15] viewed in light of the Easter "good news" that "he is risen." This gospel, which is a word of power from God (Rom. 1:16; cf. 1 Cor. 2:5) and is truth (Gal. 2:5, 14; cf. Eph. 4:21), is expressed in various terms, as God's righteousness (Rom. 1:17, "justification"), reconciliation (2 Cor. 5:18–21), and forgiveness of sins (Col. 1:14; Matt. 9:2; Luke 4:18; Acts 10:43; 13:38). Indeed Christ is himself the gospel. This is true for Paul[16] and Mark[17] in particular. One can claim, indeed, that for the first two centuries of Christianity, "gospel" denoted "the revelation of Christ."[18]

3) The Gospel (a) Proclaimed by Witnesses

9. This gospel found expression in many ways, reflecting the church's needs and the diverse cultures and literary forms of the day.[19] It was proclaimed orally and later written down. It took the shape of credal formulas and confessions of faith (1 Cor. 12:3, "Jesus Christ is Lord"; 1 Cor. 15:3–5); hymns (Col. 1:15–20); letters (e.g., 1 Thessalonians); catechetical material (1 Cor. 6:9–11; Gal. 5:19–23; Matt. 5–7); miracle stories; narratives; and eventually gospel books and apocalypses large (Revelation) and small (Mark 13). It was proclaimed in Baptism (Matt. 28:19) and the Lord's Supper (1 Cor. 11:26). It was spoken, in the New Testament period, in Aramaic, Greek, Latin, and probably other languages. It employed images from the Hebrew Scriptures and from the cultures of the ancient Near East and the Hellenistic world. The gospel addressed needs of the Christian community in preaching, teaching, worship, and every aspect of daily life.

10. The witnesses who set forth this gospel shared in the authority of Jesus Christ. During his earthly ministry Jesus had sent forth disciples to carry on his mission by proclaiming the message about the kingdom of God (Mark 3:15; 6:7; Matt. 4:23; 9:35). After Easter the risen Lord commissioned followers with his authority to go forth into all the world, to the close of the age (Matt. 28:19–20), and promised them his presence in their corporate mission as his Church (Matt. 18:20). When they proclaimed his word, they shared in the authority of Jesus himself. Jesus said, "He who hears you hears me" (Luke 10:16; cf. Matt. 10:14, 40; John 17:18, 20:21). The witnesses to Jesus are enumerated in such groupings as apostles, prophets, teachers, evangelists, pastors, etc.,[20] and in lists of names such as those of "the Twelve."[21] Although those who exercised this apostolic Ministry are

often anonymous and little is known about them, their boldness, confidence, and assurance are striking.[22] They did not hesitate at times to assert that the Holy Spirit guided the decisions they had made (Acts 15:28, "It has seemed good to the Holy Spirit and to us"); they invoked anathemas on those who preached a false gospel (Gal. 1:6–9). Their statements reflect confidence that the truth of their message is ultimately anchored in God.[23]

4) The Gospel (b) Recorded in Scripture

11. In the period before the New Testament writings were composed and collected, the authoritative gospel about Christ was a spoken message transmitted by apostolic witnesses. Hence one can speak of "the Tradition of the Gospel (the *paradosis* of the *kerygma*)" by which Christians lived.[24] To be sure, the Christian community did have a Bible in what we term the Old Testament; these Scriptures were regularly interpreted in light of Jesus Christ and the good news about him (Luke 24:27, 45).

But to meet needs of their day and to offer their testimony in a more enduring form, the early witnesses wrote letters, Gospels, and other books, beginning about A.D. 50. Within the next 50 to 100 years all 27 books eventually designated as New Testament Scripture were composed,[25] and during the second, third, and fourth centuries these were assembled into the authoritative collection of books which we call the canonical New Testament. This collection provides a written precipitate of the primitive Church's faith. It witnesses to Christ, pointing to ways in which the gospel had been set forth. It was written "that you may believe that Jesus is the Christ, the Son of God, and that believing you may have life in his name" (John 20:31). The canonical collection,[26] which includes the Old and New Testaments, is normative and authoritative for all the Church's statements of faith and teaching.

5) The Gospel (c) Made Living by the Spirit

12. The Spirit of God has been at work in every stage of the transmission of the gospel. No one can confess Jesus as Lord (1 Cor. 12:3) or witness to him (John 15:26–27) apart from the Holy Spirit. Moreover, the Spirit is associated with Jesus' promise, "When the Spirit of truth comes, he will guide you into all the truth; for he will not speak

on his own authority, but whatever he hears he will speak, and he will declare to you the things that are to come" (John 16:13). The Spirit is active not only in the inspiration of Scripture but also in the reception and further transmission of the message. The inscription of Scripture is to be understood within the setting of the early Christian community. It is a unique work of the same Spirit who through the ages enlivens Christ's people with his gifts and brings them to assurance of faith. The Spirit-filled community plays an authenticating role in the reception of Scripture and the gospel.

6) The Gospel (d) Summarized in the regula fidei

13. Brief summaries of the apostolic preaching were already developed in the first Christian generation. Some were in writing before that generation ended (cf. 1 Cor. 15:3ff.) and others were recorded in the second-generation Christian literature, including those documents that were later recognized as part of the canon of the New Testament (Titus 3:5–7; cf. 1 Clement 32:3–4). These summary statements, often used in the context of Baptism, were responses to the challenges of their day and guides to discerning the truth of the gospel. They continued to be fashioned in the second century, and the Church Fathers could describe such formulations as "the canon of the truth" (Irenaeus), "the rule of faith (*regula fidei,* esp. Tertullian). From such summary statements developed the Old Roman Symbol from which is derived the Apostles' Creed. In the third and fourth centuries these confessions of local churches grew into authoritative statements of faith, stressing central truths and affirming particular points that had become crucial. This development reached a climax in the conciliar creeds of Nicaea-Constantinople (A.D. 325, 381), which took up and reformulated credal statements of previous generations.[27]

7) The Gospel (e) Served by Ministers

14. Along with the emergence of Scriptures and credal statements in this period, forms of church leadership also developed. The apostles, prophets, teachers, *episkopoi,* deacons, presbyters, and evangelists[28] of the first century were succeeded by others who carried on their witness. There developed an idea of "succession to the apostles," which has been interpeted as succession in doctrine, or as succession in office, or both.[29]

15. Of special relevance in the light of later developments is the "Petrine function" as delineated in the New Testament.[30] Among other texts, Matt. 16:18 has served to assure the faithful that "the powers of death shall not prevail" against the Church.[31] Peter, who is presented there as the "rock" on which the Church is to be founded, is the one for whom Jesus prayed that his faith might not fail (Luke 22:32); he has thus been associated with the notion of indefectibility.[32] Power and authority have also been associated with the image of Peter, to whom the "keys of the kingdom" are entrusted (Matt. 16:19) and who has, along with others (Matt. 18:18), the task of "binding and loosing."[33] Alongside of this, the Petrine function has been seen, in the light of Luke 22:32, as one of "strengthening the brethren," a responsibility which Peter also shares with others (Acts 15:32).[34]

However such passages are interpreted,[35] Peter's role should be understood in relation to Jesus' promise to remain with his disciples until "the close of the age" (Matt. 28:20). The extent to which this promise includes a guarantee of Christian preaching and teaching is a question which Scripture does not answer.

16. Infallibility is not a New Testament term. It is used neither of the gospel nor of its proclamation, let alone of books, doctrines, or persons. Yet the New Testament is concerned with many of the issues that arise in later theological discussions of the authority and infallibility of Scripture, Church, councils, and popes.

The Pastoral Epistles in particular display a special awareness of the problem of the faithful transmission of the gospel. The author directs Titus to "amend what is defective and appoint elders in every town" (Titus 1:5), and Timothy to "charge certain persons not to teach any different doctrine" (1 Timothy 1:3). Timothy is told,"guard what has been entrusted to you" (1 Timothy 6:20; cf. 2 Timothy 1:12, 14). The key virtue of the apostolic Ministry which Timothy and Titus share is faithfulness (Titus 1:7–9; 2 Timothy 2:2). From this faithfulness should flow their bold proclamation of the gospel (Titus 2:15; 1 Timothy 4:11–16). They share in and contribute to the solid assurance that belongs to "God's firm foundation" (2 Timothy 2:19; cf. 1 Timothy 3:15).[36]

B) Gospel and Doctrinal Authority in Subsequent Centuries

17. The concern for faithful transmission did not diminish during the following centuries. The Church Fathers emphasized the normative past and the Church's task of preserving the "deposit of faith."

They trusted that the Holy Spirit would protect the gospel against false teaching. The earliest history of the appeal to an unbroken line of apostolic teaching is unclear. But in the late second century, especially in the struggle against Gnosticism, the Fathers linked the reliable transmission of apostolic teaching to episcopal sees regarded as founded by apostles. The doctrine transmitted in these sees became important for the councils, which endeavored to set forth authoritative interpretations of "the faith . . . delivered to the saints" (Jude 3).

18. Among these sees Rome gained special importance. At first the Roman bishops did not take much initiative in the doctrinal controversies, which took place mainly in the East. By the middle of the third century, however, they seem to have assumed special responsibility for preserving and interpreting the faith of "antiquity" because of the prerogatives of the See of Peter *(cathedra Petri).*[37] Some Roman emperors included the faith of the bishop of Rome in the official norm of orthodoxy, and the biblical image of the Church "without spot or wrinkle" (Eph. 5:27) began to be applied to the church of Rome. Rome became *the* apostolic see. As Pope Innocent I put it, from Rome "the other churches, like waters proceeding from their natal source . . . (like) pure streams from an uncorrupt head, should take up what they ought to enjoin."[38] As the Formula of Pope Hormisdas (A.D. 525) declared, in Rome "the catholic religion has always been preserved immaculate."[39] The conviction that Rome had always defended the purity of the faith continued on into the Middle Ages, and it found expression in such influential documents as the Pseudo-Isidorian Decretals, in statements by popes and theologians, and in collections of canon law.

19. There were, however, challenges to such claims, both in the East and in the West. Eastern Chrstians regarded Rome as one of several apostolic sees to which protection of the pure faith had been entrusted. The faithfulness of such popes as Liberius, Vigilius, and Honorius was questioned. Even in the early Middle Ages western metropolitans could see it as their duty to contradict papal decisions if necessary. Prophetic voices, from the 11th century on, warned that the pope might be an antichrist rather than the faithful preserver of the gospel.[40] It was readily admitted that individual popes of the past had been in error on specific points of doctrine, and the canonical tradition reckoned with the possibility that a pope might deviate from the faith.[41] Yet the formula that the Roman church "has never erred" survived, even though the expression *ecclesia Romana* was by no means ambiguous, particularly in its reference to the universal Church.

20. On the basis of the belief that Rome had never deviated from the truth, it came to be held that in the future Rome would be immune

from error: the Roman church or the Roman bishop cannot err. While such a claim started appearing almost casually with Pope Gelasius (A.D. 492–496),[42] it did not imply that Rome could formulate "new doctrine," since novelty was the mark of heresy. Reformulations when attempted by bishops, synods, or councils were intended to affirm what had been handed down. Reception by the Church at large was undoubtedly a major factor in establishing the authoritativeness of such statements.[43] Roman bishops from the fourth century on regarded their "confirmation" of conciliar actions as an indispensable sign of authoritative teaching. Their own doctrinal decisions, however, needed to be accepted by secular authorities, councils, and fellow bishops in order to be enforced. With the growing practice of appealing to Rome, papal decisions came to be regarded in matters of faith as the last word, from which there could be no further appeal.[44] Popes since Siricius (A.D. 384–399) appealed to the Petrine function of "strengthening the brethren" (Luke 22:32) and to "solicitude for all the churches" (2 Cor. 11:28), in order to establish their teaching authority. The legal maxim that "the first see is judged by no one,"[45] which appeared first in the sixth century, was later interpreted as ensuring the pope's highest teaching authority in matters of faith and morals. It was restated in the era of the Gregorian Reform in terms of immunity from appeal and also on the basis of Christ's unfailing prayer for the faith of Peter (Luke 22:32). Shortly thereafter, Thomas Aquinas could describe the pope as the one to whose sole authority it belongs to "edit a new version of the creed,"[46] and whose judgment in matters of faith must be followed because he represents the universal Church, which "cannot err."[47]

21. In this context the language of "infallibility" first came to be associated with the papal *magisterium.* According to some recent historical research, this usage was occasioned by the controversy over poverty in the Franciscan Order during the late 13th and early 14th centuries.[48] Advocates of a rigorist position used the word to defend the binding authority of statements by earlier popes against the decisions of their successors. A theologian of the 14th century, Guido Terreni, was the first to speak expressly of the "infallible" truth of the teaching of the Roman pontiff in matters of faith.[49]

22. To be sure, the term "infallible" had been used earlier with reference to God's truth, his revelation, the Church's normative teaching, and in similar contexts. It continued to be used with reference to the norm of the Word of God and Holy Scripture in the churches of the Reformation. But with the discussions of the 13th and 14th centuries it had taken on a new, highly technical meaning.

23. Whatever one may think about the appropriateness of the term "infallible," it points to the unavoidable issue of the faithful transmission of the gospel and its authoritative interpretation, guided by the Spirit.

C) Doctrine and the Cultural Context

24. Lutherans and Catholics share the confidence that the Spirit is present and guides Christian teaching not only in the first periods of church history but also in later developments. Both accept, for example, not only Scripture and the rule of faith *(regula fidei)* as formulated in the Apostles' Creed, but also solemn declarations by early ecumenical councils, such as the creeds of Nicaea-Constantinople, and statements of belief on a central point of doctrine, such as the so-called Athanasian Creed, which focuses on the Trinitarian faith. Further, Lutherans have their confessional writings, and Catholics, various later dogmas. The churches have traditionally attached a high degree of authority to such formulations of their teaching, so that to deny the faith confessed in these documents has been seen as amounting to a rejection of the gospel.

25. By Christ's own commission, the gospel had to be preached in diverse civilizations and cultures, and to be transmitted from generation to generation to the close of the age. This communication of the gospel has implied that the Church has the obligation and the authority to formulate its faith in such a way that this faith can be recognized and believed. Such an authority is spiritual, for it is fundamentally the authority of the Spirit guiding the faithful. It is evangelical, for it is the authority of the gospel (the evangel) itself, knowledge of which is transmitted through the Church's preaching and teaching. It is apostolic, for it is rooted in the early apostolic commission and community. It is centered upon Christ, the Word of God Incarnate who is the one mediator (1 Tim. 2:5–7) of God's self-revelation to humankind.[50] It derives from God's gracious gift and not from any human work or merit. It is not a product of human culture or philosophy.

26. For our two traditions, the saving faith by which the gospel is received and believed has a noetic or intellectual aspect. Because human persons live in concrete cultural contexts, the gospel must be proclaimed in ways that speak to their culture. As cultures evolve, new emphases in the proclamation of the gospel may be needed, new conceptualizations may take shape, new formulations may become urgent. The formulation of the gospel, therefore, presents two aspects: the par-

ticular form in which the message is presented and understood, and the truth and certainty of the message itself. On the one hand, with respect to the form in which the message is presented, human language remains inadequate to the transcendent mystery of God and to the fulness of the paschal mystery of Jesus Christ. On the other hand, with respect to the truth and certainty of the message, Christians trust that through their Scriptures, their creeds, their conciliar definitions, and their confessional writings, they are led by the Holy Spirit to the truth of the gospel and to an authentic life of faith.

27. The historical–cultural context of the Christian faith, which at times demands reformulation of the Church's teaching, makes it necessary for the Church to develop structures concerned with the task of reformulation. The members and leaders of the Church must listen carefully both to the diverse human cultures in order to be able to use their language, and to the Church's own past in order to maintain the proper continuity in the teaching of the Christian message. They must compare both the traditional understandings and contemporary reformulations of this message to the normative witness of the Scriptures.[51] Both Catholics and Lutherans believe that the Spirit will guide the process of reformulation so that the Church remains faithful to the gospel. They trust God's promise that the Church of the future will likewise be assisted by the Spirit in its missionary task.

28. This trust that the Holy Spirit guides the Church in transmitting the Christian message to new generations in fidelity to the gospel (cf. John 16:13) has given rise to the concept of the indefectibility of the Church, a term which is known to both the Lutheran and Catholic traditions. Indefectibility, like infallibility, has reference to the preservation of the Church thanks to the work of the Holy Spirit. But the two terms are not synonymous. Indefectibility refers to the continued existence of the Church in all its essential aspects, including its faith. Such fidelity is not an automatic quality of everything that the Church's leaders may say or endorse, but is the result of divine grace. It is recognized by testing the Church's faith and life by the standard of the Word of God. Infallibility has reference to an immunity from error in specific beliefs and teachings.[52] Even though protected by infallibility, such beliefs and teachings nonetheless reflect a merely partial understanding of the gospel, and may be inopportune or poorly expressed. Whatever their differences with regard to infallibility, the Lutheran and Catholic traditions share the certainty of Christian hope that the Church, established by Christ and led by his Spirit, will always remain in the truth fulfilling its mission to humanity for the sake of the gospel.

29. Thus both our communions hold that the gospel of Christ is transmitted within the body of believers, the people of God. "The Spirit dwells in the Church and in the hearts of the faithful as in a temple."[53] Through the guidance of the Spirit, who distributes different gifts for the welfare of the Church, there is a unity of fellowship and service which is a sign that Christ is building up the Church as his own body. The gospel is transmitted in a special way in preaching and the sacraments, through which Christ unites his people to himself. Yet our two communions have sought to assure this transmission of the gospel along different lines.

II
CATHOLIC AND LUTHERAN EMPHASES

A) Catholic Emphases

30. In the contemporary Roman Catholic understanding of the Church, it is emphasized that the transmission of the gospel is the responsibility of the whole people of God. Within this people the college of bishops has a special role. Working together with priests, deacons, and laity, the bishop helps the believers to hear the Word of God in the preached word, in the sacraments, and in the life of the community.

The bishop, as a member of the episcopal college, has a responsiblility not only to the local community but also to the Church universal. Each bishop represents his local Church, but all the bishops together in union with the pope represent the entire Church.[54] The episcopal college exercises its authority in a solemn way through an ecumenical council, and also in an ordinary way through the unity of the bishops dispersed throughout the world.[55]

31. Within the episcopal college the bishop of Rome has a unique function as head of the college. This function has many aspects.[56] One of these has been to supervise the transmission of doctrine in order that the faith of the people of God may be kept in its integrity and authenticity and may bear the fruit of a holy life. Teaching at the higher levels of authority has been exercised (1) through conciliar action, (2) in occasional papal statements, (3) through the guidance and supervision provided, under the pope, by the Roman congregations, secretariats, and commissions.

32. The highest authority in the transmission of doctrine has been exercised in definitions of faith made by councils or by the bishop of

Rome speaking *ex cathedra.* By virtue of divine assistance,[57] the bishop of Rome is then acting with the infallibility with which the Church is endowed. Such a definition depends on the guidance of the Holy Spirit and is "irreformable."[58]

33. The Catholic belief that such definitions can be made implies:

a) the confidence that, when the bishop of Rome is the agent of the definition, he acts subject to conditions imposed by the Word of God and the faith of the Church, with the careful investigation and study that the seriousness of the action and the conditions of the time require and permit;[59]

b) the recognition that the irreformability of definitions does not rule out further research, interpretation through the hermeneutical process, various applications to the life of worship and piety, and new formulations that are called for if fidelity to the Word of God expressed in previous Catholic definitions is to be maintained, and if the needs of new historical or cultural situations are to be met;

c) the acknowledgment that the exercise of infallibility is open to historical investigation, that points of doctrine that have been said to be infallibly proclaimed may in fact not have been so proclaimed, and there is no official list of *ex cathedra* definitions;

d) the trust that, thanks to the *sensus fidelium,* assent to a definition of faith will not be lacking.[60]

B) Lutheran Emphases

34. In protest against what were viewed as distortions of Christian truth, the Lutheran Reformers insisted on the priority, objectivity, and authority of the address of God to his creatures in his Word. The Word of God has priority: the initiative is God's. It has objectivity: God's Word comes as his address to us; it is not a figment of our mind or imagination. Authority resides ultimately in the power of the proclaimed Word to convict of sin and convince of grace. Given the depth of sin and the resultant human capacity for self-deception, it is necessary that sinners look only to God and his promise for their hope of salvation. All things are created good, but their goodness has been rendered ambiguous by sin, and therefore not even the greatest of God's gifts in the realm of creation can be trusted apart from the promise of God in the gospel of Jesus Christ. Human reason, morality, religious experience, and church structures all have their value, but can all be deceptive guides apart from God's self-disclosure in Christ.

35. The Lutheran understanding of the way that the gospel is com-

municated in the Church is expressed concisely in the Smalcald Articles. " . . . the Gospel . . . offers counsel and help against sin in more than one way, for God is surpassingly rich in grace: First, through the spoken word, by which the forgiveness of sin (the peculiar [*eigentlich*] function of the Gospel) is preached to the whole world; second, through Baptism; third, through the holy Sacrament of the Altar; fourth, through the power of the keys; and finally, through the mutual conversation and consolation of brethren. . . . "[61]

The grace of God is thus made known and communicated in several distinct ways: proclamation, Baptism, Eucharist, confession and absolution, and the mutual edification of the life of the community. Luther emphasizes that proclamation is the oral announcement of God's love and mercy in Christ by one person to others. The Church, he stresses, is a "mouth-house" and not a "book-house."[62] In his speech to us God uses things he has created: human language, rites involving words and signs, human community, and the Church itself.

36. For the Lutheran Reformers, the signs of the apostolicity or genuineness of the Church are twofold: the actual proclamation of the gospel of God's love for sinners and the administration of the sacraments according to Christ's command. Where these two signs are present, one can be sure that Christ is at work, and where Christ is, there is the Church. Recognition of both signs depends upon the Spirit's illumination and guidance. Both signs, therefore, drive the community back to the Word of God, where God grants the decisive disclosure of his will.[63]

37. For the authentication of the Church's proclamation of God's grace and love, the Lutheran Reformation looked primarily to the Word of God in Scripture. Even though modern historical study and the cultural relativity of all language complicate the process of interpretation, the Word of God as it is communicated to us in the Scriptures remains the final judge of all teaching in the Church.

38. The Reformers looked to tradition in the form of creeds and confessions as a secondary guide to the establishment of sound teaching. These texts, themselves the products of the Church's witness and often of theological controversy and struggle, show how the Scriptures were understood at certain critical periods in the life of the Church. The creeds and confessions also supply hermeneutical guidance for our reading of the Scriptures today.[64] Like the Scriptures, they too are expressed in human language, which is always relative to its culture and historical situation. They, therefore, are also in need of interpretation.

39. The traditional organs for continuing this process of interpre-

tation were largely lost to the Lutheran churches at the time of the Reformation. The Reformers had a high regard for the authority of ecumenical councils and wished to maintain the historic ecclesiastical order, although they were unable to do so because of polemical conditions in the 16th century.[65] As a result, they were forced to rely heavily upon the princes and their theological advisers not only in the governance of the church but also in the formulation and acceptance of the Lutheran confessional writings. At present, Lutheran churches are organized in many different forms, episcopal, presbyterian, and congregational, depending upon the historical circumstances of their development. Doctrinal interpretation and discipline are accordingly exercised in a great variety of ways. These provisional arrangements have provided a platform, though not the most adequate, for Lutherans in the 20th century to confess together their faith as a worldwide communion. Lutheran communities, while rejoicing that these arrangements have helped to protect them from disintegration on the one hand and from excessive centralization and the sacralization of ecclesiastical power on the other, are increasingly sensitive to the shortcomings of their structures for teaching and mission in a worldwide ministry.

C) Common Ground and Divergences

40. There are notable differences in emphasis and in structure between Lutherans and Catholics. There is also a considerable common ground. Both communities have emphasized the authority of Christ, of the gospel, of Scripture, and of subsequent tradition, though in different ways and proportions. Lutherans have stressed Christ's presence and power in the Word proclaimed and also made visible in the sacraments. Catholics have, in addition, stressed his presence and power in the continuity of the Church as his body socially present and organized. There have been correlative differences in institutional structures, especially relating to authoritative teaching. Catholics have insisted on the authority of the Church's institutions, particularly of the structures of the Ministry of bishops and priests under the primacy of the bishop of Rome. But Lutherans have had to create other institutions, which, though intended to be provisional, have become part of the contemporary Lutheran patrimony. In both churches the structures are intended as means to promote the gospel. But as institutions become established, they tend to become ends rather than means. Each

church has the responsibility of protecting its spiritual vitality against the weight of its institutions. And the two churches together have the responsibility of seeking ways of convergence, both at the level of doctrinal emphasis and at that of institutional structure.

III
CONVERGENCES

41. The context within which the Catholic doctrine of papal infallibility is understood has changed. Lutherans and Catholics now speak in increasingly similar ways about the gospel and its communication, about the authority of Christian truth, and about how to settle disputes concerning the understanding of the Christian message. One can truly speak of a convergence between our two traditions. The following instances of this convergence are significant. Our churches are agreed:

1) that Jesus Christ is the Lord of the Church, who discloses his gracious sovereignty through the proclamation of the apostolic gospel and the administration of the sacraments;

2) that the Word of God in the Scriptures is normative for all proclamation and teaching in the Church;

3) that the apostolic Tradition in which the Word of God is transmitted, while normative for all other tradition in the Church, is interpreted within the family of God with the assistance of tradition in the form of creeds, liturgies, dogma, confessions, doctrines, forms of church government and discipline, and patterns of devotion and service;

4) that in accordance with the promises given in the Scriptures and because of the continued assistance of the risen Christ through the Holy Spirit, the Church will remain to the end of time;

5) that this perpetuity of the Church includes its indefectibility, i.e., its perseverance in the truth of the gospel, in its mission, and in its life of faith;

6) that among the means by which Christ preserves the Church in the truth of the gospel, there is the Ministry of the Word and sacrament, which will never perish from the Church;

7) that there are Ministries and structures[66] charged with the teaching of Christian doctrine and with supervision and coordination of the ministry of the whole people of God, and that their task includes the mandate for bishops or other leaders to "judge doctrine and condemn doctrine that is contrary to the Gospel";[67]

8) that there may appropriately be a Ministry in the universal Church charged with primary responsibility for the unity of the people of God in their mission to the world;[68]

9) that this Ministry to the universal Church includes responsibility for overseeing both the Church's proclamation and, where necessary, the reformulation of doctrine in fidelity to the Scriptures;

10) that in the Church universal the harmony between the teaching of the Ministers and its acceptance by the faithful constitutes a sign of the fidelity of that teaching to the gospel;[69]

11) that the Church in every age is able under the guidance of the Spirit to find language and other forms of witness which can communicate the gospel to persons living in different cultures, that no human language succeeds in exhausting the diversity and richness of the gospel, and that no doctrinal definition can adequately address every historical or cultural situation.

In the light of these convergences, Catholics can better appreciate the significance of the Lutheran confession that the Church is indefectible. Specifically, the Lutheran trust that God will keep the Church in the truth of the gospel to the end has, in the context of Christian preaching and teaching, much in common with the Catholic concern for the Church's infallibility. Lutherans can recognize that Catholics affirm the supreme authority of the gospel and consider conciliar and papal infallibility as being subordinate to it.

42. This, to be sure, is not yet full agreement. Catholics, as well as many Lutherans, regret the absence in Lutheranism of a universal *magisterium* (i.e., of effective means of speaking to and for the whole Church), while Lutherans, as well as many Catholics, believe that the doctrine and practice of papal teaching authority and infallibility are not yet sufficiently protected against abuses. Catholics look upon the papacy, in view of its high responsibilities and the promises given to Peter, as especially assisted by the Holy Spirit. Lutherans think that Catholics have overconfidently identified the locus of the work of the Spirit with a particular person or office. Nevertheless, in the new context each side finds itself compelled to recognize that the other seeks to be faithful to the gospel. Further, given the convergence on the wider questions of authority and certainty in the Church, it becomes possible to hope that the two communions will be able to enter into further degrees of fellowship, while continuing to develop together their respective positions on infallibility.

43. These convergences, even though not complete, have concrete implications for the exercise of authority in the Church and for the method of settling disputes. The recognition of the primacy of the gos-

pel enables us to see that Scripture, tradition, and church structures are means of transmission in the service of the gospel. While their subordination to the gospel message has never been actually denied, it has to some extent been overlooked in the past. Lutherans have a tendency to treat Scripture as if it were identical with the gospel or the Word of God, while Catholics have shown a similar tendency with regard to tradition and church structures. We have now become more aware of the varied forms of oral and written proclamation, of practice, and of structure through which the gospel was and is handed on in the Church. The one message must often be presented in new ways in order to address specific audiences with reference to their particular problems. One cannot simply repeat Scripture and tradition in order to be faithful to the gospel, but one must be open to new ways of structuring its transmission in the Church. While this need has been recognized in the creative periods in the Church's life, it has often been ignored by theologians and church authorities, sometimes with unfortunate results.

44. Moreover, historical work has led to a better understanding of the relation of tradition and Scripture. Oral proclamation preceded the composition and collection of the writings of the New Testamant.[70] Despite the polemics of the past, "Scripture can no longer be exclusively contrasted with tradition, because the New Testament itself is a product of primitive tradition."[71] Understood as the total process in which the gospel and Scripture itself are transmitted, tradition cannot be regarded as "merely human words." From this point of view Lutherans highly value liturgies, creeds, and confessions as embodiments of tradition.

45. In the Catholic Church there is a renewed appreciation of the privileged authority of Scripture. Scripture is the fount of virtually all we know of the founding Tradition, and is moreover the primary witness to the gospel. Catholic theologians now generally agree that there is no second source alongside Scripture which witnesses to the original revelation. Scripture is normative for all later tradition, and some Catholic theologians also find it possible to speak, as did the Reformers, of Scripture as the *norma normans non normata* and thus, in a certain sense, of *sola scriptura.*[72]

46. There is also a growing recognition of the need to restructure teaching authority in the Church. Although in the 16th century Lutheran churches spoke decisively on crucial doctrinal issues through the Confessions, they are deficient in the dimension of universality today.[73] Lutherans, like other Christians in our present divided state, lack the institutional means to participate with other Christian tradi-

tions in doctrinal decision making. Thus they are confronted with the increasingly urgent need to develop new structures or adapt old ones in a way that will do justice to this universal aspect of their responsibility to the gospel.

47. Catholics increasingly recognize that all members of the people of God share in principle the responsibility for teaching and formulating doctrine. According to Vatican II, lay people "have the right and sometimes the duty to make known their opinion on things which concern the good of the Church."[74] The highest exercise of authority is itself fundamentally ecclesial, since the bishop of Rome acts in dependence on the faith of the Church.[75]

48. Moreover, structures can be developed that will make reciprocal relationships more apparent on all levels.[76] The laity should be enabled to participate in responsible discussions of doctrine, since they must witness to the faith. The clergy and theologians should be consulted, since they have a teaching responsibility. Bishops have always taken part in the consultations which have led to doctrinal definitions, but further ways of participation of the episcopal college in the definition of doctrine should be devised—for instance, through formal involvement of the episcopal conferences and of the synod of bishops.

49. The understanding of infallibility is affected not only by restructuring the process of defining doctrine but also by the new context created by the modern science of language. Whereas human languages have, at each moment, a recognizable structure, this structure does not remain stable through time. As the structure evolves, its impermanence affects all the formulations of human language. The formulations of Scripture and of doctrine also reflect the conditions prevailing at the moment when they take shape. The interpretation of such statements must accordingly take into account the historical circumstances which have called forth the formulation, the intentions of those who have drawn it up, and the religious and theological values they have attempted to assert or defend. Therefore, no statement, whether biblical or doctrinal, can be detached from its historical and cultural context if it is to be adequately understood.[77] Because the questions and concerns of our period differ from those of the 19th century, it becomes necessary to reinterpret or reformulate the concept of infallibility so that its valid theological insight may become more persuasive.

50. We already find ourselves in growing agreement on the practice of doctrinal authority. "Neither the *sola scriptura* principle alone nor formal references to the authoritativeness of the magisterial office

are sufficient."[78] It is through Scripture, tradition, and teaching authority that the Spirit enables the believing community to settle disputes about the gospel. The convergences we have outlined provide both the context and the beginning of a reinterpretation of infallibility.

IV
CONCLUSION

51. In light of the considerations mentioned above, it is clear that doctrinal definitions should be seen as decisive moments in the continuing pastoral and theological search for a deeper understanding of the mystery of Christ. They should not be viewed as bringing to an end all previous developments or as making all further discussion superfluous. The ultimate trust of Christians is in Christ and the gospel, not in a doctrine of infallibility, whether of Scripture, the Church, or the pope. Thus infallibility does not stand at the center of the Christian faith. Whatever infallibility is ascribed to Scripture, the Church, or the pope, it is wholly dependent on the power of God's Word in the gospel.

52. For Catholics, papal infallibility is now commonly discussed in the context of the infallibility of the Church and in relation to confidence in the faithful transmission of the gospel. As a consequence, the infallibility of the Church takes on greater importance than papal infallibility. Catholics, for whom the understanding of papal infallibility, though secondary, is important, should not therefore regard the Lutheran rejection of papal infallibility as equivalent to a denial of the central Christian message. What is more, the unresolved differences between Lutherans and Catholics on this matter need not, of themselves, preclude a closer union than now exists between the two churches.

53. For Lutherans, the developments of the last two decades have given a new outlook on the dogma of papal infallibility. Historical and linguistic studies on the meaning of the dogma, the emphasis since Vaitcan II on the collegial relationship of the pope and the bishops in theology and practice, and the initiation of new styles of papal leadership by Pope John and Pope Paul can help Lutherans see that the pope is not an absolute monarch. The Ministry of the bishop of Rome should be seen as a service under the authority of the Word of God. The doctrine of infallibility is an expression of confidence that the Spirit of God abides in his Church and guides it in the truth.[79] This understanding should allay Lutheran fears that papal infallibility is a

usurpation of the sovereign authority of Christ, and make clear that this dogma is not the central doctrine of the Catholic Church and that it does not displace Christ from his redemptive and mediatorial role.

54. For both Lutherans and Catholics, these convergences have implications for the exercise of teaching authority. In our discussions we have become aware of strengths and weaknesses in the existing structures of this Ministry in our churches. This leads us to ask practical questions of Catholics and Lutherans as we seek to bear witness to the gospel today, without implying that we would all answer them in the same way.

55. Has not the time come for our churches to take seriously the possibility of what we have come to call "magisterial mutuality"?[80] Should we not recognize the Spirit of Christ in each other's church and acknowledge each other's Ministers as partners in proclaiming the gospel in the unity of truth and love? Should we not listen to each other in formulating teaching, share each other's concerns, and ultimately develop a more unified voice for Christian witness in this world?

56. Specific questions are raised which Catholics ought to examine seriously:

1) What is their present understanding of the anathemas directed in the past at Luther and at Lutheran teaching? Are these condemnations relevant today? Since the trend of our times is to avoid anathemas—witness the absence of any in Vatican Council II—should not the past anathemas against Lutheranism be reviewed? Could they possibly be "committed to oblivion"[81] or even rescinded?

2) Should not Catholic theology take a new look at the Lutheran Confessions, especially those—such as the Augsburg Confession—whose original purpose was irenic? Reinterpreted in a new context which would highlight their Catholic dimension, could these Confessions be recognized as valid expressions of the Church's teaching? Could such recognition serve as an instance of magisterial mutuality?[82]

3) Should not creative efforts be made to discover a form of institutional relationship between the Catholic and the Lutheran churches which would express magisterial mutuality and would correspond to the converging state of their traditions? The present Catholic authorization of some sacramental sharing with the Orthodox, who do not acknowledge papal infallibility, shows more flexibility in Catholic thought and practice than was anticipated a few decades ago. Should the current developments in our two churches lead to analogous authorizations regarding sacramental sharing between Catholics and Lutherans?

57. Specific questions are likewise raised which Lutherans ought to examine seriously:

1) Should not Lutherans be ready to acknowledge that the polemical language traditionally used to describe the papal office is inappropriate and offensive in the context of Catholic–Lutheran relationships today?[83]

2) Should not Lutherans, as participants in a movement toward a common Christian witness in our day, be willing to consult with Catholics in framing doctrinal and social-ethical statements?

3) Should not Lutherans move to develop closer institutional relationships with the Catholic Church in respect to teaching authority which would be expressive of the converging state of their traditions?

58. Our dialogue has thus completed another stage in a search for convergence between the Catholic and Lutheran traditions. Our dialogue began to bear fruit especially in 1967 with our agreed statement on "The Eucharist as Sacrifice." Since that date we have arrived at agreements on "Eucharist and Ministry" (1970) and on "Papal Primacy and the Universal Church" (1974). With the present statement on questions raised by the Catholic doctrine of infallibility, we have found new areas of agreement in controversial matters which have for centuries separated Lutherans and Catholics. We are not in a position to state that all grounds for continuing division have been removed; we have not yet dealt at length with doctrinal issues such as justification; there are degrees of consensus which we have not yet been able to attain; there are reactions to our dialogue which we need to consider further; the agreements of theologians are not yet a consensus of the churches. It is our judgment, however, that the common grounds we have discovered in the doctrinal area point the way forward to significant changes in the lived relationships between our churches. We are convinced that our churches can overcome their past oppositions only as they become far more engaged, at all levels, through theological reflection, study of the Scriptures, worship, mission, and pastoral care, in a search for convergence along the lines developed in the work of this dialogue.

II
ROMAN CATHOLIC REFLECTIONS

INTRODUCTION

1. The Roman Catholic participants are gratified by the conver-

gence achieved in this dialogue on the questions of teaching authority and infallibility in the Church. Although the consensus is not complete, the discussion has unearthed elements in each tradition which, with cultivation, may eventually lead to an agreed ecumenical reinterpretation of these doctrines. We are pleased to have had a share in this process.

2. In what follows we intend to reflect more specifically on various aspects of the Common Statement in the light of traditional Catholic themes and to deal in greater detail with certain questions that have been put to us by the Lutherans at different times in this round of discussions.

3. The convergences with regard to the communication of the gospel, as summarized, for example, in paragraph 41 of the Common Statement, are noteworthy especially when taken in conjunction with the agreements noted in *Papal Primacy and the Universal Church.*[84] These convergences may be seen as compatible with a recognition of the universal teaching Ministry of popes and councils.[85] The most significant new agreements—partial though they are at the present stage—have to do with the emotionally laden and theologically complex question of infallibility.

4. The concept of infallibility is by no means free from difficulty. The Common Statement (16) calls attention to the fact that "infallibility is not a New Testament term." Absent also in patristic literature, it emerges only in the late medieval period. But we have to ask ourselves whether the concept and the term do not have a foundation in the data of the New Testament and in the faith of the first centuries. Examining the roots of the notion of infallibility, the Common Statement calls attention to the confidence of Christians, from the earliest times, that the Church could teach the truth of the gospel with assured authority.

5. The Common Statement (52–53) seeks to place the doctrine of infallibility in the theological categories of promise, trust, and hope rather than in the juridical categories of law, obligation, and obedience. Seen from this perspective, infallibility can be interpreted as a consequence of Christ's promise to be with the Church and to assist it "to the close of the age" (Matt. 28:20). That promise is regarded by Roman Catholics as the basis of their confidence and trust that all those who have doctrinal responsibility, and especially the pope and the episcopal college as servants of unity, will be assisted by the risen Christ.

6. It is the "gospel" that invites us as Christians to respond with faith and trust or confidence (Rom. 1:16). The Common Statement has accordingly set forth New Testament evidence about authority in doc-

trinal matters in terms of the gospel. The use of this term echoes the dynamism associated with *evangelion* by Paul (Rom. 1:16), its truth (Gal. 2:5, 14), and its relation to the Spirit (1 Thess. 1:5). It is to be understood as a brief way of referring to the proclamation of the saving revelation which comes to us in the person, message, and deeds of Jesus Christ. The term "gospel," understood in this inclusive manner, has a secure place in the Roman Catholic tradition[86] and is capable of summing up what Vatican II referred to as "the Word of God."

7. The Catholics in this dialogue understand that contemporary Lutheran thought, emphasizing the sinfulness of all human institutions and instruments, finds it difficult to recognize any episcopal see, church office, person, or officeholder as gifted with such unfailing assistance from the Spirit as to preclude error in teaching. Therefore, the Lutheran tradition does not tie to any institution the task of authentic reformulation of Christian doctrine, which Catholics assign preeminently to the episcopal college and the bishop of Rome. For the Catholic participants in these conversations, the doctrine of infallibility aims at safeguarding a basic Christian insight: that the Church, in view of its mission to preach the gospel faithfully to all nations, may be trusted to be guided by the Holy Spirit in proclaiming the original revelation and in reformulating it in new ways and languages whenever such reformulation is necessary. Such a trust, rooted in the sovereignty of God, is in our view inseparable from the Christian faith as understood and practiced in both our traditions.

8. In the following pages we propose to reflect more specifically on certain themes of the Common Statement: (1) the authority of the living Church; (2) the Catholic understanding of papal infallibility; (3) the biblical and historical background for the claim of papal infallibility; (4) noninfallible and doubtfully infallible papal teaching; (5) nonacceptance of infallible teaching; (6) conclusion.

I
THE AUTHORITY OF THE LIVING CHURCH

9. The Common Statement (28) calls attention to a major area of agreement between Lutherans and Catholics. Christ himself, who taught with the authority of the Son of God, by promising to be with his disciples to the end of the age and by bestowing the Holy Spirit, empowered the Church, as a community of faith, to abide forever in the truth of the gospel. Thanks to the divine assistance, the gospel will continue to be preached and believed, and thus the Church will endure

to the end. In other words, the Church is indefectible as a community of Christian faith and witness, even though all its members, including its pastors, continue to be subject to weakness and sin.

10. In more familiar Catholic terminology we may say, as did the medieval theologians, "The universal Church cannot err";[87] that is to say, its faith in the gospel of Jesus Christ is divinely protected against corruption. Thus Vatican II declared: "The body of the faithful as a whole, anointed as they are by the Holy One (cf. 1 John 2:20, 27), cannot err in matters of belief. Thanks to a supernatural sense of the faith which characterizes the people as a whole, it manifests this unerring quality when from the bishops down to the last member of the laity it shows universal agreement in matters of faith and morals" (*LG* 12).

11. Going further, Catholics have felt entitled to assert that those charged with the Ministry to the universal Church, in their teaching of the revelation of Christ, will not be allowed to lead the Church astray, for Christ remains with the apostolic body which teaches in his name. Accordingly, Vatican I taught that the assent of Christian faith extends to all that is contained in the Word of God and taught by the universal teaching body as divinely revealed (DS 3011).

12. The infallibility of the total Church in teaching and in believing forms, in the Catholic understanding, the context of conciliar and papal infallibility. The infallibility of popes and that of bishops gathered at ecumenical councils are particular instances of expressions of the infallibility of the whole Church, for these organs are held to represent the whole Church. Thus Vatican I, in its definition of papal infallibility, ascribed to the pope no other infallibility than that with which Christ willed the entire Church to be endowed (DS 3074). Even though Lutherans do not recognize any particular office as gifted with infallibility, we do not think this would require them to deny that the whole body of pastors or the whole body of the faithful is protected against error.[88] Indeed, the Lutheran understanding of indefectibility implies the preservation of the Church, as a community of Christian faith and proclamation in the truth of the gospel.

II
THE CATHOLIC UNDERSTANDING OF PAPAL INFALLIBILITY

13. The term "infallibility," especially when it is connected with some particular office, can easily give rise to confusion. It suggests to many that the office or officeholder is being somehow divinized and

deprived of the capacity for error that is a mark of the human condition. Thus understood, the doctrine of infallibility seems to remove the official teachers from their subjection to Christ and the gospel and to put them, in the eyes of the faithful, on a par with the divine Persons. This, however, is not the Catholic teaching on the subject.

14. Vatican Council I did not state without qualification that the pope is infallible. Rather, it taught that when performing certain very narrowly specified acts, he is gifted with the same infallibility which Christ bestowed on his Church (DS 3074). In his explanation of the meaning of the definition, given to the Fathers two days before they voted on the draft, Bishop Vincenz Gasser clearly pointed out that absolute infallibility is proper to God alone and that the infallibility of the pope is limited and conditioned. "In fact," he went on to say, "the infallibility of the Roman pontiff is restricted in respect to the *subject,* when the pope speaks as teacher of the universal Church and as supreme judge seated on the chair of Peter, i.e., in the center. It is restricted in respect to the *object,* insofar as it concerns matters of faith and morals, and in respect to the *act,* when he defines what has to be believed or rejected by all the faithful" (M 52:1214).

15. Vatican I did not define the infallibility of the successors of Peter as a permanent property, definitely attached to the person of the pope. Though a personal infallibility is ascribed to a pope, it is present, as Gasser explained, "only when he exercises in reality and in act the function of supreme judge in the controversies of faith and doctrine of the universal Church" (M 52:1213). Here "act" must not be restricted too narrowly.

16. Admittedly, several misunderstandings have been occasioned by the expressions used in the Vatican I definition. Many difficulties have arisen from the sentence, "Such definitions of the Roman pontiff are therefore irreformable by themselves *(ex sese)* and not by reason of the agreement of the Church *(non autem ex consensu ecclesiae)*" (DS 3074). This might seem to give the pope an authority independent of that of the Church, as though the pope were not a member of the Church but somehow above it.

17. Historical research, however, makes it clear that the final phrase, *non autem ex consensu ecclesiae,* was added for the purpose of excluding the tendency of some Gallicans and conciliarists, who regarded approval by the bishops as necessary in order to give infallibility to any papal definition.[89] Vatican I was here reacting against the kind of juridical language found in the fourth Gallican article of 1682, in which it was claimed that papal decrees are not irreformable until the assent of the Church *(ecclesiae consensus)* supervenes (DS 2284).

Thus it is apparent that the term *consensus* at Vatican I is to be understood in the juridical sense of official approval and not in the more general sense of agreement or acceptance by the Church as a whole, which, according to Gasser, can never be lacking (M 52:1214). As Gasser also explains, the pope's infallibility is not "separate" for he is not protected against error except when he teaches as successor of Peter, and hence as representing the universal Church (1213). The same conclusion is supported by the statement of Vatican I that the assistance of the Holy Spirit is given to the successors of Peter not that they might manifest new doctrine but that they might safeguard and explain faithfully the revelation handed down through the apostles, the deposit of faith (DS 3070).

18. Another major difficulty arising from the text of Vatican I has to do with the term "irreformable," which is sometimes understood as though it excluded any further reformulation or reinterpretation. In order to dispel this impression, the Common Statement (49) emphasizes that the formulas of faith are historically conditioned and are therefore subject to revision according to circumstances of particular times and places. In that connection it asserts that the doctrine of infallibility itself may need to be reinterpreted and newly expressed, so that its enduringly valid theological insight may better appear.

19. Our Catholic reflections on papal primacy[90] have already shown, with the help of the Declaration of the Congregation for the Doctrine of the Faith *Mysterium Ecclesiae* (1973), that definitions of doctrine are subject to a fourfold historical conditioning.[91] They are affected by the limited context of human knowledge in the situation in which they are framed, by the specific concerns that motivated the definitions, by the changeable conceptions (or thought categories) of a given epoch, and by "the expressive power of the language used at a certain point of time."[92] These four factors are critical for the proper interpretation of the Catholic teaching on papal infallibility. Application of the principles of *Mysterium Ecclesiae* to this question suggests the possibility of eventually finding new expressions faithful to the original intention and adapted to a changed cultural context. This process of reinterpretation was already at work in the way in which the doctrine of papal infallibility was treated at Vatican II, bringing new aspects to the fore. Seven factors in this reinterpretation seem noteworthy:

1) Vatican II made it clearer than had Vatican I that the infallibility of the pastors (pope and bishops) must be related to the *sensus fidelium* or the "sense of faith" possessed by the entire people of God.

The popes and bishops are infallible insofar as they are assisted in giving official expression and formulation to what is already the faith of the Church as a whole.[93] This theme of Vatican II underscores what is implicit in the assertion of Vatican I that the pope has no other infallibility than that which Christ conferred upon the Church.

2) Vatican II saw the infallibility of the pope as closely connected with that of the college of bishops. Indeed, when it described the infallibility of the Roman pontiff, it referred to him as "head of the college of bishops," a phrase not used in the constitution *Pastor aeternus* of Vatican I. This suggests that normally, when he defines a matter of faith and morals, the pope should be expected to consult his fellow bishops and proceed in a collegial manner (*LG* 25, with footnote referring to Gasser in M 52:1213 AC).

3) Vatican II pointed out that while no antecedent or subsequent juridical approval by the Church is necessary for the exercise of infallibility, the assent of the Church can never be wanting to an authentic definition "on account of the activity of that same Holy Spirit, whereby the whole flock of Christ is preserved and progresses in unity of faith" (*LG* 25). This observation, together with Vatican II's emphasis on the *sensus fidelium,* puts in proper context the assertion of Vatican I that papal definitions are irreformable *ex sese, non autem ex consensu ecclesiae* (DS 3074).

4) Vatican II placed the teaching of the pope in the context of a pilgrim church. His definitions of faith will reflect the situation of a church whose task is "to show forth the mystery of the Lord in a faithful though shadowed way until at last it will be revealed in total splendor" (*LG* 8). In other words, such definitions will inevitably suffer from a certain obscurity.[94]

5) Vatican II recognized that the Church, insofar as it is an institution on earth, is always affected by human finitude and sinfulness (*UR* 6), failings that may leave their mark even on the most solemn acts of the highest magisterium. Even while true in the technical sense, a dogmatic statement may be ambiguous, untimely, overbearing, offensive, or otherwise deficient.[95]

6) By its ecumenical orientation, Vatican II gave rise to the question: Will infallibility be able to serve the purpose for which it is intended without far more consultation with Christian communities not in full union with Rome?[96]

7) Vatican II called attention to the fact that "in Catholic teaching there exists an order or 'hierarchy' of truths, since they vary in their relationship to the foundation of the Christian faith" (*UR* 11). This

important principle suggests the possibility that authentic faith in the basic Christian message may exist without explicit belief in all defined dogmas—a question to be discussed below (Section V).

20. The state of the doctrine of papal infallibility at the end of Vatican II is not to be taken as the last word on the subject. The understanding of the doctrine will continue to be nuanced in various ways as the historical, cultural, and linguistic situations change. Recent debates may have been a factor contributing to the rather moderate statement of infallibility in the declaration *Mysterium Ecclesiae,* referred to at the beginning of paragraph 19 above.

III
BIBLICAL AND HISTORICAL BACKGROUND

21. With regard to the biblical and historical testimonies about teaching authority in the Church, no sharp differences between Lutherans and Catholics have emerged in this dialogue. Catholics have usually thought that there is a biblical and patristic basis for the doctrine of papal infallibility, but we would add that the doctrine cannot be found explicitly in these early sources, nor can it be strictly deduced from these sources by syllogistic argument.

22. The Common Statement, in our opinion, gives a satisfactory overall presentation of the testimony of the New Testament regarding authoritative teaching. Some of the texts mentioned in our Common Statement, however, have at times received greater emphasis in the Roman Catholic tradition.

23. The promise of the risen Jesus commissioning the Eleven to "make disciples of all nations, baptizing them . . . [and] teaching them to observe all that I have commanded you" (Matt. 28:19–20) has been understood as implying distinctions among Christ himself, those teaching, and those taught. While acknowledging that the function of the Eleven "represents Christ and his over-againstness to the community only insofar as it [the Ministerial office] gives expression to the gospel,"[97] many Christians—correctly, in our view—have emphasized that the very commission given here is the basis of a teaching authority as a special Ministry within the Christian community, and one that is safeguarded by the assistance of Christ himself "to the close of the age."

24. Though this Matthean passage is not related literarily to the Pastoral Epistles, the Matthean commission to teach given by the risen Christ corresponds to the view of "the Church of the living God" and

its apostolic Ministry spoken of in 1 Timothy 3:15. The phrase "the pillar and bulwark of the truth" in this text should not be heard anachronistically with jurisdictional overtones. Nevertheless, 1 Timothy 3:15 is a confident expression of the reliability of the Church—or at least of a Minister of the Church—to which the risen Christ has committed the preaching of the gospel.[98]

25. The Common Statement makes mention of the Petrine function and its relation to teaching authority in the Church. This function has to be understood with the explanations given in *Papal Primacy and the Universal Church* and in *Peter in the New Testament.*[99] As we move beyond the discussion of primary presented there to the question of infallibility and the Petrine function, we see how limited are the New Testament data on this topic. In the course of the tradition the Petrine text of Luke 22:32 was given the major emphasis. Jesus' prayer for Simon, who would prove faithless in denying him, has to be understood as efficacious: "that your faith may not fail." In virtue of this assurance of Jesus, Simon is told that he, after being converted, would have a role of strengthening his brothers. Now it is obvious that the New Testament does not make the distinction of later theologians about *fides quae* (the faith which is believed) and *fides qua* (the faith by which one believes) and that Simon's "faith" here would have to be understood in a comprehensive sense; in any case, it cannot be restricted to faith in a content sense *(fides quae).*

26. Finally, it should be noted apropos of the Petrine texts in Matt. 16:18 and Luke 22:32, which are used in the Common Statement, that they have likewise been cited in the Dogmatic Constitution of Vatican I *Pastor aeternus* (DS 3066, 3070) and used in connection with papal infallibility. Some Roman Catholic theologians have at times regarded these biblical passages as officially interpreted, or even infallibly defined, by the Council.[100] However, Vatican I did not define the sense of these verses.[101] While we recognize that these Petrine texts have played an important role in the development of the doctrine of papal infallibility, we do not claim that these texts, taken exegetically, directly assert that doctrine.

27. As regards the patristic and medieval history of teaching authority in the Church, we have noted, as have the Lutheran participants, the gradual emergence of papal primacy in doctrinal decision making through a lengthy historical process briefly summarized in the Common Statement. The doctrine of papal infallibility was not formally taught until the end of the 13th century. It continued to be disputed within the Catholic Church, with many conciliarists and Gallicans denying it, until the definition of 1870. That definition was so

restricted in scope and moderate in tone that it failed to satisfy the desires of ardent papalists, many of whom in the period after Vatican I went far beyond the letter of the Council in claiming infallibility for papal teaching that did not strictly meet the conditions for an *ex cathedra* pronouncement as set forth by Vatican I.

28. Lutherans and Catholics, of course, differ in their appraisal of the development they both recognize. However Lutherans evaluate this development, at very least they do not regard it as binding on all Christians. For Catholics, it represents an implication of the gospel or the Word of God as seen in the perspective of a long historical reflection, and as having developed in accordance with principles already present in the gospel from the beginning. Nevertheless, the doctrine has at times been too naively or rigidly understood by Catholics themselves and consequently stands in need of further nuancing. The concerns of Lutherans, as expressed in this dialogue, can help Catholics to understand papal infallibility in ways that better safeguard the primacy of the gospel and the freedom of the Christian believer.

29. It has sometimes been alleged that historical research can actually disprove the infallibility of the pope. Attention is called to various "papal errors," many of which were discussed at length both prior to and at Vatican I. There is no need, in these reflections, to review the evidence regarding the celebrated cases of Popes Liberius, Vigilius, and Honorius, which are discussed, to some degree, in our background papers.[102] In an earlier volume we published a background paper on Pope Boniface VIII and *Unam sanctam.*[103] Turning to yet another case, it need not be denied that Pope John XXII erred in his teaching regarding the beatific vision, which was corrected both by John XXII himself and by his successor Benedict XII.[104] No one doubts that popes can err in their teaching as private doctors. In none of the preceding cases can it be shown that the errors, or alleged errors, would have met the requirements specified by Vatican I for an *ex cathedra* pronouncement, and hence these historical difficulties prove nothing against the truth of the teaching of that Council on infallibility. These historical difficulties, to which the Council fathers adverted, form part of the historical context within which the definition is to be understood.[105]

IV
NONINFALLIBLE AND DOUBTFULLY INFALLIBLE PAPAL TEACHING

30. The cases just mentioned illustrate the importance of distin-

guishing between two major categories of papal teaching: that which is, and that which is not, clearly infallible. Before discussing the obligatory force of the latter, it will be helpful to clarify certain questions concerning the former. The Lutherans in this dialogue have frequently pressed us to respond to the following two questions. First, how does one distinguish which papal statements are, or are not, to be considered infallible? Second, what obligatory force attaches to noninfallible papal teaching?

31. There are only two papal pronouncements which are generally acknowledged by Catholics as having engaged papal infallibility: the dogma of the Immaculate Conception (1854) and that of the Assumption of the Blessed Virgin (1950).[106] Several other types of papal pronouncement have, however, been thought by some to be infallible. With an eye to the teaching of 20th century theological manuals, several prominent examples may here be mentioned: the solemn canonizations of saints, the condemnation of certain doctrines, papal teaching concerning certain moral matters, and the decision concerning Anglican ordinations.

32. The theological manuals of recent generations rather commonly hold that solemn canonizations of saints, as contained in papal decretal letters, are infallible.[107] The tradition in favor of infallibility in the matter has been traced back at least to the time of Thomas Aquinas,[108] but there are genuine difficulties in seeing how canonizations fall within the object of papal infallibility as taught by Vatican I or Vatican II. Certainly, the virtues of particular persons of post-biblical times, and their present situation before God, can scarcely be reckoned as part of the apostolic deposit of faith. If one looks on revelation as having become complete in Christ, holiness may reasonably be seen as a concrete way of living, in a given culture, the saving truth revealed in Christ. The Church has the power to recognize authentic Christian holiness, yet canonization would not seem of its nature to convey infallible certitude that the holiness in question was actually present in the life of this or that historical person.[109]

33. The condemnation of certain doctrinal errors—for example, those of the Jansenists or the Modernists—would seem to fall indirectly within the scope of papal infallibility, insofar as such errors deviate from basic Christian belief or previously defined doctrine. Whether a particular condemnation is an exercise of infallibility is always a factual question, and the affirmative answer to this question is not to be presumed. According to canon law, "Nothing is to be understood as dogmatically declared or defined unless this is clearly manifest" (*CIC*, can. 1323, #3). For the infallible character to be

clearly manifest, the condemnation would have to claim infallibility for itself and would have to fall within the scope of papal infallibility as set forth by the two Vatican Councils. In point of fact, none of the papal documents condemning doctrinal errors evidently meets these two criteria. Whatever clearly infallible teachings are contained in such papal condemnations have this status because other more authoritative documents or the universal and constant teaching of the Church affirm the same points.

34. With regard to the Bull *Exsurge Domine* (1520), condemning certain views attributed to Luther, the Catholic members of this dialogue are convinced that there are no solid grounds for regarding it as an exercise of papal infallibility. It embodies propositions of unequal theological weight. If some of the teachings in this Bull are infallible, this is because other more authoritative documents, such as conciliar canons, affirm the same points.[110]

35. Some authors maintain that the pope has acted infallibly in issuing certain moral teachings, notably in the case of the statements about contraception in the encyclicals of Pius XI[111] and Paul VI.[112] The solution to this question depends in part on whether the Church's infallibility extends to questions of the natural moral law, to which these documents primarily appeal. But even granted that it does so extend, there is the further point that the documents in question do not manifestly invoke infallibility. Moreover, Catholic commentators are not unanimous in regarding these teachings as infallible. Thus it seems that freedom to deny the infallibility of these documents must be allowed.

36. The principles just enunciated would hold likewise for the rejection of Anglican orders by Pope Leo XIII in the Letter *Apostolicae curae* (1896). Even granting that infallibility might extend to a "dogmatic fact" of this kind, the language of the Letter does not seem to demand that the decision be taken as infallible. In view of the lack of consensus among approved authors, the decision may be treated in practice as reformable.[113]

37. This brings us to the second question: the obligatory force of papal teaching which is not, or not evidently, infallible. Pius XII, in *Humani generis* (1950), pointed out that encyclicals, even when they do not engage the supreme teaching authority of the pope, have genuine doctrinal weight. More specifically, according to Pius XII, when the pope in such letters deliberately gives a decision on some previously controverted issue, the question may no longer be considered as one to be freely debated among theologians (DS 3885).[114]

38. *Lumen gentium* 25 restated and carried forward the essential teaching of Pius XII by its assertion:

> Religious allegiance of the will and intellect should be given in an entirely special way to the authentic teaching authority of the Roman pontiff, even when he is not speaking *ex cathedra;* this should be done in such a way that his supreme teaching authority is respectfully acknowledged, while the judgments given by him are sincerely adhered to according to his manifest intention and desire, as this is made known by the nature of the documents, or by his frequent repetition of the same judgment, or by his way of speaking.[115]

As Karl Rahner points out in his commentary on this text, it may be significant that the Council did not reassert the doctrine of *Humani generis* forbidding further public discussion of matters settled by the pope, even though this doctrine appeared in the preliminary draft of November 10, 1962.[116]

39. There exists a vast literature dealing with the highly complex question of the authority of noninfallible papal teaching and the conditions under which this or that form of silent or vocal dissent may be permitted or required.[117] To illustrate one approach, we may refer to the collective Pastoral of the German bishops issued on September 22, 1967. Using an analogy which some have found helpful, this letter compares the noninfallible teaching of the magisterium to the decisions of a judge or statesman. "In such a case, the situation of the individual with regard to the Church is somewhat like that of a man who knows that he is bound to accept the decision of an expert, even though he knows that it is not infallible."[118]

40. As regards the legitimacy of dissent, the German bishops' Pastoral says that the contrary opinion may not be taught as Catholic doctrine, but that one may properly point out to the faithful the limited authority of such revisable pronouncements.

> The Christian who believes that he has a right to his private opinion, and that he already knows what the Church will only come to grasp later, must ask himself in sober self-criticism before God and his conscience, whether he has the necessary depth and breadth to allow his private theory and practice to depart from the present doctrine of the ecclesiastical authorities.[119]

41. As this quotation illustrates, there is a very important differ-

ence between the assent of faith which is called for by infallible teaching and the religious allegiance or submission which is per se expected in the case of ordinary but noninfallible papal teaching.

V
NONACCEPTANCE OF INFALLIBLE TEACHING

42. Much of our discussion in the present round of dialogues has focused on three undoubted instances in which infallibity has been invoked: the conciliar dogma of papal infallibity itself (1870) and the two papal dogmas of the Immaculate Conception (1854) and the Assumption (1950). Questions have been raised about the implications of these three dogmas for the continuing relations between Catholics and Lutherans. To what extent does nonacceptance of these teachings preclude communion and unity?

43. First of all, the Catholic members of this dialogue must record their conviction that these dogmas refer to realities and values that are important for the Christian's response to God's word of revelation in Christ, even though they do not stand at the very center of Christian faith and teaching. In accordance with Vatican II, which presented these doctrines in a way calculated to show their relation to the mystery of the Church,[120] we are persuaded that these doctrines ought not to be viewed in isolation but in relationship to the entire Christian vision of God's saving work. We recognize, however, that the Lutherans represented in this dialogue consider that their Christian faith does not oblige them to affirm these teachings.

44. Second, we acknowledge that the community of those who accept these dogmas is not coextensive with the full number of individuals and groups that are rightly called Christian. Catholics do not hold that membership in Christ's Church is restricted to persons who formally and explicitly accept the three dogmas in question. For example, there are some Catholics today who belong to the Church even though they accept these teachings only implicitly.[121]

45. Third, the question arises about persons and groups, who after considering these doctrines, decide not to accept or even to reject them. There it may be well to recall that each of the teachings in question was accompanied by an anathema (DS 3075) or its equivalent (DS 2804, 3904). Canonically, an anathema involves an excommunication (*CIC*, can. 2257, #2), which, however, is not incurred except by persons whose disbelief is culpable, obstinate, and externally manifested. The language of the anathemas in the instances that here concern us

seems to reflect the presumption that only in rare and exceptional situations could a Christian in good faith deny these dogmas once they had been defined. However necessary presumptions are, they are understood in church law to yield to facts and to be open to change when facts so indicate. In our day it seems evident that many sincere Christians are unable to profess these dogmas with personal faith. And yet these same individuals wish very much to belong to Christ's Church; they gather together in his name to announce his death until he comes; they confess his Lordship; they accept his message as reflected in the Bible and the early Christian creeds; and they bear witness to him in their lives or service to his brothers and sisters. The questioning or denial of these dogmas should not be regarded, at least today, as presumptive evidence of a lapse from Christian faith.

46. A step in this direction was taken by Vatican II, which permited *limited* Eucharistic sharing between Catholics and Orthodox,[122] even though the latter do not normally accept (and even at times explicitly reject at least one or more of) the dogmas in question. The situation of the Orthodox and Lutherans, though different in many ways, is similar at least in the following: both find themselves for the most part unable to accept one or more of these teachings as part of the deposit of faith. If this inability on the part of the Orthodox does not preclude all Eucharistic sharing with Catholics, the same inability on the part of Lutherans should not of itself do so either. Lack of Christian faith would and should so preclude. But the operative presumption is that Christian faith sufficient for Eucharistic sharing exists in the case of Catholics and Orthodox despite the inability of the latter to accept all these particular dogmas. We believe that this presumption regarding Christian faith should be extended also to Lutherans. If so, it would not thereby follow that limited Eucharistic sharing was justified in their case too. But it would follow that such sharing ought not to be ruled out because of Lutheran failure to accept these three teachings.

47. In this connection it should be mentioned that some Catholics are at times unable to accept one or other or even all these dogmas with personal faith. We are not here considering the hypothetically possible case of someone who would claim to be a Catholic and yet believe only what he or she would find personally appealing. We restrict our remarks to the refusal to accept the three dogmas with which we are here concerned. Given the information explosion, its impact on religious communication, and the widespread influence of mass media, it is understandable that the beliefs of many Catholics have been affected. Could it be that, in their questioning or denial of

these three dogmas, not a few Catholics are reacting more against the inadequacy, incompleteness, limited expressive power, and historically-conditioned character of the official formulations than against the Word of God to which these dogmas bear witness? Would not this be especially indicated if such persons adhere to, and seek to live, their Catholic faith in other matters? We think our church leaders ought to consider whether a presumption to this effect may not be called for in our day. We do not concede that one can be a Roman Catholic Christian by simply wanting to and without thereby being committed to the acceptance of any specific teachings. We admit that at times the rejection of the three dogmas we are considering may be a sign that one has separated oneself from Catholic tradition and faith, but we think this ought not to be presumed. Indeed, a good case can be made for the opposite presumption.

48. Finally, we must say something about the question of lifting the anathemas themselves. Since the anathemas do not refer directly to the truth of the dogmas but rather to the canonical effects of their denial, they could be withdrawn without altering the truth of the dogmas or the obligation to believe them. The removal of these anathemas has in fact been suggested.[123] Such an action would serve to highlight the imperfect ecclesial communion that exists between Catholics and Lutherans despite the latter's nonacceptance of these three dogmas.

49. Nevertheless, there are grounds for hesitation in view of the historic nexus that exists between the anathema and the truth of the dogma. Given that nexus, the formal removal of the anathema might well contribute to the "take your pick among the dogmas" mentality that is already found among some Catholics (and other Christians). That anathemas were attached to such teachings in the past is something over which we, the living, have no control; past history cannot be undone. To judge the consciences of those, whether Lutheran or Catholic, who leveled anathemas at their opponents is best left to God. True, anathemas from the past might be lifted in the present. Indeed, the lifting in the case of these three dogmas might be a sign pointing to the ecclesial communion already in existence and contributing to the growth of that communion. But could this be accomplished without giving the impression that the Catholic Church no longer holds and teaches these dogmas? This is far from sure. On the question, then, whether the anathemas should be lifted, there is need for further discussion within the Catholic community. In this connection it is worth noting that Vatican II, true to its general style of teaching, reaffirmed these dogmas, in a new context, without restating the anathemas.

50. However this discussion may be resolved, we wish to stress

here two important points. First, whether the anathemas are lifted or not, the differences between Catholics and Lutherans regarding these dogmas do not of themselves exclude all Eucharistic sharing between the churches.[124] Second, the truth-implications of these dogmas must not be overlooked. We aim at mutual communion one day with Lutherans without requiring either side to give up the fundamental evangelical convictions and values of its tradition. Even if there were a mutual recognition of Ministries and limited Eucharistic sharing, we would feel that we owed it to evangelical truth, as we are given by the Spirit to understand it, to continue to pray and study with Lutherans about these questions. It would still be important to preserve a mutuality of discussion regarding the meaning of these three dogmas, their place in this hierarchy of truths, and their roles in the effective transmission of the Word of God. If our discussions were to lead one day to such recognition and such limited sharing, there would still be a task incumbent on both traditions: to search for a more shared understanding of the Word of God as it applies to Mary and to the one who continues in a unique way the Petrine office among the disciples of Jesus today.

VI
CONCLUSION

51. Considering both the progress already achieved and the task that still remains before us, we are both saddened by our inability to announce full agreement between Lutherans and Catholics regarding the infallible character of certain teaching and encouraged by the large measure of agreement that does exist regarding the nature and importance of teaching authority. Even with regard to infallibility, we have found it increasingly difficult, as our dialogue has proceeded, to specify the exact point at which, in fidelity to our respective traditions, we are bound to disagree.

52. There are certain understandings of infallibility which Lutherans, according to their own principles, would evidently have to reject. For example, if Catholics were to teach that any papal statement issued with certain juridical formalities, regardless of its basis in Scripture and tradition and its consonance with the faith of the Church, could be imposed as a matter of faith. Lutherans would legitimately protest that the primacy of the gospel was being imperiled. But as we have sought to show, such an understanding of infallibility would be a misinterpretation of the Catholic doctrine.

53. Again, if irreformability meant that the solemn teaching of popes and councils had to be accepted forever as it was understood and stated when originally promulgated, with the result that it could not be reconceptualized and reformulated according to the needs and possibilities of different times and cultures, Lutherans would have good reason to reject irreformability. But, as we have explained, irreformability does not preclude further reinterpretation, reconceptualization, or rephrasing.

54. Because of the nuanced understanding of infallibility in much contemporary Catholic theology, we find that some Lutherans, even while denying what they recognize as infallibility, come very close to affirming what some Catholics understand by that term. They can in fidelity to their own tradition accept a certain presumption in favor of the evangelical truth of the preaching of duly constituted pastors, especially when this preaching resonates with the faith of the Christian community and is seen, upon examination, to be consonant with Scripture and early tradition. This kind of presumption could tell in favor of the pope as a bishop specially charged with the Ministry of universal supervision in matters of doctrine.

55. The denial of infallibility from the Lutheran side might seem to Catholics, at first sight, to open the path to radical questioning of the inherited affirmations of faith, but we do not hear the Lutherans in this dialogue so questioning Christian tradition. They do not hold that a contemporary Christian would be entitled to interpret the Bible in a sense patently contrary to the ancient creeds and confessions which, in their estimation, reliably express the teaching of Scripture and the faith of the Church. Drawing upon this shared heritage of Christian belief, and working in the light of a new will to overcome our past divisions, this dialogue has been able to achieve a convergence about teaching authority and infallibility which could scarcely have been thought possible even a few years ago.

56. The attempt to express papal infallibility in terms of promise, trust, and hope has already brought us a long way toward agreement. As to the limits that do remain in our present agreement on teaching authority, their source may lie in other issues that have been long debated by Catholics and Lutherans. Some of our remaining differences may be rooted in the content of certain dogmas and their basis in Christian revelation (e.g., the Immaculate Conception of Mary and her Assumption). Moreover, our theologies may still differ about the way the Scriptures are normative for faith.[125] Furthermore, Lutherans and Catholics could well direct further attention to the effects of grace and sin on individuals and institutions, including the teaching Church.

We, therefore, need to discuss the doctrine of justification, a doctrine at the very root of the Reformation itself.

57. There remains an important ecumenical task incumbent on Catholics; infallibility has to be further examined in the light of the primacy of the gospel and of Christ's saving act; but it is also important to show how infallibility can render a service to God's people by giving expression to that primacy.

58. To promote a more ecumenical dimension in our Church's teaching function, we recommend:

a) that Catholics, particularly writers and teachers, observe an evangelical discretion in the titles bestowed on the papacy, avoiding that exaggerated language which tends to obscure the radical distinction between Christ or his Spirit and all other teachers within the Church, including the pope;

b) that Catholic leaders invite Lutheran church authorities to participate in the formulation of Catholic doctrine in a consultative capacity, seeking to follow and even to go beyond the precedent set by the participation of non-Catholic observers at Vatican Council II;

c) that Catholic bishops and their Lutheran counterparts seek to give joint witness (e.g., in pastoral letters) to emphasize and further Christian unity;

d) that Catholic theologians and religious educators make greater use of statements issued by Lutherans, especially when this will demonstrate and strengthen the unity of Christian faith.

The recommendations we have made refer to the Lutheran churches, because it is with them that we have been in dialogue. We trust that these recommendations offer a positive contribution to the efforts Christians are making toward greater unity in faith.

III
LUTHERAN RELFECTIONS

1. As is true of previous topics in this dialogue series, there is much that the Lutheran participants need to say to their fellow Lutherans about the question of infallibility beyond what is contained in the Common Statement. We need to explain from a Lutheran perspective the nature and reasons for both our growing agreements and our remaining disagreements with our Roman Catholic fellow Christians.

2. That we can speak of even partial agreement may seem extraordinary in view of the divisiveness of this issue in the past. The Lutheran participants were prepared for disappointments as they

approached this round of the dialogue. The issue of papal infallibility seemed to be an inner-Catholic problem to which Lutherans had little to contribute. Yet we recognized the inescapability of the theme. While not identical with papal primacy, the concept of papal infallibility is closely related to the exercise of the universal teaching office in the Roman Catholic Church and thus had to be discussed after the completion of our work on papal primacy and the universal Church. During the course of our conversations, however, we have become aware that the issues at stake in this particular doctrine are anything but a solely Roman Catholic problem. The very nature and truth of the gospel, the verification and authority of its proclamation and interpretation, and the credibility of the Church's preaching and teaching Ministry are involved in this question. Our partners in dialogue have pressed us hard on many of these points, and we are deeply grateful to them. We discovered that, as Lutherans, we were not as clear as we have traditionally supposed about how to give account of our confidence in the truth of the gospel and in the authority of a teaching office. We have also discovered that the Roman Catholics with whom we are in conversation are as concerned as we are about the Lordship of Christ and the truth of the gospel. We have been led to examine afresh some of our most fundamental assumptions and cherished emphases in the course of trying to understand what Roman Catholics mean today when they affirm the infallibility of the papal magisterium. Some of the results of our reflections must be spelled out here.

3. It seems best to start where we started as a group. Thus we shall first treat of Lutheran problems with traditional infallibility claims and language. This will provide us with the viewpoint from which, in the second and third places, Roman Catholic and Lutheran convergences and continuing difficulties in this area can be assessed. Finally, we shall discuss the possibilities and hopes for the future opened up by our growing though by no means complete agreement on the nature and function of teaching authority in the Christian churches.

I

4. Ever since its definition in 1870, the dogma of papal infallibility has been widely seen as both theologically and emotionally the most divisive of all the issues separating the Roman Catholic communion from the churches of the Reformation. To be sure, Lutherans have difficulties not only with papal infallibility but with the ascription of infallibility to any of the Church's teaching offices (including ecumen-

ical councils). Before turning to the theological core of these difficulties, however, we need to remind ourselves of the history of objections to the notion of an infallible pope.

5. From the 16th century on, Lutherans rejected what they regarded as exaggerated claims by the late medieval papacy, among them the claim to teach truth inerrantly. "Nor should that be transferred to the popes which is the prerogative of the true Church: that they are pillars of the truth and that they do not err."[126] Following an older tradition, they even called the pope the "antichrist,"[127] in part because they saw him arrogating to himself the sole authority to interpret scriptural truth without fail. Thus antipapal polemics have remained a major part of the Lutheran stance. The First Vatican Council seemed to confirm all former suspicions. Its definition of infallibility was seen by many as the final step in the direction of papal absolutism, widening the gap between Roman and Reformation churches and making the break irreparable. The attempts at reconciliation and unification which occurred before the 19th century now seemed fruitless. While much of the emotion over Vatican I had national and political overtones, Lutherans reacted against the terminology of papal infallibility primarily because they thought it contradicted their basic conviction of the fallibility of all ecclesiastical institutions and orders. To speak of the pope or any of his pronouncements as infallible suggested to them the usurpation of the place which only Christ and the Word of God could occupy in the Church's teaching Ministry.[128] Infallibility language thus became the clearest proof, in the popular Lutheran perception of the decades since 1870, of what was regarded as the autocratic, oppressive, and anti-Christian character of the Roman Catholic Church. The definition of the Marian dogma of the Assumption[129] hardened this attitude even in irenic circles.[130] Lutherans objected not only to the claim of infallibility for this dogma but also to the very notion that the Assumption of Mary could in any sense be proclaimed a doctrine of the Church. It did not serve, they believed, to protect the gospel, nor did it have the scriptural basis which is necessary for authoritative teaching.

6. It next needs to be noted, however, that the theological difficulty many Lutherans today have with infallibility language and claims is much broader and more fundamental than the specifically interconfessional problems raised by the dialogue between Lutherans and Roman Catholics. The critique of such language and claims in recent history has been directed in the first instance against certain aspects of the Lutheran tradition itself, especially against claims made about the infallibility or inerrancy of Scripture.[131] In defense of their normative

scriptural principle, the fathers of the second Lutheran generation[132] used the late medieval language of inerrancy for Holy Scripture as the Word of God and developed a doctrine of scriptural infallibility which was elaborated in ever greater detail during the period of Lutheran orthodoxy.[133] Some Lutherans even today regard the doctrine of the "inerrancy of Scripture" as the true touchstone of faithfulness to the Lutheran Confessions.

7. Others, however, have come to hold that such an emphasis on the letter of Scripture is not compatible with the doctrine of justification by faith, the article by which "the Church stands and falls."[134] Put most simply, this doctine affirms that because God justifies the ungodly, forgiving sinners for Christ's sake, nothing else can be trusted for salvation. Neither scriptural inerrancy nor, even less, the infallibility of the Church's teachers, teaching offices, and doctrines is the basis of the Christian's confidence. All these may err, but not the gospel of God's unconditional mercy in Jesus Christ to which the biblical writings are the primary witness.

8. In the light of this, Lutherans believe that the transcendence which the gospel enjoys over human truth claims consists precisely in the fact that through the gospel God declares sinners righteous for Jesus' sake. The gospel, so to speak, establishes its own transcendence. Its truth becomes known and its authority acknowledged only upon being heard through the Word, received in the sacraments, and believed through the power of the Spirit. The authority of the Church's teachings and teaching office is dependent on the degree to which these further the proclamation of the gospel in accordance with Scripture.

9. One corollary of this emphasis on the self-authenticating character of the gospel is that questions about its authority can be answered ultimately only in its proclamation and celebration in preaching and sacraments when the Word of God genuinely encounters human beings in judgment and grace. Thus the Lutheran Confessions' use of something akin to infallibility language is in connection with the promises of God, i.e., "God does not lie" in such promises.[135] This, in turn, is inseparable from the conviction that the promises of God can be received only by faith, and that faith, by definition, is trust in such promises.

10. This understanding of faith has important consequences for the Lutheran view of church doctrine. It becomes necessary to make a careful distinction between faith as trust in the divine promises and those aspects of the faith of the Church which are responses to the divine promise through confession, action, teaching, and doctrinal formulations. These responses are necessary: the gospel (the promise of

God) does indeed have a specifiable "knowledge" content. But the authority of this content, Lutherans believe, is established by its power to convict of sin and convince of grace through the work of the Holy Spirit and is not enhanced by saying that the teaching office or doctrinal formulations are themselves infallible.

11. Thus doctrinal formulations for Lutherans are, on the one hand, confessions and doxologies rather than promulgations of infallible dogma; and, on the other, they function as guides for the proper proclamation of the gospel, the administration of the sacraments, and the right praise of God rather than as statements which are themselves objects of faith. Furthermore, the scriptural witness to the gospel remains the ultimate norm for such formulations. Yet this does not exclude a high regard for their authority. Although they are the result of human responses to the word of forgiveness, church doctrines when rightly used are vitally important in order to foster, insofar as possible in changing historical contexts, the proper proclamation of the Word and the transmission of that Word in its purity. Lutherans should be supremely conscious in all this that "we have this treasure in earthen vessels, to show that the transcendent power belongs to God and not to us" (2 Cor. 4:7). The Church abides and its teachings are authoritative, yet both remain *in via* until the day of Jesus Christ.

II

12. Although Lutherans have used this view of doctrinal authority in recent times largely as a critique of aspects of their own tradition, it is natural for them to apply it also in their interconfessional discussions with Roman Catholics. This leads them, on the one hand, to resist any suggestion that attributing infallibility to persons, institutions, doctrinal formulations, or even the Church as a whole could enhance the authority of the gospel; on the other hand, they welcome the assurance of the Roman Catholics that infallibility language is not intended to add anything to the authority of the gospel, but rather to let that authority be recognized without ambiguity. They rejoice in the increasing emphasis among Catholics on the supremely normative status of the gospel as witnessed to in Scripture, and on the importance of understanding infallibility in terms of trust, confidence, and hope in God's promises.

13. Roman Catholics, like Lutherans, have been impelled by historical research, the philosophical critique of language, and the contemporary experiences of change and pluralism to recognize the cul-

turally conditioned character of all doctrinal formulations, though without surrendering convictions regarding their dimensions of abiding validity and truth. Further, changes in the understanding of the Church at Vatican II have begun to transform the monarchical features of papal infallibility into something more communal and collegial. As is made clear in both the Common Statement and the Catholic Reflections, infallibilist claims take on a very different appearance in this new context of thought and life. From the Lutheran perspective, it is now much clearer than before that Catholics also wish to place their ultimate reliance not in the teaching of popes, councils, or the Church but in God's promises in Jesus Christ.

14. One consequence of this is that Lutherans can no longer simply repeat their traditional objections to infallibility. What many Roman Catholics, including those who regard as important the acceptance of this doctrine, now affirm is not what Lutherans have in the past rejected. Our partners in dialogue deny that there is any automatic guarantee of the truth of dogmatic pronouncements. They seem to us to hold that assurance of the truth of a doctrinal pronouncement does not ultimately depend on promulgation by pope or council but on the Word of God witnessed in Scripture and interpreted in the community of faith under the unfailing guidance of the Holy Spirit. We have come to recognize that it is for them often difficult to determine whether a particular teaching is to be numbered among infallible doctrines and that there is no official list of such doctrines. We hear them saying that their confidence in the abiding truth of, for example, the ancient Trinitarian and Christological creeds (which Lutherans also accept) is ultimately based on trust in God and his promised guidance of the Church, not in juridically conceived authority. Their acceptance of infallibility sometimes seems to us little different from the affirmation which we share, that God will not permit the Church to err definitively on any issue vital to the faith: "the gates of hell shall not prevail against it" (Matt. 16:18 KJV).

15. As Lutheran theologians, we find it difficult to object to such a position. Lutherans also have a confidence, rooted in God's mercy, that the early ecumenical creeds, not to mention the Reformation decision on justification, are of abiding validity and value. As a result, it has sometimes seemed in these discussions that our disagreements over the possibility of infallible doctrines are more verbal than real.

16. Verbal disagreements, to be sure, can be important. The language of infallibility continues to seem dangerously misleading to most of us even when applied to the Bible, and to all of us when used in reference to popes, councils, or doctrinal formulations. It can too eas-

ily be abused to detract from the primacy of God's justifying act in Jesus Christ. Nevertheless, we must record our conviction that this is not the way this language is understood by the Catholic theologians with whom we have discussed these issues. There is, we are persuaded, increasing agreement between us on the centrality of the gospel and of trust in God and his promises. This has the consequence that we often find it difficult to pinpoint exactly where or how we differ from each other on the question of infallibility.[136] Yet this is an embarrassment in which we rejoice, because it grows from the convergence of Catholic concerns with those which spring from the Reformation.

17. Much, to be sure, remains to be done. Even if the difference on infallibility were overcome, there would still remain divergences between Catholics and Lutherans on specific doctrinal questions. The most manifest of those doctrinal divergences which we have not yet dealt with are the Marian dogmas of 1854 and 1950. Yet, given the convergence on the primacy of the gospel evident in our past and present discussions, it is our hope and prayer that even these need not be church-dividing.

III

18. Convergence, however, has taken place not only from the Catholic side. While Catholics are rethinking the meaning of infallibility, many Lutherans are reawakening to the importance of an ecumenical or universal teaching Ministry within the Church. This has been our experience in this dialogue. Our Catholic partners have stimulated us to consider how vital it is for the churches to speak, when occasion demands, with one voice in the world and how a universal teaching office such as that of the pope could exercise a Ministry of unity which is liberating and empowering rather than restrictive or repressive.

19. This convergence, propelled by the Lutheran confessional commitment to the cause of Christian unity,[137] occurs in the midst of conflicting claims to authority in the modern world. Lutherans, like Catholics, are called to move in creative, ecumenical ways toward an effective expression of universal teaching authority. We share the conviction that decisions about the truth of the gospel have to be made for the sake of the gospel's life in the world. Consequently, we affirm a Ministry which has the responsibility of reformulating doctrine in fidelity to the Scripture when circumstances require.[134] In order to fulfil this responsibility, we need to overcome our past difficulties in orga-

nizing an effective *magisterium* which can articulate the doctrinal concerns of Lutherans around the globe. It should be the explicit purpose of such a magisterium to break through parochial, national, and denominational barriers and share in the ecumenical responsibility of witnessing in the world.[139] Ecumenical councils in conjuction with the papacy could thus become once again the instrument through which the unity and mission of the Church are affirmed and realized. Lutherans have always recognized that, though not guaranteed against error, the doctrinal decisions of free and universal councils are, when accepted by the churches, the highest exercise of the teaching office.[140]

20. To be sure, the Lutheran characterization of such a Ministry remains distinct from the Catholic one. As has been repeatedly emphasized, we continue to question the appropriateness of speaking of the Church's teaching office or doctrines as "infallible."[141] Infallibility suggests something above and beyond that indefectibility of the Church which we also accept. For us, there is no special gift (charism) of infallibility to the *magisterium,* although there is a preaching and teaching authority which exists to serve the proclamation of the Word and for the sake of order and discipline in the Church. Such order and discipline are, in part, the responsibility of the Ministry, which exists to ensure that the gospel is transmitted and preserved. The only guarantee of this transmission is the Holy Spirit, "who works faith, when and where he pleases."[142] Doctrinal decisions of the Church are to be taken with utmost seriousness, but this means that they are to be constantly reexamined and reinterpreted in the light of God's Word. We thus return to the emphasis on God's promises, which is expressed in the affirmation that only the Word of God found in Scripture is "infallible and unalterable."[143]

IV

21. Yet, although our accord on infallibility is not complete, the convergences we have traced are of great significance. To agree on the primacy of the gospel is more than a change of climate. It calls, as the Common Statement has already noted, for "magisterial mutuality," for cooperation with Catholics in the teaching function of the Church. Concrete steps need to be taken to right old wrongs and to prepare for new directions at this crucial point in the history of our churches. Thus we recommend to our churches:

a) that they officially declare that the Lutheran commitment to the Confessions does not involve the assertion that the pope or the papacy in our day is the antichrist;[144] in this way our churches would publicly affirm that antipapal polemics should be replaced by an attitude of respect and love;

b) that they undertake an examination, with the participation of Catholics, of catechetical and other teaching materials, in order to identify and eliminate distorted accounts of historic and contemporary Roman Catholicism;

c) that in the presentation of our common Christian faith they encourage the greater use of Roman Catholic doctrinal, theological, catechetical, pastoral, and liturgical materials;

d) that they facilitate Catholic contributions to the process of formulating Lutheran positions on doctrinal and ethical issues; this might include Catholic participation in Lutheran conventions and assemblies;

e) that they develop structures for regular consultation with Catholic bishops on the local and national levels regarding matters of mutual concern;

f) that they declare their willingness to participate in a worldwide and ecumenically-based *magisterium;* this participation might take many forms, from representation in synods of bishops to joining in a fully ecumenical council.

We are aware that these recommendations are difficult to implement. They are in some respects ahead of what is at present possible. Yet, if our two traditions have indeed drawn as close in their understanding of the primacy of the gospel of Jesus Christ in relation to the Church's teaching authority as our work indicates, then it is incumbent on Lutherans to take concrete steps to bring the insights of our encounter to fruition. Only thus can Lutheranism become what it originally claimed to be: a reformation movement under the gospel within the Church catholic. We belong together with our Roman Catholic brothers and sisters in sharing the sufferings, joys, and tasks to which our common Lord calls us in God's world.

Notes

1. The previous volumes in this series are described in the list of abbreviations.
2. As noted in L/RC 4:9, "ministry" (lowercase) is used for the task of proclaiming the gospel by the whole Church and "Ministry" for that particular form of service, order, function, or gift *(charism)* within and for the sake of Christ's Church in its mission to the world.
3. DS 3074.
4. A. Vacant, L. Billot, E. Dublanchy, J. Salaverri, and J.C. Fenton, among oth-

ers, ascribed a fundamental infallibility to the ordinary magisterium of the pope. For a survey of opinions on this point, see F.M. Gallati, *Wenn die Päpste sprechen* (Vienna: Herder, 1960), pp. 41–42, 80–85; also A. Peiffer, *Die Enzykliken und ihr formaler Wert für die dogmatische Methode* (Freiburg [Switz.]: Universitätsverlag, 1968), pp. 72–100. Popular catechisms often made no distinction between the ordinary and extraordinary magisterium of the pope, stating simply that the pope is infallible when he proclaims a doctrine of faith and morals to all. See e.g. *A Catechism of Christian Doctrine Prepared and Enjoined by Order of the Third Plenary Council of Batimore* (New York: Benziger, 1886), p.30.

5. DS 3885.

6. *Lumen gentium* 25.

7. *Treatise on the Power and Primacy of the Pope;* Tappert 320–335.

8. DS 1451–1492.

9. *Ap.* 7–10; Tappert 168–180.

10. *Ap.* 7–8; Tappert 168–173.

11. *Ap.* 7–8; 33–34; Tappert 174–175; L/RC 4, pp. 18–19; L/RC 5, pp. 25ff.

12. "The Gospel and the Church" (Malta Report of the Joint Lutheran/Roman Catholic Subcommission), par. 16. German text in *Herder Korrespondenz* 25 (1971): 536–544; Eng. tr. in *Worship 46* (1972): 326–351, and *Lutheran World* 19 (1972): 259–273.

13. MR, par. 17.

14. On the work of the Holy Spirit, see further in par. 12 below.

15. E.g. his message about the kingdom (Matt. 4:17) and "all that I have commanded you" (28:20), which in Matthew's Gospel refers especially to the discourses in chaps. 5–7, 10, 13, 18, 24–25.

16. Cf. André Benoît, "The Transmission of the Gospel," *The Gospel as History,* ed. by Vilmos Vajta (Philadelphia: Fortress, 1975), p. 147. Note the equation: Christ = the power of God (1 Cor. 1:24) = the word of the cross (message about Christ crucified, 1 Cor. 1:18) = the gospel (Rom. 1:16).

17. Cf. Mark 8:35 and 10:29, where the two expressions are placed in parallel, "for my sake and the gospel's." Cf. Willi Marxsen, *Mark the Evangelist* (Nashville: Abingdon, 1969), pp. 120–121, 136–137; J.A. Fitzmyer, "The Kerygmatic and Normative Character of the Gospel," *Evangelium-Welt-Kirche,* ed. by H. Meyer (Frankfurt: Lembeck-Knecht, 1975), pp. 111–128; G. Strecker, "Literarkritische Überlegungen zum *euangelion*-Begriff im Markusevangelium," *Neues Testament und Geschichte,* Festschrift O. Cullmann (Zürich: Theologischer Verlag, 1972), pp. 91–104.

18. Damien van den Eynde, *Les normes de l'enseignement chrétien dans la littérature patristique des trois premiers siècles* (Gembloux: Duculot, 1933), pp. 32–33.

19. Cf. the Biblical Commission's *Instruction concerning the Historical Truth of the Gospels* (Rome, 1964); see TS 25 (1964); 402–408.

20. 1 Cor. 12:28; Rom. 12:6–8; Eph. 4:11. Cf. L/RC 4, p. 10, n. 6.

21. Mark 3:16–19; Matt. 10:2–4; Luke 6:14–16; Acts 1:13; 6:5.

22. Cf. Acts 2:29 and 4:13, referring to the boldness of Peter and John, who had "been with Jesus." The church in Jerusalem prayed to speak the word with boldness (4:29, cf. 31), and the Book of Acts closes with an emphasis on preaching and teaching "with boldness" (28:31). Cf. 1 Thess. 2:3; 2 Cor. 4:3; Eph. 3:12; and 1 Timothy 3:13 as examples in the Pauline corpus.

23. Paul stressed that his gospel was not "man's gospel" but came through a revelation of Jesus Christ (Gal. 1:11–12). Heb. 6:19 states that God provides "a sure and steadfast anchor." In Heb. 11:1 ff., faith is viewed as assurance. Assurance is particularly a concern in Luke-Acts; cf. Luke 1:4, " . . . that you may know the truth (assurance) concerning the things of which you have been informed."

24. *Faith and Order Findings* 2 (Montreal, 1963), sect. 45. *Kerygma* means "proclamation" and here denotes the apostolic gospel. *Paradosis* is the Greek word for "transmission" or "that which is transmitted" orally, and is used in the New Testament in a positive sense for Christian traditions in 1 Cor. 11:12 and 2 Thess. 2:15; 3:6; cf. 1 Cor.

11:23 and 15:3 for the verbal form. It was a feature of the Montreal statement to use "the Tradition" (with a capital) with references to the New Testament witnesses and "traditions" (lower case) for the subsequent individual confessional developments of various churches.

25. 1 Thessalonians is dated around A.D. 50. Most New Testament books were composed by the end of the century. Some would date 2 Peter towards the end of the first half of the second century. Cf. *Peter in the New Testament,* ed. R. Brown, K. Donfried, and J. Reumann (Minneapolis and New York: Augsburg and Paulist, 1973), p. 17.

26. The Catholic and Lutheran traditions agree on the 27 books which comprise the New Testament canon.

27. Representative texts are conveniently gathered in DS 1-75, and in Philip Schaff, *The Creeds of Christendom* 2 (New York: Funk and Wagnalls, 1890), pp. 11–41. Cf. Irenaeus, *Adversus haereses* 1, 10, 1; 3, 4, 1–2; 4, 33, 7; and further, for his salvation-history approach, *Proof of the Apostolic Preaching,* tr. J.P. Smith, in *Ancient Christian Writers* 16 (Westminster, Md.: Newman, 1952); also Tertullian, *De virginibus velandis* 1; *Adversus Praxean* 2; *De praescriptione haereticorum* 13, 36. On development from credal elements in the new Testament via the rule of faith to the Old Roman Symbol and later creeds, cf. J.N.D. Kelly, *Early Christian Creeds,* 3rd ed. (London: Longmans, Green, 1972).

28. For the development of a pattern of the threefold Ministry of deacon, presbyter (priest), bishop, cf. J.F. McCue, "Apostles and Apostolic Succession in the Patristic Era," in L/RC 4, pp. 137–171; cf. also ibid., pp. 10, n. 6, and J.D. Quinn, "Ministry in the New Testament," ibid., pp. 69–100, which has now appeared in revised form in *Biblical Studies in Contemporary Thought,* ed. by M. Ward (Somerville, Mass.: Greeno, Hadden, 1975), pp. 130–160.

29. Cf. L/RC 4, p. 12; MR, par. 15; *Anglican-Lutheran International Conversations* (London: SPCK, 1973), pp. 17ff., sect. 73–74; *Lutheran-Episcopal Dialogue: A Progress Report* (Cincinnati: Forward Movement Publications, 1973), pp. 20–22.

30. L/RC 5, p. 11; *Peter in the New Testament,* pp. 162 ff.

31. *Peter in the New Testament,* pp. 83ff.

32. Cf. Luke 22:32 Vulgate, *Ut non deficiat fides tua* ("In order that your (singular) faith may not fail").

33. *Peter in the New Testament,* pp. 95 ff.

34. *Ibid.,* 49–50.

35. *Ibid.,* 157–158.

36. The phrase at 1 Timothy 3:15, "pillar and bulwark of the truth," may be understood as referring to the church, local or universal, or to Timothy as a Minister. It was later applied to the gospel, the Spirit, the four Gospels, and even an individual Christian. For details see J.D. Quinn, "On the Terminology for Faith, Truth, Teaching, and the Spirit in the Pastoral Epistles," L/RC 6, pp. 232–237 below. The history of interpretation of the verse points to places where assurance of the truth has been sought.

37. According to the research of Pierre Batiffol, Stephen I (254–257) was apparently the first bishop of Rome to claim explicitly that he held the *cathedra Petri* by succession, but several years earlier Cyprian had argued that "Rome possessed the church instituted first of all in the person of Peter," i.e., the *ecclesia principalis,* the *cathedra Petri.* See P. Batiffol, *Cathedra Petri: Etudes d'histoire ancienne de l'église* (Paris: Cerf, 1948), pp. 13–14; cf. pp. 135–142, 150, 178–181.

38. Epistle *In requirendis* (DS 217; Mirbt-Aland [6th ed.] no. 403); E. Giles, *Documents Illustrating Papal Authority* (London: SPCK, 1952), p. 201.

39. DS 363; Mirbt-Aland, no. 470.

40. H. Grundmann, "Die Papstprophetien des Mittelalters," *Archiv für Kulturgeschichte* 19 (1929): 77–137; Horst D. Rauh, *Das Bild des Antichrist im Mittelalter, Beiträge zur Geschichte der Philosophie und Theologie des Mittelalters,* NF 9 (Münster: Aschendorff, 1973).

41. B. Tierney, *Foundations of the Conciliar Theory* (Cambridge: Cambridge University Press, 1955), pp. 57–67 and passim.

42. Epistles 1, 27, 34; 12, 6. See R. Eno, "Some Elements in the Prehistory of Papal Infallibity," L/RC 6, pp. 238–258 below.

43. See R. Eno, ibid. For the concept of "reception," also Y. Congar, "La réception comme réalité ecclésiastique," *Revue des sciences philosophiques et théologiques* 56 (1972): 369–403.

44. The earliest instances are found in letters of Pope Zosimus (417–418) and Pope Boniface I (418–422).

45. See A.M. Koeniger, ed., "Prima sedes a nemine judicatur," *Festgabe für Albert Ehrhard* (Bonn and Leipzig: K. Schroeder, 1922; reprint, Amsterdam: Rodopi, 1969), pp. 273–300.

46. *Sum.theol.* 2-2, q. 1, a. 10, corpus. See Y. Congar, "St. Thomas and the Infallibility of the Papal Magisterium (S. Th. II-II, q. 1, a. 10)," *Thomist* 38 (1974): 81–105.

47. *Quodlib.* 9, q.7, a. 16.

48. This is the thesis of the book by B. Tierney, *Origins of Papal Infallibility* (Leiden: Brill, 1972).

49. The text was published by Bartholomaeus M. Xiberta, O. Carm., under the title *Guidonis Terreni Quaestio de magisterio infallibili Romani pontificis, Opuscula et textus,* Series scholastica et mystica, fasc. 2 (Münster: Aschendorff, 1926). For other instances of this use of the term, see Paul de Vooght, "Esquisse d'une enquête sur le mot 'infaillibilité, durant la période scholastique," in O. Rousseau *et al., L'Infaillibilité de l'Eglise: Journées oecuméniques de Chevetogne,* Sept. 25–29, 1961 (Chevetogne: Editions de Chevetogne, 1963), pp. 99–146.

50. To emphasize the revelation in Christ does not detract from the revelation of God through nature or in the Old Testament.

51. *Mysterium Ecclesiae* (AAS 65 [1973]: 402–403).

52. See Avery Dulles, "Infallibility: The Terminology," L/RC 6, pp. 68–80 below.

53. *Lumen gentium* 4.

54. *Ibid.* 23.

55. *Ibid.* 22.

56. *Ibid.* 18, 22, 23, 25.

57. DS 3074. Cf. M.C. Duchaine, "Vatican I on Primacy and Infallibility," in L/RC 5, p. 148.

58. *Ibid.,* pp. 148–149.

59. *Lumen gentium* 25; Duchaine (n. 57 above), p. 149.

60. *Lumen gentium* 25.

61. *Smalcald Articles,* Part 3, art. 4; Tappert 310.

62. WA 10/1,2:48,5; 7:475, 14–18; cf. WA 10/1,1:17,8; LW 35:123; WA 10/1,1:626,6–9; 12:259,8–15.

63. CA 7; Tappert 32.

64. *Formula of Concord, Epitome* 1; Tappert 464–465; *Formula of Concord, Solid Declaration,* Summary Formulation 1–13; Tappert 503–506.

65. *Ap.* 14; Tappert 214–215.

66. E.g. ecumenical councils and synods.

67. CA 18:21; Tappert 84.

68. See L/RC 5, p. 21.

69. *Lumen gentium* 25.

70. Cf. par. 5 above.

71. MR, par. 17.

72. For an argument in favor of Scripture as final norm *(norma normans non normata)* see Walter Kasper, *Glaube und Geschichte* (Mainz: Matthias-Grünewald, 1970), pp. 188–190. Karl Rahner has repeatedly characterized Scripture as being in practice, for the contemporary believer, the only original, underived source of Christian revelation, e.g. in his *Theological Investigations* 6 (Baltimore: Helicon, 1966), pp. 91–95. In this restricted sense, but without questioning the need for the authoritative testimony of tradition and *magisterium,* Rahner is prepared to defend a Catholic *sola scriptura* principle; see ibid., pp. 98–112.

73. But note the Lutheran World Federation as an international study and service agency.

74. *Lumen gentium* 37; *Gaudium et spes* 62.

75. *Lumen gentium* 25.

76. See L/RC 5, pp. 19–23.

77. *Mysterium Ecclesiae* (AAS 65 [1973]: 402–404).

78. Cf. MR, par. 18; *Dei verbum* 10.

79. *Lumen gentium* 25.

80. Cf. E. Gritsch, "Lutheran Teaching Authority: Past and Present," L/RC 6, pp. 138–148 below. The term emerged in the discussions of the dialogue group at its New Orleans meeting, February 1972.

81. The term was used in the meeting between Pope Paul VI and the Ecumenical Patriarch Athenagoras in Istanbul with reference to the mutual excommunications of 1053. See W.M. Abbott and J. Gallagher, *The Documents of Vatican II* (New York: Guild, 1966), p. 726.

82. Cf. *Katholische Anerkennung des augsburgischen Bekenntnisses, Oekumenische Perspektiven* 9 (Frankfurt: Josef Knecht, 1977).

83. *Smalcald Articles,* Part 2, art. 4; Tappert 298–301. See also the Lutheran Reflections below, par. 21.

84. L/RC 5, pp. 21–22.

85. Whether this ministry should be regarded as of divine institution must be judged in terms of the principles and difficulties stated *ibid.,* pp. 22, 30, 31, 34.

86. In this comprehensive sense the term was used in the Tridentine decree on the canon of Sacred Scripture (DS 1501), where *puritas ipsa evangelii* was used to sum up what was promised in "Sacred Scripture" (= the OT) and promulgated by Christ himself. Compare *Dei verbum* 7.

87. E.g. see Thomas Aquinas, *Sum. theol.* 2–2, q. i, a. 9, sed contra.

88. *Ap.* 7:27; Tappert 173.

89. See Georges Dejaifve, "Ex sese, non autem ex consensu ecclesiae," *Salesianum* 24 (1962): 283–297; Eng. tr. in *Eastern Churches Quarterly* 14 (1962): 360–378; also Heinrich Fries, "Ex sese, non ex consensu ecclesiae," in *Volk Gottes,* Festgabe J. Höfer, ed. by R. Bäumer and H. Dolch (Freiburg: Herder, 1967), pp. 480–500.

90. L/RC 5, pp. 35–37.

91. Text in AAS 65 (1973): 396–408; Eng. tr. in *Catholic Mind* 71, no. 1276 (Oct. 1973); 54–64.

92. AAS 65 (1973): 402; *Catholic Mind* (n. 91 above): 58–59.

93. "Tunc enim Romanus Pontifex non ut persona privata sententiam profert, sed ut universalis ecclesiae magister supremus, in quo charisma infallibilis ipsius ecclesiae singulariter inest, doctrinam fidei catholicae exponit vel tuetur" (*Lumen gentium* 25). See J.D. Quinn, "Charisma veritatis certum': Irenaeus, *Adversus haereses* 4, 26, 2," TS 39 (1978): 520–525; also Kilian McDonnell, "Infallibility as Charism at Vatican I," L/RC 6, pp. 270–286 below.

94. This insight of Vatican II, of course, was not entirely new. It recalls the famous definition of an article of faith, used by Thomas Aquinas and many other Scholastic theologians, as a "glimpse of the divine truth toward which it tends" *(perceptio divinae veritatis tendens in ipsam);* see *Sum. theol.* 2–2, q.1, a. 6, sed contra.

95. See K. Rahner and K. Lehmann, *Kerygma and Dogma* (New York: Herder and Herder, 1969), pp. 87–88.

96. On this point see G.A. Lindbeck, *Infallibility* (Milwaukee: Marquette University Press, 1972), pp. 21–22 and 60, with references to the work of R.P. McBrien.

97. MR, par. 50.

98. On the problems of interpreting the phrase "pillar and bulwark of the truth" (1 Timothy 3:15), see above, "Common Statement," par. 16, n. 26. There are also several passages in the Fourth Gospel which could be examined further in this connection.

99. See end of n. 24 above.

100. See e.g. A. Cotter, *Theologia fundamentalis,* 2nd ed., (Weston, Mass.: Weston

College, 1947), p. 681. Cf. A. Durand, "Exégèse," *Dictionnaire apologétique de la foi catholique* 1:1838; E. Mangenot and J. Rivière, "Interprétation de l'écriture," DTC 7:2318.

101. U. Betti, a historian who has devoted much study to Vatican I and its Decree *Pastor aeternus,* has written: "The interpretation of these two texts (Matt. 16:16–19 and John 21:15–17) as proof of the two dogmas mentioned does not fall *per se* under the dogmatic definition, not only because there is no mention of them in the canon, but also because there is not a trace that the Council wanted to give an authentic interpretation of them in this sense" *(La costituzione dommatica "Pastor aeternus" del Concilio Vaticano I)* (Rome: Antonianum, 1961), p. 592. Similarly, apropos of Luke 22:32: " . . . the Council abstained from wanting to give an authentic interpretation . . . of that particular text . . . , although the request had been made in this sense by someone in the preparatory phase of the Decree and again during the concilar discussion of the Decree" (p. 628).

102. See Robert Eno, "Some Elements in the Prehistory of Papal Infallibility," L/RC 6, pp. 238–258 below.

103. See G. Tavard, "The Bull *Unam sanctam* of Boniface VIII," L/RC 5, pp. 105–119.

104. For John XXII's earlier position, see Marc Dykmans, *Les sermons de Jean XXII sur la vision béautifique* (Rome: Gregorian University, 1973), p. 96. For John XXII's subsequent retraction and the correction published by Benedict XII, see DS 990–991 and 1000–1001.

105. In his controversy with Hans Küng, Karl Rahner asserted: "All Küng's examples for such erroneous propositions seem to me either not to have been definitions or else there is question of propositions which Küng can reject as erroneous only if they are interpreted in a very definite manner which does not unambiguously impose itself" ("*Mysterium Ecclesiae:* Zur Erklärung der Glaubenskongregation über die Lehre der Kirche," *Stimmen der Zeit* 191 [1973]: 587). Cf. Y. Congar, in *Revue des sciences philosophiques et théologiques* 62 (1978): 87.

106. These definitions, contained in apostolic constitutions published in the form of bulls, are phrased in unmistakably solemn language (DS 2803, 3903) and clearly claim to be infallibly uttered.

107. In favor of the infallibility of canonizations, see I. Salaverri, *De ecclesia Christi,* 2nd ed. (Madrid: B.A.C., 1952), nos. 724–725, pp. 723–725; L. Lercher, *Institutiones theologiae dogmaticae* 1, 4th ed., rev. by F. Schlagenhaufen (Barcelona: Herder, 1945), n. 511b, p. 305; P. Molinari and A.E. Green, "Canonization of Saints," *New Catholic Encyclopedia* 3:55–61, esp. 59 and 61.

108. See M. Schenck, *Die Unfehlbarkeit des Papstes in der Heiligsprechung* (Freiburg: [Switz.]: Paulusverlag, 1965). This is an extended commentary on Thomas Aquinas, *Quodlib.* 9, a. 16.

109. P. Chirico, *Infallibility: The Crossroads of Doctrine* (Kansas City: Sheed, Andrews, and McMeel, 1977), p. 287.

110. The view that *Exsurge Domine* is an infallible document is represented by J.B. Franzelin, *Tractatus de divina traditione et scriptura* (Rome: Propaganda Fide, 1870), pp. 112–113. This view is not reflected in recent textbooks. The question whether Pius IX's *Syllabus of Errors* represents infallible teaching has been debated both pro and con by manualists.

111. *Casti connubii* (1930), which is held by F. Cappello and A. Vermeersch to contain an *ex cathedra* definition. For references see J.C. Ford and G. Kelly, *Contemporary Moral Theology* (Westminster, Md.: Newman, 1964), 2:263–271. Ford and Kelly, while holding that the Encyclical contains infallible doctrine, attribute its infallibility to the ordinary and constant teaching of the *magisterium* which this Encyclical confirms. The authority of *Casta connubii* is also discussed by J. Noonan, who inclines toward non-infallibility in his *Contraception* (Cambridge, Mass.: Harvard University, 1965), pp. 427–428.

112. *Humanae vitae* (1968). Some theologians argue that the Encyclical in its prohibition of contraception contains irreformable doctrine because in it "the Pope as

supreme teacher in the Church proclaims a truth that has constantly been taught by the Church's teaching office and corresponds to revealed doctrine." These are the words of Cardinal Pericle Felici in *Osservatore romano,* Oct. 3, 1968. Hans Küng, who quotes this in his *Infallible? An Inquiry* (Garden City: Doubleday, 1971), p. 61, also quotes on the preceding page a similar statement by Cardinal Charles Journet. Küng himself, seeking to discredit the doctrine of infallibility, argues that *Humanae vitae,* which he regards as erroneous, engages the claim of infallibility. For an opinion opposing the infallibility of the Encyclical, see K. Rahner, "On the Encyclical 'Humanae vitae,'" *Theological Investigations* 11 (New York: Seabury, 1974), pp. 263–287. See also C.E. Curran, ed., *Contraception: Authority and Dissent* (New York: Herder and Herder, 1969); J.A. Komonchak, "*Humanae vitae* and Its Reception: Ecclesiological Reflections," TS 39 (1978): 221–257; J.C. Ford and G. Grisez, "Contraception and the Infallibility of the Ordinary Magisterium," TS 39 (1978): 258–312.

113. In favor of the infallibility of this condemnation, see M. d'Herbigny, *Theologica de ecclesia* 2, 2nd ed. (Paris: Beauchesne, 1921), no. 329, pp. 210–212. For an opposing view, see L. Marchal, "Ordinations anglicaines," DTC 11:1166.

114. According to Paul VI, in an address to the College of Cardinals of June 23, 1964, this teaching of Pius XII still holds good. See AAS 56 (1964): 588–589.

115. The translation is that of J.A. Komonchak in his article "Ordinary Papal Magisterium and Religious Assent," in Curran, *Contraception,* pp. 101–126, at pp. 102–103.

116. K. Rahner, in H. Vorgrimler, ed., *Commentary on the Documents of Vatican II* (New York: Herder and Herder, 1967), 1:210. The test of the schema in question is quoted in English translation by Komonchak, "Ordinary Papal Magisterium," pp. 101–102.

117. Besides the article of Komonchak already cited, see A. Dulles, *The Resilient Church* (Garden City: Doubleday, 1977), pp. 107–112, and the various articles of R.A. McCormick there referred to.

118. Quoted by K. Rahner, "Magisterium," *Encyclopedia of Theology: The Concise 'Sacramentum mundi'* (New York: Seabury, 1975), p. 878.

119. Ibid.

120. See *Lumen gentium,* chaps. 3 and 8.

121. Regarding the implicit rather than the explicit faith of many Catholics, see J.H. Newman, *An Essay in Aid of a Grammar of Assent* (London: Longmans, Green, 1888), pp. 146, 153, 211.

122. Vatican II, *Orientalium ecclesiarum* 26–29.

123. Cf. A. Dulles, "A Proposal to Lift Anathemas," *Origins* 4 (1974): 417–421.

124. Whether such sharing is excuded on other grounds is a complicated question that cannot and need not be answered here.

125. In L/RC 1, p. 32, this dialogue already noted: "Different understandings of the movement from kerygma to dogma obtained in the two communities. Full inquiry must therefore be made into two topics: first, the nature and structure of the teaching authority of the Church; and, secondly, the role of Scripture in relation to the teaching office of the Church." The second of these inquiries has not as yet been undertaken by this group.

126. *Ap.* 7–8:27; Tappert 173.

127. "This is a powerful demonstration that the pope is the real Antichrist . . . ;" ". . . we cannot suffer his (i.e., the devil's) apostle, the pope or Antichrist, to govern us" (*Smalcald Articles,* Part 2, art. 4:10 and 1–4; Tappert 300–301. Cf. *Treatise on the Power and Primacy of the Pope* 39–42; Tappert 327–328; *Ap* 7–8:24; Tappert 172; *Ap.* 15:18–19; Tappert 217–218). This historical background is treated in Hans Preuss, *Die Vorstellungen vom Antichrist im späteren Mittelalter, bei Luther und in der konfessionellen Polemik* (Leipzig: Hinrichs, 1906). For more recent echoes, especially in the Lutheran Church-Missouri Synod, see Myron A. Marty, *Lutherans and Roman Catholicism: The Changing Conflict, 1917–1963* (Notre Dame: University of Notre Dame, 1968), pp. 146–170.

128. See the remarks on the definition of Vatican I in such standard works as Karl von Hase, *Handbook of the Controversy with Rome,* vol. 1 (London: Religious Tract

Society, 1906), pp. 24–74 and 324–329; W. von Loewenich, *Modern Catholicism* (New York: St. Martin's, 1959), pp. 49–51; Per E. Persson, *Roman and Evangelical* (Philadelphia: Fortress, 1964), pp. 57–58. For some early reactions cf. Ulrich Nembach, *Die Stellung der evangelischen Kirche und ihrer Presse zum ersten Vatikanischen Konzil* (Zurich: EVZ, 1962).

129. *Munificentissimus Deus,* Nov. 1, 1950 (DS 3900–3904).

130. See the review article by Friedrich Heiler in ThLZ 97 (1954): 1–48.

131. See e.g., the programmatic essay by Gerhard Ebeling, "The Significance of the Critical Historical Method for Church and Theology" (1950), in *Word and Faith* (Philadelphia: Fortress, 1963), pp. 17–61. An aspect of the historical origins of the historical-critical method is traced by Gottfried Hornig, *Die Anfänge der historisch-kritischen Theologie: Johann Salomo Semlers Schriftverständnis und seine Stellung zu Luther* (Göttingen: Vandenhoeck & Ruprecht, 1961). For a contemporary insistence on inerrancy, see *Crisis in Lutheran Theology: The Validity and Relevance of Historic Lutheranism vs. Its Contemporary Rivals 1: Essays by John Warwick Montgomery,* 2nd ed. (Minneapolis: Bethany Fellowship, 1973).

132. The reference is to theologians such as Matthias Flacius, Martin Chemnitz, and Nikolaus Selnecker, who were prominent in the second half of the 16th century.

133. See Robert D. Preus, *The Inspiration of Scripture: A Study of the Theology of the Seventeenth Century Lutheran Dogmaticians* (London: Oliver & Boyd, 1955); also by the same author, *The Theology of Post-Reformation Lutheranism,* vol. 1 (St. Louis: Concordia, 1970), esp. pp. 339–362.

134. Cf. *Smalcald Articles,* Part 2, art. 1:1; Tappert 292; *Formula of Concord, Solid Declaration* 3:6; Tappert 540.

135. LC, *Lord's Supper* 57; Tappert 444. Similar expressions in the same context include: God's Word cannot "deceive," "cannot err" (ibid.); Scriptures "will not lie to you" (LC, *Lord's Supper* 76; Tappert 455).

136. The "Roman Catholic Reflections" (par. 51) expresses the same sentiment: "Even with regard to infallibility, we have found it increasingly difficult, as our dialogue has proceeded, to specify the exact point at which, in fidelity to our respective traditions, we are bound to disagree."

137. Cf. CA, Preface 13: " . . . we on our part shall not omit doing anything, insofar as God and conscience allow, that may serve the cause of Christian unity" (Tappert 26).

138. "Common Statement," par. 41.

139. "Common Statement," par. 46.

140. Cf. Luther's treatise *Von den Konziliis und Kirchen,* 1539 (WA 50:509–653; LW 41:9–178) and the Common Statement, par. 23.

141. See "Common Statement," par. 28.

142. CA 5:2, Tappert 31.

143. *Book of Concord,* Preface; Tappert 8.

144. See n. 127 above and L/RC 5, p. 25. In making such a recommendation, we are aware that to the best of our knowledge there is no precedent for Lutherans to affirm officially that, in the light of changing historical circumstances, a statement in the Confessions no longer applies. Our churches, however, have long been involved in such historical interpretation of the Confessions.

Justification by Faith

INTRODUCTION

1. Since 1965 a theological dialogue between Lutherans and Roman Catholics in the United States has been taking place concerning doctrines that have united or separated their churches from one another since the sixteenth century. The degree of consensus or convergence that exists on the Nicene Creed, Baptism, the Eucharist, the Ministry, Papal Primacy, and Teaching Authority and Infallibility has been expressed in summaries and joint statements that have become important for relations between our churches and for wider ecumenical discussions.

2. The question of justification by faith, which is at the heart of the divisions inherited from the sixteenth century, has not yet, however, been directly addressed in the United States dialogue, although its implications for other topics have been noted in previous documents. The Malta Report of the International Lutheran/Catholic Study Commission said in the course of a short section on the doctrine that "today . . . a far-reaching consensus is developing in the interpretation of justification."[2] But a further treatment of the subject and its implications is needed.[3] The present relationship between the Catholic and Lutheran traditions calls for a greater clarity about the way to understand and speak of justification than has yet been achieved in official discussions, for the good news of God's justifying action in Jesus Christ stands at the center of Christian faith and life.

3. The present statement is a response to this need. It is based on discussions since 1978 of position papers drawing on a considerable body of biblical, historical, theological, and ecumenical literature.[4] It seeks to indicate how historic disagreements in the interpretation of the biblical doctrine of justification have developed and to what extent they can now be overcome. It attempts to remove obstacles to joint proclamation of the message of justification and includes a declaration proclaiming our common faith. For justification is above all a reality to be proclaimed in word and sacrament.

4. We emphatically agree that the good news of what God has done for us in Jesus Christ is the source and center of all Christian life and of the existence and work of the church. In view of this agreement, we have found it helpful to keep in mind in our reflections an affirmation which both Catholics and Lutherans can wholeheartedly accept: *our entire hope of justification and salvation rests on Christ Jesus and on the gospel whereby the good news of God's merciful action in Christ is made known; we do not place our ultimate trust in anything other than God's promise and saving work in Christ.* This excludes ultimate reliance on our faith, virtues, or merits, even though we acknowledge God working in these by grace alone *(sola gratia).* In brief, hope and trust for salvation are gifts of the Holy Spirit and finally rest solely on God in Christ. Agreement on this Christological affirmation does not necessarily involve full agreement between Catholics and Lutherans on justification by faith, but it does raise the question, as we shall see, whether the remaining differences on this doctrine need be church-dividing. Our intent in presenting this statement is to help our churches see how and why they can and should increasingly proclaim together the one, undivided gospel of God's saving mercy in Jesus Christ.

CHAPTER ONE
THE HISTORY OF THE QUESTION

5. In order to understand how disagreements over justification that were once irresolvable may now not be church-dividing, it is important to have in mind certain features not only of the Reformation conflict itself but also of its medieval background and of later developments. In sketching these features in the following historical sections, we have utilized the work of many scholars of different traditions and outlooks who have done much to overcome the confessionally and polemically biased pictures of the past, but we do not claim to have done justice to the complexity of the material and the variety of interpretations. We have attempted simply to highlight those aspects of the total story which are of particular importance for the present Lutheran-Roman Catholic discussion.

A. Before the Sixteenth Century

6. Historical research in recent generations has greatly increased our awareness of the degree to which the debate over justification in the sixteenth century was conditioned by a specifically Western and Augustinian understanding of the context of salvation which, in reliance on St. Paul, stressed the scriptural theme of *iustitia,* of righteousness. Eastern theologians, on the other hand, generally saw salvation within the framework of a cosmic process in which humanity occupies a place of honor.[5] Combining biblical allusions to divinization (e.g., Ps. 82:6; 2 Pet. 1:4; 2 Cor. 3:18) with an ascetically oriented, Neoplatonic understanding of the ascent of the soul, Eastern theologians described human salvation in terms of a return to God of a creation that had gone forth from God. This pattern is still found in Augustine's spirituality, in the Western mystical tradition influenced by Pseudo-Dionysius, and in the structures of Peter Lombard's *Sentences* and Thomas Aquinas' *Summa theologica.*

7. Yet the basic pattern of thought in the West about salvation, especially as developed in Augustine's fifth-century confrontation with Pelagius, was distinctive. Not only did Augustine emphasize Paul's teaching on justification much more than was common in the East, but he understood this primarily in terms of the transformation of the individual, as suggested by the Latin etymology of the term *justificare,* to make righteous.[6] His concern was to stress that this transformation takes place by grace, and the specific theme of the present statement, justification by faith, was not at the center of his attention. Thus at issue in the debate with Pelagius and the Pelagians was the extent to which God's grace is necessary and sovereign in this soteriological process of individual transformation. Prominent Eastern theologians had different concerns, as is shown by the attention they gave to the cosmic dimension of salvation, the divinizing character of grace, the universality of corruptibility and death, as well as freedom and responsibility, in contrast to the prominence of fate and inevitability in some pagan and gnostic thought.[7] In some later treatments of sin, grace, and predestination, Augustine stressed the total need of grace on the part of human beings and the total sovereignty of God in regard to salvation. In so doing he set much of the agenda for both medieval and Reformation theology, and with his victory the name "Pelagianism" became the label for an infamous heresy (although the degree to which Pelagius was a Pelagian is now debated by historians).[8]

8. It is thus not surprising that virtually all medieval theologians claimed to be anti-Pelagian, but this did not prevent frequent charges of Pelagianism throughout the period,[9] and the Protestant critique suspected the entire sacramental system of the medieval church of this heresy. While Augustine's stress on the absolute priority of God's initiative and the primacy of grace was often reiterated, his transformational model of justification, when set within the context of new developments in intellectual outlook, church practice, and spirituality,[10] allowed for growing speculation about the human role in the process.[11] This development is particularly evident in (1) the treatment of grace, (2) the emphasis on merit, and (3) the changing attitude toward predestination.

9. *(1) Grace.* Augustine's intention in developing the doctrine of grace was to protect the absolute priority of God's action over all human endeavor: "What do you have that you did not receive?" (1 Cor. 4:7).[12] His distinctions between "operating" and "cooperating," "prevenient" and "subsequent" grace point in this direction.[13] Early Scholasticism added further categories such as first grace, grace freely given *(gratia gratis data),* and justifying grace *(gratia gratum faciens)* in order to clarify various stages of the process and was open, as is evident in Peter Lombard, to identifying infused love with the Holy Spirit.[14] In view, however, of a growing awareness that the difference between the natural and the supernatural is not simply identical with that between creatures and God,[15] a distinction came to be made between two types of supernatural grace, the uncreated grace (*gratia increata,* i.e., God himself or the indwelling of the Holy Spirit) and the created "habit" or disposition of grace *(gratia creata).*[16]

10. Interest in the transforming effect of created grace led to discussion of the potentialities of human nature in the Aristotelian sense. For some theologians, such as Thomas Aquinas, God remained in total command as the initiator and perfecter of the movement *(motus)* from sinner to saint,[17] and for all theologians God retained the initiative in that the habit of grace is freely "infused" (cf. Rom. 5:5).[18] Yet for many the insistence on infused grace and on the presence of special assisting graces *(gratiae gratis datae)*[19] at every step of the way was combined with a strong emphasis on the ability of free will to contribute to salvation, not simply on the basis of grace, but independently, *ex suis naturalibus.*[20] This emphasis on human freedom was strong especially, though not exclusively, among those influenced by Ockham's nominalism and the *via moderna* at the end of the Middle Ages; yet there were others, including some nominalists, such as Gregory of Rimini, who attacked it as Pelagian despite the disclaimers of its proponents.[21]

11. *(2) Merit.* A similar shift can be traced in the expanding thought on merit before the Reformation. Augustine took the term from the African tradition. For him it had its basis in the biblical language of reward, but again the mature Augustine wanted to vindicate

God's absolute priority: "When God rewards our merits, he crowns his own gifts."[22] In time the shift of interest to the role of human nature led to the distinction between "congruous" and "condign" merit (*meritum de congruo* and *meritum de condigno*).[23] The former *(meritum de congruo)* in one of its meanings designated the basis for a hope that God "does not deny grace to those who do what is in them" *(facientibus quod in se est Deus non denegat gratiam).*[24] This assertion can be understood as affirming God's priority in the sense that merciful divine inspiration and direction are necessary for every good action of the human creature. It is in this sense that Thomas Aquinas speaks of doing what is in one's power *(facere quod in se est).* This preparation for justification is possible only because of the undeserved help of God's merciful providence.[25] Although Thomas describes the good works performed in the process of preparation as congruously meritorious, he does not fail to note that this involves an extended use of the term "merit." Indeed, he says one should, if pressed, concede that such works before justification do not merit any good rather than assert that they do.[26]

12. The formula *facere quod in se est,* however, can also be used in a Pelagianizing sense if "doing what is in one" is thought of as a condition which on the one hand calls for the conferral of grace and which on the other hand human beings can and must fulfill by relying on the unaided powers of their fallen nature. In the late medieval *via moderna* such a condition was commonly regarded as involving a gracious accommodation on the part of God, who precisely by accepting human efforts that are unworthy chooses to grant the grace leading to justification and thus, in this broad sense, renders these efforts meritorious. While this explanation was intended to diminish the Pelagian danger,[27] it also allowed theologians to claim that God owes it to himself to be gracious if there is any attempt to seek him, and it could be used to urge people to try ever harder to prove themselves worthy of being accepted by good works. The precept, "to do what is in one's power" *(facere quod in se est),* according to some historians contributed to the rampant scrupulosity of the late Middle Ages, and it was viewed by the Reformers as a cause of the "terrified conscience."[28]

13. *(3) Predestination.* A shift can also be observed in the treatment of predestination. Augustine's struggle in his later years to defend the primacy of grace against Pelagius led him also to stress the primacy of God's eternal will. He did not consistently teach a double predestination, but from his emphasis on God's election of some to glory it seemed logical to infer the predestination of others to eternal perdition. The regional Council of Orange, however, taught what is generally called single predestination (i.e., of the elect to glory)[29] and condemned double predestination.[30]

14. Influenced by the new interest in the powers of nature, the Scholastic theologians of the twelfth and thirteenth centuries stressed that God, in predestining to salvation, sees to it that the person receives the grace that removes sin and sanctifies the soul. God, they insisted, imposes no constraint on human freedom; yet they continued to affirm the primacy of grace. Bonaventure, for example, held that in predestination there are an eternal divine plan, a conferral of God's grace in time, and an eternal glorification; in reprobation there are again an eternal plan, an obstinacy in time, and eternal punishment. One who has been given grace in this life merits the glory of heaven just as one who sins obstinately in this life merits the punishment of hell. Nevertheless, because both predestination and reprobation involve God's eternal plan, neither can, taken as a whole, be merited.[31] Why God wishes to justify this person rather than another has not been revealed because such knowledge is not necessary for our salvation.[32]

15. Thomas Aquinas also emphasized the primacy of grace. Since eternal glory is the final gift that God bestows, it can be merited on the basis of earlier gifts of God's grace, but the grace of justification cannot itself be merited.[33] He says in the *Summa theologica* that "it is impossible that the total effect of predestination in general have any cause on our part." Further, the reason why God has "elected some to glory and condemned" others is none other than "the divine will."[34]

16. For John Duns Scotus predestination properly refers to an act of the divine will electing a rational or intellectual creature to grace and glory. With this in mind he asks whether one who is predestined can be damned. His answer is that God may predestine an individual or choose not to do so—not both simultaneously or successively but one or the other at the same instant of eternity.[35] Scotus made much of the distinction between what God could do by means of the divine power working in the present order *(de potentia ordinata)* and what God could do by absolute divine power *(de potentia absoluta)* in another order.[36]

17. Some later theologians were less careful than Scotus in maintaining that predestination, as the entire effect of God's decree, is not based on foreseen merits. They held that even in the present order God can and does predestine those who do their best by their own natural powers.[37] Yet there were also late medieval theologians who taught that all preparation for grace is the effect of predestination as an act of God's will and who viewed this position as the touchstone of true

Augustinianism against the "new Pelagians." In the Augustinian order, to which Luther later belonged, some argued this way, but others did not.[38]

18. The late medieval scene was thus characterized by a bewildering variety in which Augustinian intentions combined with competing interests arising out of an emphasis on the power and freedom of human nature within the order established by God. Everyone professed to be Augustinian and anti-Pelagian, but there was little agreement on what these terms meant. Customary labels such as *"via antiqua," "via moderna,"* "nominalism," and "Augustinian" do not correspond to specific types of the doctrine of justification,[39] and thus the Reformers of the sixteenth century, although influenced by their predecessors, cannot be aligned with any single medieval school of thought.

19. On the depravity of human nature, for example, there are parallels, recognized by Luther himself, between his teachings and those of theologians of the Augustinian order such as Giles of Rome and Gregory of Rimini.[40] The Reformers' rejection of the category of created grace may echo Peter Lombard's identification of infused love with the Holy Spirit.[41] In rejecting positions such as that of Gabriel Biel, that human beings have a natural capacity to merit grace, the Reformers resembled Aquinas and others. Their language of imputation, some scholars have argued, has similarities to the Scotist notion of acceptation and to the language of Bernardine mysticism.[42]

20. Yet, as we shall later see in more detail, fresh accents in the Reformation understanding of justification as by faith alone *(sola fide),* not simply grace alone *(sola gratia),* fundamentally challenged Augustine's transformationist thinking. The Reformation wanted to restore Augustinian emphases on sin and grace. With its stress on faith, however, it also went beyond these emphases and conceptualized salvation in a new way which, while retaining the focus on the individual, is in some respects as different from the older Augustinian and medieval patterns as these are from the ideas of divinization and cosmic redemption which prevailed in the East.

B. In the Sixteenth Century

21. In contrast to the medieval discussions, the debate over justification in the sixteenth century, with its focus on faith and not simply grace, embraced every aspect of Christian thought and practice. Further, what was central to the Reformers was often secondary to their opponents; perhaps neither side fully considered the claims of the other. In order to understand why this was so, we need to review in their historical setting the salient aspects of the Reformation doctrine[43] and the history of the controversy.[44]

1. The Reformation Doctrine

22. The two chief problems which occasioned the Reformers' appeal to St. Paul's teaching that human beings are "justified by faith apart from works of law" (Rom. 3:28 RSV) were, from their point of view, rampant Pelagianism or "works-righteousness," on the one hand, and the need to "console terrified consciences," on the other. Their attack on Pelagianism drew heavily on Augustine's theological stress on radical sinfulness, the loss of freedom, the primacy of grace, and, especially in Luther's *Bondage of the Will* (1525), predestination, but the focus of their attack was on medieval trends in piety as well as in theology. Salvation was widely viewed as something to be earned by good works, which included not only fulfillment of the moral law and the monastic counsels of perfection but also observance of a vast panoply of penitential disciplines and ecclesiastical rules and regulations. Moreover, money paid for Masses and indulgences was often thought of as automatically obtaining the remission of purgatorial penalties.

23. By protesting against such practices and attitudes, the Reformers, without initially intending to do so, threatened the source of power and income of much of the clerical establishment. They thus became involved in a struggle against ecclesiastical moral corruption which was also a widespread concern among many who did not share their theological outlook. Before changes made by the Council of Trent (1545–1563), indulgences were a major source of papal revenues, and Masses for the dead and for other purposes provided the main support for a large proportion of priests. This system of "buying" salvation, furthermore, was administered by a frequently venal hierarchy. The higher ranks of clergy, among them Renaissance popes, included members of wealthy and noble families who had purchased lucrative church offices for large sums and used ecclesiastical income to live luxuriously, enrich relatives, build splendid public works, and fight wars. Monastic orders and the lower ranks of the clergy were also often in a decadent state and resistant to changes in practices from which they profited. Thus the Reformation emphasis on justification "apart from works of law" was a challenge not simply to trends in theology and religious practice but also to powerful special interest groups. It is also true that factors such as incipient nationalism and a desire for greater freedom from ecclesiastical control of life, expressed as anticlericalism and popular rationalism, influenced some supporters of the Reformation.[45]

24. For the Reformers, however, the chief problem was neither moral laxity nor a Pelagianizing tendency to ascribe salvation partly to human effort apart from grace. In their situation the major function of justification by faith was, rather, to console anxious consciences terrified by the inability to do enough to earn or merit salvation. Even if grace is freely given "to do good works," one does not escape the perils of the anxious conscience. Thus for Luther the answer to the question "How do I get a gracious God?" must be "by faith alone," by trust in nothing but God's promises of mercy and forgiveness in Jesus Christ. Here Luther went beyond the Augustinian primacy of grace *(sola gratia)* to that of faith *(sola fide)*. In reference to this problem of the terrified conscience and the assurance of salvation, it does not suffice to say that "when God rewards our merits, he crowns his own gifts."[46] One should add that it is not on the basis of his gifts of infused grace, of inherent righteousness, or of good works that God declares sinners just and grants them eternal life, but on the basis of Jesus Christ's righteousness, a righteousness which is "alien" or "extrinsic" to sinful human beings but is received by them through faith. Thus God justifies sinners simply for Christ's sake, not because of their performance, even with the help of divine grace, of the works commanded by the law and done in love.

25. Justification by faith without the works of the law led Luther to a mode of thinking about Christian life and experience markedly different from traditional Augustinian and medieval transformationist models. Instead of a progressive transformation under the power of grace, the imputation of an alien righteousness received in faith implies a simultaneity; the justification is complete in the imputing of it so that the believer is "simultaneously a righteous person and a sinner" *(simul iustus et peccator)*. All notions of "change" and "growth" in the life of the Christian therefore receive a quite different cast. The very imputation of Christ's righteousness also reveals to the believer the depth and persistence of sin. Sin, however, is then not merely the failure to do "good works" or the despair over such failure but is, above all, the human propensity to trust in one's own righteousness. The imputed alien righteousness of Christ creates a new situation in which sin is exposed as both presumption and despair and is attacked in its totality. Only when so exposed and confessed can sin no longer reign.

26. It can be seen from this that justification *sola fide* (as Luther read Rom. 3:28)[47] is justification *propter Christum.* Nothing but faith in Christ alone makes sinners pleasing to God; their works are good in his sight only "on account of Christ" *(propter Christum).* Because faith itself is wholly the gracious work of the Spirit,[48] the Reformation teaches that God forgives and justifies by grace alone, through faith alone, on account of Christ alone.[49]

27. The doctrine of justification with its Christological focus and trinitarian presuppositions was later described by Luther in the Smalcald Articles (1537) as the "first and chief article":

> . . . Jesus Christ, our God and Lord, "was put to death for our trespasses and raised again for our justification" (Rom. 4:25). He alone is "the lamb of God, who takes away the sin of the world" (John 1:29). "God has laid upon him the iniquities of us all" (Isa. 53:6). Moreover, "all have sinned," and "they are justified by his grace as a gift, through the redemption which is in Christ Jesus, by his blood" (Rom. 3:23–25).
> Inasmuch as this must be believed and cannot be obtained or apprehended by any work, law or merit, it is clear and certain that such faith alone justifies us. . . .
> Nothing in this article can be given up or compromised, even if heaven and earth and things temporal should be destroyed. . . .
> On this article rests all that we teach and practice against the pope, the devil, and the world.[50]

As Luther still later says, "If this article stands, the church stands; if it falls, the church falls."[51]

28. To see justification by faith in this fashion as the *articulus stantis et cadentis ecclesiae* is, for the Reformers, to treat it as a criterion or corrective for all church practices, structures, and theology. They regard it as the heart of the gospel because the gospel message in its specific sense is the proclamation of God's free and merciful promises in Christ Jesus[52] which can be rightly received only through faith. All aspects of Christian life, worship, and preaching should lead to or flow from justifying faith in this gospel, and anything which opposes or substitutes for trust in God's promises alone should be abolished. The claim of the Lutheran confessional writings, especially in the Augsburg Confession and the Smalcald Articles, is that this criterion is the primary basis for the attacks on what the Reformers regarded as practical abuses and false theological teachings.

2. The History of the Controversy

29. Turning now to the history of the sixteenth-century conflict, we shall see that the problem of justification was indeed the source of the Reformation protests but often was not central in the resultant controversies, especially not for the Roman Catholics. The starting point for Luther was his inability to find peace with God as an Augustinian hermit in the Erfurt monastery. Terrified in his own conscience, he became increasingly convinced that the theology in which he had been trained and the spiritual formation which he had received did not resolve the deep spiritual struggle *(Anfechtung)* of his quest for a gracious God. By 1517 he had made known his conclusion in published academic disputations as well as in intensive dialogue with his father confessor, the Augustinian vicar general John Staupitz; his conclusion was that the theology and piety of his time had fallen victim to Pelagianism, especially in relation to the sacrament of penance.[53]

30. It was in light of this conviction that Luther reacted against John Tetzel's preaching on the indulgences to be granted by Pope Leo X for contributions to the rebuilding of St. Peter's Basilica in Rome. Tetzel's sermons promised the remission of spiritual penalties of purgatory to those who gained the indulgences. They were, moreover, sanctioned by official instructions from Archbishop Albrecht of Mainz. Luther wrote to the archbishop, asking that preachers be given other directives:[54] people were not to be lulled into false security and an absence of fear but were to be instructed that "works of piety and love are infinitely better than indulgences" and to "learn the gospel and the love of Christ." Accompanying his letter were his *Ninety-Five Theses,*[55] which attacked abuses in the practice and doctrine of indulgences. Similarly, Luther protested against the instructions which people were receiving about the confession of sins in the sacrament of penance; they were being led to believe that their own contrition and satisfaction made the difference between forgiveness and rejection by God. In the context of these controversies over indulgences and penance, Luther already occasionally insisted that justification and forgiveness of sins came solely through faith in Jesus Christ, which was for him the heart of the gospel.[56]

31. Although Luther gained much popular support, he also met strong opposition. Some of it stemmed from nontheological concerns, such as the desire of those who profited from ecclesiastical benefices to retain their gains or the efforts of princes and the emperor to keep peace in the realm. The theological opposition, as indicated by the censures passed in 1518–1521 by the theological faculties of Mainz, Cologne, Louvain, and Paris, centered not directly on the doctrine of justification by faith alone taken as a doctrine by itself but rather on questions related to free will, the alleged sinfulness of all good works, the role of contrition, confession, and satisfaction in the sacrament of penance, the *ex opere operato* efficacy of the sacraments, the sinfulness of concupiscence, and the value of indulgences. During these years the various points under debate increasingly came to be linked with the question of the teaching authority of the church and especially the teaching authority of the pope.

32. The noted theologian Tommaso de Vio (Cardinal Cajetan) was sent by the pope to deal with Luther's case and met with him at Augsburg in 1518. Arguing on the basis of Scripture, Cajetan maintained that a person's reception of forgiveness is not an object of divine faith since faith bears only on what is revealed in the word of God; that forgiveness of sin is obtained by faith only if faith is animated by charity *(fides caritate formata)*;[57] that the requisite charity is not among "the works of the law" which Paul rejected as a condition for justification; that those who do good works do so with the help of Christ's grace and truly merit under the terms of the new covenant, even though they never put God in their debt; and that good works done with Christ's grace do not satisfy for the guilt of sin, but for the temporal punishment due to sin.[58]

33. Cajetan, unwilling to accuse Luther of heresy, charged him with having made rash assertions on two points. First, he rejected Luther's assertion in the *Ninety-Five Theses* (No. 58) that the merits of Christ do not constitute a treasury for indulgences. Since Pope Clement VI had affirmed in his bull *Unigenitus Dei Filius* (1343) that Christ has acquired for the church a treasure to be dispensed by it for the remission of the temporal punishment due to sins,[59] Cajetan demanded that Luther recant.[60] For Cajetan indulgences were not simply the removal of penalties imposed by the church; in granting indulgences, the church relied on a commission to heal the wounds left in the sinner after forgiveness had been given for Christ's sake and through his merits. Thus Cajetan and others feared that an emphasis on Christ's righteouness alone would lead to minimizing the church's role in communicating his merits to sinners. The second error indicated by Cajetan was what he took to be Luther's position on the kind of faith required by the sacrament of penance. For Cajetan it was excessive to demand that penitents have the certainty of faith that their sins are actually forgiven. "This is to construct a new church."[61]

34. In November 1518 Pope Leo X, at the request of Cajetan, issued the bull *Cum postquam,* in which he set forth the current doctrine on indulgences and demanded that Luther retract any contrary opinions of his own. Before receiving the bull Luther had drafted a canonical appeal from the papacy to a future general council. Then in

July 1519, in the course of a disputation with John Eck at Leipzig, he publicly refused to submit to *Cum postquam* on the ground that it failed to meet the arguments he had advanced from Scripture, the Fathers, and the canons. The debate at Leipzig, having begun with the issues of grace and predestination, climaxed with a disagreement over the teaching authority of popes and councils.[62] Eck believed that he had exposed the tendency of Luther's positions to overthrow the structure of the church.

35. In view of these developments the Holy See determined to take further action. A papal commission, with the help of lists of Luther's errors compiled by the universities of Cologne and Louvain, began to draw up a condemnation. As a result of the commission's work in February and March 1520, Pope Leo X on June 15 issued the bull *Exsurge Domine.* Threatening excommunication, it censured forty-one of Luther's assertions on penance, indulgences, purgatory, sacramental grace, and papal teaching authority as "heretical or scandalous or false or offensive to pious ears, or seductive to simple minds and standing in the way of Catholic faith."[63] Luther's conflict with the late medieval church came to a head later in the same year when he published four reform treatises (*Treatise on Good Works, To the Christian Nobility of the German Nation, The Babylonian Captivity of the Church,* and *The Freedom of a Christian*).[64] Further Roman reaction followed in the bull of excommunication, *Decet Romanum Pontificem* (January 3, 1521). At the subsequent Diet of Worms (January 27–May 25), to which Luther had been summoned to defend his theses before the Emperor Charles V, an imperial ban was imposed on him (Edict of Worms, May 25). In that edict Luther was declared a heretic for teaching a pagan determinism which denied the doctrine of free will.[65]

36. By 1525 the Reformation movement had gained sufficient political support to threaten the unity of the Holy Roman Empire. At the Diet of Speyer in 1526 Emperor Charles V postponed the enforcement of the Edict of Worms in Lutheran territories until a general council could be called to deal with the religious conflict. Consequently the Lutheran movement expanded its influence in Germany and strengthened its foothold through catechetical and liturgical reforms, especially in electoral Saxony.[66]

37. When Charles V invited the Lutherans to present their case at the Diet of Augsburg in 1530, Philip Melanchthon was chosen to draft the Augsburg Confession, which was subsequently approved by Luther, who because of the ban was unable to attend the Diet. Read before the emperor on June 25, 1530, this Confession sought to present the Lutheran position in an irenic form, acceptable to the Roman party. Twenty-one of its articles were devoted to doctrinal questions and seven to church practices. After the first three articles on God, sins, and Christ, the fourth article asserts:

> Our churches also teach that men cannot be justified before God by their own strength, merits, or works but are freely justified for Christ's sake through faith when they believe that they are received into favor and that their sins are forgiven on account of Christ, who by his death made satisfaction for our sins. This faith God imputes for righteousness in his sight (Rom. 3, 4).[67]

Stressing the problem of abuses, the Confession claimed to uphold rather than denigrate ancient traditions and called for further dialogue on controverted matters in the hope of avoiding a schism between Lutherans and Catholics.[68] However, the Confession did not attain its goal.

38. A commission of theologians appointed by the emperor found difficulties in some of the affirmations of the Augsburg Confession. In their report of August 3, 1530, the *Confutatio,*[69] they approved ten of the doctrinal articles, accepted five others with qualifications, and rejected six as deficient. Their objections concerned Lutheran denials of Roman Catholic teachings on original sin, concupiscence, merit, faith animated by love, the necessity of confessing all serious sins one remembers, the value of satisfaction in the sacrament of penance, divinely instituted ecclesiastical order, good works, and invocation of the saints. The doctrine of justification by faith alone was, moreover, described as "diametrically opposed to the evangelical truth, which does not exclude works."[70] The differences were not, however, solely doctrinal, for they also involved church practices (e.g., celibacy, communion under two forms). Although the emperor insisted that theologians from both sides meet in order to overcome the impasse and some rapprochement ensued,[71] no full agreement was reached, and the conflict intensified.

39. Melanchthon was once again commissioned to defend the Lutheran cause. In his Apology of the Augsburg Confession (1530) he argued that "in this controversy the main doctrine of Christianity is involved," viz., the proper distinction between law and gospel grounded in Scripture.[72] Following Luther, who had called this distinction "the greatest skill in Christendom,"[73] Melanchthon explained that justification is the cornerstone of a theology which must always properly distinguish between the two ways in which God deals with the human creature: in the demands of the law God reveals human sin, whereas in his gift of the gospel he promises the righteousness of faith in Christ. Justification must be exclusively attributed to faith, not to the law. "If the doctrine of faith is omitted, it is vain to say that our works are valid by virtue of the suffering of Christ."[74] Ultimately "God pronounces righteous those who believe him from their heart and then have good fruits, which please him because of faith and therefore are a keeping of the law."[75] Frightened consciences are consoled by faith in the benefits of Christ's suffering. "Faith is not merely knowledge but rather a desire to accept and grasp what is offered in the promise of Christ."[76]

40. Melanchthon's detailed argumentation constituted an attack on what he considered to be the Scholastic doctrine, namely, that faith is saving because it is animated by love *(fides caritate formata)*. Rather, faith is saving because it clings to its object, God's promise of forgiveness in the death and resurrection of Jesus Christ. Saving or justifying faith, to be sure, is never alone, never without good works; but it does not justify for that reason. Melanchthon, in contrast to much Scholastic teaching, held that love is a work, indeed "the highest work of the law."[77] Thus the Reformers maintained that love and good works are the necessary fruits of faith, though not its perfecting form, and are the inevitable consequences of forgiveness rather than prior conditions for it. Such assertions were a reply to the accusation that justification by faith alone is an antinomian doctrine which undermines morality.

41. In contrast to a "spiritualist" *(schwärmerisch)* exaltation of the internal word *(verbum internum)*, the Lutheran understanding of justification maintained the priority of the external word *(verbum externum)* and the indispensability of the means of grace through which this faith-creating word is communicated.[78] This principle of the dependence of faith on the external word and the means of grace also enabled Lutherans to defend their retention of postbiblical traditional practices and their refusal to engage in the iconoclasm characteristic of many Protestants. Lutherans contended that some practices such as private confession and absolution should be preserved, since they can be helpful in proclaiming the word and arousing faith. Other practices, such as the use of vestments and the presence of pictures and statues in churches, are in principle *adiaphora*[79] or matters of indifference which need not be abandoned so long as they do not detract from trust in God alone. To insist on their elimination, as the iconoclasts did, was from this Lutheran perspective to fall victim to new forms of legalism and works-righteousness. Similarly, fasting and other ascetic practices and vocations, including celibacy, should not be imposed as law or thought of as earning grace but were nevertheless appropriate as voluntary responses of faith to discipline the body to "perform the duties required by one's calling."[80] Thus because justification by faith served as a criterion against puritan radicalism and not only against rigid traditionalism, Lutheranism was in some respects, as has often been observed, a conservative reforming movement. In the polemical atmosphere of the sixteenth century, however, this openness to tradition was often not emphasized by Lutherans and usually not recognized by Catholics.

42. It would be erroneous, however, to conclude that all Catholic reactions to Luther were negative. There were Catholics who, while accepting papal decisions and authority, also shared some of Luther's ideas. His call for reform of the church was in tune with the wishes of many in the early sixteenth century. The reforming movement was itself no stranger to the papal court, as one may see in the election of Adrian VI (1522–1523) to the papacy and in the creation by Paul III (1534–1549) of a commission of cardinals which made bold though unsuccessful proposals for reform in its *Consilium de emendanda ecclesia.*[81] Furthermore, Luther's conception of justification by faith found a favorable echo in spiritual movements such as those centered in the "oratories of divine love" of Italy and in circles influenced by some of the early Christian humanists. His way of reading Scripture was not uniformly rejected. There were theologians, still faithful to the pope, whose emphasis on the sufficiency of Scripture was similar to his.[82]

43. Yet this was not enough to stem a deterioration of the relationships between Lutherans and Catholics, a deterioration which was powerfully abetted by nontheological factors. In the Reformation lands princes and the rising middle classes profited from the expropriation of monastic and church property and were resistant to any reconciliation which would endanger their financial and political advantages. Violence was used by Lutherans as well as by Catholics in advancing and defending their causes. Such an outcome was perhaps inevitable in a society which had no experience of religious pluralism, in which civil authorities, no matter what their church allegiance, considered it necessary to enforce religious uniformity, and in which much political as well as ecclesiastical power was still held by churchmen. Luther's movement suffered from the traumatic disorders provoked by extremist groups and by the peasant revolts, which often claimed to implement justification by faith by rejecting any kind of church authority, all sacraments, and all political authority.[83] It is not surprising that a Catholic opponent of the Reformation, Johannes Mensing, wrote thus to Melanchthon:

> You, however, with your countless errors, tumult, and false teaching, have brought it to the point where no one believes you, even if once in a while a truthful word escapes you. . . . And truthfully, as was said, that is why we trust you so little when you say something which otherwise could perhaps be tolerated and benevolently interpreted, just as we also understand many sayings of the holy teachers in the best sense.[84]

44. After 1530 the schism between Lutherans and Catholics began to threaten Germany's political stability, and the Lutheran princes formed the Smalcald League (1531) in anticipation of the possible need to defend the Lutheran cause in a religious war. Luther himself believed that reconciliation had become impossible. Instructed by the Saxon court to state the articles of faith which could not be compromised and those which could, Luther drafted the Smalcald Articles for review by the Smalcald League at its meeting in 1537. He declared, as we have already noted,[85] that no concessions could be made on justification by faith. The Mass, practiced as a sacrificial work to earn God's favor, must be rejected, Luther held, because it was a fundamental denial of justification by faith. He further argued that "if the Mass falls, the papacy will fall with it"[86] and that the papal office could never be reformed or made acceptable.[87] On this last point Melanchthon and some of his associates disagreed, saying that they could concede to the pope "that superiority over the bishops which he possesses by human right" provided "he would allow the gospel," that is, justification by faith.[88] Thus although there were differences at Smalcald over the application of the criterion of justification by faith, there was agreement that this doctrine is the ultimate test for church unity.

45. Despite Luther's stance some Lutherans and Catholics continued their efforts at rapprochement. At least on one occasion, at the meeting arranged by Emperor Charles V during the Diet of Regensburg in the spring of 1541, they seemed to reach an understanding on justification. Catholic and Protestant teams, each consisting of three theologians, two princes and two jurists, agreed on common statements concerning the human condition before the fall, free will, the cause of sin, and original sin. After they had discussed justification, they announced on May 2, 1541, that they had agreed on this crucial doctrine.[89]

46. The agreement at Regensburg on justification asserted that no one can be reconciled to God and freed from sin except by the unique mediator Christ who makes individuals sharers *(consortes)* of the divine nature and children of God. These benefits of Christ are not available except by a prevenient motion of the Holy Spirit, moving one to detest sin. This motion is through faith by which the mind, surely believing everything revealed *(tradita)* by God, also most certainly and without doubt assents to the promises given by God.

47. The participants in the Regensburg Colloquy forged a double justification formula, speaking of "inherent righteousness" *(iustitia inhaerens)* or the infusion of charity by which the will is healed, and an "imputed righteousness" *(iustitia imputata)* which is given solely because of Christ's merits. But one may not depend upon communicated, inherent righteousness. Assurance of salvation lies only in the righteousness of Christ by which one is accounted righteous and in the promise of God by which the reborn from the moment of their rebirth are owed eternal life. Although the good works of these children of God merit a reward in this life and in the life to come, nevertheless these good works cannot earn justification. Also with regard to good works, therefore, a form of double justification is involved, for rewards are not given "according to the substance of the works, nor insofar as they are human works, but insofar as they are done in faith and are from the Holy Spirit who dwells in the faithful while our free will concurs as a partial agent."[90]

48. The Regensburg participants disagreed on teaching authority, transubstantiation, confession, and the relation of justification to hierarchical authority. Rome and Luther, however, rejected the results of the Regensburg Colloquy. A papal consistory disapproved of the double justification formula because of its ambiguity; the faithful as well as preachers could be misled.[91] Luther rejected the formula because it attempted to "glue together" *(zusammenleimen)* biblical justification and the Scholastic doctrine of "faith animated by love"; moreover, he still found in the formula traces of free will and other objectionable matters.[92] But while the Regensburg formula failed to reunite Roman Catholics and Lutherans, both the effort and the momentary agreement of theologians and princes on both sides indicate that the two ways of explaining justification are not necessarily exclusive.

49. Luther, who had appealed several times for a general council, wanted one free of papal control. The spread of Lutheran influence in Europe and the fact that many people loyal to Rome sensed the need for drastic reform in doctrinal, moral, and administrative areas eventually led to a widespread demand for a general council. Wars among Catholic rulers and the hesitations of various popes, however, continued to delay the convocation of such a council. After several frustrated attempts and postponements and to avoid an impending war between Lutheran and Catholic territories in Germany, Paul III in 1542 called a council to meet at Trent, south of the Alps. It was actually convened on December 13, 1545. The Lutherans were absent, however, because their condition that it should be "free, general, and not a papal council" had not been met.[93] Luther's death, which occurred on February 18, 1546, and the Smalcald War, which erupted in the same year, made prospects for rapprochement even less likely.

50. Twenty-five sessions were held at Trent in three periods and under three popes: 1545–1547 (sess. I–X), 1551–1552 (XI–XVI), and 1562–1563 (XVII–XXV). Addressing themselves simultaneously to right doctrine and church reform, the council fathers reaffirmed the Nicene-Constantinopolitan Creed as the basis of Catholic faith and dealt extensively with such topics as the canon of Scripture and its relation to apostolic traditions, original sin, justification, grace and merit, the sacraments, eucharistic presence, communion under both forms, the sacrifice of the Mass, purgatory, the cult of saints, and indulgences. The debate on justification began on June 22, 1546, and the decree was promulgated on January 13, 1547.

51. The Council of Trent taught that original sin is a condition affecting "the whole human race" and that such sin, and the punishment due to it, are remitted by the grace of baptism. The council fathers distinguished original sin from concupiscence, which remains in those baptized. Concupiscence "comes from sin and leads to sin," but it is not by its mere presence a sin before it is freely consented to. Here Trent thought it was standing with Augustine and against Luther.[94]

52. In its teaching on justification the Council of Trent reaffirmed the unique role of Christ who died for all and who grants grace "through the merits of his passion" to those reborn in him, and without rebirth in him one can never be justified.[95] The Council further taught that "nothing prior to justification, whether faith or works, truly merits *(promeretur)* the grace of justification."[96] Moreover, in the process leading to the justification of the adult sinner, priority belongs to "the predisposing grace of God [given] through Christ Jesus."[97] The sinner indeed cooperates with this grace, at least in the sense of not sinfully rejecting it. Influenced by grace and enlightened by the Holy Spirit, the sinner believes the truth of God's revelation and God's promises, especially that the unjustified are justified by the grace of God in Jesus Christ.[98]

53. In a central paragraph the Council of Trent expounded the nature of justification with the help of Scholastic causal categories.[99] The final cause is the glory of God and of Christ, and eternal life. The efficient cause is the merciful God who freely cleanses and sanctifies, sealing and anointing by the Holy Spirit. The meritorious cause is

Jesus Christ, who by his passion merited our justification and made satisfaction for us to God the Father. The formal cause is "the righteousness of God—not that whereby God is righteous but that whereby he makes us righteous."[100] The justified sinner is not only reckoned righteous but is truly called righteous and is righteous, since one receives righteousness according to the free generosity of the Holy Spirit and in proportion to one's own dispositions and cooperation.

54. In its description of justification Trent insisted on the primacy of faith. "'Faith is the beginning of human salvation,' the foundation and root of all justification, 'without which it is impossible to please God.'"[101] But faith, although unconditionally necessary for justification, is not living unless

> through the Holy Spirit the charity of God is poured into their hearts . . . and inheres in them. Hence in justification itself one receives through Christ, into whom one is engrafted, along with the forgiveness of sins, all these [gifts] infused at the same time: faith, hope and charity. For faith, unless hope and charity be added to it, neither unites one perfectly with Christ, nor makes one a living member of his body.[102]

Thanks to this justification, received through the grace of Christ, human beings are renewed, and "as faith cooperates with good works [cf. Jas. 2:22], they grow and are further justified."[103]

55. The council went on to affirm that a person who is justified can still fall into sin and, having sinned, cannot be sure of future repentance.[104] The identity of the predestined remains a mystery hidden in God.[105] Finally, to avoid the suspicion that stress on faith and on works performed in grace might derogate from the saving power of Christ, Trent asserted: "Far be it from Christians to trust or glory in themselves and not in the Lord [cf. 1 Cor. 1:31; 2 Cor. 10:17], whose bounty toward all is so great that he wishes his own gifts to be their merits."[106]

56. The first part of the last statement can be read as open to the central insistence of the Reformers that believers should look entirely to God and not at all to their own accumulation of merits for salvation, while the second implies (as the decree on justification elsewhere explicitly states)[107] that, faithful to his promise, God finally judges human beings "not apart from" the merits he gives them. Nonetheless Trent and later Roman Catholicism frequently failed to stress the first concern (that of the Reformation), whereas Lutherans regarded the Catholic doctrine of merit as undermining trust in God alone for salvation. The Tridentine decree on justification, with its own way of insisting on the primacy of grace *(quae virtus* [*Christi*] *bona eorum opera semper antecedit),*[108] is not necessarily incompatible with the Lutheran doctrine of *sola fide,* even though Trent excluded this phrase. Part of the reason for this exclusion was, it seems, to deny that human beings can rely for assurance of salvation on knowledge or experience of their own faith rather than on Christ. Moreover, Trent insisted that "the good deeds of one justified are gifts of God" in such a way that they are also "the good merits of that same justified person" and that the justified person "by the good deeds which are done by him, through the grace of God, and the merit of Jesus Christ (of whom he is a living member) truly merits an increase of grace, eternal life, and the attainment of that eternal life (if indeed he die in grace), as well as an increase in glory."[109]

57. In its doctrinal as well as in its reform decrees, the Council of Trent recognized that the Reformation critique of the state of the church was at least partly justified. In particular, its reaffirmation of the primacy of grace in the role of justification and salvation assured that the anti-Pelagian intention of the classic Augustinian tradition not be lost.

58. After the Council of Trent the final statements on justification and related issues in the Lutheran Confessions were not replies to that council but were concerned with intra-Lutheran problems. Following Luther's death in 1546, Lutherans in Germany were torn by conflicts over the proper interpretation of Luther's "chief article."[110] In a series of theological controversies "Gnesio-Lutherans" (disciples of the "authentic" Luther) and "Philippists" (disciples of Melanchthon) struggled for formulations which would preserve the preeminence of justification and at the same time make it of controlling importance for other doctrines, especially original sin, human freedom, good works, and the proper distinction between law and gospel. The Formula of Concord (1577) tried to settle these controversies.[111]

59. In their attempt to establish Lutheran unity, the authors of the Formula increasingly moved towards a purely forensic[112] understanding of justification as the divine reckoning which must be carefully distinguished from any intrinsic human righteousness. This was not done primarily in opposition to Roman Catholics but against some Lutherans who understood justification as the indwelling of Christ's divine nature in the believer. The Formula, on the other hand, insisted strongly on the distinction between the "imputed righteousness of faith" *(imputata fidei iustitia)* and the "inchoate righteousness of the new obedience of faith" *(inchoata iustitia novae obedientiae seu bonorum operum).* Only the former counts before God, whereas the latter follows justification. Although the latter should be preached to Christians, it is too imperfect and impure to stand before the divine tribunal.[113] Although the primary intention of the distinction was not to attack Trent, the opposition is unmistakable.

60. This tendency to objectify justification as a forensic act created difficulties for the framers of the Formula when they attempted to recast traditional teachings on original sin, human freedom, and good works. When radical Gnesio-Lutherans contended that justification by faith alone excluded any notion of natural human good, or when some Philippists, at the opposite end of the spectrum, argued that free will cooperates with the justifying and faith-creating work of the Holy Spirit, the Formula had recourse to medieval Scholastic terminology and Aristotelian philosophical categories in order to mediate this controversy over synergism. Distinctions similar to those employed by medieval theologians were made between the human "substance" *(substantia),* created in the image of God, and original sin inhering in fallen human nature as "accident" *(accidens).* In this way the Formula sought to assert a deep and unspeakable corruption of human nature in all its parts and powers but not a destruction or substantial transformation of human nature in the fall.[114] Quite aware of their inability to settle all controversies through new formulations, the authors of the Formula kept reminding the feuding factions that Lutheran theology was to be guided by Luther's injunction to distinguish between law and gospel so that Christians find true comfort in the benefits of Christ rather than in their own righteousness.[115]

61. The theological distinction between law and gospel raised questions about the relation of law to the chronology of the life of the justified. Does the distinction between divine demand and divine promise lead to an end of the law at some point in time? Luther, holding to his view of the justified person as simultaneously righteous and sinful *(simul iustus et peccator),* stressed only two uses of the law: one is for the restraint of sin through political authority *(usus legis politicus);* the other is for the disclosure of sin through accusation and exhortation (*usus legis theologicus* or *paedagogicus,* which is also called *elenchticus*). Under the pressure of antinomian controversies, the Formula of Concord, apparently fearing a separation between law and gospel, which would lead to individualistic "enthusiasm" *(Schwärmerei),* held that believers "require the teaching of the law"; under the heading of "the third function of the law," it insisted on the preaching of the law to believers "so that they will not be thrown back on their own holiness and piety and under the pretext of the Holy Spirit's guidance set up a self-elected service of God without his Word and command."[116]

62. The Formula also took a stand against what its authors understood to be the Calvinist doctrine of predestination to damnation as well as to salvation. It speaks only of "our eternal election to salvation" and insists that this should be preached only in order to console consciences: "If anyone so sets forth this teaching concerning God's gracious election that sorrowing Christians can find no comfort in it but are driven to despair, . . . then it is clearly evident that this teaching is not being set forth according to the Word and will of God."[117] Because of this focus on pastoral concerns, on consoling consciences, the Formula viewed itself as in agreement with Luther, even though it avoided the strongly predestinarian language which he employed in such treatises as the *Bondage of the Will.*[118]

63. Thus the Formula of Concord and Trent seem closer to each other on the role of morality and law in Christian life, the nature of sin, the primacy of grace, and even the role of faith than were Luther and the "Pelagianizers" whom he chiefly attacked. Yet the interconfessional polemics remained much the same. Lutheran controversialists argued that Pelagianism and works-righteousness were in fact concealed under what they regarded as Trent's specious use of biblical and Augustinian language,[119] while the Catholics, on their side, generally ignored the careful formulations of the Lutheran Confessions and continued to repeat unchanged the earlier charges of antinomianism, Manichaeism, determinism, and the denial of sacraments.[120]

C. After the Sixteenth Century

64. In the last four hundred years both the Roman Catholic and the Lutheran churches have continued to affirm their sixteenth-century pronouncements on justification. Since the Council of Trent and the *Book of Concord,* Lutheran theologians have usually claimed that the doctrine is of central importance but have interpreted it in a variety of ways; Roman Catholics, although debating the issues of sin, freedom, nature, and grace, have for the most part not made justification itself a primary object of attention. In both cases, furthermore, the discussions have been chiefly within, rather than between, the two communions.

65. Seventeenth-century Lutheran Orthodoxy attempted to bring systematic clarity to the Lutheran Confessions included in the *Book of*

Concord (1580). To solve the problem of the relationship between justification as an objective forensic act and the individual's apprehension of it (subjective justfication), Lutheran dogmaticians developed various theories about the "order of salvation" *(ordo salutis).* While justification retained its forensic character, at least in theory, attention tended to shift to more subjective aspects of the process of salvation. Melanchthon's description of faith, involving knowledge of objective truth, assent to that truth, and trust of the heart (*notitia, assensus,* and *fiducia*) was now analytically expanded into an order which introduced such categories as gospel call, illumination, conversion, regeneration, renewal, mystical union, sanctification, good works, preservation, and glorification. The teaching about justification by faith was shifted to the section in dogmatics on practical theology *(gratia applicatrix).* In the opinion of some interpreters, Lutheran Orthodoxy came to think of justification in a framework similar to that of Trent in that Orthodoxy used Scholastic terminology and viewed justification in the context of an order of salvation.[121] This was a partial return to transformationist modes of thought, but it tended to sharpen the remaining differences over the specifically forensic character of justification as an act distinct from sanctification.

66. A few Catholic theologians in the seventeenth century (e.g., Lessius, Petavius, Thomassinus), assisted by their studies in the Greek patristic tradition, expanded on Trent's teaching regarding the divinizing presence of the Holy spirit in justification. In general, however, Catholic theology in the post-Tridentine period concentrated on the nature and causes of created grace. Prolonged and bitter disputes broke out regarding the question how grace, while being infallibly efficacious, could leave intact the freedom of the recipient. Some, such as Luis de Molina, S.J., maintained that the decree of predestination to glory *(praedestinatio praecise ad gloriam)* is logically subsequent to divine foreknowledge of a person's merits, while others, such as Domingo Báñez, O.P., held that this decree is prior to any foreseen merits. The opposing schools accused one another of Pelagian and Lutheran tendencies, but Rome intervened and forbade either of these positions to be branded as heretical.[122]

67. Yet there were positions that Rome would not tolerate. Michel de Bay (Baius) and Cornelius Jansen (Jansenius), taking a very pessimistic view of the effects of the fall, emphasized divine predestination almost to the exclusion of human cooperation. Their positions were condemned by Rome in 1567 and 1653 respectively. In so doing, Rome rejected as heretical the view that Christ died only for the predestined.[123] This condemnation was an emphatic reassertion of the reality of God's universal salvific will. In 1713 Rome condemned one hundred and one propositions taken from the writings of the Jansenist Pasquier Quesnel. Some of these propositions relating to justification can be seen as similar to Lutheran statements, for example, "Without the grace of the Liberator, the sinner is not free except to do evil" and "Under the curse of the law, good is never done, for one sins either by doing evil or by avoiding it simply out of fear (Gal. 5:18)."[124]

68. Partly as a result of the voyages of discovery to the Americas and to the East, the question of the salvation of infidels became acute. The adversaries of Jansenism reached a consensus that justification lay within reach of the unevangelized, who were included in God's saving will. Agreeing that faith was necessary for salvation, theologians disputed about the kind of saving faith pagans could have. In opposition to certain liberal views, the Holy Office in 1679 denied that "faith in the broad sense *(fides late dicta),* based on the witness of creatures or some such motive, is sufficient for justification."[125]

69. Much of the spiritual literature of the seventeenth and eighteenth centuries continued to emphasize both the primacy of faith as "the only proximate means of union with God" (St. John of the Cross) and, especially in the circles influenced by Cardinal de Bérulle, the centrality of Christ.[126] Even authors who had no connection with "quietism" stressed self-abandonment to divine providence and renunciation of self, of spiritual consolations, and of personal merits. "Trust in God alone" (Henri-Marie Boudon) and "It is God who does everything" (Jean-Martin Moye)[127] often acted as correctives to an exuberant piety which sometimes took peculiar forms not unlike the decoration of rococo churches. Thus despite the prevalence of anti-Reformation themes in the dominant official theology of the period, there remained currents within Catholicism which had affinities with several of the basic ideas of the Reformers.

70. In the same centuries Lutheran Pietism called for major changes in the understanding of justification in Lutheran Orthodoxy. Thus the movement in Germany and later in Scandinavia was more concerned with the experiential impact of justification on the individual person than with a systematic description of justification in an *ordo salutis.* Emphasizing rebirth, evidenced by a conversion experience, and sanctification, measured by external tests of conduct, the Pietists in effect de-emphasized forensic justification in which an individual is *declared* righteous in favor of stressing how an individual is *made* righteous. Justification therefore was seen as identical with the rebirth of the sinner who has experienced the "penitential struggle" *(Busskampf)* precipitated by the saving work of God.[128]

71. Whereas Pietism emphasized the individual experience of justification in rebirth and sanctification, Enlightenment theologians of the eighteenth century, such as Semler, no longer viewed justification as an essential Christian doctrine. Reflecting a rationalistic anthropology which minimized sin and stressed the prowess of the natural creature and the ability of individuals to control their destiny, these theologians taught that righteous conduct, in accord with natural morality and the teaching of Jesus, brings salvation. It seemed sufficient to acknowledge God as the father of humankind, to follow Jesus as the teacher of universal moral values, and to experience the Holy Spirit as the power which prompts human beings to lead a better moral life.[129]

72. In the nineteenth and twentieth centuries, however, there has been renewed attention to the Reformation docrine of justification with its concern for sin and forgiveness. Schleiermacher, Ritschl, Kähler, Althaus, Elert, Prenter, Aulén, Tillich, and Barth, among other Protestants, have dealt extensively with the doctrine in a wide variety of ways.[130] Meanwhile, Möhler, Newman, Scheeben, Rahner, and Küng, among others, contributed to the development of Catholic thought on this topic.[131] Further, exegetes such as Schlatter, Bultmann, and Käsemann have emphasized the biblical importance of the doctrine,[132] and the renaissance of Luther studies in the last hundred years has made Catholics and Protestants increasingly aware that at the heart of the Lutheran Reformation was not a value such as freedom of conscience or individual autonomy, or even the principle *sola scriptura,* but rather justification by faith. Finally, the growth of dialogue in recent decades between Catholics and the heirs of the Reformation has stimulated research into the interconfessional aspects of justification. Each of these developments could be profitably explored at length, but for our purposes it is the recent statements of the churches and certain emphases in contemporary theology which are of primary importance. The problem of justification was addressed in indirect ways by the Second Vatican Council; the Assembly of the Lutheran World Federation in 1963 took up justification as a major theme. Some comments on these treatments and on the current theological situation are in order before we turn to our own reflections.

D. Recent History

1. Vatican Council II

73. Vatican II gave little explicit attention to the theme of justification, but it touched on the subject indirectly in its teachings on matters such as faith, grace, salvation, and the ministry of the church. By broadening the definition of faith beyond intellectualistic concepts that had been prevalent in modern Scholasticism, the council left open the possibility that faith might include the entire response of the faithful to justifying grace.[133] In its references to cooperation and merit, the council showed sensitivity to Protestant concerns and to the need of resisting any Pelagianizing tendencies that might exist among Catholics.

74. In its Constitution on the Church the council set the traditional doctrines of grace, hope, cooperation, merit, and prayer for the dead in an ecclesiological and eschatological framework. The renewal of creation is seen as anticipated in a real way, so that even in its pilgrim state the church is marked by "genuine though imperfect holiness."[134] Christians should remember, however, that their dignity is "to be attributed not to their own merits, but to the special grace of Christ."[135] Thanks to the gift of the Holy Spirit, the baptized can look forward to their salvation in hope. They are linked to the heavenly church in the hope that, when "judged according to their works," they may be numbered among the blessed.[136] The saints in heaven "show forth the merits which they won on earth through the one Mediator between God and man, Christ Jesus (cf. 1 Tim. 2:5)."[137]

75. Vatican II stressed that Christ is the one mediator[138] who made "the perfect satisfaction needed for our reconciliation."[139] Christ associates the work of the church with himself and is present by his power in the sacraments, so that the liturgy is an exercise of Christ's own priesthood.[140] He is present likewise in the proclamation of the gospel, which is seen as the principal ministry of bishops and of priests.[141] This understanding of Christ as the one who above all acts in the liturgy involves a different view of the Eucharist from the one the Reformers had in mind when they attacked the sacrifice of the Mass as a human work.

76. Further, to participate in the liturgy one must have accepted the gospel in faith and repentance.[142] The sacraments, inseparable from the ministry of the word,[143] are rightly called "sacraments of faith," for they presuppose faith and nourish, strengthen, and express it.[144] By taking part in the praise and worship offered by the church, the faithful receive the grace of Christ.[145] They are required to cooperate with that grace "lest they receive it in vain (cf. 2 Cor. 6:1)."[146] This stress on cooperation or "active participation" in worship is in some respects similar to Luther's concern for personal faith in connection with the reception of the Lord's Supper.[147] For purposes of the present dialogue it is also significant that Vatican II envisaged the church as "embracing sinners in her bosom" and as "always in need of being purified."[148] It pursues "the path of penance and renewal,"[149] for, as an earthly and human institution, it stands in need of "continual reformation," whether in conduct, in discipline, or in the formulation of doctrine.[150]

77. Of no less significance is the emphasis placed by Vatican II on the word of God and especially on Scripture as sources of life and energy for the church.[151] Paul is quoted as teaching that the gospel "is the power of God unto salvation to everyone who believes, to Jew first and then to Greek (Rom. 1:16)."[152] The church and its *magisterium* are held to be under the word of God.[153] Holy Scripture, as the word of God "consigned to writing under the inspiration of the Holy Spirit,"[154] is accorded a certain priority over tradition. While acknowledging the supremacy of Christ and the gospel over all that could be set against them, the council did not anticipate that there could be ultimate conflicts between gospel and church. Vatican II embodies the traditional Catholic position that Christ, by the assistance promised in the gospel, keeps the teaching of the church faithful to revelation by the power of the Holy Spirit.[155]

2. Catholic Theology Since World War II

78. In the features just noted Vatican II reflects the general character of Catholic theology since the Second World War. Without making any radical break with earlier Catholic tradition and the doctrine of Trent, recent Catholic theologians have sought to distance themselves from the thought forms of late Scholasticism as being too individualistic, intellectualistic, abstract, and legalistic. Catholic theology has been seeking to renew itself through a return to biblical categories together with a more personalistic and historical emphasis. The contemporary tendency is to look upon conversion as a conscious response of the whole person to God's gracious call in Christ; to view grace primarily as the loving self-communication of the triune God; to stress that in sacramental worship the faithful share in the communal life of Christ's mystical body; and to regard merit and satisfaction as features of the pilgrim existence of believers as they are drawn by God to eternal life. This changing climate in Catholic theology has opened up new possibilities of encountering, and profiting from, the Reformation theology of justification.[156] The adequacy of polemical statements made in the atmosphere of the Counter Reformation can no longer be taken for granted.

79. Among influential contemporary Catholic theologians, Karl Rahner may be given special mention. His theology emphasizes the primacy and centrality of Christ in the whole order of creation and redemption. Grace is not to be understood primarily as a created quality (i.e., as sanctifying grace), but rather as God making himself personally present in the Spirit in merciful love (and thus as "uncreated grace"). Insofar as the human subject is never fully delivered from the deleterious effects of the fall, there is a sense in which one may speak of the justified as *simul iustus et peccator.* The free human response to grace, for Rahner, does not diminish the primacy of grace, for the act whereby grace is accepted is itself a gift of grace.[157] Without holding that explicit faith in the gospel is essential for the justification of adults, he maintains that every movement toward justification, sanctification, or salvation is a free gift of God through Christ, transforming human consciousness and thus involving the active receptivity of faith. Proceeding from a *solus Christus,* Rahner believes that he has affirmed in a Catholic context much of what has traditionally been understood by the Reformation principles of *sola gratia* and *sola fide.*[158] His Christocentric approach offers some parallels to the Reformation view that the article of justification is nothing other than "applied Christology" and contributes to significant convergences between Lutheran and Catholic theologians.

80. A number of Catholic theologians, including Rahner, have attempted to build into Catholic theology a more vivid appreciation of the word of God. They depict the word not simply as a preliminary condition for the sacramental conferral of grace, but as a dialogic event in which God's justifying power is made present and active under the conditions of history.[159] This position represents a conscious rapprochement with certain strands in Lutheran theology.

81. The most recent Catholic theology is marked by a growing concern to overcome any suspicion of individualism or privatism in the theology of grace. The free and gracious gift of justification, according to Edward Schillebeeckx, cannot be experienced except by those who lose themselves for the sake of others.[160] The Uruguayan liberation theologian, Juan Luis Segundo, warns that a paralyzing concern for one's personal justification could distract one from the communal task of building the kingdom.[161] The Brazilian Leonardo Boff, although concerned to remain in continuity with the Council of Trent, prefers to speak of liberation rather than justification. The term *liberation,* he holds, designates the same reality, but "now elaborated in terms of its dynamic, historical dimensions."[162] These themes from contemporary

Catholic political theology and liberation theology converge, as we shall presently see, with the stress on corporate service in certain recent Lutheran theologies of justification.

3. The Helsinki Assembly of the Lutheran World Federation

82. World Lutheranism has had no counterpart to Vatican II, but the Fourth Assembly of the Lutheran World Federation in Helsinki, Finland (1963), gave particular attention to justification. Considerable work was done by its Commission of Theology from 1952 on, and the Assembly itself dealt with the topic in addresses, discussions, and its report.

83. Although official dialogue between the Lutheran and Roman Catholic churches had not begun,[163] a preparatory *Study Document "On Justification"*[164] noted that, while the Reformation doctrine had been hammered out in debate with the Church of Rome, Rome was now changing, as can be seen in "the renewal of biblical studies" and the "liturgical movement." Furthermore, problems were posed for traditional Lutheran understandings, it was said, by historical study of the Bible, the "greater variety and diversity among the biblical writers" which "we now see," erosion of theological terms, changes in cultural climate (including a more anthropocentric emphasis and the loss of eschatology), and the fact that "the Gospel can be proclaimed without . . . the word Justification." Exposition of the doctrine followed the approach of the Augsburg Confession; new accents were provided by the stress on the Old Testament (¶¶ 46–48), Jesus (¶¶ 49–51), and "use of the terms 'justify' and 'justification' in the earliest period of the Christian community" prior to Paul (¶ 52). The theological analysis showed that Lutherans now, as in the sixteenth century, do not understand the *sola fide* as minimizing the means of grace; faith takes shape in a church with Ministry and sacraments. Not surprisingly, the social dimension of the good works which flow from faith was emphasized more than in the past; the "new obedience" includes opposition to the materialism of modern culture, to nationalism, and to divisions of race and caste.

84. At Helsinki addresses and discussion groups took up the theme.[165] The Reformation witness to justification was said to have been in a threefold "Babylonian captivity" of "doctrinalization, individualization, and spiritualization." Hence justification should be understood as focusing on the entire human race and on "amnesty for all." God's power "takes hold of the whole world . . . and subjects it to his righteousness." This universalist emphasis parallels a similar concern on the Catholic side (see above, 78). The opposition between forensic and transformationist views of justification was questioned: "The old alternative whether the sinner is considered justified . . . 'forensically'—or . . . 'effectively'—is begging the question," for God's action brings about "rebirth." Another address insisted that the "act through which God forgives is at the same time that act through which God renews."[166]

85. It has sometimes been concluded that at Helsinki Lutherans failed to agree or say anything significant about justification. A summary statement prepared during the sessions was presented to the Assembly but was merely "received" rather than approved, though the next year it was published by the Commission with only minor revisions.[167] In part, the negative reactions at the Assembly stemmed from procedural matters, over what the status of such a statement would be (the *magisterium* question), and whether this particular draft represented fully the twenty-six group discussions. In part, the concern was also with structure and tone.[168] Some found fault with the traditional language, the absence of attention to the Old Testament,[169] or the lack of emphasis on fresh approaches from the New Testament exegetes.

86. The resulting document from Helsinki, *Justification Today,* suggests that the world's current question is no longer about "a gracious God" but about the "meaning of life" (¶¶ 1–4). Yet justification is still said to be central, for the fact "that Christ is with sinners and lives as true man in the midst of the godless, . . . gives courage to believe in the justification of man before God" (¶¶ 5–8). The church with its sacraments is built upon such faith (¶¶ 9–10). Justification creates fellowship, a church in service to the world (¶¶ 11–15). A new life lived in faith must follow (¶¶ 16–24), "a new courage to be" which conquers meaninglessness (¶¶ 25–29).

87. Some of the insights expressed at Helsinki have proved fruitful in later discussions, including our own, but perhaps the main importance of the Assembly is that it alerted Lutherans to a need for further consideration of the cardinal theme of justification. This need was apparent from the "free and persistent expressions of differences of opinion" by voices from around the world, especially "Africa and Asia, desirous of bridging immediately the gap between the timely Augsburg Confession of 430 years ago and an explication of the faith of Lutherans for the man of today."[170] What "made it impossible to write a satisfactory theological document on such an important subject in a mere ten days" was the very "vigor and involvement of the assembly." "A healthy discussion had begun" and, according to one prediction, "It will continue. . . ." One may regard the present dialogue between Lutherans and Catholics as part of that continuation.

4. A Lutheran Hermeneutical Perspective

88. A further development in the understanding of the Reformation doctrine of justification is rooted in such historical studies of Luther's hermeneutics as those of Karl Holl and Gerhard Ebeling.[171] Although of little direct importance at Helsinki, this development has since become increasingly influential. It focuses on the hermeneutical insights which lay at the root of Luther's proposal of justification by faith alone and helps clarify why this doctrine functions as a critical principle in judging all thought and practice. The central point is that the proclamation of God's grace in word and sacrament is itself the saving event in that it announces the death and resurrection of Jesus Christ. God's word does what it proclaims or, in modern terminology, the gospel message is performative; it effects the reality of which it speaks. The preaching of the gospel has the force of decreeing the forgiveness of sins for Christ's sake. Like a will or testament, it makes human beings heirs of the promise quite apart from what they deserve. God's word accomplishes what it says in the very act of being proclaimed.

89. In this hermeneutical perspective even the faith which receives the promise is not a condition for justification. It is not a human achievement, but it is rather a free gift created and bestowed in the power of the Holy Spirit by the justifying word to which it clings. Justification is unconditional in the sense that the justifying word effects its own reception. In a similar vein, the Apology says: "For if the promise were conditional upon our merits and the law, which we never keep, it would follow that the promise is useless. Since we obtain justification through a free promise, however, it follows that we cannot justify ourselves. Otherwise, why would a promise be necessary?"[172]

90. This hermeneutical understanding of justification can be termed forensic but not in the sense that it gives exclusive primacy to one image for the saving action of God in Christ over others. Particular images, however, are of special usefulness for particular purposes, and judicial or forensic ones are of prime importance when emphasizing the proclamatory character of justification. There are various ways of expressing that God's promises are themselves unconditional, but this is done with particular pointedness by saying that God declares or imputes an alien righteousness, that of Christ, to wholly undeserving sinners.

91. Whatever the imagery, the affirmation that God's word saves by being declared introduces sharp discontinuities into theologies that are centered on justification by faith. When, for example, justification is seen wholly as a liberating gift bestowed in proclamation, the will cannot be said to have any freedom in itself; it is in bondage, as Luther says, in relation "to those things which are above us."[173] Similarly, it is in hearing the gospel that believers recognize the gravity of sin and their situation as *simul iusti et peccatores.* Because they look only to the promise of forgiveness in Christ, they can see nothing in themselves that is good before God *(coram deo).* To be sure, when human beings are viewed in comparison with one other *(coram hominibus),* it is appropriate to speak of them as having free will and varying degrees of goodness, but before God all "righteousnesses are filthy rags" (Isa. 64:6 KJV). Thus salvation as a product of God's creative word is, in this perspective, radically discontinuous with fallen nature.[174] It is a new creation, not a transformation or perfecting of the old.

92. This emphasis on the proclamatory character of justification does not result in an uncatholic narrowing of the Christian reality. Faith is not excluded, for the justifying promise is received by faith alone. The word and sacraments are not excluded, for it is through them that the promise is declared. "Love and good works must also follow faith. So they are not excluded. . . . "[175]

The doctrines of justification, of the word and sacraments, and of the church (which for Luther was a "mouth house" that exists to proclaim the gospel)[176] are inseparable. Justification by faith is emphasized not primarily by speaking of the doctrine but by so teaching and acting within the church that Christians are constantly directed to God's promises in word and sacrament from which all else flows. Thus Luther says little directly about the doctrine of justification in his sermons and catechisms, but the doctrine is nevertheless constantly present as the hermeneutical guide for the presentation of all other teachings. This hermeneutical guide, furthermore, may be operative even when the doctrine of justification by faith alone is not articulated. Such saints as Gregory, Bernard, Francis, and Bonaventure, Luther says, ultimately relied wholly on God for salvation despite their errors in theology and practice.[177]

93. While this hermeneutical interpretation of the doctrine of justification is suggested especially by Luther's early writings, it was largely forgotten in later Lutheranism and even now is often not understood. Yet it is important for our purposes because, while it conflicts with Scholastic approaches, whether Catholic or Lutheran, it also converges in part with certain recent trends in Catholic sacramental and kerygmatic theology (cf. 77 and 80, above).

CHAPTER TWO
REFLECTION AND INTERPRETATION

94. As we now turn from historical considerations to an examination of the contemporary relations of Roman Catholics and Lutherans on the question of justification, it is evident that many of the difficulties have arisen from the contrasting concerns and patterns of thought in the two traditions. In the polemical atmosphere of the past, these differences gave rise to fears and were interpreted as conflicts, but the development of ecumenical dialogue, historical research, and new modes of theological thinking enable us to consider the possibility that these patterns may in part be complementary and, even if at times in unavoidable tension, not necessarily divisive. In this second part of the report, therefore, we shall describe and interpret the historical concerns and thought patterns of Lutheran and Catholic understandings of justification before we turn in the third part to a consideration of convergences in biblical exegesis and theological understanding.

95. Lutherans generally emphasize God's address to sinners in the good news of Christ's life, death, and resurrection; theology and doctrine should serve proclamation so as to exclude reliance on self for salvation. They therefore focus on safeguarding the absolute priority of God's redeeming word in Jesus Christ. The unconditionality of God's love for fallen humankind implies that the fulfillment of the promise of salvation depends on nothing else but the gift of faith by which believers trust in God. Catholics, while not rejecting the absolute priority of God's saving action, are generally speaking more concerned with acknowledging the efficacy of God's saving work in the renewal and sanctification of the created order, an efficacy which Lutherans, for their part, do not deny.

96. These different concerns entail notably different patterns of thought and discourse. The Catholic concerns are most easily expressed in the transformationist language appropriate to describing a process in which human beings, created good but now sinful, are brought to new life through God's infusion of saving grace.[178] Grace, as the medieval adage has it, does not destroy but perfects nature.[179] Lutheran ways of speaking, on the other hand, are shaped by the situation of sinners standing before God *(coram deo)* and hearing at one and the same time God's words of judgment and forgiveness in law and gospel. Attention is here focused on this discontinuous, paradoxical, and simultaneous double relation of God to the justified, not the continuous process of God's transforming work.

97. These different concerns and thought patterns entail different ways of speaking and thinking about points such as (1) the imputational or forensic character of justification, (2) the sinfulness of the justified, (3) the sufficiency of faith, (4) merit, (5) satisfaction, and (6) the criteria by which Christian life and doctrine are to be judged. On each of these questions we shall make brief observations, while fully recognizing that our generalizations cannot do justice to the complexity of the questions and the variety of theological positions that are possible within each tradition.

98. *1. Forensic Justification.* Lutherans describe justification as the imputation to sinners of a righteousness which is that of Christ himself *(iustitia aliena),* received in faith. Justification therefore is the forensic act whereby God declares the sinner just; it is an act performed outside of us *(extra nos)* by which faith is accounted as righteousness. Looking on God's declaration as efficacious, Lutherans also affirm the reality of sanctification and good works, but they regard these effects as fruits rather than parts of justification itself. In this sense the Lutheran doctrine of imputed righteousness is intended to safeguard the unconditional character of God's promises in Christ.

99. Catholics agree that God's saving will has no cause outside himself and that therefore salvation in its totality, as an effect of that will, is unconditional.[180] But they see this totality as including a number of elements, some of which are conditional upon others. Thus justification depends on faith, which in turn depends on the word of God, mediated through the Scriptures and the church (cf. Rom. 10:13–17). Receptivity to God's saving word requires that the seed fall on good soil and that the hearer be not deaf (cf. Matt. 13:1–9 par.). In the execution of God's saving plan, therefore, there may be conditions, which, without restricting God's power and freedom, condition the created effects of his powerful decrees. In efficaciously willing the effect, of course, God also wills the conditions and provides for their realization. With regard to the centrality of justification, Catholics agree with the Lutheran insistence that the truth of the gospel is saving truth and that Christology must be seen not statically but dynamically as God's deed "for us and for our salvation." But Catholics hesitate to trace everything to justification considered simply as a forensic act. They are often inclined to emphasize other images or concepts such as the remission of sin, adoption, redemption, regeneration, healing, sanctification, reconciliation, new creation, and salvation.

100. Although Catholics recognize the possibility of organizing one's theology about the theme of justification, they commonly fear that emphasis on forensic justification or imputed righteousness, if not accompanied by other themes, could unintentionally encourage a certain disregard of the benefits actually imparted through God's loving deed in Christ. Lutherans, conversely, fear that the Catholic emphasis on the non-forensic aspects could tend to throw believers back on their own resources. On this, as on other points, each tradition wishes to guard against what the other sees as weaknesses and is convinced that it can do so within its own framework.

101. Characteristic of the two traditions are different approaches to the relationship between the remission of sins and the transformation wrought by grace. Catholics have tended to look on the infusion of grace as a cause of the forgiveness of sins and sanctification.[181] Lutherans can admit that this Catholic understanding of the infusion of grace does not necessarily imply that justification is dependent on sanctification in such a way as to undermine confidence in God and induce an anxiety-ridden reliance on the uncertain signs of grace in one's own life. Yet they are likely to think that the traditional Catholic emphasis on the infusion of grace makes it difficult to express adequately the unmerited character of God's forgiving mercy. For them God's justifying act of forgiveness is itself the cause or constant power of renewal throughout the life of the believer. Catholics, conversely, may think that the Lutheran position is too narrowly focused on the "consolation of terrified consciences" and does not take sufficient account of the doxological dimension of the response of faith, i.e., of the praise of God for his transformative indwelling.

102. *2. Sinfulness of the Justified.* Lutherans maintain that the sinfulness of the justified is revealed simultaneously with the forensic act of justification. Thus the justified see themselves as in a true sense sinners *(simul iusti et peccatores).* While granting that justification unfailingly effects inner renewal (including the gifts of the Holy Spirit, sanctification, and good works), Lutherans see this renewal as a lifelong struggle against sin both as unrighteousness and self-righteousness. Because God's justifying act is itself the attack on the sin it exposes, original sin and its effects can no longer reign in those who continue to hear and trust the justifying proclamation. Sin nevertheless remains and is in need of continued forgiveness.[182] Catholics, on the other hand, hold that the sanctifying action of the Holy Spirit removes the guilt of sin *(reatus culpae)* and renders the justified pleasing in God's sight. The concupiscence which remains is not "truly and properly sin in those born again."[183] As a result it is possible, Catholics maintain, for the justified to avoid mortal sins, which involve the loss of the Holy Spirit. Grace enables the justified to avoid venial sins as well, although lifelong success in this struggle can be achieved only by a special divine favor.[184] For however just and holy, they fall from time to time into the sins that are those of daily existence.[185] What is more, the Spirit's action does not exempt believers from the lifelong struggle against sinful tendencies. Concupiscence and other effects of original and personal sin, according to Catholic doctrine, remain in the justified, who therefore must pray daily to God for forgiveness.[186]

103. Lutherans fear that the Catholic doctrine of inherent righteousness may cause the Christian to be anxious or complacent, and in either case insufficiently reliant on God's promise of mercy. Catholics fear that the Lutheran position may lead to a certain neglect of good works or may not adequately motivate the believer to give praise and thanks to God for the healing and transforming effects of his redemptive action in us. To describe this transformation, Catholics sometimes appeal to the concept of divinization *(theosis),* which occupied such an important place in the Greek patristic tradition, and thereby stress that the "inherent righteousness" of believers is primarily God's gift of himself, i.e., primarily *gratia increata* and only secondarily *gratia creata.*[187] Ordinarily Lutherans have not employed the language of divinization, though at times Luther approximated it. But they do follow him in speaking of the believer's participation in the glory of the resurrected Christ and of the continously operative presence in believers of the Holy Spirit, who "calls, gathers, enlightens, and sanctifies the whole Christian church on earth and preserves it in union with Jesus Christ in the one true faith."[188]

104. Recent ecumenical discussion, by calling attention to the common elements within different structures of thought, makes it difficult for Catholics to accuse Lutherans of diminishing the importance of sanctification or of the Holy Spirit and at the same time makes it difficult for Lutherans to accuse Catholics of overlooking the abiding effects of sin in the baptized. Nonetheless, the divergent ways in which the two traditions usually talk about the sinfulness of the justified are symptoms of continuing differences in their concerns.

105. *3. Sufficiency of Faith.* Catholics can speak of justification by faith or even of justification by faith alone insofar as they teach, as do Lutherans, that nothing prior to the free gift of faith merits justification and that all of God's saving gifts come through Christ alone. Catholics stress, however, that the indwelling Holy Spirit brings about in believers not only assent and trust but also a loving commitment that issues in good works. In Catholic theology it has therefore been customary to hold that faith, to be justifying, must be accompanied (or, perhaps better, intrinsically qualified) by the gift of love *(caritas).* This traditional position is somewhat technically summed up in the Scholastic formula, "faith animated by love" *(fides caritate formata).* Only when love qualifies faith does faith unite believers perfectly to Christ and make them living members of his body.[189] By consenting to sin and allowing it to reign in oneself, it is possible, according to the Catholic view, to be outside the realm of righteousness even while continuing to believe and hope in Christ; in this sense faith can exist without love and without justifying grace.

106. Lutherans, for their part, recognize without difficulty that the faith that justifies is living and operative. They also deny that faith as mere assent (called in their theological tradition *fides historica*) can be justifying. They stress that faith is living, and it alone justifies because it clings to Christ and the promise of the gospel. Love always springs from such faith, but is among the works of the law, which do not justify. Thus Lutherans are dissatisfied with the Catholic teaching that infused faith (i.e., faith as a gift produced in the soul by God) can be dead and sterile. They suspect that in making a distinction between dead faith and living faith Catholics teach by implication that believers can move themselves from a state of sin to righteousness, thus in effect justifying themselves. Lutherans' fears are increased when they find Catholics speaking of sinners actively cooperating in their own justification. Although Catholics maintain that cooperation is itself a gift of grace and that the love which makes faith live is totally God's gift, Lutherans find that thinking in terms of such a process is liable to Pelagian distortions.[190] The Catholic doctrine that faith alone is insufficient, some Lutherans maintain, tempts Christians to rely on their own activity rather than on the saving work of Christ.

107. The past controversies about the sufficiency of faith alone were aggravated by differences in terminology emerging from late medieval Scholasticism and by the then prevalent tendency to read the New Testament in the light of Scholastic problems and concepts. In recent decades the common approach to exegesis and the shift from Scholastic to modern categories of thought (personal and existential rather than physical or metaphysical) have greatly narrowed the differences. But the theological differences regarding the relation of faith to love have not been fully transcended, even though faith is now recognized on both sides as incomplete without trust in Christ and loving obedience to him.

108. *4. Merit.* Both Lutherans and Catholics hold that, thanks to the inner renewal that comes from justification, the justified can, do, and must perform good works. Lutherans, however, associate merit with law. Asserting that Christians "are justified before they keep the law,"[191] they deny that good works merit salvation. They grant in their

Confessions, on the other hand, that the good works of the justified are meritorious "not for the forgiveness of sins, grace, and justification (for we obtain these only by faith) but for other spiritual and physical rewards in this life and in that which is to come."[192] Lutherans, however, have generally considered it misleading to speak of any rewards as "merited."

109. Catholics, convinced that justification removes whatever is hateful to God in the justified, hold that the good works of the righteous give a title to salvation itself in the sense that God has covenanted to save those who, prompted by grace, obey his will. Catholics recognize, to be sure, that the merit of the creature before God differs radically from that whereby one human being merits from another. Any merit which the creature can have in the sight of God, they point out, is predicated on God's free promises in Christ. Meritorious works, moreover, necessarily presuppose grace and bring to fruition what God's grace has initiated. They have their meritorious value because the Holy Spirit is present and active in those who do such works.

110. Even when these reservations are made, Lutherans are inclined to hold that Catholic ways of thinking and speaking about merit can lead to a legalism that derogates from the unconditional character of God's justifying word. They speak of reward, new obedience, and good fruits, but avoid the language of merit.

111. Catholics readily admit that merit has often been preached in a self-righteous way bordering on legalism, but they deny that the abuse of the doctrine invalidates the doctrine itself. To minimize God's gifts, Catholics assert, is not a way of magnifying the giver. It must never be forgotten, they observe, that in crowning our merits God crowns his own gifts. Meritorious works, moreover, cannot derive from a mere desire to accumulate spiritual treasures for oneself. Such works presuppose a charity that proceeds from God and goes out to God. For any assurance of final perseverance and salvation, Catholics believe, one must not trust in one's own merits but rather hope in God's continued mercy.

112. Thus the essential intentions behind both the Catholic doctrine of merit *ex gratia* and the Lutheran doctrine of promise may be compatible, but the two sides have difficulty in finding a common language. The differences of language here again reflect differences in concern. Lutherans are primarily intent on stressing the saving character of the unconditional promises God addresses to human beings and on preventing Christians from being left to their own resources, whereas the Catholic preoccupation is to make sure that the full range of God's gifts, even the crowning gift of a merited destiny, is acknowledged. Both concerns reflect aspects of the gospel, but the tension nevertheless remains.

113. *5. Satisfaction.* The disagreements regarding satisfaction are hard to specify since this theme has been less prominent in modern theological discussion than the other themes mentioned here. In the sixteenth century both Lutherans and Catholics were convinced that, as far as eternal punishments were concerned, Christ through his sufferings and death gave full satisfaction for all sin, original or personal. Lutherans, furthermore, agreed that the good works which are the fruit of repentance and of faith include mortification of the flesh, i.e., "the amendment of life and the forsaking of sin."[193] While they did not themselves call this mortification of the flesh "satisfaction," they agreed with the statement ascribed to Augustine that "true satisfaction means cutting off the causes of sin, that is, mortifying and restraining the flesh, not to pay for eternal punishments but to keep the flesh from alluring us to sin."[194]

114. Catholics, however, held that the sufferings of the saints, united in a mysterious way with those of Christ himself, could "fill up" what was lacking in Christ's sufferings (cf. Col. 1:24), not as regards intrinsic value but as regards the application to particular times, places, and persons. They held that believers who were living in the grace of God could participate in the sufferings of Christ, in his expiation of their sins, and in his intercession for the spiritual needs of others.

115. The Catholic doctrine, often poorly presented and wrongly understood, was used in support of a variety of abuses that were rightly denounced by the Lutherans and by many reforming Catholics. Many of these abuses were corrected by the reforms of the Council of Trent; others have gradually died out, but some, no doubt, still remain.

116. In spite of these abuses, Catholics generally continue to hold that the sufferings of penitent sinners and of the innocent can be prayerfully applied, in union with the immeasurable satisfaction given by Christ, to beseech God's mercy and pardon. Although it may be impossible to know exactly what such an entreaty implies, it need not involve the "works-righteousness" attacked by the Reformers. Properly interpreted, the Catholic doctrine of satisfaction can give a Christian meaning to suffering and to solidarity in the communion of saints. Further study will be needed to determine whether and how far Lutherans and Catholics can agree on these points, which have far-reaching ramifications for traditionally disputed doctrines such as the sacrament of penance, Masses for special intentions, indulgences, and purgatory. These questions demand more thorough exploration than they have yet received in this or other dialogues.[195]

117. *6. Criteria of Authenticity.* The Lutheran movement, founded at a time when superstition and corruption were rampant, was legitimately concerned to find a critical principle by which to test what is authentically Christian. The principle of justirfication by faith, understood as the correlative of the sole mediatorship of Christ, was accepted as the article by which the church must stand or fall. Lutherans believe that this principle has continuing validity, since the tendency of Christians to rely on their own devices rather than on Christ is unabating. While granting that the principle of justification by faith alone must not be employed to erode the fullness of the apostolic heritage and of the means whereby this heritage is to be mediated in any given time and place, they believe that this principle retains its critical importance.

118. Catholics, on their side, are wary of using any one doctrine as the absolute principle by which to purify from outside, so to speak, the catholic heritage. They recognize, to be sure, the danger of absolutizing merely human ecclesiastical structures. While conceding that the church stands under the gospel and is to be judged by it, Catholics insist that the gospel cannot be rightly interpreted without drawing on the full resources available within the church. To speak of "Christ alone" or "faith alone," they contend, could lead, contrary to the intentions of Lutherans themselves, to the position that the grace of Christ is given apart from the external word of Scripture, Christian preaching, the sacraments, and the ordained ministry.

119. Here, as on other points, there is much common ground. Lutherans are aware of the dangers of neglecting the means of grace and of fostering individualism in the church. They recognize the importance of the canonical Scripture, sacraments, ritual, devotion, and of the ordained ministry.[196] They have recently been recovering valuable elements in the ancient liturgical tradition of the church. But they continue to ask whether, even in modern Catholicism, it has been made sufficiently evident that (as the Malta Report expressed the Lutheran position) "the rites and orders of the church are not to be imposed as conditions for salvation, but are valid only as the free unfolding of the obedience of faith."[197] They suspect that the papacy and magisterial infallibility remain in need of reinterpretation and restructuring in order to make them unmistakably subordinate to the gospel.[198] Finally, to mention a problem this dialogue has not discussed, they wonder whether official teachings on Mary and the cult of the saints, despite protestations to the contrary, do not detract from the principle that Christ alone is to be trusted for salvation because all God's saving gifts come through him alone.

120. In the existing divergences concerning the principles and methods of church reform, we see once again the consequences of two different sets of concerns. Lutherans, primarily intent upon emphasizing God's unconditional saving promises and upon purifying the church from superstition, corruption, and self-glorification, continue to press for a more thoroughgoing application of justification by faith as a critical principle. Catholics, concerned with protecting the fullness of God's gifts as granted through Christ in the Holy Spirit, are on guard against criticism that might erode the catholic heritage. In spite of their different concerns, both traditions agree that the church is subject to criticism and judgment in light of the gospel and that the gospel is always to be heard and interpreted by Christians in the church, where God's word is explicitly proclaimed.

121. *Conclusion.* If this interpretation is correct, Lutherans and Catholics can share in each others' concerns in regard to justification and can to some degree acknowledge the legitimacy of the contrasting theological perspectives and structures of thought. Yet, on the other hand, some of the consequences of the different outlooks seem irreconcilable, especially in reference to particular applications of justification by faith as a criterion of all church proclamation and practice. In order to move beyond this impasse, it is necessary for both sides to take seriously the concerns of the other and to strive to think jointly about the problems. It is to such an effort that we now turn, first, by looking at the biblical data on justification, and, second, by summarizing and reflecting on the convergences of past and present.

CHAPTER THREE
PERSPECTIVES FOR RECONSTRUCTION

A. The Biblical Data

122. In recent decades developments in the study of Scripture have brought Catholics and Lutherans to a fuller agreement about the meaning of many passages controverted at least since the sixteenth century. Of special importance has been, within general Roman Catholic biblical emphasis, the encouragement given by church authority to Catholic interpreters in the last fifty years to make use of historical-critical methods, thus sharing in a mode of interpretation employed by Protestants for a longer time. In particular, this approach to the Bible lays emphasis on the context of each book or passage and on the theology of each individual writer. In that way readers are encouraged to avoid misusing isolated verses out of context as "proof-texts" in a bad sense and so to respect the meanings of the biblical authors. This common concern for what the biblical texts in their situations affirm has also influenced Lutheran and Catholic systematic theologians in their work.

123. As part of our diaglogue, extensive attention has been given to biblical passages bearing on righteousness/justification by faith and its relation to the love and good works expected of a Christian. A detailed and comprehensive survey, impossible to summarize fully here, is available in a separate volume entitled *"Righteousness" in the New Testament* as well as in related essays on merit.[199] Here we shall accent the contributions from our joint study that bear on the historically divisive issue of how to interpret the biblical data on justification by faith. Overall it may be said that Catholics have come to acknowledge that "righteousness/justification is more prevalent in NT teaching than has normally been suspected in earlier centuries or among earlier commentators, and that it is an image of prime importance for our expression of the Christ-event or even the gospel" (*Righteousness,* ‡ 423); and Lutherans acknowledge that this theme has more nuances and, some would say, limitations in expressing the gospel (pp. 347–49) than has been generally supposed in their tradition.

124. Our examination of the scriptural evidence has brought out not merely a number of convergences and outright agreements already existing in the work of Catholic and non-Catholic exegetes[200] but also some particular emphases and new insights not previously highlighted in ecumenical discussions on righteousness/justification. The *first* of these involves the fact that it is the Hebrew Scriptures (or Old Testament) which provide the proper setting for any such discussion (‡‡ 27–48; 358–64). That point is readily apparent even from a casual perusal of Paul, for Paul's appeal, in his dispute with his opponents, is to Hab. 2:4 (cf. Gal. 3:11; Rom. 1:17, "he who through faith is righteous shall live") and to Gen. 15:6 (Gal. 3:6; Rom. 4:3, "Abraham 'believed God, and it was reckoned to him as righteousness'"; cf. also Rom. 3:21, "the law and the prophets bear witness"). Many of the varied meanings of the New Testament Greek term *dikaiosynē* (and related words) stem from the nuances of the Hebrew root *ṣdq.*

125. The biblical terms "righteousness" and "justification" have a rich background and a wide variety of uses. As images they are drawn from juridical, forensic (law court) settings and are employed to describe the right relationship of human beings to God or to one another and the mode or process by which such a relationship comes about. Thus the term "righteous" may denote a human being as innocent or acquitted before a judge's tribunal. It may also suggest a complex of right relationships and, according to many interpreters, covenant behavior and loyalty, and, according to some, even a relation to the cosmic order.

126. When predicated of human beings, biblical "righteousness" is understood as justice in ruling or judging, ethical uprightness, covenantal loyalty, obedience to the Torah, or forensic innocence. The descriptions of the way in which a person is brought to righteousness in the sight of God vary among the OT authors and in the NT, especially in the writings of Paul.

127. When predicated of God, "righteousness" is understood as his fundamental uprightness; his triumph(s) in a holy war, in a lawcourt dispute *(rîb)* with Israel, or in legal decisions (Ps. 9:5); but above all, especially in the postexilic period, as his gracious salvific activity, manifest in a just judgment (Isa. 46:3; 51:5–8; 56:1; cf. Hos. 2:18–19; Pss 40:9–10, 98:2). We are made especially aware of such nuances associated with God's "righteousness" when the Hebrew for that term *(ṣdq)* appears in the Greek translation of the Old Testament as his "mercy" (Isa. 56:1, RSV "deliverance") or when his "steadfast love" (Hebrew *ḥesed*) is rendered as his "righteousness" (*dikaiosynē;* LXX Ex. 34:7; Isa. 63:7).

128. The *second* area of discovery for the present dialogue lay in the possibility of determining the earliest Christian use of righteousness/justification terminology. While Jesus himself is not normally attested as having employed such language (‡‡ 49–54, 365–67), the words and associated forensic imagery seem first to have appeared in creedal summaries or confessions of faith now embedded in the Pauline and other epistles but pre-Pauline in origin (‡‡ 55–76, 368–75). Examples include 1 Cor. 6:11 ("justified in the name of the Lord Jesus Christ"); Rom. 4:24–25 ("Jesus our Lord, who was put to death for our trespasses and raised for our justification"); and Rom. 3:24–26a (cf. also 1 Cor. 1:30; 1 Pet. 3:18; 1 Tim. 3:16, and possibly 2 Cor. 5:21). Clearly in the thirties and forties of the first century the early Christian community was making use of this Old Testament imagery to express the claim that by Christ's death and resurrection human beings stand righteous before God's tribunal. These formulations do not specifically mention "faith" or "works," but they show, as part of a common expression of the apostolic faith, that Paul was not the first to formulate the meaning of the Christ event in terms of righteousness/justification.

129. What Paul did do, in inheriting the righteousness/justification language of the Old Testament and its previous applications to Christ, was to sharpen the meaning, especially though not exclusively, in Galatians, Romans, and Philippians. He related the process of justification to "grace" and set forth the theme of "justified through faith, not by works of the law," though he also insisted on "the obedience of faith" (Rom. 1:5) and response to the gospel in believers' lives (see §§ 132–36 below). The Pauline data became for us a *third* area containing a number of new insights (‡‡ 77–162, 376–99).

130. (*a*) In the face of disputes since the Reformation, our understanding of what Paul meant when he wrote that his gospel revealed "the righteousness of God . . . through faith for faith" (Rom. 1:17) has been greatly helped first of all by consideration of the rich Old Testament and pre-Pauline background which has opened up concerning "the righteousness of God."

131. Luther at times attributed to his predecessors an identification of the biblical "justice of God" (Vulgate, *iustitia dei*) with God's punitive, vindictive justice.[201] He himself preferred to speak of "the righteousness of God" as an alien righteousness *(iustitia aliena)* that God gives on account of faith in Christ. It alone is *"die Gerechtigkeit die vor Gott gilt."*[202] Historians of doctrine today usually admit that Luther's medieval predecessors did not as a rule identify *iustitia dei* with a punitive justice.[203] In any case, recent biblical scholarship sees the righteousness of which Paul speaks both as a gift from God[204] and, in some passages, as an attribute or quality of God, a power exercised on behalf of sinful humanity to save and justify *(heilsetzende Macht).*[205] This widespread consensus in the modern understanding of *dikaiosynē theou,* according to which it is an attribute of God, but also his power present in his gift, should help us further to go beyond the divisive issues of the sixteenth century. At that time Paul's texts were interpreted in polemical debates about sin and grace, faith and good works; his use of the notion of "righteousness of God" was often translated into categories other than his own and categories that were mutually exclusive. Moreover, each side then suspected the other's intentions when appealing to Paul.

132. (*b*) A second way in which we have been helped in grasping what Paul says on justification is by relating this theme to other images which he employed to describe God's salvific activity toward human beings. While righteousness/justification is the primary way the apostle describes what God has done for us in Christ, it is complemented by other images which express aspects of God's activity in a nonforensic terminology that refers to personal and corporate transformation. Paul recognized that Christ had "once for all" (Rom. 6:10) died to sin and had justified human beings (Gal. 2:16; Rom. 3:26–28; 4:25; 5:18), but he freely described what this involves under such other images as salvation (2 Cor. 7:10; Rom. 1:16; 10:10; 13:11), expiation of sins (Rom. 3:25), redemption of sinners (1 Cor. 1:30; Rom. 3:24; 8:32), reconcilation of sinners to God (2 Cor. 5:18–20; Rom. 5:10–11; 11:15), adoption (Gal. 4:5; Rom. 8:15; 23), sanctification (1 Cor. 1:2, 30; 6:11), freedom (Gal. 5:1, 13; Rom. 8:1–2, 21), transformation (2 Cor. 3:18; Rom. 12:20), glorification (2 Cor. 3:10; Rom. 8:30), and a new creation (Gal. 6:15; 2 Cor. 5:17; cf. 1 Cor. 15:45). Though sometimes intertwined with righteousness/justification, these images point to dimensions of God's saving activity that cannot easily be denoted by forensic terminology, even though the forensic emphasis may be needed for their proper interpretation.

133. (*c*) While, as already noted, Paul inherited righteousness/justification terminology as a biblical way of describing what Christ Jesus had done for human beings, he also more clearly related it to grace and faith than had been done previously. Yet in all seven of his uncontested letters he makes use of righteousness terms in a generic sense as though their meaning could be presumed. Hence it appears that this way of articulating what Christ's death and resurrection means is not merely the result of debates with Judaizers in Galatia, though such confrontation may have been the occasion for sharpening his formulation in terms of "faith" and in contrast to "works of the law." Paul's classic thesis is set forth in Gal. 2:16: "a human being is not justified [*dikaioutai*] because of deeds [i.e., observances] of [the] law, but rather through faith in Jesus Christ" (cf. Rom. 3:21). The verb "is justified" is surely used in a declarative, forensic sense; whether there is also an effective sense here (i.e., that the person is made, as well as declared righteous) is not resolvable by philological analysis alone. Yet since justification has not only a forensic sense but also represents God's power at work, sinners are "rendered righteous" (cf. Rom. 5:19); this involves righteousness both in an ethical sense and before God (‡‡ 100, 382).

134. In any case, according to Paul, this justification takes place by "the grace of God," through faith, not through the law (Gal. 2:21; Rom. 3:22, 24), as Paul's argument from the Abraham story in Galatians 3–4 and Romans 4 shows. For Paul faith in Christ is a response to the gospel; it comes from hearing the gospel (Gal. 3:2, 8; Rom. 10:17) and results in personal "obedience" (Rom. 1:5; cf. 16:26). Faith is also something "which works itself out through love" (Gal. 5:6), a concise Pauline phrase expressing the relation of faith and loving

Christian service (unless *agape* might here refer to God's love for us). Such an understanding (‡‡ 105, 106, 384) avoids much of the sixteenth-century acrimony over the interpretation of Gal. 5:6.[206]

135. Without doubt Paul emphasizes in the Letter to the Romans the argument that righteousness comes through faith and by grace (1:17; 3:22ff.). Yet even in this letter there have been problems over "judgment" and "works." For Paul states that "God's righteous judgment" (Rom. 2:5; *dikaiokrisia* as distinct from his *dikaiosynē*) will be revealed; "[God] 'will render to everyone according to his works' (Ps. 62:12); to those who by persistence in a good deed seek glory and honor and immortality [he will give] eternal life"; for those who sin, his furious wrath waits (Rom. 2:6–8). Whether Rom. 2:6–11 refers to Christians or not is debated by exegetes (‡‡ 125–29, 390–91). Compare also 2 Cor. 5:10, "For we must all appear before the judgment seat of Christ, so that each one may receive good or evil, according to what he has done in the body." We note that from such passages some Protestant interpreters have come to reckon more fully in Paul with a judgment based on works and some Catholics with the likelihood that this need not be understood as contrary to justification by faith (‡ 129).

136. (*d*) With regard to such passages, we realize today that Paul's statements about the appearance of human beings before God's tribunal have to be understood in the larger context of his insistence on God's gracious justification offered to all men and women through faith in Christ Jesus, a justification accomplished through Christ's death for sins "once for all," yet one for which believers wait in "the hope of righteousness" through the Spirit (Gal. 5:5; cf. Rom. 8:23, 25). It is moreover an effective declaration, happening now, when one is justified and lives at peace in Christ, having in effect heard the judgment of God and his justifying word (Gal. 2:15–20; Rom. 5:1–2; 8:28–37). Thus justification is not simply a future or past event, but is an eschatological reality which stretches from the past through the present and into the future (‡‡ 147, 398). Hence Paul, in writing to the Philippians, can enjoin, "Work out your own salvation with fear and trembling," and then immediately add, "For God is at work in you, both to will and to work for his good pleasure" (2:12–13). "God does everything, therefore we have to do everything. And we shall receive everything."[207] The "good deed" (cf. Rom. 2:7; 1 Thess. 1:3) that Christians, justified by faith in Christ Jesus, will bring to the tribunal of God will be done because God is at work in them (‡‡ 83, 125, 377, 390). In brief, it seems that Paul's eschatological outlook enabled him to speak of both judgment in accordance with works and justification by faith apart from works of the law.

137. A *fourth* area where there is now greater agreement because of modern scholarly attention to the specific contexts within which biblical passages need to be interpreted concerns those Pauline epistles widely conceded to be the product of Paul's pupils and the Pauline school. The emphasis in Paul's own letters on justification by faith becomes less pronounced in the changed situations of the Deutero-Paulines and Pastorals. There is less interest in the mode by which believers are justified and a rising emphasis upon the effects of justification in their lives. Thus Col. 4:1, and Eph. 5:9; 6:14 take up righteousness terminology in urging the ethical effects of justification. Even Eph. 4:24 presupposes rather than argues that justification causes holiness. Eph. 2:4–10 echoes Pauline teaching about being "*saved* by grace through faith," but Ephesians does not use "righteousness/justification" terminology to make this point. Moreover, the eschatology changes, for there is no future reference, and while salvation is "not by works" (2:9), the "good works" in which Christians are to walk have been "prepared beforehand" by God (2:10; cf. ‡‡ 171–74, 401).

138. The Pastoral Epistles are similar in tone. On one occasion (Titus 3:5–7) the mode of justification is expounded in connection with baptism ("justified by his grace," "not because of deeds done by us in righteousness"). Elsewhere the three letters emphasize the effects of God's grace and mercy (undeserved by merely human works) in terms of the "good *(agatha)* deeds" or the "fine *(kala)* deeds" of believers. The latter phrase, unprecedented in Paul and very rare in the Greek biblical tradition, lends a missionary orientation to the effects of justification (‡‡ 178–91, esp. 185; 402; 428–47, esp. 432 and 434). As a body of literature the Deutero-Paulines (and the Pastorals specifically) illustrate the living reality that justification introduces into the believer's existence. Thus methods of analysis unavailable in the sixteenth century show to a greater degree than has been possible in the past how Paul's doctrine was further developed in the Pastoral Epistles.

139. The *fifth* area of insights is provided by a full survey of the other New Testament writings on righteousness/justification, the Synoptics and Acts, the Johannine literature, Hebrews, and the Petrine epistles (‡‡ 223–318, 409–20), and gives further support to the overall trends noted above (§ 123): righteousness terminology and expressions of the concept of justification are more prevalent than has often been suspected, but the usages vary, differing especially from Paul's. Some examples follow.

140. Among the Synoptic evangelists Matthew has especially used the noun *dikaiosynē* to refer to God's way of salvation (e.g., 5:6, 6:33) or human ethical response (e.g., 5:10; 6:1) or both (cf. 21:32; ‡‡ 226–43; 410). Whereas Paul regarded "righteouness" as God's gift and "faith" as human response, Matthew speaks at times of "the kingdom" as the gift from God and "righteousness" especially as the response. The few occurrences of the terms in Luke (18:14) and Acts (15:10–11; 13:38–39) are akin but not identical to Paul's usages and represent another type of development (‡‡ 244–53, 411).

141. What examples there are of righteousness terminology in John, 1 John, and Revelation reflect Old Testament, especially ethical nuances, though Christ is "the Righteousness One" who is the expiation for sins (1 John 2:1–2; ‡‡ 254–65; 412). Hebrews interprets the Christ event at times in terms of righteousness (1:9; 5:13; 10:37–38) but scarcely with the Pauline sense of justification and with a different sense for faith (11:1ff.; ‡‡ 285–99, 415–17). The modest use of righteousness terms in 1 Peter puts that document in the Pauline or, better, pre-Pauline apostolic Christian orbit; in 2 Peter, "the righteousness of our God and Savior, Jesus Christ" (1:1) suggests use of inherited language to meet a new threat from false teaching in a pluralistic Hellenistic environment (‡‡ 305–14, 418–20).

142. The Letter of James constitutes a *sixth* area of exegetical understanding (‡‡ 266–83, 413–14), an area which has been of neuralgic significance in Lutheran-Catholic debates. Some usages are not controversial: Jas. 1:20 speaks of the "righteousness of God" in the sense of God's unshakable fidelity understood as a norm for Christian conduct, and "righteous(ness)" in an ethical sense also occurs (3:18; 5:6, 16). In Jas. 2:14–26, however, we encounter the famous discussion of faith and works, which argues that justification is not by faith alone but by works that complete it. One widespread contemporary interpretation sees this part of the letter as not directed against Paul himself or his teaching on justification by faith.[208] It is rather an attempt to correct a caricature of his teaching which seemingly advocated some form of libertinism, a caricature with which Paul himself at times had to contend (see Rom. 3:8; 6:1, 15). "You see that a human being is justified by works and not by faith alone" (Ja. 2:24) may seem to contradict Gal. 2:16 or Rom. 3:28. Yet we recognize that for Paul "works" regularly means "works of the [Mosaic] law" (see Rom. 3:21) and "faith" means a faith which "works itself out through love" (Gal. 5:6, see § 134). Such faith is for Paul no "dead" faith; it is akin to that "faith which is completed by works" (Jas. 2:22b). Moreover, for Paul the pregnant sense of faith includes both allegiance to God in Christ and the inescapability of good deeds flowing therefrom. It thus differs greatly from what "faith" denotes in Jas. 2:19—acceptance of revelation without corresponding behavior. (It may be noted that in the New Testament the phrase *sola fide* occurs in Jas. 2:24, not in a Pauline writing.) Thus it can now be agreed that James did not directly attack Paul's concept of faith or of justification by faith, although it may be difficult to reconcile James' overall understanding of law, works, and sin with Paul's teaching on the same themes.

143. The topic of merit provides a *seventh* area where modern examination of the biblical data sheds some light on what was another divisive issue in the sixteenth-century controversies of Rome with Luther and his colleagues. "Merit" is a technical Western theological term for a concept that has no single terminological equivalent in the original texts of the Bible. Even in the Vulgate *meritum* occurs at only two or three places in Ecclesiasticus (10:31; 16:15; 38:18 [?]), translating a variety of Greek or Hebrew terms (see LXX Sirach 10:28; 16:14; 38:17), none of which has much to do with "merit."

144. However, the notion can be related to, though it is not exactly the same as, the biblical idea of the "recompense" or "retribution" that the God of Israel gives for human conduct. Under a variety of images drawn from nature (e.g., "produce," "fruit," "harvest") and from human relationships (particularly of a contractual or competitive character, e.g., "wages" and "prizes"), the Old Testament literature, from the Torah through the prophets, psalms, and sapiential books, often sets forth this aspect of life and conduct, the relationship between what men and women do for (or against) God and what they in turn receive from him (See Gen. 2–12; Deut. 28; Jer. 31:29–30; Ezek. 18:1–32; Pss. 1; 37:25–26; Prov. 13:13; 19:16–17; the Book of Job; cf. Tob. 4:7–11; 12:5–6; Wis. 2:22; 3:14–15; 5:15–16; Sir. 51:30). Paul can write of death as "the wages of sin," but he does so in contrast to eternal life as "God's free gift" (*charisma;* never "wages of good works," Rom. 6:23; cf. Gal. 6:7–9) which has been effected by the all-sufficing act of the Christ who died for us (cf. Rom. 5:9–11 with vv. 15–17). Eph. 2:1–10 (see § 137 above) describes this act of Christ in terms of the immeasurable riches that the Father has freely given through his Son (cf. 1 Pet. 1:18–19, on believers ransomed "with the precious blood of Christ"). Using such biblical data, the Latin theological and liturgical tradition interpreted the immeasurable riches of Christ's work as his "infinite merits" and compared them with the lesser or nonexistent "merit" of merely human or Christian works;[209] in Lutheran and Protestant hymnody the merits of Christ, in contrast to human lack of merits, are often mentioned.[210]

145. The images and parables that the New Testament uses to designate the recompense that God gives to each person for his conduct (e.g., Mark 10:29–30 and parallels: Matt. 19:29; Luke 18:29–30)[211] when considered together with those which stress the "unprofitableness" of works (Matt. 20:1–10; Luke 17:7–10) remind us how complex are the questions that stand under the heading of "merit." There is no easy, systematic transfer of our human ethical schemata (including those of natural or commutative justice) into the divine judgment. Matthew, to take one example, depicts the Son of man separating sheep from goats and granting rewards for human conduct (Matt. 25:31–46; cf. 16:27). John, to take another, portrays the consequences of faithful and unfaithful discipleship through the image of the vine and the branches (John 15:1–11; cf. John 3:19–21; 5:25–29). In still other ways Hebrews (4:1; 6:7–8, 10–12; 10:26–36) and the book of Revelation (14:13; 22:11–12) articulate the same teaching, illustrating the paradoxical incalculability of a divine recompense which, in the last analysis, is, for those who do good, God himself, and for those who do evil, the eternal loss of God. One dare not overlook this aspect of biblical teaching, though it must always be set within the framework of God's merciful action on behalf of humankind in Christ.

146. Yet it is righteousness/justification which emerges in Paul and elsewhere as an image and concept of prime importance, at times, as in Romans, the central or dominant image, for expressing what God has done in Christ and thus for expressing the gospel. Along with this emphasis there is also found in the New Testament writings a stress, though on the whole not as great, on the consequent deeds of the righteous Christian and on the recompense that awaits them. "Righteousness" and "justification" in other New Testament writings are not always qualified, as they are in the Pauline writings, with the phrases "by grace" and "through faith." Yet the classic formulation of the doctrine of *iustitia dei* has come to us through Paul. It is he among biblical authors who most fully and carefully discussed "righteousness" and "faith" and who, in the light of his understanding of these terms, thinks of justification as simply "by grace" and "through faith" without additions or qualifications. Paul was not, he tells us, "ashamed of the gospel," because "in it the righteousness of God is revealed through faith for faith" and "it is the power of God for the salvation of everyone who believes" (Rom. 1:16–17). In brief, a faith centered and forensically conceived picture of justification is of major importance for Paul and, in a sense, for the Bible as a whole, although it is by no means the only biblical or Pauline way of representing God's saving work.

147. The significance of these exegetical findings depends in part on the attitude adopted toward the theological problem of "the center of Scripture," which is related to that of a "canon within the canon." When a principle such as justification by faith is taken as the key to the interpretation of all Scripture, those biblical books, especially Paul's major letters, which stress this doctrine are sometimes regarded as canonical in a special sense, while others (e.g., James) may be viewed as of secondary or even doubtful canonicity. Luther sometimes spoke in this way, but the issue of a canon within the canon has become a major one chiefly in recent times, in part because of our greater awareness of the theological differences among biblical authors.

148. The problem is not entirely new. Medieval authors commonly agreed that there was a hierarchy among the books of the New Testament, the four Gospels coming first in importance (a view reiterated by Vatican Council II).[212] The "spiritual" senses of Scripture often led to a Christocentric reading of it, as is patent in this formula of Bonaventure: " . . . by faith Christ dwells in our hearts. Such is the knowledge of Jesus Christ, from which the certainty and understanding of all the Holy Scripture derives."[213] This Bonaventurean statement may be compared to Luther's view that Scripture is *was Christum treibet,*[214] an approach which for Luther meant, among other things, that Scripture should be interpreted in terms of justification by faith.

149. In view of this history it is possible for Lutherans and Catholics to agree that for purposes of theological interpretation Scripture has a Christological center which should control the interpretation of those parts of the Bible which focus on matters other than the center itself and which are therefore of secondary rank in the canonical hierarchy. Their lesser rank, however, does not mean that they lack all importance or authority; on that both Lutheran and Catholic confessional traditions are agreed.[215] When it is thus granted that all Scripture must be taken seriously, it becomes clear from the exegetical findings we have summarized that the biblical witness to the gospel of God's saving work in Christ is richer and more varied than has been encompassed in either traditional Catholic or Lutheran approaches to justification. Both sides need to treat each other's concerns and ways of interpreting Scripture with greater respect and willingness to learn than has been done in the past.

B. Growing Convergences

150. The interpretation of Scripture is crucial, but it is not the only factor which contributes to the theological convergences we shall now review. These convergences have been facilitated by the widespread disappearance of nontheological sources of division. The crowns of princes, the incomes of priests and pastors, the standings of social classes are no longer intertwined, as they were in the sixteenth century, with the conflict over justification. The disestablishment of the churches and their detachment from the struggle for worldly power make it easier to discern and acknowledge agreements between them.

151. In light of these developments Lutherans and Catholics have drawn closer together. Theology in both churches is influenced by modern scriptural studies and intellectual developments in the humanities, social studies, and the natural sciences. Both churches are affected by the liturgical renewal, with its emphasis on early Christian patterns of worship different from those of the Middle Ages and post-Reformation Protestantism. The abuses which occasioned the Reformation have for the most part been condemned by Trent and by the Second Vatican Council; in four hundred years of history Lutherans on their side have acquired their own burden of unfaithfulness to the gospel. Both communions acknowledge the need for continual reformation, and both are learning to work together towards that end. They increasingly cooperate in the service of human needs and, to a lesser though important extent, in educational efforts and in bringing the gospel to the world. Lutherans and Catholics are at home with each other and in each other's churches as never before in their divided histories. It is scarely surprising that they are now closer on the doctrine of justification than at any time since the collapse of their last extended official discussion of the topic at Regensburg in 1541 (§§ 45–48 above.)

152. What has emerged from the present study is a convergence (though not uniformity) on justification by faith considered in and of itself, and a significant though lesser convergence on the applications of the doctrine as a criterion of authenticity for the church's proclamation and practice (§ 121). We shall comment first (1) on the incomplete convergence on the use of the criterion and then (2) on the material convergence.

1. Use of the Criterion

153. Catholics as well as Lutherans can acknowledge the need to test the practices, structures, and theologies of the church by the extent to which they help or hinder "the proclamation of God's free and merciful promises in Christ Jesus which can be rightly received only through faith" (§ 28). This accord, however, does not always imply agreement on the applications of the criterion, i.e., which beliefs, practices, and structures pass the test. Catholics and Lutherans, for example, traditionally differ on purgatory, the papacy, and the cult of the saints (§§ 116, 119). Lutherans, however, do not exclude the possibility that such teachings can be understood and used in ways consistent with justification by faith; if such teachings are preached and practiced in accord with this doctrine, they need not, from this Lutheran perspective, divide the churches even though Lutherans do not accept them. Catholics, on their side, admit the legitimacy of the test and hold that their doctrines do foster the "obedience of faith" (cf. Rom. 1:5), but they are open to different opinions regarding the degree to which these traditionally Catholic positions must be accepted by others on the way to closer communion. The ecumenical rapprochement that has already occurred during and since Vatican II is evidence that greater church union, including a limited admission to the Eucharist, is possible without explicit adherence to all Roman Catholic dogmas.[216] The problems regarding the acceptability of post-Reformation developments in each tradition cannot be solved simply by reference to justification by faith as a doctrine per se. Each development must be assessed in its own right and in connection with other outstanding issues such as the relation between Scripture and tradition.

154. It is apparent from our discussion that differences in thought structures play a considerable role in causing tension between Catholic and Lutheran views on justification. Reference has been made (25) to Augustinian and medieval "transformationist models" in contrast to "a model of simultaneity" that reinterprets all notions of change and growth. The Lutheran hermeneutical understanding of justification by faith (88–93) in some ways heightens the tension with Catholic positions. It does so by excluding from the gospel proclamation all reference to the freedom and goodness of fallen human beings on the ground that this would undermine the unconditionality of God's promises in Christ. Such interpretation raises even more questions from Lutherans regarding Catholic descriptions of justification as a process of ontological transformation. Catholics, on their side, continue to ask whether Lutheran formulations of this kind do justice to God's respect for human freedom and to the idea of a real change wrought by the Holy Spirit (98–104). These problems are complicated, no doubt, by differing thought structures within Lutheran and Catholic theological "camps" as well as between them. The conflict between thought structures raises a number of issues we have not resolved and points to the need for further dialogue. We believe, however, that here too Lutherans and Catholics can acknowledge the legitimacy of concerns that come to expression in different ways. In view of the convergences to which we now turn, theological disagreements about structures of thought in relation to the proclamation of the gospel, though serious, need not be church-dividing.

2. Material Convergences

155. The convergence on the use of justification by faith as a criterion depends on prior and fuller material convergences on the doctrine itself. It is only because Catholics and Lutherans share fundamental convictions regarding justification and faith that they can be in increasing accord on criteria of Christian authenticity and accept justification as an *articulus stantis et cadentis ecclesiae* protective of the *solus Christus* (cf. 160). Some of their common convictions are longstanding, others have come to light more recently, and all remain subject to different interpretations and formulations in each tradition. Yet, when looked at as a whole, they constitute a very significant agreement.

156. Elements in this agreement may be formulated as follows:

1) Christ and his gospel are the source, center, and norm of Christian life, individual and corporate, in church and world. Christians have no other basis for eternal life and hope of final salvation than God's free gift in Jesus Christ, extended to them in the Holy Spirit.

2) The prerequisite of final salvation is righteousness. To be saved one must be judged righteous and be righteous.

3) As a consequence of original sin all human beings stand in need of justification even before they commit personal sins. Those in whom sin reigns can do nothing to merit justification, which is the free gift of God's grace. Even the beginnings of justification, for example, repentance, prayer for grace, and desire for forgiveness, must be God's work in us.

4) We remain God's creatures even when ruled by sin. We retain the human freedom to make choices among created goods, but we lack the capacity to turn to God without divine help.

5) Justification, as a transition from disfavor and unrighteousness to favor and righteousness in God's sight, is totally God's work. By justification we are both declared and made righteous. Justification, therefore, is not a legal fiction. God, in justifying, effects what he promises; he forgives sin and makes us truly righteous.

6) Scripture, the proclamation of the word, and the sacraments are means whereby the gospel, as the power of God for salvation, comes concretely to individuals to awaken and strengthen justifying faith.

7) In justification we receive by faith the effects of Christ's action

on our behalf. Justifying faith is not merely historical knowledge or intellectual conviction, but a trustful, self-involving response to the gospel.

8) Justifying faith cannot exist without hope and love; it necessarily issues in good works. Yet the justified cannot rely on their own good works or boast of their own merits as though they were not still in need of mercy.

9) Sin no longer reigns in the justified, yet they remain subject to sinful inclinations and the assaults of sin so that, when left to their own powers, they fall repeatedly. Of themselves they remain capable of losing justification, but, because of the great mercy of God in Christ, they may firmly trust and hope that God will bring them to final salvation.

10) The eternal reward promised to the righteous is a gift, for it depends wholly on God's grace in Christ, the one mediator between God and fallen humanity.

11) The good works of the justified, performed in grace, will be recompensed by God, the righteous judge, who, true to his promises, "will render to everyone according to his works" (Rom. 2:6) (cf. § 108).

12) The priority of God's redeeming will over every human action in bringing about ultimate salvation is recognized in both our traditions by the classic doctrine of predestination.

157. Involved in this agreement as is apparent from 6), 7) and 8) is a fundamental affirmation which was noted in the introduction (4) as particularly helpful for our discussions: *our entire hope of justification and salvation rests on Christ Jesus and on the gospel whereby the good news of God's merciful action in Christ is made known; we do not place our ultimate trust in anything other than God's promise and saving work in Christ.* Such an affirmation is not fully equivalent to the Reformation teaching on justification according to which God accepts sinners as righteous for Christ's sake on the basis of faith alone; but by its insistence that reliance for salvation should be placed entirely on God, it expresses a central concern of that doctrine. Yet it does not exclude the traditional Catholic position that the grace-wrought transformation of sinners is a necessary preparation for final salvation. The agreement, in short, is on the nature of trust or assurance of salvation, on the fundamental experiential attitude of the justified in relation to God *(coram deo).* There are, however, remaining differences on theological formulations and on the relation between theology and proclamation (cf. 88, 154).

158. It must be emphasized that our common affirmation that it is God in Christ alone whom believers ultimately trust does not necessitate any one particular way of conceptualizing or picturing God's saving work. That work can be expressed in the imagery of God as judge who pronounces sinners innocent and righteous (cf. 90), and also in a transformist view which emphasizes the change wrought in sinners by infused grace. Further, as the Malta Report puts it, "The event of salvation to which the gospel testifies can also be expressed comprehensively in other representations derived from the New Testament, such as reconciliation, freedom, redemption, new life and new creation."[217] Yet whatever the aspect of God's saving action one is led to highlight by the needs of gospel proclamation in each age, the affirmation holds that ultimate hope and trust for salvation are to be placed in the God of our Lord Jesus Christ, and not in our own goodness, even when this is God-given, or in our religious experience, even when this is the experience of faith.

159. Wherever this affirmation is maintained, it is possible to allow great variety in describing salvation and in interpreting God's justifying declaration without destroying unity. There may still be debate over the best way to proclaim or evoke reliance on God's gift of himself in Christ Jesus. The belief that the assurance of salvation and the certainty of hope are to be found (as Thomas Aquinas puts it) "chiefly" *(principaliter)* by looking at God's mercy, not at oneself, does not decide such disputes.[218] But where the affirmation is accepted, Lutherans and Catholics can recognize each other as sharing a commitment to the same gospel of redemptive love received in faith.

160. This affirmation, like the Reformation doctrine of justification by faith alone, serves as a criterion for judging all church practices, structures, and traditions precisely because its counterpart is "Christ alone" *(solus Christus).* He alone is to be ultimately trusted as the one mediator through whom God in the Holy Spirit pours out his saving gifts. All of us in this dialogue affirm that all Christian teachings, practices, and offices should so function as to foster "the obedience of faith" (Rom. 1:5) in God's saving action in Christ Jesus alone through the Holy Spirit, for the salvation of the faithful and the praise and honor of the heavenly Father.

DECLARATION

161. Thus we can make together, in fidelity to the gospel we share, the following declaration:

> We believe that God's creative graciousness is offered to us and to everyone for healing and reconciliation so that through the Word

made flesh, Jesus Christ, "who was put to death for our transgressions and raised for our justification" (Rom. 4:25), we are all called to pass from the alienation and oppression of sin to freedom and fellowship with God in the Holy Spirit. It is not through our own initiative that we respond to this call, but only through an undeserved gift which is granted and made known in faith, and which comes to fruition in our love of God and neighbor, as we are led by the Spirit in faith to bear witness to the divine gift in all aspects of our lives. This faith gives us hope for ourselves and for all humanity and gives us confidence that salvation in Christ will always be proclaimed as the gospel, the good news for which the world is searching.

162. This gospel frees us in God's sight from slavery to sin and self (Rom. 6:6). We are willing to be judged by it in all our thoughts and actions, our philosophies and projects, our theologies and religious practices. Since there is no aspect of the Christian community or of its life in the world that is not challenged by this gospel, there is none that cannot be renewed or reformed in its light or by its power.

163. We have encountered this gospel in our churches' sacraments and liturgies, in their preaching and teaching, in their doctrines and exhortations. Yet we also recognize that in both our churches the gospel has not always been proclaimed, that it has been blunted by reinterpretation, that it has been transformed by various means into self-satisfying systems of commands and prohibitions.

164. We are grateful at this time to be able to confess together what our Catholic and Lutheran ancestors tried to affirm as they responded in different ways to the biblical message of justification. A fundamental consensus on the gospel is necessary to give credibility to our previous agreed statements on baptism, on the Eucharist, and on forms of church authority. We believe that we have reached such a consensus.

165. We submit this statement to our churches for study, with the hope that it will serve them as they face the need to make appropriate decisions for the purpose of confessing their faith as one. We also trust that Christian believers of all traditions may find in it an invitation to new hope and new love in the grace that is offered to humanity by God through his Word, Jesus Christ, in the Holy Spirit.

Notes

Part I. Justification by Faith (Common Statement)

1. Lutherans and Catholics in Dialogue, 6 vols. 1. *The Status of the Nicene Creed as Dogma of the Church* (1965); 2. *One Baptism for the Remission of Sins* (1966); 3. *The Eucharist as Sacrifice* (1967); 4. *Eucharist and Ministry* (1970); 5. *Papal Primacy and the Universal Church* (Minneapolis: Augsburg, 1974); 6. *Teaching Authority and Infallibility in the Church* (Minneapolis: Augsburg, 1980). Vols. 1–4 were originally published by the Bishops' Committee for Ecumenical and Interreligious Affairs, Washington, D.C., and the U.S.A. National Committee of the Lutheran World Federation, New York, N.Y. Vols. 1–3 have been reprinted together in one volume by Augsburg Publishing House (n.d.), as has vol. 4 (1979).

2. The common statement of the Joint Study Commission appointed by the Lutheran World Federation, Geneva, and the Secretariat for Promoting Christian Unity, "The Gospel and the Church," was published in *Worship* 46 (1972) 326–51; and *Lutheran World* 19 (1972) 259–73. The text of it in German and English, along with position papers which were discussed over five years, can be found in H. Meyer, ed., *Evangelium—Welt—Kirche: Schlussbericht und Referate der römisch-katholisch/evangelisch-lutherischen Studienkommission "Das Evangelium und die Kirche," 1967–1971* (Frankfurt am M.: O. Lembeck/J. Knecht, 1975). The final drafting of the statement was done in San Anton, Malta (1971), whence the commonly used name for it. See especially section 26; L/RC 2:61–68, 74–75, 82, where the topic of justification by faith is also briefly mentioned.

3. For an assessment of the treatment of justification in the Malta Report and the view that fuller treatment is needed, see *Ecumenical Relations of the Lutheran World Federation: Report of the Working Group on the Interrelations between the Various Bilateral Dialogues* (Geneva: Lutheran World Federation, 1977) 117–23, 131–32. Further, *Lutheran-Episcopal Dialogue Report and Recommendations, Second Series, 1976–1980* (Cincinnati: Forward Movement Publications, 1981) 22–24.

4. A complete list of the essays and when they were discussed is found in this volume, 10–12.

5. William G. Rusch, "How the Eastern Fathers Understood What the Western Church Meant by Justification," in this volume, 131–42.

6. Augustine, *De Spiritu et Littera* 26, 45: *"Quid est enim aliud, justificati, quam justi facti, ab illo scilicet qui justificat impium ut ex impio fit justus"* ("What does the word 'justified' mean except 'made just,' i.e., by him who justifies the ungodly so that one who was ungodly becomes just"). This meaning of *dikaioun/justificare* can also be found in Greek writers. See John Chrysostom, *In ep. ad Rom. hom.* 8.2 (PG 60:456): *". . . dynatai ho theos ton en asebeia bebiōkota touton exaiphnēs ouchi kilaseōs eleutherōsai monon, alla kai dikaion poiēsai . . ."* (" . . . God is able of a sudden not only to free someone who has lived in impiety from punishment, but even to make him righteous") (Chrysostom's comment on Rom. 4:5). See also John Chrysostom, *In ep. II ad Cor. hom.* 11.3 (PG 61:478).

7. These concerns are summarized in Jaroslav Pelikan, *The Christian Tradition, Vol. 1: The Emergence of the Catholic Tradition* (Chicago: University of Chicago Press, 1971) 280–86.

8. Modern studies have argued that Pelagius' concerns were not totally contrary to those of Augustine. His appeal to human responsibility was not intended to belittle God's initiative but to encourage human response. See R. F. Evans, *Pelagius. Inquiries and Reappraisals* (New York: Seabury, 1968), and G. Greshake, *Gnade als konkrete Freiheit. Eine Untersuchung zur Gnadenlehre des Pelagius* (Mainz: Matthias-Grünewald, 1972).

9. This does not mean that the accusers were consistently Augustinian and lacking in Pelagian tendencies. See A. E. McGrath, "Augustinianism? A Critical Assessment

of the So-Called 'Medieval Augustinian Tradition' on Justification," *Augustiniana* 31 (1981) 247–67.

10. The situation was complex due to the context of a sophisticated Scholastic theology and was further complicated by several historical factors. Knowledge of the so-called semi-Pelagian controversy and of the important decisions of the regional Council of Orange (A.D. 529) was for the most part lost after the Carolingian period. Only in the mid-sixteenth century did the texts of Orange reappear and start to be used. See H. Bouillard, *Conversion et grâce chez S. Thomas d'Aquin* (Paris: Aubier, 1944) 99–123; M. Seckler, *Instinkt und Glaubenswille nach Thomas von Aquin* (Mainz: Matthias-Grünewald, 1961) 90–133. Furthermore, Pelagius' own commentary on the Pauline Epistles circulated under orthodox names in only slightly revised form and was widely read; see the *Introduction* to the critical edition by A. Souter, *Pelagius' Expositions of Thirteen Epistles of St. Paul* I (Texts and Studies 9; London: Cambridge Univ. Press, 1922); also H. A. Frede, *Ein neuer unbekannter Paulustext und Kommentar* (Vetus Latina, Aus der Geschichte der lateinischen Bibel 7; 2 vols.; Freiburg: Herder, 1973–74). Finally, rising monastic-ascetic fervor as well as the humanism of the late Middle Ages reinforced not only Eastern soteriological accents but also a general confidence in the powers of human nature.

11. The shift to new accents of this kind cannot be traced easily in the development of justification language itself. The term was not important and was discussed incidentally within various other contexts such as the doctrines of grace, of the work of Christ, and of the sacrament of penance. (Cf. Karlfried Froehlich, "Justification Language in the Middle Ages," in this volume, 143–61). Nor do the medieval treatments of sin or faith reveal much of the shift, because the Augustinian notion of original sin and the patristic understanding of faith with its emphasis on an assent to credal content *(fides quae),* which is completed by being active in love (cf. Gal. 5:6), remained normative.

12. Augustine, *De praedestinatione sanctorum* 3, 7 (PL 44:964).

13. For the following, see the accounts in O. H. Pesch and A. Peters, *Einführung in die Lehre von Gnade und Rechtfertigung* (Darmstadt: Wissenschaftliche Buchgesellschaft, 1981) 15–54; P. Fransen, "Dogmengeschichtliche Entfaltung der Gnadenlehre," in *Mysterium Salutis* (ed. J. Feiner and M. Löhrer; Einsiedeln: Benziger, 1973) 4/2:631–772.

14. Peter Lombard, *Sent.* I. d. 17, c. 1 and 6.

15. See H. de Lubac, *Surnaturel: Études historiques* (Paris: Aubier, 1946); B. Stoeckle, *Gratia supponit naturam. Geschichte und Analyse eines theologischen Axioms* (Rome: Herder, 1962).

16. The distinction between *gratia creata* and *gratia increata* first appears in the commentaries on I. *Sent.* d. 17. See J. Auer, *Die Entwicklung der Gnadenlehre in der Hochscholastik* (Freiburg: Herder, 1942) 1:86–123. The systematic use of the term *habitus* probably goes back to Philip the Chancellor (12th century); a first official reference to grace as habit occurs at the Council of Vienne in 1312 (DS 904). See Fransen, "Dogmengeschichtliche Entfaltung," 672–79.

17. This is certainly the intention of Aquinas' doctrine of grace. See Pesch and Peters, *Einführung,* 64–107 (cited above, n. 13).

18. After the Council of Trent the technical term for the infused habit of grace was "sanctifying" grace.

19. Sometimes *gratia gratis data* meant a gift bestowed by God on one person for the sake of assisting others on the way to salvation. At other times the term was used more widely to include what is today called actual grace, i.e., a transient divine assistance moving an individual toward a salutary operation. Thomas Aquinas knew how to combine both meanings (*De Ver.* q. 24, a. 15, c.) when he asked about the need of grace to prepare oneself for sanctifying grace *(gratia gratum faciens).*

20. *Ex suis naturalibus* or *ex puris naturalibus* referred in the *via moderna* to the natural abilities remaining in fallen human beings and should not be confused with the later concept of *natura pura* introduced by Cajetan. Cf. de Lubac, *Surnaturel,* 105 (cited above, n. 15).

21. Paul Vignaux, *Justification et Prédestination au XIVe Siècle* (Paris: Presses Universitaires de France, 1934), esp. 97–175 on William of Ockham and Gregory of Rimini. For Ockham's understanding of Pelagianism and consequent denial that he favored that heresy, see 126–27.

22. *". . . cum Deus coronat merita nostra, nihil aliud coronet quam munera sua,"* Augustine, Ep. 194:5, 19 (CSEL 57:190).

23. The term "congruous" merit seems to have its root in the Porretan school of the late 12th century. "Condign" merit (cf. Rom. 8:18) appears at about the same time. See B. Hamm, *Promissio, Pactum, Ordinatio: Freiheit und Selbstbindung Gottes in der scholastischen Gnadenlehre* (Tübingen: Mohr-Siebeck, 1977) 445–62.

24. See A. M. Landgraf, *Dogmengeschichte der Frühscholastik* (Regensburg: Pustet, 1952) 1/1:238–302; Auer, *Entwicklung der Gnadenlehre,* 1:229–61.

25. *In IV Sent.,* d. 17, q. 1, a. 2, sol. 1, c.; *De Ver.* q. 24, a. 15, c.

26. *In IV Sent.,* d. 15, q. 1, a. 3, sol. 4, c: *". . . ex merito congrui dicitur aliquis mereri aliquod bonum per opera extra caritatem facta . . . Quia tamen hoc meritum non proprie meritum dicitur ideo magis concedendum est quod hujusmodi opera non sint alicujus meritoria quam quod sint."*

27. See W. Dettloff, *Die Lehre von der acceptatio divina bei Johannes Duns Scotus mit besonderer Berücksichtigung der Rechtfertigungslehre* (Franziskanische Forschungen 10; Werl: Dietrich-Coelde Verlag, 1954); *Die Entwicklung der Akzeptations- und Verdienstlehre von Duns Scotus bis Luther mit besonderer Berücksichtigung der Franziskanertheologen* (Beiträge zur Geschichte der Philosophie und Theologie des Mittelalters 40/2; Münster: Aschendorff, 1964); "Die antipelagianische Grundstruktur der scotistischen Rechtfertigungslehre," *Franziskanische Studien* 48 (1966) 266–70.

28. Ap 4:19–20; BS 163; BC 109–110.

29. DS 387.

30. Both the monk Gottschalk in the 9th century (DS 621) and probably the presbyter Lucidus in the 5th century (DS 330–42) taught double predestination; they were condemned.

31. *In I Sent.,* d. 41, a. 1, q. 1c.

32. Ibid., q. 2c.

33. *In I Sent.,* d. 41, q. 1, a. 3, c. and ad 2; *In II Sent.,* d. 27, q. 1, a. 4, c. and ad 4.

34. *"Et sic impossible est quod totus praedestinationis effectus in communi habeat aliquam causam ex parte nostra"* (S.T., I, q. 23 a. 5). *"Sed quare hos elegit in gloriam et illos reprobavit, non habet rationem nisi divinam voluntatem"* (ad 3).

35. *Ordinatio* I, d. 40, c.

36. *Ordinatio* I, d. 44, c.

37. Heiko Oberman, *The Harvest of Medieval Theology* (Cambridge: Harvard Univ. Press, 1967) 185–96, esp. 189–92, discusses the role of foreseen merits in predestination for Gabriel Biel in relation to William of Ockham. It should be noted that for these authors and for the many late medieval theologians who agree with them, God does in some exceptional cases, such as those of St. Paul and the Virgin Mary, elect to eternal life apart from foreseen merits, but ordinarily *(regulariter)* God requires "that one must do his very best" (192).

38. McGrath, "Augustinianism?" (see above, n. 9) 256–266.

39. McGrath, "Augustinianism?" (see above, n. 9).

40. See A. Zumkeller, "Erbsünde, Gnade und Rechtfertigung im Verständnis der Erfurter Augustinertheologen des Spätmittelalters," *Zeitschrift für Kirchengeschichte* 92 (1981) 39–59.

41. P. Vignaux, *Luther, Commentateur des Sentences* (Livre I, Distinction XVII) (Paris: J. Vrin, 1935).

42. Cf. K. Froehlich, "Aspects of Justification Language in the Middle Ages," in this volume, 143–61.

43. See §§22–28 below.

44. See §§29–63 below.

45. See §43 below.

46. See n. 22 above.

47. The *sola*, added by Luther in his translation of Rom. 3:29, was to express the exclusion of good works in justification. See *On Translating,* 1530 (WA 20/2:636, 11-638, 22; LW 35:187–89). On Luther's doctrine of faith, see Walter von Loewenich, *Luther's Theology of the Cross* (Minneapolis: Augsburg, 1976), ch. 2. Melanchthon regarded the *sola* as an "exclusive particle" denying "trust in the merit of love or works" (Ap. 4:73–74; BS 175; BC 117).

48. CA 3:4; BS 54; BC 30; CA 5:2; BS 58; BC 31.

49. Cf. CA 4, where "alone" is implied rather than expressed (BS 56; BC 30).

50. See SA 2/1:1–5; BS 415; BC 292.

51. *". . . quia isto articulo stante stat Ecclesia, ruente ruit Ecclesia," Exposition of Ps. 130:4,* 1538 (WA 40/3:352, 3). Luther used similar formulations elsewhere. This statement and similar ones caused later Lutheran theologians to call the article of justification by faith "the article on which the church stands and falls" *("articulus stantis et cadentis ecclesiae").* Valentin E. Löscher seems to have been the first to employ this phrase in his anti-pietist essay, *Timotheus Verinus* (Wittenberg, 1718). See Friedrich Loofs, *"Der articulus stantis et cadentis ecclesiae," Theologische Studien und Kritiken* 90 (1917) 345.

52. FC SD 5:20–21; BS 958–59; BC 561–62.

53. Luther expounded these views in the *Disputation Against Scholastic Theology,* 1517 (WA 1:221–28; LW 31:9–16); in the *Ninety-Five Theses,* 1517 (WA 1:233–38; LW 31:25–33), and in *The Heidelberg Disputation,* 1518 (WA 1:353–74; LW 31:39–70). See also Thomas N. Tentler, *Sin and Confession on the Eve of the Reformation* (Princeton: Princeton Univ. Press, 1977) 351–63. On the influence of Staupitz on Luther, see David C. Steinmetz, *Luther and Staupitz* (Duke Monographs in Medieval and Renaissance Studies 4; Durham, N.C.: Duke Univ. Press, 1980) 141–44.

54. Letter of October 31, 1517 (WA Br 1:111, 37–46; LW 48:47).

55. WA 1:233–38; LW 31:25–33.

56. See, for example, Thesis 25 in *The Heidelberg Disputation,* 1518 (WA 1:364, 1–16; LW 31:55–56). Luther had already dealt with justification in his *Lectures on Romans,* 1515–16. See Karl Holl, "Die Rechtfertigungslehre in Luthers Vorlesung über den Römerbrief mit besonderer Rücksicht auf die Frage der Heilsgewissheit" in *Gesammelte Aufsätze zur Kirchengeschichte, I: Luther* (4th and 5th eds; Tübingen: Mohr, 1927: reprinted, Darmstadt: Wissenschaftliche Buchgesellschaft, 1965) 111–54.

57. In much of the Scholasticism of the day *caritas* was understood as a divinely infused virtue whereby the believer is brought into union with God. The formula *fides caritate formata* was meant to interpret the Vulgate version of Gal. 5:6, *"fides quae per caritatem operatur,"* transposing it into Aristotelian thought categories: "faith formed [in the Aristotelian sense of formal causality] by charity," i.e., a faith animated by love. The Greek of Gal. 5:6 is usually translated "faith working through love" (RSV), but another possible meaning is "faith inspired by [God's] love [toward us]." Contemporary Scholastic usage is indicated by the statement of Johannes Altenstaig, *Vocabularius theologiae* (Hagenau, 1517) I: Fol. XXXI: "Charity . . . is the form of the virtues inasmuch as through charity the act of virtue is made perfect, because through charity they [the acts of the virtues] are referred to their last end, which is God. For it is more perfect for an act to be related to God than to any other end." Altenstaig is here speaking of infused charity, poured into the human heart by God.

58. See Jared Wicks, *Cajetan Responds. A Reader in Reformation Controversy* (Washington, D.C.: Catholic University of America, 1978) 56–58 et passim. In greater detail see J. Wicks, "Roman Reactions to Luther: The First Year (1518)," *Catholic Historical Review* 69 (1983) 561–62 esp. 549–50; also Gerhard Hennig, *Cajetan und Luther. Ein historischer Beitrag zur Begegnung von Thomismus und Reformation* (Arbeiten zur Theologie 7; ed. Alfred Jepsen et al.; Stuttgart: Calwer, 1966) 67–69.

59. DS 1025–26.

60. See Luther's own account of the Proceedings at Augsburg, 1518 (WA 2:7, 29–34; LW 31:261). For Cajetan's view see n. 58 above. For a review of this encounter in the context of Luther's doctrine of justification, see Ernst Bizer, *Fides ex auditu: Eine Untersuchung über die Entdeckung der Gerechtigkeit Gottes durch Martin Luther* (Neukirchen-Vluyn: Verlag der Buchhandlung des Erziehungsvereins, 1958) 115–23.

61. Cf. Cajetan, *Opuscula* (Lyons, 1562) 111a: *"Hoc enim est novam ecclesiam construere."* Quotation translated in Wicks, *Cajetan Responds,* 55; cf. 22–23.

62. Luther summarized his view of the papacy in thesis 13. See the *Leipzig Debate,* 1519 (WA 2:161, 35–38; LW 31:318). Cf. the analysis of Scott H. Hendrix, *Luther and the Papacy: Stages in a Reformation Conflict* (Philadelphia: Fortress, 1981) 81–85.

63. DS 1451–92.

64. See WA 6:202–76; LW 44:21–114. WA 6:381–469; LW 44:123–217. WA 6:497–673; LW 36:5–126. WA 7:49–73; LW 31:333–77.

65. See A. Kluckholm et al., eds., *Deutsche Reichstagsakten unter Karl V* (Göttingen: Vandenhoeck & Ruprecht, 1962 [reprint]) 2:647, 1–3. English text in DeLamar Jensen, *Confrontation at Worms* (Provo, Utah: Brigham Young Univ., 1973) 86–87. For a detailed account of events, see E. Gordon Rupp, *Luther's Progress to the Diet of Worms* (New York: Harper, 1964). On Luther's trial, see Daniel Olivier, *The Trial of Luther* (tr. John Tonkin; St. Louis: Concordia, 1978); Remigius Bäumer, ed., *Lutherprozess und Lutherbann* (Corpus Catholicorum 32; Münster: Aschendorff, 1972).

66. These reforms were started by Luther. See *The Basic Liturgical Writings,* 1523–26 (WA 12:35–37, 205–20; 18:417–21; 19:72–113; LW 53:5–90); *The Large and Small Catechisms,* 1529 (BS 501–733; BC 337–461).

67. Translation of Latin text (BS 56; BC 30). Compare the German text of this article.

68. "The dispute and dissension are concerned chiefly with various traditions and abuses" (Conclusion of Part I; BS 83d, 5; BC 48:2).

69. Text in *Melanthonis Opera,* CR 27:6–244. See also Herbert Immenkötter, *Die Confutatio der Confessio Augustana vom 3. August 1530* (Corpus Catholicorum 33; Münster: Aschendorff, 1979). English translation in J. M. Reu, ed., *The Augsburg Confession: A Collection of Sources with An Historical Introduction* (Chicago: Wartburg Publ. House, 1930; reprinted, St. Louis: Concordia Seminary Press, 1966) *348–83.

70. *". . . ex diametro pugnat cum evangelica veritate opera non excludente," Confutatio* 6, 3 (CR 27:99; Immenkötter, *Confutatio,* 90, 18–21; Reu, *The Augsburg Confession,* 352).

71. For a detailed analysis of these negotiations, see Vinzenz Pfnür, *Einig in der Rechtfertigungslehre? Die Rechtfertigungslehre der "Confessio Augustana" (1530) und die Stellungnahme der katholischen Kontroverstheologie zwischen 1530 und 1535* (Wiesbaden: Franz Steiner, 1970). Cf. J. Raitt, "From Augsburg to Trent," in this volume, 200–17.

72. Ap. 4:2–8; BS 158–60; BC 107–08.

73. "Die höchste Kunst im Christentum," Sermon on Gal. 3, January 1, 1532 (WA 36:9, 28–29).

74. Ap 4:382; BS 232; BC 165.

75. Ap 4:252; BS 209; BC 143.

76. Ap 4:227; BS 209; BC 139.

77. Ap 4:229; BS 204 *("summum opus legis")*; BC 139.

78. CA 5:2; BS 58; BC 31.

79. "Things that make no difference," or things neither commanded nor prohibited; "things in the middle" *(Mitteldinge).* The concept originated in Stoic philosophy referring to ethically neutral matters not necessary for true wisdom. Lutherans used the concept as an equivalent for items which fall under the headings of *ius ecclesiasticum.* See FC SD 10:5–9; BS 1055–57; BC 611–12. See also Arthur C. Piepkorn, "*Ius Divinum* and *Adiaphoron* in Relation to Structural Problems in the Church: The Position of the Lutheran Symbolical Books," L/RC 5:123–26; and Bernard J. Verkamp, "The Limits

Upon Adiaphorist Freedom: Luther and Melanchthon," *Theological Studies* 36 (1975) 52–76.

80. CA 26:39; BS 106; BC 69.

81. Recommendtions of a select committee of nine cardinals and prelates to Pope Paul III. See Colman J. Barry, ed., *Readings in Church History* (Westminster: Newman, 1965) 2:96–102. Barry gives 1538 as the date of this document, though some others date it a year or two earlier.

82. See, for example, the notions of the supremacy of Scripture in the works of Kaspar Schatzgeyer (1463–1527), Johann Dietenberger (d. 1534), and Ambrose Catarinus Politi (1484–1553). Cf. George H. Tavard, *Holy Writ and Holy Church* (New York: Harper and Row, 1959) 173–84.

83. See, e.g., Hubert Kirchner, *Luther and the Peasants' War* (Facet Books, Historical Series 22; Philadelphia: Fortress, 1972). On the "left wing" in general, see George H. Williams, *The Radical Reformation* (Philadelphia: Westminster, 1962), esp. chs. 4 and 13.

84. Mensing, *Antapologie* (Frankfurt/Oder, 1533), fol. 13, r.v.; cited by Pfnür, *Einig in der Rechtfertigungslehre . . .* , 328 (cited above, n. 71). Mensing, a Dominican adversary of Luther, received his licentiate in theology at Wittenberg in 1517, became provincial of Saxony in 1534, and suffragan bishop of Halberstadt in 1539. He died about 1541.

85. See above, §27.

86. SA 2/2:10; BS 419; BC 294.

87. SA 2/4:7; BS 429; BC 299.

88. Appendix to SA; BS 464:7; BC 316–17.

89. The text of the "Regensburg Book" *(Liber Ratisbonensis)* can be found in *Melanthonis Opera,* CR 4:190–238. The colloquy met from April 17 to May 31, 1541. For a detailed account of Luther's influence on the Regensburg meeting, see Walter von Loewenich, *Duplex iustitia: Luthers Stellung zu einer Unionsformel des 16. Jahrhunderts* (Veröffentlichungen des Instituts für europäische Geschichte, Mainz 68; Wiesbaden: Franz Steiner, 1972) 23–55. On the problems generated at Regensburg, see Vinzenz Pfnür, *Die Einigung bei den Religionsgesprächen von Worms und Regensburg 1540/41: Eine Täuschung?* (Schriften des Vereins für Reformationsgeschichte 191; Gütersloh: Gerd Mohn, 1980).

90. CR 4:201.

91. Hubert Jedin, *A History of the Council of Trent* (tr. Dom E. Graf; London: Nelson and Sons, 1954) 1:382.

92. Letter to John Frederick, May 10 or 11, 1541 (WA Br 9:406, 8). See also Loewenich, *Duplex iustitia,* 54. The Protestant participants submitted their objections to the Catholic side on May 31, 1541. See *Melanthonis Opera,* CR 4:348–76.

93. This was the principal condition of the Smalcald League. Luther had proposed the condition during a meeting with the papal emissary Paul Vergerio in Wittenberg in 1535. See *Melanthonis Opera,* CR 2:987.

94. DS 1515. Cf. Augustine, *Ctr. duas ep. Pelagianorum,* bk. 1, ch. 13, #26 (CSEL 60:445; PL 44:562).

95. DS 1523.

96. DS 1532. Heiko Oberman maintains that the verb *promeretur* (translated in our text as "truly merits") indicates the council *did not exclude* that acts of the sinner posited with divine grace may prepare for or merit justification congruously, i.e., not in the strict sense *(de condigno),* but in a lesser or partial way *(de congruo).* If so, this passage does not exclude (though it also does not endorse) the Ockhamist thesis. See H. Oberman, "Das tridentinische Rechtfertigungsdekret im Licht spätmittelalterlicher Theologie," *Zeitschrift für Theologie und Kirche* 61 (1964) 251–82 (tr., "The Tridentine Decree on Justification in the Light of Late Medieval Theology," *Journal for Theology and the Church 3, Distinctive Protestant and Catholic Themes Reconsidered* [ed. R. W. Funk; New York: Harper & Row, 1967] 28–54, esp. 38–39). Thus the text, in Oberman's

opinion, leaves room for justification to be *partim* a work of God and *partim* a work of the still unjustified human being. Oberman thinks that Roman Catholic scholars are themselves divided in the way they interpret *promeretur* in this context and knows that not all concede his reading as plausible. Lutherans may fear that failure to exclude any and all types of merit prior to justification will engender false confidence and works-righteousness. Catholics may suspect that this fear discounts Trent's insistence on the prevenience of God's grace and its description of human cooperation in terms of a failure to do what humans could do by their own devices (namely, reject the grace and thus sin). For a Catholic reaction to Oberman's article, see Eduard Schillebeeckx, "The Tridentine View on Justification," in F. Böckle, ed., *Moral Problems and Christian Personalism* (Concilium 5, 1965) 176–79.

97. DS 1525.

98. DS 1526.

99. DS 1529.

100. Ibid. The council is here quoting Augustine, *De Trinitate,* bk. 14, ch. 12, #15 (PL 42:1048).

101. DS 1532, with quotations from Roman Ritual *Ordo Baptismi* n. 1 and from Heb. 11:6.

102. DS 1530–31.

103. DS 1535.

104. DS 1540.

105. DS 1540, 1565–66.

106. DS 1548. Cf. Augustine, quoted in n. 22 above.

107. DS 1549.

108. DS 1546.

109. DS 1582.

110. See §27 above.

111. FC SD 1–6; BS 843–99; BC 508–68. See also Eric W. Gritsch and Robert W. Jenson, *Lutheranism* (Philadelphia: Fortress, 1976), ch. 5.

112. "Forensic" (from Latin *forum,* the marketplace where judicial and other business was conducted) is a designation used by Luther and other Reformers to emphasize the justification *(Rechtfertigung)* of the sinner on account of Christ rather than on account of merit by fulfilling God's law *(Recht)* through good works. In this sense "forensic" denotes the *pronouncing* or *declaring* righteous of the sinner who stands before God's judicial tribunal without, however, excluding the necessity of good works as the fruit of justification. Luther used the designation in analogy to old German judicial practices. See Werner Elert, "Deutschrechtliche Züge in Luthers Rechtfertigungslehre," *Zeitschrift für systematische Theologie* 12 (1935) 22–35. See also Melanchthon, Ap 4:252–53; BS 209; BC 143. FC SD 3:32; BS 925; BC 544. Cf. G. Forde, "Forensic Justification and the Law in Lutheran Theology," in this volume, 278–303.

113. FC SD 3:32; BS 925; BC 544–45. These statements were directed against such theologians as Andreas Osiander, who spoke of justification as the "indwelling" *(Einwohnung)* of the divine nature in the believer. See FC SD 3:54; BS 923–33; BC 548–49.

114. FC SD 2:60–62; BS 864–65; BC 519.

115. FC SD 5:27; BS 961; BC 563.

116. FC SD 6:20; BS 968; BC 567.

117. FC SD 11:28; BS 1071; BC 620. FC SD 11:91; BS 1089–90; BC 631–32.

118. *De servo arbitrio,* WA 18:600–787; LW 33:15–295. Cf. also Luther's "Preface to the Epistle of St. Paul to the Romans" 1546 (1522), WA DB 7:22–25; LW 35:378: "In chapters 9, 10, 11 he teaches of God's eternal predestination . . . in order that our salvation may be taken entirely out of our hands and put in the hand of God alone. . . . But you had better follow the order of this epistle. Worry first about Christ and the gospel. . . . Then, when you have reached the eighth chapter and are under the cross and suffering, this will teach you correctly of predestination in chapters 9, 10, and 11, and how comforting it is."

119. Martin Chemnitz, *Examen Concilii Tridentini* I–IV (ed. Eduard Preuss: Leipzig: Hinrichs, 1975) Part I, Locus Eighth, sec. I, art. 1–3, pp. 147–99 (*Examination of the Council of Trent* [tr. Fred Kramer; St. Louis: Concordia Publ. House, 1971], Eighth Topic, Concerning Justification, Sec. I, art. 1–3, 1:465–92).

120. A. Hasler, *Luther in der katholischen Dogmatik* (Munich: Max Hueber Verlag, 1968) 58–98.

121. This is the judgment of critical analysts of Lutheran Orthodoxy. See, for example, Wilhelm Dantine, *The Justification of the Ungodly* (tr. Eric W. Gritsch and Ruth C. Gritsch; St. Louis: Concordia Publ. House, 1968), chs. 1–2, esp. 24. Hans E. Weber, *Reformation, Orthodoxie und Rationalismus* (2nd ed.; Gütersloh: Gerd Mohn, 1937; reprinted, Darmstadt: Wissenschaftliche Buchgesellschaft, n.d.) I/1:126.

122. DS 1997, 2008, 2509–10, 2564–65. The controversy is referred to as *"de auxiliis (divinae gratiae)"* ["on the aids (of divine grace)"]. A position similar to the Molinist view was taken by the Danish Lutheran Bishop Erik Pontoppidan in his explanation to Luther's Small Catechism, *Truth unto Godliness (Sanhed til gudfrygtighed . . . forklarung over Luthers Liden catechismo,* 1737); in answer to question 548, "What is election?," he wrote, "God has appointed all those to eternal life who He from eternity has foreseen would accept the offered grace, believe in Christ, and remain constant in this faith unto the end" (as cited from the "Madison Agreement" among U.S. Norwegian Lutheran groups, in R. C. Wolf, ed., *Documents of Lutheran Unity in America* [Philadelphia: Fortress, 1966] document 100, p. 233). On the ongoing influence of Pontoppidan's formulation, cf. T. R. Skarsten, "Erik Pontoppidan and His Asiatic Prince Menoza," *Church History* 50 (1981) 33–34.

123. DS 2005–6.

124. DS 2438, 2464.

125. DS 2123. *Fides late dicta,* a term coined by Juan Ripalda, S.J. (1594–1648), means faith based on the so-called "natural" revelation of God through the created order. Ripalda held that such faith, in the case of the unevangelized, could be justifying provided it was elicited in response to divine grace. The condemnation was apparently directed at Gilles Estrix, S.J., who is reported to have taught Ripalda's opinion at Louvain in 1670. The Holy Office did not state that Ripalda was in error but that Estrix's thesis in the form quoted was "at least scandalous and harmful in its practical effects" (DS 2166). See S. Harent, art. "Infidèles (salut des)," DThC 7:1759–60, 1792–98.

126. See *Ascent of Mount Carmel,* II, ch. 9, in Kieran Kavanaugh and Otilio Rodriguez, eds., *The Collected Works of St. John of the Cross* (Washington, D.C.: Institute of Carmelite Studies, 1973) 129–30. On Bérulle and his classical work, *Discours de l'état et des grandeurs de Jésus* (1623), see Fernando Guileen Preckler, *Bérulle aujourd'hui. Pour une spiritualité de l'humanité du Christ* (Paris: Beauchesne, 1978).

127. Henri-Marie Boudon (1624–1702), *Oeuvres completes* (Paris: Migne, 1856) 1:406; similar expressions recur in all his writings. Jean-Martin Moye (1730–1793), *Lettres* (Gap, 1962) 59; see Georges Tavard, *L'Expérience de Jean-Martin Moye. Mystique et mission* (Paris: Beauchesne, 1978) 67–68, 145. Other formulations along the same lines will be found in many authors of the period, e.g., in Jean-Pierre de Caussade, *L'Abandon à la providence divine* (Paris: Desclée de Brouwer, 1966), composed between 1730 and 1740; in English: *The Sacrament of the Present Moment* (tr. Kitty Muggeridge; San Francisco: Harper & Row, 1981). See also the prayers from Teresa of the Child Jesus, from Claude de la Colombière, and from the Roman Liturgy (collect for the fifth Sunday after Epiphany) cited in H. Küng, *Justification: The Doctrine of Karl Barth and a Catholic Reflection* (tr. T. Collins, E. E. Tolk, and D. Granskou; New York: Thomas Nelson, 1964; 2nd ed., Philadelphia: Westminster, 1981) 274.

128. See, for example, the Pietist August Hermann Francke (1663–1727) in Gerhard Müller, *Die Rechtfertigungslehre, Geschichte und Probleme* (Studienbücher, Kirchen und Dogmengeschichte; Gütersloh: Gerd Mohn, 1977) 81, cf. 77–83 (bibliography).

129. See, for example, the Lutheran theologian Johann Salomo Semler (1725–91), in Müller, *Rechtfertigungslehre,* 85, cf. 83–88 (bibliography) (cited above, n. 128).

130. Friedrich Schleiermacher, *The Christian Faith* (English tr. of the 2nd German edition, 1830; ed. H. R. Mackintosh and J. J. Stewart; Philadelphia: Fortress, 1976) 478–505, 484; justification is treated as part of regeneration. Albrecht Ritschl, *The Christian Doctrine of Justification and Reconciliation* (ed. and tr. H. R. Mackintosh and A. B. Macaulay; Library of Religious and Philosophical Thought; Clifton, N.J.: Reference Book Publishers, Inc., 1966), chs. 1–3: "The Conception of Justification and Its Relations." How Ritschl influenced later theologians, among them Wilhelm Herrmann (1846–1922) and Adolf von Harnack (1851–1930), is shown by Walther von Loewenich, *Luther und der Neuprotestantismus* (Witten: Luther-Verlag, 1963) 111–29. For a summary of Schleiermacher's and Ritschl's treatments of justification, see Müller, *Rechtfertigungslehre,* 89–100 (cited above, n. 128).

M. Kähler, *Die Wissenschaft der christlichen Lehre von dem evangelischen Grundartikel aus im Abrisse dargestellt* (3 vols.; Erlangen: Andreas Deichert, 1883).

P. Althaus, *The Theology of Martin Luther* (tr. Robert C. Schultz; Philadelphia: Fortress, 1966), esp. 224–50; *Die christliche Wahrheit: Lehrbuch der Dogmatik* (3rd ed.; Gütersloh: Bertelsmann , 1952), esp. section 61.

W. Elert, *Der christliche Glaube. Grundlinien der lutherischen Dogmatik* (2nd ed. rev.; Hamburg: Furche Verlag, 1960); on Elert, see Müller, *Rechtfertigungslehre,* 107–12 (cited above, n. 128). R. Prenter, *Creation and Redemption* (tr. Theodor I. Jensen; Philadelphia: Fortress, 1967); *Spiritus Creator* (tr. John M. Jenson: Philadelphia: Muhlenberg, 1953).

G. Aulén, *The Faith of the Christian Church* (tr. E. H. Wahlstrom and G. E. Arden; Philadelphia: Muhlenberg, 1948).

P. Tillich, *Systematic Theology* (3 vols. in one; Chicago: University of Chicago Press, 1967) I:49–50, 222–28; K. Barth, *Church Dogmatics,* 4: *The Doctrine of Reconciliation,* Part I (tr. G. W. Bromiley; Edinburgh: Clark, 1956) 514–642.

For an overview see Ernst Kinder, ed., *Die evangelische Lehre von der Rechtfertigung* (Quellen zur Konfessionskunde, Reihe B, Protestantische Quellen 1; Lüneburg: Heliand-Verlag, 1957) 12–13, 83–105; A. Peters, in O. H. Pesch and A. Peters, *Einführung in die Lehre von Gnade and Rechtfertigung* (Darmstadt: Wissenschaftliche Buchgesellschaft, 1981) 284–365; Robert Bertram, "Recent Lutheran Theologies on Justification by Faith: A Sampling," in this volume, 241–55. H. G. Pöhlmann, *Rechtfertigung: Die gegenwärtige kontroverstheologische Problematik der Rechtfertigungslehre zwischen der evangelisch-lutherischen und der römisch-katholischen Kirche* (Gütersloh: Gerd Mohn, 1971). Arthur B. Crabtree, *The Restored Relationship: A Study in Justification and Reconciliation* (Valley Forge, Pa.; Judson, 1963) 160–86. Vittorio Subilia, *La Giustificazione Per Fede* ("Biblioteca Di Cultura Religiosa"; Brescia: Paideia Editrice, 1976) (in German: *Die Rechtfertigung aus Glauben: Gestalt und Wirkung vom Neuen Testament bis heute* [tr. Max Krumbach; Göttinger theologische Lehrbücher; Göttingen: Vandenhoeck & Ruprecht, 1981]).

131. J. A. Möhler, *Symbolism, or Exposition of the Doctrinal Differences between Catholics and Protestants as Evidenced by Their Symbolical Writings* (first German ed., 1832; tr. James B. Robertson; 5th English ed.; London: Gibbins and Co., 1906), ch. 3, "Opposite Views on the Doctrine of Justification."

John Henry Newman, *Lectures on the Doctrine of Justification* (Westminster, Md.; Christian Classics, 1966; first ed. 1838; reprint of ed. of 1900) 348, 278.

M. J. Scheeben, *The Mysteries of Christianity* (first German ed. 1865; tr. Cyril Vollert; St. Louis: B. Herder, 1946) 625–628; *Nature and Grace* (first German ed., 1861; tr. C. Vollert; St. Louis: B. Herder, 1954).

On K. Rahner, see below, I. D. 2, "Catholic Theology since World War II," §79.

H. Küng, *Justification* (cited above, n. 127). Cf. also George Tavard, "Catholic Views on Karl Barth," *Christian Century* 76, 5 (February 4, 1969) 132–33; Müller, *Rechtfertigungslehre,* 100–106 (cited above, n. 128).

For developments among Catholic theologians, see also Wilfried Joest, ed., *Die katholische Lehre von der Rechtfertigung und von der Gnade* (Quellen zur Konfessionskunde, Reihe A. Römisch-Katholische Quellen 2; Lüneburg; Heliand-Verlag, 1954);

and Avery Dulles, "Justification in Contemporary Catholic Theology," in this volume, 256–77.

132. A. Schlatter, *Gottes Gerechtigkeit: Ein Kommentar zum Römerbrief* (Stuttgart: Calwer, 1935; 3rd ed. 1959) 42–43, 117. Schlatter's son Theodor felt constrained to explain in the preface to the 4th ed. that the commentary's aim was not criticism of Luther's interpretation but to "go beyond Luther forward to Paul" in order to show how Paul saw God's saving work.

R. Bultmann, *Theology of the New Testament* (tr. K. Grobel; New York: Scribner's 1951) 1:270–85: *"Dikaiosyne Theou," Journal of Biblical Literature* 83 (1964) 12–16. A different approach was offered by Krister Stendahl, who warned against narrowing the gospel to an introspective interpretation of justification but has subsequently shown his interest to be not against justification so much as in favor of a salvation-history approach. Cf. his "The Apostle Paul and the Introspective Conscience of the West," *Harvard Theological Review* 56 (1963) 199–215; reprinted in *Ecumenical Dialogue at Harvard* (ed. S. H. Miller and G. E. Wright: Cambridge, Mass.: Harvard Univ. Press, 1964) 236–56; and most recently in Stendahl's *Paul Among Jews and Gentiles* (Philadelphia: Fortress, 1976) 78–96; cf. 23–40 and 129–32.

E. Käsemann, "The 'Righteousness of God' in Paul," in *New Testament Questions of Today* (Philadelphia: Fortress, 1969) 168–82. Note also the dissertations done under Käsemann: Christian Müller, *Gottesgerechtigkeit und Gottes Volk: Eine Untersuchung zu Römer 9–11* (FRLANT 86; Göttingen: Vandenhoeck & Ruprecht, 1964); and Peter Stuhlmacher, *Gerechtigkeit Gottes bei Paulus* (FRLANT 87; Göttingen: Vandenhoeck & Ruprecht, 1965).

See further n. 200 below for Catholic exegetes such as Lyonnet and Kertelge.

133. *Dei verbum* 5 implies such a broader definition when it describes the obedience of faith as one "by which man entrusts his whole self freely to God offering 'the full submission of intellect and will to God who reveals' [Vatican I] and freely assenting to the truth revealed by Him." The Council of Trent had already referred to faith as *fundamentum et radix omnis justificationis* (DS 1526) but in the sixth chapter of its decree on justification it described faith rather as the gift whereby we believe the truth of what God has revealed and promised (DS 1532). Trent, therefore, favored a more strictly intellectual concept of faith than that which prevailed at Vatican II.

134. *Lumen gentium* 48.

135. Ibid., 14.

136. Ibid., 48.

137. Ibid., 49.

138. In addition to the text just quoted, see *Ad gentes* 7 and *Lumen gentium* 8, 14, 28, 41, 60, and 62.

139. *Sacrosanctum concilium* 5.

140. Ibid., 7.

141. On bishops, see *Lumen gentium* 25 and *Christus Dominus* 12. On presbyters (priests), see *Lumen gentium* 28 and *Presbyterorum ordinis* 4.

142. *Sacrosanctum concilium* 9.

143. Ibid., 10.

144. Ibid., 59.

145. Ibid., 10.

146. Ibid., 11.

147. See Vilmos Vajta, "Renewal of Worship: *De sacra Liturgia,*" in *Dialogue on the Way* (ed. G. Lindbeck; Minneapolis: Augsburg, 1965) 101–128, esp. 108–113.

148. *Lumen gentium* 8.

149. Ibid.

150. *Unitatis redintegratio* 6.

151. "For in the sacred books, the Father who is in heaven meets His children with great love and speaks with them; and the force and power in the word of God is so great that it remains the support and energy of the Church, the strength of faith for her sons, the food of the soul, and pure and perennial source of spiritual life" (*Dei verbum* 21).

152. Ibid.

153. *Dei verbum* 10.

154. Ibid. 9. In 21 it is noted that the Scriptures "impart the word of God Himself without change." In 24 it is stated: "The sacred Scriptures contain the word of God and, since they are inspired, really are the word of God; and so the study of the sacred page is, as it were, the soul of sacred theology."

155. According to *Lumen gentium* 25 all definitions by popes and councils will win acceptance in the church "on account of the activity of that same Holy Spirit, whereby the whole flock of Christ is preserved and progresses in unity of faith." The Catholic doctrine of the assistance promised to the hierarchical *magisterium* was discussed in volume 6 of this dialogue, L/RC 6:26–27, 44–45.

156. See, for example, L. Bouyer, *The Spirit and Forms of Protestantism* (tr. A. V. Littledale; Westminster, Md.: Newman, 1956); H. Küng, *Justification* (cited above, n. 127); H. U. von Balthasar, *The Theology of Karl Barth* (tr. John Drury; New York: Holt, Rinehart and Winston, 1971); G. Söhngen, *Gesetz und Evangelium* (Freiburg and Munich: K. Alber, 1957); P. Fransen, *The New Life of Grace* (tr. G. Dupont; New York: Herder and Herder, 1972). For other references see A. Dulles, "Justification in Contemporary Catholic Theology," in this volume 256–77.

157. K. Rahner, *Foundations of Christian Faith* (tr. W. Dych; New York: Seabury [Crossroad], 1978) 359–69. Cf. his "Questions of Controversial Theology on Justification," *Theological Investigations* (tr. K. Smyth; Baltimore: Helicon, 1966) 4:189–218.

158. " . . . [N]ot only the grace of divinization, but even the acceptance of this gift must according to all theological sources be characterized as grace. Hence the acceptance of the divine gift of justification is itself part of the gift. . . . " (Rahner, "The Word and the Eucharist," *Theological Investigations* 4:257).

159. "This word of God (as inner moment of the salvific action of God on man and so with it and because of it) is the salutary word which brings with it what it affirms. It is itself therefore salvific event, which, in its outward, historical and social aspect, displays what happens in it and under it, and brings about what it displays. It renders the grace of God present" (ibid., 259–60). For a sampling of recent Catholic "word" theology, see *The Word: Readings in Theology* (compiled at the Canisianum, Innsbruck; New York: P. J. Kenedy, 1964).

160. E. Schillebeeckx, *Christ: The Experience of Jesus as Lord* (tr. John Bowman; New York: Seabury [Crossroad], 1980) 838.

161. J. L. Segundo, "Capitalism—Socialism: A Theological Crux," in *The Mystical and Political Dimension of the Christian Faith* (ed. C. Geffre and G. Gutiérrez; Concilium 96; New York: Herder and Herder, 1974) 122.

162. L. Boff, *Liberating Grace* (tr. John Drury; Maryknoll, N.Y.: Orbis, 1979) 151–52.

163. Earlier in Germany important discussions on justification had taken place between Roman Catholic and Lutheran theologians. Cf. esp. the essays in *Pro Veritate* (ed. H. Volk and E. Schlink; Münster: Aschendorff, 1963) by P. Brunner, pp. 59–96, and H. Volk, pp. 96–131.

164. *A Study Document "On Justification,"* prepared by the Commission on Theology for the Lutheran World Federation Assembly in Helsinki, July 30–August 11, 1963 (New York: National Lutheran Council, n.d.).

165. *Proceedings of the Fourth Assembly of the Lutheran World Federation Helsinki, July 30–August 11, 1963,* published by the Lutheran World Federation (Berlin and Hamburg: Lutherisches Verlagshaus, 1965). Cf. "Helsinki 1963," *Lutheran World* 11 (1964) 1–36, esp. 4–10.

166. *Proceedings,* ¶¶ 77 and 83 for the quotations from an address by Gerhard Gloege; 95, cf. ¶¶ 97 and 89 for that by Helge Brattgård, who refers to FC SD 3:41; BS 928; BC 546, *"sola fides est, quae apprehendit benedictionem sine operibus, et tamen numquam est sola"* (cf Luther, WA 43:255, 38; LW 4:166).

167. "'Justification Today,' Document 75—Assembly and Final Versions," *Lutheran World* 12, 1, Supplement (1965) 1–11. The supplement includes "The Meaning

of Justification 1958–1963," by Jorg Rothermund, "The Discussion since Helsinki," and "Questions for Further Study and Discussion." On the development of the Helsinki texts on justification, see also Peter Kjeseth and Paul Hoffman, "Document 75," *Lutheran World* 11 (1964) 83–86.

168. "Justification Today," 1.

169. Cf. Henning Graf Reventlow, *Rechtfertigung im Horizont des Alten Testaments* (Beiträge zur evangelischen Theologie 58; Munich: Kaiser, 1971).

170. A. R. Wentz, "Lutheran World Federation," in *The Encyclopedia of the Lutheran Church* (ed. Julius Bodensieck; Minneapolis: Augsburg, 1965) 2:1428–29, for this and the following quotations. For a summary of further, subsequent interpretation, see Albrecht Peters, "Systematische Besinnung zu einer Neuinterpretation der reformatorischen Rechtfertigungslehre," in *Rechtfertigung im neuzeitlichen Lebenszusammenhang. Studien zur Neuinterpretation der Rechtfertigungslehre* (ed. W. Lohff and C. Walther; Gütersloh: Gerd Mohn, 1974) 107–25; and in Pesch and Peters, *Einführung,* 332–33 (see n. 130 above).

171. K. Holl, "Luthers Bedeutung für den Fortschritt der Auslegungskunst," *Gesammelte Aufsätze* (cited above, n. 56) 1:544–82. Gerhard Ebeling, "Die Anfänge von Luthers Hermeneutik," *Zeitschrift für Theologie und Kirche* 48 (1951) 172–230; "The New Hermeneutics and the Young Luther," *Theology Today* 21 (1964) 34–45. Cf. also James S. Preus' study of Luther's hermeneutic, *From Shadow to Promise* (Cambridge, Mass.: Harvard Univ. Press, 1969).

172. Ap 4:42–43; BS 168; BC 113. This unconditionality of the promise, to be sure, does not exclude "the Word and sacraments" (see below, §92).

173. *Luther and Erasmus: Free Will and Salvation* (ed. E. G. Rupp and D. Watson; Library of Christian Classics 17; Philadelphia: Westminster, 1969) 143.

174. Cf., e.g., FC SD 2:20–21; BS 879–80; BC 524–25. This passage, pieced together from a number of Luther's writings, was a favorite target of Catholic controversialists. See Hasler, *Luther* (cited above, n. 120) 175–76.

175. Ap 4:73–74; BS 175; BC 117.

176. Advent Postil, 1522, WA 10/1, 2:48, 5; WA 7:475, 14–18; WA 18:638; LW 33:70.

177. For Luther's view that these saints were saved by faith despite their errors on justification, see WA 40/1:687; LW 26:459–60; WA 39/2:107–8; 7:774; 8:451–2. Cf. John M. Headley, *Luther's View of Church History* (New Haven: Yale Univ. Press, 1963) 191, 212, 220–1.

178. In speaking of the state of historical humanity Pope John Paul II has recently used the phrase, *"status naturae lapsae simul et redemptae"* (*L'Osservatore Romano,* Eng. ed., Feb. 18, 1980, p. 1).

179. Thomas Aquinas, S. T., I, q. 1, a. 8, ad 2.

180. "Catholic theologians also emphasize in reference to justification that God's gift of salvation for the believer is unconditional as far as human accomplishments are concerned" (MR #26).

181. According to Trent (DS 1528–30) the infusion of grace, the forgiveness of sins, and sanctification are simultaneous. For St. Thomas the process of justification, of its nature, requires that in the justified person liberation from sin precede the attainment of justifying grace. But he holds that in relation to God, who justifies, the order is reversed. *"Et quia infusio gratiae et remissio culpae dicuntur ex parte Dei iustificantis, ideo ordine naturae prior est gratiae infusio quam culpae remissio. Sed si sumantur ea, quae sunt ex parte hominis iustificati, est e converso; nam prius est naturae ordine liberatio a culpa, quam consecutio gratiae iustificantis"* (S.T., I–II, q. 113, a. 8, ad 1).

182. SA 3/3:43–45; BS 448; BC 310. See also Ap 4:48; BS 169; BC 114.

183. Council of Trent, Session VI, chap. 5 (DS 1515).

184. Ibid., can. 23 (DS 1573).

185. Ibid., ch. 11 (DS 1537).

186. Ibid.

187. Karl Rahner in particular has emphasized that created grace is "a consequence" rather than "the basis" of uncreated grace, i.e., of God's communication of himself (*Theological Investigations* 1 [tr. Cornelius Ernst; Baltimore: Helicon, 1961] 325).

188. Luther, Small Catechism, 2 (Creed) 6; BS 512; BC 345. Luther spoke of faith as the power which "unites the soul with Christ as a bride is united with her bridegroom." He called this communion "a joyous struggle and exchange" *(fröhlicher Streit und Wechsel),* WA 7:25, 34; 55:8; LW 31:351. See also *Lectures on Galatians,* 1535, where Luther speaks of faith "consummating the Deity" *(consummat divinitatem)* not in the substance of God but in us, WA 40/1, 360:24–25; LW 26:227. A comparable notion appears in FC SD 9 (Person of Christ), 96: " . . . that our flesh and blood have in Christ been made to sit so high at the right hand of the majesty and almighty power of God" (BS 1049; BC 610).

189. DS 1531. See above §54.

190. A contemporary Lutheran, Robert W. Jenson, has coined the term "anti-Pelagian codicil" to describe the efforts of medieval theology to evade the Pelagian consequences he holds to be implicit in the Scholastic doctrine of cooperation. See Gritsch and Jenson, *Lutheranism* (cited above, n. 111) 39; also R. W. Jenson, "On Recognizing the Augsburg Confession" in *The Role of the Augsburg Confession* (ed. J. A. Burgress et al.; Philadelphia: Fortress, 1980) 160–62. In a parallel way some Catholics seem to find something resembling an anti-Manichaean or anti-Antinomian codicil in certain formulations of Lutheran Orthodoxy. See Avery Dulles, "Luther's Theology: A Modern Catholic Reflection," unpublished paper for the convocation on Luther and the Modern World held at the Lutheran School of Theology at Chicago, October 20, 1980; manuscript p. 19.

191. Ap 4:366; BS 229; BC 163.

192. Ap 4:194; BS 198; BC 133; cf. Ap 4:365–69; BS 229–30; BC 163. See also M. Luther, *Rhapsodia seu Concepta in Librum de loco Iustificationis* (1530), WA 30/2:670; and his *Wochenpredigten über Matt. 5–7* (1530–32), WA 32:543; LW 21:292–94.

193. CA 12:6; BS 67; BC 35. Cf. Ap 12:45–46, 164–66, 174; BS 260, 288, 290; BC 188, 208, 210.

194. Ap. 12:168; BS 288; BC 209. See H. Fagerberg and H. Jorissen, "Penance and Confession," in *Confessing One Faith: A Joint Commentary on the Augsburg Confession by Lutheran and Catholic Theologians* (ed. G. W. Forell and J. F. McCue; Minneapolis: Augsburg, 1982) 234–61, esp. 244–47.

195. See in this connection the statement of the Lutheran/Roman Catholic Joint Commission, *The Eucharist* (Geneva: Lutheran World Federation, 1980), especially the fourth Supplementary Study, "The Mass as Sacrifice for Atonement for the Living and the Dead *ex opere operato,*" by Vinzenz Pfnür, 76–80 and the fifth Supplementary Study, "The Eucharist as a Communal Meal," by Harding Meyer, 81–83.

196. See §41 above.

197. MR #29.

198. See L/RC 5:21–3, 31–3; 6:32, § 42.

199. Fuller discussion of the New Testament material which bears on the topic of justification by faith has been provided in the volume developed within the dialogue, *"Righteousness" in the New Testament: "Justification" in Lutheran-Catholic Dialogue,* by John Reumann, with responses by Joseph A. Fitzmyer, S.J., and Jerome D. Quinn (Philadelphia: Fortress; New York: Paulist, 1982). This material was discussed by dialogue members in the plenary sessions. It is cited above with the sections of the book indicated by the symbol ‡. See also Jerome D. Quinn, "The Scriptures on Merit," and Joseph A. Burgess, "Rewards, But in a Very Different Sense" in this volume, pp. 82–93 and 94–110.

200. E.g., A Schlatter, *Gottes Gerechtigkeit* (cited above, n. 132) 35–39, 117; E. Käsemann, "'The Righteousness of God' in Paul" (cited above, n. 132); *Commentary on Romans* (Grand Rapids, Mich.: Eerdmans, 1980) 21–32 et passim; P. Stuhlmacher, *Gerechtigkeit Gottes bei Paulus* (cited above, n. 132); K. Kertelge, *"Rechtfertigung" bei*

Paulus: Studien zur Struktur und zum Bedeutungsgehalt des paulinischen Rechtfertigungsbegriffs (Neutestamentliche Abhandlungen ns 3; Münster in W.: Aschendorff, 1967); S. Lyonnet, "De 'iustitia Dei' in epistola ad Romanos," *Verbum Domini* 25 (1947) 23–34, 118–21, 129–44, 193–203, 257–63; K. Kertelge, *"Dikaiosyne, etc.," Exegetisches Wörterbuch zum Neuen Testament* (Stuttgart: Kohlhammer, 1980) 1:784–810. Other literature is cited in *"Righteousness" in the New Testament.*

201. See Luther's *Preface to the Complete Edition of the Latin Writings,* 1545 (WA 54:185–86; LW 34:336–37). Luther ascribed "the formal or active righteousness . . . with which God is righteous and punishes the unrighteous sinner" to "all the teachers" (WA 54:185; LW 34:336). On Luther's "tower experience" *(Turmerlebnis),* reference to which follows in his *Preface,* see also the Table Talk passage, WA TR 3: Nr. 3232a, b, c; LW 54:193–94; further, in O. Scheel, ed. *Dokumente zu Luthers Entwicklung* (2nd ed.; Tübingen: J. C. B. Mohr [Paul Siebeck], 1929) 91, and K. G. Hagen, "Changes in the Understanding of Luther: The Development of the Young Luther," *Theological Studies* 29 (1968) 472–96, esp. 478–81. Joseph A. Fitzmyer, "Brief Remarks on Luther's Interpretation of Pauline Justification" (unpublished paper).

202. Literally, "the righteousness which matters (or holds up, or is valid) before God"; thus in the Luther Bible at Rom. 1:17; 3:21; 2 Cor. 5:21. Cf. the literature cited in n. 201.

203. Heinrich Denifle, O. P., *Die abendländischen Schriftausleger bis Luther über "Justitia Dei" (Rom. 1, 17) und "Justificatio"* (vol. 1, part 2; 2nd ed.; Mainz: F. Kirchheim, 1905). Karl Holl, "Die *iustitia dei* in der vorlutherischen Bibelauslegung des Abendlandes" (1921), reprinted in *Gesammelte Aufsätze, III: Der Westen* (1928; reprinted 1965) 171–88. Gordon Rupp, *The Righteousness of God: Luther Studies* (New York: Philosophical Library, 1953) 123–26.

204. See esp. Phil. 3:9 "the righteousness from God that depends on faith." Cf. 2 Cor. 5:21: " . . . so that in him [Christ] we might become the righteousness of God"; if not pre-Pauline (see above, §128), then it is Paul's own phrase expressing what Luther means by *"die Gerechtigkeit die vor Gott gilt."* On the righteousness of God as "gift," see esp. R. Bultmann, *Theology* and *"Dikaiosyne Theou,"* as cited above in n. 132.

205. See esp. Rom. 3:5 and Käsemann, as cited above in n. 127; *Righteousness* ‡‡ 93, 381.

206. See above, n. 57.

207. Burgess, "Rewards . . . ," p. 104 in this volume.

208. See *"Righteousness" in the New Testament,* pp. 280–83, cf. 413–14, and contrast 275; to the dissenting literature there cited can be added P. Stuhlmacher, "Schriftauslegung in der Confessio Augustana," *Kerygma und Dogma* 26 (1980) 201–202 (the texts, Stuhlmacher holds, cannot be reconciled; instead there must be a more systematic relating to the mission and death of Jesus for sinners from a Pauline perspective), and Jürgen Roloff, *Neues Testament* (Neukirchen-Vluyn: Neukirchener, 1977) 165–66. Cf. D. Lührmann, "Glaube," *Reallexikon für Antike und Christentum* 11 (1979) 78; *Glaube im Frühen Christentum* (Gütersloh: Gütersloher Verlagshaus Gerd Mohn, 1976).

209. Merit language appears frequently in the texts of the Roman liturgy, but words such as *"meritum," "dignus,"* and *"iuste"* are often used in vague and poetical senses that do not lend themselves to precise theological interpretation. For example, the *praeconium paschale* in the Easter Vigil praises the sin of Adam *"quae talem ac tantum meruit redemptorem"* ("which merited such and so great a redeemer"). On Good Friday the wood of the cross is hailed for being *"digna ferre mundi victimam"* ("worthy to bear the victim of the world") (hymn, *"Pange lingua"* in the *Missale Romanum,* commonly called the Tridentine missal). In many of the old Roman collect prayers God is petitioned to grant favors in view of the merits of the saints. Very frequently God or Christ is acknowledged as the giver of all our merits and is implored to grant us merits we do not have. Frequently also the faithful confess their own lack of mertis, their unworthiness, and their need of mercy, as they do, for instance, in the *"Domine, non sum dignus"* ("Lord, I am not worthy") regularly recited before the reception of Holy Communion.

There are also some texts in which God is acknowledged as justly giving to sinners and saints the rewards of their respective deeds.

Illustrative texts from the contemporary Roman liturgy would include the following: *" . . . et omnium sanctorum tuorum; quorum meritis precibusque concedas, ut in omnibus protectionis tuae muniamur auxilio"* (" . . . and of all your saints; may their merits and prayers gain us your constant help and protection" [or more literally, " . . . and of all your saints; grant that through their merits and prayers we may be fortified by your protection in all things"]); Prex Eucharistica I, *Missale Romanum* (Editio typica; Typis Polyglottis Vaticanis, 1971) 448. The first translations given are those of ICEL (International Commission on English in the Liturgy) in *The Sacramentary* (New York: Catholic Book Publishing Co., 1974), followed by a more literal rendering *"Non aestimator meriti sed veniae quaesumus largitor admitte"* ("Do not consider our merits but grant us your forgiveness" [or "Receive us, we beg, not as a judge of merit but as a giver of mercy"]); ibid., 455. *"Gratias agentes quia nos dignos habuisti astare coram te et tibi ministrare"* ("We thank you for counting us worthy to stand in your presence and serve you"); Prex Eucharistica II, ibid., 458. Other texts: First Sunday of Advent, Opening Prayer: *Missale Romanum,* 129; Ash Wednesday, Prayer after Communion: ibid., 180; Wednesday of First Week of Lent, Opening Prayer: ibid., 188; Friday of Second Week of Lent, Opening Prayer: ibid., 198. Also pertinent is the final antiphon of the Blessed Virgin Mary starting with Saturday after the octave of Pentecost: *"Ora pro nobis, sancta Dei Genetrix, ut digni efficiamur promissionibus Christi"* ("Pray for us, holy Mother of God, that we may be made worthy of the promises of Christ"); *The Hours of the Divine Office in English and Latin* (Collegeville, Minn.: Liturgical Press, 1964) 3:4 of the supplementary material.

Regarding the collect which became the opening prayer for the fifth Sunday in Ordinary Time, A. Baumstark (*Comparative Liturgy* [Westminster, Md.: Newman, 1958] 61) observes that it was precisely the Pelagian and semi-Pelagian controversies that marked such collects in the ancient sacramentaries, particularly in the season after Pentecost. Some texts indicating a convergence between Catholic and Lutheran prayer language have been listed in L/RC 4:18–19. For additional texts consult the liturgical concordances such as Andre Pflieger, *Liturgicae Orationis Concordantia Verbalia: Prima Pars, Missale Romanum* (Freiburg: Herder, 1964); Thaddeus A. Schnitker and Wolfgang A. Slaby, *Concordantia Verbalia Missalis Romani* (Münster: Aschendorff, 1983).

210. Examples in recent American Lutheran hymnals, *The Lutheran Hymnal* (1941, LH); *Service Book and Hymnal* (1958, SBH); and *Lutheran Book of Worship* (1978, LBW), include the following: Luther (*"Aus tiefer Not,"* v. 3), *"Darum auf Gott will hoffen ich, auf mein Verdienst nicht bauen"* (LBW 295, 3, "It is in God that we shall hope, and not in our own merit"); (*"Nun Freut Euch,"* 3), *"Mein guten Werk die galten nicht, es war mit ihn' verdorben"* (LBW 299, 3, "My own good works all came to nought, No grace or merit gaining"); LBW 374, 3, " . . . forgiveness and salvation/Daily come through Jesus' merit" (LH expanded trans. of Luther's *"Wir Glauben All"*). Paul Speratus (*"Es ist das Heil,"* 1523, v. 11), *"Der woll mit Gnad erfüllen, was er in uns angfangen hat"* (LBW 297, 5, "The God who saved us by his grace, all glory to his merit"). J. Major (*"Ach Gott und Herr,"* 1613, v. 3), *"Zu dir flieh ich; verstoss mich nicht, wie ichs wohl hab verdienet"* (LH 317, 3, "Lord, Thee I seek, I merit nought"). E. C. Homberg (*"Jesu, Meines Lebens Leben,"* 1659, v. 1), *"in das aüsserste Verderben, nur dasz ich nicht möchte sterben"* (LBW 97, 1 [tr. Catherine Winkworth], "Through your suff'ring, death, and merit/Life eternal I inherit"). J. Neander (*"Gott ist gegenwärtig,"* 1680), as translated in LH 4 and SBH 164, v. 3, "trusting only in thy merit."

Isaac Watts (Congregationalist; "Blest is the man," 1719), "He pleads no merit of reward/And not on works but grace relies" (LH 392, 2). Edward Mote (Baptist; ca. 1834), "My hope is built on nothing less/Than Jesus' blood and righteousness; No merit of my own I claim, But wholly lean on Jesus' name" (LBW 294, 1). J. M. Neale (Anglican; "Blessed Savior, who hast taught me," 1842), "Resting in my Savior's merit" (LH 333, 3; SBH 290, 3). K. J. P. Spitta (Lutheran: *"Wir sind des Herrn,"* 1843), trans. C. T. Astley

(Anglican), "We are the Lord's. His all-sufficient merit . . . this grace accords" (LH 453, 1; LBW 399, 1). H. W. Baker (Anglican; "Ransomed, Restored, Forgiven," 1876), "Not ours, not ours the merit" (LH 32, 2); ("O Perfect Life of Love," 1875), "Thy works, O Lamb of God, I'll plead, Thy merits, not mine own" (LH 170, 6). LH 437, 3, "Who Trusts in God," " . . . Until we stand at Thy right hand/Thro' Jesus' saving merit."

For many more examples, see E. V. Haserodt, *Concordance to The Lutheran Hymnal* (St. Louis: Concordia, 1956) 404–5, *s.v.* "merit, merits," noun and verb.

211. Quinn, "Merit," 89–90; Burgess, "Rewards . . . ," 107–108 in this volume.

212. *Dei verbum* 18.

213. *Breviloquium,* prol., n. 2. See George H. Tavard, *Transiency and Permanence. The Nature of Theology according to St. Bonaventure* (St. Bonaventure, N.Y.: Franciscan Institute, 1974); Renato Russo, *La Metodologia del sapere nel sermone di S. Bonaventura. Unus est Magister Vester Christus* (Grottaferrata: Collegio S. Bonaventurae, 1982).

214. Luther used the German phrase (sometimes translated "what inculcates Christ," LW 35:396) to indicate that the "genuine, sacred books" always preach and teach Christ; Preface to the Epistles of St. James and St. Jude, 1546 (1522); WA DB 7:385, 27; LW 35:396. Such preaching and teaching must be normed by justification, i.e., by the way in which Christ made right the relationship between God and sinners (Rom. 3:21; 1 Cor. 2:2, quoted ibid.). *"Treiben"* is an old German verb which may have been widely used by seafarers. It may have been related to "*propellere*—to drive, to propel" and to "*trudere*—to thrust, to impel"; see Friedrich Kluge, *Etymologisches Wörterbuch der deutschen Sprache* (21st ed.; Berlin: de Gruyter, 1975) 788.

215. The disagreement over the canonical status of the so-called Apocrypha or deuterocanonical books of the Old Testament is irrelevant to our present topic because, with the exception of a single passage (2 Macc. 12:42–45) purportedly referring to the tangential question of purgatory, these books have not been cited in the disputes relating to justification.

216. L/RC 6:37, 52–56 deals with the question of the acceptance of all church dogmas as a condition for church union. Page 54, §46, takes note of the limited eucharistic sharing that can exist between Roman Catholics and Orthodox notwithstanding the nonacceptance by the Orthodox of certain Roman Catholic dogmas such as papal infallibility and the Immaculate Conception.

217. MR #27.

218. S.T. II–II, q. 19, a. 4, ad 2. For discussions of the parallelism between Thomas Aquinas and Martin Luther on the assurance of salvation (ascribed by the former to hope and by the latter to faith), see S. Pfürtner, *Luther and Aquinas—A Conversation: Our Salvation, Its Certainty and Peril* (tr. Edward Quinn; New York: Sheed & Ward, 1965) and, more briefly, O. H. Pesch, *Theologie der Rechtfertigung bei Martin Luther und Thomas von Aquin: Versuch eines systematisch-theologischen Dialogs* (Walberger Studien der Albertus-Magnus Akademie, theologische Reihe 4; Mainz: Matthias-Grünewald, 1967) 262–83, 748–57.

UNITED METHODIST–ROMAN CATHOLIC DIALOGUES

Introduction

The United Methodist Church was formed in 1968 by the union of The Methodist Church and The Evangelical United Brethren Church. The two churches shared a common historical and spiritual heritage. The Methodist Church resulted in 1939 from the merger of three branches: the Methodist Episcopal Church; the Methodist Episcopal Church, South; and the Methodist Protestant Church. The Methodist movement began in eighteenth century England with the preaching of John Wesley, but the so-called Christmas Conference of 1784 in Baltimore is regarded as the date on which the organized Methodist Church was founded as an ecclesiastical organization. There Francis Asbury was elected the first bishop in the U.S.A. The evangelical United Brethren Church was founded in 1946 with the merger of the Evangelical Church and the United Brethren in Christ. Both had their beginnings in Pennsylvania in the evangelistic movement of the eighteenth century.

The United Methodist/Roman Catholic dialogue[1] began in the United States in 1966. The first round of seven years discussed salvation, faith, good works, the Holy Spirit, the Church, government aid to education, religious concerns and the educational crisis, sacraments, ministries, and communion. The document on education is published in this volume. The next series discussed spirituality, holiness and ministry, with its report published here. A third round (1977–1981) produced the document on celebration, also published in this collection. The present series (1982–present) has taken up the theme of biomedical ethics.

Note

1. Cf. R. L. Stewart, "A Survey of Catholic/Methodist Dialogue: 1971–1981," *OIC,* 18 (1982), pp. 223–236, "Toward a Statement on the Church: Report of the Joint Commission between the Roman Catholic Church and the World Methodist Council, 1982–1986," *OIC,* 12:3 (1986), pp. 241–265, IS "Report of the Joint Commission between the

Roman Catholic Church and the World Methodist Council, 1972–75," 1977, 34:II, 11–20, "Catholic/Methodist International Commission: Report on Third Series of Conversations, 1977–1981," 1981, 46:II, 84–96, "Catholic-Methodist Commission, Milan, November 1983," 1983, 53:IV, 102–103, "Catholic/Methodist International Commission, Venice, October/November, 1985," 1985, 59:III-IV, 42.

Shared Convictions about Education

December 16, 1970

1. An adequate education is one of the most indispensable achievements for life in the modern world, and it is a crucial responsibility of the entire society to make it possible for every child to obtain such an education.

2. The public school is the chief instrument by means of which our society attempts to make an adequate education available to all children. It is not the only agency of education, but if others fail, it must take up their task. It must be open to all on an equal basis, without discrimination because of race, religion, national origin, sex, or economic class.

3. It is the right and responsibility of parents to choose the kind of education their children shall have, particularly what understanding of the nature and duty of man they shall be taught. Parents may delegate this responsibility to teachers in public or private schools, but it remains the parents' right and should not be usurped by others.

4. Our entire society is and should be taxed for the expenses of education through various modes of taxation, local, state and federal. Taxes paid by all the people under duress of law must be used in ways that are essentially and actually amenable to public control for benefits that are available to all without discrimination.

5. Resources obtained from the entire society by taxation cannot be used to finance the teaching or practice of religion, whether in public schools or private. What constitutes financing the teaching or practice of religion in public and private schools is still a subject of disagreement and litigation.

6. Parents may arrange for their children to be taught a particular understanding of the nature and duty of man and the meaning of existence, at their own direction and expense, in church schools, summer camps, and private schools of general education.

7. Any (non-public) school which provides the type of education

which parents want for their children (and which meets certain minimal standards and does not actually jeopardize public health or safety) is a legitimate part of the total education enterprise of the Americn society, and deserves recognition, protection, consideration, and encouragement as such.

8. Children in private as well as public schools are entitled to welfare benefits provided by government to all children without discrimination, irrespective of what schools they may attend. These welfare benefits clearly include school lunches, medical and dental care, and may include bus transportation, secular textbooks, and certain other services, the extent of which is still a subject of disagreement, experiment and litigation.

9. Teachers and administrators of private schools are entitled to respect and encouragement as important contributors to the common good. Their counsel and cooperation should be sought and valued in any efforts to improve the total educational enterprise. They should enjoy the same professional standards and opportunities as those in public schools within the limits of nos. 4 and 5 above.

10. Certain subjects that are deemed to be entirely "secular" in significance should be offered by public schools to children enrolled for the rest of their instruction in private schools, through such arrangements as shared time and educational television, thus making possible significant economies for private schools and a mingling of school-children with their peers of varying persuasions.

11. In situations where public schools cannot or do not provide an adequate education for children or where they cannot or do not meet the expectations of parents, other kinds of schools may be needed to supply what the public schools are not supplying. How they may be enabled to assume this extra burden is a matter for continuing exploration and experiment. It is conceivable that some way can be found to enable private institutions to serve a public purpose with public resources without losing their autonomy or distinctiveness, without sacrificing public control of public funds, and without risking discrimination among children.

Holiness and Spirituality of the Ordained Ministry

January, 1976

I. National bilateral conversations sponsored by committees of The United Methodist Church[1] and the National Conference of Catholic Bishops[2] have been in progress since 1966. Over the years these have dealt with a wide variety of subjects of mutual interest and concern. In 1971, the decision was reached to focus the dialogue for a time on an issue of special interest to both churches, namely, "Spirituality in the Ministry." The findings of our sustained study of this subject are the concern of this report.

Several reasons dictated the choice of this particular theme for this dialogue. Both our communions emphasize the importance of a life style which authentically derives from relationship with the Spirit of Christ. This emphasis is not in contradiction to others, such as a confessional emphasis on the faith, but can be perceived as a dimension of Christianity, the importance of which is distinctively underscored in our respective traditions. The subject seemed all the more fruitful as it touches our common emphasis on holiness and spirituality as well as our noticeably different ways of expressing this in life and conduct. It has been experienced by Catholics and United Methodists as a source of sympathetic contact and, at times, of puzzlement or uncertainty with respect to one another. Questions have been raised as to whether distorting pietism, individualism, clericalism, cultic ritualism or triumphalism might lurk in our traditions under the guise of holiness. These questions needed to be explored—and, we hope, resolved—in order to set aside one barrier, real even when only subliminally perceived, to further Roman Catholic-United Methodist understanding and the quest for a more profound reconciliation between us.

Another key reason for our emphasis was the supposition that it would open the way to wider reflections on the life of our churches, and so indeed it has. By focusing on the theme of holiness and spirituality with reference to the ministry, and especially to the ordained ministry, the dialogue did not seek to bypass the even more fundamental question of holiness as lived by the whole church. While our churches may have given more concentrated attention to the holiness and spirituality expected of those ordained in the service of the people, we could see that what has been said and encouraged in regard to ordained persons is illustrative of the holiness to which all members of the church are called.

At the same time, the theme is pertinent to an area in which both of our churches have evidenced the need to achieve new perceptions in our time. The concurrent concerns in both churches[3] suggested that the subject was more than merely timely. It indicated as well a vigorous search for ways of life which are in accord with the values of our traditions and in keeping with the shape of society and the needs of changing cultures.

Finally, we observed that our concerns in this dialogue are equally felt in the larger framework of the ecumenical movement as a whole. By concentrating on the complexities of spirituality in relationship to the ministry, we hoped to contribute a new element to the very rich discussion in other ecumenical forums of other aspects of the ministry.

Among the specific questions our consultation has had to face and has sought to answer in the following report are these:

- Is the holiness and spirituality to which the ordained ministers are called different in either kind or degree from that to which all Christians are called?
- What is the source of the efficacy of the ordained ministry as it is exercised in our communions?
- Are new spiritual disciplines, in some ways different from those followed by priests and ministers in the past, needed today to express and support more clearly the holiness and spirituality of the ministers of the church?

As Roman Catholics and United Methodists, we face together the changing needs of people to whom the ministry seeks to respond. We recognize that just as there is no genuine ecumenism, so there can be no effective ministry, without a willingness for changes of heart. Our report comes out of some experience of warmth and insight into such changes.

II. The vocation of the Christian community as a whole and of each person is to accept the gift of holiness and to employ it as God intends. The requirement of Christian spirituality is conformity of the church and its members to the holiness of God. Each person is to celebrate the coming of the new age in the dying and rising Christ, and to receive his Spirit. Becoming a new creation, they are selected by God to be holy before him. Ministers, therefore, stand among the people of God as men and women who serve and who thereby exemplify the call of all to servanthood. Whether we refer to God as Father, Son, or Spirit, we are speaking equally of the One Whose divine holiness is communicated to our human condition. The holiness of the triune God is known and conceived by us through His gracious revelation.

First, God is the eternal Creator and Sustainer of all that is. Thus, our most appropriate attitude toward Him is one of reverence, awe and love.

Second, God makes himself known as the Holy One of Israel (Isaiah 6; 9; 54:5; 55:5), the Maker and Redeemer of all people and all creation (Isaiah 40:25–26; 41:20; Acts 17:24–26). He chose the People Israel to be a holy community, priestly and prophetic, and bound to himself by a lasting covenant (Exodus 19:5–6).

Through the incarnation, ministry, death and resurrection of Jesus Christ, God constituted the universal church as the first fruit of the new creation which he is still bringing to reality (II Cor. 5:17).

Third, God communicates to us that mystery of his holiness and makes us heirs of Israel's faith and joint-heirs with Christ (Rom. 8:17). Three dimensions of God's holiness bear upon our own holiness:

a) Separateness
The Holy God is one; he alone is God (Deuteronomy 5:7 and 6:4). He is not to be confused with any divinities, ideologies or value systems of human devising. The church, too, is to avoid those destructive temptations of the world which distract it from the vocation of holiness: not for fear of pollution of a holy life but of dilution of a holy mission (II Cor. 6:16–18). That is to say, the derived holiness of the church is not to be regarded as the basis for a moral superiority over other human beings; it is the holiness of divine intention, the instrumentality of God's own saving mission in history to all people (Mt. 28:19; Acts 1:8; Jn. 17:18).

b) Love
The Holy God is love (1 Jn. 4:8); the highest gift of God, the Holy Spirit, is love (1 Cor. 13:13). God's love which became incarnate in Jesus Christ, bridges the separation between God and humanity, heals the estrangement caused by sin

and achieves reconciliation. The church and its members who received the gift are not only summoned to love as He loves: as both Roman Catholic and Methodist traditions emphasize, they are made holy in love by the Holy Spirit working amongst us. By sanctification we mean that the grace and power of divine love are displacing the sin of pride and faithlessness in our hearts and minds.

c) Righteousness
The Holy God is righteous (Isaiah 6). God's holiness is manifested in Jesus Christ who is our righteousness and sanctification and who calls us to obedience in grace (1 Cor. 1:30). Persons and communities that delight in experiencing and expressing the love of God must likewise delight in the righteous law of the Lord (Ps. 1:2) or else fear the consequences of deliberate disregard of it (Mt. 7:21–23). Love without law is sentimental; law without love is tyrannical. The holiness which the Church receives from God includes both law and love. (Rom. 8:2–4)

III. The church's holiness is a *gift* derived from and dependent on God. It has been accented by our two traditions in different ways. While United Methodists and Catholics are at one in their confession that the church is holy, there is divergence both within and between the two traditions regarding the meaning of the church's holiness and its realization in practice. Such divergence can be partially explained by the respective emphases on different models of the church within the two traditions. For example, in the United Methodist tradition, the church is frequently seen as the herald of God's word; accordingly, the holiness of the church is seen as the personal response to the preaching of the Gospel. For example, in the Catholic tradition, the church is frequently seen as a sacrament, a visible sign conveying God's grace; accordingly, emphasis is given to the necessity of visible signs as means of grace and holiness.

Both these (and other) models of the church are necessary in a comprehensive ecclesiology, which views the different emphases regarding the church's holiness as complementary, not incompatible. Nonetheless, it should be candidly acknowledged that it is not always obvious how the divergent aspects of ecclesiological models can be harmonized either in theory or in practice.

Both Catholics and United Methodists agree that God's holiness is communicated to the church. While the Incarnation is the primary reality of this communication, Biblical sources and Christian history indicate that God communicates himself through a variety of channels. The variety and plurality of God's gifts overwhelm us; particularly so when it comes to theoretical appreciation of them. We do agree that manifold persons and events have been used by the Holy Spirit to actualize God's holiness in the life of the Christian community. If the two traditions sometimes diverge in their respective views of the nature of these gifts and its relation to the individual Christian's holiness, nevertheless it should be recognized that this divergence is not pervasive, since each tradition has shared elements of the other.

Both the Catholic and the United Methodist traditions recognize that the Church's holiness is general and the means of holiness in particular challenge individual Christians to a personal appropriation and manifestation of holiness in their daily lives. Both the wide-ranging diversity of gifts as well as the individuality of each Christian imply that the quest for holiness is uniquely personal. Although the holiness of Christians is quite diverse in practice, it is possible to recognize a number of trends or "schools" in the practice of holiness, in Christian life style, in spirituality. While such diversity is both legitimate and desirable as a personal appropriation and manifestation of God's holiness in Christ through the church, it should not be allowed to cloud, much less to negate, the common quest for holiness that is characteristic of both traditions.

IV. The church's holiness is also a *task*. In the design of God, the church's members are called to serve. In the power of the Spirit, Christians are called to offer themselves to God in praise and worship, always giving thanks for his glory. They likewise devote their energies to sharing with the human family the fruits of redemption. They served God by their life of prayer and surrender to divine grace, and by their compassionate attention to the needs of all their brothers and sisters. Guided by the Word of God, they witness to the liberating action of Christ and bring hope to humanity in its struggle for true freedom.

V. The Lord of the church calls his people to be holy in the totality of their lives. The people of God are assisted in their response to this call by their ordained ministers (priests). Our discussions revealed to us that the basic functions of our clergy are the same, namely, to announce the good news of Christ, to interpret the Scriptures, to exhort the faithful to live in *agapê,* to lead the people in prayer, to invite the faithful to meet the Lord in the sacraments, to preside at the eucharistic worship, to exercise pastoral care, to develop Christian education, and to administer the parish. Furthermore, the ordained attempt, in ecumenical dialogue, to arrive at a vision of Christian truth which will establish the authority of this truth within the whole fellowship of the disciples of Christ. They must give special attention to the specific needs of our day: the promotion of peace and reconciliation within and among families, races, classes and nations. Often at the cost of their own comfort they must show compassion for those who suffer, provide assistance to the needy, defend the victims of oppression, and participate in the struggle to achieve political, social and economic justice.

VI. The responsibilities of the ordained ministers have been performed in multiform ways through the centuries, but the fundamental purpose has remained the same: to be instruments of the Spirit in symbolizing and actualizing the community's holiness, apostolicity, catholicity and unity. No one of these four notes of the church can be understood apart from the others. The church's holiness must be seen in relation to its apostolicity, for it stands in continuity with the new age first experienced in the apostolic church. Nor can it be understood apart from its catholicity and unity. Within the church, the Spirit seeks to transform and unify Christians with one another. Through the church the Spirit reaches out to transform and unify the whole human family and all realms of society by his gracious power; the collegial exercise of ministerial oversight of the church's holiness should thus be a reminder and a symbol of the church's unity in the service of the Gospel.

VII. Ordination is a sacramental act by which the church recognizes and authenticates the Spirit's call of certain persons to fulfill the particular functions enumerated above. Accordingly, the church prays that the Spirit impart the gift of grace for the fulfilling of its ministers' apostolic stewardship. The Spirit holds up the ministry, death and resurrection of Jesus Christ as the source and norm of ministerial service and contemplation. As High Priest, he sanctifies them and their actions by his continued empowering presence. We agree that there is no difference between the holiness of the ordained and that of the whole people of God. The minister's manner of being and acting should, from that fact, be in harmony with his or her high calling to be a symbol of the church's holiness, apostolicity, catholicity, and unity. The clergy knows its own frailty and dependence upon the whole company of the faithful. Its members can therefore live out their call to holiness in fellowship with one another and with the people whom they serve.

VIII. The Catholic and United Methodist traditions, in different ways and with different stresses, have both insisted upon the ordained minister's duty to lead a holy life in the service of the Lord. The minister of the word and sacraments, in addition to directing prayer and preaching about it, must be a person of prayer whose life is marked by simplicity and humility.

In the Catholic tradition, celebrating the eucharist usually has been identified as the chief source of spiritual strength for bishops and presbyters. Their mode of access to the means of Christian holiness, however, should not set them apart from the people they serve. Also, a commitment to lifelong celibacy as a means to service has been regarded as a means to holiness, although it is not cited as an absolute in recent official reports to the National Conference of Catholic Bishops. Deacons, bishops and presbyters are committed to approachability, not aloofness or privilege.

In the United Methodist tradition, ordained ministers are required to make an earnest and visible commitment to the pursuit of Christian perfection, in the expectation that the Spirit would empower their growth into holiness of life. In its finest expression this love for God and neighbor has taken the form of challenging the evils of one's time and of meeting the pressing needs of one's contemporaries. If this pattern has sometimes tended to degenerate into a legalizing moralism replacing the disciplined freedom of the Christian individual, it has in general served to remind United Methodist Christians of God's sovereign, sanctifying purpose. Personal restraint has been a constant characteristic. This ministry is open to men and women, married and single persons. The means to Christian holiness in the life of a United Methodist minister are not as specified as those of a Catholic minister, although some daily life of prayer and devotion is assumed. In the past it has often had an individual character and is only now becoming identified as communal or ecclesial.

These examples of holiness patterns so briefly provided are not intended as counters to play one against another. While the means of Christian holiness are or have been quite different in the two traditions, the end for both is that perfection which is love for God and neighbor. We join in seeking new models of expression to that end.

IX. The forms of Christian holiness have necessarily been influenced by the diverse cultures in the many places in which the church has taken root. Today, various African and Asian religious traditions are making claims on the modes of expressing Christian faith and life. Along with other Christians who live in these places, Catholics and United Methodists are seeing that adaptations to indigenous cultures are indispensable if faith in Christ is to be a religious reality for all peoples. Likewise, in both hemispheres the rapid changes occurring in technological societies create new problems for persons seeking authentic holiness of life. Ministers need the gift to discern in their situations the signs of the Spirit's direction of the human quest for a more spiritually abundant and holy life.

X. The ministers and members of the church should take a positive interest in all contemporary paths to Christian holiness. The spiritual realm, in traditional Christian speech, relates to God's Spirit and his action on the human community and the individual human spirit. The present age is marked by many characteristics not always easily reconcilable. Among them are a widespread search for personal authenticity, a return to simple ways of living, the investigation in depth of human motives, and the adoption of practices like fasting and meditation, often without any reference to Christianity. Such manifestations of the power of the human spirit are to be viewed positively so long as the danger of bondage to the elements of this world is discerned. Christian ministers should be alert to the human potential for good (as for evil) and should share in the struggle for justice against poverty and oppression, as well as for the liberation and full equality of both sexes. In no case may a thing that is good for humanity be impugned by those serving in Christian ministry or preparing for it. At the same time, every striving of the human spirit must be subjected to God's Spirit if it is to prosper as contributing to the reign of God.

XI. Ministerial authority needs to be conceived and practiced as service, not as dominion. Its chief characteristic will be an evident solidarity between ministers and those to whom they minister. For example, the poor and other oppressed should be joined in the struggle against the evils of an oppressive society. Frequently, the need is to identify and attack corporate evil: the demonic spirit of power embedded in institutions, such as the unbridled amassing of wealth and its concomitants of war and economic exploitation. The holiness of the individual, whether minister or lay person, is no sufficient answer to the evil operating in institutions.

XII. A simple way of life best befits Christian ministers, who cannot escape completely the social or individual evils they are bound by. Simplicity may go to the extreme of poverty; poverty, however, is creative only when it is voluntarily chosen or accepted. Ministry, after all, is a service, not a servitude. Therefore, neither ostentatious consumption nor an inequitable return for services fittingly characterizes the minister of the gospel.

XIII. The commitment of our traditions to the holiness of the church and of its ministers carries with it the danger of falling into hypocrisy or arrogance. Much of the modern world reacts negatively to the assertion of the holiness of the church because of its apparent hypocrisy. Hence, the need to emphasize that real compassion and true humility are an integral part of holiness. If they are honest, the church's ministers will acknowledge that they share the anguish of men and women who, like them, are unable to live up to the Gospel and to achieve in themselves the holiness to which they aspire.

XIV. There is great urgency in today's world for mankind's needs and awesome earthly powers to be challenged by moral and humane values. A central part of the church's mission is to facilitate that process. Ministers should be at the forefront of this movement, helping to allow the realities of this world to be directed and transformed by placing them at the service of Christ. In a world marked by growing separation of the secular and the religious and by the conflict of peoples against peoples and class against class, the ordained ministry should be an example of wholeness. Essential to this wholeness is the recognition of the importance of the role of women in the church. Such concern encompasses the need of the two churches to work toward full utilization of and respect for women in all forms of ministry.

XV. As it is only in Christ that the church is holy, ministers will manifest the church's holiness in their own spirituality only if they live their lives as a gift from Christ and as a task for Christ. As they discover the Lord deeper in their own lives, they will find new strength for their service and new joy in their calling.

XVI. In the course of our dialogue we have become keenly aware that our two churches share much common ground. We have attempted to articulate afresh those common elements and convictions about the role the ordained ministry plays in the service of the holiness to which God calls his people. Our report is offered to the many persons in our two churches—as well as to the many beyond them—who sense a need to formulate and to live a spirituality that is both faithful to the gospel and appropriate to our time.

Implicit in this consensus statement is indebtedness to the ecumenical impetus provided by the Second Vatican Council; awareness that mutual criticism of ecclesiologies is necessary if the form of the church is to remain secondary in importance to the Spirit of its Lord; commitment to the idea that Christian unity is not an end in itself; commitment to the value of ecumenical honesty and clarity; rejoicing at convergences and mutual growth and a sense of the unique opportunity that has been afforded the participants. The sense of excitement and joy which frequently has been the experience of those who have contributed to this statement is not easily communicated in writing. It can be found, however, by those who will in the same spirit engage in their own dialogues and in "collaboration according to conscience." Hopefully, others will be enticed to an increase in holiness of heart and life which would further the pastoral need yet to be met adequately by our churches.

Notes

1. Begun by the former Commission on Ecumenical Affairs and continued since 1972 by the Ecumenical and Interreligious Concerns Division, Board of Global Ministries (EICD).

2. Bishops' Committee on Ecumenical & Interreligious Affairs (BCEIA).

3. In the United Methodist Church, through several commissions on the ministry authorized by the General Conferences of 1964, 1968 and 1972, the nature of the ministry has been probed. In particular, these commissions have contributed important data and reflection on the questions related to ordination. The current studies are examining the relationship between ordination and the connectional polity of appointing clergy to pastoral and other ministry posts.

In the Roman Catholic Church the Synod of Bishops addressed the subject of the ministerial priesthood in 1971. This followed the earlier papal encyclical of 1967 and the (U.S.) National Conference of Catholic Bishops' statement of 1969, and the Sacred Congregation for Catholic Education's document of 1974, all on the celibacy of priests. In 1972, the National Conference of Catholic Bishops received the results of weighty studies of the Catholic priesthood from sociological, historical and psychological but not theological perspectives. One of these studies concentrated entirely on the spirituality of the ordained ministers of the church.

Eucharistic Celebration: Converging Theology—Divergent Practice

December, 1981

Part 1: Converging toward the Unity God Wills

"Because there is one loaf," wrote the Apostle Paul, "we who are many are one body, for we all partake of the same loaf." (1 Corinthians 10:17) The symbol of one bread designates not only the unity of the sacrament of the Eucharist (Holy Communion), but also beyond that the unity of the whole church. This includes, among many others, all Roman Catholics and United Methodists.

To be divided is sinful. But by using our human will and intelligence, empowered by the Holy Spirit, we can keep removing barriers to eucharistic unity. We honor one another's faith and conscience. We respect one another's doctrine insofar as we understand it to be faithful to the one Spirit. In seeking to manifest unity, we also learn to appreciate the beauty, holiness and spiritual power of the Eucharist in the whole range of human experience.

Within the context of many national and international ecumenical dialogues, the United Methodist Church and the Roman Catholic Church have been in conversation in the United States since 1966 through officially appointed representatives.[1] The first formal harvest of this common enterprise was *Holiness and Spirituality of the Ordained Ministry,* 1976.[2]

Encouraged by the level of agreement attained during the first phases, a new team was asked to study the meaning and practice of the Lord's Supper, or Eucharist as it is now widely called. This was hardly a pioneering venture. Earlier ecumenical studies in liturgy had established a precedent for theological agreement on a number of aspects of this sacrament. In particular, the official international dialogues between the World Methodist Council and the Roman Catholic Church on this subject had reached substantial accord in the reports given at sessions of the World Methodist Council at Denver (1971) and Dublin (1976). Also, the maturing studies of the Commission on Faith and Order of the World Council of Churches, involving almost all the churches over several decades, proved to be stimulating in our probe of questions and issues not covered previously in these discussions. Now we are pleased to offer this report to our two communions and to the ecumenical community at large.

We feel a profound gratitude for the ecumenical dialogues generated by the Second Vatican Council, for the gracious opportunity to inquire after the deeper sources of our unity, for the honest meeting of representative voices from our respective traditions, and for the fruit of common ecumenical experience and research among Roman Catholics and United Methodists during the past two decades. While this statement cannot be regarded as official teaching for either Roman Catholics or United Methodists, it expresses new levels of insight born of extensive dialogue concerning the theology and practice of the Eucharist in our churches.

During the course of our work we have shared the word of God, prayed and sung together in common non-eucharistic worship, and have come to know and appreciate one another as pastors, theologians and liturgical leaders in our churches. Mutual respect and love born of discovery of new dimensions in each other's traditions have grown as we have explored points of surprising convergence as well as remaining differences in teaching and practice concerning the Eucharist. Painful awareness of our separation and growing joyful recognition of common ground beyond the language of the renewed texts of our eucharistic rites mark our progress and characterize our point of view.

One of the distinctive features of this dialogue involved the study, comparison and contrast of the most recent liturgical reforms generated within our traditions. The revised Roman Catholic Sacramentary and Lectionary were explored. Also, some of the most recent United Methodist texts were shared: *Word and Table;* the 1980 edition of the text of the *Sacrament of the Lord's Supper;* further elaborations of the lectionary resources as found in *Seasons of the Gospel* (1979) and *From Ashes to Fire* (1979); and *At the Lord's Table* (1981)—a cycle of seasonal eucharistic prayers for official use through the entire year—all parts of the new worship and teaching resources.

After studying our historical development, we analyzed and compared actual texts and current shifts in practice and theology in both traditions. In keeping with post-Vatican Council development, we examined key concepts such as "memorial," "sacrifice" and "presence." Our study of the interrelatedness of word and sign-actions of the community gave definition to our inquiry. We gave full attention to the two churches' sacramental teaching, noting the lack of magisterial authority for regulating the details of doctrine and practice of the Eucharist in Methodism. We described how we actually celebrate the sacrament, noting varieties of practice, and discussed shifts in theology implicit (and explicit) in the prayer texts we are currently using, and how these contrast with earlier usages. The findings of our dialogue and these reflections upon them attempt to present a comprehensive view which, we hope, will set a future agenda in light of the convergence in theology and practice expressed in the next two sections of this report.

The Dublin Report reminds us that "Roman Catholics and Methodists approach the Eucharist without a history of explicit disagreement. Our traditions have indeed developed in separation from each other but not in direct historical conflict." (Par. 48). Yet we have been able to discern that other disagreements lie beyond our mutual understanding of the elements of eucharistic theology. In the concluding section of this report we cite work to be done on questions concerning the nature both of the church and of ministry in relation to our quest for eucharistic unity.

We are in a period of historical development even during the writing of this report. Since Roman Catholics and United Methodists are fully involved in the reform and renewal of eucharistic rites, in both churches issues of sacramental theology are now being reexamined in the context of living celebration of the gathered people of God. Therefore it is appropriate that issues of church authority and ministry also be illumined by continued exploration of authentic proclamation of God's word and the communal celebration of the "mystery of faith." Proper and adequate understanding of true celebration of the Eucharist will shed light on doctrines about ministry and authority, and would alter the procedure of simply applying antecedent understanding of ministry and authority to issues in sacramental theology. The same procedure applies to such questions as intercommunion and the unity in faith which permits of plural rites and traditions.

Yves M.-J. Congar, writing on the phrase "post-ecumenism" in *Concilium* (Vol. 54, 1970), cites two decisive experiences which we have begun to live through together as Christians in the mid-twentieth century:

> (1) the experience of returning to the sources, especially the Bible, leaving aside all strictly confessional positions (though without thereby rejecting them); (2) the experience of the fact that the same

> questions which the world is asking today through its tragic tensions and its secularism face us all, and that since we all have the *same* origin, we are led to give the same answers and adopt the same commitments. (page 17)

Our dialogue acknowledges this insight of Congar, and has struggled with the significance of these experiences. It is both disturbing and promising to become aware that in respect to biblical, theological and liturgical matters we may share more in common with our dialogue partners than we do with many persons within our own communions. This raises acute questions about being in accord with authority within one's tradition. We have been forced to mark the differences at places other than those we first expected. Thus, difficult questions are asked about the nature of unity of belief and practice within each of our respective traditions. We are reminded that matters of unity—more specifically of eucharistic faith and practice—are never simply theological or simply liturgical. They are political and historical as well.

Heartened by the deepened level of constructive discussion, we search for a common language which will allow us to recognize true and efficacious elements in each other's tradition of teaching and celebration. Out of our study and appropriation of the living prayer of the renewed eucharistic liturgies, this common language is emerging.

Part II: Structure of the Eucharistic Celebration

Remarkable unity and agreement on the structure of the eucharistic celebration and on the central eucharistic prayer have been discovered in our dialogue. This is in large measure a result of the background of shared scholarship in the areas of biblical studies, liturgical history, and theology which contributed to the restored texts. The broader liturgical reforms, including the modes of celebrating eucharistic rites, also reflect these shared understandings.

First, we declare our mutual recognition of the underlying unity of the whole eucharistic service: both the liturgy of the word and the liturgy of the table (in Roman Catholic usage, "of the Eucharist"). Vatican II gave Roman Catholics a new awareness of this important truth: "The two parts which, in a certain sense, go to make up the Mass, namely, the liturgy of the word and the eucharistic liturgy, are so closely connected with each other that they form but a single act of worship." (*Constitution on the Liturgy,* 56) This awareness helps Roman Catholics avoid an imbalance which has often been struck between word and sacrament. The Eucharist is not indifferent to the word, but is seen as the thanksgiving precisely for the things portrayed as God's wondrous gifts in the word proclaimed and sung. Analogously, in *Word and Table* United Methodists, who have traditionally stressed the importance of the word, often to the neglect of the eucharistic celebration, have returned to a more balanced understanding of the structure of the Sunday worship service. The new orders of service (Alternate Text, 1972, rev. 1980) manifest this very structure.

Secondly, we recognize that the sixteenth century liturgical reformers, both Catholic and Protestant, had insufficient knowledge of the earliest prayers of praise and thanksgiving which were the Christian sequel to Jewish liturgical practice. Rather than simply repeating the Protestant polemic and its Counter-Reformation counterpoint, eucharistic dialogue among us returns to common roots, especially in the pattern and content in biblical and patristic sources.

Early Christian practice of the Eucharist has been described as having a fourfold action:

1) bread and wine are taken and the table prepared;

2) the presiding minister gives thanks to God over bread and wine;

3) the bread is broken;

4) the bread and wine are distributed and consumed.

Dom Gregory Dix says: "In that form and in that order these four actions constituted the absolutely invariable nucleus of every eucharistic rite known to us throughout antiquity from the Euphrates to Gaul." (*The Shape of the Liturgy,* p. 48) This fourfold action has its origins in Jesus' own actions at table with his disciples. Both churches understand this shape of the liturgy as his command to "do this in memory of me," which is reflected in our eucharistic practices.

Having accepted this common background, we discussed the elements essential to Christian eucharistic prayer. We found structural agreement in comparing: Paragraph 55 of the *General Instruction of the Roman Missal* and chapter four, "The Great Thanksgiving: Its Essential Elements," in *Word and Table,* pp. 44–46. These elements are schematized as follows:

GENERAL INSTRUCTION OF THE ROMAN MISSAL (par. 55)

The chief elements of the eucharistic prayer are these:

a) Thanksgiving (expressed especially in the preface): in the name of the entire people of God, the priest praises the Father and gives him thanks for the work of salvation or for some special aspect of it in keeping with the day, feast, or season.

b) Acclamation: united with the angels, the congregation sings or recites the Sanctus. This acclamation forms part of the eucharistic prayer, and all the people join with the priest in singing or reciting it.

c) Epiclesis: in special invocations the Church calls on God's power and asks that the gifts offered by men may be consecrated, that is, become the body and blood of Christ and that the victim may become a source of salvation for those who are to share in communion.

d) Narrative of the institution and consecration: in the words and actions of Christ, the sacrifice he instituted at the Last Supper is celebrated, when under the appearances of bread and wine he offered his body and blood, gave them to his Apostles to eat and drink, and commanded them to carry on this mystery.

e) Anamnesis: in fulfillment of the command received from Christ through the Apostles, the Church keeps his memorial by recalling especially his passion, resurrection, and ascension.

f) Offering: in this memorial, the Church—and in particular the Church here and now assembled—offers the victim to the Father in the Holy Spirit. The Church's intention is that the faithful not only offer the spotless victim but also learn to offer themselves and daily to be drawn into ever more perfect union, through Christ the Mediator, with the Father and with each other, so that at last God may be all in all.

g) Intercessions: the intercessions make it clear that the eucharist is celebrated in communion with the whole church of heaven and earth, and that the offering is made for the Church and all its members, living and dead, who are called to share in the salvation and redemption acquired by the body and blood of Christ.

h) Final doxology: the praise of God is expressed in the doxology which is confirmed and concluded by the acclamation of the people.

THE GREAT THANKSGIVING: ITS ESSENTIAL ELEMENTS (From *At The Lord's Table,* The Methodist Publishing House, 1981)

The Great Thanksgiving is a hymn of praise and a creed as much as it is a prayer. It is trinitarian, though it is addressed throughout to the first Person of the Trinity. It begins in thanksgiving to God the Father, narrates the work of God the Christ, and invokes the Father to send God the Holy Spirit for our benefit. The concluding doxology, though addressed to God the Father, ties together the trinitarian nature of the whole prayer.

The Great Thanksgiving opens with (1) a *dialogue* of greeting between the presiding minister and people and invites them to join in the giving of thanks, just as we might introduce grace before an ordinary meal.

Then comes (2) a joyful thanksgiving called the *preface,* which usually recites either a specific work of Christ (varying according to season or occasion) or a general narration of salvation history.

This thankful recalling of God's mighty acts is punctuated by (3) a *congregational acclamation* of praise: "Holy, holy, holy" *(Sanctus)* from Isaiah 6:3 and Revelation 4:8 and "Blessed is he who comes in the name of the Lord" *(Benedictus qui venit)* from Psalm 118:26 and Matthew 21:9. In some Christian traditions, God's mighty acts under the old covenant are recited before this acclamation, and the new covenant follows. In other traditions, this acclamation comes either at the beginning or at the end of the whole recitation.

This is followed and culminated by (4) the *words of institution*—the commemoration of the events in which Jesus instituted the Lord's Supper. Some traditions locate the words of institution at their chronological place in the recitation of salvation history, but in any event these words are not neglected.

Some recent liturgies employ another *congregational acclamation* after the words of institution, such as "Christ has died, Christ is risen, Christ will come again."

Then occurs (5) the remembering *(anamnesis)* before God of what Jesus has done as we offer this memorial of his sacrifice *(oblation).* Usually this segment of the prayer refers concisely to Christ's death, resurrection, and ascension, offering these before God for our benefit.

Next comes (6) an invocation *(epiclesis)* in which God is asked to send the Holy Spirit upon the gifts and on the assembled congregation. Benefits desired from communion are prayed for. Intercessions for the living and dead have sometimes occurred at this point.

Triumphantly and joyfully all concludes with (7) a trinitarian *doxology* and *amen.* The doxology sums up in praise the trinitarian theme of the whole prayer.

Frequently (8) *the Lord's Prayer* follows as a congregational act in which we address with familiar confidence the God who has done all these wonderful things simply as "Our Father."

(Adapted from the chapter of the same title written by James F. White in *Word and Table* [1st ed. only], Abingdon, 1976.)

Part III: Theological Understanding Emerging from the Structure

Recognizing the convergent understandings of the inner structure of the eucharistic prayer, we affirm the possibility of more substantial theological agreement concerning the nature of the eucharistic action. At the same time, the understanding of the structural parts of the eucharistic celebration is not always the same in the two churches, especially when considered on the level of popular piety and liturgical practice. Following the lead of the Dublin Report, we divide our consideration into the questions of the presence of Christ and of the sacrifice of Christ, to which we add that of faith and Eucharist.

Presence of Christ

In modern times the concept of the presence of Christ has been reevaluated. The whole question of eucharistic presence in the elements has been placed in the broader context of Christ being present through his Spirit in the gathered people, in prayer, song and in the reading and proclaiming of the word.[3] The Denver Report to the World Methodist Conference raises the question of the contrast often made between Christ's presence in the Eucharist and his presence in other means of grace. This contrast, however, is somewhat misleading. "While there are different emphases, we both affirm that wherever Christ is present he is present in his fullness." (Par. 56)

This statement is understood differently in the two churches. We understand that the popular piety of the two churches views the presence of Christ from differing perspectives. Most Roman Catholics emphasize the presence of Christ in the eucharistic elements. Most United Methodists emphasize the presence of Christ in the proclaimed word enlivened by the Holy Spirit. An agreed-upon position concerning presence, then, realistically will have to allow for varying preferences at the level of popular piety and for specific theological accents on the part of the two churches. We affirm that the presence of Christ in the Eucharist must be understood as manifold, as indicated above. There is a pluralism of belief within the Methodist tradition which is not anchored in a tradition of explicit theological formulation. Belief in real presence is, however, powerfully expressed in the eucharistic hymns of John and Charles Wesley. There is little doubt that a claim to real presence is consistent with John Wesley's belief and is expressed in the new United Methodist texts. The Holy Spirit is implored to "help us know, in the breaking of this bread and the drinking of this wine, the presence of Christ who gave his body and blood for all." Thus, increasingly many United Methodists understand the elements to have a determinative relation to how Christ is present distinctively in the Eucharist. For their part, Roman Catholics have begun to see that the doctrine of transubstantiation is itself an historically conditioned theological formulation that seeks to avoid misunderstanding about Christ's eucharistic presence.

Sacrifice of Christ

The area of sacrifice presents even more complexity. The Dublin Report acknowledged: "The term sacrifice is not used so readily by Methodists as by Roman Catholics when speaking of the eucharist." (Par. 64) Also quoting the Denver Report and the Anglican-Roman Catholic Windsor Statement (1971), the Dublin Report stated:

> We are one in affirming that "The eucharist is the celebration of Christ's full, perfect and sufficient sacrifice, once and for all, for the whole world." It is a memorial *(anamnesis)*. It is not a mere calling to mind of a past historical event or of its significance, but the church's effectual proclamation of God's mighty acts. Some would wish to link this dynamic view not with "a reenactment of Christ's triumphant sacrifice," but with Christ's being present and bringing with him all the benefits of his once-for-all sacrifice for us. (Par. 63)

Our conversations brought out the fact that many United Methodists mean by "sacrifice" the once-for-all sacrifice of Christ on the cross, while many Roman Catholics think primarily of the sacrifice that the church has offered down through the centuries, which is that one sacrifice. Both sides are being aided now by recent biblical and historical studies which discuss the early church's understanding of sacrifice in both its cultic and ethical dimensions.

By interpreting "sacrifice" in terms of memorial, both traditions affirm the once-for-all-ness of Christ's self-offering on the cross. Both affirm that the benefits of his passion and death are present to the faithful now. Nevertheless this explanation by itself bypasses certain other important issues. The role played by the church in the offering of this sacrifice remains a problem. The answer to the question "Who offers what?" is far from clear. United Methodists are not comfortable with such terminology of Vatican II as the Eucharist's "perpetuating the sacrifice of the Cross throughout the centuries." (*Constitution on the Liturgy*, no. 47)

A related problem concerns the frequency of celebration. Does not a radical diversity of practice between United Methodists and Roman Catholics express real differences in theological understanding? One church stresses the uniqueness of Christ's sacrifice, the other the need for the church to make the fruits of the sacrifice of Christ its own. Infrequency of celebrating the Eucharist—quarterly or even less among some United Methodists—indicates the idea that Eucharist is an occasional act of worship which the church does, whereas frequency of celebration—as practiced by Roman Catholics—indicates that the Eucharist constitutes the church, determining what the church is.

A way forward is found in the inner connection between Christ's sacrifice and our continuing self-offering. The new United Methodist text makes this explicit: As we remember and "experience anew" the reality of Jesus Christ in the sacramental sign-action we pray that God will accept "this, our sacrifice of praise and thanksgiving, which we offer in union with Christ's offering for us, a living and holy surrender of ourselves." This is characteristically Wesleyan; but it is also clearly expressed in the *Constitution on the Sacred Liturgy,* par. 48. Our offering is always in union with Christ's offering. We both understand that as Christ offers himself, so our response in the communal enactment of his memorial *(anamnesis)* is itself sacrificial in character. It is sacrificial in the senses of both Christian worship and behavior. Only through Christ's sacrificial offering in his full life, passion and death and resurrection is the church able to offer any sacrifice of praise and thanksgiving. Both Roman Catholic and United Methodist understanding stresses that the church's offering of Christ's sacrifice does not repeat the death, but rather proclaims and shows forth the redemptive mystery of Christ's self-giving for us.

The worship character of eucharistic sacrifice, expressed by traditional Roman Catholic teaching, is thus joined more clearly to the United Methodist accent on ethical sacrifice—the self-surrender to God in service of neighbor. Both accents are necessary for a deeper understanding of Christ's continuing, active and redeeming presence, and his intercession for the world. This belief is acknowledged and enacted by the church's eucharistic celebrations.

The two churches do not have doctrinal agreement about the specific sense in which the offering of the church is the full offering of Christ. Yet it is clear for both churches that the Holy Spirit in the gathered community makes real what Christ has gained for us (as "all benefits of his passion"). This understanding is the basis for exploring the relationship between ecclesiology and the nature of the eucharistic sacrifice. For both word and sacrament are made efficacious, are "realized," as Wesley said, by the action of God the Holy Spirit.

Faith and the Eucharist

We acknowledge in both traditions the centrality of faith in the celebration of the Eucharist. We affirm that Christ is present to the church, in both word and Eucharist, independently of the faith of individuals. We assert both the primacy of God's act in Christ, and the continuing activity of the Holy Spirit in animating and realizing the saving work of God in Christ. The offering of grace in the Eucharist is God's free gift. Yet, faith is necessary for a life-giving encounter. In the language of the 1971 Anglican-Roman Catholic Windsor Statement, "When this offering is met by faith, a life-giving encounter results." (Par. 8)

Roman Catholic teaching avoids the "receptionist doctrine" that sacramental reality is a matter of personal faith-experience only. United Methodists, in devotional piety, emphasize experience, especially the need to experience the presence of Christ. However, the language of their new texts makes clear that faith is located both in the church as community by the operation of the Holy Spirit and in the hearts of the believers. For United Methodists, faith is not located solely in the individual believer's response. It is the faith of the church which is the ongoing context of "the word rightly preached and the sacraments duly celebrated."

United Methodists welcome the new and strong stress by Roman Catholics on "full and active participation" in the liturgy. Attentive and active faith on the part of believers has been the hallmark of Wesleyan evangelicalism, stressing worship "in spirit and truth." At the same time, Roman Catholics welcome the new United Methodist theological accent on the Eucharist as a corporate offering of the whole church. Both communions are correcting the long-prevailing imbalance between word and sacrament. Indeed we both acknowledge their mutual interdependence.

Our understanding of what constitutes eucharistic devotion and practice differs. Yet there is clear convergence between Roman Catholics and United Methodists in understanding how grace, God's free offer of salvation in preaching and the Eucharist, both activates and elicits a faith response.

If our common theological consensus expressed in these pages were fully reflected in the practice of piety and common worship we would be far closer to the deeper unity we seek, the unresolved questions concerning authority and ministry notwithstanding. We must live with the gaps between theological and liturgical convergence, and the differences of practice in our traditions. We are both in the process of change and development in practice. For both churches there is still some ambiguity in the understanding of "being in accord with the faith and practice of the church." This is especially unclear for the United Methodist Church which does not have the authoritative structure for teaching uniform doctrine of eucharistic faith and practice in local churches. Because Methodism is a non-confessional tradition, any definitive understanding by the people is precluded, at least at the level of explicit doctrinal assent. The disciplinary understandings of Methodism do not require unanimity in the mode of celebration by the clergy. The Roman Catholic Church is currently engaged in a profound recatechesis of the laity.

Thus while historical expressions of doctrinal differences regarding the Eucharist have separated us, we are both appealing to the practice of liturgical reform and renewed formation of the faithful based in large measure upon common biblical and patristic principles of reform. Such common grounding in the re-education of clergy and laity, when it issues in a more vivid and mature celebrating community, in itself marks a more deeply shared theological agreement in faith. At the heart of reform and renewal is a dynamic conception of the eucharistic mystery which cannot be confined to debates over real presence in the elements. Indeed, our reformed rites both express the fullness of Christ's offering and the whole sweep of the life, death, resurrection and coming in glory of the Christ more adequately than in previous eucharistic texts.

Part IV: Work Begun and Unfinished: Questions toward the Future

Our mutual exploration of Roman Catholic and United Methodist eucharistic practice and theology has suggested a continuing agenda that is at once challenging and promising. The agenda contains two kinds of considerations. The first concerns additional shared theological themes which we now recognize as crucial but which need more thorough investigation; the second concerns certain fundamental questions which we did not explore. The theological themes are: Eucharist and eschatology; worship and ethics, the mission of the church and our evangelical witness; Eucharist and the Holy Spirit. The questions yet to be pursued are those of church order, authority and ministry, on which our differences are considerable.

Theological Themes

(1) Both traditions have begun to rediscover and to articulate the eschatological and ethical implications of the Eucharist rightly cele-

brated and understood by the people. The recovery of Eucharist as a resurrection meal and foretaste of the messianic banquet manifests a central meaning of the sacrament. We rejoice in this development, and call for further study of its significance for mutual understanding. We have much yet to discover in theology and spirituality from this perception of solidarity with all God's people on earth and in heaven in expectancy of the unambiguous Reign of God. Such an understanding cannot be confined to certain Sundays of the year, but should permeate our fundamental understanding of what it means to be eucharistic people formed by God's word and enlivened by God's Spirit.

We recognize and affirm that both churches are beginning to reinterpret and teach the Eucharist as an eschatological meal, in addition to its meaning as memorial and sacrifice. Every act of the worshiping community around pulpit and altar, in remembering the death and resurrection of Christ, is always oriented toward our future, and that of the whole creation, with God. Such an eschatological emphasis is signified in the people's acclamations and at other points in the new rites. We profess together that participation in the saving power of Christ's body and blood involves living for the coming Kingdom which has already broken into our history.

Our common recognition of the eschatological character of all Christian prayer enables both Roman Catholics and United Methodists to know why the Kingdom of God and the church can never be fully identified. Nevertheless, by virtue of the saving activity of God manifest through the church's faithful proclamation and celebration of the Gospel sacraments, as well as its faithful evangelical witness in service to all the world in Christ's name, the church is forever ordered toward the Kingdom of God.

(2) Another crucial theme emerging in our discussion concerns the necessary link between the Eucharist and ethics, namely our life of service as Christ's Body in the world. The Wesleys and early Methodism understood an intrinsic connection between receiving the sacramental means of grace and doing good works which flow from faith in Christ. This insight has been recently regained by United Methodists, and is given explicit expression liturgically in the post-communion prayers, as found in the 1980 United Methodist order: "You have given yourself for us, Lord. Now we give ourselves for others. . . . Help us to glorify you in all things." Similarly, recent Roman Catholic theological commentary on the Eucharist has stressed the inner relation between bread of the eucharistic table and "bread for the world." In both cases we anticipate a deepening understanding of this connection between our "sacrifice of praise and thanksgiving" and our ethical

responsibilities and mission as God's people in a suffering and hungry world.

We welcome renewed interest in the experience and doctrine of the Holy Spirit, especially in relation to the sanctification of human life and its liberation from many kinds of bondage. Roman Catholics and United Methodists alike have long emphasized growth in grace and the centrality of the life of personal holiness.[4] The distinctive Wesleyan stress on exercising the means of grace in the Eucharist, in prayer and in scriptural holiness is similar to the Roman Catholic emphasis upon authentic liturgical spirituality. With the recovery of the more primitive shape of the liturgy and the new understanding and practice of active participation in the prayer of the church, both churches find themselves sharing common resources—liturgical and devotional—which reveal new dimensions of Eucharist and sanctification.

Our recovered appreciation of the Holy Spirit in the eucharistic celebration signals a growing area of common understanding about the work of the Spirit in the church and in the world. Both traditions have made explicit the prayers for work of the Spirit in word and eucharistic presence. The centrality of the prayer invoking the Spirit *(epiclesis)* is the most striking case in point. United Methodists have contributed to full, active participation in the Eucharist by witnessing to the Spirit's work in gathering the fellowship, in vital preaching, in spontaneous prayer, and in congregational song. Roman Catholics have steadfastly witnessed to the presence and work of the Spirit who enables the church to make the sacrifice of Christ her own. Both are now discovering that the manifold presence of Christ is made real by the Holy Spirit, in the faith and teaching of the church as well as in the enkindled piety of the people in lives of discipline, obedience and love. Out of the riches of these resources in our traditions, it remains for us to explore the interrelation of the Spirit and ecclesial life and order.

We acknowledge that differences in our respective conceptions of the church and its authority in matters of faith and doctrine bear directly upon our theological differences concerning the nature and meaning of sacramental discipline and participation. In our dialogue we have discerned that ecclesiological differences, while real, need not govern what can be learned from the deepest and most faithful aspects of each other's recovery of Eucharist in its fullness.

Questions to be Pursued

These recently discovered aspects of agreement concerning the Eucharist have made all the more imperative the need to state unresolved questions which need further exploration in future dialogues between Roman Catholics and United Methodists. Despite our deepening consensus on the interrelation of word and Eucharist, the presence of Christ in its various aspects, the meaning of memorial *(anamnesis)*, sacrifice, prayer of invoking the Spirit *(epiclesis)* and the meal context of the Eucharist, we must face questions concerning authority and ministry.

(1) There remains a lack of clarity about the teaching authority concerning eucharistic and baptismal faith and practice within the United Methodist Church. The recently published "Supplemental Worship Resources" series is a sign of hope for United Methodists. We may expect a growing acceptance of the liturgical documents and their accompanying pastoral instruction, which reflect some of the foundational ecumenical elements noted in this report. It is true in both churches that eucharistic practice and understanding will mature gradually as the new eucharistic prayers are better understood, and more adequately taught and celebrated in their richness and variety in both seminaries and congregations.

(2) We have not explored the problems concerning our different understandings of ordained ministry in relation to sacramental celebration. Eucharistic sharing awaits our mutual understanding of the nature and authority of church order and ministry. This includes the question of the ordination of women. Our conversations showed that recovery of a more authentic conception of the Eucharist will assist us with issues concerning ministry and its importance in the midst of the priestly people.

(3) During our discussions we asked: Who authorizes? Who may celebrate? What does it mean to be in communion with one another? This brings us face to face with the question of how the church can claim to offer what Christ offers. This is rooted in the unresolved problems of church authority and structure. For Roman Catholics the challenge is to appropriate the images of the church articulated in the documents of the Second Vatican Council and highlighted in recent liturgical reforms. For United Methodists, the challenge is to appropriate a more ecumenical understanding of the church in light of their Anglican, Reformed and Wesleyan roots. United Methodists must deal with some conflicting concepts of the church inherited from the American experience of the past two centuries. Also, there is a need to address those factors that inhibit a more sacramentally informed understanding of the nature of the church and its ministry.

A Summons

Out of the harvest of mutual understanding, we urge the continuance of the formal Roman Catholic/United Methodist dialogue. Further, we encourage our churches and their local congregations to extend dialogue by sharing a common lectionary, joining in a common commitment to serve one another and the world in Christ's name, and practicing all such common prayer and study of God's word that opens our lives to the unity implied in our common baptism into the death and resurrection of Jesus Christ our Lord.

We pray that congregations will experience a renewed life together; that they will commit themselves to evangelization and service to the world, empowered by a eucharistic life of prayer, consistent with recent reforms in both traditions. We too, in this dialogue, have experienced the joy and graced surprise of deeper union in Christ as we explored the growing convergences and sensed the varied richness preserved in our different expressions of eucharistic theology and piety. Our work and prayer have led us to respect more deeply our differences and our similarities as these constitute a call to deeper sharing.

We long for the day when all shall gather at the one table. In the meantime, we will share the word and work of Christ, and in profound gratitude and great hope cry out, "Come, Holy Spirit."

Notes

1. In the United Methodist Church these conversations were begun by the former Commission on Ecumenical Affairs and continued since 1972 by the Ecumenical and Interreligious Concerns Division, Board of Global Ministries (EICD). On the Roman Catholic side, the dialogue is sponsored by the Bishops' Committee for Ecumenical and Interreligious Affairs (BCEIA) of the National Conference of Catholic Bishops.

2. Publications Office, United States Catholic Conference, 1312 Massachusetts Avenue, N.W., Washington, D.C. 20005.

3. See the RC/World Methodist Council report on the Holy Spirit, 1979.

4. Cf. *Holiness and Spirituality of the Ordained Ministry,* 1976, United Methodist/ Roman Catholic Report.

EASTERN ORTHODOX–
ROMAN CATHOLIC
DIALOGUES

Introduction

Roman Catholics and Eastern Orthodox Christians live in the United States as neighbors in a unique situation. Although they have been estranged for centuries, theological work and careful historical scholarship has laid a groundwork for the reconciling progress.[1]

Co-sponsored by the BCEIA and the Standing Conference of Canonical Orthodox Bishops in America, the dialogue in the United States began in September, 1965. It continues to meet regularly.[2] While the documents have no official status, they provide an instructive basis for mutual understanding and pastoral approaches. This work has preceded the opening of the international Roman Catholic/Eastern Orthodox Dialogue in 1980.[3] In addition to the results of the national dialogue, one regional dialogue has been included. The concentration of Orthodox in certain urban areas, such as New York and Boston, provides such regions with important resources for ecumenical leadership.

Notes

1. Edward Kilmartin, *Toward Reunion: The Orthodox and Roman Catholic Churches* (Paulist Press, 1979); cf. also Stransky and Sheerin, eds., *Doing the Truth in Charity* (Ecumenical Documents I; New York: Paulist Press, 1982), pp. 177–229.

2. IS "Coordinating Committee of Catholic/Orthodox Dialogue, Venice, May 1981," 1981, 46:II, "Catholic/Orthodox Joint Commission: The Mystery of the Church and of the Eucharist in the Light of the Mystery of the Holy Trinity." 1982, 49:II, III; "Coordinating Committee of Catholic/Orthodox Commission, Cyprus, June 1983," 1983, 52:III; cf. John Meyendorff, "Orthodox-Roman Catholic Dialogue Faces Snags," *St. Vladimir's Theological Quarterly* (1986), 30:4, 351–356.

3. For further information on Orthodox ecumenical involvement cf. *Orthodox America 1794–1976: Development of the Orthodox Church in America,* Constance Tarasar, ed. (Syosset, NY: Orthodox Church in America, 1975); *Orthodox Perspectives on Baptism, Eucharist and Ministry,* Gennadios Limouris and Nomikos Michael Vaporis, eds., Faith and Order Paper No. 128 (Brookline: Holy Cross Orthodox Press, 1986); S. Surrency, *The Quest for Orthodox Church Unity in America* (New York: Sts. Boris and Gleb Press, 1973); Fotios Litsas, ed., *A Companion to the Greek Orthodox Church* (New York: The Greek Orthodox Archdiocese of North and South America, 1984); E.J. Stormon, SJ, ed., *Towards the Healing of Schism: The Sees of Rome and Constantinople,* Ecumenical Documents III (New York: Paulist Press, 1987).

An Agreed Statement on Mixed Marriages

The recent dialogue between the Orthodox and Catholic Churches has led to a deeper appreciation of their common tradition of faith. This exploration has helped us to reassess some specific theological and pastoral problems in the area of Christian marriage. We recognize the practical difficulties which couples continue to face when they enter a mixed marriage as long as their churches are divided on matters of doctrine and styles of Christian life. Because of these difficulties both of our churches discourage mixed marriages.

I. Pastoral Problems

1. We recognize that under the conditions of modern life these mixed marriages will continue to take place. For this reason counseling of couples entering such unions by pastors of both churches is imperative. In this counseling the sincerely held religious convictions of each party, based upon their church's tradition, must be respected, especially as regards the nature of marriage and the style of life in marriage.

2. One area in which counseling by the pastors is desirable concerns the Christian upbringing of the children. We recognize the responsibility of each partner to raise their children in the faith of their respective churches. We encourage the pastors of both churches to counsel these couples in the hope of helping to resolve the problem which this responsibility creates. Specific decisions should be made by the couple only after informed and serious deliberation. Whether the decision is made to raise the children in the Orthodox or Catholic tradition, both partners should take an active role in the Christian upbringing of the children and in establishing their marriage as a stable Christian union. The basis for this pastoral counsel is not religious indifferentism, but our conviction of a common participation in the mystery of Christ and his Church.

3. Each partner should be reminded of the obligation to respect

the religious convictions and practice of the other and mutually to support and encourage the other in growing into the fullness of the Christian life.

II. Theological Problems

1. According to the view of the Orthodox Church the marriage of an Orthodox can only be performed by an Orthodox priest as the minister of the sacrament. In the view of the Catholic Church the contracting partners are the ministers of the sacrament, and the required presence of a Catholic major cleric as witness of the Church can be dispensed with for weighty reasons. In view of this, we recommend that the Catholic Church, as a normative practice, allow the Catholic party of a proposed marriage with an Orthodox to be married with the Orthodox priest officiating. This procedure should, however, take place only after consultation by the partners with both pastors.

2. We plan the further study of the Orthodox and Catholic traditional teaching concerning marriage.

New York City
May 20, 1970

An Agreed Statement on Respect for Life

We, the members of the Orthodox-Roman Catholic Bilateral Consultation in the United States, after extensive discussions on the sanctity of marriage, feel compelled to make a statement concerning the inviolability of human life in all its forms.

We recognize that human life is a gift of God entrusted to mankind and so feel the necessity of expressing our shared conviction about its sacred character in concrete and active ways. It is true that the Christian community's concern has recently seemed to be selective and disproportionate in this regard, e.g., in the anti-abortion campaign. Too often human life has been threatened or even destroyed, especially during times of war, internal strife, and violence, with little or no protestation from the Christian leadership. Unfortunately, the impression has frequently been given that churchmen are more concerned with establishing the legitimacy of war or capital punishment than with the preservation of human life. We know that this has been a scandal for many, both believers and unbelievers.

We feel constrained at this point in history to affirm that the "right to life" implies a right to a decent life and to full human development, not merely to a marginal existence.

We affirm that the furthering of this goal for the unborn, the mentally retarded, the aging, and the underprivileged is our duty on a global as well as a domestic scale.

We deplore in particular the U.S. Supreme Court's decision failing to recognize the rights of the unborn—a decision which has led to widespread indiscriminate early abortion.

We affirm our common Christian tradition with regard to the right of the unborn to life.

We acknowledge our responsibility to mediate the love of Christ, especially to the troubled expectant mother, and thus make possible the transmission and nurturing of new life and its fully human development.

We urge our churches and all believers to take a concrete stand on this matter at this time and to exemplify this evangelical imperative in their personal lives and professional decisions.

Washington, D.C.
May 24, 1974

An Agreed Statement on the Church

Issued by the Orthodox-Roman Catholic Bilateral Consultation in the U.S.A.

1. Christianity is distinguished by its faith in the Blessed Trinity. In the light of this revelation Christianity must interpret the world and every aspect of it. This revelation has obvious implications for the interpretation of the nature of the church.

2. The church is the communion of believers living in Jesus Christ and the Spirit with the Father. It has its origin and prototype in the Trinity in which there is both distinction of persons and unity based on love, not subordination.

3. Since the church in history is constituted by the Spirit as the body of Christ, the continuity of the church with its origin results from the active presence of the Spirit. This continuity is expressed in and by historical forms (such as Scripture and sacraments) which give visibility to the continuing presence of the Spirit but it does not result merely from a historical process.

4. Sharing in Christ and the Spirit, the local church is at once independent in its corporate existence: a church, and at the same time interdependent in relation to other churches.

The independent existence of the local church is expressed best in its eucharistic celebration. The sacramental celebration of the Lord's presence in the midst of his people through the working of the Spirit both proclaims the most profound realization of the church and realizes what it proclaims in the measure that the community opens itself to the Spirit.

5. The independence of local eucharistic communities, in the disciplinary and constitutional spheres, was curtailed in the early church as soon as priests became leaders of the local churches. The dependence of local churches on the territorial bishop found its counterpart in the dependence of bishops on the "first" bishop (archbishop, metropolitan, patriarch) as territories were divided among bishops.

The interplay of independence and communality on the local, territorial, and patriarchal levels mirrors the church's prototype: the Trinity, which the church can only approach.

6. The fundamental equality of all local churches is based on their historical and pneumatological continuity with the church of the apostles. However, a real hierarchy of churches was recognized in response to the demands of the mission of the church. Still this did not and cannot exclude the fundamental equality of all churches.

7. The Catholic and Orthodox Churches explain differently the meaning of this hierarchy of churches.

The Catholic Church recognizes that the position of Peter in the college of the apostles finds visible expression in the Bishop of Rome who exercises those prerogatives defined by Vatican Council I within the whole church of Christ in virtue of this primacy.

The Orthodox Church finds this teaching at variance with its understanding of primacy within the whole church. It appears to destroy the tension between independence and collegiality. For interdependence, a basic condition for collegiality, appears to be removed as a consequence of the jurisdictional and teaching role attributed to the Patriarch of the West by Vatican Council I. The Orthodox believe that a necessary primacy in the church depends on the consent of the church and is at present exercised by the Patriarch of Constantinople.

8. Our two traditions are not easily harmonized. Yet we believe that the Spirit is ever active to show us the way by which we can live together as one and many. We have the hope that we will be open to his promptings wherever they may lead. "For only so will harmony reign, in order that God through the Lord in the Holy Spirit may be glorified, the Father and the Son and the Holy Spirit" (Apostolic Canons, Cn. 34).

New York City
December 10, 1974

The Principle of Economy: A Joint Statement

1. Members of the Orthodox-Roman Catholic Bilateral Consultation in the United States, having met since 1965, have examined openly, in a spirit of Christian faith and fraternal charity, a wide spectrum of theological questions judged to be crucial for mutual understanding between our two churches.

2. One topic which has been discussed with particular interest, especially during 1975 and 1976, has been *oikonomia* or ecclesiastical "economy." Because of the possible relevance of economy to the question of mutual recognition of churches, this topic, which has been important for the Orthodox, has received increasing attention among Anglicans and Roman Catholics in recent years.

3. In its discussion of economy the Consultation considered an introductory report prepared in 1971 by the Inter-Orthodox Preparatory Commission for the forthcoming Great Council of the Orthodox Church. Some Orthodox and Roman Catholic members were dissatisfied with the interpretation it gave to certain texts and historical incidents but found it a useful beginning for further discussion.

4. Our investigation has shown:

(a) The wealth of meanings which economy has had over the centuries;
(b) Some weaknesses in recent presentations of economy;
(c) The significance of economy for our ongoing ecumenical discussion.

5. At the most basic level, the Greek word *oikonomia* means management, arrangement, or determination in the strictly literal sense. A few overtones add to this basic meaning. *Oikonomia* may imply accommodation, prudent adaptation of means to an end, diplomacy and strategy and even dissimulation and the "pious lie." But *oiko-*

nomia can also have highly positive connotations. It suggests the idea of stewardship, of management on behalf of another, on behalf of a superior.

6. In the New Testament the word *oikonomia* occurs nine times: Luke 16:2, 3, 4; 1 Corinthians 9:17; Ephesians 1:10, 3:2; 3:9; Colossians 1:25, and 1 Timothy 1:4. In the Parable of the Steward, Luke 16, the word refers generically to stewardship, house management. In other New Testament usages such as Ephesians 3:9, the word is used to refer to God's purpose or *prothesis,* the economy of the mystery hidden for ages in God who created all things.

Also in Ephesians 1:8–10 we read that God "has made known to us in all wisdom and insight the mystery of his will, according to his purpose which he set forth in Christ as a plan for the fullness of time *(oikonomian tou pleromatos ton kairon)* to unite all things in him, things in heaven and things on earth." This usage is closely related to the patristic idea that in and through his person the incarnate and risen Christ brings to fulfillment all of creation *(anakephalaiosis).* The Pauline corpus of letters uses *oikonomia* to refer to Paul's own ministry or pastoral office to make the word of God fully known.

7. These New Testament usages of *oikonomia* are further expanded by the fathers' understanding as summarized by the Inter-orthodox Preparatory Commission's report which states: "Apart from the meaning which concerns us here, the term *oikonomia* also denotes the divine purpose of *prothesis* (Eph. 1:10, 3:9–11), the mode of existence of the one Godhead in Trinity through mutual indwelling *(perichoresis),* its broad action in the world through the church, divine providence, the savior's incarnation, the whole redeeming work of our Lord Jesus Christ and all the operations through which human nature was made manifest in the Son, from the time of his incarnation to his ascension into heaven."

God is seen as arranging all for the purpose of man's salvation and eternal well-being; and man fashioned in the image and likeness of God is viewed as being called to imitate this divine activity.

8. The word *oikonomia* later acquired additional uses in ecclesiastical contexts, in particular:

(a) The administration of penance, the arranging or managing of a penitent's reconciliation to the church;
(b) The reception of those turning to the church from heresy or schism;
(c) The restoration of repentant clergy and the reception of heretical or schismatic clergy as ordained.

In all these areas, however, the understanding of economy as responsible stewardship, imitating the divine economy, is maintained, excluding arbitrariness or capriciousness.

9. Recent presentations of economy often have included the following elements:

(a) Economy understood as a departure from or suspension of strict application *(akribeia)* of the church's canons and disciplinary norms, in many respects analogous to the West's *dispensatio.*

(b) Economy applied not only to canon law and church discipline, but to the sacraments as well. In this context, it has been argued, for example, that all non-Orthodox sacraments, from the point of view of strictness, are null and void but that the Orthodox Church can, by economy, treat non-Orthodox sacraments as valid. These views imply that the application of economy to the sacraments may vary according to circumstances, including such pastoral considerations as the attitude of the non-Orthodox group toward Orthodoxy, the well-being of the Orthodox flock, and the ultimate salvation of the person or groups that contemplate entering Orthodoxy.

10. These recent interpretations do not, in the judgment of the Consultation, do justice to the genuine whole tradition underlying the concept and practice of economy. The church of Christ is not a legalistic system whereby every prescription has identical importance, especially when ancient canons do not directly address contemporary issues. Nor can the application of economy make something invalid to be valid, or what is valid to be invalid. Because the risen Christ has entrusted to the church a stewardship of prudence and freedom to listen to the promptings of the Holy Spirit about today's problems of church unity, a proper understanding of economy involves the exercise of spiritual discernment.

We hope and pray therefore that our churches can come to discern in each other the same faith, that they can come to recognize each other as sister churches celebrating the same sacraments, and thus enter into full ecclesial communion.

Washington, D.C.
May 19, 1976

An Agreed Statement on the Sanctity of Marriage

Introduction

At a time when the sacred character of married life is radically threatened by contrary lifestyles, we the members of the Orthodox-Roman Catholic Consultation feel called by the Lord to speak from the depth of our common faith and to affirm the profound meaning, the "glory and honor," of married life in Christ.

I. The Sacramental Character of Marriage

For Christians of both the Orthodox and Roman Catholic Churches marriage is a sacrament. Through the prayers and actions of our wedding rites we profess the presence of Christ in the Spirit and believe that it is the Lord who unites a man and a woman in a life of mutual love. In this sacred union, husband and wife are called by Christ not only to live and work together, but also to share their Christian life so that each with the aid of the other may progress through the Holy Spirit in the life of holiness and so achieve Christian perfection. This relationship between husband and wife is established and sanctified by the Lord. As a sacred vocation, marriage mirrors the union of Christ and the church (Eph. 5:23).

Christ affirmed and blessed the oneness and profound significance of marriage. Christian tradition, following his teaching, has always proclaimed the sanctity of marriage. It has defined marriage as the fundamental relationship in which a man and a woman, by total sharing with each other, seek their own growth in holiness and that of their children, and thus show forth the presence on earth of God's kingdom.

II. Enduring Vocation

The special character of the human relationship established through marriage has always been recognized in the Christian tradition. By sanctifying the marital bond, the church affirms a permanent commitment to personal union, which is expressed in the free giving and acceptance of each other by a man and a woman. The sacrament of marriage serves as an admirable example of the union which exists between God and the believer. The Old Testament uses marriage to describe the covenant relationship between God and his people (Hosea). The Letter to the Ephesians sees marriage as the type of relationship which exists between Christ and his church (Eph. 5:31–35). Consequently both the Orthodox and Roman Catholic churches affirm the permanent character of Christian marriage: "What God has joined together, let no man put asunder" (Mt. 19:6).

However, the Orthodox Church, out of consideration of the human realities, permits divorces, after it exhausts all possible efforts to save the marriage and tolerates remarriages in order to avoid further human tragedies. The Roman Catholic Church recognizes the dissolution of sacramental nonconsummated marriages either through solemn religious profession or by papal dispensation. To resolve the personal and pastoral issues of failed marriages which have been consummated an inquiry is often undertaken to uncover whether there exists some initial defect in the marraige covenant which would render the marriage invalid.

III. The Redeeming Effect of Marital Love

A total sharing of a life of love and concern is not possible apart from God. The limitations of human relationships do not allow for a giving and receiving which fulfill the partners. However, in the life of the church, God gives the possibility of continual progress in the deepening of human relationships. By opening the eyes of faith to the vision that these relationships have as their goal, God offers a more intimate union with himself. Through the liberating effect of divine love, experienced through human love, believers are led away from self-centeredness and self-idolatry. The Gospel indicates the direction that this love must ultimately take: toward intimate union with the One Who alone can satisfy the fundamental yearning of people for self-fulfillment.

Given this vision of reality, Christian tradition recognizes that the total devotion of the married partners implies as its goal a relationship with God. It teaches, moreover, that the love which liberates them to seek union with God and which is the source of sanctification for them is made possible through the presence of the Spirit of God within them.

Through the love manifested in marriage, an important witness is given to the world of the love of God in Christ for all people. The partners in Christian marriage have the task, as witnesses of redemption, to accept as the inner law of their personal relationship that love which determines the relationship between Christ and the church: "Husbands, love your wives as Christ loved the church and gave himself up for her" (Eph. 5:25). Through this love which liberates believers from selfish interests and sanctifies their relationships, the Christian husband and wife find the inspiration in turn to minister in loving service to others.

IV. Theological Clarifications on Christian Marriage

In the teaching of the Orthodox and Roman Catholic Churches a sacramental marriage requires both the mutual consent of the believing Christian partners and God's blessing imparted through the ministry of the church.

At present there are differences in the concrete ways in which this ministry must be exercised in order to fulfill the theological and canonical norms for marriage in our two churches. There are also differences in the theological interpretation of this diversity. Thus the Orthodox Church accepts as sacramental only those marriages sanctified in the liturgical life of the church by being blessed by an Orthodox priest.

The Catholic Church accepts as sacramental the marriages which are celebrated before a Catholic priest or even a deacon, but it also envisions some exceptional cases in which, by reason of a dispensation or the unavailability of a priest or deacon, Catholics may enter into a sacramental marriage in the absence of an ordained minister of the church.

An examination of the diversities of practice and theology concerning the required ecclesial context for Christian marriage that have existed in both traditions demonstrates that the present differences must be considered to pertain more to the level of secondary theological reflection than to that of dogma. Both churches have always agreed that the ecclesial context is constitutive of the Christian sacrament of marriage. Within this fundamental agreement various possibilities of realization are possible as history has shown and no one form of this realization can be considered to be absolutely normative in all circumstances.

V. Plans for Further Study

The members of the Orthodox-Roman Catholic Consultation gives thanks to God for this common faith in the sanctity of marriage which we share in our sister churches. We recognize however that pastoral problems remain to be studied in depth, such as the liturgical celebration of weddings between Orthodox and Roman Catholic partners and the religious upbringing of children in such families. We continue to explore these questions out of a common vision of marriage and with confidence in the guidance of the Holy Spirit.

New York, N.Y.
December 8, 1978

Joint Recommendations on the Spiritual Formation of Children of Marriages Between Orthodox and Roman Catholics

Introduction

1. In this consultation's *Agreed Statement on Mixed Marriages* (New York City, May 20, 1970) reference was made to the spiritual formation of children of marriages involving Orthodox and Roman Catholic partners. The consultation affirms the position taken in that statement but now presents a more detailed explanation of its reasons for it.

Christian Marriage and the Spiritual Formation of Children

2. Our understanding of the spiritual formation of children is based on our common understanding of Christian marriage as a sacrament, as expressed in our *Agreed Statement on the Sanctity of Marriage* (New York, December 8, 1978). Christian marriage is a vocation from God in which the liberating effect of divine love is experienced through human love. This love expresses itself in permanent commitment to mutual fidelity, help and support in all aspects of life, spiritual as well as physical. It also expresses itself in the generation of new life—that is, in the procreation and nurture of children—again, on both the spiritual and physical levels. A primary responsibility of parents therefore is the spiritual formation of their children, a task which is not limited to church membership and formal religious education but extends to all aspects of their lives.

Church Community and the Spiritual Formation of Children

3. Christian marriage also has a social dimension which extends beyond the partners and their relatives. Through marriage the partners are integrated in a new way into the church community. Just as the marriage partners have a responsibility for the building up of the church, so the church community itself has a responsibility to each Christian family to foster its life of faith. In particular the community shares in the responsibility for the spiritual formation of children.

Current Practice

4. Practical difficulties often arise in discharging this responsibility, especially in mixed marriages. Today each of our churches insists that the children of such marriages be raised within its own communion, on the grounds that this is in the best interests of the child's spiritual welfare, thus presuming that one of the parents will relinquish the chief responsibility to the other. Yet if the purpose of the general law is indeed the child's spiritual welfare, its application should be guided by a prudent judgment concerning what is better for the child in the concrete situation.

Practical Recommendations

5. The Orthodox/Roman Catholic couple contemplating marriage should discuss the problem of the spiritual formation of children with both their pastors. Both parents should be urged to take an active role in their children's spiritual formation in all its aspects. Pastors should counsel the parents, and their children as well, against indifference in religious matters, which so often masks itself as tolerance. Since unity in Christ through the Spirit is the ultimate basis and goal of family life, all members of the family should be willing, in a spirit of love, trust, and freedom, to learn more about their faith. They should agree to pray, study, discuss, and seek unity in Christ, and to express their commitment to this unity in all aspects of their lives.

6. Decisions, including the initial and very important one of the children's church membership, rest with both husband and wife and should take into account the good of the children, the strength of the religious convictions of the parents and other relatives, the demands of their consciences, the unity and stability of the family, and other

aspects of the specific context. In some cases, when it appears certain that only one of the partners will fulfill his or her responsibility, it seems clear that the children should be raised in that partner's church. In other cases, however, the children's spiritual formation may include a fuller participation in the life and traditions of both churches, respecting, however, the canonical order of each church. Here particularly the decision of the children's church membership is more difficult to make. Yet we believe that this decision can be made in good conscience. This is possible because of the proximity of doctrine and practice of our churches, which enables each to a high degree to see the other precisely as *Church,* as the locus for the communion of men and women with God and with each other through Jesus Christ in the Holy Spirit.

Conclusion

7. In no way do we mean to minimize differences that still exist between our churches; and we are well aware of the difficulties which these differences may present for those in mixed marriages. Yet we are convinced that such marriages can be a means of spiritual growth both for the partners and for their children.

8. We are also aware that our joint recommendations on the formation of children of marriages between Orthodox and Roman Catholics differ in certain respects from the present legislation and practice of our churches. Yet we believe that our position is theologically and pastorally sound. Therefore we would urge our respective hierarchies to consider ways of reformulating legislation and pastoral guidelines in this area and of communicating this on the parish level, so that the spiritual growth of both the partners and the children of such marriages may better be fostered.

New York City
October 11, 1980

Agreed Statement on Orthodox–Roman Catholic Marriages

Preamble

This paper is the result of nearly four years of Orthodox–Roman Catholic discussions in the metropolitan New York/New Jersey region. Beginning with an initial meeting in November 1981 between the ecumenical staffs of the Greek Orthodox Archdiocese of North and South America and the Roman Catholic Archdiocese of New York, the dialogue has expanded to include a number of dioceses. Representatives of the Antiochian Orthodox Christian Archdiocese, the Orthodox Church in America, the Roman Catholic Archdiocese of Newark, the Roman Catholic Diocese of Brooklyn, and the Roman Catholic Diocese of Rockville Centre have participated in these discussions. In addition, until his assignment away from the region, a representative of the Serbian Orthodox Church in the U.S.A. and Canada participated regularly.

Meeting five times a year, the dialogue group has examined extensively documents and Church laws relating to Orthodox–Roman Catholic marriages. After much deliberation, the dialogue group mandated a subcommittee to draft a joint statement with pastoral recommendations. The entire dialogue group revised the drafted statement extensively in a series of three meetings.

All meetings of the Metropolitan New York/New Jersey Orthodox–Roman Catholic Dialogue have been candid and open discussions of the actual situation of Orthodox–Roman Catholic marriages in the region. The dialogue has benefited from the pastoral experience of many participants as well as from the ecumenical expertise of several participants who also serve on national and international committees, consultations, and dialogues. The ten points, jointly recommended in the conclusion and representing the consensus of this dialogue, are realistic and merit prompt attention. Their implementation would well serve Orthodox–Roman Catholic couples entering marriage and would promote Orthodox–Roman Catholic relations in the United States.

I. Introduction

To articulate a theology of marriage is a complex task which has engaged both the Orthodox and Roman Catholic Churches over the centuries down to the present day. One cannot find in the New Testament a clear and systematic doctrine of the sacrament of marriage. In the New Testament Churches, marriage is more often mentioned in the context of anticipating the imminent end of the world and the Parousia.

Christians derive a significant understanding of the theology of marriage from the Old Testament. In Genesis, God is shown to be the author of holy matrimony, in which a man and a woman are united to help each other achieve their salvation. Although the injunction of Genesis 1:28 to increase and multiply and subdue the earth does not completely describe the nature and purpose of marriage, it does indicate an important characteristic of the marital relationship.

In Old Testament references to marriage, the concept of spousal love appears in virtually every passage. Attraction and love are the subject of the Song of Songs in which God's relationship to his people is imaged in the marriage of a man and a woman. The same theme appears in Hosea 2:19–20, Isaiah 54:5, and Ezekiel 16:8. This authentic love of a man and a woman in marriage reflects the compassionate love God has for his people. God's fidelity to his people, despite their faithlessness to him, is striking. The image of husband and wife is also carried into the New Testament to describe God's love for his people. In Ephesians 5:32 and Revelation 19:7, the relationship between husband and wife is perceived as the relationship between Christ and the Church.

As the celebration of the marriage rite unfolds in both Churches, Old Testament references to the marriages of Abraham and Sarah, Isaac and Rebekah, Jacob and Rachel, and other biblical couples are made. It is easy for a bridal pair in the marriage rites of both Churches to understand their marriage as being in continuity with the scriptural foundations of marriage. The joining of hands, the exchanging of rings, and the exchanging of crowns are descriptive of the spiritual union and interdependence that the couple shares.

A couple's free decision to marry must be made in accordance with God's design for marriage. Their decision requires the couple to be constant in their care, sacrifice, protection, and love for one another. Orthodox Christians and Roman Catholics share a common understanding of the glory and honor of married life in Christ. The marriage between an Orthodox and a Roman Catholic is unique because of a common participation in the mystery of Christ and his Church. Marriage is a sacrament through which Christ unites a man and a woman in mutual love for the ultimate sake of the salvation of each.

Although in some societies marriage is especially encouraged and almost expected of everyone, the two Churches believe that marriage is not mandatory. It is a divine gift and must flow from God's invitation to accept this particular grace. An authentic Christian marriage carries with it the gift of discerning God's will for the couple and the gift of healing whatever may wound the marriage. In the Kingdom to come the marriage union will be brought into the perfect relationship that is fulfilled totally and completely in Christ.

The marital bond is by nature indissoluble. Both the Orthodox and Roman Catholic Churches affirm the permanent character of Christian marriage: "What God has joined together, let no man put asunder" (Mt 19:6). (See: *An Agreed Statement on the Sanctity of Marriage,* 1978.) The revised *Code of Canon Law* for the Latin Church reminds pastors to aid spouses in the unity of conjugal and family life and to see to it that the children of a mixed marriage do not lack spiritual assistance in fulfilling their obligations (Canon 1128). If this is carried out, the faithful of both communions are assured that children born of such marriages will be initiated into and spiritually nourished by the sacramental mysteries of Christ. Their formation in authentic Christian doctrine and ways of Christian living would be very similar in either Church. Differences in liturgical life and private devotion need not be a stumbling block to family prayer.

Without denying the existence of certain dogmatic differences which, in fact, do impede full sacramental and canonical communion between the two Churches, it is clear that certain of these dogmatic differences, real as they are, between Orthodox Christians and Roman Catholics, do not have a major influence on the everyday Christian lives of our people. Since these Christians are privileged to have such a mutual understanding, it is pastorally prudent to emphasize and uphold the sound and consistent teaching of both Churches. This should be the first, and perhaps most important, principle to underscore and uphold in pastoral preparation of couples involved in Orthodox–Roman Catholic marriages.

II. Consideration of Canonical Discipline

Both Churches have established canonical disciplines regarding impediments to marriage, the formalities of marriage, and matrimonial consent.

III. Pastoral Concerns

One of the objectives of this paper is to indicate the problem areas concerning marriages between Orthodox Christians and Roman Catholics which take place in this region and to suggest guidelines for the pastoral care of these marriages within the framework of the theological understanding, canonical discipline, and pastoral experience of the two Churches. Toward this end, an effort has been made in this paper to identify and clarify as much as possible those areas of agreement which already do exist. Now this paper will try to indicate common practices and recommendations for future developments in the area of pastoral care, especially in those cases where differences still exist between us.

This Orthodox–Roman Catholic dialogue recognizes a common concern for the problems of family life and the spiritual formation of the young people of both Churches. Common Christian witness, personal spirituality, mutual respect, and socio-sexual morality, as well as particular problems such as chemical dependency, child abuse, family violence, and divorce, are not merely Orthodox or Roman Catholic issues. These two communions offer some very specific and similar positions based on shared and complementary traditions.

Specific attention can be given to the relationship of the Churches in the Americas. The situation here offers some distinct advantages. The political, ethnic, and cultural differences which, in the old countries, often nourished mistrust, and even hatred, are disappearing. In the Americas, Christians are engaged in an effort to construct a society which is pluri-traditional and yet reflects a unity and harmony among us. The variety in the Orthodox communities carries with it a variety of ecclesiastical practices regarding marriages between their own communicants as well as marriages with Roman Catholics. This variety offers a spectrum of solutions which should make it possible to treat individual cases according to the circumstances of each case. The revised *Code of Canon Law* also contributes to this process since it provides much more flexibility than has existed in the past and is explicitly conscious of the particular relationships existing between the two Churches. It is with this in mind that the following pastoral guidelines are offered for counseling couples entering into Orthodox–Roman Catholic marriages.

A. General Norms of Premarital Counseling

Marriage within the same faith community is the ideal for both Churches. Increasing contacts among people of various religious backgrounds and the growth of genuine love among them clearly show that mixed marriages have become a fact and indeed have become frequent. Attempts to discourage such marriages, for example, by strong family opposition or strict application of canonical discipline, have often resulted in the alienation of one or both partners from Church life and have led to instances where persons have given up Church practice and may have even lost their faith. The fact that the couple is conscious of their genuine Christian love and wishes to celebrate it in a sacrament should be the occasion for positive pastoral encouragement. The disciplines of the two Churches, therefore, should serve as pastoral aids to their people who wish to remain in their respective Churches and to pass on an authenic Christian heritage to their children. Marriage is an occasion of joy and an expression of mutual love and commitment. Its positive aspects should be stressed rather than its negative aspects or feelings.

The engaged couple, as a couple, should seek the premarital counseling of the pastors of both Churches. Priests of both Churches have a pastoral obligation to meet with the couple to discuss the various spiritual aspects and serious responsibilities of their proposed marriage. Each priest has an obligation to encourage the couple to meet with the other pastor. In addition to this personal contact, appropriate reading material and other media aids should be provided for couples planning to marry, especially those materials which emphasize theological positions shared by both Churches. In premarital counseling the religious convictions of each partner and the teachings and practices of both Churches should be respected.

Both priests ought to counsel against religious indifference and encourage each partner to retain real commitment to his/her own Church and to participate fully in its life. Given this commitment, sharing frequently in the liturgical life of the other Church according to the discipline of that Church is recommended, especially where this would foster the unity of family life.

B. The Planning and Celebration of the Marriage Ceremony

The planning and celebration of the marriage ceremony itself poses certain difficulties because of the differences in canonical discipline in this regard. According to Roman Catholic discipline, given the proper dispensations, marriage can take place in either the Roman Catholic or Orthodox Church. While most Orthodox ecclesiastical provinces require that the marriage take place in the Orthodox Church only, recent synodal decisions of two (the Patriarchate of Moscow and the Church of Poland) recognize the validity of the sacrament of marriage performed by Roman Catholic priests provided that the Orthodox bishop gives his permission. (See: *Diakonia* II:2/67, p. 202 and III:1/68, p. 43).

The priests of both Churches are responsible for carrying out the rite of marriage according to their respective disciplines. Both Churches permit the presence of both the Roman Catholic and Orthodox priest at the same ceremony. However, the roles that each fulfills may differ according to varying disciplines. These facts should be recognized and explained to the couple so as to assist in promoting mutual understanding, if not mutual agreement. If the couple requests the special presence of a priest of the other Church, the invitation should be extended to him through the officiating priest. The following specific regulations of each Church should be noted.

In the Orthodox Church (in agreement with the *Guidelines for Orthodox Christians in Ecumenical Relations,* the Standing Conference of Canonical Orthodox Bishops in the Americas, 1973, pp. 19–22):

1. The active participation of the Roman Catholic priest within the marriage rite is not permitted at this time, and this should be made explicit to him at the time of the invitation.
2. The Roman Catholic priest should be invited to wear his liturgical vesture (choir dress or alb).
3. He should be given a place which distinguishes him from the congregation.
4. At the conclusion of the Orthodox ceremony, the Roman Catholic priest will be properly acknowledged and intro-

duced. He then may give a benediction to the couple and address to them words of exhortation and good wishes.

5. Mixed marriages are never celebrated within the context of a Eucharistic Liturgy.
6. Announcement and publication of the marriage should clearly indicate the distinction between the Orthodox celebrant and the guest Roman Catholic priest, avoiding confusing terms as "assisted" or "participated," but rather indicating that the Roman Catholic priest "was present and gave a blessing."

In the Roman Catholic Church:

1. When the Roman Catholic priest officiates, the active participation of the Orthodox priest within the marriage rite is permitted, for example, reading the Scriptures, giving the homily, offering prayers, and giving a blessing. However, out of respect for the current discipline which does not permit an Orthodox priest to participate in this way, the officiating Roman Catholic should not invite him to do so.
2. The Orthodox priest who accepts an invitation to be present at the marriage rite should be invited to wear the liturgical vesture permitted by his discipline.
3. He should be given a place of honor in the sanctuary.
4. The Roman Catholic priest should acknowledge and welcome the Orthodox priest, preferably at the start of the marriage ceremony; at the conclusion of the ceremony, he should invite the Orthodox priest to offer prayer and words of good wishes to the couple.
5. While Orthodox–Roman Catholic marriages may be celebrated at a Eucharistic Liturgy, such a choice should be strongly discouraged in view of current prohibitions regarding Eucharistic sharing.
6. Announcement and publication of the marriage should clearly indicate the distinction between the Roman Catholic celebrant and the guest Orthodox priest, avoiding confusing terms like "a double ceremony" or "an ecumenical marriage," but rather indicating that the Orthodox priest "was present and offered prayers."

Particular note should be taken of the fact that in the case of Orthodox–Roman Catholic marriages, Roman Catholic discipline (revised *Code of Canon Law* 1127, 1) recognizes the validity of the marriage of an Orthodox and a Roman Catholic performed by an Orthodox priest. Indeed, if a proper dispensation from the canonical form is secured, the marriage is also licit. While Roman Catholic policy allows an Orthodox priest to be a marriage officiant in a Roman Catholic church building, Orthodox practice requires the specific permission of the Orthodox bishop.

Neither the Orthodox Church nor the Roman Catholic Church permits two separate marriage ceremonies. The common consent of two people baptized into Christ creates a new sacramental union whose root significance would be destroyed by the repetition of the wedding ceremony. Both adhere to Christ in faith; both share the Church's sacramental life; both pray in the same Spirit; both are guided by the same Holy Scripture. All this converges to make this most important moment a sacred event for the bride and groom. Three requirements must be observed in Orthodox–Roman Catholic marriages:

1. The marriage rite can be performed only once, and all indication of two distinct religious ceremonies should be avoided.
2. The ceremony should take place in an Orthodox or Roman Catholic church building.
3. The rite of the celebration is that of the officiating priest, and it should be made clear that one person is officiating in the name of that Church.

It is the recommendation of the Metropolitan New York/New Jersey Orthodox–Roman Catholic Dialogue that some canonical provision be made to resolve the problem which has great pastoral implications for Orthodox Christians marrying in the Roman Catholic Church. When an Orthodox Christian marries a Roman Catholic in a Roman Catholic ceremony, the Orthodox partner usually is separated from the participation in the sacraments of the Orthodox Church. In order to rectify the canonical situation of the Orthodox partner, current discipline requires that the marriage be regularized in the Orthodox Church. Any form of regularization should avoid giving the impression that the marriage which has taken place in the Roman Catholic Church does not have a fundamental sacramental character. Nor should it imply that a "new" ceremony is taking place. The goal is to reintegrate the Orthodox communicant into the full life of his/her own Church and to restore him/her to full canonical standing within the Church. In the hope of alleviating this canonical problem, this dialogue offers some recommendations further on for consideration by the appropriate authorities.

C. Counseling Those Entering into Orthodox–Roman Catholic Marriages Concerning Family Life and Rearing of Children

The religious education of children is the responsibility of both parents. The couple ought to be counseled to give serious consideration prior to the wedding to the religious upbringing of their children. It is recognized that each Church desires that every reasonable effort be made on the part of its own member to raise the children within its own community. It is hoped, however, that no prior agreement which would exclude the possibility of raising the children in either the Orthodox or Roman Catholic faith be entered into by either party. Within the context of the agreement which takes place before the marriage, the following norms are to be maintained:

1. A free decision must be made by the couple to raise the children either in the Orthodox or the Roman Catholic Church. The practice of raising some of the children in one Church and others in the other Church is wrong. It divides the family, fails to reflect the theology and practice of either Church, and could lead to an attitude of indifference. It is equally unacceptable to neglect to baptize and catechize children under the presumption that they will "decide for themselves" when they are older. Such a procedure very often results in those children having only a weak and confused faith and spiritual life.
2. Children should be taught to love and respect the Church and religious traditions of the other parent. Toward this end they should be able to worship occasionally at the liturgy and to participate in the devotional life of that parent's Church. However, every impression should be avoided of rearing the children in a "Christian" faith without identifying them with a concrete ecclesial community and spiritual tradition.
3. Where one partner is uncommitted to his/her faith and apparently will give little encouragement to the religious training of the children or become involved in it, then the children should be reared in the Church of the committed parent rather than have no connection with the sacramental life of either Church. (See *Joint Recommendations on the*

Spiritual Formation of Children of Marriages between Orthodox and Roman Catholics, 1980.)

While exposure to and participation in both traditions is desirable for the sake of the unity of the family, there are a number of points where differences in practice between the Orthodox and Roman Catholic Churches may very well pose problems and ought to be discussed during pastoral counseling, such as:

1. Church attendance,
2. Family worship at home,
3. Fasts (more numerous and probably more strictly observed in the Orthodox Church),
4. Feasts, especially Pascha/Easter and Christmas, which may or may not differ in the date of celebration and in the customs and concomitant demands made by them.

Both priests should counsel the couple on moral issues concerning family life, stressing commonality of beliefs and tradition, in order to bring about as much unity as possible in the faith and morals of the family. Topics in counseling should include: mutual respect, marital morality (including premarital and extramarital conduct), accepted means of family planning, family violence, divorce, chemical dependencies. Particular attention should be given to the subjects of Christian witness in a mixed marriage and personal spirituality. Whenever necessary, priests should be ready to recommend professional counseling or therapy in addition to their own pastoral counseling. It is particularly recommended that joint materials concerning Christian marriage and family life and especially the Christian rearing of children be developed and produced jointly for the guidance of the clergy and for the use of people involved in Orthodox–Roman Catholic marriages.

IV. Conclusion

This document has included a number of concrete recommendations which are presented to the two Churches for implementation. Some of them are immediately applicable. However, since others may not coincide in detail with current discipline and practices in the respective Churches, the following points are presented to the Churches for their particular consideration and action:

1. That canonical procedures for marriages between Orthodox and Roman Catholics be made uniform and obligatory in both Churches;
2. That the two Churches formally recognize the sacramentality of marriage in each other's Church;
3. That, in the light of examples given by the present canonical discipline of the Roman Catholic Church and synodal decisions of the Patriarchate of Moscow and the Church of Poland, measures of reciprocity be taken for recognizing the validity and liceity of all Orthodox–Roman Catholic marriages taking place in this country, as long as the proper canonical procedures are observed;
4. That the two Churches work toward eliminating the canonical institute of the formal promises to baptize and educate the children in a particular Church, as an absolute requirement for Orthodox–Roman Catholic marriages. (See: *Joint Recommendations on the Spiritual Formation of Children of Marriages between Orthodox and Roman Catholics,* 1980.)
5. That there be only one marriage ceremony in which either one or both priests are present, with the rite being that of the officiating priest and with specific parts of the service being offered to the guest priest in accordance with accepted norms;
6. That the marriage be recorded in both Churches' registries;
7. That if a Church judges that some supplementary liturgical action is needed so that its own member may be readmitted to full sacramental and disciplinary communion, care should be taken that the liturgical form of this celebration not give the impression of being another marriage ceremony, or that the marriage which had already taken place is not being recognized;
8. That both Churches seek to safeguard the richness and integrity of each tradition by cautioning the couple and their respective pastors against attempts to absorb one partner into the other's Church;
9. That the two Churches give full consideration to the marriage and dissolution/annulment requirements and procedures of each Church, recognizing that, when the canonical disciplines differ, any unclear case should be brought to the appropriate authorities of both Churches who, in common consultation, will seek to arrive at a solution; and

10. That materials for Christian marriage and family life and especially the spiritual formation of children be jointly developed and produced both for the guidance of the clergy and for the use of the people involved in Orthodox–Roman Catholic marriages.

Epilogue

We, the Metropolitan New York/New Jersey Orthodox–Roman Catholic Dialogue, offer this statement as a vision for improving pastoral care for our people in Orthodox–Roman Catholic marriages. In a spirit of cooperation, we have pinpointed the essential areas of difference which are in need of resolution.

We give glory to the Triune God for the continuing opportunity to engage in dialogue. Through the prayers of the Holy Mother of God and all the saints, may this statement be another step towards achieving Christian unity.

METROPOLITAN NEW YORK/NEW JERSEY ORTHODOX–
ROMAN CATHOLIC DIALOGUE
January 6, 1986

Agreed Statement on Apostolicity: God's Gift to the Church

October, 1986

1. In the creed we confess the Church to be "one, holy, catholic, and **apostolic.**" What is meant by this term? Modern scholarship, reflected in many joint and common statements of the ecumenical dialogue, has advanced discussion of this question in several important areas. For example, historical critical study of the Bible has called attention to the ways in which the word **apostolos** is used in the New Testament as well as to the distinctive role of the Twelve and to the place of Peter in the New Testament. So also, historians of doctrine have called attention to the importance of the struggle against gnosticism in the second century for the development of the concept of apostolic succession.

2. In 1985 the North American Orthodox/Roman Catholic Bilateral Consultation took up the study of apostolicity. Our papers and discussions prompted the following reflections, which we offer now particularly with the hope that they will help to advance the work of the International Orthodox/Roman Catholic Consultation as it moves forward in its own discussion of apostolicity.

3. It is not our intention simply to repeat or even to summarize the many scholarly foundational studies on apostolicity, though at times we shall call attention to points raised in them. Rather, we wish to examine certain other aspects of this subject, for we are convinced that, as Orthodox and Roman Catholics, we share a perception of apostolicity and of its implications for church structures which in some sense has united us even during periods of mutual antagonism. By trying to articulate this shared perception, we hope to carry our own discussion of apostolicity beyond the points of agreement and convergence already reached by others involved in ecumenical dialogue.

4. Biblical scholarship has drawn our attention to the fact that the

New Testament understanding of apostolicity is not so one-dimensional as both our traditions have sometimes appeared to presume. The differing theological emphases found there—St. Paul's claim to apostolic title or the tendency in Luke—Acts to identify the apostles with the Twelve—suggest that there is a continuing need for theological reflection on apostolicity, a task to which we today are also called.

5. In biblical language, apostles are those who have been sent out to perform a task in the name of another. They are endowed with the authority and freedom to act authentically on behalf of the one who sent them. Apostles in the New Testament are witnesses to the risen Christ who are explicitly commissioned by him to spread the gospel of his resurrection to the world and to promote, in his name, the active presence and power of God's kingdom. We call the Church apostolic first of all because the Church continues to share this mission in history, continues to be authorized by the risen Lord, through its continuing structures, as his legitimate representative.

6. For Orthodox and Roman Catholics, therefore, that the Church is apostolic is not simply a statement of fact, but an object of faith. The creed says, "I **believe** in one only, catholic and apostolic church." Like the Christ-event, this apostolicity is a gift from God given once for all; its content is not of our making. As biblical scholars have observed, the apostles were unique and irreplaceable in their witness to God's decisive intervention in human history. At the same time, this apostolic gift has an eschatological dimension, particularly—but not exclusively—when the Twelve are identified as apostles. The apostle appears as a uniquely authoritative figure, not only at the foundation of the Church but also as a companion of the eschatological Christ at the judgment of the last day. This eschatological dimension does not only mean that the Church, founded on the Twelve, awaits its perfect form at the end of God's plan for history. It also means that the Church shares now in the finality, the irrevocable fullness of God's action within the changes of history, precisely because the Twelve have passed on to the Church their witness to the presence of God's kingdom in the risen Lord and their role as authoritative heralds of his coming in history.

7. These two dimensions of apostolicity—the historical and the eschatological—cannot be separated, and certainly in our lived experience as Orthodox and Roman Catholics they have always been held together. Indeed, one of the characteristics of God's gift of apostolicity is that it manifests the events of the **end** to the present time. This is seen clearly in the pattern of the eucharist, where the Holy Spirit brings the reality of the resurrected Christ to the Church, and it is visible also

in the tradition of iconography, which brings to bear upon the present life of the Church both the historical past and the power of the world to come. Apostolicity thus is not reduced to simple reference to the past, nor is it referred only to the reality of a future age. It means that here and now the life of the Church—whether expressed in authoritative teaching, in judgment and discipline, or in the eucharist itself—is being moulded, corrected, and governed by what has been received from the past **and** by what is awaited at the last day.

8. We frequently speak of our faith as apostolic, by this usually stressing that its content has been received from the apostles. This understanding of the apostolic faith took on particular importance in the Church's struggle against gnosticism in the second century, when it came to be described as a deposit left by the apostles and handed down within the communities founded by them. But there has never been any need to understand this deposit as an inert object, relayed in purely mechanical fashion from generation to generation by duly authorized ministers. Rather, it remains a living confession. We see the paradigm of this in Peter's response to Christ's question, "Who do men say that I am? . . . Who do you say that I am?" The apostolic faith of Peter appears not only in the content of the confession—"Thou art the Christ, the son of the living God"—but also in the very act of confessing.

9. It is primordially within the mystery of Christian initiation that apostolicity is continually experienced in the life of the Church and in the life of each Christian. The baptismal act of receiving and giving back the Church's confession of faith (**traditio/redditio**) marks each Christian's entry into the appropriation of the apostolic life and faith of the Church. As an essential element in the life of the whole Church and of every Christian, apostolicity therefore is by no means unique to or limited to the realm of hierarchical ministry. For just as we share by baptism in the royal and prophetic priesthood, so also by this baptismal confession we too become bearers of the Church's apostolicity.

10. In our consultation attention was drawn to at least two corollaries which may follow from this understanding of apostolic faith: (a) The apostolicity of ministry is generally seen as derived from the continuity of the community as a whole in apostolic life and faith; the succession of ministers in offfice is normally agreed to be subordinate to that ecclesial apostolicity. (b) Apostolicity seems to consist more in fidelity to the apostles' proclamation and mission than in any one form of handing on community office. These observations alert us once again to reducing apostolicity simply to forms and institutional structures. Yet we also must resist any temptation to locate apostolicity in

what is merely individual or in what falls outside the mediated nature of the divine economy—as happened and still happens, for example, in the gnostic claim to immediate experience. Apostolicity is experienced not in a-temporal isolation but rather in the Church's social nature as a community of faith and in its historical continuity and permanence—even in concrete forms and patterns once again the Church's life by its relation to the civilization of the Greco-Roman world.

11. Within this social and historical experience of the apostolic Church, how do we as Orthodox and Roman Catholics conceive of those structures which attest to and assure the unity of the churches in their apostolic confession? Here historians have called attention to certain differences of approach which may characterize our churches. Yet we are uncomfortable with any assessment that would too sharply polarize differences, as though at every point—even those on which at first glance we would appear to be united—we were in fact divided by hopelessly irreconcilable mentalities.

12. In the Eastern churches there has frequently been an emphasis on the fullness of each church's apostolicity and, indeed, "petrinity," and there has been criticism of the Roman Church, for tending to localize these qualities in a single see. The Roman Church, on the other hand, has strongly emphasized the need to express the unity of the Church's apostolic faith through concrete structures and practice and has criticized the Eastern churches for losing sight of this need. Such differences of approach should not, however, be presented as evidence of an irreducible opposition between "local church" and "universal Church." This dilemma is an artificial one which arises at least in part when we are unwilling to see the same qualities present in both the local and the universal, albeit realized in different ways. The image of Peter within the apostolic college is reflected in the life of each local church; it is also reflected in the visible communion of all the local churches. There is no intrinsic opposition between these two approaches.

13. In examining the Church's historical relationship to civil society, scholars have also contrasted a "principle of accommodation" in the East to a "principle of apostolicity" in the West. Yet at a time when East and West were united in one Christian Roman Empire, neither approach necessarily excluded the other, for both pointed and aspired to universality. It was in Rome after all, the imperial capital, that Peter and Paul, "first enthroned of the apostles, teachers of the **oikumene,**" bore witness to the apostolic faith even unto death (Troparion of the feast of SS. Peter and Paul in the Byzantine Liturgy). And in the East,

it was no abstract principle of conformity to civil structures that prevailed. Rather, the concrete structures of a universal empire were used to express the Church's universality. Also instructive here are ways in which the themes of diversity-in-unity and ordered harmony are developed in the many Byzantine treatises on the pentarchy. What is envisioned is by no means simply an institutional unity, but an organic unity.

14. These points are offered in the hope that they will clarify and facilitate our common approach not only to the question of apostolicity but also to the question of primacy. Taken together, they call us to exercise particular caution in our use of theological language. When distinctions have been made or noted—as was done above, for example, in distinguishing the content and the act of apostolic faith—we must resist the temptation to leave them in a state of opposition. Unless the distinguished elements are recombined in their proper relationship and proportion, the integrity of the underlying theological reality is lost and the spiritual experience of this reality in both our traditions is travestied. There is no need to claim that what may characterize one tradition in a particular way exhausts the content of that tradition or, in turn, must be absent from another tradition as a matter of course.

15. The historical study of apostolicity also calls us to examine carefully the ways in which we present our respective histories. This has particular importance when we are speaking of that historical continuity we each claim as bearers of the apostolic faith, or when we recount those particular incidents in our histories—for example, the monothelite controversy in the seventh century—which may reflect different understandings of apostolicity. In such contexts we can easily forget the achievements of our common theological reflection and retreat once again—consciously or unconsciously—into what is less than the fullness of truth. We must not be too quick to identify this kind of retreat with that fearless confession of the apostolic faith "in season and out of season" which binds us all as Orthodox and Catholic Christians.

ORIENTAL ORTHODOX–
ROMAN CATHOLIC
DIALOGUES

Introduction

Since the Council of Chalcedon (451), the Coptic and Syrian Churches and their daughter churches in Ethiopia and India respectively, as well as the Church of Armenia, have been separated from the Byzantine Orthodox and Western churches. The doctrinal issue at the time of the separation was the definition of the person and nature of Christ.[1] These churches now have members throughout most of the world. Careful theological work has been done to heal the Christological divisions, and subsequent ecclesiological alienation between these churches and those of the Orthodox East and the Protestant and Roman Catholic West.[2]

The Oriental Orthodox Churches are much smaller and less well known in the United States. However, significant theological work has been produced by dialogues in the United States which have relied also on international agreements.[3] This dialogue with the BCEIA was inaugurated by the Armenian Church of America, in collaboration with the Syrian Orthodox, Syrian Orthodox of India, Coptic Orthodox, and Ethiopian Orthodox Churches. A priority in this dialogue has been pastoral support and mutual understanding.

Notes

1. Robert F. Taft, ed., *The Oriental Orthodox Churches in the United States* (United States Catholic Conference, 1986).

2. *Wort und Wahrheit* (in English, *Revue for Religion and Culture*) (Supplementary Issues No. 1 [December 1972], 2 [December 1974], 3 [December 1976], 4 [December 1978]; Paulos Gregorios, William Lazareth and Nikos Nissiotis, eds., *Does Chalcedon Divide or Unite? Towards Convergence in Orthodox Christology* (Geneva: World Council of Churches, 1981).

3. Archbishiop Tiran Nersoyan and Paul Fries, eds., *Christ in East and West* (Macon, GA: Mercer University Press, 1987).

Purpose, Scope and Method of the Dialogue Between the Oriental Orthodox and Roman Catholic Churches

1980

Introduction

The Oriental Orthodox and Roman Catholic Churches share in the same Spirit, the Incarnate Son and the Father through saving faith. For this profound reason our churches have much to contribute to one another from the spiritual treasures which they derive from their holy traditions. The responsibility to open channels of communication which may serve to facilitate this spiritual exchange derives from the Gospel command given to all Christians to love one another both in word and act after the example of the Father who "gave His only Son" (Jn 3:16) and Jesus Christ who "loved his own . . . to the end" (Jn 13:1). To share our lives with one another, ourselves and our spiritual and material riches, in the cause of strengthening the faith of those who are in Christ, this is the only adequate response to the one who calls us to "love one another as I have loved you" (Jn 15:12).

It is in this spirit that we begin our dialogue. We recognize that the church is called to be the community of those who live a common life like the Trinity; a world-wide community in which no single member or local church is foreign to any other member or local church but rather one in which each have their measure to receive and give. Hence this dialogue aims at contributing to the establishment of the conditions which make possible the visible manifestation of the love which already exists between our churches. The goal of the dialogue, therefore, is to work toward the realization of a mutually acceptable profession of faith which embraces the whole range of the life of faith and a corresponding communion of ecclesial life which respects the freedom of Christian communities in all things which do not pertain to the essentials of the life of faith.

As a step in this direction this dialogue intends to promote 1) mutual growth of our churches through the reciprocal sharing in doctrinal and spiritual traditions as well as liturgical life; 2) cooperation in their common responsibility for the furthering of the unity of all Christian churches and the preaching of the Gospel to the world; 3) unity of action between the churches in responding to the various problems and questions which arise in the numerous Christian communities and the world at large.

In brief, since the main concern of this dialogue is the fostering of conditions which favor full communion between our churches, it has both a practical and doctrinal orientation. It looks to ways of deepening unity in Christ through both concrete acts of love and theological discourse. For the dialogue in love which nourishes unity includes both word and act.

I. Dialogue in Love—Practice of Love

As a consequence of the estrangement between our churches which took place many centuries ago, and the accompanying insensitivity toward the ecclesial status of one another, both churches have attempted to proselytize individual members and particular local communities of the other church. Such activity has been especially detrimental to the stability and growth of certain Oriental Orthodox churches. Moreover this practice is contrary to the demands of an ecclesial dialogue in love which assumes that both churches, as churches of Jesus Christ, should live in a communion which respects the ancient traditions and styles of life of one another.

The long history of estrangement, intensified by well-meaning though at times self-serving ecclesiastical activity, must come to an end. This can only be achieved through a dialogue in love which leads us to seek new ways to remedy the effects of actions of the past which do not harmonize with the new experience of the ecclesial status of both churches; concrete acts of love, especially when costly, demonstrate that both churches recognize one another as true churches of Jesus Christ deserving of the right to life, respect, and support. Therefore the daily life of the two churches commands our attention. We intend to consider what practical means of cooperation are possible in the social, moral, and political spheres; whatever means can be employed to afford the faithful of both churches the experience of their oneness in Christ. Beyond this the dialogue intends to respond, where possible, to the needs of other churches, especially in lending support to heal schisms wherever they exist. Finally it accepts the task of developing practical suggestions for ways by which the two churches can effectively cooperate in common witness to the Gospel before the world.

II. Dialogue in Love—Theological Dialogue

Theological dialogue is a requirement of the dialogue in love. For one of the aspects of the dialogue in love is the mutual commitment to seek the truth together in order that both partners may live more fully in the truth.

This mutual commitment to seek the truth is not based on speculation concerning the possibility of arriving at knowledge of God and the mystery of the human person. It is grounded on the conviction that divine revelation of these mysteries has occurred in history, reaching its fullness in Jesus Christ; that the Holy Spirit was sent to make this revelation accessible to all people until Christ's Second Coming by sustaining and nourishing the church of Jesus Christ in the truth.

The church is the place where God's word always remains present and affirmed. But it is the "tent of the word of God" and, in its proper activity, sacrament of the truth: the way which gives all people access to God. This means that the dogmas, by which the church formulates its experience of the mystery of God acting in history, function as introduction into the mystery of faith: God the Father revealing himself in Jesus Christ through the Spirit. The totality of the mystery cannot be expressed adequately in any of its dogmatic formulations. Dogmatic statements are historically conditioned expressions of the divine truth. Although affirming divine truth, they remain in need of continual reinterpretation so as to be made more fully intelligible in changing historical and cultural contexts. Therefore Christian theology has the task of continually re-reading dogmas in the light of Scripture and Tradition as well as the newer insights and expressions of the life of the church. Just as in the early undivided church, so now the written Scripture is accepted as our norm of faith in the context of the living church which interprets it in the light of the past and present ecclesial self-understanding. Since we believe that our churches possess the Spirit of God, we are also convinced that our mutual witness of faith in dialogue can contribute to a deeper knowledge of the divine truth.

However this dialogue can only be carried on in the atmosphere of love. For charity furnishes the insight that the Spirit dwells in each of us and that we can only expect the other to accept the witness of faith insofar as he is convinced in faith, and this means in the Spirit. This conviction of the presence of the Spirit in the partners in dialogue, grounded on the experience of mutual love, determines the style of the dialogue. It is only properly conducted in a non-authoritarian, open and discoursive way. Since there exists in all truly Christian dialogue the presence of Christ in the Spirit the partners should maintain an openness to receive from one another the liberating power of the Gospel and share with one another their personal understanding of the truth as the Spirit reveals it.

1. Conditions for Theological Dialogue

The word *dialogue* means a speaking together with the accent on togetherness. By its very nature it aims at broadening areas of mutual agreement. Consequently it is imperative that the partners be open to one another *(reciprocity)* and ready to learn from one another and change ways of thinking and acting when the truth discovered through the conversations leads in a new direction *(mutual commitment).* In brief, dialogue aims at mutual enrichment and unity at as many levels as possible: communication of self to the other on all levels (human relations, truth, practical collaboration).

What is demanded of dialogue in general must be found in this dialogue between members of the churches of the Oriental and Roman Catholic traditions. The partners of the dialogue should consider each other as "equals." This means that 1) each should view the other as faithful to the Gospel according to his lights; 2) each should regard the other as possessing the Spirit and so capable of teaching or learning in speaking or listening through the Spirit; 3) both partners share in common the fundamental spiritual goods which are the mutual possession of both churches.

2. Differences Between Churches and Theological Dialogue

While the principle of equality between the members of the dialogue must be affirmed, the churches which they represent have developed characteristic theological approaches to the Christian economy of salvation to which correspond differences in the organizational form of church life, liturgy and spirituality. Many of the differences are clearly superficial but others are more substantial. Since we reject that form of doctrinal indifferentism which claims that all positions held by the churches of Jesus Christ have equal validity, the partners of this dialogue are committed to seek together resolutions to those seemingly incompatible divergences in content and expression of doctrine and the variations in the concrete style of ecclesiastical life which derive from them.

In this connection we recognize the existence of a hierarchy of truths within the diverse formulations of Christian faith. The partners of this dialogue, therefore, accept the task of articulating this hierarchy of truths and explaining the relationships between these truths as they see it. Here the problem of language inevitably arises. Since it is a question of establishing communication between two theological traditions, it is clear that the partners must submit the language they use to critical study. To avoid traveling along parallel lines wherein the same thing is meant by different words, the mutual effort must be made to discover the mentality, the genius of the culture, the philosophical outlook, traditions and styles of life which lie behind what is being said.

3. Methodology of the Theological Dialogue

The method of the dialogue involves several elements which can operate in succession or concurrently: 1) exchange of ideas where each one presents a point of view on the subject under discussion; 2) comparison of ideas to bring out differences and likenesses; 3) further investigation of shared positions; 4) highlighting aspects of the subject previously unnoticed which lead to further investigation.

Concerning the subjects of the dialogue a distinction must be made between 1) truths confessed in common; 2) truths obscured in one community but developed in the other; 3) religious insights even in areas of divergence (e.g., particular forms of worship; emphasis on certain aspects of Christian life).

Once this distinction is established, the following approach is recommended:

1) Begin the dialogue with elements which unite the two churches. This will foster a positive spirit which, it may be hoped, will prevail when dealing with areas of disagreement. Moreover it will afford a yardstick by which the partners are in a better position to evaluate differences and make changes where necessary.
2) An exposition of doctrine should be made in a constructive way which avoids defining by opposition, a process which leads to overstressing or hardening of certain positions.
3) In the discussion of doctrine an effort should be made in the direction of a constructive synthesis which attempts to take into account the whole scope of revealed truth.

4) In examining theological problems which exist between the Oriental Orthodox and Roman Catholic Churches, the historical developments since the New Testament and Patristic periods, as well as the current theological developments and ecclesial practices in both churches, should not be ignored. Also account should be taken of the fact that the Spirit of the church is both a conserving and renewing Spirit.
5) In examining problems which exist between the two churches a distinction should be made between divergences which are compatible and those which are seemingly incompatible with reference to full communion.

4. Themes of the Theological Dialogue

The ways by which our knowledge of Christian faith comes to us are varied. They parallel the ways in which we reach out for and allow reality to enter our consciousness. The world is laid open to us by our moods and feelings (sentient field), by our interaction with people (interpersonal field), by the personal and social stories which serve to organize our feelings and to form a sense of continuous identity (narrative field). In these primal fields the knowing subject is not consciously detached from the object known. However the subject may consciously detach himself from the object to be known and seek to know the real in itself (theoretic field).

Corresponding to these ways by which knowledge of the faith is obtained and expressed, theologians distinguish between two types of theological statement: 1) those which derive more directly from the experience of the life of faith and are expressed in self-involving language; 2) those which attempt to formulate in a scientific way the doctrinal content of the more direct expressions of faith. Since the liturgy, with its self-involving language, is the best expression of the ecclesial experience of the life of faith, it provides an indispensable source of the dogmatic statements of the official church and the theological reflection of scientific theology. Thus it is fitting that this dialogue begin with the study of the liturgies of the two churches and, in particular, with the sacraments of the church.

Moreover since the Mystery of Christ, in which all Christian theology is grounded, is expressed and realized in the church most perfectly through the celebration of the Divine Liturgy, the Eucharist, it seems most appropriate that this dialogue begin with and continually return to this theme. For the value of particular theological positions and practices of the church can be measured by the harmony they display with the faith expressed in the celebration of the Eucharist.

In the discussions about the Eucharist, or whatever topic is singled out for analysis, the participants are resolved to adopt as a working principle the one which Pope John XXIII formulated in his opening address to the participants of Vatican Council II:

> For the deposit of faith itself, namely the truths contained in our venerable teaching, is one thing; the way of expressing them is another.

There already exists a concrete example of the application of this principle which has brought our churches closer together. The joint statement published by the Syrian Orthodox Patriarch Ignatius Jacoub III and Pope Paul VI at the end of the Patriarch's visit, October 1971, reads in part:

> Pope Paul VI and the Patriarch Mar Ignatius Jacoub III are in agreement that there is no difference in the faith they profess concerning the mystery of the Word of God made flesh and become really man, even if over the centuries difficulties have arisen out of different theological expressions by which this faith was expressed.

This agreement provides us with a solid base for the hope that in "speaking the truth in love" (Eph 4:15a) this dialogue will make a contribution to our further growth together "into him who is the head, into Christ, from whom the whole body, joined and knit together by every joint with which it is supplied, when each part is working properly, makes bodily growth and upbuilds itself in love" (Eph 4:15b–16).

Agreed Statement on the Eucharist

Oriental Orthodox/Roman Catholic Dialogue
June 9, 1983

1. We agree that in the Eucharist the Church assembled is carrying out the injunction of the Lord to do what He did in the Last Supper, in commemoration of Him.
2. We agree that just as bread and wine became Christ's body and blood at the Last Supper, so do bread and wine become the body and blood of Christ when the Eucharist is celebrated by our churches.
3. We agree that the power of the triune God effects the change of bread and wine into the body and blood of Christ in the Eucharist. Traditionally this has been attributed either to the Word or to the Spirit.
4. We agree that the exercise of this divine power most properly is attributed to the Holy Spirit as source of God's action and grace in the Church. This corresponds well with the Spirit's role as life-giver, as overshadower in the incarnation, as sanctifier who sanctifies the bread and wine, become the body and blood of Christ, so that it sanctifies us when we receive it.
5. We further agree that the consecration of the elements is effected through Christ, the risen Lord, true God and true man, who operates through the Spirit in the life of the Church. This corresponds well with Christ's role in the Last Supper.
6. We recognize that some Fathers of the Church, such as John Chrysostom, Severus of Antioch and Ambrose of Milan, have taught that the eucharist is effected by the words of Christ, "This is my body . . . ; This is my blood." For when the priest pronounces these words during the anaphora, he does not do so in his own name but as representative of Christ and the Church.

But since what Christ did, once and for all, is made present now through the work of the Holy Spirit, other Fathers have held that the eucharist is effected when the Holy Spirit has been invoked upon the gifts of bread and wine.

7. We agree that in the anaphora or canon the account of institution, the anamnesis, and the epicletic prayers are all integral parts of a functional unity, and that the function of each can be properly understood only in the context of their mutual relations.

PRESBYTERIAN & REFORMED–
ROMAN CATHOLIC
DIALOGUES

Introduction

The Presbyterian Church, which in 1983 merged the United Presbyterian and Presbyterian Church US, the Reformed Church in America, the United Church of Christ, the Hungarian Reformed and the Cumberland Presbyterian Churches are among the communions represented in the World Alliance of Reformed Churches (WARC). These represent the dominant Calvinist churches with Scottish, Puritan and Dutch heritage in the USA. Their standards of faith are grounded in the Reformed confessions. One of these churches, the United Church of Christ, represents a union of churches with Lutheran, Calvinist and Disciples traditions (1957).

In July, 1965, an exploratory meeting opened a consultation between the BCEIA and the North American section of the WARC. This consultation divided into two sections, one on theology and one on worship and mission. Meeting twice a year between 1965 and 1967, the dialogue discussed the Holy Spirit in the Church, Scripture and tradition, development and reform of doctrine, ministry and order, mixed marriage, and worship and witness. Many of these papers appeared in *Reconsiderations.*[1] The dialogue continued to meet twice a year (1968–1971), on the themes of ministry[2] and on interchurch marriage.[3]

In 1972 the dialogue was restructured. One section incorporated sociologists and historians, and used the case study method to complement the theological section. After meeting twice a year, in 1976 the consultation produced a proposal, "The Unity We Seek," published in this volume. Four of the background papers have also been included with the full proposal.[4]

The third round (1976–79) dealt with morality and ethics. The two statements from this dialogue are also published here. The full document, *Ethics and the Search for Christian Unity,* includes an interpretive report and a commentary from the perspectives of the two traditions.[5]

The fourth round (1980–85) continued the discussion on ethical issues. The report on education and peace is published here.[6] None of the results of these dialogues have been submitted to the churches for action or formal response.

These discussions are supplemented by worldwide dialogues between the Secretariat for Promoting Christian Unity and the World Alliance of Reformed Churches.[7] This dialogue is also well developed in many other parts of the world.[8]

Notes

1. *Reconsiderations: Roman Catholic/Presbyterian and Reformed Theological Conversations 1966–67* (New York: World Horizons, Inc., 1967), 13–45.

2. "The Ministry of the Church," *Journal of Ecumenical Studies* (hereafter JES) 5 (1968) 462–65, John Charlot, "Validation of Ministries in the New Testament," Kilian McDonnell, "Ways of Validating Ministry," JES 7 (1970) 209–65, "Ministry in the Church," "Women in Church and Society," JES 7 (1970) 686–91.

3. Glenn Baumann, "The Churches and Their Attitudes Toward Inter-Christian Marriages," Henry Beck, "Proposed Pastoral Guidelines for Interchristian Marriages," *Worship* 42 (1968) 609–16, 43 (1969) 159–65, Christopher Kiesling, "Light and Shadow: A Theological View of Christian Marriage," *Cross and Crown* 21 (1969) 24–39.

4. Ernest Unterkoefler and Andrew Harsanyi, eds., *The Unity We Seek* (New York: Paulist Press, 1977).

5. *Ethics and the Search for Christian Unity* (Washington: United States Catholic Conference, 1981). The dialogue between Roman Catholics and the United Church of Canada also addressed the abortion issues: "The Churches on Abortion," *Ecumenism* 83 (September, 1986).

6. *Partners in Peace and Education:* Presbyterian–Reformed/Roman Catholic Bilateral Consultation. Ronald C. White, Jr. and Eugene J. Fisher, eds. (Grand Rapids: Eerdmans, 1987).

7. GIA 433–465, IS "The Theology of Marriage and the Problems of Mixed Marriages: Dialogue Between the Lutheran World Federation, the World Alliance of Reformed Churches, the Secretariat for Promoting Christian Unity–Roman Catholic Church, 1971–1978," IS 1978, 36:I, "Catholic/Reformed Dialogue: Report of Evaluation Group," 1981, 45:I, 46–48.

8. Lukas Vischer, Andreas Karrer, ed., *Reformed and Roman Catholic in Dialogue,* Geneva: World Alliance of Reformed Churches, 1988.

Women in the Church

Christian faith acknowledges the equal dignity of man and woman. We, the members of the Worship and Mission Section of the Roman Catholic/Presbyterian and Reformed Consultation, have studied the life of women in Church and society in our meetings at Morristown, N. J., May, 1970; Princeton, N. J., October, 1970; Columbus, Ohio, May, 1971; and Richmond, Va., October, 1971. As a result of this study, we are moved to make some recommendations to our parent bodies—the Bishops' Committee on Ecumenical and Interreligious Affairs and the North American Area Council, World Alliance of Reformed Churches—in regard to women in the Churches served by our parent bodies.

Our own, personally conducted theological investigation is not the basis for these recommendations, for we are not this consultation's Theological Section, charged with the task of theological research. We are moved to present these recommendations because of several facts which have been brought to our attention in the course of our study.

The first fact is the injustice imposed upon women in both society and the Churches. We have heard and weighed the grievances and aspirations of women of wide experience who have devoted many years of service to the Churches and to the world: Margaret Kuhn (Presbyterian) and Arlene Swidler (Roman Catholic) at Morristown; Frances McGillicuddy (Roman Catholic), the Reverend Patricia Doyle (Presbyterian), and Suzanne Hiatt (Anglican) at Princeton; Grace Howard (Presbyterian), Sheila Collins (Methodist), Theodora Sweeney and Sister Jane Pank, H.M., (Roman Catholics) at Columbus. At Princeton we also heard the observations of the sociologist, the Reverend Joseph Fichter, S.J.

As a result of their testimony, we have been led to see such injustices as: Men are usually hired for jobs in preference to women, even when the women are equally or better qualified for the job; women are generally paid less than men for the same work; woman's identity is so dependent upon a man that the unmarried woman is regarded as strange or unsuccessful by society and is frequently excluded from participation in society's affairs. That this exclusion is often the result of oversight only confirms the affirmation that in society's eyes a woman's identity comes from her relationship to some man rather than from her own person. Married women are identified by their husband's name rather than their own, as if they were pieces of their husband's property.

Within the fellowship of the Church, it would appear that we have obliged women to exercise a secondary and often demeaning ministry. Women have been excluded from making decisions in the Churches, even in an advisory capacity, although many of those decisions determined the disposition of their own lives. Even when women are involved in decision-making, more often than not their voice is not significant in relation to their contribution to the life of the Church. We have either denied women part in the ordained ministry or have granted them part with reluctance, and then have proceeded to hedge their ministry with severe limitations. Very few ordained women, in those Churches which admit them to ordination, have been accepted as pastors by local communities.

This list of obvious injustices could be extended. More subtle ones could be added, for "our way of life, our folk cultures, and even the very idiom of our speech have assigned to women a secondary and, at best, supportive role . . . " ("Women in Church and Society," statement of the Worship and Mission Section of the Roman Catholic/Presbyterian and Reformed Consultation, Morristown, May 15, 1970, in *Journal of Ecumenical Studies* 7 [1970]:690).

Of the many injustices of our age, the injustice inflicted upon women is surely one of the most massive, for it affects one-half of the human race—and one-half of the Churches' membership! The unjust conditions under which women are (often subtly) compelled to live affects adversely the personal development of men as well as women. No human being is truly and fully free as long as even one other human being is in bondage. "More and more women today feel strongly that they wish to share fully with men in all human responsibilities" ("Ministry in the Church," draft paper of the Theological Section of the Roman Catholic/Presbyterian and Reformed Consultation, Richmond, October, 1971). This aspiration of women today is frustrated by the accepted status of women in society and the Church. We judge this status quo to be sinful and immoral.

> True, all men are not alike from the point of view of varying physical power and the diversity of intellectual and moral resources. Nevertheless, with respect to the fundamental rights of the person,

> every type of discrimination, whether social or cultural, whether based on sex, race, color, social condition, language, or religion, is to be overcome and eradicated as contrary to God's intent. For in truth it must still be regretted that fundamental personal rights are not yet being universally honored. Such is the case of a woman who is denied the right and freedom to choose a husband, to embrace a state of life, or to acquire an education or cultural benefits equal to those recognized for men (Vatican Council II, *Pastoral Constitution on the Church in the Modern World,* no. 29).

In the light of the Gospel of Jesus Christ, Christians could have, and very often should have, known and acted otherwise than we have in regard to the treatment of women in Church and society. We acknowledge our sins of commission and omission which contribute to the unjust conditions to which women are subjected. Therefore we acknowledge our need for conversion, for finally recognizing and ensuring women's personal identity, dignity, freedom, and rights to human fulfillment, especially in the Church. "The whole Christian community must summon the will and discover ways whereby the equality of the sexes is boldly confessed before God and man—confessed both in word and in deed. This equality of personhood, whether male or female, married or unmarried, can no longer be stifled" ("Women in Church and Society," Morristown).

The world will attach little credibility to the call of the People of God for justice for every human being, if the People of God within their own fellowship continue to regard and treat women as inferior human beings, discriminating against them because of their sex and thereby depriving them of fundamental personal rights.

A second fact is the women's liberation movement which is gaining momentum in society today. "The People of God . . . labors to decipher authentic signs of God's presence and purpose in the happenings, needs, and desires in which this People has a part along with other men of our age" (Vatican Council II, *Pastoral Constitution on the Church in the Modern World,* no. 11). Thus, penetrating through the excesses which sometimes accompany the women's liberation movement, we discern a sign of God's presence and purpose in its basic cause of justice, freedom, and full personal dignity for women. The Churches will be unfaithful to the Spirit of the Lord if they fail to take up this cause, especially within their own fellowship.

Many Churches were slow in exercising leadership in the civil rights and peace movements of the 1960's. The credibility of the Churches will be damaged further if they fail to demonstrate creative leadership in the movement for women's rights in the 1970's. Given the current alienation of so many young people from the institutional Church, this matter of the credibility of the Churches cannot be taken lightly.

A third fact is that an ever growing number of theological investigations have been made in recent decades in various Churches and have repeatedly come to the conclusion that there are no conclusive, Biblical, doctrinal, or theological reasons why women cannot exercise decision-making positions in the Church and receive ordination. (A list of such studies and pertinent ecclesiastical decisions is in the appendix to this statement.) Christian theology demands certain steps which will correct a patently unjust situation which is intolerable in the light of the Gospel. We urge readers of this statement to consider the theological studies which have been made concerning women in the Church, and in particular certain sections of the study on "Ministry in the Church" of the Theological Section of this consultation.

We have become starkly aware of the gap between the status accorded to women in our Churches and in the Word of God. The status of women in our Churches often lags behind that accorded to them in society at large. For example, in some Churches women are not involved in decision-making positions. This noninvolvement may arise from conditioning in childhood not to desire involvement. Both the conditioning and the resultant noninvolvement reflect the pattern formerly followed in secular society and long since outmoded. The criterion for the status of women in our Churches is the Word of God in Jesus Christ.

St. Paul bears witness to this revelation of God when he writes: "For as many of you as were baptized into Christ have put on Christ. There is neither Jew nor Greek, there is neither slave nor free, there is neither male nor female; for you are all one in Christ Jesus. And if you are Christ's, then you are Abraham's offspring, heirs according to promise" (Gal. 3:27–29 RSV). In this passage and others (Rom. 10:12; I Cor. 12:13; Eph. 4:24; Col. 3:11), the Word of God, alive and active, cuts like any two-edged sword, but more finely (cf. Heb. 4:12), into the assumptions of the ancient synagogue and societies of every age with regard to women's status. The Christian life as such, both in its individual and corporate manifestation, is grounded in baptism in Christ, not in this or that ethnic origin, this or that social status, or this or that sex. Human beings are "Abraham's offspring, heirs according to promise," not by being male or female, but by belonging to Christ. The place accorded to women in the Churches should stand in prophetic judgment on the place accorded to them in society and not simply give divine sanction to society's values.

It is, indeed, true that there are certain statements in the New Testament which treat women as unequal to men, v.g., I Cor. 14:34; I Tim. 2:11–15 ("women should keep silence in the churches . . . " RSV). Here, it may be suggested, the Apostles mirror the culture of their times, reflecting a sociology which de facto made women subordinate. Just as the Apostles could accept slavery yet at the same time unleash spiritual insights which finally found slavery incompatible with the Gospel, so their seminal affirmations, v.g., Gal. 3:27–29 and I Cor. 11:11 ("nevertheless in the Lord woman is not independent of man nor man of woman" RSV) would, in the end, point toward the integral Christian vision of women as fully equal to men.

Finally, we are prompted to make our recommendations for ecumenical reasons. All our Churches are confronted by the same challenge: To recognize, promote, and safeguard the personal dignity, freedom, and rights to human fulfillment of the women who constitute half of their membership. Our various Churches have made different degrees of progress toward this common goal. Those Churches which have made little progress can benefit from the experience of those which have advanced farther, and these latter can find corroboration of their efforts in the undertakings of the former.

> Cooperation among all Christians vividly expresses that bond which already unites them, and it sets in clearer relief the features of Christ the Servant. Such cooperation . . . should be ever increasingly developed. . . . It should contribute to a just appreciation of the dignity of the human person, the promotion of the blessings of peace, the application of gospel principles to social life, and the advancement of the arts and sciences in a Christian spirit. Christians should also work together in the use of every possible means to relieve the afflictions of our times, such as famine and natural disasters, illiteracy and poverty, lack of housing, and unequal distribution of wealth. Through such cooperation, all believers in Christ are able to learn easily how they can understand each other better and esteem each other more, and how the road to the unity of Christians may be made smooth (Vatican Council II, *Decree on Ecumenism,* no. 12).

If the Churches can advance toward the unity willed by Christ for his Church by working together to secure justice in the world-at-large, how much more fruitful for Christian unity will be their working together for justice for women, not only in the world, but especially in the Church!

Recommendations

Because we are concerned about the worship and mission of the Church, because unjust and unchristian conditions prevent women from full participation in the worship and mission of the Church, because the Church is broken, because different theologies, customs and practices exist in regard to women in the worship and mission of the Church, and because we are placed in a position to make suggestions to the Churches which we represent, we recommend:

(1) *That qualified women be given full and equal participation in policy- and decision-making, and voice in places of power, in the Churches on local, regional, national, and world levels.*

The first and most obvious reason for admitting women to policy- and decision-making positions and to voice in places of power in the Churches is the fact that the policies and decisions made and the power exercised frequently determine the lives of women. Unless they have an effective part to play in these policies and decisions and this exercise of power, they are being treated as children and manifestly deprived of their rights as adults to determine their own lives. Until women have such an effective part to play in the determination of their lives in the Churches, it is difficult to avoid the accusation that in the Churches they are oppressed in a kind of bondage or slavery.

The second and more profound reason why women ought to participate in decision-making and the exercise of power in the Churches is for the sake of the total life of the Church, both men and women. "We are to grow up in every way into him who is the head, into Christ, from whom the whole body, joined and knit together by every joint with which it is supplied, when each part is working properly, makes bodily growth and upbuilds itself in love" (Eph. 4:15–16 RSV). "If one member suffers, all suffer together; if one member is honored, all rejoice together" (I Cor. 12:26 RSV).

Our recommendation is supported by voices within our Churches. For example, the *Report of the Standing Committee on Women to the 183rd General Assembly (1971) of the United Presbyterian Church, U.S.A.* enunciates this principle: "Since women are called to be partners with men, they must accept all forms of service in the Church, including leadership positions in the decision-making processes. The

Church must encourage and enable women to assume ecclesiastical and societal responsibilities" (Introduction, principle no. 3).

The draft document "Justice in the World," prepared for the Third World Synod of Bishops (October, 1971), speaks of the various rights which must be honored. Among these rights, "a third series of rights regards the active participation of all men in the various decision-making institutions which control social, economic, cultural, political, and religious life" (in the *National Catholic Reporter,* 13 August 1971, p. 7).

The Theological Section of the Roman Catholic/Presbyterian and Reformed Consultation, in its statement "Ministry in the Church" (Richmond, 1971), recommends: "All offices in the Church, ordained and unordained, be opened to qualified women, and that a major effort be undertaken to place qualified women, ordained and unordained, in offices and positions of leadership and decision-making in something approaching their proportion in Church membership."

(2) *(A) That seminary education in all the Churches be opened to qualified women; (B) that qualified women be admitted to ordination; (C) that in those Churches where the ordination of women presents theological difficulties and no theological study of the matter has been made, a theological committee be established immediately to investigate the problem and make recommendations.*

(A) The basic reasons for this recommendation are the same ones mentioned above. The following additional reasons may be added:

First, many women desire to serve the Church and the world with that theological and pastoral expertise which men enjoy as a result of seminary education. To prevent the fulfillment of this desire is to deny "the right and freedom" of women "to acquire an education or cultural benefits equal to those recognized for men" (Vatican Council II, *Pastoral Constitution on the Church in the Modern World,* no. 29).

Second, the needs of today's world call for the theological and pastoral expertise which seminaries alone are geared to provide. If the Churches are going to respond adequately to this call, they must make use of all the human resources at their disposal, whatever the sex of those human resources. Therefore the Churches should open seminary education to women as well as men.

Third, the Churches' seminaries were for a long time exclusively the domain of men and are still overwhelmingly dominated by them. Welcoming women into the seminaries of all the Churches would be a sign to the Churches' membership and to society that the Churches take seriously their proclamation that in Christ there is neither male nor female and that women ought to be accorded personal rights and freedoms equally with men. Admission of women to seminary education would signify that the Church is willing to back up its proclamation by deeds.

Finally, the admission of women to seminary education would benefit not only women but men. Future male ministers and priests would learn the woman's point of view in those areas of life where women have specialized knowledge and often exclusive experience, e.g., pregnancy, childbirth, motherhood, sexual discrimination, etc. Seminary students would have the opportunity to learn to relate to men and women on the basis of their equal ability to think theologically and function skillfully in pastoral situations.

(B) Since the Churches have need of all available human resources for carrying out their mission to mankind, it is unreasonable to deny ordination to women simply because women have not been admitted to ordination in the past. Several thorough theological investigations made in various Churches have found no Biblical, doctrinal, or theological obstacles to the ordination of women. Moreover, some qualified women believe themselves called by God to ordination.

(C) Some of the Churches which we represent are not willing to accept the theological investigations conducted in other Churches and concluding that women may be ordained. Yet in those Churches unwilling to accept these theological investigations, there are women who desire to be ordained and believe that the Holy Spirit is the source of their desire. The least that should be done is to test this desire and belief in accord with 1 Thess. 5:19, 21. The will of the Holy Spirit may be at stake here, as well as the personal rights of women members of these Churches. We should also consider the need of the Churches to use all available human resources in the mission of Christ. It would be a serious neglect before God and man for any Church to delay to make that rigorous theological investigation which would settle the question of the ordination of women. To hesitate to take up the question in the most serious, competent, and formal manner would suggest indifference to the will of the Holy Spirit, the personal rights of women, and the needs of the Church in its mission to the world.

(3) *That the North American Area Council, World Alliance of Reformed Churches and the Bishops' Committee on Ecumenical and Interreligious Affairs establish and fund an Ecumenical Commission on Women, inviting other Churches involved in bilateral consultations with the Roman Catholic Church to join them on an equal basis in responsibility and funding for this commission and in sharing the fruits of its labors; that the members of this commission be predominantly*

women from all the sponsoring Churches who are actively engaged in the lives of their Churches and also positively concerned for women's dignity, freedom, and rights; that the purpose of this commission be to facilitate the fulfillment of the first two recommendations and to safeguard and extend the gains made.

Such a commission would be a concrete step in implementing our first recommendation, namely, that qualified women be given full and equal participation in policy- and decision-making, and voice in places of power, in the Churches on local, regional, national, and world levels. It would be charged with making recommendations to the leaders of the Churches in pursuit of justice, dignity, and freedom for women in all the Churches and in pursuit of unity among the Churches in regard to women's rights. The commission would give valuable guidance to the Churches and would greatly encourage women to assume their full responsibility in the life and mission of the Church.

We do not wish to prescribe as a priority what projects this commission should undertake, but we make the following suggestions of the sort of projects that could be profitable.

(1) The development of criteria for guiding children, adolescents, and adults in attaining a healthy attitude toward their own sexuality and a joyous celebration of their manhood and womanhood.

(2) The exploration of additional forms of innovative ministries for both women and men, unordained and ordained—ministries which would be ecumenical in nature, and recognized and supported by the Churches.

(3) A study of means of encouraging and preparing congregations to receive women as pastors.

(4) A thorough study of the Churches' influence, through their teachings, customs, and the unexamined attitudes of their members, upon both men and women in the development of their attitudes about being men or women and in their fulfillment as persons.

(5) A careful study of the conditioning to which the young are subjected through the educational materials which the Churches use, in order to determine what attitudes about being male or female this conditioning produces.

The Unity We Seek

I. The Mission and Nature of the One Church of Christ

"Christ is the visible likeness of the invisible God. He is the first-born Son, superior to all created things. For by him God created everything in heaven and on earth, the seen and the unseen things, including spiritual powers, lords, rulers, and authorities. God created the whole universe through him and for him. He existed before all things, and in union with him all things have their proper place. He is the head of his body, the Church; he is the source of the body's life; he is the firstborn Son who was raised from death, in order that he alone might have the first place in all things. For it was by God's own decision that the Son has in himself the full nature of God. Through the Son, then, God decided to bring the whole universe back to himself. God made peace through his Son's death on the cross, and so brought back to himself all things, both on earth and in heaven" (Col. 1:15–20).

Proclaimed here is the complete sufficiency of Christ as the center of humanity's history and as the head of the Church. For the fullness of God, his wisdom and power are in Christ who shares these with the Church which, in turn, affects all humanity through the preaching of the Gospel. Thus the Church is the visible, historical, socially articulated manifestation of God's eternal decree in Christ. By that decree the Father calls all humanity to communion with himself, the Son, and the Spirit. The Church is willed and called into being to witness to this divine universal love and mercy. Hence by Word and sacrament, by every possible service of reconciliation, the Church must seek to be a sign of this mission and endeavor to accomplish it effectively.

Yet the existence of consultations such as ours sorrowfully testifies to the many failures of the Christian Church as it has sought to accomplish this mission. Consciousness of these evident failures led from the world mission movement to the ecumenical movement. This same deepening awareness has more and more permeated the discussions of the Roman Catholic/Presbyterian-Reformed Bilateral Consultation.

This common conviction concerning the mission of the Church of Christ, the history of our bitter and rending discords, the vocation of the Church to be a sign of unity and a witness to God's love—all these have led us to choose the theme of this joint statement: the shape of the unity we seek.

The Problem

If we maintain—we believe we must—that ecclesial unity is possible, then can we describe this possibility realistically? Can we so give shape to this possibility of Christian unity that we will be able to state future goals with Christian realism? Our very existence as a consultation underlies our affirmative approach. This does not mean a claim to spell out each step. Nor does it mean that we can define in clear and complete detail a future Christian Church which is authentically one. What we do affirm is that in the present biblical, historical, theological, and sociological resources it is possible to construct a working model that can be projected into the future.[1] In taking this theme we are aware that we are undertaking to come to grips with the ultimate concern of ecumenism as well as of this consultation. Basically our theme entails a real response to the question: What do we mean when we say "one Church"? It also obliges us to try to describe in the concrete the ecclesial unity we seek.

The People of God

Our consensus is that the first step in understanding the shape of the unity we seek is an understanding of the Church as the people of God. In treating the Church as the people of God we realize that it is only one aspect of the total mystery of the Church of Christ. By beginning with this dimension, however, we intend to give primacy to what is the beginning and abiding core of the Christian life—our oneness in Christ through faith and baptism. It affirms that this faith and baptism are the cause and initiation of our unity; any distinction is subordinate to this unity and to be judged by the priority of our commitment to Christ. Accepting the Church as the people of God also puts in the forefront one of the basic characteristics of biblical revelation—the corporate or communal character of salvation. Finally, it gives strong stress to the visible historical character of God's Church and the historical character of God's dialogue with his people. So it points firmly to the role of historical event and human experience—the historicity of man—in God's salvific design.

Our understanding of the Church as the people of God is rooted in both Testaments. St. Paul begins with the idea of Israel as the people of God. It is a people chosen by God and given his covenanted promises and love. Yet, as prophetically understood, it is imperfect, awaiting a new and universal covenant in the future. So, for St. Paul, the Church is the new people, linked with Israel but founded by Jesus Christ, ministering to the advance of God's reign and the salvation and reconciliation of all humanity. It has been called together through Christ and is an essential element of God's plan of salvation. It possesses a new covenant that consecrates this new people to God. Like Israel, it too is imperfect, a "pilgrim Church," beset by historical tensions and the weakness of the flesh, but, "moved by the Spirit, it may never cease to renew itself until through the cross it arrives at that light that knows no setting."[2]

To this new people of God the Spirit gives his gifts in abundance, because this whole people shares the prophetic office of Christ. Each member is called to be a living witness through a life of faith and love. All the gifts are given for the building up of the Church. Each member has a Christian ministry. Each ministry is a gift of the Spirit. Each ministry has a necessary role to play in the wholeness of the unity of the Church.[3] The ultimate quality of these gifts is the love that informs and motivates them.[4] These charisms are a continuing reality and an integral dimension of the structure of the Church. In affirming this Pauline doctrine we are only reaffirming a basic element of his ecclesiology and so more effectively indicating the shape of the unity we seek.[5]

Implicit in an ecclesiology modeled on the people of God of the new covenant is the principle of catholicity. For this people of God of the new covenant *is* the principle of catholicity. This new people of God looks to all humanity, since the reason for this people's existence in Jesus Christ is to be a bearer of the good news to all humanity. Thus we cannot attempt to define the future unless we also affirm that diversity and unity are not mutually exclusive. Pluralism is endemic to human beings and has richly positive dynamisms and creative possibilities. So also for God's people. Diversities of language, of culture, of religious and historical experience are not by nature divisive. Rather they are called to be part of a rich and manifold expression of that total reality of our reconciliation with God in Christ.

In saying this, however, we must contritely take into full account our Christian past and present and so our failure to live with diversity. We must acknowledge that the power of religious passion has again and again created a mentality that looks upon any diversity as contrary to the will of Christ. Yet, if we are to give a future unity shape, we are convinced that we must also accept diversity on many levels and in many aspects. Otherwise our goal is impossible, and this we as Christians do not believe.

In the light of this principle of catholicity, we propose for consideration the theological "tentative" of a typology of churches.[6] "Type" *(typos)* here means general form or character. The assertion is that there can be a plurality of types *(typoi)* within the communion of the church of Christ. In the words of Cardinal Willebrands: " . . . the notion . . . of a *typos* of a Church does not primarily designate a diocese or a national church. . . . It is a notion which has its own phenomenological aspects with their own theological meaning."[7] Thus, "where there is a long, coherent tradition commanding men's [and women's] love and loyalty, creating and sustaining a harmonious and organic whole of complementary elements, each of which supports and strengthens the other, you have the reality of a *typos*."[8]

We see, then, as the shape of our future unity, a communion of communions *(communio communiorum),* a Church of churches *(Ecclesia ecclesiarum),* each communion in the whole being a living, historical community gathered together in the name of Christ by faith and baptism. Each gathering has a tradition that embodies an enduring Christian commitment and an experience proper to itself. Out of this comes a theological, liturgical, and spiritual tradition which is accepted by the community and through which the community endeavors to live the Christian life. Each communion, as the whole Christian Church, accepts as the wellspring of its unity and the heart of its common loyalty the person and message of Jesus Christ and the graced conviction that he is God and Savior.

Our mutual conviction is that the shape of unity conceived in terms of a communion of communions is a very fruitful approach to future unity. It avoids the abstraction of a superchurch that transcends all diversities and denominationalism. Such an abstraction tends to ignore the continuing human experience of catholicity. We are sharply aware from historical experience that this approach of a communion of communions has its own dangers. Excessive denominationalism and consequent sectarianism must be constantly guarded against. As has been pionted out to us, denominationalism can readily involve "misconstrued priorities" whereby the denomination is first and the Church is second.[9] Denominationalism leads to a strong negative reaction to any larger, positive overseeship. History also makes us aware that large-scale oversight runs the real danger of negating diversity and emphasizing uniformity for the sake of efficiency and unanimity of action.

While we have chosen the model of the Church as the people of

God as primary to our ecumenical purpose, we recognize that it cannot totally suffice for the full explication of our theme. For the emphasis on this dimension of the Church's visible and historical character and its catholicity may well obscure the transcendent unity of all Christians. For what distinguishes the unity of the Christian community from any other community is that it is the body of Christ—another Pauline model. In this latter model we see the divine life revealed in Jesus Christ and communicated to believers by the Holy Spirit. The Christian Church, of course, has visible and social bonds, but the bonds are engendered by the spiritual community of grace and charity by which Christ becomes the head of the Church, his body. This spiritual bond constitutes the whole Christ—head and members.

Sign of the Unity of All Humanity

As we have reflected together on our common quest for unity, it has become increasingly evident that the unity Christ willed for his Church he also willed for all humanity. As Christians, we believe that Christ's redemptive mission encompasses the entire human community. In this belief so many in the ecumenical movement find their most powerful motivation that Christian unity may be the harbinger of that peace and unity it seeks to promote. For this reason we see the Church as called to be a sign—a sacrament—of that unity which God has willed for his creation and disclosed in Jesus Christ. Yet, again, we have been confronted with the history of our separations and divisions and the tragic sign that they are. We must acknowledge that only God's grace can make us the instrument of unity. Nonetheless, this very consciousness of our failure has animated our efforts toward unity. At this moment we see Christians as having a charismatic ministry to press toward unity with every effort. It becomes, then, an integral part of the Christian vocation to pray and to demand that Christian leaders will work together to unite the Church of Christ, so that it will become a fruitful sign and instrument of that unity to which God has called the total human family.

As part of the total human community, the ministry of the Church must play a real and vital role in the needs of that community. In the grim actualities of our day, the public proclamation of the need for peace and justice does not suffice. Oppression, lack of education, malnutrition, and famine are not abstractions but agonizing and mortal problems in our own nation and in the world community.

We must not forget that these problems have found their most tragic and complex dimensions in countries that have been the object of Christian missionary effort for generations and even centuries. Here in a special way the Church is called to be not only a sign but an effective bearer of hope, performing a Christian ministry of reconciliation. But we Christians will not be able to effectuate such a ministry unless first of all we show ourselves aware that we have failed in many ways. Perhaps unwittingly and despite good intentions, all too often Christian missionaries have become instruments of colonial establishments. We realize that we cannot begin over again, but we also see that evangelical realism must accept the principle of catholicity.

A genuine and unmistakable commitment to the concrete human needs of our day is an inescapable obligation of the Christian Church seeking for unity. Only when this commitment is evident to what has been called the Third World can the Church effectively carry out its ministry of reconciliation and become a prophet of a better hope.

This ministry of reconciliation must witness that the dynamic power of an authentic Christian ministry to human needs is the proclamation of the person and message of Jesus Christ. It is the crucified and risen Christ that we must preach if humanity's hope is to be engendered. Under no circumstances should the Church appear as just another social agency. But to proclaim the Gospel with believable conviction and authenticity, we need to show ourselves committed to giving concrete form to the evangelical imperatives of freedom, justice, peace, and mutual love.

A Pilgrim Church

Finally, in our general thematic—the shape of the unity we seek—we are cognizant of the eschatological nature of the Church and its mission. We accept the fact that the Christian Church is a pilgrim Church always in need of reform and renewal. Hence, we must view the Church in the eschatological perspectives of salvation history. "The unity and catholicity of the Church are always and in every case in process; they will always remain a task. The solution cannot lie either in mutual absorption or in a simple integration of individual Christian communities but only in the constant conversion of all, that is, in the readiness to let the event of unity, already anticipated in grace and sign, occur over and over again in obedience to the one Gospel as the final norm in and over the Church."[10]

II. The Unity We Seek in Belief

As Christians we all believe it has been divinely revealed that

Jesus is God and Savior, sent by the Father to lead all creation under the guidance of the Spirit to salvation,[11] to liberation,[12] "to reconcile everything in his person" (Col. 1:20). Our trust in Jesus assures us that God the Father has sent him, and still continues to work through him in the power of the Spirit.

In this or a like statement we have the two basic elements of our Christian belief, our creed. One element is the act by *which (fides qua)* we articulate our faith, namely, our trusting in Jesus and God the Father through the power of the Spirit. This is our "faith as act." The second element is that *about which (fides quae)* we affirm our trust, namely, that Jesus is God and Savior and so forth. This is our "faith as content."

All Christians clearly have the first element, the faith as act, in common. All also doubtless have the fundamental portions of the second element, the faith as content, in common. But because the Christian community (the Church) was from the beginning a living community, that is, a community which attempted to live according to its beliefs, it naturally reflected on the faith as content in light of its ongoing living experience, applied it to that experience with varying success, and handed on *(tra-ditio)* the results of its reflections and applications.[13] Hence, the faith as content—those things which Christians trusted that God the Father had done in Jesus for us, those "truths" of the faith—became ever more refined and applied.

In time and in space not all Christians agreed fully on all such refinements and applications. When this lack of agreement reached sufficient intensity, the unity of the faith was rent, that is, in effect one group of Christians stated that another group's lack of affirming certain "essential" elements of the faith as content was so fundamental as to seem to imply that their trusting in God, their faith as act, was also essentially not Christian. But it is impossible for one group of Christians to assert with certitude that only they are in good faith, that is, have an authentic faith as act, as trust in God. Yet it is to such an attempt that we Christians, including Reformed and Roman Catholic Christians, have often turned.

To regain an essential Christian unity in the areas of belief, all Christians must first clearly recognize and affirm that all Christians "in good faith" do indeed share the same trust in God who has wrought all creation's liberation in Jesus, the same faith as act. With this mighty fulcrum of a consciously shared faith in Christ (faith as act), we Christians should be able to remove all obstacles to essential Christian unity resulting from reflections on, and applications of, the faith as content.

What Is Essential in Christian Belief?

Central in Christian belief is Jesus as God and Savior. Outside of the first witnesses, all Christians come to know Jesus through the Christian proclamation, the Christian story; Paul says that we come to faith through hearing (Rom. 10:17). Here then is the common essential core of our Christian belief—the person of Jesus as handed on ("traditioned") through the Christian story as told primarily in the Scriptures and reverberated subsequently in various Christian communities throughout history.

But when Christians move beyond perceiving Jesus as God and Savior through the Christian story and attempt to live according to this perception, that is, attempt to say in their own actions and words what they understand, then human, historical, cultural conditions and limitations enter visibly. Indeed, they were necessarily present from the beginning of Christian belief, for there can be no talk of the perception of Jesus as God and Savior except in terms of the dialectic of the perceiver and the perceived. But when the perceiver, here the Christian believer, takes the next step and expresses what he or she perceives, believes, then naturally the particular stance of the perceiver (believer) essentially affects the statements (beliefs, creeds).

Of course, some persons and groups have greater clarity and strength of perception (belief) on some issues than others, and some have more effective powers of expression (statement of "truths," creeds) than others. Hence the statements of belief or creeds (faith as content) of such Christians will come to be seen by the community, or large portions of it, as helpful expressions of the reflections on, and applications of, the Christian story which echo the more or less unexpressed perceptions, beliefs, of the less articulate members of the community. Not all such statements will be equally helpful to all Christians of all times and places.

This kind of relativity is not only not surprising, but even greatly to be desired. Each individual and each community of Christians could be satisfied with simply repeating identically the same statements of other Christian communities only if their experienced situation in the world were totally the same as that of the other groups. This is a clear impossibility since every individual and every community is unique in a significant sense. If the revelation that Jesus is God and Savior is to affect the lives of Christians, individually and communally, Christians must reflect on and apply what they have perceived and believed. When the stance in the world of enough Christians changes sufficiently, they will naturally feel the need to express proportionately their new perception (belief) in communal fashion in accordance with their new situation.

All this quite naturally happens not only to individuals and small groups of Christians, but also to large communities within the universal Church, and at times even to the whole Church, as it moves through history. This trusting response of faith (faith as act) on the part of the Christian Church, or large portions of it, spells out through a variety of organs the newly perceived or newly applied dimensions (faith as content) of the Christian revelation at various times and places in Christian history, leading the community of believers, the Church, to an ever richer expression of the Christian faith. Christians trust that this process occurs under the guidance of the Spirit, who is the Spirit of truth and, as Jesus promised, "will guide you unto all the truth" (Jn. 16:13). This growth is what theologians refer to as development of doctrine.

Handling Differences of Belief

But such new expressions (creeds, theologies) need not mean the rejection of other expressions that were, or are, found helpful by other groups of Christians, or by the same group at another time.[14] Christians would do well to seek the truth wherever they can find it, that is, in this context, seek that which is helpful in the Christian statements of belief of other Christians. This approach would eliminate many, if not most, of the obstacles to essential Christian unity arising from differences in beliefs (faith as content). However, if the differences become so fundamental as to seem to approach mutual exclusivity, then an effective means must be found which would allow (indeed, facilitate) all Christians to arrive at an expression of Christian belief that will be acceptable, that is, truly helpful, to all.

For several centuries after the beginning of the fourth century A.D., the ecumenical councils seemed to be a more or less effective instrument for resolving conflicts, although they were not without their faults of polemics, schisms, and other scandals. Perhaps the insights of group dynamics and the broader and longer experience in representative and participatory democratic procedures and structures of the modern period would help to make councils an even more effective means of arriving at generally (ecumenically) helpful expressions of Christian belief. So also would the newly developed cross-fertilization of Protestant and Roman Catholic Scripture scholarship, which would greatly facilitate the testing of all faith statements against the original Christ event as revealed and "traditioned" in the Scriptures.

So too would the Roman Catholic insight that there is a hierarchy of doctrine, whereby certain faith affirmations provide the perspective within which other faith elements are to be understood and interpreted[15]—an insight very like that of "the core of the Gospel"[16] of the Reformed tradition. At any rate, such an instrument or instruments must be sought and then constantly employed and improved.

Our two Christian traditions, Roman Catholic and Reformed, have in their history several communal statements of Christian belief of accepted major significance. Some are held jointly from the earlier centuries of the history of the Christian Church, for example, the Apostles' Creed and the Nicene Creed; some are held separately, for example, the creedal portions of the Council of Trent for Roman Catholics, the Westminster Confession, Heidelberg Catechism, Second Helvetic Confession, and the Confession of 1967 for the Reformed. Such major expressions of Christian belief, and others not listed here, should be cherished as a sacred trust in our Christian heritage and should be used as wellsprings of an ever deeper and broader understanding of the Christ event. Surely this is true of the mutually shared creedal statements and the statements of one's own tradition; but can and should it not also be true of most of the other traditions' statements as well?

An intense study of the faith statements of both traditions undertaken jointly would probably show that there is a vast area of congruence and a further large area of mutually inclusive complementarity. If significant elements still appeared to remain mutually exclusive, they could then be presented to the accepted instruments designed to resolve creatively such oppositions, for example, local, regional, national, and international dialogue groups, and ultimately a fully ecumenical, that is, universal, council.

Indeed, in an extremely important manner this has already been taking place. It is most apparent in the joint statements issued by dialogue groups such as this one,[17] and other consultations.[18] But the reconciliation of portions of faith statements which previously appeared mutually exclusive has also been occurring internally in the sense that the separate traditions have themselves moved beyond the positions of certain earlier perceptions. For example, the papacy is no longer described as the anti-Christ in all official versions of the Westminster Confession,[19] and the Roman Catholic Church officially no longer refuses to refer to Protestant communities as churches.[20] This process needs to be broadened, deepened, and accelerated.

Thus, seen in historical perspective, the creedal statements of the Christian Church, and specifically our Roman Catholic and Reformed communions, fall largely into three periods: first, jointly held statements, then separately held statements, and now in part jointly and in part separately held statements. It is hoped that this period will give way to a fourth, and last, period of statements held jointly on an even more profound level.

We see then the kind of unity in the area of belief that is essential to a united Christian Church to be one which recognizes and encourages a multiplicity of mutually complementary statements of faith (and the many theological cultures, that is, patterns of worship, Church structures, styles of living, etc., that will reflect, and in turn will affect, them). At the same time this unity must also work through effective instruments at first to hold apparently mutually exclusive basic elements in a creative tension, and eventually to reconcile them. Important touchstones in this creative process of reconciliation would be the *whole* Scripture, the *whole* tradition, and the voice of the *whole* contemporary living Church. This insistence on wholeness will be the safeguard against heresy, which is a "choosing of a part."

Recommendations

This consultation, therefore, recommends to its parent bodies, the National Conference of Catholic Bishops and the North American Area of the World Alliance of Reformed Churches, that they commission a thoroughgoing scholarly study of each other's major faith statements, as well as the various subsequent internal revisions and joint statements, with a view to analyzing them as described above, that is, into those elements which are held jointly, those which are complementary, and those which appear to be mutually exclusive. The team of scholars appointed would have to include at least one Reformed and one Roman Catholic Christian for each statement chosen to be studied. The results of these studies should then be both sent to the parent bodies with recommendations for actions and also filtered into all the levels of the several churches' educational operations from that of the preschool through the parish, adult education, college, and the seminary.

This consultation also wishes to urge all Roman Catholic and Reformed scholars, clergy, and laity to begin immediately or to continue to take up these joint studies of each other's understandings of faith on all levels, whether in congregational study groups, clergy dialogue groups, university sponsored symposia, councils of churches' projects, or other forums. Only thus can all Christians fully reflect on and apply their faith to their living.

III. The Unity We Seek in Structure

What we say about the unity of the Church must be translated into specific recommendations concerning its structures. In the process of convergence each church will bring to this unity the distinctive richness of its own experience and hope. The Spirit will enable the churches to grow together as they come closer. Our task now is to clarify the process by which we may move toward unity in structure.

The center of the Church's unity and life is Jesus, who is God's self-disclosure and therefore our Lord and Savior. For this reason we seek to conform all the structures of our faith and life to his mind and Gospel, not modeling ourselves on the world around us but by the new mind that we have received from him. Our starting point is, therefore, our readiness for that repentance which is critical reflection upon our previous practices and the renewed orientation of all our structures to the mind and Gospel of Christ.

Principles for a Period of Transition

In passing from our present structures to those future forms which are not yet clear to us, we can roughly indicate a direction which reflects our separated pasts as well as our common hope, our disparate traditions as well as our shared future. The following principles are offered as guidelines for those changes for which we can hope. But we must also be alert to discern the prophetic word and act for which we have not prepared, and the sign which has not been reckoned on.

The first need is to plan for a period of gradual transition, reflection, and shared experience. In this process the whole Church must examine not only the depths that it sees in "the mystery of Christ" (Eph. 3:4) but also the social reality which likewise belongs to its nature in history; not only its mission to the world but also what has been grasped and lived out and is being embodied in concrete new patterns of life together.

The process should occur at all levels. The entire Church should be prepared to accept and advocate this transition, reflection, and experience. Initiatives taken at the local level are of first importance. A unique responsibility therefore resides in the local church, in full consultation with the other local churches of the ecclesiastical province or judicatory. Any change that is going to take place will involve an interchange between various manifestations of the Church, in the local congregations as well as at regional, national, and ecumenical or world levels. Any initiatives or changes that help to achieve the transition or broaden the shared experience should be permitted and encouraged, where they are found to be appropriate.

Since the Church is summoned to reveal to the world the mystery of Christ, *all its structures are to be subordinated to the mission of the Son and of the Holy Spirit.* In the biblical witness the Spirit is both a divine, dynamic force as well as the principle of life and activity proper to the Christian. There is therefore both an interior and exterior relation between the Spirit and Church order. The Spirit has many fruits, and the structures of the Church, as it passes through a period of transition to a fullness of unity, will be fruitful as they create the ministries by which the mission of the Church is carried out. The mission and the structures of the Church are integral to one another. In the period of transition our concern with structures flows from our call to discipleship among all peoples.

The catholicity of the Church implies and is properly expressed in a communion of communions. Within the organic whole of the one Church there are and always have been complementary elements or empirically contributory factors, each of which supports and strengthens the others. These elements are the living, historical Christian communities gathered in the name of Christ, each with its tradition that articulates its faith and hope and its experience proper to itself.

Christian experience in contemporary cultures, and nowhere more than in the United States, has shown that, while pluralism has its own inherent dangers, it is inherent in our society with its diversity, conflict, and enrichment. With appropriate translations, we can expect a like pluralism within the Church. Indeed, the pluralism which we already see within the various communions indicates that we can expect a comparable pluralism within the coming Church. This suggests to us that we need to keep open to diversity of structure, while conserving those forms that are needed and effective.

The shape of the unity we seek will be wrought out in both freedom and order. The complexity and fragmentation of the world is for us the given situation, the milieu within which we shall move to new structures. What is called for is that we respond to the impulse of the Spirit which will enable us to break free of many of our present structures. The Spirit can never be contained.

The Church as a social system is also an orderly vehicle by which people are nurtured in their participation in God's act of creating and reintegrating the world. It is a social entity with all the human infrastructures that make up the whole. Unfailingly present, therefore, are the dynamisms and laws which make up the structure of the Church, with all its ambivalences and ambiguities. Tensions may lead to conflicts between freedom and orderliness, to disagreement and divison especially on moral issues and long-range policies. But the tensions may also be positive goods. Because the Church is a human structure it will show political divisions. A society that looks for unanimous consent on all points at issue is artificial or moribund. A lively society should expect to see strong differences, and these differences need not necessarily rend its unity. Indeed, where there are no clearly articulated divisions in the freedom of the Gospel, we can suspect that they are being either stifled or driven below the surface.

This structure of freedom and order will typically be seen in its local manifestations. The task of leadership within the Church will be to facilitate this growth, not to oppose it, and to link it with other creative expressions in such a way that a larger unity may emerge. In the unity we seek, structures will not have firm and unyielding boundaries, but will aid the churches to see their relation to a common center. Often it may appear that the Church at a local level is hindered by people of narrow vision. But their focus on the local level may be a strength as much as a weakness. Faith, hope, and love always have to be translated into common words and actions. If they cannot be expressed in such daily concerns as job or family, they have no meaning. So the boundaries of which we speak, though discernible, should be regarded as flexible rather than as fixed. To be sure, the Church must have an articulated, corporate, and visible reality to it. God has really called us to redemption in Christ. If ever the Church is to have an impact on its members, it will be through its identity as the body of Christ. Yet we must always be concerned not only with the articulated center but also with the boundaries where we stand beside those who are in quest of a meaning for their lives.

How Can We Make the Transition?

What measures can the churches begin to take at present in changing, adapting, or modifying their strucutres? Our separate traditions and histories provide us already with patterns of Church order from which we may draw guiding principles. The patterns which we have known and used, even of irreducible ecclesial elements, are partial and transient. In ever fresh obedience to Christ we must open them to reflect the ecumenical character of the world mission of the Word of God. As the Church lives in preparation for the Advent presence of Christ, it becomes more ready to alter what is essentially incomplete in its structural forms.

A first stage in the transition to the fullness of Church unity should be a continuing process of general and comprehensive ecumenical con-

sultation. The ecumenical movement of the modern period has been one of the decisive factors in our common life as Christians. Only if all the churches are committed to one another and determined by the Word of God can they address the theological questions about human existence and the ecclesial questions about Church structures.

Joint studies of movements for human liberation in and beyond the churches can foster imaginative action in hard or intractable problems. Collaborations in the concerns of fairness and equity in government, economic life, education, and the administration of justice can engender cooperation also in Church reform and renewal.

We can also pray together and for one another. A sign of this commitment to one another could be a covenanting agreement between particular churches in city, rural, or suburban areas to do as much together as possible. Two or more parishes, entering into conversation with one another, yoke themselves together in a common covenant. They may work together, for example, on a joint statement of their common faith. They may witness together by deed and word to the Gospel of the saving presence, activity, and teaching of the Lord. We also need agencies to deal with these questions at all levels beyond the local.

In various ways we seek possibilities of deepening trust in one another and learning from one another. Again at a local level, Roman Catholic and Presbyterian-Reformed churches could plan to let a given number of people, selected by their pastors, meet together regularly for a year to share their thoughts and hopes on the meaning of Christian faith and life today. Such an undertaking would not only be a real step, taken in the light of our commitment to the people of God, but would also help us to come to understand one another better. At such meetings the central question might be: What is so basic in our faith that we must pass it on to others?

Another stage in the transition will be a time of coalescence of ecclesial and organizational styles. Various styles of Church order and organization will be necessary for the life of the Church in a pluralistic society.

In the Reformed churches, the ministers of the Word exercise a corporate authority in worship, doctrine, and discipline, along with lay elders associated with them. In the courts of the churches, they together maintain continuity of ordination and jurisdiction. In the Roman Catholic Church, the hierarchical structures of orders and of Petrine and episcopal ministries are constitutive elements of the people of God, along with the renewed principles of collegiality and subsidiarity, as the sign of salvation in the world. These divergencies, which have caused separation in the past, may also, nevertheless, be a means of movement along fresh lines in the future. On the Reformed side there is a growing willingness on the part of many to discuss the corporate functioning of the Church in worship, doctrine, and pastoral oversight through a creative fusing of the episcopal, presbyteral, and congregational traditions. On the Roman Catholic side there have been great efforts to emphasize the role of the papacy as one of unity through service, carried out in collegiality with ever more levels of the Church.

There is abundant agreement in this consultation about the changes to which we are willing to come as a result of our living together. We can collaborate already in planning for change and improvement. We can share a number of ministries already. To become socialized into any kind of Christian community implies more than a matter of rational understanding. It is the acceptance and experiencing of the Christian faith in symbolic ways through rite and Church order. Among the Reformed and Presbyterian churches an increase in the number of eucharistic observances would be of significance in the course of our growing together. The Roman Catholic Church has much to learn from the experience of lay representation and government in the other communions.

Recommendations

In our approach to the unification of structure through the acceptance of a pluralism of ecclesial and organizational styles and mutual adaptation, members of this consultation refer to the recommendations which were appended to the statement made by the Theological Section of this consultation on October 30, 1971. These are:

A. That this Statement on Ministry in the Church be received and acted upon appropriately.
B. That proper steps be taken to have the appropriate organs of our respective churches at the highest level officially affirm in some appropriate way that Christ is present and at work in the ministries and Eucharist of each of our traditions.
C. That although *general* eucharistic sharing is not to be recommended for the present, these same appropriate organs designate *specific* occasions on which invitations to a eucharistic sharing may be extended.
D. That areas of ministry be opened, as far as possible, to qual-

ified women, and that a major effort be undertaken to place qualified women, ordained and unordained, in offices and positions of leadership and decision-making; accordingly, that an ecumenical commission composed of women and men be constituted by our churches: to study the role of women in Church and society, especially the full involvement of women in all offices and leadership functions, both clerical and lay; to recommend corrective and innovative actions and programs in these areas; and to monitor their implementation.

E. That encouragement be given to explorations at the parish, diocesan, national, and world levels which would further the *practical* fusing, both within and between our churches, of the unifying role of individual leadership in service and of collegial, democratic responsibility, and that appropriate groups be commissioned both within and between our churches to implement this recommendation.

F. That effective Church action be taken to initiate or to intensify and broaden ecumenical learning and experiences on the grass-roots level, so that the lives of all of our Church members may be touched and significantly changed by the movement toward Christian understanding and unity; that committees which would provide effective programming in this area be set up or strengthened both on the national and local levels; specifically, that on the Roman Catholic side, the Committee on Education for Ecumenism of the Bishops' Committee on Ecumenical and Interreligious Affairs be reactivated to work closely with appropriate ecumenical education and programming committees of the Presbyterian-Reformed churches.

G. That an ecumenical consultation be constituted among our churches, and perhaps others, which would investigate basic moral issues of our time and ascertain as clearly as possible what the Christian Gospel has to say to them, such a consultation to be composed of women and men with the necessary range of experience, knowledge, and concern, among them persons with expertise in such areas as ethics, Scripture, theology, history, psychology, sociology, and political science.

H. That an ecumenical commission be constituted by our churches to study the evangelical values both of celibacy and of a married clergy.[21]

Ways of Expressing Structural Unity

On both sides we see the goal as that of realizing ecclesial and eucharistic communion. The goal is not unattainable. Many positive influences have helped us to lose suspicions and gain a sense of what it means for the pilgrim Church to live in the time between what has come and what has yet to come. Warm and cordial relations have developed between us, awareness of the catholicity we share has deepened, and our experience has convinced us that the oneness of Christ's Church must be demonstrated in fact.

The acceptance of one another's members. As they prepare themselves for a fullness of relationship between all the people of God, the churches meanwhile seek to bring their members into mutual acceptance of one another. The Church of the future may be expected to be "a communion of communions," and there is likely to emerge a variety of worshiping communities, liturgical styles, and modes of response to ethical issues. Appropriate discussion should take place within and beyond the churches about both the possibilities and the limits of such freedom.

The responsibility of all Christians for the life of the church. No group can function for long effectively without organization. People do not move purposefully in any direction unless their resources are channeled and directed by a leadership that includes both the creative enthusiasts and the bureaucrats. Though important, efficient administration may be less so than the task of symbolizing the goals and values of an organization in its very structure. In all the churches today the tasks of forming, serving, developing, and integrating a Christian community require a variety of forms of leadership.

Increasingly, the people of God in the local community are coming to experience and express the priestly and prophetic function and the participation in God's reign which they have received from Christ. At each level in the life of the Church they are making their own decisions. A much more thorough reform of the structures of communication and decision-making is necessary in order that a full representation of those who are involved, women and men alike, may replace authoritarian exercise of power. No one group or person is in charge without qualification. Thus leadership is increasingly shared in the churches today: goals are set out of the needs and perceptions of what is at issue and what are the priorities. This increased emphasis on shared authority and the real needs of the churches imply that the people of God in a particular place (the parish or congregation, the diocese or region) participate fully both in leadership and in the choice of leaders.

The ordained ministry. Within the general ministry of the whole Church, ministers are called and ordained to represent Christ to the community and the community before Christ. Through the proclamation of the Gospel and the celebration of the sacraments this ministry has endeavored to unite and order the Church for the ministry of the whole people of God. Setting a person apart for this ministry situates that person in the community of the whole priestly people. It confers a special mission for the sake of that community, viz., the building up of the community.

The function of the ordained ministry is to see to it that the Word of God is proclaimed, the sacraments celebrated, individuals led to Christian maturity, and the Christian community built up. He or she may not necessarily do all of these things personally, but is publicly responsible in view of ordination for seeing to it that they are done. Each member of the Church is thus encouraged to use the gift or gifts which the Spirit bestows on each one for the edification of the whole body of Christ.

Apostolic succession and primacy. The Church is apostolic in that it lives the faith of the apostles and continues the mission which Christ gave to the apostles. The canonical Scriptures are the normative expression of this apostolicity. Within the general ministry of the whole Church the setting apart of some to the administration of the Word and sacrament includes the invocation of the Holy Spirit and the laying on of hands by other ordained ministers. The continuity of this special ministry of Word and sacrament arises in Christ's original commission to the apostles but depends also on his continual call and action. The invocation of the Holy Spirit reminds us that Jesus Christ is present and at work through the continual operation of his Holy Spirit. The laying on of hands is an effective sign that initiates and confirms the believer in the ministry which is conferred.

We believe in apostolic succession within the Church, though from our different standpoints we locate that succession in different ways. Apostolic succession consists at least in the continuity of the apostles' teaching, and this understanding is not in opposition to the idea of succession through continuity of ordained ministry. The two elements already described both inhere in apostolic succession: historical continuity with the apostles and the contemporary action of Christ through the Holy Spirit.

There are two main aspects of the papacy with which the Reformed churches have had difficulty: its claims to primacy and universal jurisdiction in Church government, and to infallibility in teaching. Our earlier statement of October 30, 1971 thus summarizes our discussion of these questions:

> The growing awareness in the Reformed churches of the need for effective worldwide unifying forms, and in Roman Catholicism of the collegial context and pastoral character of the papal role, opens the way to new possibilities in the first problem area. On the local level the contemporary Church needs a creative fusing of the episcopal and presbyteral/congregational traditions. So, too, on a much wider scale the Church needs, in a spirit of pastoral service, to blend the unifying drive which a papacy of the future might provide, with the vitalizing growth which can come from the "collegial" or representative spirit inherent in the Reformed tradition. Hence, one of the main questions may prove to be how effectively the conciliar and representative pattern can be fused at the world level with individual personal leadership. There will also need to be careful exploration as to precisely what kinds and what degree of ecclesiastical jurisdication are appropriate at each level: regional, national, and worldwide. Consequently, although our churches are presently divided in habits of thought and practice, as is true of both Roman Catholics and Presbyterian-Reformed Christians among themselves, it is clearly to the advantage both of the universal Church and also of the world to which it witnesses and ministers that we learn from each other and act jointly in this regard.[22]

IV. The Unity We Seek in Worship

The major features of the shape of the unity we seek in worship are: (1) recognition of a plurality of forms of worship as authentically Christian, (2) new communities of worship, (3) active participation of all, and (4) integrity of Christian worship. These features are explained in the following paragraphs.

1. *Recognition of a plurality of forms of worship as authentically Christian.* By "plurality of forms" we do not mean simply various services of worship such as baptism, the Eucharist, confirmation, proclamation of the Word, morning prayer, and so forth. Assuming these, we intend primarily a variety of forms resulting from different experiences and understandings of Christian faith and acceptable within individual Christian traditions. Thus there should be forms of worship reflecting the Roman Catholic tradition, the Presbyterian-Reformed tradition, and other Christian traditions, both Eastern and Western.

One communion should recognize as authentically Christian the worship of another communion—for example, the Roman Catholic Church should recognize the worship of the Presbyterian-Reformed churches and vice versa. Within each communion there should be willingness to adopt new forms of worship in keeping with its tradition. There should also be newly created ecumenical forms in which all communions can recognize authentic Christian worship.

Such a plurality of forms of worship is justifiably expected. The New Testament bears witness to slightly different forms of eucharistic celebration.[23] Free prayer seems to have been especially vigorous in Pauline churches.[24] Whatever the New Testament evidence, the history of the Church provides ample witness to a multiplicity of liturgies. Theology testifies that this plurality of forms serves to bring out the richness of God's revelation in Jesus Christ, facilitates appropriation of revelation through faith by men and women of diverse cultures, and enables men and women to express their faith in worship suited to their mentality and needs.

Those forms which meet the criteria for the authenticity and integrity of Christian worship should be recognized in the unity we seek. This recognition should be official, that is, explicitly and formally stated by the competent overseeing persons of bodies of each of the churches, so that there will be no question in the minds of the members of any Church about the worth of the worship of any other Church. This recognition should also be popular, that is, the members of all churches, clerical and lay, should acknowledge and respect the value of the worship of every Church and feel free to participate in it.

Acceptance should extend to the many forms of worship as legitimate expressions of faith as the act by which we trust in Jesus and of faith as what we affirm in trusting in Jesus. (For further clarification of this distinction and its implications, see Section II on the unity we seek in belief. That section also offers grounds for the possibility of this recognition.)

Authentic Christian worship presupposes "the reality of ministry and priesthood of Word and sacraments as having their source in the Spirit and the risen Lord."[25] Lack of mutual recognition of this reality by the churches vis-à-vis one another has been and continues to be a major source of separation in worship. For these reasons, official and popular recognition should extend to the many forms of worship as grounded in mutually recognized ministries. For the possibility of this mutual acceptance, see the statement "Ministry in the Church" of this consultation,[26] also *Reconsiderations* by this consultation,[27] and Kilian McDonnell's "Ways of Validating Ministry."[28]

The many forms of worship should be recognized as instruments of God's saving action, in contrast to the centuries-long doubt, suspicion, and even denial of the efficacy of various Christian churches' worship. The possibility of this recognition is demonstrated by its partial realization, for example, among the various churches in the Presbyterian-Reformed tradition, and in Vatican II's statement: "The brethren divided from us also carry out many of the sacred actions of the Christian religion. Undoubtedly, in ways that vary according to the conditions of each church or community, these actions can truly engender a life of grace, and can be rightly described as capable of providing access to the community of salvation."[29]

A current obstacle to worship together is the sense of obligation which Christians feel to participate in their own denomination's worship. This feeling may arise from respect for the legislation of one's Church, from loyalty to one's own Church, or from suspicion of other churches' worship. In the unity we seek in worship, this narrow sense of obligation should no longer exist because the churches should recognize officially and popularly the many forms of Christian worship as satisfying obligations and expectations which may arise from belonging to one or another denomination. The possibility of this recognition lies in the previous acknowledgments and in a new understanding of the Church which cuts through denominational divisions and is articulated in this statement's Section I on the unity we seek in the Church as the people of God.

The many qualifiying forms of worship should be recognized as fulfillments of personal and ecumenical needs. Thus, in good conscience, members of a denomination may choose the worship they will participate in on a given day. Because a person needs a supporting community for his or her Christian life and has actually become a member of a particular Church, he or she should usually share in that Church's worship. But because he or she needs to celebrate with a relative on the occasion of the latter's wedding, he or she may participate fully in the worship of another community on that day.

The possibility of this kind of recognition is manifested in the acknowledgment by many churches of the right of their members to participate in the worship of other churches as they see fit. Even the Roman Catholic Church, generally reserved in this matter, permits and even encourages its members to participate, under certain conditions, in the worship of Eastern Orthodox churches to satisfy a variety of personal needs.[30]

2. *New communities of worship.* The worship in the unity we seek should sometimes be celebrated, not by denominational congrega-

tions, but by groups of Christians from several denominations who experience together in a special way Christian proclamation *(kerygma),* service *(diakonia),* and fellowship *(koinonia)* and desire to express and nourish this experience in worship. These communities will be more associational than familial in character, that is, based upon conscious choice of specific objectives by the members rather than upon kinship, friendship, or intimacy, although the impetus of Christian love will open them to and perhaps even lead them to friendship and intimacy.[31] Obviously these groups will not be territorial parishes of any particular denomination.

The possibility of such communities flows from the recognition of a plurality of forms of worship which we have just described, and from what is proposed about the people of God, unity in belief, and cooperative organization in other sections of this statement.

3. *Active participation.* For a developed explanation of this feature, see the exploratory paper, "Toward the Unity We Seek in Worship," prepared for this consultation.[32] Here it is sufficient to point out that this active participation extends beyond the actual celebration of worship to include both planning the manner in which received forms of worship are celebrated and creating new forms of worship which meet the criteria of authentic Christian worship. Participation to this extent, involving laity as well as clergy, women as well as men, young and old, and other groups hitherto excluded from a say in the form of their own worship, will result in forms of worship more clearly related to Christian life and mission in the world, and more expressive of the equality of all in Christ, regardless of sex, race, ethnic background, and social or ecclesiastical status.

The possibility of such participation is evident in the steps which various churches have taken in recent years in this direction, in accord with growing awareness of the Church as the people of God, all members sharing in some way in the priesthood of Jesus.

4. *Integrity of Christian worship.* Naturally we expect the worship we seek in unity to possess those qualities which will make it authentically Christian and effective for Christian life and mission. Thus the worship we seek should be characterized not only by active participation of all but also by a combination of structure and freedom, an involvement of the whole person, a sense of transcendence, an orientation to mission, a balance of Word and sacraments, and a shared understanding of Christian worship. These characteristics are explained in detail in the paper "Toward the Unity We Seek in Worship" mentioned in no. 3, above, on active participation.

Steps Toward Unity in Worship

Evidence of the need for the kind of worship just described can be found in the local scene, as this consultation found it in Columbus, Ohio.[33] Responsible steps should be taken, therefore, to advance our respective churches toward such unity in worship. Such steps should be encouraged by those entrusted with leadership positions.

The Eucharist, or Lord's Supper, continues to be a vexing problem in our relationship. Presbyterian-Reformed and Roman Catholic Christians are often experiencing profound unity in marriages, in theological schools, in spiritual retreats, in cooperative action for social justice. Yet they are suffering because they are prevented from sealing their common Christian experience, witness, and mission by sharing in one another's Holy Communion or a common ecumenical one. The situation begets frustration, anger, and—it should be faced—disregard for Church discipline behind closed doors. Presbyterian-Reformed Christians feel insulted by Roman Catholic suspicion of the authenticity and integrity of their Reformed Holy Communion; Roman Catholic Christians fear that Reformed eucharistic doctrine underplays important themes and that, consequently, Reformed discipline is too liberal in its admission to the Lord's Supper and too casual in its treatment of the elements used in the celebration. These festering feelings of insult and of fear threaten to poison ecumenical relations.

Clearly, steps must be taken to clarify misunderstandings, resolve genuine disagreements, and move toward shared Eucharists. Toward this end, we wish to indicate first our agreement in regard to the Lord's Supper, then note differences, and finally make some recommendations in regard to both Holy Communion and other forms of worship.

We Roman Catholic and Presbyterian-Reformed Christians profess in faith that the Eucharist is the sacramental meal which Christ has given to his disciples. It is the effective sign of Christ's gift of himself as the Bread of Life through his offering of his life and death and through his resurrection. It is the great thanksgiving to the Father for all that he has done in creation and redemption, for all that he does today in the Church and the world, and for all that he will accomplish in the consummation of his reign. In the Eucharist the Church celebrates the unrepeatable sacrifice of Christ and shares in its saving power.

Christ instituted the Eucharist as the memorial *(anamnesis)* of his whole life, especially his death and resurrection. Christ himself, with all he accomplished for us and all creation, is present in this memorial, which is also a foretaste of his coming reign. This memorial, in which Christ acts upon his Church through its joyful celebration, implies this presence and anticipation. It is not merely a mental or spiritual recollection of a past event or its significance, but the proclamation-making-present the whole of God's great work in Christ Jesus, enabling the Church through its fellowship with Christ to share in that reality.

As the Church carries out this memorial of the suffering, death, and exaltation of Christ, our high priest and intercessor, we receive from the Father the fruits of the unique and perfect sacrifice of his Son and beg the Father to apply its saving power to every human being. Thus, united with our Lord who offers himself to the Father, and in union with the universal Church in heaven and on earth, we renew and offer ourselves in a living and holy sacrifice, which we must express also in our daily lives.

The memorial of Christ is the content of the preached Word as it is of Holy Communion. The celebration of the Eucharist supposes the preaching of the Word, for the Eucharist is meaningless without faith, and the preaching of the Word is the call to faith. On the other hand, the Lord's Supper completes the preaching of the Word. The preaching of the Word is not merely an occasional service of the Church but pertains to its very nature as sent by the Lord; similarly the Eucharist is not merely a convenient service provided by the Church for individuals, but belongs to and manifests the very nature of the Church as a participant in the mystery of Christ.

This memorial, in its fullest sense, includes the invocation of the Spirit *(epiclesis).* Christ in his heavenly intercession asks the Father to send his Spirit upon his children. The Spirit, called upon the assembly and upon the bread and wine, makes Christ really present for us, gives him to us, and enables us to discern him. The memorial and invocation find their fulfillment in partaking of Holy Communion.

In the Eucharist the Lord himself says: "Take and eat; this is my body which will be given up for you. Take and drink; this is the cup of my blood of the new covenant which shall be shed for many for the forgiveness of sin." We profess, therefore, the real, living, active presence of Christ in this sacrament.

The discernment of the body and blood of Christ requires faith. The real presence of Christ in the Eucharist, however, does not depend upon the belief of each individual, but on the power of Christ's Word mentioned above and upon his promise to bind himself to the sacramental event as the sign of his person given to us.[34]

In this consultation's study of ministry in the Church, we reached agreement that "each church's ministry had been real long before members of the other church or churches came to admit it, indeed notwithstanding its denial for centuries. Our respective ministries derive their efficacy from the presence of Jesus Christ, who is operative in them through his Spirit, and not from the recognition accorded by other Christian communities. . . . We cannot but recognize the risen Christ present and at work for the healing of his people in the ministry and Eucharist of each of our traditions."[35] We deemed it "a grace to have come to the realization that Christ is operative, however differently, in the ministries of both churches, and further ask that this realization be publicly recognized."[36]

We are united in affirming in faith the mystery of Christ's real presence in the Lord's Supper in virtue of his Word and the power of the Holy Spirit. We diverge, however, when we begin to articulate this faith, as the following paragraphs illustrate.

On both sides, the real presence of Christ is affirmed in the assembled community, in the community's praise and thanksgiving, in the proclamation of the Word, in the speaking of the words of institution in the name, authority, and power of Christ, and in the partaking of the bread and wine.

But there are different ways of expressing Christ's presence in relation to the elements. Presbyterian-Reformed Christians prefer to speak of Christ's giving himself with the bread and wine. Roman Catholics say that through the conversion of the bread and wine Christ is really present under the appearances of bread and wine. These expressions reflect different appropriations of "how" Christ is present in relation to one factor in the total eucharistic event; they do not indicate a difference about the fact of his real presence in the total event. The different expressions have, however, resulted in different liturgical practices and attitudes toward the elements. The doctrinal implications of these differences should be explored.

This difference, which along with others provoked considerable discussion in this recent phase of our consultation, illustrates that in regard to the Eucharist much still remains to be clarified and, in some cases, to be worked through from disagreement to accord. Our differences and questions may reveal divergence in the articulation of faith rather than in faith itself. But in practice that distinction is not easy to observe; different articulations of faith may indicate different faiths by which people are actually living. Moreover, the distinction can be abused: people can worship together and yet hold different views difficult to reconcile, so that the witness to unity by worship is betrayed by disunity in everything from doctrine to moral decisions. We found this phenomenon occurring even with our denominations.[37]

Recommendations

We conclude with several recommendations that will promote the unity we seek in worship.

1. *Dialogue on the Eucharist.* We recommend dialogue on the Lord's Supper between our respective churches to resolve the many questions which still exist about one another's celebration of the sacrament and generally hinder shared Eucharists. Members of our churches in a variety of ecumenical endeavors or on special occasions, such as weddings, desire strongly to share Holy Communion but are unable to do so for a variety of reasons, some doctrinal, some disciplinary, some attitudinal. This inability to share Holy Communion prevents participation together in full Christian worship, namely, worship through Word *and* Eucharist. It hinders our missionary witness to Jesus Christ as the one in whom humanity is united.

If the Roman Catholic Church still has doubts about the authenticity of the Lord's Supper in the Presbyterian-Reformed churches, then the Roman Church should immediately, humbly, with open mind, and in dialogue with brothers and sisters in Christ, examine the texts of Presbyterian and Reformed eucharistic liturgies, resolving the doubts or indicating precisely what is wanting.

Likewise, doubts which remain in many Presbyterian-Reformed circles regarding Roman Catholic teaching and practice should be honestly examined. It should be determined if in fact there are grounds for the fears that non-scriptural speculations have been raised to the status of dogmas and that the veneration of the saints, especially the Blessed Virgin Mary, has detracted from the unique honor of Christ. The actual teaching of the Roman Catholic Church, especially since Vatican Council II, and the devotional tradition associated with the Mass need understanding among Protestants.

2. *Re-education in teaching about the Eucharist.* We recommend comprehensive re-education of the members—lay and clerical—of our respective churches in regard to the Lord's Supper. Generally the eucharistic faith of the majority of the members of our churches does not possess the balance and fullness of eucharistic understanding which has emerged in scholarly study in recent decades. Many Christians have simple, clear-cut but overly simplistic faith in the Eucharist, focused on the "real presence of Christ" narrowly conceived and on the question whether it is or is not a sacrifice, with little appreciation of the ultimate reality, or grace, signified and intended by the sacrament. Many other Christians have such vague ideas about Holy Communion that one may wonder if their faith really embraces the Eucha-

rist. Neither of our communions can boast of the integrity and fullness of the eucharistic faith of its members. Nothing will be accomplished on the pastoral level in terms of eventual shared Eucharists if our churches settle for consensus on the Lord's Supper among an elite of scholars in dialogue and do very little to re-educate the laity and clergy at large.

3. *Occasional shared Eucharists.* We recommend occasional shared Eucharists for members of our churches. We reiterate our proposal adopted in our statement "Ministry in the Church":

> It must be faced, as we have seen, that serious divisions remain between Roman Catholic and Reformed Christians, divisions serious enough to preclude *general* eucharistic sharing for the present. Nevertheless, since we have moved significantly toward a greater recognition of each other's ministry and a common eucharistic faith, we believe that our churches should act not only with a consciousness of their own distinct identity, but also with a practical recognition of the common bonds already uniting them with one another. They should designate specific occasions on which invitations may be offered to celebrate together in the Eucharist the unity of faith which we have found in common and should provide effective means of striving toward the greater ecclesial union yet to be achieved. We therefore recommend to the ecclesiastical authorities to whom we are responsible the implementation of such *limited* eucharistic sharing.[38]

As a sign of unity, the Lord's Supper presupposes loyalty to Christ which, in practice, requires agreement on faith and order. But as this consultation notes elsewhere in this statement, the point at which differences in the articulation of faith become essential differences in faith itself is not always clear. In the case of Holy Communion, moreover, we are faced with a mystery attained only by faith and never exhaustively grasped in our frail human concepts and words. Before judging another's eucharistic faith inadequate, we ought to be mindful of our own limitations before this mystery of God's love.

We do have much in common as a basis for shared Eucharist. We have one baptism which makes us brothers and sisters in the one body of Christ, who is our common Lord and whom we both regard as the Lord who presides over our Eucharists. Together we are members of the one people of God in the new covenant founded upon and sealed by the one sacrifice of Christ efficaciously proclaimed, we both believe, in our Eucharists. We confess together the faith expressed in the Apostles' Creed and in the Nicene Creed, and we do not inquire beyond these creeds from communicants in our own churches when they approach the Table of the Lord. We profess together the eucharistic faith enunciated at the beginning of this section on the Eucharist.

The purpose of Holy Communion is to build up the body of Christ, to effect as well as signify the unity of the Church. Presbyterian-Reformed churches have communion open to all baptized believers in Jesus Christ as Lord and Savior, provided they are repentant.[39] Within the Roman Catholic Church, exceptions to the principle that the Eucharist is a sign of unity are already made for Protestants to share in the Catholic Eucharist on the basis that the Eucharist is also a source of nourishing grace for baptized individuals on their way to personal salvation.[40] Exception can be made as well on the basis that the Eucharist is a source of unifying grace for the divided pilgrim Church on its journey toward oneness in Christ.[41]

Even though differences remain to be resolved, sufficient grounds exist for occasional shared Eucharists, most especially where Roman Catholic and Presbyterian-Reformed Christians have discussed, or have been instructed about, the extent as well as the limitations of accord in regard to the Eucharist and about the meaning and implications of such shared Eucharists.

4. *Congregations' covenanting worship together.* In Section III of this statement, covenanting between congregations of our respective churches is explained. Here we wish to note that a particularly suitable and important matter for covenant agreements is worship. Roman Catholic parishes on the one side and, on the other, Presbyterian-Reformed congregations may covenant to have: representatives from each side attend the Sunday worship of the other once a month, even though this may exclude reception of Holy Communion for the present; joint services of worship on special days, for example, on the Fourth of July and Thanksgiving in the civil year, on Pentecost and the First Sunday of Advent in the ecclesiastical year, on special occasions such as weddings and ordinations, and during the Week of Prayer for Christian Unity; joint study groups to learn more about one another's values, spirit, and traditions of worship; informal prayer groups; observers from the partner congregation at meetings of the session or parish committee concerned with worship; instruction of children about one another's worship in Sunday school, parochial school, and religious education programs. This list is only illustrative of possibilities.

5. *Education in one another's worship.* Religious educational materials (books, audio-visuals), curricula, programs, and actual

instructions prepared in our respective churches, whether by local, regional, or national agencies or by individuals, should include instruction on each other's worship. This applies for all levels of education, namely, for children, youth, and adults. It is especially crucial for the education of those preparing for public ministry in the Church as ordained ministers or priests, religious educators, social workers, and so forth. Responsibility for taking initiative in this ecumenical education rests upon individual pastors, teachers, heads of schools or regional programs, as well as upon official local, regional, and national agencies. Publishers of educational materials can exercise great influence by requiring inclusion of such content in materials they publish.

6. *A Year of Ecumenical Worship.* Our respective churches could commit themselves, covenant, to sponsor a Year of Ecumenical Worship in 1980. Another year is possible provided it allows time for preparation. During this year our churches would cooperate in making known to one another and learning from one another our different heritages of Christian worship in the unity we seek. Sermon and homily aids could be jointly prepared to assist preachers in our churches on this theme. Agencies devoted to preparing religious instruction materials and religious publishing houses could be asked to develop the theme in their publications. Local congregations of our respective churches could enter into covenants, as described above, for the year. Roman Catholic bishops could encourage their people to fulfill their canonical Sunday obligation on special occasions by attendance at worship in Presbyterian-Reformed churches. Presbyterian-Reformed pastors could encourage their people to attend Roman Catholic worship on special occasions. Centers of liturgical study in both our communions could be asked to devote their programs to exploring the possibilities of worship between churches of the Roman Catholic and Presbyterian-Reformed traditions. The North American Academy of Liturgy, the North American Academy of Ecumenists, the Liturgical Conference, the Federation of Diocesan Liturgical Commissions, the National Ecumenical Workshop, the Commission on Interim Eucharistic Fellowship of COCU, and the Theological Committee of the World Alliance of Reformed Churches, North American Area, could be asked to take up this theme at their annual national and regional meetings. During this year, jointly prepared and officially approved rites of baptism and marriage could be introduced for common use, especially in celebrations involving members of our denominations.

This list of activities for a Year of Ecumenical Worship seems necessary to pull people out of their denominational preoccupations and raise the level of everyone's consciousness with regard to the problems, possibilities, and imperatives of worship together. More modest proposals often fail to capture the imagination and break through inward-looking institutional routine.

Notes

1. "When an image is employed reflectively and critically to deepen one's understanding of reality, it becomes what today is called a 'model'"—Avery Dulles, *Models of the Church* (Garden City, N.Y.: Doubleday, 1974), p. 21.

2. Vatican Council II, *Dogmatic Constitution on the Church,* no. 9, in Walter M. Abbott, ed., *The Documents of Vatican II* (New York: Guild Press, 1966), p. 26. See also: Yves Congar, "The Church: The People of God," in E. Schillebeeckx, ed., *The Church and Mankind,* Concilium 1 (Glen Rock, N.J.: Paulist Press, 1965), pp. 11–37; Eugene Burke, "The Shape of the Unity We Seek," paper submitted to the Roman Catholic/Presbyterian-Reformed Consultation, May 30, 1973, Columbus, Ohio.

3. Cf. infra: "The Shape of the Unity We Seek," Eugene Burke, pp. 83–84.

4. 1 Cor. 13.

5. See: *The Interpreter's Bible,* X, pp. 149–214; *The Jerome Biblical Commentary,* 51:73–81.

6. Vatican Council II, *Dogmatic Constitution on the Church,* no. 13, in Abbott, *op. cit.,* pp. 3–32; "tentative" = hypothesis (eds.).

7. Cardinal Jan Willebrands, "Moving Toward a Typology of Churches," *Catholic Mind* 68 (April 1970):35–42. See also: ARC-DOC 1 (Washington, D.C., 1971), p. 39.

8. *Ibid.,* p. 41.

9. Arleon Kelley, "Community and Institutional Factors in the Shape of the Unity We Seek," no. 2.4.1, paper presented to the Roman Catholic/Presbyterian-Reformed Consultation, May 30, 1973, p. 12.

10. Walter Kaspar, "Der ekklesiologische Charakter der nichtkatholischen Kirchen," *Theologische Quartalschrift* 145 (1965):62.

11. At New Delhi in 1961 the World Council of Churches stated that it is "a fellowship of churches which confess the Lord Jesus Christ as God and Savior according to the Scriptures and therefore seek to fulfill together their common calling to the glory of one God, Father, Son, and Holy Spirit. Our message to you is that 'God was in Christ, reconciling the world to himself, not counting against men their transgressions, and has given us the message of reconciliation' (2 Cor. 5:19)." From "Message to Member Churches" by the Nairobi General Council of the World Alliance of Reformed Churches, printed in *God Reconciles and Makes Free,* Reports from Nairobi (Geneva, August 1970), p. 41; W. Visser't Hooft, ed., *The New Delhi Report* (New York, 1962), p. 152.

12. "I am the truth" (John 14:6) and "The truth shall make you free" (John 8:32).

13. It should be noted here that both Protestant and Catholic Scripture scholars recognize that the New Testament itself is also the written form of several "traditions" of the beliefs, the faith statements, of several of the first Christian communities.

14. Vatican II's *Decree on Ecumenism* makes a similar point when speaking of Eastern and Western Christianity: "It is hardly surprising, then, if sometimes one tradition has come nearer than the other to an apt appreciation of certain aspects of a revealed mystery, or has expressed them in a clearer manner. As a result, these various theological formulations are often to be considered as complementary rather than conflicting" (no. 17, in Abbott, *op. cit.,* p. 360).

15. In no.11 of chapter 2 of the *Decree on Ecumenism* from the Second Vatican Council it is stated: "When comparing doctrines, they should remember that in Catholic teaching there exists an order or 'hierarchy' of truths, since they vary in their relationship to the foundation of the Christian faith. Thus the way will be opened for this kind of

fraternal rivalry to incite all to a deeper realization and a clearer expression of the unfathomable riches of Christ (cf. Eph. 3:8)" (in Abbott, *op. cit.,* p. 354).

16. Writing on repentance and forgiveness, Calvin states: "Now if it is true—a fact abundantly clear—that the whole of the Gospel is contained under these two headings, repentance and forgiveness of sins, do we not see that the Lord freely justifies his own in order that he may at the same time restore them to true righteousness by sanctification of his Spirit? . . . Christ entered upon his preaching: 'The Kingdom of God has come near; repent, and believe in the Gospel' (Mk. 1:15)" (*Institutes* III, 3:19).

"The idea of the Kingdom of God, the sovereignty of God, was a conception which was central and basic to the message of Jesus. He emerged upon men with the message that the Kingdom was at hand (Mt. 4:17; Mk. 1:15). To preach the Kingdom was an obligation that was laid upon him (Lk. 4:4). It was with the message of the Kingdom that he went through the towns and villages of Galilee (Lk. 8:1). The announcement of the Kingdom was the central element in the teaching of Jesus" (William Barclay, *The Mind of Jesus* [New York: Harper & Brothers, 1961], p. 47).

"Calvin was the only one of the original reformers to make a clear distinction between doctrinal articles concerning necessary elements of the faith and other articles concerning points of doctrine about which different opinions can be held without endangering the unity of the Church (*Inst.* IV.1:12). On this basis later Reformed theologians (Junius, Jurieu, Turrettini) developed the theory of the fundamental articles which were to serve as a sufficient foundation for the reunion of the Churches.

"This theory was worked out in such a rationalistic way that it did not find wide acceptance. But the underlying conception of a hierarchy of truths has slowly but surely made its way. It is reflected in the Basis of the World Council of Churches (where the fundamental articles have become the God-given Person). It has now even been recognized in the Roman Catholic Church. For the very first time an official Roman Catholic document has declared that there exists a hierarchy of truths since they vary in their relation to the foundation of the Christian faith (*De Ecumenismo* II, 11)" (W. Visser't Hooft, "Relevant Characteristics of the Reformed Position," *Bulletin of the Department of Theology of the World Alliance of Reformed Churches* 9, no. 4 [Summer 1969]:6–7).

17. For example, "Women in the Church," *Journal of Ecumenical Studies* 9 (1972):235–241; "Ministry in the Church," *ibid.,* pp. 589–612.

18. For example, "Most Important Statement Since Reformation for Anglicans and Catholics—Agreed Statement on Eucharistic Doctrine," *ibid.,* pp. 222–26; *Documents on Anglican/Roman Catholic Relations II* (United States Catholic Conference, Washington, D.C., 1973); *Lutherans and Catholics in Dialogue I-III,* ed. by Paul C. Empie and T. Austin Murphy (Augsburg Publishing House, Minneapolis, 1974); *Lutherans and Catholics in Dialogue IV* (Augsburg Publishing House, Minneapolis, n.d.); *Papal Primacy and the Universal Church,* ed. by Paul C. Empie and T. Austin Murphy (Augsburg Publishing House, Minneapolis, 1974); *Lutheran–Episcopal Dialogue* (FM Maxi Book, n.d.); *Modern Ecumenical Documents on the Ministry* (SPCK, London, 1975).

19. The 1647 edition of the Westminster Confession reads: "There is no other Head of the Church, but the Lord Jesus Christ: Nor can the Pope of Rome, in any sense, be head thereof: but is, that Antichrist, that Man of sin and Son of Perdition, that exalteth himself, in the Church, against Christ, and all that is called God." The present edition, adopted by the United Presbyterian Church in the United States of America in 1958, reads: "The Lord Jesus Christ is the only head of the Church, and the claim of any man to be the vicar of Christ and the head of the Church is unscriptural, without warrant in fact, and is a usurpation dishonoring to the Lord Jesus Christ" (*The Book of Confessions* [Philadelphia: Office of the General Assembly of the United Presbyterian Church in the United States of America, 1970], Chapter XXV, paragraph 6). The derogatory term "popish" is also dropped from the 1958 edition in Chapter XXII, paragraph 7, and Chapter XXIX, paragraph 2.

20. Vatican Council II, *Decree on Ecumenism,* no. 19, in Abbott, *op. cit.,* p. 361.

21. "Ministry in the Church," *Journal of Ecumenical Studies* 9 (1972):611–12.

22. *Ibid.,* p. 604.

23. The Pauline and Lucan accounts imply that a meal intervenes between the sharing of the bread and partaking of the cup, while the Marcan and Matthean accounts imply that the two acts have been brought together (cf. 1 Cor. 11:25; Lk. 22:20; Mk. 14:23; Mt. 26:27).

24. Chapters 12–14 of 1 Corinthians are devoted to the problems occasioned by spontaneous prayer in the gatherings of the Corinthian church.

25. "Ministry in the Church," no. 10, *Journal of Ecumenical Studies* 9 (1972):608.

26. See note 21, *ibid.*, pp. 589–612.

27. *Reconsiderations: Roman Catholic/Presbyterian and Reformed Theological Conversations 1966–67* (New York: World Horizons, Inc., 1967), pp. 122–37, 139–53.

28. *Journal of Ecumenical Studies* 7 (1970):209–65. See also Franz Josef van Beeck, "Towards an Ecumenical Understanding of the Sacraments," *Journal of Ecumenical Studies* 3 (1966):57–112.

29. *Decree on Ecumenism,* no. 3, in Abbott, *op. cit.*, p. 346.

30. Secretariat for Promoting Christian Unity, *Directory 1967,* nos. 44–50.

31. See Raymond H. Potvin, "The Religious Group as Community," paper presented to the Roman Catholic/Presbyterian-Reformed Consultation, May 9, 1974, Columbus, Ohio.

32. Meeting of October 24–26, 1974.

33. See papers prepared for this consultation at its meeting May 30–June 2, 1973, namely: Arleon L. Kelley, "Community and Institutional Factors in the Shape of the Unity We Seek: Sociological Input, Bi-Lateral Consultation, Columbus, Ohio"; Eugene M. Burke, "Report on Presbyterian-Roman Catholic Task Force, Columbus, Ohio"; Sally Cunneen, "Report on Ecumenical Task Force Visit to Columbus, Ohio, Jan. 11–17."

34. As the basis for our discussion and statement regarding the Eucharist, this consultation used the agreement composed by a group of Reformed, Roman Catholic, and Lutheran theologians meeting at the Trappist Monastery in Les Dombes, France, September 6–9, 1971; see: "Accord doctrinal entre catholiques et protestantes sur l'Eucharistie," *Documentation catholique,* no. 1606 (April 2, 1972):334–38. In the short time allowed for our discussion of the Lord's Supper we were unable to reach mutual understanding on all the aspects of the Eucharist which the Europeans did, as comparison of our statement with theirs reveals. The eucharistic portions of this consultation's statement "Ministry in the Church" should not be overlooked, however. Other bilateral consultations in the United States, moreover, have reached significant agreement with regard to the Lord's Supper; see the Anglican-Roman Catholic Consultation, U.S.A., "Comment on the 'Agreed Statement on Eucharistic Doctrine' of the Anglican-Roman Catholic International Commission" (*Journal of Ecumenical Studies* 9 [1972]:690–91); also *Lutherans and Catholics in Dialogue, III: The Eucharist as Sacrifice* (1967) and *IV: Eucharist and Ministry* (1970).

35. "Ministry in the Church," no. 10, *Journal of Ecumenical Studies* 9 (1972):608.

36. *Ibid.*, p. 609.

37. " . . . it is a fact that within our respective churches members of the same communion often are drifting farther and farther apart, not living together at all, though they are frequently worshiping together" (no. 9, *ibid.*, p. 608).

38. No. 11, *ibid.*, p. 610, emphasis in original.

39. For example: "An invitation to partake shall be extended to all who confess their faith in Jesus Christ as Lord and Savior, and may include baptized children when their families deem it appropriate, if the session authorizes" (United Presbyterian Church in the U.S.A., *Directory for the Worship of God,* 21.04).

40. "As for common worship *(communicatio in sacris)* . . . it may not be regarded as a means to be used indiscriminately for the restoration of unity among Christians. Such worship depends chiefly on two principles: it should signify the unity of the Church; it should provide a sharing in the means of grace. The fact that it should signify unity generally rules out common worship. Yet the gaining of needed grace sometimes

commends it" (Vatican Council II, *Decree on Ecumenism,* no. 8, in Abbott, *op. cit.,* p. 352).

For application of these principles in regard to Eastern churches and in regard to other churches and ecclesial communions, see Secretariat for Promoting Christian Unity, *Directory 1967,* nos. 38–65, and *Instruction Concerning Cases When Other Christians May Be Admitted to Eucharistic Communion in the Catholic Church,* May 25, 1972, no. 4, where it is stated: "The *Directorium Oecumenicum* has already shown how we must safeguard simultaneously the integrity of ecclesial communion and the good of souls. Behind the *Directorium* lie two main governing ideas: (a) the strict relationship between the mystery of the Church and the mystery of the Eucharist can never be altered, whatever pastoral measures we may be led to take in given cases. Of its very nature celebration of the Eucharist signifies the fullness of profession of faith and the fullness of ecclesial communion. This principle must not be obscured and must remain our guide in the field. (b) The principle will not be obscured if admission to Catholic eucharistic communion is confined to particular cases of those Christians who have a faith in the sacrament in conformity with that of the Church, who experience a serious spiritual need for the eucharistic sustenance, who for a prolonged period are unable to have recourse to a minister of their own community and who ask for the sacrament of their own accord. This spiritual need should be understood in the sense defined above (No. 3, b and c): a need for an increase in spiritual life, and a need for a deeper involvement in the mystery of the Church and of its unity."

41. "Yet though it is a spiritual food whose effect is to unite the Christian man to Jesus Christ, the Eucharist is far from being simply a means of satisfying exclusively personal aspirations, however lofty these may be. The union of the faithful with Christ, the head of the mystical body, brings about the union of the faithful themselves with each other. It is on their sharing of the eucharistic bread that St. Paul bases the union of all the faithful, 'Because there is one loaf' (1 Cor. 10:17). By this sacrament 'man is incorporated in Christ and united with his members.' By frequent receiving of the Eucharist the faithful are incorporated more and more in the body of Christ and share increasingly in the mystery of the Church" (Secretariat for Promoting Christian Unity, *Instruction,* May 25, 1972, no. 3, b).

Remarkable is the fact that Roman Catholic Documents avoid, though they do not deny, application of the principle that the Eucharist is the cause of the grace which unites the Church as well as the expression of the grace of unity. In regard to the Eucharist as cause of grace, they apply that principle only in regard to the grace necessary for individuals' salvation, neither affirming nor denying explicitly its application in regard to the grace necessary to unify the Church.

Washington, D.C.
May 24, 1976

Ethics and the Search for Christian Unity

1980

THE STATEMENT ON ABORTION

Touched by the tragic personal and social dimensions of decisions regarding abortion, the members of the Roman Catholic/Presbyterian-Reformed Consultation wish to express our common concerns. We are conscious of the need for our churches to call attention to the profound moral dimensions of the situation and to identify the individual and societal factors which give rise to the issue and make resolutions so difficult. We believe that our differing traditions have much to contribute through dialogue towards the clarification of principles and the exercise of charity in this matter.

We live in a moral universe. Our human capacity and even willingness to know or apply moral principles in situations of conflict are limited and make us conscious of our human finitude and brokenness and of our need for graced guidance and open inquiry.

These limitations have sometimes prevented us from recognizing the wealth of Christian resources for pastoral guidance concerning responsible sexuality, family planning, and public witness on moral issues. At the same time, we affirm the importance of drawing upon our traditions in dealing with these issues. The proper structuring of family life, the honoring of the gift of the covenant of marriage, the demands of caring for future generations, and the protecting of the weak and vulnerable must be part of any discerning moral position.

Abortion decisions exist in a milieu of closely related social evils which limit peoples' choices. Social, educational, and economical inequities suffered by women are part of the problem. Any discussion of abortion in our times should proceed with a recognition of the pervasive bias of cultural and ecclesial traditions which devalue women.

Until these factors are acknowledged there will not be a climate in which a morally and humanly satisfactory resolution to abortion can be effected. Women are too narrowly regarded in terms of their reproductive functions. Women encounter problems of poverty, inequality of opportunity, and sexual exploitation. If our churches are to be credible in addressing abortion, they must take the lead in accepting women as full and contributing members of the human and ecclesial communities. They must work to develop supportive networks to which pregnant women have a rightful claim. We recommend extensive, open discussion in the churches on the reproductive functions, on responsible sexuality, on the social aspects of pregnancy and child rearing, and on the new problems raised by prenatal diagnostic information as well as the pervasive sexual bias influencing many of our ecclesial and societal structures and institutions.

Moral and spiritual formation of conscience, in which the churches have an important role, pertains to many questions concerning the value of life, of which abortion is only one. Those who face abortion decisions are moral agents and therefore free to make responsible decisions with the due regard for the unborn, the pregnant woman, the family, the society, and the faith community. Considering an abortion places on everyone involved a serious moral responsibility.

Some of the basic principles on which the Consultation was able to reach agreement include the following:

1. the transcendent basis for respect for human life is the image and likeness of God in which human beings are created;
2. the ultimate responsibility for moral decision making rests with the individual conscience guided by reason and grace;
3. authentic moral decisions can never be exclusively subjective or individualistic but must take account of the insights and concerns of the broader religious, social, and familial community;
4. judicial and legislative standards are not always coterminous with moral demands, and therefore the legalization of abortion does not of itself absolve the Christian conscience from moral responsibility; and
5. religious groups have the right to use licit means to influence civil policy regarding abortion.

Some of the areas in which substantial differences were discovered and which call for further dialogue between our two traditions including the following:

1. the moment and meaning of personhood;
2. the rights of the unborn in situations where rights are in conflict;
3. the role of civil law in matters pertaining to abortion; and
4. the interrelation of individual versus communal factors in decision making.

In the light of our common Christian heritage and in recognition of our real differences, our ministry, with regard to abortion, will be characterized by the following: we will attempt to clarify the basic principles pertinent to decision making in this area. We will always respect the personal dignity of those involved in making decisions about abortion. Regardless of the ultimate decision reached, we will offer pastoral support insofar as our personal conscience and moral convictions allow. We will not resort to stereotypes and abusive language. We will work to transform societal arrangements which press people into untenable moral dilemmas. We will attempt to create compassionate community which overcomes alienation, loneliness, and rejection and which makes real a genuine community of moral discourse and decision. We will take responsibility as part of the mission of the church to create an ethos which values all life and which works toward a society where abortion need not occur.

THE STATEMENT ON HUMAN RIGHTS

The people of God are called in every age to proclaim righteousness, to struggle against injustice, and to care for one another, for the structures of civilization, and for creation. In our age, human rights is a particular way of speaking of the ethical demands of righteousness and justice under God's rule. At their deepest point, all human rights are grounded in nothing else then God's righteousness, which we know through Jesus Christ. It is under the grace of God's righteousness that humans speak of a universal and reliable moral law that is known by revelation and reason. It is engraved on the human heart in such a way that no one and no group is excused from recognizing the claim that other humans must be treated with justice, and that societies must be arranged on the basis of freedom and equity.

We confess that as humans we have not always been obedient to God's call, to that which we know in our hearts. We further confess that our churches in their divisions have failed to be truly reformed and truly catholic, and hence have not always led people of conscience, civilizations, or even the worshipping communities to obedience to the universal moral law. We are too often guided by the interests of material, ethnic, national, sexual, and even religious domination. Thus, we can only rejoice when humanists and groups such as the United Nations speak for human rights. We affirm that such efforts are theologically as well as humanly valid and are rooted in God even if God is not fully acknowledged. Human rights, as a reflection of God's will known to humanity by graced reason, are a proper guide to legal entitlements and protections which are to be heeded by individuals and enacted in civil, political, and economic areas by governments.

Human rights have two aspects. One is primarily personal and involves both the right to live with dignity and the duty to respect others in all things. Humans bear within them the image of God, which is the basis for their claims and duties. Therefore, individuals ought not be arbitrarily deprived of their rights of life, liberty, or the means of sustenance, growth, and creativity.

The other is primarily social. Family, cultural, scientific, political, ethnic, and religious groups have a right and a duty to organize, assemble, speak, and manage their internal affairs in responsible ways. Freedom of religion is especially necessary for the preservation of human rights in society. Communities of faith which are free to influence persons and to exercise prophetic witness prevent individualisms which neglect the common good and prevent political authority from becoming a conspiracy of the few against the many.

In the West, the constant and continuing struggles between Christ and Caesar, between *ecclesia* and *imperium,* between pastors and magistrates, between church and state, between faithful believers and loyal citizens, have established a tradition which demands that political power and individual interest is to be limited and subject to universal moral law. This tradition is shared by the Roman Catholic and the Reformed churches in principle if not always in practice, and these branches of Christianity have provided historical contexts in which the possibilities for human rights have come to a fuller expression. Advocates of human rights also arose at times outside these traditions. These advocates sometimes advanced the recognition of a universal moral law for peoples and nations and, at other times, confused the issues with the interests of specific nations and classes. Distorted communities, both bourgeois and proletarian, have appeared whenever human rights have been undercut by absolute individualisms or absolute collectivisms at the hands of either religious or secular forces.

The universal character of human rights, although developed or discovered in a particular history, means that individuals have public duties to, as well as claims on, society. This also means that governments, as the custodians of coercive power, must be limited and restrained. Government under law, with protection of minorities, with guarantees of basic freedoms, and with the rights of opposition, is normative for all societies. While states must have sufficient power to control overt wrong, protect persons, provide for defense against aggressors and rebels, and promote the common good, no government is fully competent in interpreting the universal moral law for all areas of life. Each familial, cultural, scientific, and especially religious organization, for example, has a right and duty to discern and carry out the moral law in its own sphere as a vocation from God. Hence, civil governments must allow them freedom in organization, belief, and practice. Further, no state may prevent these parts of society and its peoples from working politically toward reform of government when that government fails to live up to the universal moral law or overtly subverts it. When a regime becomes the aggressor against its own members and when other means of reform are closed, revolution may be a necessity to reconstitute a society under moral law.

As Christians we know that a heavy moral burden rests on those who advocate and implement change by violent means. Several modern developments influence moral action in these extreme situations. The global interdependence in technology, economics, and communications allows new transnational pressures to be brought to bear on governments which attempt to stop reform from within. And both massive modern weaponry and divisive ideological tension make conflict liable to escalate destruction.

The study of human rights, its theological rootage, its history and principles, is sharpened by a close look at particular cases. In our study we turned to the crisis in southern Africa, a troubled area deeply influenced by branches of the Christian tradition, yet one where many features of human rights are violated. The failure to apply human rights to economic and racial questions is dramatic. Southern Africa illustrates one failure of people to carry out these universal principles, but it is by no means the only case present or past. Indeed, it only typifies pathologies of state absolutism and of economic and racial injustice that are present in less dramatic forms in many parts of the world under many flags and ideologies. Moreover, in South Africa, the regime is sustained by a distorted form of imperial Calvinist doctrine that operates as a legitimizer of tyranny, much as a misguided form of authoritarian Catholicism has done in other ages and in other parts of the world. Fuller understanding of the theological foundations of human rights, and a fuller obedience to God's will, can serve to correct these distortions.

In the case of South Africa, with its documented denial of civil, political, familial, economic, and religious rights of black people at the hands of a white minority, we see no alternative, as a matter of human and theological principle, but the support of those liberation movements which respect human rights and bear the promise of religious and civil freedom with economic justice for all. Failure to support such movements is likely to produce a liberation movement which itself ignores principles of moral law in civil, political, and religious matters. We recognize the moral obligations which this places on persons, governments, and some corporation leadership and urge them not to retreat from these matters of moral principle.

To all Reformed and Roman Catholic Christians in South Africa and to all those victimized by the present situation, we commend the "Koinonia Declaration" drawn up by Reformed Christians and the several statements by the Southern African Catholic Bishops' Conference as sources of inspiration and genuine teaching. Any person or institution, secular or ecclesial, which interacts with southern Africa must bear the burden of proof that its action fosters freedom and equity for all.

Under other social and historical conditions, liberation from the particular pathologies that reign will take many forms, and the resolution of conflicting rights may vary in view of specific contexts; but all forms of struggle for liberation, and all specific resolutions of conflicting rights, we jointly affirm, must be in those directions which keep alive the prospect of fulfilling basic and universal human rights in all areas of human existence and society.

As Christians in the Roman Catholic and Reformed traditions, we urge all persons of conscience, all those in authority, and especially our member churches to reflect on the meanings and implications of human rights and to apply them to their practices and policies, for the development of all people, for the upbuilding of civilization, and to the glory of God.

Partners in Peace and Education

June 27, 1985

In 1980, the sponsors of the consultation, the National Conference of Catholic Bishops' Committee on Ecumenical and Interreligious Affairs, and the Caribbean and North American Area Council of the World Alliance of Reformed Churches, approved the main theme of Round IV of these continuing bilateral consultations. The theme was an ecumenical approach to the relationship of church and state. The steering committee of the consultation refined this definition and determined that we should explore "The Church and the Kingdom: Church—State—Society."

The first part of our document ("Theological Context") considers our common biblical and patristic heritage on these matters, and describes points of agreement and disagreement in Catholic and Presbyterian/Reformed theologies on issues of kingdom, church and state. Then as a way of exploring further these theological perspectives, we have focused on two topics relating church and state in contemporary American society: the peril of nuclear warfare ("Church and Nuclear Warfare") and the role of government in matters of education ("Church and School").

Theological Context

Whenever Christians from divided traditions take up the complex questions of the relations between kingdom, church and state, they find, as we have, that sooner or later their discussions must be tested against the witness of Scripture. From the very beginning, Scripture proclaims the sovereignty of God over all creation, tells how the practical consequences of God's reign were made manifest at Sinai, and traces the history of God's covenant and the people's often imperfect attempts at respecting God's sovereignty. Ancient Israel's experience of God led it both to recognize the importance of social realities for religious life and to insist, as the prophets did, on the relative character of every social and political institution in the light of God's reign. As the story of God's people proceeds, the "kingdom of God" is gradually revealed to refer to God's future display of power and judgment, to the future moment when all creation will acknowledge God's rule and when the promises to God's people will be fulfilled. Jesus, as heir to the tradition of Jewish law, prophecy and wisdom, has taught us also to look for anticipations of God's kingdom in the present. The life, death and resurrection of Jesus shine forth as the dramatic anticipation of the fullness of God's reign. In the present the kingdom confronts us as God's constant rule, sovereignty and loving dominion.

The church is in principle the community of those who believe in Jesus Christ and his proclamation of God's kingdom. It preserves the spirit of Jesus and tries to be faithful to it. It prays and yearns for the fullness of the kingdom and works in service of the kingdom. It lives its life against the horizon of the kingdom. It is the sign and symbol of hope for the fullness of God's kingdom in the future. It announces the kingdom and encourages God's people to live in accord with the standards of the kingdom, though it cannot claim to be the fullness of the kingdom. The early church had much in common with Jewish and Greco-Roman groups of its time; what set it apart from them was its faith in the power of Jesus' death and resurrection as God's decisive self-disclosure in human history and decisive inauguration of the fullness of the kingdom.

The early Christians knew what it means to be a minority with respect to state and society. Through his proclamation of the kingdom of God, Jesus challenged assumptions of his society and so came into conflict with religious and political leaders. This challenge led to his death at the hands of the governmental officials.

Neither Jesus nor his first-century followers were in a position to influence directly the political and military policies of the Roman Empire. Nor could they transform immediately the cultural and moral attitudes of the peoples around them. Their general policy toward the empire was acceptance and even cooperation (see Mk. 12:13–17 parr.; Rom. 13:1–7; 1 Pt. 2:13–17), resisting only when the state interfered unjustly in their religious lives (see Acts 5:27–32; Rv. 17). The early Christians did not negate political life any more than they negated family or economic life; they relativized it. That is, they saw that membership in the kingdom and in the church meant that political and governmental authority was not ultimate and could not finally save humanity.

Over time, the extension of this principle eventuated in notions of government as not absolute. The early Christians' missionary strategy was to share the good news of God's kingdom anticipated in Jesus and to show by their good example what a difference the good news could make in their everyday lives. Yet even the cautious steps in the New Testament give some hints about the Gospel's power to influence governments and transform lives. In the changing circumstances of the church throughout history, there have been moments of great success on the church's part and times of great failure in these tasks.

History has taught us to beware of all claims identifying the kingdom with particular political, social or ecclesiastical structures. However, it has also shown the danger of an exclusively future, otherworldly or individualistic understanding of the coming kingdom. God's full exercise of the divine reign over creation involves radical conversion of human hearts, relationships and social structures, and thus is a process of redemption going on in the course of history. This is a work of divine initiative welcomed and implemented within human freedom.

As representatives of the Catholic and Presbyterian/Reformed traditions in the United States of America in the late 20th century, we have greater opportunities and responsibilities with respect to our government and our society than the early Christians had. We are also more directly involved in the difficult task of discerning when the church must say yes to the state and when it must say no. For all the faults of this society, and they are many, Christians in this land are grateful for the theological ancestors who struggled to preserve a society in which religious people can influence popular consciousness, change laws, organize communities and exercise political power. Many of our brothers and sisters in other lands are not nearly so fortunate in their opportunities to affect state and society. As Christians, we understand our political and public activities as flowing from our commitment to God's kingdom and church. We wish neither to neglect our responsibilities to our fellow citizens (and to the world) nor to reduce our faith to merely political action.

From the earliest days of American history, Presbyterians/Reformed Christians have been prominent in shaping our state and society. Viewing the commonwealth as an imperfect but anticipatory expression of God's kingdom, Presbyterian/Reformed Christians have undertaken political and public activities as grateful and obedient responses to God's call. They have taught all of us about reforming society through laws, the need for voluntary associations, respect for human wisdom, the formulation of just standards and their applications, the regulation of political systems, checks and balances, and the separation of church and state. In the midst of these positive activities, Presbyterian/Reformed Christians have never ceased recalling the ambiguity of political and public activities on account of their roots in fallen human nature.

Since the settlement of Maryland in 1634, Catholics in America have also developed a spirit of pluralism and toleration, one which over time allowed selective but highly significant embracing of principles also held by Reformed Christians on public matters. Catholics have made important contributions in enabling various immigrant groups to participate responsibly in American society, in developing labor unions and in energizing urban politics. For various historical reasons, American Catholics have been somewhat less prominent than Presbyterians/Reformed Christians in shaping our governmental and social institutions. That situation has changed, however, and the full range of political and social opportunities and responsibilities is now open to most American Catholics. This development coincided with the renewal of biblical studies in the Catholic Church, Vatican II's declarations on religious freedom *(Dignitatis Humanae)* and the church in the modern world *(Gaudium et Spes)*, and the theological re-evaluation of the venerable tradition of natural law.

The time is ripe for American representatives of the Catholic and Presbyterian/Reformed traditions to express their common theological understanding of kingdom, church and state, and to explore what this means with regard to some highly sensitive issues facing American society and what it means for our shared hopes for Christians in communion.

The long traditions of the Catholic and Presbyterian/Reformed churches, both when they were united in one communion from the early church through the late Middle Ages and since their division in the West into discrete bodies, agree on many aspects of a theological frame of reference regarding kingdom, church and state. They agree that not only the communities of faith rooted in Jesus Christ, but also the political orders of the world exist in relation to the kingdom of God. That is, they understand church, society and state to exist under the rule of God and governed by the laws of God; they live toward the ends and purposes of reconciliation, peace and justice for all humanity; and they bear within them, at least in partial ways, the marks and clues of the kingdom as it is already at work in history.

With this understanding the churches have the fundamental responsibility to identify, preach, teach and exemplify the power of this kingdom and, on this basis, call all members of society to responsible participation in church and political life. Failure to acknowledge or heed these laws leads to disaster and destruction. Society has priority, and the state is a temporal institution organized to protect society and the church. To put it another way, the kingdom may find its marks not only in the church, but also in some aspects of society, even if rarely in any state.

The churches have a vocation to preach, teach and exemplify by word, sacrament and deed the promises and the present power of divine life in the world. Their efforts at improving the quality of human life here and now are signs of their faith in God's promise to bring about the fullness of the kingdom. They try to facilitate the social reign of God in all aspects of civilization, insofar as this is possible within the limits of human history. The Christian tradition asserts that political authorities and institutions likewise have a responsibility under God both to protect the freedom of religious bodies to fulfill their vocation and to order the structures of social life in accord with the common good.

There is a necessary distinction between church and state. Christians maintain that the church's existence and goal derive from God in Christ, not from human efforts or historical conditions alone. The modern state has immense powers of taxation, regulation, judicial determination and administration, all reinforced by coercive power. The churches in the United States work in society without these powers. Governance in the state may require the use of coercive power, especially in controlling illegitimate violence and securing justice, whereas the church violates its own nature when it relies on such coercion as an instrument in ensuring obedience to its laws and ends. Moreover, the church is committed to values and principles that extend to all humanity, whereas the state is inevitably focused on the interests and well-being of the nation.

The church also supports, guides and defends the rights of institutions in society not directly controlled by the state—families, schools, unions, hospitals and various community organizations—so that state coercive powers can never become the sole comprehensive determinant for social policy. The use of coercive power must always be limited. Political authority must be guided by concern for the preservation and improvement of all non-governmental institutions. State power must serve the society and all humanity, not simply control them.

As American Christians today, we are discovering that we share a common biblical heritage, a common set of opportunities and responsibilities, and a common theological framework. We are also discovering that we share the task of discerning when to speak the prophetic word of the Gospel to our government and our society. Nevertheless, some real differences in approach and expression remain. As a way of understanding these differences, while acknowledging the great progress already made toward theological convergence, we have focused on two issues: how our churches speak to American government and society, and how American government and society shape and sometimes subvert our churches. In exploring the first issue, we have focused on official statements by our churches regarding nuclear warfare. In investigating the second issue, we have looked especially at legal rulings regarding state aid to church schools and related matters. On nuclear warfare, our conclusions are similar but our ways of approach and expression differ. On the second issue both our conclusions and our approaches differ somewhat (though not strictly along denominational lines).

Church and Nuclear Warfare

Since this round of the consultation began, the U.S. Catholic bishops have discussed, revised and finally approved their pastoral letter on war and peace, titled "The Challenge of Peace: God's Promise and Our Response." During this time, nearly all of the related Reformed and Presbyterian denominations have also debated and passed statements regarding Christian responsibilities as we face the growing perils of nuclear warfare and international political-military confrontation. In both the Catholic and Presbyterian/Reformed treatments of these matters, key issues about church and state, and about Christian understandings of kingdom, society and political life generally have been central. More and more of our bilateral conversations focused on issues of church and state especially as they involve the use and the limits of coercive power in and by political authority in the context of the present nuclear perils. Thus, our discussions were conducted with a sense of urgency and with a desire to find agreement wherever possible.

It was frequently and widely acknowledged in our discussions that the U.S. Catholic bishops' pastoral letter on war and peace is one of the most discerning and prophetic statements on the issue in recent years. In terms of both its substance and its impact on public discourse, this letter may well do for this issue in the American context what Martin Luther King Jr. did for the issues of racism: The conscience of the nation, and not only that of a specific communion, is given a new level of cogent expression by religious leadership. Several of the Presbyterian/Reformed national bodies have endorsed this letter and commend it to their congregations for study along with the various denominational statements. This signals a new level of joint witness to the society by the churches which exceeded our original expectations and encouraged the further work of our bilateral consultations.

In our consultations we have studied various Presbyterian/Reformed statements on war and peace along with the pastoral letter and a series of discerning background papers written by the participants. We explored the history of our traditions, both as churches separated from one another and as heirs of a common history prior to the Reformation, and have been made aware again of the spiritual, moral and political dangers of a too-intimate relationship between piety and coercive force. We confess that both our traditions have at times violated Christian principles and damaged political justice in this regard. Yet because religion and politics seem inevitably to influence one another, past errors are no reason to avoid confrontation with the problems anew. Indeed, the awareness of dangers to church and to state when these relationships are false or ill-considered prompts us to deepen and broaden our dialogue, and to identify questions needing greater clarity. The following are key questions that emerged from the discussions and from study of the various documents.

In modern life, the instruments of coercive power reach devastating proportions. The traditional vocation of the church to see that the use of military power be restrained is intensified. Churches are called to see that "common good" extends beyond national boundaries to all humanity and to see that temporal power remains constrained by universal moral principles. All believers and communions who share this heritage are to give regular and sustained witness to those principles which promote peace. Political authorities are to conduct their responsibilities so that the prospects for peace are increased. The churches have the responsibility to teach and clarify the principles of moral life in such a way that the citizenry, especially those who are members of the churches, can exercise the duties of citizenship with moral and spiritual discernment.

The discussion of church-state issues, in the context of the various denominational positions on war and peace in our nuclear age, indicates that common emphases, stated somewhat differently in different branches of our churches, have their characteristic theological groundings and particular implications.

The core logic of the bishop's pastoral letter, like that of the Presbyterian/Reformed statements, uses a combination of arguments from Scripture, from the traditional discussions of just war theory and from social-ethical analysis of the contemporary situation. These communions of the Christian family recognize that there are strong impulses toward nonviolence in the New Testament and that it is a primary duty of Christians to be peacemakers. Both communions recognize that in political affairs the limited use of coercive power may be required in order to maintain civil order, protect the neighbor from arbitrary violence and serve the common good. In contrast to some Christian communions, both the Roman Catholic and Presbyterian/Reformed traditions have held over the centuries that it is possible to be a Christian soldier or magistrate. In other words, one may be a faithful communicant and exercise coercive power—or even participate in some kinds of war as a conscientious combatant. That is to say that although there is always a pressure toward non-violence in these traditions, unqualified pacifism is not the only ethical posture for the Christian. It may be the vocation of some.

In the historic traditions of these two communions of Christianity, the arguments justifying this common stance have been somewhat different. The Western Catholic tradition, for the most part, has been dependent on criteria for reluctant but justifiable uses of coercive power developed by Augustine and others under the somewhat confusing heading "the just war theory." The phrase does not mean that war is just. It reflects the encounter of Christianity with complex political civilizations in which Christians are also citizens and magistrates. Distinctions between justifiable and unjustifiable uses of coercive activity by political authority have to be made.

The Presbyterian/Reformed churches share much of the heritage that derives from the days of the old Roman Empire. Often they also articulate the "just war" criteria as guidelines for believers. More often, however, they turn to the Old Testament and see analogies between the responsibilities placed by God upon the Israelites to engage in battle for justice and righteousness' sake, and the responsibilities of Christians to see that governments do not exploit innocent and defenseless peoples or prevent the people from worshiping God. The perils of state idolatry and quest for ultimate security in military response to crises are also frequently accented.

The two modes of argument are quite similar in result and allow for considerable convergence in our ethical witness in society. Yet some differences of note remain. The Catholic tradition modulates the tendencies of some to read the New Testament in absolutist ways by placing a high value on the faithfulness of church leaders who attempted to apply New Testament motifs to a complex Roman civilization and thereby produced an authoritative "tradition." The Presbyterian/Reformed churches tend to rely more on the Hebrew Scriptures and the application of these biblical accents to modern civilizations.

Both ways of working tend to put the pacifist tendencies of some New Testament passages into a larger historical, ethical and civilizational context of interpretation, although the different historical and civilizational understandings bring about distinctive styles of ethical judgment as the Gospel is related to complex socio-political problems. For example, the Catholic tradition draws heavily on principles adopted into canon law or promulgated by official pronouncements by councils and popes. Presbyterian/Reformed traditions, by contrast, often utilize biblical phrases, such as Christ's disarming of the "principalities and powers" (Eph. 6:12) to state analogous principles. Both communions tend to disagree with those traditions which see pacifism as the only response of a Christian, and call for responsible Christian engagement in political life, even as it may require the use of coercive means, as a proper vocation of magistrate and citizen. Both communions see peacemaking as a mandate of a Christ-informed conscience and community.

At moments in the past, individuals or groups in both the Catholic and Presbyterian/Reformed churches have misappropriated both tradition and Scripture in ways that have turned "just war" and biblical analogies to "holy war," that is, into legitimations of morally unjustifiable "crusade." At such moments the New Testament witness toward non-violence has been obscured or forgotten. In the pastoral letter and in the current Presbyterian/Reformed statements, efforts are now being made to recover and retain that witness, not in a way that excludes or denies the legitimacy of limited coercive power as a necessary instrument of the state, but as a governing priority which should be set forth as the norm of those who live under and toward the kingdom.

The new urgency of nuclear confrontation has evoked a more holistic reappropriation of the heritage. The pacifists and those who recognize the states' right to defensive war under certain conditions unite in denouncing nuclear war. Preparation for nuclear war is morally intolerable. Nuclear deterrence must be transformed into nuclear cooperation and disarmament.

Non-violent, peaceful human cooperation is the law and purpose of God. The burden of moral proof rests on those who use armed force, even the state. Peace within a state requires justice. States have no right to ignore justice and to defend particular governments with a reign of terror under the claims of national security. Nor do superpowers have the right to intervene in neighboring states to thwart domestic struggles for social change under the banners of national interest or national security. There is growing agreement that justifiable revolutions, such as certain "wars of liberation," also come under these terms and have to bear the burden of proof. Even these can never become unqualified "holy wars."

These matters are worth noting in the context of the discussion of church and state. They reveal that these two communions of the Christian family have a similar understanding. Neither believes Christianity requires disengagement from problems of power in civilization; and neither can allow "reasons of state" such as "national interest" or "defense security" or even "liberation" to become sovereign over conscience or society. Christians, we hold in common, live in the real world of power politics, but the norms of political life come from Christian ethics founded in Scripture, church tradition and reason. The latter must form and inform the former.

The above motifs lead us to a second point of comparison and contrast. The United Presbyterian Church statements and the United Church of Christ statements, particularly, accent a theme also strongly present in the Catholic pastoral letter: Christians are to be peacemakers, and the peace that is to be made by faithful and obedient action is *shalom*—a "just peace" that reflects spiritual joy. "Peace" is not simply the absence of violent conflicts, but involves both structures of justice and the realizing of spiritual wholeness. This peace disarms structures of oppression and destruction both in the institutions of society and in the human heart.

Several Presbyterian/Reformed bodies affirm that peace cannot be achieved by ending the arms race unless there is economic reform, extension of human rights to those now denied them, the establishment of democratic political institutions and the liberation of minorities, women and Third World peoples in all areas of ecclesiastical, social and civil life. Comparable motifs can be found in Catholic opinion, particularly in the papal encyclicals of the last hundred years. But there is also a stronger emphasis in the Catholic tradition on that dimension of peace which has to do with the inner, spiritual cultivation of the response to God. To be sure, this is present in several of the Presbyterian/Reformed contributions to our consultations, but it is less overt. This is an area where convergence is probably necessary to have a fully catholic, fully evangelical, fully reformed and fully orthodox community of faith. Nothing in either tradition inhibits convergence at this point. All seem to be aware that without real social justice and without inner spirituality lasting peace is unlikely even if we avoid the immediate perils of pending nuclear destruction.

One way in which the church is distinguished from the state is that it knows that "justice," as a precondition of peace, is ultimately rooted in that form of spirituality which brings "joy" and empowers persons to become peacemakers. The church also knows that spirituality of this sort has the best chance to flourish and grow where injustice does not stunt human development and force people to attend only to the struggle of survival. Justice and joy require one another as mutual preconditions to *shalom.*

In the Presbyterian/Reformed discussions of the bishops' pastoral letter a very important point emerged that has many implications for our topic. It was a series of scattered, but substantial and enthusiastic comments about the way in which the pastoral letter was developed. The process whereby the letter moved from early proposals to final draft involved open hearings with Protestant as well as Catholic theological and ethical scholars, circulation of several drafts with open invitations for comment, discussions with laity in government and defense, experts in political and nuclear affairs, and discussion at congregational levels.

The sensitive inclusion of diverse opinion, especially as it involves openness to the "ministries" and insights of laity, appears to many Reformed and Presbyterian members to be a "post-Vatican II" indicator of possible convergence in the understanding of authority and polity in the churches. Not only has this helped overcome some of the authoritarian stereotypes by which many Presbyterian and Reformed Christians tend to view Catholic ecclesiology, but it seems to have implications for the whole church's role in the shaping of conscience on political affairs.

In this connection the mode of address of the bishops' letter is to Catholics, to other Christians and to all those who seek a world free of nuclear threat. It is not in the first instance a statement directly to the U.S. government—although there are many indications that governmental leadership was quite interested in how the discussions came out. Policy-makers in American political and military affairs were not ignored nor are the more concrete political judgments to which these documents come binding in all their detail.

What is presumed by the documents on nuclear armaments by Catholics and Presbyterian/Reformed alike is that a committed, informed and ethically secure population will work through democratic channels to see that morally questionable policies will be modified. Such a presumption will seem unremarkable to a great number of people. In the context of critical Catholic and Presbyterian/Reformed reflections on church and state, the implications are significant.

Church leadership has a responsibility to work with and through the people. The people have the responsibility to use their informed consciences to shape the use of political and military power. Persuasion and the authority of the word in preaching and teaching operate through the consciences of the people, who will then see that political authority (including that which determines military policy) is the servant and not the master of human existence. To be sure, all are "to be obedient to the governing authorities" (see Rom. 13:1–7), but when authorities become a terror to good, the people through free discussion, persuasion and open democratic processes may—indeed, must—see that these policies or the leadership promulgating them are altered.

It is possible to identify some of the main theological motifs that lie behind our discussions of church and state with reference to the specific crisis of nuclear peril:

1. Creation is a gift of God. Even if it is tainted with sin since the Fall, it is not to be destroyed by any armaments contrived by human persons. No political or military policy which portends devastation of the world can be approved by the church, whatever political philosophies and interests may be involved.

2. The churches are called not only to see that creation is regarded, but to contribute to redemption from the Fall and its effects, even though every church has fallen elements within it. The church is able to do this because the kingdom of God is over, beyond and in the church. The methods of the church are primarily by preaching, teaching and sacrament, and by social action, social service and political engagement. Rightly understood, these are never merely political and never without spiritual-moral content with political implications. The ministries of the church transcend national boundaries, representing an international community seeking peace.

3. The state is an instrument of society and must serve humanity. Every political order or government involves the possible use of coercive, even lethal, power to protect and preserve human societies. In those moments when the state brings about the conditions which allow freedom, justice, joy and peace, the state may serve God's redemptive purposes. Particpation in political life as responsible citizens or leaders is a high office to be honored and encouraged. When political authorities or structures become more destructive than preservative and redemptive, Christians may withdraw their obedience to clearly unjust

civil laws and conscientiously engage in civil disobedience, being willing to suffer prosecution by the state for the sake of reforming state policy and bringing its law to accord with a just order. Should this civil disobedience and active non-violence fail and the state respond only with arbitrary violence and perpetuation or increase of an unjust order, the state may well forfeit its claim to legitimate governance. It may become, instead, a highly organized rebellion against right order, just peace and the common good. Then Christian citizens may commit themselves to the reconstruction of a preservative and redemptive government by the use of force against the rebellion of officials masking as a government.

4. Christians live in church and society in hope. The eschatological awareness brought by the threat of nuclear apocalypse invites us to act for *shalom* in the face of despair. We know that only God can bring the fulfillment of the kingdom promise and deliver us from the perils we have made for ourselves. Yet by grace we place ourselves under God, as people of God, to be witnesses to and servants of the purposes of God in the world. In all that we do, therefore, we bring our faith and our theology, our love experienced in Christian fellowship and from Christ, to the realistic analysis of political and military questions that we may actualize our hopes for the kingdom of God wisely.

On these matters, we agree and urge all in our member churches to work more closely together to make these motives active in this land. Whatever other differences and divisions remain and will remain for a time, these common elements of witness on church, state and peace are points of convergence to be celebrated at local, pastoral, regional, national and international levels and, we pray, also in heaven.

Church and School

Education was a second area in which we tested our understandings of kingdom, church and state in the American context. As our discussion progressed, we realized that we were treating different, although related, issues: policies of the churches and of the government with regard to education generally, religiously sponsored schools and the place of religion in the public schools. These issues entail, naturally, church attitudes and influences on governmental policies in education and the ways in which governmental policies permit, enhance or inhibit the capacities of the churches to follow the mandates of their faiths. Before those issues can be addressed directly, it is necessary to identify some presuppositions about the nature of education according to our religious traditions. It is also important to define the terms of our discussions.

Both the Catholic and the Presbyterian/Reformed traditions have strong commitments to education in theory and practice. Both traditions encourage education as a service to the mind and its gifts, helping young men and women to understand this world and themselves. As Christians we esteem education as one way of enhancing our readiness for the kingdom and for union with the Lord. With faith as motivation and perspective, education can lead us to appreciate this world as God's creation and to learn how to live and serve one another here as companions. We both stress the importance of education as a necessary instrument enabling persons to fulfill their vocations, to participate as good citizens in their society and to contribute to the common good.

Both the Catholic and the Presbyterian/Reformed traditions view religion as penetrating all areas of life and so look on all areas of life as religiously significant. Therefore, all human studies and scientific endeavors are to be conducted with deep regard for the most profound moral and spiritual values necessary to human well-being. Moreover, all education must be conducted with the recognition that religious and ethical questions may well be involved in the selection, presentation and evaluation of such materials. Because of the intimate relationship of knowing and believing, and of ethics and preparing for life, both traditions look on teaching as an especially significant vocation; they encourage people to undertake teaching as a profession; and they promote learning and study as a lifelong activity. Historically these traditions have been among the leading founders of schools, colleges and universities. Of special significance to both traditions is the nature and character of the early stages of education which, we hold, must foster a sacred regard for truth, a love of humanity, a principled view of morality and justice, a personal commitment to responsible labor, community life, civility and culture.

While we have rejoiced in discovering our common enthusiasm for and commitment to education, we have also noted points at which our perspectives regarding kingdom, church and society may lead us to differ on educational matters and on public-policy questions that influence education. Acknowledging the great investments that both traditions have made in higher education, we have nevertheless focused our conversations on the more sensitive areas of primary and secondary education. We have talked chiefly about grades one through 12; that is, the period in which most states in the United States have stipulated a legal obligation for children to attend school (at least to the age of 16). Most children fulfill this obligation within the state-sponsored or public school system. All taxpayers must support this system even if their own children do not attend or even if they have no children at all. It is against the U.S. Constitution, as interpreted by the Supreme Court, to use the public school curriculum or resources to propagate or show preference to any specific religion. Although the historical, literary, cultural and philosophical study of religion is permitted, the common, although dubious, interpretation of the separation of church and state makes such study rare. Thus most American children attend state-sponsored schools which are funded by all taxpayers and which are not only prevented from promoting any particular religion, but which avoid those permitted treatments of religion which are surely necessary for a complete education.

Some American children attend schools under the direction of religious bodies (dioceses, religious orders, parishes, denominations, judicatories, congregations, etc.). The Catholic primary and secondary school system consists of approximately 9,500 schools and serves over 3 million students. Few Presbyterian/Reformed churches in the United States sponsor schools. In this respect, however, the Christian Reformed parent societies have been a notable exception. Evangelical Protestant schools, some connected to the Presbyterian or Reformed traditions, are growing rapidly; in the last three years, they are being founded at the rate of about 300 per year. The religiously sponsored schools generally give preference to members of their own churches, but many welcome children from other (or no) religious backgrounds, and some use their private, parochial or diocesan systems to provide quality education to disadvantaged groups where public systems are weak. From the legal perspective, the state must treat religiously sponsored schools in the same way that it treats private independent secular schools. Catholic schools include about half of the total number of teachers and 56 percent of the students enrolled in U.S. non-public, all-day schools.

Christians in America have had their own distinctive motivation for founding religiously affiliated schools. The impartiality of the U.S. Constitution has been applied to government-sponsored schools by obliging them to be neutral toward religion. That has caused difficulties for some Christians in many traditions. At various times and places this requirement has not been honored, and parents found their children subjected to what they regarded as objectionable sectarian influences by teachers. And when neutrality was enforced, parents found that when matters of great importance were being taught, the elimination of religious viewpoints and teaching, while all other viewpoints (including those opposed by believers) were set forth, left pupils at a disadvantage. Only in religiously committed schools, they concluded, could the full range of the believer's mind and interests be freely explored, with the benefit of the Christian community's insight and wisdom.

Within this context we have discussed a number of controversial issues. On some questions we find much agreement; on others we tend to divide by communion; and on still others we find agreements and disagreements that do not neatly follow our particular traditional divisions. For example, we tend to agree that a state-authored prayer, to be offered in the public schools, is not to be recommended on either religious or constitutional grounds. Not only must the rights of minorities be protected, but government bodies are seldom theologically competent for performing the task which belongs to churches and families and individuals. Further, we agree that while the government has a right and a duty to support public education, it is important that provisions which allow taxfree, non-profit private and religious schools to exist and to develop patterns of education outside of or beyond those provided for by the common purse be sustained, provided only that they meet health, safety and minimal academic standards proper for government to protect. And we tend to agree that when it is deemed unnecessary or impossible for children who are religious or come from religious families to attend religiously sponsored schools, churches must provide supplementary programs to prepare the youth for faithful adulthood. Finally, we agree that teaching "about" religion is constitutionally possible, important for a holistic educational experience and too seldom carried out. Children who are not exposed to the great faith traditions of the world with at least as much objectivity and detail as they are now exposed to economic and political ideologies, to artistic perspectives and to scientific theories and hypotheses, are educationally deprived.

On one issue, however, we tend to disagree according to whether we are rooted in the Catholic or the Presbyterian/Reformed traditions, although there are exceptions even here. Most striking in this regard is the sensitive question of whether government at the national, state or local levels should provide some form of tax relief, direct aid or subsidy for parents to use in the education of their children if the parents decide to send their children to a private or religiously sponsored school.

This current and much-debated issue is a concrete way of exploring similarities and differences in Catholic and Presbyterian/Reformed approaches to education in the context of our theologies of kingdom, church and state. It is important to observe at the outset that we are stating common, perhaps even majority, viewpoints, but not monolithic or unanimous opinions of all our church members or leaders.

With that caution stated, it is fair to say that many Catholics and some Presbyterian/Reformed Christians (especially members of the Christian Reformed Church) argue that the government should provide tax relief for parents of children enrolled in religiously sponsored schools. The following are arguments in favor of such tax relief:

1. Parents have the primary responsibility for educating their children, though they may require the help of the state in certain aspects of education. The principle of subsidiarity suggests that tax relief would increase the freedom of parents in educating their children with the least interference in the precise mode and content of education.

2. At present, parents pay for both the public schools through their taxes and the religiously sponsored schools through their tuitions and contributions. As a matter of equity, many argue, parents deserve and need such tax relief as a just response to this double burden.

3. The proposed tax relief, parental aid or subsidy may be understood to be a transaction between the government and the parents, and not one directly between the government and the church or between the government and the religiously sponsored schools.

4. The consequence would be the pluralization of educational efforts and would encourage innovation in educational designs according to the particular needs of the students and their families. In this pluralism, religiously sponsored schools could develop even better forms of education in explicitly religious atmospheres. Students would be encouraged to relate their studies more directly to their faith commitments, and the benefits of a richly pluralistic society would be more widely gained.

Most Presbyterians, many Reformed Christians and some Catholics oppose tax relief for parents of those enrolled in religious and other private schools. The following are arguments against such tax relief:

1. The education of the next generation is a responsibility of all the citizenry and is best effected through public schools in a democratic society. Parents may have special faith commitments that require the right to organize schools outside of the publicly provided systems of education, but the public has no responsibility to subsidize, directly or indirectly, these special commitments.

2. Such tax relief, aid to parents and subsidy are in fact devices to bypass present prohibitions against entanglement of the government

in religiously sponsored education and would, in effect, promote the religious bodies that sponsor the schools. It is therefore a violation of the Constitution.

3. Such proposals might well reduce commitment to the common good in sustaining quality public schools both by diverting funds from public education and even more by eroding the concern among the voting population to commit major tax dollars to public schools. The public schools could become underfunded custodial institutions for those segments of the population which have the least resources, financially, emotionally, politically and institutionally.

4. Pluralism in educational design and program may more easily and equitably be worked out through modification of present public school curricula, etc., without promoting a pluralism which tends to segregate faith communities during the formative years of education. In this connection the churches must promote responsible participation in the common problems of the education of our youth and insist on quality of instruction "about" religion in the public schools without detracting from the specific vocations of churches and families, and trying to get schools to do their jobs for them.

The Catholic approach to this issue is based on the individual's right to an education, the primacy of the parents in educating their children and the principle of subsidiarity whereby the larger unit of the common life, the state, supplements the efforts of parents to carry out their tasks. The Presbyterian/Reformed approach, where it conflicts with the Catholic one on this issue, is based on the duty of all the citizenry to provide quality education for the next generation through common institutions and democratic participation, on a firm adherence to the separation of church and state in form and consequence, and on a vision of the church as a witness within public institutions and structures rather than the architect of private alternatives.

Both traditions affirm that religion permeates every facet of life. They differ with regard to what is the best way of educating children and to recognize and appreciate this reality—through the total environment of the religiously sponsored school or through the public school as supplemented and given a religious framework by the church? Both traditions agree that parents bear the primary weight of the public's responsibility for educating children. They differ on the role that the state should play in the educational process—promoting the education of youth as a subsidiary to parents and church or primary provider of education for most children? Both traditions affirm that freedom and justice are involved in this issue. The usual Catholic position is that tax relief is a matter of justice that would enhance the freedom of parents. A frequent Presbyterian/Reformed position argues that not using the public schools is a free choice for which parents should be willing to pay, and that equality of opportunity and quality of education are best provided by the common public administration of the schools.

A major historical factor in leading Catholics in the United States to develop their own school system was the perception that the public schools in some areas at least were rooted in Protestantism and promoting Protestant values. Even then, however, there was an articulate body of support for Catholics being educated in public schools and thus bringing about a change in the ethos of those schools. At a later period, some Protestants called for the disentanglement of public schools from all religious doctrines or observances, in part out of fear that the growing Catholic population might impose its own religious program on the public schools.

Today Catholics and Presbyterian/Reformed Christians are probably more concerned about the alleged neutrality of the public schools toward religion. Our discussions have indicated how widely the public schools in certain geographical areas vary with regard to religion. Depending on the administration and faculty and on the religious atmosphere of the community, the local public school may be perceived as friendly or hostile toward religion. The official policy, however, is neutrality. The same discussions have raised the questions of religious people about this alleged neutrality: Does neutrality lead to disregard for religion as a historical and cultural force? Does neutrality suggest that religion is not very important? Does neutrality hasten the process of secularization and even promote so-called "secular humanism"?

The religious neutrality of the public school is the context in which most American Catholic and Presbyterian/Reformed children are educated. Even though the American Catholic Church is strongly committed to its religious school system, the Catholic Church assumes that governments may establish their own schools insofar as the common good requires them. Since the vast majority of Catholic students in the United States attend public schools, there is naturally strong support for and influence on the public school system by Catholic parents. Moreover, the Catholic Church encourages Catholics who teach in public schools to give a good example of their religious commitment and Catholic students to share their faith with others. Presbyterian/Reformed Christians look upon the public schools as offering an experience of pluralism that prepares children for adult life in the United States. Both communions affirm that religious people—teachers and students—make important contributions to American society through their presence and participation in public schools. We wonder whether it would be good for our society and for our churches if all children of religious parents were studying in religiously sponsored schools. Such a situation might deprive our public schools of any religious presence and might marginalize our churches with respect to the larger society.

Our churches see the need to supplement, integrate and at times correct public school education with explicitly Christian education. The most obvious supplement is the religious education program sponsored by local congregations. Some churches also provide remedial help for public school students through various tutoring programs. There are always practical problems regarding the limited amount of time available for religious education and the quality of the programs that are available. The principles, however, are that all Christians have a right to a Christian education, that parents have the primary responsibility for assuring and providing such an education, and that our churches must make available an education enabling children to relate their faith to the materials and experiences comprising the rest of their educational program. Our two traditions doubt that the study of life, the world and human thought can be fully enriching and complete without awareness that these are to be understood in the context of God's law, God's purposes and God's love, and without recognition that the people of God have the responsibility to proclaim the kingdom of God in all areas of human existence, including education. We are untrue to our theological traditions if we fail to show our children how faith can be integrated into their everyday lives.

Public schools have been the ground on which intense political and legal debates regarding church and state have taken place. These debates concern prayer in public schools, teaching about religion in public schools, the access of religious groups to public school facilities and the rights of public schools to provide sex education and so-called values clarification. While there is not much vocal opposition to prayer in public schools from our churches, there is not much positive enthusiasm for the idea either. Too many Catholic adults recall readings from a "Protestant" Bible and the recitation of "Protestant" prayers; too many Presbyterian/Reformed Christians fear the inroads of fundamentalism.

Teaching about religion in public schools is a new phenomenon in the United States. Our concern is the manner in which it is done: The presentation should be as accurate and objective as possible, without giving the impression that religion is irrelevant or outdated, while not promoting any one religious perspective. The question of the access of religious groups to public school facilities depends on the circumstances of use (time, nature of the activity, etc.). Here our discussion tended to divide on familiar grounds, with Catholics arguing that justice required such access to all taxpayers, and Presbyterian/Reformed participants expressing caution about entanglement and state promotion of religion.

The right of public schools to provide sex education is accepted (with some reservation) by both traditions. The reservation is that this sex education be positive, accurate and prudent, guided throughout by fundamental ethical principles necessary to the formation of personal responsibility and viable relationships in all sexual behavior. Our traditions agree that sex is never, for humans, simply a matter of physiology or even of psychology. We agree that human sexuality involves moral and spiritual values at every point, and that, according to the teachings of both our traditions, sexual activity is to be carried out in the context of stable, loving, monogamous, heterosexual relationships that are sacramental or covenantal in character. Insofar as these perspectives are not allowed or emphasized in sex education courses in the public schools, tension will remain between them and the churches. Catholic and Presbyterian/Reformed Christians disagree among themselves on particular moral judgments regarding sexual matters, but combine in declaring that sexuality is of profound moral significance.

A similar problem arises with regard to "values clarification" or "values education." We agree that it is important to clarify values, but we also agree that the values held by people, once clarified, need to be evaluated. And that requires the recognition and articulation of things that are basically and "objectively" right and good. Neither of our traditions will be satisifed with values clarification which denies the possibility of discussing such ethical matters, as much of current values clarification seems to. Whose values will be taught? Will these values be Christian or religious? Will they be inimical to religion?

Our conversations about church and school have made us aware of our common commitment to education, our differing approaches to church-and-state relationships in the American context and the challenges we share in transmitting religious values to the next generation.

Challenges Ahead

Our conversations on the kingdom-church-state relationship have sharpened our consciousness of the biblical and theological framework we share on these matters. They have also made us aware of the opportunities and responsibilities facing us as committed Christians in the United States who seek to be both good citizens and faithful to our religious commitments.

A. Reflection on our churches' official statements about nuclear warfare has revealed that we can reach similar conclusions on the basis of similar theological underpinnings (about creation, kingdom, church and state) by somewhat different theological emphases (biblical teachings, "just war" criteria) and in different literary forms (the varied and concise Presbyterian/Reformed statements, the massive letter of the U.S. Catholic bishops).

It should also be noted that there is a growing acceptance of non-violent options in Catholic circles similar to non-violent trends in Presbyterian/Reformed churches. In addition, there is a deepening reliance on the biblical tradition within the Catholic community as a whole. On the other hand, there is increasing interest in some Presbyterian/Reformed circles in the interpretation of the classical "just war" theory.

Study of one another's statements on the nuclear issue leads us to offer the following suggestions:

1. Catholic and Presbyterian/Reformed Christians should be encouraged to read one another's official statements on the nuclear issue (and indeed on other issues also). Attention to their differing emphases, methods and literary forms is enlightening and can promote ecumenical understanding.

2. These statements also challenge our churches to reflect on the positive nature of the peace that we seek and perhaps come to a more holistic vision of peace (social, personal, spiritual, etc.).

3. As religious people in the United States, we must make our fellow citizens more conscious of the nuclear danger and find creative ways of influencing the political process toward just peace through global reconciliation.

4. We strongly recommend to our respective denominations that other churches be consulted, their representatives be integrated into the drafting process and that wherever feasible we speak together in joint official statements on peace and other major social issues.

B. Consideration of issues related to education has increased awareness of our common commitment to education. Our theological traditions have impelled us to encourage Christians to embrace education and even to found schools, colleges and universities. In the American context, we share perspectives on certain issues: the right of private schools to exist, the value of religiously oriented people in public schools, the importance of learning about religion, wariness regarding government-authored or government-imposed prayers, etc. Our conversations on the education issue lead us to the following suggestions:

1. The matter of tax relief brings forward deeply felt and powerful attitudes regarding church and state. There is need for proponents of both positions to listen carefully. Presbyterian/Reformed Christians need to understand why American Catholics have been so reluctant to accept the state as the adequate or exclusive provider of education. Catholics need to understand better why Presbyterians/Reformed Christians are so vigilant about government entanglement in religion. Both of us must assess the roots of our differences: Are they theological or historical-sociological? Is change possible?

2. There is also serious need for religious people to reflect across denominational lines on what their participation or non-participation in public schools may mean. The major issues for such reflection include the nature of Christian witness in American society, the kind of religious education needed to supplement, integrate or correct the academic program, the appropriate attitudes toward specific issues (school prayer, access to facilities, sex education, values clarification), and the implications for the larger society, especially for the poor, of any weakening of communal commitment to the welfare of the public schools.

3. In the course of our discussion on the church and state-supported schools, we have recognized the growing power of forces in contemporary American society that directly or indirectly would render religious values and hence religious education peripheral at best to an authentic sense of human existence. This is especially true with respect to those institutions that shape our popular culture. While there is no consensus among us on how best to deal with these disturbing trends (e.g. by improving programs in public schools, increased commitment to church schools, more effective integrative efforts), we are convinced that joint discussions of this critical feature of American public life must continue in earnest in the days ahead.

Conclusion

Our allegiances to church and to state are stressful; they are not divided. We do not see the church as presiding over God's claim on us, while the state is left to manage the affairs of this world. We do not construe the one as inward, the other as outward. We do not yield to either a governance over the other. We believe and we hope in the conformity of ourselves, as individuals and as a people, to the loving rule of God—the kingdom—through the way we live and interact within these two societies.

The United States of America has afforded us Christians almost unprecedented freedom to proclaim our faith, to worship as we choose and to enjoy immunity from civil control or taxation. Our attitude toward the state, however, goes well beyond mere appreciation for this liberty. It is in the public order that we fulfill the Lord's relentless call to feed, house, clothe, heal, defend and, in every needed way, to sustain our sisters and brothers. Our energetic participation in the civil state and its policies and institutions is an indispensable sequel to our love of neighbor for the love of God.

And here arises the stress. It is right, we claim, for us to act as citizens in the political order on the strength of the perspectives and criticisms that our religious faith affords us. Our review of the debate over warfare and nuclear arms has reinforced our conviction that we will not have our religious judgments disallowed in the public forum. It is only as Christians that we properly and fully understand the peace we seek in the civil order. We have not accepted the liberty to believe as we will at the price of cloistering those beliefs in the privacy of the church. We cannot be faithful Americans except as publicly and articulately Christian. And the peace movement has been a particular reminder to us that ecumenical collaboration yields not only political alliances, but a repossessed understanding of Jesus' call that makes us better believers, better citizens.

There is another stress. Precisely because the decisions of state bear so heavily on human welfare which we see to be of eternal significance, and because our American civil government is constrained from submitting to the doctrine of any church, we Christians are inveterately distrustful of yielding much authority to state control in matters of the mind and conscience.

We conclude with a blessed irony. What is most remarkably congenial to the Christian churches in American civil policy is due partly to persons and to philosophies that were hardly Christian. Yet it is only if we are most reflectively and pragmatically Christian that we, in the Catholic and Presbyterian/Reformed churches, will contribute most as American citizens. Thus may we serve the coming of the kingdom.

NATIONAL COUNCIL OF THE CHURCHES OF CHRIST, FAITH AND ORDER DIALOGUE

Introduction

When in 1957 the North American Conference on Faith and Order moved to establish a Commission in the USA and to locate it in the National Council of Churches of Christ, Roman Catholics were present as consultants. Since 1968 they have been full members. The Commission's work has embraced a wide range of topics, including human rights, the ecclesiological significance of Councils of Churches, spirituality in the ecumenical movement, bilateral dialogues, the community of women and men in the Church, the Unification Church, and the highly popular *Living Room Dialogues*.[1]

As examples of three very different types of dialogue, the conciliar fellowship study, the call to dialogue on controversial ethical questions and the reports on a dialogue with the Pentecostal churches have been published here. The World Council of Churches has proposed the model of conciliar fellowship as the vision of visible unity for the churches. Studies on baptism, eucharist and ministry (BEM), and common ways of deciding and acting together are among the necessary elements before such a fellowship "in each place and in every place" can come into existence. The NCC Faith and Order has taken up the BEM document to provide studies to assist the churches.[2]

A third study, "Toward a Common Expression of the Apostolic Faith," explores the bases in faith necessary for such councils.[3] The NCC has also published several explorations in this area.[4] The Pentecostal consultation is reported here.[5] The Secretariat for Promoting Christian Unity has also carried on an extensive dialogue with the Pentecostals.[6]

In addition, the work on sexuality has assisted the study on the application of the Universal Fellowship of Metropolitan Churches for membership in the NCCC.[7]

Notes

1. "The Quest for Christian Consensus: A Study of Bilateral Theological Dialogue in the Ecumenical Movement," *Journal of Ecumenical Studies* 23:3 (1986); Frederick

Borsch, *Coming Together in the Spirit* (Cincinnati: Forward Movement Publications, 1980); Letty Russell, ed., *Changing Contexts of Our Faith* (Philadelphia: Fortress Press, 1985); Lewis Mudge, *The Crumbling Walls* (Philadelphia: The Westminster Press, 1970).

2. *Baptism and Church:* A Believers' Church Vision, Merle D. Strege, ed. (Grand Rapids: Sagamore Books, 1986); Jeffrey Gros, ed., *The Search for Visible Unity* (New York: Pilgrim Press, 1984); "Baptism, Eucharist and Ministry Conference," *Midstream* 25:3 (July, 1986) 322–329.

3. Hans-Georg Link, ed., *Apostolic Faith Today: A Handbook for Study* (Geneva: World Council of Churches, 1985).

4. "Gender and Language in the Creeds," *Union Seminary Quarterly Review* (Vol. 40, No. 3, August 1985); "Toward a Common Expression of Faith: A Black North American Perspective," *Midstream,* Vol. 24, No. 4 (October, 1985), pp. 389–397; Theodore Stylianopoulos and Mark Heim, eds., *Spirit of Truth: Ecumenical Perspectives on the Holy Spirit* (Brookline: Holy Cross Orthodox Press, 1986); *Christ in East and West,* Archbishop Tiran Nersoyan and Paul Fries, eds. (Macon, GA: Mercer University Press, 1987).

5. "Confessing the Apostolic Faith from the Perspective of the Pentecostal Churches," *Pneuma* 9:1 (Spring, 1987); "Confessing the Apostolic Faith from the Perspective of the Pentecostal Churches," *OIC,* Vol. XXIII (1987 #1–2): 61–156.

6. Roman Catholic/Pentecostal Dialogues, *IS* 1974, 25:III, 20; 1975, 27:2, 24; 1975, 28:III, 14; "Final Report of the Dialogue: 1972–1976," 1976, 32:III, 31–36; 1977, 33:I, 22; 1979, 41:IV, 9; 1982, 50:IV, 128; 1985, 57:I, 14; 1986, 62:IV, p. 199; Jerry L. Sandidge, *Roman Catholic/Pentecostal Dialogue (1977–1982): A Study in Developing Ecumenism,* Volumes I and II (Frankfurt: Verlag Peter Lang, 1987).

7. Jeffrey Gros, "The Church, The Churches and the Metropolitan Church," *The Ecumenical Review,* Vol. 36, No. 1 (January 1984), pp. 71–81; "Ecumenical Documents: Report to the Governing Board," *Midstream,* Vol. XXII, Nos. 3 & 4 (July/October, 1983).

A Call to Responsible Ecumenical Debate on Controversial Issues: Abortion and Homosexuality

Prefactory Note:
This document is issued by the Commission on Faith and Order of the National Council of Churches of Christ in the U.S.A. It is a Study Document; it is not a Policy Statement. It is not to be construed as an official statement of attitudes or policies of the National Council.

Concerned as it is with all that disrupts or enhances the oneness of the Church of Jesus Christ, the Commission on Faith and Order of the National Council of Churches has watched with dismay the growing division of Christians on the questions of homosexuality and abortion. It has not viewed the turmoil from a stance of undisturbed inner tranquillity. The same conflicting views on these two issues present in the broader Christian community exist within the Commission's own membership. Hence it has seemed urgent that this Commission, comprising as it does the most inclusive American ecumenical group doing theology for the sake of Christian unity, assist its own members and other Christians in discovering God's will in these thorny matters. While we have formulated these guidelines out of an ecumenical sensitivity which aspires to a more reasonable, more edifying, and more faithful handling of opposing views on homosexuality and abortion, we offer them in the hope that they will apply equally in other issues on which the Christian community is divided, though, of course, we have not tested them in every instance.

The issues of abortion and homosexuality are dividing families, friends, congregations, and communities. Polarized positions on these issues of public policy and personal behavior reflect the absence of a moral consensus in the society and the presence of conflicting moral principles. The issues raise questions about the meaning and value of human life; individual people are affected in their private and public lives. At the same time the issues raise questions about the common welfare and the proper use of law and the political process in preserving the civil order in the midst of moral diversity. It is essential that such issues be discussed publicly and fully. Unfortunately, positions on these issues have become so hardened, emotions so inflamed, reason so confused that careful public debate is very rare. Personal suffering, anger, and fear disrupt human relationships. Intensity of commitment has turned in some cases to violence. Some see every question of the public welfare through the lens of one issue, and the abundance and complexity of life in community is then reduced to a single burning question.

Denominations and individual Christians are part of this conflict. Here, too, there are sets of moral principles which are in tension or opposition. Some of this diversity is simply a reflection of Christian freedom in responding to God's call to us to live according to God's will. But there is also diversity which reflects a deep division among Christians in understanding God's will. The unity of the Church, the Body of Christ, is a gift of God which we are called to live in fact. There is a mutual interdependence of Christians, all born into the same Body through baptism. We are called to "maintain the unity of the Spirit in the bond of peace" (Ephesians 4:3). Denominations and individual Christians are held accountable when division over any issue fractures or tears that Body.

We are now divided on the issues of abortion and homosexuality, as well as on the larger questions of the nature and meaning of human sexuality and responsible relationships among women and men. Indeed this division has already undone some of the ecumenical advances of recent decades and is disrupting life within denominations and congregations. The division reflects some deep differences in our understanding of how we are to be faithful to God's will in and for the world. These differences dare not be ignored. No part of the Body possesses complete and faultless insight into God's will. Dialogue must be established and maintained. The discernment of God's will for human beings and all creation is not a private or parochial task; it is the task of all members of the Church. The dialogue must be carried on across the lines of denominations and differing traditions, lines which all too often act as barriers or entrenchments. The following guidelines for ecumenical debate on controversial issues are offered in the hope that Christian unity may grow and be maintained.

Ecumenical Discussion of Theological and Ethical Differences

1) Christians, by virtue of their unity in baptism, are obliged individually and corporately to discuss and attempt to resolve conflicts of theology and ethics. The lack of widespread and intensive ecumenical discussion on divisive social issues is an offense and stumbling block to the unity of the Church; it weakens the announcement and inhibits the acceptance of the Gospel of Jesus Christ.

2) There are significant differences among Christians in their understanding of God, the whole creation, and the moral responsibility of human beings. Christians must hold each other accountable for the adequacy and appropriateness of their respective understandings to ensure that the debate is grounded in the faith of the community.

a) Such adequacy and appropriateness must always be tested over against these sources: the Scriptures, Christian tradition, philosophical methods and principles, scientific information and principles, and the experience of human beings.
b) Choices are made in selecting the content from each of these sources. In ecumenical discussion the reasons for these choices must be openly acknowledged.
c) Much of the conflict within the Church over issues of social ethics arises when different groups give different weight or interpretation to one of these sources. All too often, however, the debate does not reveal this level; the assumptions remain hidden.
d) The ecumenical discussion must consider the validity and relevance of each of the sources and how each is weighted when conflicts arise.

3) This method of evaluating stances on issues of social ethics would serve to keep the debate open and calls us beyond premature and partial answers to issues of social justice. Fundamental conflicts in our understanding of God's will challenge the illusion of security in firm stances on these issues.

4) Discussion must be carried on by laity and clergy, women and men, young and old, in seminaries and among church leadership. It must be ecumenical, with participants fully informed of the position of their denominations and fully aware as well of their own understanding of God, the creation, and the moral responsibility of human beings.

Public Policy

1) Political activity which seeks to bring the social order into line with ethical convictions based on religious commitment does not violate the separation of church and state. Christians individually and corporately have a right and a responsibility, as do all citizens, to influence public policy by participation in the political process.

2) Political activity and decision are not an appropriate substitute for necessary ecumenical debate on theological differences with social policy implications.

3) When extensive theological and moral differences preclude consensus on issues of public policy, it is unwise for individual Christians and denominations to advocate the closing of debate through restrictive laws.

4) When individual Christians and denominations seek to influence public policy, they have an obligation to examine and make explicit both the religious principles and the principles of reason upon which they base the public policy they advocate. Freedom of religion demands that public policy be based on a consensus of reason, not a consensus of religious principles.

5) Individual Christians and denominations have a responsibility in public policy debates to use language which is a true witness to their own positions and to the positions of opposing parties in the debate. Stereotyped notions and caricatures of people and positions must be avoided.

6) In ecumenical debates over public policy individual Christians and denominations have a responsibility to enable various perspectives on controversial issues to be heard fairly and fully.

7) The determination and protection of civil rights are of utmost importance. Individual Christians and denominations must call the State to account when the rights of citizens are denied or violated.

Some Critical Issues in the Debate over Abortion and Homosexuality

1) In our understanding of individual human beings, how much weight should be given to physical nature and how much to emotional, social, and other characteristics having to do with the personal quality of human relationships? In what way are the sanctity and quality of life related to both?

2) What is a responsible method of interpreting Scripture within

ecumenical debates: How does the Word of God challenge entrenched and competing uses of Scripture in debates on social issues?

3) What sources are appropriate and adequate in determining that a given behavior or attitude is "unnatural"? Is it appropriate that scientific insights and human experience offer correctives to assumptions about Scriptural or traditional understandings of natural law?

4) How do our differing views of nature and grace affect our stances on abortion and homosexuality? With respect to social ethics, in what way is human nature, including reason, affected by sin, and what effect does grace have?

5) How can the experiences of women be constitutive of a more inclusive understanding of the nature of human sexuality? How can we correct the long tradition that masculinity is normative for human nature?

6) Is our understanding of human nature too much a function of scientific definitions?

7) Can we reach agreement on the nature and role of reason in discerning justice in public policy questions? Does reason discern an objective moral order in the universe?

8) What considerations should be taken into account in deciding that an immoral action should also be illegal?

January 1979

Conciliar Fellowship

A Study of the Commission on Faith and Order of the National Council of the Churches of Christ in the U.S.A.

A key topic of the ecumenical movement is the nature and mission of the church. While the churches have not reached a consensus on the basis on which they can accept each other's ordained ministries, there are other topics on which they might move toward consensus. This study explores one such topic. Conciliar fellowship is not, of course, a substitute for consensus on ecclesiology, the nature and mission of the Church. There are further issues of ecclesiology which will not be healed by consensus on conciliar fellowship, or, indeed, the ordained ministry. The Study Group hopes that this brief report will contribute to understanding and consensus among the churches and stimulate further studies on the nature and mission of the Church.

A BRIEF SUMMARY OF THE STUDY

Stimulated by a proposal of the Nairobi Assembly of the World Council of Churches in 1975, the National Council of Churches Commission on Faith and Order initiated a "Study on Conciliarity" in March 1977 to last for four years. The study group's final meeting was in February 1981. The final report was delivered to the entire Commission in November 1981.

A. CONCILIAR FELLOWSHIP AND A UNIVERSAL COUNCIL OF THE CHURCH: THEIR MEANING AND NECESSITY

1. Preliminary Considerations

This report rests on several assumptions of varying importance, a few of which will be discussed here. First, the terms "conciliarity" and "conciliar fellowship," as used in this report, refer explicitly to the Church of Jesus Christ. That is, these terms are essentially *ecclesiological* in reference; they concern the self-understanding of the Church. Elsewhere, such terms may be used in quite different ways. How one comprehends "conciliarity" and "conciliar fellowship" will therefore depend, in large part, on how one understands the Church of Jesus Christ, its nature, and its characteristics. "Conciliarity" is the general concept, of which "conciliar fellowship" is the concrete expression.

In any case, as used in the pertinent documents of the World Council of Churches,[1] "conciliarity" and "conciliar fellowship" are ecclesiological and, therefore, theological terms. They may, and do have quite different meanings in sociology, economics, and psychology, for example. These several meanings are not, of course, mutually exclusive. Indeed, they complement one another, providing a context in which and through which the ecclesiology expressed in the World Council documents may be understood.

Second, "conciliarity" and "conciliar fellowship" refer to the Church of Jesus Christ as "sign and instrument of Christ's mission to all of humankind" (Bangalore, II, A, 14). That is, these terms refer to the *sacramental* and *eschatological* aspects of the Church of Jesus Christ. They have sacramental reference in the widest sense of the word "sacrament" of God. Patently, the word "sacrament" is not being used here in the limited sense of a ritual or liturgical action such as Baptism or Eucharist, but rather in the wider sense of a sign which points to and conveys a reality beyond itself.

Further, "conciliarity" and "conciliar fellowship" concern the apostolic and eschatological character of the Church of Jesus Christ. That is, the words refer to the Church as "being sent," the Church in mission, the Church as sign of God's Kingdom, already established in Jesus Christ, but yet to be achieved in its fullness. The proleptic nature of the Church prevents any complete identification of the Church with the Kingdom of God in the present age, therefore.

Third, "conciliarity" and "conciliar fellowship" refer to the Church of Jesus Christ precisely as *one* and more specifically as *visibly* one. That is, the words refer not to the mere theoretical unity of the Church of Jesus Christ, but to a unity that can be both perceived and experienced by human beings with the aid of their senses. Such visible unity consists in "unity in one faith and in one eucharistic fellowship expressed in worship and in common life in Christ . . . in order that the world may believe" (*Constitution* of the World Council of Churches, Article 3, paragraph 1). Moreover, "the one church is to be envisioned as a conciliar fellowship of local churches which are themselves truly united. . . . " (Fifth Assembly of the World Council of Churches [Nairobi], *Report of Section II,* 3).

Further, such visible unity means that the united churches "will all recognize each other's ministries; they will share the bread and the cup of their Lord: they will acknowledge each other as belonging to the body of Christ at all places and at all times; they will proclaim the Gospel to the world with one mind and purpose; they will serve the needs of humankind with mutual trust and dedication. And for these ends they will plan and decide together in assemblies constituted by authorized representatives whenever this is required" (Bangalore, I, 4). More briefly, the goal toward which the World Council of Churches now points is "unity in conciliar community in one apostolic faith and in one eucharistic fellowship . . . " (Ibid., I, 6). Therefore, "conciliarity" and "conciliar fellowship" are by no means vacuous terms.

2. The Meaning of Council in the Church

In light of these preliminary considerations concerning some of the assumptions and presuppositions underlying the topic of this report, it is possible to proceed toward an exposition of the meaning and the need for conciliar fellowship and a universal council of the Church. The following brief remarks will not attempt to construct a theology of an ecumenical council but will, instead, try to relate "conciliarity," "conciliar fellowship," and "universal council" in reference to the meaning and the need for such a council. First, it is essential to determine as precisely as possible what relationship there is between and among the terms under examination.

Both "conciliarity" and "conciliar" have the Latin noun *concilium* as their basic linguistic root. The Latin verb *conciliare* from which the Latin noun *concilium* is derived means "to call together." *Concilium* is "that which is called together." In the English language, it means, very roughly, an assembly of some kind. Here it is important, for our purposes, to note that the Latin noun *concilium* is not the Latin noun *consilium,* which has an entirely different linguistic base and a quite different meaning. From *consilium* comes the English word "counsel," which has an Indo-European root meaning "to sell" or, derivatively, "to persuade" by means of advice or advocacy. It becomes apparent merely on the basis of linguistics that *concilium* and *consilium* are not the same and do not have the same meaning even in their original forms. For example, one may give "counsel" in a "council," or one may call a "council" in order to receive "counsel."

Words have more than a linguistic history, of course. They also have political, economic, and social histories. In this report, it would be impossible to pursue at length these other aspects of the words *concilium* and *consilium*. Suffice it to say here that the noun *concilium* gradually developed in its meaning and interpretation over a long period of time. By the end of the seventh century of the Christian era, for example, *concilium* had come to mean a representative assembly summoned by an authority vested with the juridical right, indeed duty to convoke such an assembly. By that time in church history, *concilium* meant a representative assembly of local churches convoked on the authority of the emperor to consider doctrinal and disciplinary matters. Representation of the various local churches in the assembly was usually assured through the presence of a bishop from each local church acting in his capacity as leader and teacher. As time passed, the word *concilium* gained still further meanings, nuances, and interpretations, especially after the division of the church between East and West. It is impossible in the confines of this brief report to detail those developments any further.

What is essential to note, however, is that the understanding of *concilium* in the history of the Christian Church has been by no means univocal. In any case, during the early centuries of church history, *concilium* meant the kind of representative and authorized assembly described above. Such formal assemblies of representatives, duly authorized and convoked, traditionally have been called "councils," indeed councils of the Church, assemblies of the Assembly. The words "council," "conciliar," and "conciliarity," therefore, have common origins, both linguistically and historically.

The documents of the World Council of Churches attempt to make that commonality apparent by distinguishing between a council of the church and councils of churches. A council is defined as "a gathering/assembly of official representatives of local churches within a fully united sacramental fellowship" (Bangalore, II, C, 18). Councils of churches, at least as we know them in the modern ecumenical movement, are "not within one fully united sacramental fellowship" and therefore are *not* councils of the Church, although they "display many features of conciliarity" (Ibid., C, 18). The operative difference between a council of the Church and a council of churches appears to lie in the words, "within a fully united sacramental fellowship." That is, the difference lies in the areas of ecclesiology and sacramentology. To note that in Christian history, as well as in our own day, there have been and are several ecclesiologies and sacramentologies between and within the various local churches is merely to indicate the magnitude of the task of further definition and comprehension which still lies ahead.

With the relationship between "conciliarity" and "council" in mind, we can proceed to explicate in more detailed fashion the key text from the World Council Nairobi Assembly: " . . . the one Church is to be envisioned as a conciliar fellowship of local churches which are themselves truly united." What does this statement mean? According to the documents, the local churches, in order to be truly united (which is the will of God revealed in Jesus Christ and evidenced in the Scriptures), "must realize 'a visible unity in one faith and in one eucharistic fellowship, expressed in worship and in common life in Christ'" (*Constitution* of the World Council of Churches, Article III). It is important to note here that, according to the documents, the local churches (however these are defined and described) *must* realize such a visible unity in accord with the will of Jesus Christ. That the churches should seek to realize such a visible unity is not, therefore, a mere option for the local churches.

The basis upon which the local churches will realize such a unity is as follows: "We are bound to this task because we are summoned to it by Jesus Christ. Him we confess as the centre of our lives. Hence, the unity for which he prayed is a central command to us, too. The oneness of mind, the communion *(koinonia)* of the Church with Christ and of Christians with one another is an essential component of the Gospel. Therefore, we dare not regard it as . . . accidental . . . " (Bangalore, I, 6). Moreover, such a visible unity "should take the form of a 'conciliar fellowship' in the sense of a community that is capable of holding an assembly of authorized representatives coming from the different local ('local' referring to various levels of church life and structure) churches within the one church of God" (Bangalore, II, A, 12).

3. The Importance of a Universal Council of the Church

Here it should be noted that the language of the Bangalore document shifts from an imperative ("must") to a conditional ("should"). It might be inferred that such visible unity would not necessarily have to be expressed in the form of a council, although a council evidently is a preferred form for expressing such visible unity. That granted, conciliar fellowship is described in terms of a *community* that would have the *capacity,* the *ability* to convoke "an assembly of authorized representatives" from the different local churches within the One Church. Nothing further is stated in the World Council documents concerning the details of authorization and representation.

The further task of determining authorization will be difficult if only because some of the necessary conditions in the classical model of a council, especially the presence of an emperor, no longer exist or seem likely ever again to exist. The further task of determining representation will also be arduous if only because modern consciousness has been expanded by the experience of political democracy and has been heightened by greater sensitivity to human rights, the rights of minorities, the needs of the impoverished and alienated, and the legitimate demands of women, to cite only a few examples.

Nonetheless, a visibly united church would find itself in a situation in which it would be at least possible, although not absolutely necessary, to hold such a representative and authorized assembly. The preliminary conditions for holding a council would exist, precisely because the church would be united in one faith and one eucharistic fellowship which would find expression both in worship and in a common life in Christ. Such an assembly would, of course, be recognized as a universal council of the Church through the assent of the entire people of God. Indeed, an authentic council has a special role in bringing about such assent. By subsequent reception, moreover, the entire Church would affirm that a council has safeguarded the truth of the Gospel. The mechanics and details of the process of assent, affirmation, and reception, of course, await further exploration and explanation.

The importance of a council for the One Church is that both the possibility of a council and its actual occurrence would constitute a fulfillment of the Church's nature as universal sign and instrument of Christ's mission to the world: "The Church, by its very nature, is a sign of Christ's mission to all humankind" (Bangalore, II, A, 14). In other words, a universal council would be a function and a reflection of the Church's sacramental character in the sense of being a revelatory sign and instrument of God's will for humanity shown to us in Jesus Christ and through the Holy Spirit. Although it is not explicitly stated as such in the World Council documents, a universal council of the united Church would be one of the possible ways by which the Church could express its sacramental character in a universal manner.

Conciliarity would, of course, be expressed locally and regionally as well. Indeed, universal conciliarity would be a reflection and expression of local and regional conciliarity. Exactly how and by what means local and regional conciliarity would be expressed in the concrete is uncertain for now and will require further exploration. Apparently, such concrete local and regional expression would incorporate the content described for "conciliarity" and "conciliar fellowship" for universal conciliarity, namely, unity in a common faith, common recognition of members, mutual recognition of ministries, common celebration of the Eucharist, common mission, the ability to plan and to decide together in assemblies that are both duly authorized and truly representative. To achieve those realities would also be to achieve "conciliar fellowhsip," a not inconsiderable task. That is why "conciliar fellowship" is both a *goal* and a *process*.

"Conciliar fellowship" achieved in the mode of a universal council of the Church would demand more than the convocation of representatives from the local churches for the sole purpose of gathering together, a considerable achievement in itself. These are some of the functions which a universal council of the Church might perform:

- foster the unity of faith and the unity of communion within the Church itself;
- consider matters that appear to threaten doctrinal integrity and disciplinary order, at the same time as it respects personal freedom and legitimate diversity;
- promote the shaping and sharing of Christian values in the world;
- listen to the cry of the world and speak to the world compassionately about justice, peace, truth and humanity;
- insure that the Church, which is continually in need of reform, would continue to be an authentic sign and instrument of Christ's mission to the world;
- remind the Church that there is a relationship between the unity of the Church and the unity of humankind in the Kingdom of God, already present but yet to be fulfilled.

The goal of "full, visible unity in conciliar community" is thus a present challenge to all Christians: "The choice laid before us is whether we should continue to obscure the sign by remaining divided and fragmented people or whether we should clearly exhibit the sign as a people of God united in mutual forgiving and reconciliation and thus begin to represent that new humanity which Christ has inaugurated and which he will complete when his Kingdom comes" (Bangalore, II, A, 14). And again, "to be a sign and instrument is one way of expressing our common calling to be faithful stewards of God's gifts *(charismata)* so that the world may believe" (Bangalore, II, A, 15). A council of a united church, beyond and besides its practical purposes, would be a radical, faithful, and traditional way by which the Church might express itself as a sign to the nations of God's will once revealed in Jesus Christ and now continued through the Holy Spirit.

B. A UNIVERSAL COUNCIL OF THE CHURCH CREATING THE CONDITIONS THROUGH CONCILIAR FELLOWSHIP

The World Council of Churches' Assembly at Uppsala, 1968, proposed "a genuinely universal council" as the goal of the ecumenical movement.[1] This has been widely discussed and has gained support among member and non-member churches. The Assembly at Nairobi, 1975, further urged consideration of the concept "conciliarity" and "conciliar fellowship" as a guide to making visible the unity of the Church. The Assembly at Vancouver, 1983, may further contribute to the topic. Although the World Council, like other inter-church consultative bodies and assemblies, is not a church and should not be confused with a council of the Church, it can have a positive influence on the development of historical forms of conciliar life in individual churches or between churches.

Together with regional and national councils, the World Council needs to help the churches, including the Roman Catholic Church and other non-member bodies, to create the conditions in which a genuinely universal council of the Church may be able to lead the way into the future. The presence of the conditions would signify that the World Council had successfully fulfilled its purpose and should give way to new forms of Christian unity. The organizational forms of developing Christian unity are the responsibility of the churches themselves, depending on direct agreements between them.

Before any decisive reconciliation and unity, the churches themselves could convene or form a general Christian conference to be a sign of the unity achieved while simultaneously serving as a preparatory commission for the convening of a pre-council or a council. The council would be the responsibility and right of the Church itself—the One, Holy, Catholic and Apostolic Church—in which all Christians or the majority of Christians would be reconciled and liberated for the future.

Preparation of conditions for a universal council of the Church involves four things:[2]

Ending prejudices and hostilities;

Sharing one faith which includes both overcoming the anathemas of the past and finding ways of confessing together the apostolic faith;

Accepting, on the basis of agreed understanding, each other's celebration of baptism and the eucharist and the ordained ministry;

Agreeing on ways of deciding and acting together.

Creating of these conditions is not purely a future event; in varying degrees they are already present.

1. Ending Prejudices and Hostilities

The most awesome sign of the Holy Spirit's acitivity in the ecumenical movement is the decline of prejudices and hostilities between Christians of different traditions. We were enemies who failed to obey one of the most challenging precepts of the Gospel, namely to love our enemy, and went further in sanctifying our hostilities as loyalty to Jesus Christ. The pressures of meeting to pray, learn, and work together are replacing hostilities with attitudes of love. Closer acquaintance is destroying prejudices and leading to stronger affections. Increased commitment to removing the causes is needed if the first condition of a universal council is to be fulfilled.

The causes of prejudices and hostilities have to do with the question, who can claim the Christian symbols? Symbols are bound up with peoples' sense of meaning and their relation to the community. The churches are discovering that in spite of separations the Spirit of God kept in each one many of the same essential features. Yet the common features that we discover in our traditions cannot remain only the subject of official declarations. Even if the agreed statements of joint commissions are accepted by authorities of our communions, we shall not be ready for full unity. Centuries of division cannot be superseded in a few years and cannot be resolved only by decision of authorities. Even if consciousness on the necessity of real communion between the churches and the desire to build it up are growing, a premature claim to accomplishment of full unity would be either too political or too superficial to be the unity God desires.

We rightly speak of unity by stages. In view of the actual situation, the first stage is coming together in the Holy Spirit. There will be true reconciliation and full unity only when they are spiritually prepared and received. This spiritual and mystical dimension of unity is realized when in each community—and in each person—there is real reconciliation. This is not something added to the normal Christian life; it belongs to the deepest level of the life with Christ and stems from it. Only the Spirit of God can reconcile, but the Spirit will not do it without our wholehearted quest for unity.

A people proposing reconciliation among all women and men while not earnestly seeking reconciliation and unity between all Christians will increasingly be a scandal and spectacle to the world. As we see more clearly the essential links between the unity and the mission of the Church, we go beyond any superficial understanding of ecumenism as an optional exercise in ecclesiastical relationships. The Church has to offer people the community to live as sisters and brothers, able to praise God together and to commit themselves in common service.

Reconciliation coming from God is made visible when all who are baptized and confess Jesus Christ as Lord and Savior devote themselves "to the apostles' teaching and fellowship, to the breaking of bread and the prayers" (Acts 2:42). The apostle declares that God sent his Son to break down the wall of separation. "And all who believed were together and had all things in common" (Acts 3:44). The heart of evangelical life is the law of a mutual love stemming from the forgiveness of the trespasses and wrongs. Christian love is nourished by the constant forgiveness of offenses, because it is the fruit in us of the love of Christ, who came down in order to reconcile humankind in one body through the cross. Without forgiveness, Christian love cannot exist; without love, Christianity loses its identity.

This is a serious responsibility. Christians are not only to receive the gift of reconciliation from Christ. They are to transform their attitudes and their relationships in such a way that they too become, through Christ and in Christ, agents of the reconciliation coming from God (John 11:52). On the spiritual state of Christians depends the health and proper functioning of the entire body of the Church. Here is the link between the unity of the church and moral striving. This was understood by John Chrysostom in the early church: "The ship of the Church is rocked by constant storms; apart from being encountered without, these storms also arise within and demand great care and attention. . . . "

Consciousness of catholicity is linked with the awakening responsibility and activity of every member of the Church. Catholicity is the voice and conscience of the whole of the Church, freely and unitedly solving problems in the spirit of love and respect for one another, in full obedience to the truth in Jesus Christ, in full obedience to the Holy Spirit, who lives and acts in the Church and directs its conciliar mind and will. It is indispensable for Christians to develop awareness of their responsiblity before God and their neighbor for their Christian vocation, for deeds of justice, peace, and love performed in the name of Christ. This in itself will lead to increasing fellowship in the One, Holy, Catholic, and Apostolic Church, to the restoration and consolidation of essential elements of a truly Christian life. This unity is built up through faith in Christ.

2. Sharing One Faith which Includes both Overcoming the Anathemas of the Past and Finding Ways of Confessing Together the Apostolic Faith

The Holy Spirit leads people to confess Jesus Christ as Lord and Savior. The gifts of the Spirit, given to women and men of all races, nations, and social classes, build up the body in unity. The Spirit, who thus calls the Church into being and leads the pilgrim people of God into the future, is the same Spirit who, in continuity with the apostles and their teaching, guides the Church into all truth (John 16:13).

The divine initiative needs to be stressed in our particular culture, where attention is focused on individual human options. Sharing one faith is not to be reduced simply to an individual identity with Jesus Christ nor simply to a formal act of baptism or creedal affirmation. Baptism with confession of faith is initiation into the Church, the community of discipleship following the way of Jesus the suffering servant, and establishes a new quality of life (Rom. 6:3–4). The lived community of faith reflects the Triune God to whom the ancient creeds bear witness and the "basis" of the World Council reflects:

> The World Council of Churches is a fellowship of churches which confess the Lord Jesus Christ as God and Saviour according to the Scriptures and therefore seek to fulfill together their common calling to the glory of the one God, Father, Son, and Holy Spirit.[3]

Only in recent history has the Church come face to face with the dilemma of religious liberty and pluralism. This is the context in which we understand the problem of agreement between the churches as well as agreement within churches. Recently the churches have been seeking to share one faith through a complex of multilateral and bilateral dialogues. They seek ways to overcome the doctrinal divisions and condemnations of the past and at the same time to articulate the apostolic faith in language understood in our time and situation. Significant progess can be seen in the transition from an earlier period of comparative study of questions essential for the achievement of unity to the present period of elaboration of consensus in agreed statements. Attempts to implement these statements in the churches' liturgical and canonical life are encountering difficulties, which give rise to caution, procrastination, and irresolution. The present situation, however, is not cause for pessimism, as it may be a necessary gathering of strength before the transition from theological discourse and agreement to mutual forgiveness, practical conclusions, and application in the churches.

Moreover, churches are seeking to share one faith with the peoples of the world. By seeking to interpret the meaning of faith in Jesus Christ and in God's acts in history, Christians are learning more about God. The event of Jesus Christ has deep meanings which have to be unfolded and expressed in every culture for every time and place. These expressions are tested by what we know of Jesus and the apostles' teaching in Scripture.

Unity in faith is not necessarily the same as uniform expression of faith. When it is clear that Christians profess the same faith, there is room for different visible expressions of that faith. Indeed, a vital aspect of conciliar fellowship and a universal council would be to share the diverse faith resources of African, Latin American, North American, Asian, and European churches. Nevertheless, agreements between separated churches are required on what they understand to be essential to unity. When such agreements are affirmed or adopted, they may be used to overcome anathemas of the past, for catechetical instruction, and for future reference, but they will not themselves be creeds or confessions of faith. When communion is reestablished by the churches, they may turn to problems continually arising from without and from within. Common praise and prayer will then be the context of confessing together the apostolic faith.

3. Accepting, on the Basis of Agreed Understanding, Each Other's Celebration of Baptism and the Eucharist and the Ordained Ministry

Baptism is basic to any discussion about conditions for a universal council. A common understanding of baptism and the process of Christian initiation, including confirmation, has been growing. Moreover, many churches have acted to implement acceptance of other churches' baptism, notably churches participating in the Consultation on Church Union. Even where baptisms have been accepted, however, the consequences of this step are variously understood and need further study, for the act of Christian initiation is not generally viewed apart from a process of nurture and growth in particular traditions or churches. Many other churches, of course, practice only believers' or adult baptism and may or may not recognize other baptisms. The charismatic movement, moreover, raises questions about the relation of baptism of water and baptism of the Spirit.

A common understanding of the eucharist has grown also, but here again, differences remain. Even agreement on eucharistic doctrine may not result in full eucharistic communion between churches. For some, there can be communion only within the one Church, and for this it is necesary that there be agreement in essentials of faith and order. For others the eucharist expresses not only oneness of the Church in faith and life but also the gathering of the people of God, so it is legitimate to share the sacrament before full agreement in faith and order.

This difference calls for deeper study and reflection. The way to unity is not merely to overcome different theological formulas on the eucharist and other issues which have divided Christianity, replacing them with new formulas which are themselves incapable of leading to full unity. Participation in the sacrament establishes a mysterious relationship between the Christian and God, what the apostle means when he speaks of life in Christ Jesus (I Cor. 1:9), and a new mysterious relationship among Christians themselves, a people united in the unity of the Trinity. The eucharist is even now a sign and means of unity in the life of each separate communion and potentially of the communions together.

While there is growing agreement that the eucharist (word-sacrament) is the central, regular expression of the common life of the church, and while there are encouraging trends toward its more frequent celebration, there is discontinuity between theological agreements about its centrality and the practice of the churches. In many places it is still celebrated quarterly and the focus of worship is the sermon. This may lead to over-reliance on verbal formulation, with the result that the experience of grace, which is not limited to verbal formulation, may sometimes be suppressed. All of this suggests there is confusion about eucharistic theology and practice. Perhaps the greatest sign of confusion is that the practice of churches which offer the hospitality of the Lord's Table to persons from other churches not in full communion (usually with carefully regulated conditions) is seen by some as promoting reconciliation between churches seeking to overcome their differences, and by others as obscuring the nature of the sacrament. The question is, what is implied by sharing the Eucharist? What are the demands of God's gift?

Various bilateral and multilateral dialogues have considered how the separate ordained ministries might be reconciled. A common understanding has begun to appear on such matters as the link between baptism and the general and ordained ministry, the importance of continuity of ordained ministry for unity of the Church, and recognition of a threefold ordained ministry. By and large, however, the churches have not yet fully accepted one another's ministries. To be sure, there are levels of mutual acceptance, but most do not include reciprocal exercise of ministry. None necessarily implies a denial of the efficacy of other ordained ministries as instruments used by the Holy Spirit. Recently within certain communions not all members recognize as ordained ministers all who have been ordained in their church. Even when one church does fully accept the ordained ministry of another and proceeds to authorize the exercise of the other's ministers in its own body, there remain pastoral and practical questions of responsibility, placement, pensions, etc.

The full acceptance of ordained ministries has taken place or could take place in several ways according to circumstances: (1) Some church unions have entailed a mutual laying-on of hands of bishops and other ministers elected to be bishops. (2) Some church unions provided for a mutual declaration of acceptance of ordained ministries. (3) Acceptance of ministries has been declared and implemented when two Christian world communions agreed and appropriate authorities within them affirmed full communion. (4) Acceptance could take place at the assembly of a universal council.

4. Agreeing on Ways of Deciding and Acting Together

Centuries after our historic divisions occurred, when many of the factors responsible for them no longer apply, a universal council is becoming a possibility. The matter at stake is not merely a federation of churches nor an administrative merger of denominations nor even unity of action in some field or other, but genuine union of Christians in the Church, which, as the Body of Christ, represents our union in Christ. Particular united churches through their experience are among the forces fostering the desire for such union. There are many serious obstacles in the way of such sacramental union, but a major one is surely disagreement on the teaching regarding the Church itself. Without a common understanding of the nature, notes, authority, and mission of the Church, there will be no genuine visible unity. At the same time, we learn more about the Church in the struggle for visible unity and in working together.

Conciliarity must not be narrowed down to the concept of a system of administration and ecclesiastical communion. It is not simply discussion of all the most important questions at ecumenical or local councils. It does not mean establishing permanent councils. It is not identical with a collection of councils to which functions are assigned and powers delegated. Conciliarity is rather the profoundly organic result of the conciliar self-awareness of the people of the Church. Conciliarity is the genuine catholicity which develops from the participation in the fullness of church life and this gives rise to conciliar forms of administration and renewal. As a sign, conciliarity is an expression and manifestation of the communion that is required between and among local churches. At the same time it is a chief means for sustaining and deepening that communion. Through the gathering of all the local churches, the common mind of the Church, guided by the Holy Spirit, resolves at every historical moment when it is necessary the most important doctrinal questions and implements the apostolic testimony: "For it seemed good to the Holy Spirit and to us" (Acts 15:28).

While there has been speculation as well as some experience, it is impossible to know the forms to which the growth of conciliar self-awareness will lead. A major problem is the understanding of the local church, sometimes perceived as congregation, sometimes a special ministry, sometimes a diocese, sometimes a grouping of these in a nation or region. We conclude: (1) The local church embraces a rich diversity of types and sizes in both a geographical and existential sense. (2) No present manifestation of the local church is either necessarily expendable or always immutable. (3) The condition and quality of the fullness of catholicity are intended to be realized by local churches of all varieties.

We also conclude that all centers, zones, or levels of the Church are to provide for day-to-day mutual care, support, and responsibility. The modern words "interdependence" and "interrelationship" best convey this aspect of conciliarity. Even as the churches maintain and develop their particular traditions or heritages, they will require recognized organs of regular periodic communion, consultation, and communication to express and renew the unity of the Church and to enable common action. Additionally, it should be possible to call extraordinary gatherings, local councils of persons responsible for their "flocks" nationally or regionally, for a particular need or purpose.

Given the realities of our present situation in the United States, of numerous parishes, ministries, jurisdictions, it is impossible blindly to apply formulae which come from another time and age. A new, workable, and practical solution must be found which respects the tradition of the unity of the church in each place, but at the same time, does not ignore the real pastoral and cultural needs of the various jurisdictions. Further, the historic relationship of American churches with several Christian world communions must somehow be respected, even while the responsibility of the local church to deal with its own problems and issues is embodied in new conciliar forms.

A related problem is the understanding of the "universal" Church, the unity of all the "local" churches, sometimes perceived as a communion of national or regional churches, sometimes as a communion of communions proceeding from historic "types" of Christianity, sometimes as a communion of communions with the successor of Peter presiding. It is difficult even to conceive of a "universal" Church which does not gather universally when it is needed. Again, the "universal" Church will need regular periodic communion, consultation, and communication between global structures to enable collegiality, though central direction in matters of detail that should be decided locally would not be understood or welcomed. Additionally, councils of the universal Church as exceptional or prophetic events could be called for a particular need or purpose. They would be assemblies of authorized representatives of local churches called for some definite purposes, not simply to speculate or have a council. It may be doubted whether any formal definition of a universal council, using former models, is possible. It may also be doubted whether a council can be guaranteed to have authority before it occurs and without testing its results.

At the deepest level, authority is the ability to mediate to others what has been accomplished in such a way that they can intelligently and freely choose to unite themselves to that accomplishment. In the flesh Jesus Christ opened the way to eternal life, which He wishes each human to enter, but each human must be presented with this life so that he or she can choose it. He gave the ability to do that to his disciples, who manifest this divine presence in human life through the many gifts the Spirit pours out, each its own kind of authority, each a way of mediating life in Christ. It is this kind of authority, mediating Christ's risen life, which a true universal council transmits, and is received by the people of the Church.

Finally, what is to be the attitude in the Church to differences of various kinds? How do we appropriate the gifts of all for all? Within churches differentiation is vitally important and yet difficult to achieve. It tends to be either unduly subordinate to unity or else stressed in such a way as to disrupt unity. Neither unity nor differentiation should be neglected, for each is complementary and essential to the other. One needs to be able to handle disagreement without denying it is there, or there may be pressure to conformity, which is an attempt to deny that there are any such differences. Or there may be expulsion or voluntary separation, which mark the regretful acknowledgment that differences have not been resolved.

There may, of course, be differences that are fundamentally incompatible with unity, but even so, we have not begun to realize the full meaning of unity in diversity. The Church is ever newly presented with theological issues of justice and peace from without as well as within, locally as well as universally. Issues of work, family life, community, politics are all part of the Church's mission to build the kingdom. Reckoning with such issues, the local churches and the universal Church are to reflect the Christian understanding of God as personal and as love, which imply relationships. While exercising this mission of reconciliation and liberation, Christians today, like the unsaintly saints at Corinth, are called to maintain the Temple in unity, free from destructive rivalries, hostile parties, and divisive sects which drive out the Spirit, and yet serve one another's nature, situation, resources, aspirations, and needs.

What we seek is visible unity, but it must be truly the manifestation of unity, not the mere semblance of it. The appearance of unity may or may not express the truth of a situation. We must not forget our differences, we must not neglect or minimize our concern for differentiation, since without it genuine unity cannot be achieved. For God is one, not as a rationalist might conceive of oneness, a monad, but as revealed to us, the Trinity one and undivided. The common goal, for which all are responsible, is the kingdom of God, the promise and call to restore all people to unity with God and each other in Christ.

C. THE AMERICAN WAY OF LIFE, CONCILIAR FELLOWSHIP, AND A UNIVERSAL COUNCIL

The increasing realization of conciliar fellowship and the hope for a truly universal council of the Church would be affected by the differentiations peculiar to the Christians of a given nation. It is within that basic assumption that we attempt to look at a few of the prominent features of the "American Way of Life" that might condition the readiness or unreadiness of United States Christians to participate in a universal council. This brief analysis may help us see in bolder relief the assets and liabilities of the United States Christian community in relation to the four conditions listed in Chapter II (B).

1. A Brief Analysis.

a. A Nation of Nations

A fundamental reality of the United States is its extraordinary heterogeneity. With the possible exception of Brazil, no country has a national population that can trace lines of origin to all other areas and religions of the planet. In spite of powerful nativist pressures toward a melting pot policy, and despite the amazing assimilative power of the mechanisms of Americanization (language, work ethic, patriotism, national symbols, intermarriage, cultural religion, etc.), national origins have not been homogenized and ties are strong with many nations. The ethnic and racial consciousness movements of the last two decades and continuing immigration have in fact stimulated interest in national and ethnic origins, a phenomenon more inclusive than generally recognized.

The phenomenon is ambiguous, of course. Despite much civil rights legislation, the farther away one's community is from the white, male, Protestant, dominant group, the greater the social and economic liabilities are likely to be. We may sing hymns of praise to our cosmopolitanism or to the ideal of "E Pluribus Unum" ("out of the many one"), but the fact remains that worship is still one of the most segregated aspects of our national life.

Still the prospects are tantalizing. Precisely because of this diversity and the incalculable enrichment which it has brought to the nation, especially in the humanities, this nation of nations is a natural laboratory for conciliar fellowship and for testing the conditions of a universal council.

b. Religious Vitality

A fact that is often startling to Christians from abroad for whom the United States represents a dynamo of materialism and secularization, is the amazing vitality of American religion. By comparison, United States church attendance dwarfs that of the countries of Europe. Latin America also registers considerably lower *regular* attendance at public worship than in the United States. Recent studies on U.S. unchurched population reflect a remarkable phenomenon. The sixty or so million designated by this classification do not significantly differ in their beliefs from their churched counterparts. They are rightly called, therefore, "those who believe but do not belong." For them, basic Christian doctrine and institutional religion do not necessarily go together. They can exist independently of each other.

It would be an oversimplification to equate such widespread religion with culture or civil religion. For the religion of churched and unchurched is marked by a specifically Christian set of beliefs: God as Creator, Jesus Christ as Savior, the need for conversion, life beyond death, Christ's resurrection, the Bible as God's Word, etc. If anything, one might say that there is in the U.S., in and out of the churches, something of an "ecumenical" faith, perhaps of the least common denominator, but possibly more substantial.

c. Civil or Culture Religion

However one defines these terms, there is a core of beliefs of Judaeo-Christian (and Enlightenment) extraction that rally millions around their loyalty to the nation. As Robert Bellah and many others contend, this has positive signficance when it makes the country accountable to a higher criterion than itself.[1] The pledge of allegiance to the U.S. flag best illustrates this kind of religion. Much cooperation in humanitarian endeavors can be elicited by it. Indeed, much that passes for ecumenical cooperation stems more from such sort of religion than from orthodox classical faith.

d. The Principle of Voluntary Association

Deep in the U.S. psyche is the libertarian principle that one associates for the sake of self-interest. This is true when one seeks to protect the tenets of religious orthodoxy, or when one joins a group to enjoy common status and kindred values, or when one links up with others to combat the enemies of community morality or national security.

Self-interest does not exclude authority or even authoritarianism, so long as the libertarian threshold of the individual is not violated. Cults or any other kind of high-intensity religion capitalize on collectivized self-interest (a new beginning for the person within a community of kindred seekers, plus notions of saving others, even the world). But the moment authority is perceived as narrowing, not enhancing, self-interest, the time has come to leave, to be a believer in another association, or simply to keep on believing without belonging. Sociologically, this has much to say about church polity. Where laity and clergy share not only tasks but also authority, the long-range coherence of the religious group is greatly enhanced, and its capacity for good works and cooperation with others can lead to a definite sense of enlightened self-interest. Theologically speaking, sharing of this kind has enough resemblance with Christian notions of freedom for community that it may transmute self-interest into life for others, a beatitude high in the hierarchy of Christian spiritual formation.

e. Transdenominational Communities

Another version of voluntary association with characteristics of enlightened self-interest or freedom for community, is the phenomenon of Christian and trans-Christian affinity groups which for experiential and religious reasons transcend confessional lines. Prime examples are ethnic and racial movements, the feminist movement, the charismatic fellowships, and large associations gathered around issues of justice and peace. Some combine Christian orthodoxy together with Christian orthopraxis, without abandoning a continuing sacramental relationship with the religious traditions represented among them. In such instances we have an ecumenical authenticity among Christians which far outstrips the shy ecumenism of still divided ecclesial communities.

f. Entrepreneurial Denominationalism

Sociologists of knowledge have taught us the high correlation between modes of association and modes of economics and political organization. In a society such as ours where success is largely determined by competition and attainment, it should not surprise us to see denominations busy at competing and out-attaining. It may be too much to speak of salvation by numbers, but it is not too much to speak of justification by statistics. In a society so full of religion, the market is too tempting not to verify denominational strength by numbers. Only in America could the Church Growth Movement develop into serious ecclesiological theory and practice. Why should denominations seek heterogeneity when market research amply documents that growth is closely related to homogeneous groupings, among other things? Why should related denominations unite when by the very fact of uniting competition is lessened? Why unity when denominations are thriving? At this point it is not inappropriate to reflect on the danger faced by homogeneous transconfessional groups. While they avoid competitive denominationalism, they may produce a paradoxical "ecumenical sectarianism."

g. A People on the Move

One out of five U.S. families moves in the course of a calendar year; some of them overseas. It is by no means the case that in the new community the family will join a church of the same denomination. Factors such as proximity, homogeneity, music, or preaching will probably determine the choice of a new congregation. Except for those within the "catholic" side of the Christian spectrum, the others will experience little or no disruption in the ecclesial shift. Is this ecumenism by default? People experienced in this kind of church mobility wonder what all the ecumenical fuss is about. Before one dismisses them as cafeteria-style Christians or followers of a culture religion, one should ask if perhaps there is something deeper here.

At the level of the congregation, many mainline Protestant believers have hardly been pressed to adhere to a distinctive denominational theology or mode of worship. Even curriculum materials used in Sunday Schools have been more emphatic on Bible study, classical beliefs and basic Christian ethics than differentiation according to this or that tradition. Meanwhile, also, theological seminaries have been training pastors in common Protestant doctrine and pastoral skills rather than in distinctly denominational practices. Hence, congregants can easily cross denominational lines when they move with a minimum of discontinuity. We seem to have here a kind of *sensus fidei* which, while not profound, may nevertheless qualify as basic for Christian understanding and action. Do we not perceive, therefore, in such mobility potential for an ecumenical foundation to build on, or at least for the lessening of competitive denominationalism?

h. Optimism and Hope

Few nations in the history of humankind have been more devoted to the mythology of progress than the United States. The nation was born at the intersection of an optimistic Enlightenment and the opening up of a vast new continent. Until Vietnam and Watergate, the country mistakenly perceived itself as going from one experience of success to another. The ugly reality of racism was ignored. Even the wrenching tragedy of the War Between the States seemed to confirm its power to transcend the impossible. Its military and economic conquests propelled it to the status of the world's greatest power. An article of the American creed was that all problems were capable of solution. A corollary article was that that which works is true and dependable. The nation thought of itself as proof that such a faith works, hence its missionary fervor in trying to recast the whole of humanity in some facsimile of itself.

Vietnam, Watergate, Teheran, and Afghanistan, plus captivity to

OPEC, have rudely shaken American optimism. Optimism is based on success upon success. Hope, on the other hand, is confidence in spite of failure. Ours is not a hopeful nation, but it continues to be confident by a resolve to make its reversals temporary. The only way it has found to do that is by cranking itself into a position of greater power. But calling ourselves a "nation under God," power must be exercised with the legitimation of religion. The 1980 presidential election is a case in point. *Excélsior,* Mexico City's largest daily, summarized the election in this heading, "The United States Chooses Power: Reagan Is Elected."

The conjunction of power and religion often leads to the prostitution of both. But there is that accountability to a higher Power. A wise understanding of power "under God," might yet teach the reversal from optimism to hope. For some, that was the lesson of Vietnam, Iran, and Nicaragua.

The years ahead might become the occasion for millions of U.S. Christians to probe more deeply into the responsibility of national power in relation to other nations. The ecumenical movement in the United States has an unparalleled opportunity to speak prophetically, to act humbly, and to show its patriotism by not demanding of the nation what it cannot provide: ultimate security. G.K. Chesterton characterizes the United States as "the nation with the soul of a church." There lies the dilemma: either the idolatry of the nation or the subservience of the nation to the will of God who favors the humble, the repentant, and the self-giving.

2. Looking at the Conditions for a Universal Council

a. Ending Prejudices and Hostilities

The extraordinary diversity which characterizes our nation of nations can result in opposite outcomes: deepening of prejudice or learning understanding. We wish to expand our world but we fear the unknown. After the significant legislative and societal changes of the last two decades, few Americans can plead ignorance about those from whom they differ as to color, status, sex, politics, and even religion. If we continue to be hostile to the "others," our sins are more persistent than we assumed. Sins we commit as individuals are of course to be acknowledged. But greater sins are committed because of the basic principle of competitiveness built into the very core of all our institutions. The "American Way" has developed noble traditions of humanitarianism but they have not been enough to override the logic of a system in which the very definition of success is winning at the expense of someone else's loss.

Religion comes from the Latin *re-ligare,* to bind back. Reconciliation, the heart of Christian living, is that kind of religion that binds *after removing the causes of conflict.* Only cynics would deny the gains made in transcending divisions of confession, race, and sex in many of our relationships as American Christians in recent years. The gains, however, because of their modesty and their human cost, impel us to recognize two things: that we have much farther to go, but also that we have enough positive experiences amidst our heterogeneity to be more confident about the future. Perhaps in the future our greatest *intra*-Christian conflict will be over moral issues, including the economic and political. Perhaps that will unmask to what extent what we think is theological is ultimately ideological. But that, too, can be faced with confidence. The Gospel carries with it the power not only to denounce but also to announce. As a nation we need to hear the announcement that our hope is not in power but in justice. We should be grateful that among the carriers of that announcement are our own abused Christians speaking for themselves and for the millions throughout the world who would rather become our companions than our foes or our victims.

b. Sharing One Faith which Includes both Overcoming the Anathemas of the Past and Finding Ways of Confessing Together the Apostolic Faith

Groups who fanatically exclude all others from Christian fellowship on the basis of arcane biblical interpretations and commercialize their position are inevitable in a climate of entrepreneurial religion. They are in the United States one equivalent to the ancient pronouncers of anathemas. Another, no less subtle or powerful, is the sectarian spirit present in highly politicized Christian groups who judge others by an orthodoxy of a narrow ethics or a religion of national security on the basis of biblical sanctions. Confessing together the apostolic faith is not just maintaining fidelity to ancient scripture and tradition but also joining in the full catholicity of Christian wisdom emanating from the Holy Spirit in all Christian communities in all continents. Only such a catholic faith can free Christ's Church from narrow loyalties and grant to it the riches of a pluralistic dialogue between dominant and formerly excluded voices.

Again, though our U.S. record may be unimpressive, our situation is of such extreme differentiation as to test the integrity of our oft-repeated commitment to unity in diversity. In this regard American feminist, Black, and ethnic theologians put us on the cutting edge of the quest for confessing in authentic pluralism the faith of the one Church of Jesus Christ. Both our accomplishments and failures should be seen as a contribution to a universal council. A parallel observation could be made about our growing doctrinal agreements in the Consultation on Church Union (COCU) and the numerous bilateral conversations in which American theologians figure so prominently.

c. Accepting, on the Basis of Agreed Understanding, Each Other's Celebration of Baptism and the Eucharist and the Ordained Ministry

In the U.S. the practical experience of highly mobile laity and mature Christian transdenominational groups is considerably ahead of the official teaching of the churches in issues of sacraments and ministry. This is problematic. It may even render more difficult formal agreements, but the pressure may impress greater urgency on the authorities. Issues of justice may in fact accelerate the need for agreements on sacramental theology and church authority. There is urgent need in the U.S. for narrowing the gap between formal declarations of unity (COCU, the bilaterals) and the actual recognition of each other's sacraments and ministries.

It should be readily recognized that the greatest doctrinal failure of American Christianity as a whole is the virtual absence of a theology of the Church. The Church as a divine-human institution is so often considered dispensable. The deeply entrenched principle of a voluntary association is the practical equivalent of church membership or ecclesial identity.

Yet, the people of God must not be blamed for a theological lacuna resulting from formalistic notions of the Church which they have received as orthodox ecclesiology. It is not just American pragmatism that makes people ask what the Church is for. A Church that is Christ-centered, biblically informed, theologically renewed, inclusive in membership and authority, busy about the works of justice and living as a witness of God's Kingdom would not be dispensable but indispensable. In such a Church, baptism would be indeed incorporation into Christ and not into a community of self-interest. In such a Church, the Lord's Table would be a gathering of both the spiritually and the physically hungry. In such a Church, ministry would be the Lord's presence through his people as the One who serves.

Ecclesiology is, of course, a matter of high doctrine, but the more important the doctrine the greater the reality it should be in people's lives. Throughout the U.S. "intentional communities" have come into being as a search for that kind of incorporation, mutuality, and service. Another form of such a search has been the Interim Eucharistic Fellowships of COCU.[2] These are a few evidences of how much the doctrine of the Church does matter.

d. Agreeing on Ways of Deciding and Acting Together

One is afraid of suggesting that God has given this or that other nation a value desirable for church life. But one is also afraid of not recognizing that a tradition, even if full of ambiguities, may not be pressed into the service of God.

There is in the United States a pronounced proclivity to egalitarianism, if not in practice at least in intention. We have one of the most participatory societies in the world. If we have put it to selfish and unworthy purposes, that is not an inevitable outcome. It can also be directed toward "agreeing on ways of deciding and acting together." What is at stake here is something noted earlier in this paper, namely, that where laity and clergy share not only tasks but also authority, the long-range coherence of a religious group is greatly enhanced, and what might appear as enlightened self-interest may in actuality be transmuted into freedom for community.

People in the United States are not adverse to authority. In fact, there have been times when the citizenry nearly gave up its freedoms in exchange for the security of authority. But deep within, Americans are ultimately anti-authoritarian (one wishes they would respect the same freedom in others). The assumption that such libertarian spirit must inevitably issue in license is cynical.

For the last two decades, church boards and agencies have been considerably more participatory. This creates untidiness in the early stages and a nostalgia for the days when the "old boys' club" could make decisions quickly and effectively. In subsequent years, we have come to appreciate the greater fairness and authenticity in decisions made by a cross-representation of the whole membership. Let it also be said that through such practices the churches have reaped a whole new harvest of superb leaders among the young and the old, the handicapped, the women, and the minority groups. In this area of "agreeing on ways of deciding and acting together," the American Christian community could make one of the most valuable contributions to a universal council of the Church catholic.

Notes

A. Conciliar Fellowship and a Universal Council of the Church: Their Meaning and Necessity

1. For further study of the concept of conciliar fellowship as a way of describing the unity of the Church, we recommend the following materials produced by the World Council of Churches either in its world assemblies or through its Commission on Faith and Order:

"The Holy Spirit and the Catholicity of the Church," *The Uppsala Report 1968* (WCC, Geneva, 1968), p. 17.

Councils in the Ecumenical Movement (WCC Studies #5), 1968.

"Conciliarity and the Furture of the Ecumenical Movement," *Faith and Order* (Faith and Order Commission, Louvain, 1971), FOC Paper 59, pp. 225–229.

"The Unity of the Church—Next Steps," *What Kind of Unity?* (Faith and Order Commission, Salamanca, 1973), FOC Paper 69 (1974), pp. 119–130.

Councils, Conciliarity and A Genuinely, Universal Council (Study Encounter Vol. X, No. 2), 1974.

"What Unity Requires—A Comment," *What Unity Requires* (WCC, Nairobi, 1975), FOC Paper 77 (1976), pp. 14–17.

In Each Place: Towards a Fellowship of Churches Truly United (WCC, Geneva, 1976), 1977, pp. 3–12.

"The Meaning of Conciliar Fellowship—Report of Committee I" (Faith and Order Commission, Bangalore, 1978).

The following articles are also helpful:

Bishop Maximos Aghiorgoussis, "Theological and Historical Aspects of Conciliarity: Some Propositions for Discussion," *Greek Orthodox Theological Review,* 24:1 (Spring, 1979).

Pierre Duprey, WF, "The Unity We Seek," *Journal of Ecumenical Studies,* 16:2 (Spring, 1979).

J. Robert Nelson, "Conciliarity/Conciliar Fellowship," *Midstream,* 17:2 (April, 1978).

B. A Universal Council of the Church Creating the Conditions through Conciliar Fellowship

1. *The Uppsala Report,* 1968, p. 17.
2. *The Report of the Second Forum on Bilateral Conversations.* Faith and Order Paper 96.
3. World Council of Churches, Constitution.

C. The American Way of Life, Conciliar Fellowship, and a Universal Council

1. Robert N. Bellah, "Civil Religion in America," *Daedalus,* Winter, 1967, pp. 1–21; and *The Broken Covenant: American Civil Religion in Time of Trial.* New York: Seabury Press, 1975.
2. Ecumenical eucharistic fellowships gathering regularly though occasionally at the Lord's Table in various communities across the U.S. For information contact the Consultation on Church Union, 151 Wall Street, Princeton, NJ 08540.

A Consultation: Confessing the Apostolic Faith from the Perspective of the Pentecostal Churches

Fuller Theological Seminary, October 22–24, 1986

A CONSULTATION SUMMARY

by Jerry L. Sandidge (Assemblies of God)

My brother-in-law spent many years as a missionary in Africa. One of the things he liked to do was collect African proverbs. Many of these he has shared with me. My favorite one is applicable, it seems to me, for this Consultation. It says: "You never jump a chasm in *two* leaps." In some ways we have tried to jump the chasm in *one* leap and, in this context, that too is impossible. What we need is to build a bridge and for that we need time, teamwork, and a plan.

This Consultation has been a very special "divine moment" in the history of the conciliar movement. For the National Council of Churches' Commission on Faith and Order to meet on the campus of one of America's leading Evangelical seminaries to discuss "the Apostolic Faith from the perspective of the Pentecostal churches" and to be co-sponsored by Fuller's newly organized "David J. du Plessis Center for Christian Spirituality"—that is history-making, pure and simple. I am grateful to have been a part of it.

The over-riding message of our two days together was "more, *More,* MORE!" More minutes to inquire, clarify, and inform. More opportunities to dissect the timely issues raised on both sides of the question. More discussion of the Pentecostal movement and its relationship to the larger Christian family.

Pentecostals need "bridge people" who will step into the ecumenical arena with their gloves on, confronting all the issues of the conciliar movement. Those same people, then, must enter the "sweat box" of their own tradition to explain that it is good to be in the ring. Somehow, leadership in the classical Pentecostal denominations must be shown, enticed, encouraged—in some way convinced—into seeing the value and necessity of participation in the ecumenical family.

Pentecostals are already engaged in an important theological exchange with Roman Catholics. This dialogue is on an international scale, but continental dialogues (such as in Central or South America) or national dialogues (such as in Canada or the USA) should also be considered. Something should be initiated between Pentecostals and Orthodox Christians, especially for the purpose of discussing such things as the theology of the Holy Spirit, the *experience* of the Holy Spirit in relation to the role of the Creeds and sacramental life of the Church. Pentecostals should not forsake the National Association of Evangelicals and their other Evangelical partners; but with their commitment to the NAE, Pentecostals should also feel free to participate in the World Council of Churches and the National Council of Churches. Pentecostal contribution is needed in speaking about expressive and creative worship; the role of the charismata in worship; the importance of quality evangelization in Christianized areas as well as places where the Christ-event has never been presented or not in a convincing way; and the "second vocation" of all Christians to be evangelists, whether priest or parent, minister or lay, male or female.

The conciliar movement needs to nudge the Pentecostals into expressing a greater concern for threatening world issues; aching social problems; human rights—including minorities, ethnic groups, women, poor, and economically and culturally marginalized peoples; discussion of areas of common witness, possibilities for the mutual recognition of ministry, and the sharing of theological insights.

Pentecostals could use a crash course in sacramental theology. Conciliar Christians could use a few lessons on church growth. Pentecostals need not fear the inclusion of the historic creeds into their moments of worship. Participants in the ecumenical dialogue could open up more to the grace of personal encounter with the Holy Spirit. Pentecostals need to take care that their Trinitarian theology be more vocal and precise. Non-Pentecostals need to realize how important it is for them to take the initiative in establishing a meaningful ongoing relationship with Pentecostals.

Yes, the problem of proselytism must be addressed. The Pentecostal misunderstanding of the ecumenical movement as a super world-church needs to be corrected into the image of it as a "communion of communions." We Pentecostals have declared our willingness to change if it is necessary in being more closely aligned with the Gospel of Jesus Christ. Help us change where changes are needed, but do not push us to the point of compromising who we are and what we see as necessary to the true faith. We think we have learned that you in the conciliar movement are inviting us, in most cases, to join you at the Lord's Table, i.e., to seek a sacramental unity more than some form of institutional unity.

Finally, I have a suggestion, for what it is worth. I recall the words of Cardinal Bea, when he said, "The door to unity is entered on our knees." I also remember the interview I had eleven years ago with the Vice-Rector of the Catholic University of Louvain in Belgium. We were discussing the ecumenical dimension of the Roman Catholic charismatic renewal. He said, simply but profoundly, "The work of the Spirit *is* conducive to unity."

We need to repent of our sin—on both sides—of pride, theological elitism or spiritual elitism, criticism, judgment, and so on. I would like to see conducted a great repentance service, a liturgy of penitence in which we pray that the Body of Christ be healed. I would like to participate in such a common prayer meeting, where we forgive each other, ask for guidance from the Lord, and leaders demonstrate to their constituency the practicality and spiritual dimension of all our theological discussions.

This Consultation has been informative, direct, gently confrontational, and stimulating. But is is not enough. There must be follow-up. There must be something more, to push farther, step closer together, and tackle the burning separating issues. May God give us the strength and commitment to continue. This Consultation has contributed greatly to me as a Pentecostal, to lead me to become an *incurable ecumaniac.* I pray this would happen to many of my brethren, so we can begin soon to build bridges across the chasm of division.

THE NCCCUSA COMMISSION ON FAITH AND ORDER RECORDER'S REPORT

by Thaddeus Horgan, SA (Roman Catholic)

At a consultation on Confessing the Apostolic Faith from the perspective of the Pentecostal Churches co-sponsored by the David du Plessis Center for Christian Spirituality at Fuller Theological Seminary and the Commission on Faith and Order of the National Council of Churches of Christ, USA, we have gathered as Christians to witness to the power of God's reconciling Spirit. The Spirit leads us to appreciate that we all should be one "so that the world may believe." We are Confessional Protestants, Holiness, Evangelical, and Pentecostal Protestants, Orthodox, and Roman Catholic Christians. With contrite hearts, yet also with praise, we have gathered. We are contrite because of the sin of disunity. In the past we viewed our distinctiveness as something that kept us divided. Our past historical heritage and religious experience, and our lack of mutual appreciation for what has shaped and formed us, accounts for our divisions.

With gratitude to God we also profess that we are in Christ by the power of the Spirit. We already have a unity, not full unity, but unity nonetheless. And today we perceive our distinctiveness as Scripture indicates (1 Corinthians 12), namely as a gift for our mutual enrichment for the upbuilding of the worldwide Church. No longer should distinctiveness divide us. This gathering is one way to move toward overcoming our individual and corporate sinfulness which has kept us apart. We prayerfully hope that our gathering will enable us to move toward fuller unity blessed with that diversity which reflects the wonderful and multiple creative power of God.

Therefore we have gathered formally, although not officially as designated representatives of Churches. Our general purpose has been to express and to proclaim the ancient Apostolic Faith in our day. At this meeting we have sought to appreciate better how that Apostolic Faith is confessed by the Pentecostal Churches here and in Latin America. But, it must be said, the primary result of the meeting was our recognition of the continuing need to learn who we are, what we believe, and how we express that. This has to be done directly. There is no usefulness in attempting to learn about each other as we, from within our own traditions, perceive the other to be. Ongoing dialogue is necessary for this and for pinpointing what may be differences that in fact fracture unity.

The great gifts to the worldwide Church represented by the Pentecostal Churches were recognized as:

1) the renewed manifestation of the charismata,
2) expressive worship and spontaneous prayer,
3) creative forms for living Christian life in small communities,
4) and the opportunity at the grass roots which they provide for new encounters that "the power of the Spirit" invites people to share.

Issues were also identified that need further clarification between Pentecostal Churches and Churches involved in the ecumenical movement. These are:

1) the individual and corporate role of the Holy Spirit in and on the Church,

2) the relationship between Pneumatology and Christology and "functional subordinationism" in Trinitarian Theology,
3) the relationship between the charismata and the Church as institution, and
4) the role of behavior as an expression of faith. This final point was seen as particularly significant to the way Pentecostal Christians manifest faith.

From Churches in the ecumenical movement, Pentecostals sought a clarification of its object which was said to be visible unity. Visible unity, it was explained, does not imply constructing a monolithically structured super-church which would absorb particular churches. The Church's unity is God-like, one yet triune; it is unity with diversity.

The Pentecostal emphasis on evangelization was also explained, and the role of women in their Churches especially in the past was praised by many as prophetic. The sometime accusation of Pentecostal anti-intellectualism and their attitudes concerning social witness and outreach were candidly faced, and with equal candor, discussed. While agreement would not be claimed as the result of these conversations, greater understanding was.

A Pentecostal assessment of the ecumenical enterprise surfaced the following concerns which could block their participation:

1) the meaning of *koinōnia* in other Churches. *Koinōnia* is the basis of Christian unity for Pentecostals, the result of the Holy Spirit's work which presupposes a personal relationship with God through Christ,
2) the significance of doctrine which in Pentecostal experience has caused past division,
3) fear that spiritual vitality gets lost in the cerebral approach to faith employed in discussions within the ecumenical movement;
4) bearing false witness, or being ridiculed by other Christians, something that has occurred in the past;
5) and negative criticism because of preferred Pentecostal priorities. For them, issues in any possible dialogue must be those that are suggested and profoundly influenced by the Gospel.

Nevertheless there are reasons to be optimistic about future possible Pentecostal ecumenical involvement. Foremost here is the rise of the charismatic renewal movement. The source for this renewal vigor within many churches in the ecumenical movement and the source of the Pentecostal Churches' life is singular, the Holy Spirit. Interest by the World Council of Churches in charismatic developments through three consultations over the past ten years, the Vatican dialogue with some Pentecostals, and the National Council of Churches' inclusive attitude which has involved Pentecostals in the studies of its Faith and Order Commission all indicate a Pentecostal capacity for participation in the ecumenical movement and a warm welcome for them there. This Consultation itself not only witnesses to that but can be considered paradigmatic for other churches not yet either officially or formally involved in the ecumenical movement. These also demonstrate that ecumenical involvement means genuine dialogue and not some sort of comparison of particular churches' messages.

But ecumenical involvement cannot just simply happen. Attitudes need to change. Instead of seeing differences immediately, all involved should first *know and appreciate* where they agree. *Patience* is required in face of disagreements about teaching, polity, and lifestyles. *Mutual support* and affirmation need to be more prominent than defensiveness and airs of superiority. But above all, ongoing repentance for the sin of disunity and mutual *forgiveness,* given and asked for, are required if we are to get beyond past alienations and to break down presumed barriers. All of this, it was acknowledged, is dependent on the continued reference to the power of the Holy Spirit.

A renewed awareness of the developed meaning of the word "ecumenical," based on John 17:20–21, was proposed as a necessity, not only for this possible dialogue, but for all future dialogues. In Jesus' prayer, mission and unity are joined. Unity enables the church to fulfill its task in the world. While acknowledging that Pentecostals could contribute a sense of the power of the Spirit within the ecumenical movement, some urged them only to do so when they committed themselves to the total mission of the Church which is to embrace all nations, all races, all classes and all cultures. Pentecostals, in turn, affirmed their commitment to evangelization, to the charismatic renewal of existing churches and to Christian unity. They also asserted that social concern has always been a reality in their churches, a reality not always acknowledged by others.

In a series of open discussions, issues like visible unity versus spiritual unity, human-made unity or Spirit-given unity, fidelity to tradition and apparent compromise in ecumenical mergers, popularism and spiritual elitism were all addressed. Very sensitive questions like the value of creedal statements, having an implied theology, the need for a clear ecclesiology, and having experienced faith and/or cerebral faith were brought up. In a word, we shared our impressions with one another and raised delicate questions. All of this manifested our desire to be open to the Spirit and to one another. This meeting's purpose was to explore how the Pentecostal Churches confess the Apostolic Faith today. It resulted, however, in the participants manifesting their desire to know one another and to engage in dialogue.

David du Plessis said, "The ecumenical movement must be pentecostal, and the pentecostal movement must be ecumenical because the Holy Spirit cannot be contained and operates everywhere." We responded to this by coming to a consensus about our possible future. We felt we should continue similar consultations, but on specific issues, first the less sensitive and then the more sensitive. As a beginning three topics were proposed: the meaning of Christian unity, the charismata and their effects, and evangelization. We felt we had to build bridges to one another and want our respective leadership to exercise their role here. We acknowledge the essential need for ongoing repentance and continued prayer. So we prayed. And we sang, fittingly, the hymn "They'll know we are Christians by our love."

Index

Ecumenical Documents Series

Volume I: Doing the Truth in Charity, eds. Thomas F. Stransky and John B. Sheerin

Contents

The Decree on Ecumenism and other Vatican II texts • The two-part Directory concerning ecumenical matters and ecumenism in higher education • Ecumenical collaboration at the regional, national and local levels • Sacramental sharing • Marriages between Catholics and other Christians • Reception of adult baptized Christians into the Catholic Church • Principles for interconfessional cooperation in bible translations • Common calendar and fixed Easter date • Relations with the Orthodox Churches, and with the Anglican and Protestant Communions • Extracts from papal letters, sermons, etc. • Relations with the Jews

Volume II: Growth in Agreement, eds. Harding Meyer and Lukas Vischer

Contents

Anglican conversations with Lutherans, with Old Catholics, with Orthodox, with Roman Catholics • Baptist-Reformed • Disciples-Roman Catholic • Lutheran-Roman Catholic • Lutheran-Reformed-Roman Catholic • Methodist-Roman Catholic • Old Catholic-Orthodox • Pentecostal-Roman Catholic • Reformed-Roman Catholic • WCC Faith and Order Report on Baptism, Eucharist and Ministry

Volume III: Towards the Healing of Schism, ed. and trans. E.J. Stormon

Contents

Correspondence, Public Statements, Official Visits, Joint Prayer Services, and Common Declarations between the Holy See and the Ecumenical Patriarchate. Among the many important matters fully documented here are: The initiatives of Pope John XXIII and Patriarch Athenagoras • Orthodox observer delegates at Vatican II • The historic meeting of Pope Paul VI and Patriarch Athenagoras on the Mount of Olives • The official cancellation of the ancient anathemas between the two Sees • The creation under Pope John Paul II and Patriarch Dimitrios of a Joint Commission for Theological Dialogue • The exchange of delegations between Rome and Constantinople which carry forth a "dialogue of charity" and form the background for ongoing theological discussions